W9-BKY-469

THE OFFICIAL GUIDE TO

RACIAL
AND ETHNIC
DIVERSITY

RACIAL AND ETHNIC DIVERSITY

Asians,
Blacks,
Hispanics,
Native
Americans,
and
Whites

by Cheryl Russell

New Strategist Publications, Inc.
Ithaca, New York

WINGATE UNIVERSITY LIBRARY

New Strategist Publications, Inc.
P.O. Box 242, Ithaca, New York 14851
607 / 273-0913

copyright 1996, New Strategist Publications, Inc.

All rights reserved. No part of this book may be reproduced, stored in a retrieval system, or transmitted in any form or by any means, electronic, mechanical, photocopying, recording, or otherwise, without the prior written permission of the publisher and the copyright holder. Further information may be obtained from New Strategist Publications, Inc., P.O. Box 242, Ithaca, NY 14851.

Cheryl Russell, 1953—
The Official Guide to Racial & Ethnic Diversity

ISBN 0-885070-03-9

Printed in the United States of America

for Mom and Dad, who taught me to respect diversity and enjoy change

Table of Contents

Tables

Chapter 1. **Asians**

Population

Chapter 2. **Blacks**

Education

Health

Population

Wealth and Spending

Chapter 3. **Hispanics**

Education

Health

Households and Living Arrangements

Chapter 4. **Native Americans**

Chapter 5. **Whites**

Health

Households and Living Arrangements

Housing

Income

Labor Force

Chapter 6. **Total Population**

Households and Living Arrangements

Housing

Income

Labor Force

Population

Chapter 7. **Attitudes**

Introduction

With the diversity of the American population increasing rapidly, it has become vital to track America's racial and ethnic groups. *The Official Guide to Racial & Ethnic Diversity* provides the building blocks for examining the wants and needs of whites and blacks, Hispanics and non-Hispanics, Asians and Native Americans.

For many businesses, grappling with diversity is now critical for developing new products, advertising strategies, and marketing campaigns. Statistics for the total population are no longer enough, because the totals mask the many differences by race and ethnicity. The living arrangements of Hispanics are different from those of whites or blacks in ways that affect consumer behavior. The educational level of some Asian ethnic groups makes them more sophisticated consumers than the average American.

The Official Guide to Racial & Ethnic Diversity examines the characteristics of the four racial groups in the U.S: Asians, whites, blacks, and Native Americans. It also examines the characteristics of Hispanics, who may be of any race (see page xxiv for a breakdown of the racial composition of Hispanics). For Asians and Hispanics, the book presents detailed demographic information on the largest ethnic groups, such as Chinese Americans for Asians and Mexican Americans for Hispanics.

The Official Guide to Racial & Ethnic Diversity is as complete and up-to-date as possible, given the constraints of the data. In the best of all worlds, the demographic data available for each group would be identical. In the real world, this is not possible because the government collects information on the smaller racial and ethnic groups less frequently and in less detail. For Native Americans and for Asians by ethnic group, for example, most of the latest available data are from the 1990 census. There are no spending or wealth data for Asians or Native Americans. The government has only recently begun to examine non-Hispanic whites separately from the white population as a whole, and non-Hispanic whites are shown separately only for some topics.

Racial/Ethnic Classifications

The government classifies Americans by race through self-identification. On both the census and the Current Population Survey, which are the primary sources used in this book, respondents themselves indicate their race and Hispanic origin on questionnaires. The four racial groups described in *The Official Guide to Racial & Ethnic Diversity* are defined as follows:

Asian The term "Asian" includes both Asians and Pacific Islanders. The Current Population Survey classifies as Asian or Pacific Islander anyone who identifies his or her race as "Asian or Pacific Islander." The 1990 census went further, asking Asian or Pacific Islanders to specify their ethnic origin, such as Chinese, Filipino, Japanese, Asian Indian, Korean, Vietnamese, Samoan, Tahitian, and so on. Anyone who named a Far Eastern or Pacific Island nation as his or her country of origin was classified as "Asian or Pacific Islander." The only exception to this definition of Asian is in the immigration tables in the Asian and Total Population sections. The Immigration and Naturalization Service includes people from the Middle East—such as Israel, Lebanon, and Iran—as immigrants from the Asian world region. They are included as Asian immigrants in the immigration tables.

Black The black racial category includes those who identify themselves as "black" on the Current Population Survey, or as "black or Negro" on the 1990 census, or who wrote in an ancestry or ethnic origin on the 1990 census that included African American, Jamaican, Nigerian, West Indian, or Haitian.

Native American The Native American statistics in this book include people who indicated they were American Indian, Eskimo, or Aleut in the 1990 census. Some of the tables in the Native American chapter do not include Eskimos or Aleuts, a fact noted at the bottom of those tables. The American Indian category includes persons who reported their race as American Indian and/or entered the name of an American Indian tribe. The tribal data shown in this book are from the written entries on the 1990 census questionnaire.

White The white racial category includes those who identify themselves as "white" on the Current Population Survey or on the 1990 census. In addition, it includes those who report an ancestry or ethnic origin that includes Canadian, German, Italian, Lebanese, Near Easterner, Arab, or Polish, or other countries that are primarily white. The only exception to this definition of white is in the immigration tables in the Asian and Total Population sections where the Immigration and Naturalization Service classifies people from the Middle East as from the Asian world region. They are included as Asian immigrants in the immigration tables, although the Census Bureau would classify them as white.

Hispanic The government classifies people as Hispanic through self-identification in questions that are separate from those about race. Because "Hispanic" is an ethnic origin rather than a race, Hispanics may be of any race. While most are white, there are a considerable number of black, Asian, and even Native American Hispanics.

The Hispanic statistics in this book include those who identified themselves as Hispanic on the Current Population Survey or on the 1990 census. Hispanics include those who identify themselves as Mexican, Puerto Rican, Cuban, or of "other" Spanish/Hispanic origin. Persons of "other" Hispanic origin include those from Spain, the Spanish-speaking countries of Central and South America, and the Dominican Republic. They also include those who identify themselves as Spanish, Spanish American, Latino, and so on. The only exception to this definition of Hispanic is in the immigration table in the Hispanic chapter, where people from Brazil are classified as Hispanic because they are from South America.

Non-Hispanic People who did not indicate that they were Hispanic on the Current Population Survey or on the 1990 census are classified as non-Hispanic. Most of the non-Hispanic statistics are for whites and are in the White chapter. There are few statistics available for non-Hispanic blacks, Asians, or Native Americans.

A breakdown of the Hispanic composition of racial groups and the racial composition of Hispanics is shown on the next page.

How To Use This Book

The Official Guide to Racial & Ethnic Diversity is divided into seven chapters, including one for each racial group and one for Hispanics. In addition, there is a chapter showing comparable statistics for the total population. When comparable statistics for the total population are included in the individual racial or ethnic sections, no table on the topic is included in the Total Population chapter.

Hispanic Composition of Racial Groups, 1996

(number of persons by race and Hispanic origin, 1996; numbers in thousands)

	total		white		black		Asian		Native American	
	number	percent	number	percent	number	percent	number	percent	number	percent
Total persons	265,253	100.0%	219,641	100.0%	33,611	100.0%	9,728	100.0%	2,273	100.0%
Non-Hispanic	237,449	89.5	194,353	88.5	31,999	95.2	9,141	94.0	1,956	86.1
Hispanic	27,804	10.5	25,288	11.5	1,612	4.8	587	6.0	317	13.9

Racial Composition of Hispanics, 1996

(number of Hispanics by race, 1996; numbers in thousands)

	Hispanic	
	number	percent
Total persons	27,804	100.0%
White	25,288	91.0
Black	1,612	5.8
Asian	587	2.1
Native American	317	1.1

Source: Bureau of the Census, Population Projections of the United States, by Age, Sex, Race, and Hispanic Origin: 1995 to 2050, *Current Population Reports, P25-1130, 1996*

Within each chapter, sections on demographic topics are arranged alphabetically, beginning with Education and ending with Wealth and Spending. If a table on a particular topic is available for blacks, an identical table will be shown for Hispanics, Asians, whites, and so on if the data are available. When tables are not identical, it means identical data are not available for that racial or ethnic group.

The Attitudes section follows the Total Population section. The tables in the Attitudes section examine what Americans think about a range of diversity issues. The data are from the 1994 General Social Survey (GSS) of the National Opinion Research Center of the University of Chicago. Because the GSS divides respondents into three racial groups (white, black, and other), responses to diversity questions can only be shown for those groups. It is important to remember that the "other" race category in the Attitudes tables includes not only Asians and Native Americans, but also any Hispanics who did not identify themselves as either white or black.

Data Sources

The data in *The Official Guide to Racial & Ethnic Diversity* are from publicly available sources of information, identified at the bottom of each table. The two sources appearing most frequently are the Census Bureau's Current Population Survey and the 1990 census.

Most of the data in this book are from published reports. Because the government is cutting back on printed reports due to the high cost of printing and distribution, increasing amounts of demographic data are available only in unpublished form such as print-outs. To obtain these data directly, you must call the right government employees and ask the right questions—an often frustrating and time-consuming task for researchers. New Strategist publishes this and other books in its American Consumer Series to make consumer research more efficient. Any tables in the book that are based on unpublished documents are noted as "unpublished tables." Some of the data presented in this book are available only on-line, at the Census Bureau's worldwide web site. When a table's data are from the bureau's web site, that is noted at the bottom of the table. The address of the web site is given on each table so that readers can connect to the web site themselves and see the many things it has to offer (http://www.census.gov).

As yet, there is no substitute for a good book. And that is what *The Official Guide to Racial & Ethnic Diversity* is—a book full of meaningful numbers about the most important trend in the United States, the growing diversity of our population.

1

Asians

■ The Asian-American population is projected to grow from about 10 million in 1996 to nearly 20 million by 2020, when Asians will account for 6 percent of the total U.S. population.

■ Asians are much better educated than the population as a whole. Forty-one percent were college graduates in 1994, versus 22 percent of the total population.

■ For all but a few health conditions, Asians fare much better than the average American. At birth, life expectancy for Asian males is seven years longer than average, while for females it is six years longer.

■ Asian households are far more likely to be headed by married couples than are households in the nation as a whole—64 percent versus 55 percent. Forty percent of Asian households are married couples with children.

■ The median income of Asian households fell by 7 percent between 1990 and 1994. Despite this decline, the median income of Asian households was 25 percent higher than the median income of all households.

■ A 53 percent majority of Asian households have at least two earners. This compares with 45 percent of all households and is the highest proportion among all racial groups.

Note: There are no spending or wealth data for Asians.

Asians:
Education

Asians are much better educated than the population as a whole. As of 1994, 85 percent of Asians were high school graduates, versus 81 percent of the total population. Fully 41 percent of Asians were college graduates, much higher than the 22 percent of the total population that have a bachelor's degree. Among Asians, Vietnamese Americans are the least educated because many are refugees who fled Vietnam after the war. Only 61 percent of Vietnamese Americans had a high school diploma as of 1990.

Not only are Asians better educated than the average person, they are more likely to be enrolled in school. Overall, 37 percent of Asians aged 3 or older are in school, versus 27 percent of all Americans. Asians account for 5 percent of undergraduate enrollment and for nearly 9 percent of enrollment at the first-professional degree level.

More than 51,000 bachelor's degrees were awarded to Asian Americans in 1992-93. Asians earned 11 percent of bachelor's degrees awarded in biological science and in engineering. They also earned from 12 to 19 percent of first-professional degrees in the fields of dentistry, medicine, optometry, and pharmacy.

Educational Attainment of Asians by Sex, 1994

(number and percent distribution of Asians aged 25 or older by educational attainment and sex, 1994; numbers in thousands)

	total		men		women	
	number	*percent*	*number*	*percent*	*number*	*percent*
Total, aged 25 or older	4,545	100.0%	2,103	100.0%	2,442	100.0%
Not a high school graduate	691	15.2	240	11.4	452	18.5
High school graduate or more	3,854	84.8	1,863	88.6	1,990	81.5
Some college or associate's degree	868	19.1	437	20.8	427	17.5
Bachelor's degree or more	1,873	41.2	963	45.8	908	37.2

Source: Bureau of the Census, Internet web site, http://www.census.gov

Educational Attainment of Asians by Ethnicity and Sex, 1990

(total number of Asians aged 25 or older and percent who are high school or college graduates by ethnicity and sex, 1990; numbers in thousands)

	total	high school	college
TOTAL			
Total, aged 25 or older	4,316	77.5%	36.6%
Chinese	1,077	73.6	40.7
Filipino	865	82.6	39.3
Japanese	626	87.5	34.5
Asian Indian	464	84.7	58.1
Korean	456	80.2	34.5
Vietnamese	304	61.2	17.4
MEN			
Total, aged 25 or older	2,034	81.5	41.9
Chinese	525	77.2	46.7
Filipino	372	84.2	36.2
Japanese	276	89.9	42.6
Asian Indian	257	89.4	65.7
Korean	186	89.1	46.9
Vietnamese	157	68.5	22.3
WOMEN			
Total, aged 25 or older	2,283	74.0	31.8
Chinese	551	70.2	35.0
Filipino	493	81.4	41.6
Japanese	350	85.6	28.2
Asian Indian	208	79.0	48.7
Korean	269	74.1	25.9
Vietnamese	147	53.3	12.2

Note: Numbers will not add to total because not all ethnicities are shown.
Source: U.S. Bureau of the Census, Asians and Pacific Islanders in the United States, 1990 Census of Population, 1990 CP-3-5, 1993

Educational Attainment of Asians by State, 1990

(percent of Asians aged 25 or older who are high school or college graduates, by state, 1990)

	high school graduate or more	college graduate		high school graduate or more	college graduate
United States	77.5%	36.6%	Missouri	81.5%	47.3%
Alabama	78.9	43.7	Montana	78.5	32.1
Alaska	75.4	20.5	Nebraska	80.0	39.5
Arizona	80.2	37.5	Nevada	74.1	21.9
Arkansas	66.4	24.6	New Hampshire	82.7	26.1
California	77.2	34.1	New Jersey	86.8	57.1
Colorado	78.3	32.1	New Mexico	80.8	38.7
Connecticut	81.9	50.8	New York	72.4	38.7
Delaware	86.1	55.9	North Carolina	77.9	39.3
District of Columbia	80.2	50.9	North Dakota	83.7	37.8
Florida	77.8	33.6	Ohio	83.5	53.2
Georgia	77.5	38.6	Oklahoma	76.1	34.7
Hawaii	74.7	19.4	Oregon	79.4	32.3
Idaho	80.3	27.6	Pennsylvania	77.1	45.2
Illinois	83.9	49.8	Rhode Island	59.6	30.6
Indiana	85.8	53.1	South Carolina	77.4	34.4
Iowa	76.4	47.3	South Dakota	74.3	33.1
Kansas	73.6	39.9	Tennessee	79.3	42.6
Kentucky	77.9	44.2	Texas	79.1	41.3
Louisiana	68.1	31.4	Utah	80.7	29.4
Maine	74.3	44.9	Vermont	87.1	52.1
Maryland	84.8	50.3	Virginia	82.1	40.2
Massachusetts	74.1	44.9	Washington	77.3	30.2
Michigan	83.3	54.1	West Virginia	88.8	63.3
Minnesota	69.7	33.5	Wisconsin	71.5	40.4
Mississippi	68.2	35.1	Wyoming	77.5	28.6

Source: National Center for Education Statistics, Digest of Education Statistics 1993, *NCES 93-292, 1993*

School Enrollment of Asians by Age and Ethnicity, 1990

(number and percent of Asians aged 3 or older enrolled in school by age and ethnicity, April 1990)

	total		Chinese		Filipino		Japanese		Asian Indian		Vietnamese	
	number	percent	number	percent	number	percent	number	percent	number	percent	number	percent
Total, aged 3 or older	2,552,671	37.1%	589,888	37.3%	444,857	32.7%	228,551	27.3%	285,362	38.1%	252,144	44.7%
Aged 3 and 4	70,729	30.4	17,228	41.3	9,092	21.9	8,696	46.4	9,088	34.5	3,745	18.9
Aged 5 to 14	1,059,662	93.0	198,265	94.6	201,521	92.8	82,176	94.6	126,525	94.7	98,328	91.3
Aged 15 to 19	532,968	90.2	115,181	94.5	103,122	87.5	40,761	90.9	53,633	93.2	64,268	91.0
Aged 20 to 24	355,538	58.6	93,166	70.6	54,169	46.4	38,611	63.5	41,423	62.4	36,795	59.5
Aged 25 to 34	316,058	22.4	105,274	30.4	36,792	14.5	33,023	19.6	34,966	21.4	28,658	23.6
Aged 35 or older	217,716	7.5	60,774	8.3	40,161	6.6	25,284	5.5	19,727	6.6	20,350	11.1

Note: Numbers by ethnicity will not add to total because not all ethnicities are shown.
Source: U.S. Bureau of the Census, 1990 Census of Population, 1990 CP-3-5, 1993

College Enrollment of Asians by Sex, 1993

(number of Asians enrolled in institutions of higher education by level of study and sex, and Asian enrollment as a percent of total enrollment, fall 1993; numbers in thousands)

	total		men		women	
	number	*percent of total enrollment*	*number*	*percent of total men enrolled*	*number*	*percent of total women enrolled*
Total enrolled	724	5.2%	363	5.6%	361	4.6%
Undergraduate	634	5.3	314	5.7	320	4.7
Graduate	65	4.3	35	4.5	30	3.3
First-professional	25	8.8	14	8.1	11	9.2

Source: National Center for Education Statistics, Digest of Education Statistics 1995, *NCES 95-029, 1995*

Bachelor's, Master's, and Doctoral Degrees
Earned by Asians by Field of Study, 1992-93

(number and percent of bachelor's, master's, and doctoral degrees earned by Asians, by field of study, 1992-93)

	bachelor's		master's		doctoral	
	number	percent	number	percent	number	percent
Total degrees	51,463	4.4%	13,866	3.8%	1,582	3.8%
Agriculture and natural resources	318	1.9	80	2.0	23	2.0
Architecture and related programs	667	7.3	206	5.4	5	3.4
Area, ethnic, and cultural studies	463	8.4	86	5.6	13	7.3
Biological/life sciences	5,203	11.1	317	6.7	265	6.0
Business, management, and admin. services	11,780	4.6	4,304	4.8	45	3.3
Communications	1,178	2.2	151	3.2	12	4.1
Communications technologies	12	1.4	7	1.5	-	-
Computer and information sciences	2,294	9.5	1,163	11.4	56	7.0
Construction trades	2	2.9	-	-	-	-
Education	1,100	1.0	1,391	1.4	123	1.7
Engineering	6,542	10.6	2,405	8.7	379	6.5
Engineering related technologies	765	4.8	36	3.3	2	10.0
English language and literature	1,583	2.8	158	2.0	23	1.7
Foreign languages and literature	526	3.7	108	3.4	26	3.1
Health professions and related sciences	2,513	3.7	864	3.4	64	3.6
Home economics	475	3.1	52	2.1	6	1.7
Law and legal studies	71	3.5	66	3.0	-	-
Liberal arts and sciences	1,004	3.0	34	1.4	-	-
Library science	-	-	118	2.4	2	2.6
Mathematics	929	6.3	212	5.2	57	4.8
Mechanics and repairers	14	13.3	-	-	-	-
Multi/interdisciplinary studies	1,188	5.0	63	2.5	2	1.0
Parks, recreation, leisure and fitness	103	1.0	14	1.0	2	1.9
Philosophy and religion	314	4.0	50	3.5	12	2.7
Physical sciences	1,124	6.4	262	4.9	215	4.9
Precision production trades	4	1.0	-	-	-	-
Protective services	325	1.6	17	1.3	-	-
Psychology	2,596	3.9	203	1.9	63	1.7
Public administration and services	327	1.9	466	2.3	10	2.2
R.O.T.C. and military sciences	-	-	5	4.6	-	-
Social sciences and history	5,712	4.2	422	3.1	111	3.2
Theological studies/religious vocations	128	2.4	207	4.2	38	2.7
Transportation and material moving	73	1.9	6	1.2	-	-
Visual and performing arts	2,130	4.5	393	4.2	28	3.2

Source: National Center for Education Statistics, Digest of Education Statistics 1995, *NCES 95-029, 1995*

First-Professional Degrees Earned by Asians by Field of Study, 1992-93

(number and percent of first-professional degrees earned by Asians by field of study, 1992-93)

	number	percent
Total degrees	5,160	6.9%
Dentistry (D.D.S. or D.M.D.)	532	14.8
Medicine (M.D.)	2,001	12.9
Optometry (O.D.)	139	12.1
Osteopathic medicine (D.O.)	132	8.1
Pharmacy (Pharm. D.)	369	19.4
Podiatry (Pod. D. or D.P. or D.P.M.)	35	7.4
Veterinary medicine (D.V.M.)	39	1.9
Chiropractic medicine (D.C. or D.C.M.)	115	4.1
Law (LL.B. or J.D.)	1,550	3.8
Theology (M.Div., M.H.L., B.D., or Ord.)	246	4.5
Other	2	3.1

Source: National Center for Education Statistics, Digest of Education Statistics 1995, *NCES 95-029, 1995*

Asians:
Health

For all but a few health conditions, Asians fare much better than the average American. Infant mortality and death rates for accidents, heart disease, and cancer are all far lower for Asians than for the population as a whole. Tuberculosis is more common for Asians than it is for the total population, however. Many Asians are immigrants, some of whom live in cramped quarters where tuberculosis can spread easily. Because Asians are more metropolitan than other racial or ethnic groups in the U.S., they are more likely to live in counties with poor air quality.

Asians are much less likely to be disabled than are Americans as a whole, in part because the Asian population is, on average, younger than the total population. Only 10 percent of Asians are disabled, versus 19 percent of the total population.

Life expectancy for Asians is well above average. At birth, Asian males can expect to live to age 79, or seven years longer than average. Asian females can expect to live to age 85, nearly six years longer than average. Even at age 65, Asian life expectancy remains three to four years greater than the life expectancy of the average American.

Health Indicators for Asians, 1992

(selected indicators of total and Asian health status, and index of Asian health indicators to total, 1992 except where otherwise noted)

	total population indicator	Asian indicator	index
Infant mortality rate (deaths < age 1 per 1,000 live births, 1991)	8.6	5.8	67
Total deaths per 100,000 population	504.5	285.8	57
Motor vehicle crash deaths per 100,000 population	15.8	9.9	63
Work-related injury deaths per 100,000 people aged 16 or older, 1993	3.2	2.9	91
Suicides per 100,000 population	11.1	6.0	54
Homicides per 100,000 population	10.5	5.7	54
Lung cancer deaths per 100,000 population	39.3	17.9	46
Female breast cancer deaths per 100,000 women	21.9	9.3	42
Cardiovascular disease deaths per 100,000 population	180.4	107.4	60
Heart disease deaths per 100,000 population	144.3	77.8	54
Stroke deaths per 100,000 population	26.2	23.5	90
Reported incidence of AIDS per 100,000 population, 1993*	31.2	7.4	24
Reported incidence of tuberculosis per 100,000 population, 1993*	9.8	44.5	454
Reported incidence of syphilis per 100,000 population, 1993*	10.4	1.0	10
Prevalence of low birth weight, as percent of total live births	7.1	6.6	93
Births to females aged 10 to 17, as percent of total live births	4.9	2.0	41
Percent of mothers without care, first trimester of pregnancy	22.3	23.4	105
Percent < age 18 living in poverty, 1993	22.7	-	-
Percent living in counties exceeding U.S. air quality standards, 1993	23.5	37.2	158

* Data are for the non-Hispanic population.
Note: The index is calculated by dividing the Asian figure by the total figure for each indicator and multiplying by 100. For example, the index of 67 indicates that the Asian infant mortality rate is 33 percent below the rate for all infants.
Source: National Center for Health Statistics, Health Status Indicators: Differentials by Race and Hispanic Origin, *Healthy People 2000, Number 10, 1995*

Asians With Disabilities, 1991-92

(total number of Asians, number and percent with a disability, and number and percent with a severe disability, by selected characteristics, 1991-92; numbers in thousands)

	total	with a disability		with a severe disability	
		number	percent	number	percent
Total persons	7,855	778	9.9%	382	4.9%
AGE					
Under age 6	794	17	2.1	6	0.8
Aged 6 to 14	1,191	37	3.1	6	0.5
Aged 15 to 17	408	21	5.1	-	-
Aged 18 to 24	926	46	5.0	25	2.7
Aged 25 to 34	1,401	97	7.0	36	2.6
Aged 35 to 44	1,295	103	8.0	47	3.7
Aged 45 to 54	762	111	14.6	51	6.7
Aged 55 to 64	599	137	22.8	85	14.2
Aged 65 to 74	320	124	38.7	74	23.2
Aged 75 or older	159	85	53.5	52	33.0
HOUSEHOLD TYPE					
Family householder or spouse	3,378	409	12.1	215	6.4
With children under age 18	1,919	149	7.8	85	4.4
Married, spouse present	3,034	350	11.5	184	6.1
With children under age 18	1,749	132	7.6	76	4.4
No spouse present	343	59	17.3	31	9.0
With children under age 18	170	17	10.3	9	5.5
Nonfamily householder	491	69	14.0	39	8.0
Living alone	399	54	13.6	37	9.3
REGION					
Northeast	1,371	82	6.0	48	3.5
Midwest	660	82	12.5	19	2.8
South	1,390	89	6.4	40	2.9
West	4,435	524	11.8	277	6.3

Note: (-) means number in sample is too small to make a reliable estimate.
Source: Bureau of the Census, Americans with Disabilities: 1991-92, *Current Population Reports, P70-33, 1993*

Life Expectancy of Asians at Birth and Age 65, 1995 to 2020

(average number of years of life remaining at birth and at age 65 for Asian males and females, 1995-2050; difference between Asian life expectancy and total life expectancy for males and females at birth and at age 65, 1995 and 2020)

	life expectancy (years)	
	males	*females*
AT BIRTH		
1995	79.3	84.9
2000	79.5	85.0
2005	79.8	85.2
2010	80.2	85.5
2015	80.6	85.8
2020	81.1	86.2
Life exp. of Asians minus		
life exp. of total Americans		
1995	6.8	5.6
2020	5.6	4.7
AT AGE 65		
1995	18.8	22.9
2000	19.0	23.0
2005	19.2	23.2
2010	19.5	23.4
2015	19.8	23.6
2020	20.1	23.9
Life exp. of Asians minus		
life exp. of total Americans		
1995	3.3	3.7
2020	2.5	3.3

Source: Bureau of the Census, Population Projections of the United States, by Age, Sex, Race, and Hispanic Origin: 1995 to 2050, *Current Population Reports, P25-1130, 1996*

Asians:
Households and Living Arrangements

Because of immigration, Asian householders are much younger than house-holders in the nation as a whole. Fifty-five percent are aged 25 to 44, versus 43 percent of total householders. Only 10 percent of Asian householders are aged 65 or older, versus 21 percent of total householders.

Partly because of this age distribution, Asian households are far more likely to be headed by married couples than are households in the nation as a whole, 64 percent versus 55 percent. While only 26 percent of total households are nuclear families, 40 percent of Asian households are married couples with children. Among Asian Indians, fully 54 percent of households are nuclear families. Because so many Asian households are headed by married couples, Asian children are more likely than the average child to live with both parents, 82 percent versus 72 percent.

Asians are more likely to be married than are men and women in the U.S. as a whole. Overall, 60 percent of Asian women are married, a proportion that reaches 70 percent among Asian Indians. Fifty-seven percent of Asian men are married, including 65 percent of Asian-Indian men.

Asian Households by Age of Householder, 1990

(number and percent distribution of Asian households by age of householder, 1990; numbers in thousands)

	number	percent
Total households	2,020	100.0%
Under age 25	111	5.5
Aged 25 to 34	516	25.5
Aged 35 to 44	592	29.3
Aged 45 to 54	384	19.0
Aged 55 to 64	220	10.9
Aged 65 to 74	132	6.5
Aged 75 or older	66	3.3

Source: Bureau of the Census, 1990 census STF3 CD-ROM, and TGE Demographics, Inc., Honeoye Falls, New York

Asian Households by Household Type, 1994

(number and percent distribution of Asian households by type of household, 1994; numbers in thousands)

	number	percent
Total households	2,233	100.0%
Family households	1,737	77.8
Married-couple families	1,425	63.8
Female householder, no spouse present	232	10.4
Male householder, no spouse present	80	3.6
Nonfamily households	496	22.2
Female householder	248	11.1
Male householder	250	11.2

Source: Bureau of the Census, Internet web site, http://www.census.gov

Asian Households by Size, 1994

(number and percent distribution of Asian households by size, 1994; numbers in thousands)

	number	percent
Total households	2,233	100.0%
One person	368	16.5
Two persons	543	24.3
Three persons	429	19.2
Four persons	485	21.7
Five persons	246	11.0
Six persons	94	4.2
Seven or more persons	69	3.1

Source: Bureau of the Census, Internet web site, http://www.census.gov

Asian Households by Household Type and Ethnicity, 1990

(number and percent distribution of Asian households by type of household and ethnicity of householder, 1990; numbers in thousands)

	total	Chinese	Filipino	Japanese	Asian Indian	Korean	Vietnamese
TOTAL, NUMBER	2,020	509	356	316	234	202	141
Family households	1,578	390	293	208	193	163	118
With children <18	938	209	176	87	132	102	82
Without children <18	640	181	117	121	61	61	36
Married-couple families	1,295	331	231	174	175	137	85
With children <18	816	190	148	76	126	90	65
Without children <18	479	141	83	98	49	47	20
Female householder,							
no spouse present	186	37	44	25	9	18	19
With children <18	94	14	22	8	5	10	12
Without children <18	92	23	22	17	4	8	7
Male householder,							
no spouse present	97	22	18	9	9	8	14
Nonfamily households	443	120	63	108	41	39	22
People living alone	325	90	44	88	28	29	14
TOTAL, PERCENT	100.0%	100.0%	100.0%	100.0%	100.0%	100.0%	100.0%
Family households	78.1	76.6	82.3	65.8	82.5	80.7	83.7
With children <18	46.4	41.1	49.4	27.5	56.4	50.5	58.2
Without children <18	31.7	35.6	32.9	38.3	26.1	30.2	25.5
Married-couple families	64.1	65.0	64.9	55.1	74.8	67.8	60.3
With children <18	40.4	37.3	41.6	24.1	53.8	44.6	46.1
Without children <18	23.7	27.7	23.3	31.0	20.9	23.3	14.2
Female householder,							
no spouse present	9.2	7.3	12.4	7.9	3.8	8.9	13.5
With children <18	4.7	2.8	6.2	2.5	2.1	5.0	8.5
Without children <18	4.6	4.5	6.2	5.4	1.7	4.0	5.0
Male householder,							
no spouse present	4.8	4.3	5.1	2.8	3.8	4.0	9.9
Nonfamily households	21.9	23.6	17.7	34.2	17.5	19.3	15.6
People living alone	16.1	17.7	12.4	27.8	12.0	14.4	9.9

Note: Numbers by ethnicity will not add to total because not all ethnicities are shown.
Source: Bureau of the Census, Asians and Pacific Islanders in the United States, *1990 Census of Population, 1990 CP-3-5, 1993*

Living Arrangements of Asian Children, 1994

(number and percent distribution of Asian children under age 18 by living arrangement, 1994; numbers in thousands)

	number	percent
Total children	2,045	100.0%
Living with two parents	1,685	82.4
Living with one parent	284	13.9
Mother only	223	10.9
Father only	61	3.0
Living with neither parent	74	3.6

Source: Bureau of the Census, Internet web site, http://www.census.gov

Marital Status of Asians by Sex and Ethnicity, 1990

(number and percent distribution of Asians aged 15 or older by sex, marital status, and ethnicity, 1990; numbers in thousands)

	total	Chinese	Filipino	Japanese	Asian Indian	Korean	Vietnamese
Women, number	2,864	675	610	403	266	340	205
Never married	769	189	164	95	58	81	72
Married	1,709	404	358	241	187	211	108
Separated	50	8	13	5	3	5	6
Widowed	203	51	43	36	13	24	12
Divorced	132	22	31	26	6	18	8
Women, percent	100.0%	100.0%	100.0%	100.0%	100.0%	100.0%	100.0%
Never married	26.9	28.0	26.9	23.6	21.8	23.8	35.1
Married	59.7	59.9	58.7	59.8	70.3	62.1	52.7
Separated	1.7	1.2	2.1	1.2	1.1	1.5	2.9
Widowed	7.1	7.6	7.0	8.9	4.9	7.1	5.9
Divorced	4.6	3.3	5.1	6.5	2.3	5.3	3.9
Men, number	2,649	656	490	329	322	253	231
Never married	984	234	171	121	101	89	118
Married	1,519	392	286	185	209	153	101
Separated	34	6	8	3	3	3	5
Widowed	33	9	8	6	3	2	2
Divorced	79	15	18	14	6	6	5
Men, percent	100.0%	100.0%	100.0%	100.0%	100.0%	100.0%	100.0%
Never married	37.1	35.7	34.9	36.8	31.4	35.2	51.1
Married	57.3	59.8	58.4	56.2	64.9	60.5	43.7
Separated	1.3	0.9	1.6	0.9	0.9	1.2	2.2
Widowed	1.2	1.4	1.6	1.8	0.9	0.8	0.9
Divorced	3.0	2.3	3.7	4.3	1.9	2.4	2.2

Note: Numbers by ethnicity will not add to total because not all ethnicities are shown.
Source: Bureau of the Census, Asians and Pacific Islanders in the United States, *1990 Census of Population, 1990 CP-3-5, 1993*

Asians:
Housing

Asian Americans own some of the most highly valued homes in the nation, in large part because so many Asians live in the two states with the most expensive housing—Hawaii and California. Overall, homes owned by Asians had a median value of $178,300 in 1990, compared with a median value of $78,300 for the average American home. But Asians are less likely to own a home than are average Americans. Fifty-two percent of Asians own their homes, versus a homeownership rate of 64 percent for all Americans.

The largest number of Asian households is in Los Angeles-Long Beach, California, followed by New York City, Honolulu, and San Francisco. These four metropolitan areas account for 35 percent of all Asian households in the nation. Among the 25 metropolitan areas with the most Asian households, homeownership rates are greatest in Nassau-Suffolk, New York, at 77 percent. Housing values for Asian households are highest in San Francisco, with a median value of $304,100.

Among the homes occupied by Asians, only 48 percent are single-family detached homes. For householders in the nation as a whole, 62 percent live in single-family detached homes.

Characteristics of Asian Households
by Metropolitan Status, 1990

*(number of Asian households, percent of total households that are Asian, percent of Asian house-
holds that are owner occupied, and median value of owner-occupied Asian households, by metropolitan status, 1990; numbers in thousands)*

	number	Asian share of total households	owner-occupied	
			percent	median value
Asian households	2,014	2.2%	52.2%	$178,300
Inside metropolitan areas	1,896	2.7	52.0	184,000
Central cities	983	3.3	40.4	169,100
Suburbs*	914	2.2	64.5	191,700
Outside metropolitan areas	117	0.6	54.6	106,900

* The suburbs are the portion of a metropolitan area that is outside the central city.
Source: Bureau of the Census, Housing in Metropolitan Areas—Asian and Pacific Islander Households,
Statistical Brief, SB/95-6, 1995

Asian Homeownership in the 25 Metropolitan Areas With the Most Asian Households, 1990

(number of Asian households, percent of total households that are Asian, percent of Asian house-holds that are owner occupied, and median value of owner-occupied Asian households, in the U.S. and in the 25 metropolitan areas with the most Asian households, ranked alphabetically, 1990; numbers in thousands)

	number	Asian share of total households	owner-occupied percent	owner-occupied median value
Total Asian households	2,014	2.2%	52.2%	$178,300
Anaheim-Santa Ana, CA	64	7.7	60.2	256,300
Atlanta, GA	14	1.3	46.7	98,500
Bergen-Passaic, NJ	18	3.9	52.8	247,700
Boston, MA	27	2.5	39.2	203,900
Chicago, IL	66	3.0	52.6	140,000
Dallas, TX	20	2.1	43.9	92,300
Detroit, MI	16	1.0	59.1	111,000
Honolulu, HI	155	58.5	62.2	274,000
Houston, TX	36	3.1	55.2	68,100
Los Angeles-Long Beach, CA	277	9.3	51.3	246,300
Middlesex-Somerset-Hunterdon, NJ	15	4.2	66.5	194,700
Minneapolis-St. Paul, MN-WI	15	1.6	41.7	92,500
Nassau-Suffolk, NY	15	1.7	76.8	224,400
New York, NY	167	5.1	32.6	220,700
Newark, NJ	14	2.2	61.2	221,900
Oakland, CA	77	9.9	61.3	240,600
Philadelphia, PA	28	1.6	56.1	121,000
Riverside-San Bernardino, CA	26	3.0	64.6	162,500
Sacramento, CA	32	5.8	55.4	140,000
San Diego, CA	48	5.4	53.2	177,200
San Francisco, CA	96	15.0	50.7	304,100
San Jose, CA	70	13.4	60.4	282,000
Seattle, WA	40	5.1	54.7	134,200
Stockton, CA	14	8.8	47.4	111,600
Washington, DC-MD-VA	56	3.8	61.1	183,600

Source: Bureau of the Census, Housing in Metropolitan Areas—Asian or Pacific Islander Households, *Statistical Brief, SB/05-6, 1995*

Characteristics of Housing Units Occupied by Asians, 1990

(number and percent distribution of housing units occupied by Asians, by number of units in structure, 1990; numbers in thousands)

	number	percent
Total occupied housing units	1,983	100.0%
Number of units in structure		
1, detached	942	47.5
1, attached	157	7.9
2 to 4	222	11.2
5 to 9	145	7.3
10 to 19	160	8.1
20 to 49	145	7.3
50 or more	168	8.5
Mobile home or trailer	18	0.9
Other	26	1.3

Source: Bureau of the Census, Asians and Pacific Islanders in the United States, *1990 CP-3-5, 1993*

Asians:
Income

The median income of Asian households fell by 7 percent between 1990 and 1994 as the recession of the early 1990s cut into earnings. Despite this decline, Asian median household income was 25 percent greater than the median income of total households in 1994.

Nearly 20 percent of Asian households had incomes of $75,000 or more in 1993. Asian couples had the highest incomes, with a median of nearly $50,000. More than one in four Asian couples had an income of $75,000 or more. Interestingly, Asian families headed by women without a spouse have a higher median income than those headed by men without a spouse.

Asian men working year-round, full-time earned a median of $32,601 in 1994, up about 6 percent since 1990, after adjusting for inflation. Asian women earned a median of $24,452, up 1 percent since 1990. Asian men and women earn slightly more than the average full-time worker because they are better educated. Overall, about half of Asians aged 25 or older who work full-time have a bachelor's degree.

Because many Asians are recent immigrants, a relatively large proportion are poor. Fully 41 percent of Asian families with a householder who did not graduate from high school are poor. The proportion who are poor falls to just 7 percent among those with bachelor's degrees. Twelve percent of Asian married couples are poor, versus just 6 percent of all married couples.

Median Income of Asian Households, 1988 to 1994

(median income of Asian households, and ratio of Asian to total median income, 1988-1994; percent change in income and ratio, selected years; in 1994 dollars)

	median income	ratio Asian/total
1994	$40,482	1.25
1993	39,329	1.23
1992	39,930	1.23
1991	39,660	1.21
1990	43,598	1.28
1989	43,147	1.25
1988	40,422	1.19
Percent change		
1990-1994	-7.1%	-2.3%
1988-1994	0.1	5.9

Note: The ratio is calculated by dividing the median income of Asian households by the median for total households.
Source: Bureau of the Census, unpublished tables from the 1995 Current Population Survey

Income Distribution of Asian Households, 1993

(number and percent distribution of Asian households by income, 1993; households in thousands as of 1994)

	number	percent
Total households	2,233	100.0%
Under $10,000	304	13.6
$10,000 to $19,999	317	14.2
$20,000 to $34,999	442	19.8
$35,000 to $49,999	288	12.9
$50,000 to $59,999	210	9.4
$60,000 to $74,999	237	10.6
$75,000 or more	435	19.5
Median income	$38,346	-

Source: Bureau of the Census, Internet web site, http://www.census.gov

Income Distribution of Asian Families by Family Type, 1993

(number and percent distribution of Asian families by income and type of family, 1993; families in thousands as of 1994)

	total	married couples	female householder, no spouse present	male householder, no spouse present
Total	1,737	1,426	232	79
Under $10,000	179	127	38	13
$10,000 to $19,999	224	163	48	14
$20,000 to $34,999	305	235	50	19
$35,000 to $49,999	243	195	31	17
$50,000 to $74,999	391	334	50	7
$75,000 or more	393	369	15	8
Median income	$44,456	$49,507	$28,922	$23,128
Percent distribution	100.0%	100.0%	100.0%	100.0%
Under $10,000	10.3	8.9	16.4	16.7
$10,000 to $19,999	12.9	11.4	20.8	18.0
$20,000 to $34,999	17.6	16.5	21.7	24.2
$35,000 to $49,999	14.0	13.7	13.2	21.9
$50,000 to $74,999	22.5	23.4	21.5	8.6
$75,000 or more	22.6	25.9	6.4	10.4

Source: Bureau of the Census, Internet web site, http://www.census.gov

Median Earnings of Asian Men and Women
Who Work Full-Time, 1988 to 1994

(median earnings of Asian men and women aged 15 or older who work year-round, full-time; ratio of Asian to total median earnings, and ratio of Asian female to Asian male median earnings, 1988-1994; percent change in earnings and ratios for selected years; in 1994 dollars)

	Asian men		Asian women		
	median earnings	ratio Asian/total	median earnings	ratio Asian/total	ratio Asian female/male
1994	$32,061	1.04	$24,452	1.10	0.76
1993	31,694	1.02	24,968	1.12	0.79
1992	32,241	1.01	24,085	1.07	0.75
1991	32,816	1.03	23,040	1.03	0.70
1990	30,349	0.97	24,179	1.08	0.80
1989	33,645	1.03	25,531	1.14	0.76
1988	33,976	1.02	24,238	1.10	0.71
Percent change					
1990-1994	5.6%	7.5%	1.1%	2.4%	-4.3%
1988-1994	-5.6	2.1	0.9	0.2	6.9

Note: The Asian/total ratios are calculated by dividing the median earnings of Asian men and women by the median for total men and women. The female/male ratio is calculated by dividing the median earnings of Asian women by the median earnings of Asian men.
Source: Bureau of the Census, unpublished tables from the 1995 Current Population Survey

Earnings of Asian Men and Women
Who Work Full-Time by Education, 1993

(number of Asian year-round, full-time workers aged 25 or older with earnings by sex and educational attainment, and percent distribution by earnings, 1993; men and women in thousands as of 1994)

	total	not a high school grad	high school graduate	some college or associate's degree	bachelor's degree or more
MEN	1,303	79	282	277	665
Percent distribution	100.0%	100.0%	100.0%	100.0%	100.0%
Under $10,000	5.6	17.4	6.9	5.6	3.7
$10,000 to $19,999	17.5	57.5	24.3	15.5	10.8
$20,000 to $29,999	21.8	17.2	31.9	23.8	17.2
$30,000 to $39,999	17.7	4.9	16.6	28.0	15.3
$40,000 to $49,999	12.1	-	6.5	15.4	14.5
$50,000 to $74,999	16.2	1.9	12.7	9.8	22.0
$75,000 or more	9.0	1.0	1.1	1.6	16.4
Median earnings	$31,560	$15,213	$23,494	$31,092	$41,221
WOMEN	985	75	228	190	492
Percent distribution	100.0%	100.0%	100.0%	100.0%	100.0%
Under $10,000	7.1	28.2	10.8	3.5	3.7
$10,000 to $19,999	29.0	41.8	51.2	29.8	16.5
$20,000 to $29,999	24.7	23.1	24.9	26.6	24.0
$30,000 to $39,999	15.8	3.0	5.0	20.3	21.1
$40,000 to $49,999	12.8	3.9	3.4	15.2	17.7
$50,000 to $74,999	7.1	-	2.1	3.9	11.7
$75,000 or more	3.4	-	2.7	0.8	5.2
Median earnings	$25,427	$12,166	$17,331	$25,070	$31,780

Note: (-) means number in sample is too small to make a reliable estimate.
Source: Bureau of the Census web site, http://www.census.gov

Poverty Status of Asian Families, 1993

(total number of Asian families, and number and percent below poverty level by type of family and by education of householder, 1993; families in thousands as of 1994)

		in poverty	
	total	number	percent
Family type, householders aged 15+			
Total families	1,737	235	13.5%
Married couples	1,426	177	12.4
Female householder, no spouse present	232	43	18.6
Male householder, no spouse present	79	15	19.1
Education, householders aged 25+			
Not a high school graduate	219	90	41.0
High school graduate	365	49	13.4
Bachelor's degree or more	788	55	7.0

Source: Bureau of the Census, Internet web site, http://www.census.gov

Asians:
Labor Force

More than 3.5 million Asians were in the civilian labor force in 1994, or 64 percent of all Asian Americans aged 16 or older. Nearly 72 percent of Asian men are in the labor force, as are 50 percent of Asian women. The labor force participation rates of Asians are slightly below those for the total population.

Among Asian men, labor force participation rates are highest for Asian Indians, at 84 percent in 1990. Among Asian women, rates are highest for Filipinos, at 72 percent (1990 is the latest year available for data on labor force participation rates by Asian ethnicity).

A 53 percent majority of Asian households have at least two earners. This compares with 45 percent of total households and is the highest proportion among all racial groups.

One-third of employed Asian men and women are in managerial or professional specialty occupations. This compares with 27 percent of men and 29 percent of women in the nation as a whole. Asians account for 2.8 percent of the nation's workers, but for 3.4 percent of managers and professionals.

The number of workers who are Asian or "other" race (primarily Native Americans) will grow by 39 percent between 1994 and 2005, according to projections by the Bureau of Labor Statistics. The Asian and "other" share of the labor force will reach 5.2 percent by 2005.

Employment Status of Asians by Sex, 1994

(employment status of the civilian noninstitutional Asian population aged 16 or older, by sex, 1994; numbers in thousands)

	total	men	women
Civilian labor force	3,540	1,883	1,657
Employed	3,310	1,762	1,548
Unemployed	230	121	109
Not in labor force	2,022	737	1,285
Percent in labor force	63.7%	71.9%	56.3%
Percent unemployed	6.5	6.4	6.6
Percent not in labor force	36.4	28.1	43.7

Note: The civilian labor force equals the number employed plus the number unemployed. The civilian population equals the number in the labor force plus the number not in the labor force.
Source: Bureau of the Census, Internet web site, http://www.census.gov

Employment Status of Asians by Sex and Ethnicity, 1990

(employment status of the civilian noninstitutional Asian population aged 16 or older, by sex and ethnicity, 1990; numbers in thousands)

	Chinese	Filipino	Japanese	Asian Indian	Korean	Vietnamese
MEN						
Civilian labor force	468	359	242	263	180	160
Employed	447	339	237	251	172	148
Unemployed	21	20	6	12	8	13
Not in labor force	174	99	80	52	65	62
Percent in labor force	72.9%	79.3%	75.5%	83.5%	73.8%	72.3%
Percent unemployed	4.5	5.6	2.4	4.5	4.3	8.0
Percent not in labor force	27.1	20.7	24.5	16.5	26.2	27.7
WOMEN						
Civilian labor force	393	432	221	153	185	111
Employed	373	411	215	141	173	101
Unemployed	20	20	6	12	11	10
Not in labor force	271	166	178	108	148	88
Percent in labor force	59.2%	72.0%	55.4%	58.6%	55.5%	55.8%
Percent unemployed	5.0	4.7	2.7	7.6	6.1	8.9
Percent not in labor force	40.8	27.7	44.5	41.4	44.5	44.2

Note: The civilian labor force equals the number employed plus the number unemployed. The civilian population equals the number in the labor force plus the number not in the labor force.
Source: Bureau of the Census, Asians and Pacific Islanders in the United States, *1990 Census of Population, 1990 CP-3-5, 1993*

Asian Households by Number of Earners, 1994

(number and percent distribution of Asian households by number of earners, 1994; numbers in thousands)

	number	percent
Total households	2,233	100.0%
No earners	364	16.3
One earner	694	31.1
Two or more earners	1,175	52.6
Two earners	891	39.9
Three earners	179	8.0
Four or more earners	105	4.7

Source: Bureau of the Census, Internet web site, http://www.census.gov

Occupations of Asians by Sex, 1994

(number and percent distribution of employed Asians aged 16 or older in the civilian labor force by occupation and sex, 1994; numbers in thousands)

	men		women	
	number	*percent*	*number*	*percent*
Total employed	1,762	100.0%	1,548	100.0%
Managerial and professional specialty	631	35.8	505	32.6
Technical, sales, and administrative support	442	25.1	587	37.9
Service	222	12.6	271	17.5
Farming, forestry, and fishing	41	2.3	2	0.1
Precision production, craft, and repair	189	10.7	50	3.2
Operators, fabricators, and laborers	240	13.6	135	8.7

Note: Numbers may not add to total due to rounding.
Source: Bureau of the Census, Internet web site, http://www.census.gov

Asian Share of Workers by Occupation, 1994

(number of Asians aged 16 or older employed in the civilian labor force by occupation, and Asian share of total employed by occupation, 1994; numbers in thousands)

	number	*share of total employed*
Total employed	3,310	2.8%
Managerial and professional specialty	1,136	3.4
Technical, sales, and administrative support	1,029	2.8
Service	493	2.9
Farming, forestry, and fishing	43	1.3
Precision production, craft, and repair	239	1.9
Operators, fabricators, and laborers	375	2.2

Note: Numbers may not add to total due to rounding.
Source: Bureau of the Census, Internet web site, http://www.census.gov

Asian Labor Force Projections by Sex, 1994 to 2005

(number of persons of Asian or "other" race aged 16 or older in the civilian labor force in 1994 and 2005, labor force participation rate of Asians and "others" in 1994 and 2005, and Asian and "other" share of the total labor force in 1994 and 2005; by sex; percent change in number and percentage point change in share; numbers in thousands)

	1994	2005	percent change 1994-2005
Number in labor force			
Total	5,474	7,632	39.4%
Men	3,002	4,054	35.1
Women	2,471	3,578	44.8
			percentage point change 1994-2005
Labor force participation rate			
Total	65.3%	64.0%	-1.3
Men	74.3	72.3	-2.0
Women	56.9	56.7	-0.2
Percent of labor force			
Total	4.2	5.2	1.0
Men	4.2	5.3	1.1
Women	4.1	5.1	1.0

Note: Persons of "other" race are primarily Native Americans.
Source: Bureau of Labor Statistics, Monthly Labor Review, *November 1995*

Asians:
Population

The Asian-American population is projected to grow from about 10 million in 1996 to nearly 20 million by 2020, when Asians will account for 6 percent of the total U.S. population.

Driving much of this growth is immigration. The Asian world region accounted for 45 percent of all immigrants to the U.S. in 1994, with the largest numbers coming from China, the Philippines, and Vietnam. Fully 63 percent of Asian Americans are foreign-born, according to the 1990 census.

Most Asian Americans speak English "very well." Only 38 percent of those aged 5 or older do not speak English fluently. But among those aged 65 or older, more than half do not speak English "very well."

More than half of Asian Americans live in the West, where they account for nearly 10 percent of the population of the Pacific division, which includes California and Hawaii. California is home to 39 percent of the nation's Asian population, including 52 percent of Filipinos and 46 percent of Vietnamese. Los Angeles has more Asians than any other metropolitan area.

Nearly 153,000 babies were born to Asian-American mothers in 1993, or just under 4 percent of all babies born that year. This proportion should rise to nearly 7 percent by 2020. In 1993, Asians accounted for fully 67 percent of all births in Hawaii and 10 percent of births in California.

Asians by Age, 1990 to 2020

(number of Asians by age, selected years 1990-2020; percent change 1990-2000 and 2000-2010; numbers in thousands)

	1990	1996	2000	2010	2020	percent change 1990-2000	percent change 2000-2010
Total persons	7,570	9,728	11,245	15,265	19,651	48.5%	35.7%
Under 5	656	850	926	1,170	1,476	41.2	26.3
5 to 9	619	772	925	1,145	1,440	49.4	23.8
10 to 14	575	797	901	1,233	1,524	56.7	36.8
15 to 19	626	733	894	1,248	1,502	42.8	39.6
20 to 24	670	738	811	1,141	1,473	21.0	40.7
25 to 29	728	849	895	1,164	1,515	22.9	30.1
30 to 34	754	892	968	1,119	1,452	28.4	15.6
35 to 39	687	875	975	1,148	1,417	41.9	17.7
40 to 44	587	788	919	1,142	1,298	56.6	24.3
45 to 49	413	658	779	1,065	1,238	88.6	36.7
50 to 54	318	464	630	941	1,153	98.1	49.4
55 to 59	256	357	447	779	1,043	74.6	74.3
60 to 64	223	292	356	633	913	59.6	77.8
65 to 69	182	249	290	457	748	59.3	57.6
70 to 74	123	192	232	345	582	88.6	48.7
75 to 79	81	118	159	246	384	96.3	54.7
80 to 84	43	65	83	160	241	93.0	92.8
85 or older	30	39	55	130	250	83.3	136.4
18 to 24	938	1,010	1,158	1,632	2,058	23.5	40.9
18 or older	5,362	6,848	7,946	10,961	14,292	48.2	37.9
65 or older	459	664	819	1,338	2,206	78.4	63.4

Source: Bureau of the Census, Population Projections of the United States, by Age, Sex, Race, and Hispanic Origin: 1995 to 2050, *Current Population Reports, P25-1130, 1996; and* U.S. Population Estimates, by Age, Sex, Race, and Hispanic Origin: 1980 to 1991, *Current Population Reports, P25-1095, 1993*

Asian Share of the Total Population by Age, 1990 to 2020

(Asians as a percent of the total population by age, selected years 1990-2020)

	1990	*1996*	*2000*	*2010*	*2020*
Total persons	3.0%	3.7%	4.1%	5.1%	6.1%
Under age 5	3.5	4.4	4.9	5.8	6.7
Aged 5 to 9	3.4	3.9	4.6	5.9	6.7
Aged 10 to 14	3.3	4.2	4.5	6.1	7.1
Aged 15 to 19	3.5	3.9	4.5	5.7	7.0
Aged 20 to 24	3.5	4.3	4.4	5.4	6.9
Aged 25 to 29	3.4	4.5	5.1	5.9	7.0
Aged 30 to 34	3.4	4.2	5.0	6.0	6.8
Aged 35 to 39	3.4	3.9	4.4	6.2	6.9
Aged 40 to 44	3.3	3.8	4.1	5.7	6.8
Aged 45 to 49	3.0	3.6	3.9	4.9	6.7
Aged 50 to 54	2.8	3.3	3.7	4.3	6.0
Aged 55 to 59	2.4	3.1	3.4	4.1	4.9
Aged 60 to 64	2.1	2.9	3.3	3.9	4.4
Aged 65 to 69	1.8	2.5	3.1	3.8	4.3
Aged 70 to 74	1.5	2.2	2.7	3.9	4.2
Aged 75 to 79	1.3	1.7	2.1	3.5	4.1
Aged 80 to 84	1.1	1.4	1.7	2.9	4.1
Aged 85 or older	1.0	1.0	1.3	2.3	3.9
Aged 18 to 24	3.5	4.1	4.4	5.4	6.9
Aged 18 or older	2.9	3.5	3.9	4.9	5.8
Aged 65 or older	1.5	2.0	2.4	3.4	4.1

Source: Bureau of the Census, Population Projections of the United States, by Age, Sex, Race, and Hispanic Origin: 1995 to 2050, *Current Population Reports, P25-1130, 1996; and* U.S. Population Estimates, by Age, Sex, Race, and Hispanic Origin: 1980 to 1991, *Current Population Reports, P25-1095, 1993*

Non-Hispanic Asians by Age, 1990 to 2020

(number of non-Hispanic Asians by age, selected years 1990-2020; percent change 1990-2000 and 2000-2010; numbers in thousands)

	1990	1996	2000	2010	2020	percent change 1990-2000	percent change 2000-2010
Total persons	7,096	9,141	10,584	14,402	18,557	49.2%	36.1%
Under 5	604	790	867	1,093	1,381	43.5	26.1
5 to 9	572	712	859	1,072	1,347	50.2	24.8
10 to 14	533	740	834	1,158	1,427	56.5	38.8
15 to 19	582	683	835	1,165	1,411	43.5	39.5
20 to 24	621	688	756	1,063	1,385	21.7	40.6
25 to 29	678	789	836	1,089	1,418	23.3	30.3
30 to 34	709	838	907	1,052	1,362	27.9	16.0
35 to 39	649	828	921	1,085	1,338	41.9	17.8
40 to 44	557	748	873	1,080	1,230	56.7	23.7
45 to 49	392	628	742	1,013	1,177	89.3	36.5
50 to 54	302	442	602	898	1,096	99.3	49.2
55 to 59	244	341	428	745	996	75.4	74.1
60 to 64	213	279	342	608	875	60.6	77.8
65 to 69	175	239	278	440	719	58.9	58.3
70 to 74	119	184	222	331	559	86.6	49.1
75 to 79	78	113	152	235	368	94.9	54.6
80 to 84	41	62	79	152	231	92.7	92.4
85 or older	28	37	51	123	237	82.1	141.2
18 to 24	870	942	1,081	1,521	1,933	24.3	40.7
18 or older	5,054	6,470	7,514	10,372	13,539	48.7	38.0
65 or older	440	635	783	1,281	2,113	78.0	63.6

Note: Hispanics may be of any race and most are white. For a breakdown of the Hispanic composition of racial groups and the racial composition of Hispanics, see the introduction to this book.
Source: Bureau of the Census, Population Projections of the United States, by Age, Sex, Race, and Hispanic Origin: 1995 to 2050, *Current Population Reports, P25-1130, 1996; and* U.S. Population Estimates, by Age, Sex, Race, and Hispanic Origin: 1980 to 1991, *Current Population Reports, P25-1095, 1993*

Asians by Age and Sex, 1996

(number of Asians by age and sex, and sex ratio by age, 1996; numbers in thousands)

	total	male	female	sex ratio*
Total persons	9,728	4,690	5,038	93
Under age 5	850	434	415	105
Aged 5 to 9	772	396	376	105
Aged 10 to 14	797	404	393	103
Aged 15 to 19	733	370	363	102
Aged 20 to 24	738	363	374	97
Aged 25 to 29	849	409	439	93
Aged 30 to 34	892	429	463	93
Aged 35 to 39	875	420	455	92
Aged 40 to 44	788	368	420	88
Aged 45 to 49	658	304	355	86
Aged 50 to 54	464	217	247	88
Aged 55 to 59	357	168	189	89
Aged 60 to 64	292	130	162	80
Aged 65 to 69	249	104	145	72
Aged 70 to 74	192	81	111	73
Aged 75 to 79	118	49	69	71
Aged 80 to 84	65	28	37	76
Aged 85 or older	39	15	24	63
Aged 18 to 24	1,010	500	510	98
Aged 18 or older	6,848	3,222	3,626	89
Aged 65 or older	664	278	386	72

* The sex ratio is the number of males per 100 females.
Source: Bureau of the Census, Population Projections of the United States, by Age, Sex, Race, and Hispanic Origin: 1995 to 2050, *Current Population Reports, P25-1130, 1996*

Asians by Age and Foreign-Born Status, 1990

(total number of Asians, and number and percent who are foreign born, by age; 1990; numbers in thousands)

	total	foreign born	
		number	percent
Total persons	7,227	4,559	63.1%
Under age 5	574	56	9.8
Aged 5 to 9	588	131	22.4
Aged 10 to 14	551	226	41.0
Aged 15 to 19	591	336	56.9
Aged 20 to 24	606	418	69.0
Aged 25 to 34	1,414	1,093	77.3
Aged 35 to 44	1,258	1,028	81.7
Aged 45 to 54	736	613	83.2
Aged 55 to 64	466	349	74.9
Aged 65 to 74	295	197	66.9
Aged 75 to 84	118	88	74.1
Aged 85 or older	29	23	80.7
Aged 18 or older	5,175	3,961	76.5
Aged 65 or older	443	308	69.7

Note: The 1990 figures are from the April 1, 1990, census sample.
Source: Bureau of the Census, Asians and Pacific Islanders in the United States, *1990 Census of Population, CP-3-5, 1990*

Asians by Age, Ethnicity, and Foreign-Born Status, 1990

(total number of Asians, and number and percent who are foreign born, by age and ethnicity, 1990; for six largest Asian ethnic groups, 1990; numbers in thousands)

	Chinese			Filipino			Japanese		
		foreign born			foreign born			foreign born	
	total	number	percent	total	number	percent	total	number	percent
Total									
persons	1,649	1,143	69.3%	1,420	914	64.4%	866	281	32.4%
Under 5	108	8	7.3	103	6	5.4	47	8	17.5
5 to 9	102	21	20.5	107	18	16.8	47	11	22.6
10 to 14	107	48	44.6	110	33	29.9	40	9	21.5
15 to 19	122	74	60.6	118	52	43.8	45	11	24.8
20 to 24	132	92	69.8	117	72	61.9	61	20	33.5
25 to 34	346	281	81.3	255	194	76.2	168	60	35.5
35 to 44	312	261	83.7	254	218	85.8	150	61	40.8
45 to 54	164	145	88.2	162	145	89.3	94	38	40.8
55 to 64	123	103	83.5	94	81	86.7	108	44	40.9
65 to 74	87	72	82.8	61	57	93.1	74	8	11.3
75 to 84	36	31	85.1	34	32	97.0	23	3	14.9
85 or older	9	7	83.3	7	6	97.5	9	7	70.0
18 or older	1,264	1,026	81.2	1,033	830	80.4	708	248	35.0
65 or older	132	110	83.5	101	96	94.6	106	18	17.2

(continued)

(continued from previous page)

Total	Korean			Asian Indian			Vietnamese		
		foreign born			foreign born			foreign born	
	total	number	percent	total	number	percent	total	number	percent
persons	797	579	72.7%	787	593	75.4%	593	474	79.9%
Under 5	70	7	9.4	65	8	11.7	49	5	10.3
5 to 9	70	14	20.4	68	17	24.6	54	14	25.3
10 to 14	63	25	39.4	66	27	41.1	54	36	66.1
15 to 19	74	46	61.7	58	36	62.5	71	63	88.8
20 to 24	64	52	81.8	66	57	85.3	62	58	94.0
25 to 34	154	145	94.0	164	156	95.7	121	119	98.0
35 to 44	129	125	96.9	155	152	97.7	98	96	98.8
45 to 54	96	93	97.7	91	89	97.9	46	45	98.5
55 to 64	43	41	95.5	34	33	96.8	22	22	98.2
65 to 74	24	22	91.2	15	15	95.3	11	11	97.7
75 to 84	9	8	92.7	5	4	94.4	5	4	97.3
85 or older	1	1	94.8	1	1	85.9	1	1	93.8
18 or older	552	510	92.5	554	522	94.3	394	382	97.1
65 or older	34	31	91.7	21	20	94.7	17	16	97.4

Note: The 1990 population figures are from the April 1, 1990, census sample.
Source: Bureau of the Census, Asians and Pacific Islanders in the United States, *1990 Census of Population, CP-3-5, 1990*

Asians by Age, Ethnicity, and Ability to Speak English, 1990

(number and percent of Asians aged 5 or older who do not speak English "very well" by age and ethnicity, for six largest Asian ethnic groups, 1990; numbers in thousands)

	total		Chinese		Filipino		Japanese	
	number	*percent*	*number*	*percent*	*number*	*percent*	*number*	*percent*
Total, aged 5 or older	2,555	38.4%	777	50.5%	318	24.2%	206	25.2%
Aged 5 to 17	379	25.7	90	32.6	32	11.2	21	18.8
Aged 18 to 64	1,912	40.4	589	52.1	228	24.4	148	24.5
Aged 65 to 74	168	56.9	64	73.1	34	56.6	21	28.0
Aged 75 or older	96	65.4	34	76.8	24	60.2	17	53.0

	Korean		Asian Indian		Vietnamese	
	number	*percent*	*number*	*percent*	*number*	*percent*
Total, aged 5 or older	376	51.6%	169	23.5%	331	60.8%
Aged 5 to 17	40	22.5	25	14.7	67	44.6
Aged 18 to 64	308	59.5	133	24.9	249	66.1
Aged 65 to 74	20	81.9	9	55.3	10	88.2
Aged 75 or older	8	85.2	3	59.3	5	87.0

Source: Bureau of the Census, Asians and Pacific Islanders in the United States, *1990 Census of Population, CP-3-5, 1990*

Asian Immigrants by Country of Birth, 1994

(total number of immigrants and number of Asian immigrants for countries sending at least 1,000 immigrants to the U.S., Asian immigrants as a percent of total immigrants by country of birth, 1994)

	number	percent
Total immigrants	804,416	100.0%
Total Asian immigrants	358,047	44.5
China, Mainland	53,985	6.7
Philippines	53,535	6.7
Vietnam	41,345	5.1
India	34,921	4.3
Korea	16,011	2.0
Iran	11,422	1.4
Taiwan	10,032	1.2
Pakistan	8,698	1.1
Hong Kong	7,731	1.0
Japan	6,093	0.8
Iraq	6,025	0.7
Thailand	5,489	0.7
Laos	5,089	0.6
Lebanon	4,319	0.5
Jordan	3,990	0.5
Bangladesh	3,434	0.4
Israel	3,425	0.4
Syria	2,426	0.3
Afghanistan	2,344	0.3
Turkey	1,840	0.2
Malaysia	1,480	0.2
Cambodia	1,404	0.2
Indonesia	1,367	0.2
Kuwait	1,065	0.1

Source: U.S. Immigration and Naturalization Service, Statistical Yearbook of the Immigration and Naturalization Service, *1995*

Characteristics of the Asian Foreign-Born Population, 1994

(number and percent distribution of the Asian foreign-born population by age, sex, education, region of residence, metropolitan status, and selected countries of origin, 1994; countries in order of size of foreign-born population; numbers in thousands)

	Philippines		China		Korea		Vietnam		India	
	number	percent	number	percent	number	percent	number	percent	number	percent
Total foreign born	1,033	100.0%	565	100.0%	533	100.0%	496	100.0%	493	100.0%
Age										
Under age 5	4	0.4	4	0.7	7	1.3	7	1.4	4	0.8
Aged 5 to 15	72	7.0	19	3.4	65	12.2	65	13.1	29	5.9
Aged 16 or 17	15	1.5	5	0.9	21	3.9	22	4.4	11	2.2
Aged 18 to 24	87	8.4	37	6.5	52	9.8	105	21.2	40	8.1
Aged 25 to 29	107	10.4	39	6.9	48	9.0	40	8.1	79	16.0
Aged 30 to 34	107	10.4	65	11.5	60	11.3	43	8.7	80	16.2
Aged 35 to 44	257	24.9	126	22.3	105	19.7	92	18.5	105	21.3
Aged 45 to 64	280	27.1	166	29.4	126	23.6	96	19.4	123	24.9
Aged 65 or older	105	10.2	104	18.4	49	9.2	27	5.4	25	5.1
Sex										
Male	468	45.3	284	50.3	230	43.2	237	47.8	285	57.8
Female	565	54.7	282	49.9	303	56.8	259	52.2	209	42.4
Education, aged 25 or older										
Not high school grad.	111	13.0	138	27.6	54	13.9	117	39.4	40	9.8
High school grad. or some college	352	41.1	149	29.8	194	50.0	136	45.8	101	24.6
Bachelor's degree	339	39.6	121	24.2	98	25.3	37	12.5	137	33.4
Graduate degree	54	6.3	92	18.4	42	10.8	7	2.4	132	32.2
Region										
Northeast	121	11.7	182	32.2	99	18.6	51	10.3	207	42.0
Midwest	73	7.1	61	10.8	47	8.8	36	7.3	64	13.0
South	103	10.0	72	12.7	108	20.3	116	23.4	92	18.7
West	736	71.2	252	44.6	279	52.3	293	59.1	131	26.6
Metropolitan status										
Metropolitan, total	1,007	97.5	545	96.5	520	97.6	482	97.2	465	94.3
Central city	452	43.8	313	55.4	215	40.3	198	39.9	159	32.3
Suburbs*	555	53.7	232	41.1	305	57.2	284	57.3	306	62.1
Nonmetropolitan	26	2.5	20	3.5	14	2.6	14	2.8	28	5.7

* The suburbs are the portion of a metropolitan area that is outside the central city.
Source: Bureau of the Census, Internet web site, http://www.census.gov

Asians by Region, Division, and Ethnicity, 1990

(number and percent distribution of Asians, and Asian share of the total population, by region, division, and ethnicity, 1990; numbers in thousands)

	total	Chinese	Filipino	Japanese	Asian Indian	Korean	Vietnamese
Number							
UNITED STATES	7,274	1,645	1,407	848	815	799	615
Northeast	1,335	445	143	74	285	182	61
New England	232	72	15	15	36	21	22
Middle Atlantic	1,104	373	128	59	249	161	39
Midwest	768	133	113	63	146	109	52
East North Central	573	103	97	50	123	80	26
West North Central	195	30	17	13	23	29	26
South	1,122	204	159	67	196	153	169
South Atlantic	631	114	108	39	114	101	62
East South Central	84	15	9	9	15	12	10
West South Central	407	76	43	20	67	40	97
West	4,048	863	991	643	189	355	334
Mountain	217	40	32	34	15	28	20
Pacific	3,831	823	960	609	173	327	314
Percent distribution							
UNITED STATES	100.0%	100.0%	100.0%	100.0%	100.0%	100.0%	100.0%
Northeast	18.4	27.1	10.2	8.7	35.0	22.8	9.9
New England	3.2	4.4	1.1	1.8	4.4	2.6	3.6
Middle Atlantic	15.2	22.7	9.1	7.0	30.6	20.2	6.3
Midwest	10.6	8.1	8.0	7.4	17.9	13.6	8.5
East North Central	7.9	6.3	6.9	5.9	15.1	10.0	4.2
West North Central	2.7	1.8	1.2	1.5	2.8	3.6	4.2
South	15.4	12.4	11.3	7.9	24.0	19.1	27.5
South Atlantic	8.7	6.9	7.7	4.6	14.0	12.6	10.1
East South Central	1.2	0.9	0.6	1.1	1.8	1.5	1.6
West South Central	5.6	4.6	3.1	2.4	8.2	5.0	15.8
West	55.7	52.5	70.4	75.8	23.2	44.4	54.3
Mountain	3.0	2.4	2.3	4.0	1.8	3.5	3.3
Pacific	52.7	50.0	68.2	71.8	21.2	40.9	51.1

(continued)

(continued from previous page)

Percent share	total	Chinese	Filipino	Japanese	Asian Indian	Korean	Vietnamese
UNITED STATES	2.9%	0.7%	0.6%	0.3%	0.3%	0.3%	0.2%
Northeast	2.6	0.9	0.3	0.1	0.6	0.4	0.1
New England	1.8	0.5	0.1	0.1	0.3	0.2	0.2
Middle Atlantic	2.9	1.0	0.3	0.2	0.7	0.4	0.1
Midwest	1.3	0.2	0.2	0.1	0.2	0.2	0.1
East North Central	1.4	0.2	0.2	0.1	0.3	0.2	0.1
West North Central	1.1	0.2	0.1	0.1	0.1	0.2	0.1
South	1.3	0.2	0.2	0.1	0.2	0.2	0.2
South Atlantic	1.4	0.3	0.2	0.1	0.3	0.2	0.1
East South Central	0.6	0.1	0.1	0.1	0.1	0.1	0.1
West South Central	1.5	0.3	0.2	0.1	0.3	0.1	0.4
West	7.7	1.6	1.9	1.2	0.4	0.7	0.6
Mountain	1.6	0.3	0.2	0.2	0.1	0.2	0.1
Pacific	9.8	2.1	2.5	1.6	0.4	0.8	0.8

Note: The 1990 figures are for April 1, 1990.
Source: Bureau of the Census, General Population Characteristics, *1990 Census of Population, CP-1-1, 1992*

Asians by Region and Division, 1990 to 2020

(number and percent distribution of Asians and Asian share of the total population by region and division, selected years 1990-2020; percent change in number and percentage point change in distribution and share, 1990-2000 and 2000-2010; numbers in thousands)

Number	1990	1995	2000	2010	2020	percent change 1990-2000	2000-2010
UNITED STATES	7,458	9,756	12,125	17,191	22,658	62.6%	41.8%
Northeast	1,362	1,678	1,991	2,668	3,372	46.2	34.0
New England	236	291	349	506	681	47.9	45.0
Middle Atlantic	1,126	1,387	1,642	2,162	2,691	45.8	31.7
Midwest	781	1,057	1,345	1,902	2,474	72.2	41.4
East North Central	583	777	977	1,355	1,737	67.6	38.7
West North Central	198	280	368	547	736	85.9	48.6
South	1,145	1,621	2,095	3,025	3,964	83.0	44.4
South Atlantic	640	909	1,174	1,692	2,212	83.4	44.1
East South Central	85	120	155	219	287	82.4	41.3
West South Central	420	593	766	1,114	1,465	82.4	45.4
West	4,170	5,400	6,694	9,595	12,844	60.5	43.3
Mountain	225	355	490	748	1,019	117.8	52.7
Pacific	3,945	5,045	6,203	8,846	11,825	57.2	42.6

Percent distribution	1990	1995	2000	2010	2020	percentage point change 1990-2000	2000-2010
UNITED STATES	100.0%	100.0%	100.0%	100.0%	100.0%	-	-
Northeast	18.3	17.2	16.4	15.5	14.9	-1.9	-0.9
New England	3.2	3.0	2.9	2.9	3.0	-0.3	0.0
Middle Atlantic	15.1	14.2	13.5	12.6	11.9	-1.6	-0.9
Midwest	10.5	10.8	11.1	11.1	10.9	0.6	0.0
East North Central	7.8	8.0	8.1	7.9	7.7	0.3	-0.2
West North Central	2.7	2.9	3.0	3.2	3.2	0.3	0.2
South	15.4	16.6	17.3	17.6	17.5	1.9	0.3
South Atlantic	8.6	9.3	9.7	9.8	9.8	1.1	0.1
East South Central	1.1	1.2	1.3	1.3	1.3	0.2	0.0
West South Central	5.6	6.1	6.3	6.5	6.5	0.7	0.2
West	55.9	55.4	55.2	55.8	56.7	-0.7	0.6
Mountain	3.0	3.6	4.0	4.4	4.5	1.0	0.4
Pacific	52.9	51.7	51.2	51.5	52.2	-1.7	0.3

(continued)

(continued from previous page)

Percent share	1990	1995	2000	2010	2020	percentage point change 1990-2000	2000-2010
UNITED STATES	3.0%	3.7%	4.4%	5.7%	7.0%	1.4	1.3
Northeast	2.7	3.3	3.8	5.0	6.1	1.1	1.2
New England	1.8	2.2	2.6	3.7	4.7	0.8	1.1
Middle Atlantic	3.0	3.6	4.2	5.5	6.6	1.2	1.3
Midwest	1.3	1.7	2.1	2.9	3.6	0.8	0.8
East North Central	1.4	1.8	2.2	2.9	3.6	0.8	0.7
West North Central	1.1	1.5	1.9	2.7	3.5	0.8	0.8
South	1.3	1.8	2.2	2.8	3.4	0.9	0.6
South Atlantic	1.5	1.9	2.3	3.1	3.6	0.8	0.8
East South Central	0.6	0.7	0.9	1.2	1.5	0.3	0.3
West South Central	1.6	2.1	2.5	3.3	3.9	0.9	0.8
West	7.9	9.3	10.6	13.1	15.3	2.7	2.5
Mountain	1.6	2.3	2.9	3.9	4.8	1.3	1.0
Pacific	10.1	11.8	13.4	16.3	18.8	3.3	2.9

Note: The 1990 figures are for April 1, 1990 and have been modified to correct for Asians who reported "other" race. Projections of total Asians for 2000, 2010, and 2020 are different from those at the beginning of the population section because they are from an earlier report for states and regions.
Source: Bureau of the Census, Population Projections for States, by Age, Sex, Race, and Hispanic Origin: 1993 to 2020, Current Population Reports, P25-1111, 1994

Asians by State and Ethnicity, 1990

(number of Asians by state and ethnicity, 1990; numbers in thousands)

	total	Chinese	Filipino	Japanese	Asian Indian	Korean	Vietnamese
United States	7,274	1,645	1,407	848	815	799	615
Alabama	22	4	2	2	4	3	2
Alaska	20	1	8	2	-	4	1
Arizona	55	14	8	6	6	6	5
Arkansas	13	2	2	1	1	1	2
California	2,846	705	732	313	160	260	280
Colorado	60	9	5	11	4	11	7
Connecticut	51	11	5	4	12	5	4
Delaware	9	2	1	1	2	1	-
District of Columbia	11	3	2	1	2	1	1
Florida	154	31	32	9	31	12	16
Georgia	76	13	6	6	14	15	8
Hawaii	685	69	169	247	1	24	5
Idaho	9	1	1	3	-	1	1
Illinois	285	50	64	22	64	42	10
Indiana	38	7	5	5	7	5	2
Iowa	25	4	2	2	3	5	3
Kansas	32	5	3	2	4	4	7
Kentucky	18	3	2	3	3	3	2
Louisiana	41	5	4	2	5	3	18
Maine	7	1	1	1	1	1	1
Maryland	140	31	19	7	28	30	9
Massachusetts	143	54	6	9	20	12	15
Michigan	105	19	14	11	24	16	6
Minnesota	78	9	4	4	8	12	9
Mississippi	13	3	2	1	2	1	4
Missouri	41	9	6	3	6	6	4
Montana	4	1	1	1	-	1	-
Nebraska	12	2	1	2	1	2	2
Nevada	38	7	12	4	2	4	2
New Hampshire	9	2	1	1	2	2	1
New Jersey	273	59	53	17	79	39	7
New Mexico	14	3	2	2	2	1	1
New York	694	284	62	35	141	96	16
North Carolina	52	9	5	5	10	7	5

(continued)

(continued from previous page)

	total	Chinese	Filipino	Japanese	Asian Indian	Korean	Vietnamese
North Dakota	3	1	1	-	-	1	-
Ohio	91	19	10	10	21	11	5
Oklahoma	34	5	3	2	5	5	7
Oregon	69	14	7	12	4	9	9
Pennsylvania	137	30	12	7	28	27	16
Rhode Island	18	3	2	1	2	1	1
South Carolina	22	3	6	2	4	3	2
South Dakota	3	-	1	-	-	1	-
Tennessee	32	6	3	3	6	5	2
Texas	319	63	34	15	56	32	70
Utah	33	5	2	7	2	3	3
Vermont	3	1	-	-	1	1	-
Virginia	159	21	35	8	20	30	21
Washington	211	34	44	34	8	30	19
West Virginia	7	1	2	1	2	1	-
Wisconsin	54	7	4	3	7	6	2
Wyoming	3	1	-	1	-	-	-

Note: Numbers may not add to total because not all Asian ethnicities are shown. The 1990 figures are for April 1, 1990.
Source: U.S. Bureau of the Census, Internet web site, http://www.census.gov

Distribution of Asians by State and Ethnicity, 1990

(percent distribution of Asians by state and ethnicity, 1990)

	total	Chinese	Filipino	Japanese	Asian Indian	Korean	Vietnamese
United States	100.0%	100.0%	100.0%	100.0%	100.0%	100.0%	100.0%
Alabama	0.3	0.2	0.1	0.2	0.5	0.4	0.4
Alaska	0.3	0.1	0.6	0.2	0.1	0.5	0.1
Arizona	0.8	0.9	0.6	0.7	0.7	0.7	0.9
Arkansas	0.2	0.1	0.1	0.1	0.2	0.1	0.4
California	39.1	42.8	52.0	36.9	19.6	32.5	45.6
Colorado	0.8	0.5	0.4	1.3	0.5	1.4	1.2
Connecticut	0.7	0.7	0.4	0.4	1.4	0.6	0.7
Delaware	0.1	0.1	0.1	0.1	0.3	0.2	0.1
District of Columbia	0.2	0.2	0.1	0.1	0.2	0.1	0.1
Florida	2.1	1.9	2.3	1.0	3.9	1.6	2.7
Georgia	1.0	0.8	0.4	0.8	1.7	1.9	1.3
Hawaii	9.4	4.2	12.0	29.2	0.1	3.1	0.9
Idaho	0.1	0.1	0.1	0.3	0.1	0.1	0.1
Illinois	3.9	3.0	4.6	2.6	7.9	5.2	1.7
Indiana	0.5	0.4	0.3	0.6	0.9	0.7	0.4
Iowa	0.4	0.3	0.1	0.2	0.4	0.6	0.5
Kansas	0.4	0.3	0.2	0.2	0.5	0.5	1.1
Kentucky	0.2	0.2	0.2	0.3	0.4	0.4	0.2
Louisiana	0.6	0.3	0.3	0.2	0.6	0.3	2.9
Maine	0.1	0.1	0.1	0.1	0.1	0.1	0.1
Maryland	1.9	1.9	1.4	0.8	3.5	3.8	1.4
Massachusetts	2.0	3.3	0.4	1.0	2.4	1.5	2.5
Michigan	1.4	1.2	1.0	1.3	2.9	2.0	1.0
Minnesota	1.1	0.5	0.3	0.4	1.0	1.4	1.5
Mississippi	0.2	0.2	0.1	0.1	0.2	0.1	0.6
Missouri	0.6	0.5	0.4	0.4	0.7	0.7	0.7
Montana	0.1	0.0	0.1	0.1	0.0	0.1	0.0
Nebraska	0.2	0.1	0.1	0.2	0.1	0.2	0.3
Nevada	0.5	0.4	0.9	0.5	0.2	0.5	0.3
New Hampshire	0.1	0.1	0.1	0.1	0.2	0.2	0.1
New Jersey	3.7	3.6	3.8	2.0	9.7	4.8	1.2
New Mexico	0.2	0.2	0.1	0.2	0.2	0.2	0.2
New York	9.5	17.3	4.4	4.2	17.3	12.0	2.5
North Carolina	0.7	0.5	0.4	0.6	1.2	0.9	0.8

(continued)

(continued from previous page)

	total	Chinese	Filipino	Japanese	Asian Indian	Korean	Vietnamese
North Dakota	0.0%	0.0%	0.1%	0.0%	0.1%	0.1%	0.0%
Ohio	1.3	1.2	0.7	1.2	2.6	1.4	0.8
Oklahoma	0.5	0.3	0.2	0.3	0.6	0.6	1.2
Oregon	1.0	0.8	0.5	1.4	0.4	1.1	1.5
Pennsylvania	1.9	1.8	0.9	0.8	3.5	3.4	2.6
Rhode Island	0.3	0.2	0.1	0.1	0.2	0.2	0.1
South Carolina	0.3	0.2	0.4	0.2	0.5	0.3	0.3
South Dakota	0.0	0.0	0.0	0.0	0.0	0.1	0.0
Tennessee	0.4	0.3	0.2	0.4	0.7	0.6	0.3
Texas	4.4	3.8	2.4	1.7	6.8	4.0	11.3
Utah	0.5	0.3	0.1	0.8	0.2	0.3	0.5
Vermont	0.0	0.0	0.0	0.0	0.1	0.1	0.0
Virginia	2.2	1.3	2.5	0.9	2.5	3.8	3.4
Washington	2.9	2.1	3.1	4.1	1.0	3.7	3.0
West Virginia	0.1	0.1	0.1	0.1	0.2	0.1	0.0
Wisconsin	0.7	0.4	0.3	0.3	0.8	0.7	0.4
Wyoming	0.0	0.0	0.0	0.1	0.0	0.1	0.0

Source: U.S. Bureau of the Census, Internet web site, http://www.census.gov

Asian Share of the Total Population by State and Ethnicity, 1990

(Asians as a percent of state populations by ethnicity, 1990)

	total	Chinese	Filipino	Japanese	Asian Indian	Korean	Vietnamese
United States	2.9%	0.7%	0.6%	0.3%	0.3%	0.3%	0.2%
Alabama	0.5	0.1	0.0	0.1	0.1	0.1	0.1
Alaska	3.6	0.2	1.5	0.4	0.1	0.8	0.1
Arizona	1.5	0.4	0.2	0.2	0.2	0.2	0.1
Arkansas	0.5	0.1	0.1	0.0	0.1	0.0	0.1
California	9.6	2.4	2.5	1.1	0.5	0.9	0.9
Colorado	1.8	0.3	0.2	0.3	0.1	0.3	0.2
Connecticut	1.5	0.3	0.2	0.1	0.4	0.2	0.1
Delaware	1.4	0.3	0.2	0.1	0.3	0.2	0.1
District of Columbia	1.8	0.5	0.3	0.2	0.3	0.1	0.1
Florida	1.2	0.2	0.2	0.1	0.2	0.1	0.1
Georgia	1.2	0.2	0.1	0.1	0.2	0.2	0.1
Hawaii	61.8	6.2	15.2	22.3	0.1	2.2	0.5
Idaho	0.9	0.1	0.1	0.3	0.0	0.1	0.1
Illinois	2.5	0.4	0.6	0.2	0.6	0.4	0.1
Indiana	0.7	0.1	0.1	0.1	0.1	0.1	0.0
Iowa	0.9	0.2	0.1	0.1	0.1	0.2	0.1
Kansas	1.3	0.2	0.1	0.1	0.2	0.2	0.3
Kentucky	0.5	0.1	0.1	0.1	0.1	0.1	0.0
Louisiana	1.0	0.1	0.1	0.0	0.1	0.1	0.4
Maine	0.5	0.1	0.1	0.0	0.0	0.1	0.1
Maryland	2.9	0.6	0.4	0.1	0.6	0.6	0.2
Massachusetts	2.4	0.9	0.1	0.1	0.3	0.2	0.3
Michigan	1.1	0.2	0.1	0.1	0.3	0.2	0.1
Minnesota	1.8	0.2	0.1	0.1	0.2	0.3	0.2
Mississippi	0.5	0.1	0.1	0.0	0.1	0.0	0.1
Missouri	0.8	0.2	0.1	0.1	0.1	0.1	0.1
Montana	0.5	0.1	0.1	0.1	0.0	0.1	0.0
Nebraska	0.8	0.1	0.1	0.1	0.1	0.1	0.1
Nevada	3.2	0.6	1.0	0.3	0.2	0.4	0.2
New Hampshire	0.8	0.2	0.1	0.1	0.2	0.1	0.0
New Jersey	3.5	0.8	0.7	0.2	1.0	0.5	0.1
New Mexico	0.9	0.2	0.1	0.1	0.1	0.1	0.1
New York	3.9	1.6	0.3	0.2	0.8	0.5	0.1
North Carolina	0.8	0.1	0.1	0.1	0.1	0.1	0.1

(continued)

(continued from previous page)

	total Asian	Chinese	Filipino	Japanese	Asian Indian	Korean	Vietnamese
North Dakota	0.5%	0.1%	0.1%	0.0%	0.1%	0.1%	0.0%
Ohio	0.8	0.2	0.1	0.1	0.2	0.1	0.0
Oklahoma	1.1	0.2	0.1	0.1	0.1	0.1	0.2
Oregon	2.4	0.5	0.3	0.4	0.1	0.3	0.3
Pennsylvania	1.2	0.2	0.1	0.1	0.2	0.2	0.1
Rhode Island	1.8	0.3	0.2	0.1	0.2	0.1	0.1
South Carolina	0.6	0.1	0.2	0.1	0.1	0.1	0.1
South Dakota	0.4	0.1	0.1	0.0	0.0	0.1	0.0
Tennessee	0.7	0.1	0.1	0.1	0.1	0.1	0.0
Texas	1.9	0.4	0.2	0.1	0.3	0.2	0.4
Utah	1.9	0.3	0.1	0.4	0.1	0.2	0.2
Vermont	0.6	0.1	0.0	0.1	0.1	0.1	0.0
Virginia	2.6	0.3	0.6	0.1	0.3	0.5	0.3
Washington	4.3	0.7	0.9	0.7	0.2	0.6	0.4
West Virginia	0.4	0.1	0.1	0.0	0.1	0.0	0.0
Wisconsin	1.1	0.2	0.1	0.1	0.1	0.1	0.1
Wyoming	0.6	0.1	0.1	0.1	0.1	0.1	0.0

Source: U.S. Bureau of the Census, Internet web site, http://www.census.gov

Asians by State, 1995 to 2020

(number of Asians by state, selected years 1995-2020; percent change 1995 to 2020; numbers in thousands)

	1995	2000	2010	2020	percent change 1995-2020
United States	9,756	12,125	17,191	22,653	132.2%
Alabama	33	44	65	86	160.6
Alaska	29	39	59	81	179.3
Arizona	91	127	204	287	215.4
Arkansas	20	27	41	56	180.0
California	3,908	4,906	7,169	9,685	147.8
Colorado	89	117	166	216	142.7
Connecticut	60	70	99	130	116.7
Delaware	14	18	28	37	164.3
District of Columbia	11	12	16	21	90.9
Florida	231	303	443	585	153.2
Georgia	109	140	199	257	135.8
Hawaii	679	681	746	875	28.9
Idaho	15	21	31	41	173.3
Illinois	383	476	648	819	113.8
Indiana	55	72	102	131	138.2
Iowa	33	41	53	67	103.0
Kansas	50	69	103	138	176.0
Kentucky	24	30	40	51	112.5
Louisiana	60	78	119	161	168.3
Maine	8	9	14	20	150.0
Maryland	196	249	361	474	141.8
Massachusetts	180	215	307	411	128.3
Michigan	140	176	253	334	138.6
Minnesota	113	151	232	320	183.2
Mississippi	17	22	31	41	141.2
Missouri	56	72	105	140	150.0
Montana	6	8	12	15	150.0
Nebraska	17	22	31	40	135.3
Nevada	70	99	148	197	181.4
New Hampshire	14	18	31	46	228.6
New Jersey	356	435	591	743	108.7
New Mexico	25	35	56	78	212.0
New York	846	977	1,257	1,546	82.7

(continued)

(continued from previous page)

	1995	2000	2010	2020	percent change 1995-2020
North Carolina	88	123	190	257	192.0%
North Dakota	5	7	11	16	220.0
Ohio	122	152	206	261	113.9
Oklahoma	52	71	115	161	209.6
Oregon	111	153	238	326	193.7
Pennsylvania	185	229	315	402	117.3
Rhode Island	25	31	46	62	148.0
South Carolina	31	39	56	73	135.5
South Dakota	5	7	11	15	200.0
Tennessee	46	59	83	109	137.0
Texas	461	590	839	1,086	135.6
Utah	54	77	122	171	216.7
Vermont	4	5	9	12	200.0
Virginia	220	275	378	481	118.6
Washington	318	424	635	859	170.1
West Virginia	11	14	20	27	145.5
Wisconsin	76	100	145	192	152.6
Wyoming	4	6	9	13	225.0

Note: Projections of total Asians for 2000, 2010, and 2020 are different from those at the beginning of the population section because they are from an earlier report for states and regions.
Source: Bureau of the Census, Population Projections for States, by Age, Sex, Race, and Hispanic Origin: 1993 to 2020, *Current Population Reports, P25-1111, 1994*

Distribution of Asians by State, 1995 to 2020

(percent distribution of Asians by state, selected years 1995-2020)

	1995	2000	2010	2020
United States	100.0%	100.0%	100.0%	100.0%
Alabama	0.3	0.4	0.4	0.4
Alaska	0.3	0.3	0.3	0.4
Arizona	0.9	1.0	1.2	1.3
Arkansas	0.2	0.2	0.2	0.2
California	40.1	40.5	41.7	42.8
Colorado	0.9	1.0	1.0	1.0
Connecticut	0.6	0.6	0.6	0.6
Delaware	0.1	0.1	0.2	0.2
District of Columbia	0.1	0.1	0.1	0.1
Florida	2.4	2.5	2.6	2.6
Georgia	1.1	1.2	1.2	1.1
Hawaii	7.0	5.6	4.3	3.9
Idaho	0.2	0.2	0.2	0.2
Illinois	3.9	3.9	3.8	3.6
Indiana	0.6	0.6	0.6	0.6
Iowa	0.3	0.3	0.3	0.3
Kansas	0.5	0.6	0.6	0.6
Kentucky	0.2	0.2	0.2	0.2
Louisiana	0.6	0.6	0.7	0.7
Maine	0.1	0.1	0.1	0.1
Maryland	2.0	2.1	2.1	2.1
Massachusetts	1.8	1.8	1.8	1.8
Michigan	1.4	1.5	1.5	1.5
Minnesota	1.2	1.2	1.3	1.4
Mississippi	0.2	0.2	0.2	0.2
Missouri	0.6	0.6	0.6	0.6
Montana	0.1	0.1	0.1	0.1
Nebraska	0.2	0.2	0.2	0.2
Nevada	0.7	0.8	0.9	0.9
New Hampshire	0.1	0.1	0.2	0.2
New Jersey	3.6	3.6	3.4	3.3
New Mexico	0.3	0.3	0.3	0.3
New York	8.7	8.1	7.3	6.8
North Carolina	0.9	1.0	1.1	1.1

(continued)

(continued from previous page)

	1995	2000	2010	2020
North Dakota	0.1%	0.1%	0.1%	0.1%
Ohio	1.3	1.3	1.2	1.2
Oklahoma	0.5	0.6	0.7	0.7
Oregon	1.1	1.3	1.4	1.4
Pennsylvania	1.9	1.9	1.8	1.8
Rhode Island	0.3	0.3	0.3	0.3
South Carolina	0.3	0.3	0.3	0.3
South Dakota	0.1	0.1	0.1	0.1
Tennessee	0.5	0.5	0.5	0.5
Texas	4.7	4.9	4.9	4.8
Utah	0.6	0.6	0.7	0.8
Vermont	0.0	0.0	0.1	0.1
Virginia	2.3	2.3	2.2	2.1
Washington	3.3	3.5	3.7	3.8
West Virginia	0.1	0.1	0.1	0.1
Wisconsin	0.8	0.8	0.8	0.8
Wyoming	0.0	0.0	0.1	0.1

Source: Bureau of the Census, Population Projections for States, by Age, Sex, Race, and Hispanic Origin: 1993 to 2020, *Current Population Reports, P25-1111, 1994*

Asian Share of State Populations, 1995 to 2020

(Asians as a percent of state populations, selected years 1995-2020; percentage point change in share, 1995-2020)

	1995	2000	2010	2020	percentage point change 1995-2020
United States	3.7%	4.4%	5.7%	7.0%	3.3
Alabama	0.8	1.0	1.3	1.6	0.8
Alaska	4.6	5.6	7.6	9.4	4.8
Arizona	2.2	2.9	4.0	5.0	2.8
Arkansas	0.8	1.0	1.5	1.9	1.1
California	12.1	14.1	17.4	20.2	8.1
Colorado	2.4	2.9	3.7	4.4	2.0
Connecticut	1.8	2.1	2.9	3.6	1.8
Delaware	1.9	2.4	3.4	4.2	2.3
District of Columbia	2.0	2.2	2.8	3.3	1.3
Florida	1.6	2.0	2.6	3.0	1.4
Georgia	1.5	1.8	2.3	2.7	1.2
Hawaii	55.6	51.3	48.1	48.2	-7.4
Idaho	1.3	1.6	2.1	2.6	1.3
Illinois	3.2	3.9	5.1	6.2	3.0
Indiana	0.9	1.2	1.6	2.0	1.1
Iowa	1.2	1.4	1.8	2.2	1.1
Kansas	1.9	2.5	3.5	4.4	2.5
Kentucky	0.6	0.8	1.0	1.2	0.6
Louisiana	1.4	1.7	2.5	3.1	1.7
Maine	0.6	0.7	1.1	1.4	0.8
Maryland	3.9	4.7	6.2	7.5	3.6
Massachusetts	3.0	3.6	5.0	6.5	3.5
Michigan	1.5	1.8	2.5	3.2	1.7
Minnesota	2.4	3.1	4.5	5.9	3.5
Mississippi	0.6	0.8	1.1	1.3	0.7
Missouri	1.1	1.3	1.8	2.3	1.2
Montana	0.7	0.9	1.2	1.4	0.7
Nebraska	1.0	1.3	1.7	2.1	1.1
Nevada	4.7	5.9	7.6	9.2	4.5
New Hampshire	1.2	1.5	2.4	3.3	2.1
New Jersey	4.5	5.3	6.9	8.2	3.7
New Mexico	1.5	1.9	2.7	3.3	1.8
New York	4.7	5.4	6.8	8.1	3.4
North Carolina	1.2	1.6	2.3	2.9	1.6

(continued)

(continued from previous page)

	1995	2000	2010	2020	percentage point change 1995-2020
North Dakota	0.8%	1.1%	1.6%	2.2%	1.7
Ohio	1.1	1.3	1.8	2.2	1.1
Oklahoma	1.6	2.1	3.1	4.0	2.4
Oregon	3.5	4.5	6.1	7.5	4.0
Pennsylvania	1.5	1.9	2.5	3.2	1.7
Rhode Island	2.5	3.1	4.4	5.7	3.2
South Carolina	0.8	1.0	1.3	1.6	0.8
South Dakota	0.7	0.9	1.3	1.7	1.0
Tennessee	0.9	1.1	1.4	1.7	0.8
Texas	2.5	2.9	3.7	4.2	1.7
Utah	2.8	3.6	5.0	6.2	3.3
Vermont	0.7	0.8	1.4	1.8	1.1
Virginia	3.3	3.9	4.9	5.7	2.4
Washington	5.8	7.0	9.0	10.8	5.0
West Virginia	0.6	0.8	1.1	1.5	0.9
Wisconsin	1.5	1.9	2.6	3.3	1.8
Wyoming	0.8	1.1	1.5	2.0	1.2

Source: Bureau of the Census, Population Projections for States, by Age, Sex, Race, and Hispanic Origin: 1993 to 2020, *Current Population Reports, P25-1111, 1994*

Metropolitan Areas With the Most Asians, 1990

(metropolitan areas with at least 100,000 Asians ranked by size of Asian population; number of Asians and Asian share of total metropolitan population, 1990; numbers in thousands)

		number	percent
1.	Los Angeles-Riverside-Orange County, CA	1,339	9.2%
2.	San Francisco-Oakland-San Jose, CA	927	14.8
3.	New York-Northern New Jersey-Long Island, NY-NJ-CT-PA	898	4.6
4.	Honolulu, HI	526	63.0
5.	Chicago-Gary-Kenosha, IL-IN-WI	258	3.1
6.	Washington-Baltimore, DC-MD-VA-WV	248	3.7
7.	San Diego, CA	198	7.9
8.	Seattle-Tacoma-Bremerton, WA	181	6.1
9.	Boston-Brockton-Nashua, MA-NH-ME-CT	137	2.5
10.	Houston-Galveston-Brazoria, TX	132	3.5
11.	Philadelphia-Wilmington-Atlantic City, PA-NJ-DE-MD	119	2.0
12.	Sacramento-Yolo, CA	115	7.7

Source: Bureau of the Census, Statistical Abstract of the United States 1993

Asian Births by Age of Mother, 1993

(number and percent distribution of births to Asian women, by age of mother, 1993)

	number	percent
Total births	152,800	100.0%
Under age 15	225	0.1
Aged 15 to 19	8,409	5.5
Aged 20 to 24	27,216	17.8
Aged 25 to 29	47,052	30.8
Aged 30 to 34	44,829	29.3
Aged 35 to 39	20,603	13.5
Aged 40 or older	4,466	2.9

Source: National Center for Health Statistics, Advance Report of Final Natality Statistics, 1993, Vol. 44, No. 3 Supplement, 1995

Births to Asian Teenagers and Unmarried Women by Ethnicity, 1993

(percent of births to Asian women under age 20, and percent to unmarried Asian women, by ethnicity; 1993)

	percent of births to women	
	under age 20	unmarried
Total Asian births	5.7%	15.7%
Chinese	1.0	6.7
Filipino	5.8	17.7
Japanese	2.7	10.0
Hawaiian	18.5	47.8
Other	6.5	16.1

Source: National Center for Health Statistics, Advance Report of Final Natality Statistics, 1993, Vol. 44, No. 3 Supplement, 1995

Asian Births by Age and Ethnicity of Mother, 1992

(number and percent distribution of births to Asian women by age and ethnicity of mother, 1992)

	total*	Chinese	Filipino	Japanese	Korean	Asian Indian	Vietnamese
Total, number	108,295	19,497	24,482	7,383	8,772	9,173	10,870
Under age 15	162	-	17	1	-	3	6
Aged 15 to 19	5,781	144	1,353	194	110	135	639
Aged 20 to 24	18,841	1,426	4,474	581	883	1,599	2,582
Aged 25 to 29	33,309	6,122	6,959	1,819	3,499	3,821	3,060
Aged 30 to 34	32,002	7,648	6,816	2,964	3,222	2,648	2,646
Aged 35 to 39	15,098	3,561	4,046	1,555	933	849	1,500
Aged 40 or older	3,102	596	817	269	125	118	437
Total, percent	100.0%	18.0%	22.6%	6.8%	8.1%	8.5%	10.0%
Under age 15	100.0	0.0	10.5	0.6	0.0	1.9	3.7
Aged 15 to 19	100.0	2.5	23.4	3.4	1.9	2.3	11.1
Aged 20 to 24	100.0	7.6	23.7	3.1	4.7	8.5	13.7
Aged 25 to 29	100.0	18.4	20.9	5.5	10.5	11.5	9.2
Aged 30 to 34	100.0	23.9	21.3	9.3	10.1	8.3	8.3
Aged 35 to 39	100.0	23.6	26.8	10.3	6.2	5.6	9.9
Aged 40 or older	100.0	19.2	26.3	8.7	4.0	3.8	14.1

* Asian births by ethnicity are for seven reporting states only, accounting for 72 percent of all Asian and Pacific Islander births. The seven states are California, Hawaii, Illinois, New Jersey, New York, Texas, and Washington.
Note: Numbers will not add to total because not all Asian ethnicities are shown. (-) means number in sample is too small to make a reliable estimate.
Source: National Center for Health Statistics, Birth Characteristics for Asian or Pacific Islander Subgroups, 1992, Vol. 43, No. 10 Supplement, 1995

Asian Births by State, 1993

(number and percent distribution of Asian births by state, and Asian births as a percent of total births by state, 1993)

	number	percent	Asian share of total births
United States	152,800	100.0%	3.8%
Alabama	493	0.3	0.8
Alaska	520	0.3	4.7
Arizona	1,168	0.8	1.7
Arkansas	258	0.2	0.8
California	58,543	38.3	10.0
Colorado	1,294	0.8	2.4
Connecticut	1,095	0.7	2.3
Delaware	193	0.1	1.8
District of Columbia	524	0.3	4.9
Florida	3,126	2.0	1.6
Georgia	1,879	1.2	1.7
Hawaii	13,186	8.6	67.3
Idaho	217	0.1	1.2
Illinois	5,482	3.6	2.9
Indiana	772	0.5	0.9
Iowa	587	0.4	1.6
Kansas	780	0.5	2.1
Kentucky	431	0.3	0.8
Louisiana	919	0.6	1.3
Maine	138	0.1	0.9
Maryland	3,297	2.2	4.4
Massachusetts	3,356	2.2	4.0
Michigan	1,599	1.0	1.1
Minnesota	2,379	1.6	3.7
Mississippi	287	0.2	0.7
Missouri	972	0.6	1.3
Montana	85	0.1	0.7
Nebraska	360	0.2	1.6
Nevada	964	0.6	4.3
New Hampshire	153	0.1	1.0
New Jersey	5,321	3.5	4.5
New Mexico	337	0.2	1.2
New York	13,277	8.7	4.7
North Carolina	1,406	0.9	1.4

(continued)

(continued from previous page)

	number	percent	Asian share of total births
North Dakota	96	0.1%	1.1%
Ohio	1,680	1.1	1.1
Oklahoma	734	0.5	1.6
Oregon	1,406	0.9	3.4
Pennsylvania	3,109	2.0	1.9
Rhode Island	489	0.3	3.5
South Carolina	520	0.3	1.0
South Dakota	94	0.1	0.9
Tennessee	704	0.5	1.0
Texas	7,466	4.9	2.3
Utah	975	0.6	2.6
Vermont	71	0.0	1.0
Virginia	3,131	2.0	3.3
Washington	4,882	3.2	6.2
West Virginia	125	0.1	0.6
Wisconsin	1,853	1.2	2.7
Wyoming	67	0.0	1.0

Source: National Center for Health Statistics, Advance Report of Final Natality Statistics, 1993, *Vol. 44, No. 3 Supplement, 1995*

Asian Births by State and Ethnicity, 1992

(number and percent distribution of Asian births by state and ethnicity of mother, for seven reporting states; 1992)

	total	Chinese	Filipino	Japanese	Korean	Asian Indian	Vietnamese
Number, 7 reporting states	108,295	19,497	24,482	7,383	8,772	9,173	10,870
California	59,519	11,673	15,669	3,497	4,449	3,375	7,410
Hawaii	13,258	737	3,700	2,421	422	10	179
Illinois	5,367	654	955	260	527	1,255	252
New Jersey	5,384	889	1,068	269	576	1,442	181
New York	13,252	4,087	1,376	487	1,512	2,075	370
Texas	6,953	1,032	801	175	748	866	1,817
Washington	4,562	425	913	274	538	150	661
Percent, 7 reporting states	100.0%	18.0%	22.6%	6.8%	8.1%	8.5%	10.0%
California	100.0	19.6	26.3	5.9	7.5	5.7	12.4
Hawaii	100.0	5.6	27.9	18.3	3.2	0.1	1.4
Illinois	100.0	12.2	17.8	4.8	9.8	23.4	4.7
New Jersey	100.0	16.5	19.8	5.0	10.7	26.8	3.4
New York	100.0	30.8	10.4	3.7	11.4	15.7	2.8
Texas	100.0	14.8	11.5	2.5	10.8	12.5	26.1
Washington	100.0	9.3	20.0	6.0	11.8	3.3	14.5

Note: Number of births by ethnic group will not add to total because not all ethnicities are shown.
Source: National Center for Health Statistics, Birth Characteristics for Asian or Pacific Islander Subgroups, 1992, Vol. 43, No. 10 Supplement, 1995

Projections of Asian Births, 1995 to 2020

(number of Asian births, and Asian births as a percent of total births, 1995-2020; numbers in thousands)

	number	Asian share of total births
1995	162	4.1%
1996	167	4.3
1997	172	4.4
1998	176	4.5
1999	181	4.6
2000	186	4.8
2001	191	4.9
2002	196	5.0
2003	202	5.1
2004	207	5.2
2005	212	5.3
2006	218	5.4
2007	224	5.5
2008	230	5.6
2009	236	5.6
2010	243	5.7
2011	249	5.8
2012	256	5.9
2013	262	6.0
2014	269	6.1
2015	275	6.2
2016	282	6.3
2017	288	6.4
2018	295	6.5
2019	302	6.6
2020	308	6.7

Source: Bureau of the Census, Population Projections of the United States, by Age, Sex, Race, and Hispanic Origin: 1995 to 2050, *Current Population Reports, P25-1130, 1996*

2

Blacks

■ The black population is projected to grow from 34 million in 1996 to more than 45 million by 2020. Blacks will remain the largest minority in the U.S. until 2009, when Hispanics begin to outnumber them.

■ Seventy percent of blacks were high school graduates in 1993. While this is less than among the total population, blacks are rapidly gaining on whites in educational attainment.

■ A 56 percent majority of blacks say they are in excellent or very good health. Only 15 percent say they are in fair or poor health.

■ Just 17 percent of black households are married couples with children. Fifty-nine percent of black children live with their mother only.

■ Few blacks think their neighborhood has a crime problem—only 11 percent of homeowners and 18 percent of renters say crime is a problem in their area.

■ Black household income was just 65 percent of the median for all households in 1994. The lower median household income of blacks is due to the fact that only 33 percent of black households are married couples—typically the most affluent household type.

■ Blacks spend more than the average household on many items, including fish and seafood, fresh fruit juices, and telephone services.

Blacks:
Education

Seventy percent of blacks were high school graduates in 1993. While this proportion is about 10 percentage points lower than the share of the total population with a high school diploma, blacks are rapidly gaining on whites.

Over the past few decades, blacks have made great strides in educational attainment. As recently as 1980, barely half of blacks had graduated from high school. The surge in educational attainment is due to the much greater educational level of younger blacks. Among blacks in their 20s and 30s, 83 percent are high school graduates.

Twelve percent of blacks had a bachelor's degree in 1993, compared with 22 percent of the total population. Among black families with children aged 18 to 24, 28 percent have a child in college full-time. This proportion rises to 56 percent among black families with incomes of $75,000 or more. Over 1.5 million blacks were in college in 1993, 43 percent of them full-time students at four-year schools.

Blacks earned 7 percent of bachelor's degrees, 5 percent of master's degrees, and 3 percent of doctorates awarded in 1992-93. Blacks earned 8 percent of first-professional degrees awarded in theology and 9 percent of those awarded in podiatry in 1992-93.

Black High School and College Graduates, 1980 to 1993

(percent of blacks aged 25 or older who are high school or college graduates, by sex, 1980-93)

	total	men	women
High school graduates			
1993	70.4%	69.6%	71.1%
1990	66.2	65.8	66.5
1985	59.8	58.4	60.8
1980	51.2	51.1	51.3
College graduates			
1993	12.2	11.9	12.4
1990	11.3	11.9	10.8
1985	11.1	11.2	11.0
1980	7.9	7.7	8.1

Source: Bureau of the Census, Educational Attainment in the United States: March 1993 and 1992, *Current Population Reports, P20-476, 1994*

Educational Attainment of Blacks by Sex, 1993

(number and percent distribution of blacks aged 25 or older, by educational attainment and sex, 1993; numbers in thousands)

	total		men		women	
	number	percent	number	percent	number	percent
Total, aged 25 or older	17,786	100.0%	7,953	100.0%	9,833	100.0%
Not a high school graduate	5,261	29.6	2,418	30.4	2,843	28.9
High school graduate or more	12,526	70.4	5,535	69.6	6,990	71.1
Some college or associate's degree	3,910	22.0	1,650	20.7	2,259	23.0
Bachelor's degree or more	2,165	12.2	948	11.9	1,215	12.4

Source: Bureau of the Census, Educational Attainment in the United States: March 1993 and 1992, *Current Population Reports, P20-476, 1994*

Educational Attainment of Blacks by Age and Sex, 1993

(percent of blacks aged 25 or older who are high school or college graduates, by age and sex, 1993)

	total	men	women
HIGH SCHOOL GRADUATES			
Total, aged 25 or older	70.4%	69.6%	71.1%
Aged 25 to 29	82.8	85.0	80.9
Aged 30 to 34	83.6	84.1	83.1
Aged 35 to 39	83.0	80.4	85.3
Aged 40 to 44	82.1	82.2	82.0
Aged 45 to 49	74.8	69.9	78.8
Aged 50 to 54	68.1	64.9	70.7
Aged 55 to 59	63.4	59.2	66.8
Aged 60 to 64	49.6	47.8	51.1
Aged 65 to 69	40.0	31.6	46.0
Aged 70 to 74	36.9	32.7	40.4
Aged 75 or older	23.2	23.6	22.9
COLLEGE GRADUATES			
Total, aged 25 or older	12.2	11.9	12.4
Aged 25 to 29	13.2	12.6	13.8
Aged 30 to 34	12.8	12.0	13.5
Aged 35 to 39	15.3	15.3	15.3
Aged 40 to 44	15.9	15.8	15.9
Aged 45 to 49	14.4	12.4	16.1
Aged 50 to 54	11.4	9.4	12.9
Aged 55 to 59	9.8	12.2	7.8
Aged 60 to 64	8.8	9.7	8.1
Aged 65 to 69	6.3	5.2	7.1
Aged 70 to 74	6.5	6.7	6.3
Aged 75 or older	5.1	6.0	4.6

Source: Bureau of the Census, Educational Attainment in the United States: March 1993 and 1992, *Current Population Reports, P20-476, 1994*

Educational Attainment of Blacks by Age and Region, 1993

(percent of blacks aged 25 or older who are high school or college graduates, by age and region, 1993)

	Northeast	Midwest	South	West
HIGH SCHOOL GRADUATES				
Total, aged 25 or older	73.8%	71.1%	67.1%	83.5%
Aged 25 to 34	84.7	81.8	82.0	90.3
Aged 35 to 44	82.2	82.3	81.5	91.5
Aged 45 to 54	75.3	77.0	66.0	86.1
Aged 55 to 64	60.8	58.2	51.4	80.2
Aged 65 or older	45.7	34.7	26.7	50.4
COLLEGE GRADUATES				
Total, aged 25 or older	13.7	11.8	11.6	13.7
Aged 25 to 34	17.5	12.5	11.8	12.9
Aged 35 to 44	14.8	14.9	16.4	12.5
Aged 45 to 54	13.6	13.5	11.5	19.7
Aged 55 to 64	9.0	10.8	7.8	16.9
Aged 65 or older	8.2	4.3	5.7	6.9

Source: Bureau of the Census, Educational Attainment in the United States: March 1993 and 1992, *Current Population Reports, P20-476, 1994*

Educational Attainment of Blacks by State, 1990

(percent of blacks aged 25 or older who are high school or college graduates, by state, 1990)

	high school graduate or more	college graduate		high school graduate or more	college graduate
United States	63.1%	11.4%	Missouri	65.1%	11.2%
Alabama	54.6	9.3	Montana	80.9	18.4
Alaska	88.2	14.1	Nebraska	73.2	12.4
Arizona	75.1	14.3	Nevada	70.8	9.0
Arkansas	51.5	8.4	New Hampshire	86.1	25.7
California	75.6	14.8	New Jersey	67.0	13.6
Colorado	80.8	17.1	New Mexico	74.7	14.2
Connecticut	67.0	12.3	New York	64.7	12.6
Delaware	63.2	10.6	North Carolina	58.1	9.5
District of Columbia	63.8	15.3	North Dakota	95.9	17.1
Florida	56.4	9.8	Ohio	64.6	9.1
Georgia	58.6	11.0	Oklahoma	70.1	12.0
Hawaii	94.2	15.2	Oregon	75.0	9.1
Idaho	82.8	15.8	Pennsylvania	63.5	10.0
Illinois	65.2	11.4	Rhode Island	65.9	12.7
Indiana	65.4	9.3	South Carolina	53.3	7.6
Iowa	70.1	12.8	South Dakota	82.2	24.1
Kansas	71.0	11.6	Tennessee	59.4	10.2
Kentucky	61.7	7.7	Texas	66.1	12.0
Louisiana	53.1	9.1	Utah	77.0	15.9
Maine	87.6	22.3	Vermont	82.9	30.5
Maryland	70.6	16.1	Virginia	60.3	11.1
Massachusetts	70.0	17.0	Washington	81.2	15.4
Michigan	64.9	10.1	West Virginia	64.7	10.9
Minnesota	76.2	17.5	Wisconsin	61.3	8.3
Mississippi	47.3	8.8	Wyoming	81.2	9.5

Source: National Center for Education Statistics, Digest of Education Statistics 1993, *NCES 93-292, 1993*

School Enrollment of Blacks by Age and Sex, 1993

(number and percent of blacks aged 3 or older enrolled in school as of October 1993, by age and sex; numbers in thousands)

	total		male		female	
	number	percent	number	percent	number	percent
Total, aged 3 or older	9,791	32.4%	4,899	34.8%	4,891	30.4%
Aged 3 and 4	526	39.8	287	41.7	239	37.8
Aged 5 and 6	1,139	94.6	607	96.9	532	92.1
Aged 7 to 9	1,706	99.0	860	99.3	847	98.7
Aged 10 to 13	2,375	99.8	1,213	100.0	1,162	99.7
Aged 14 and 15	1,111	98.5	565	99.0	547	97.9
Aged 16 and 17	1,024	94.7	526	96.0	498	93.4
Aged 18 and 19	600	57.7	329	63.6	272	51.9
Aged 20 and 21	308	30.0	112	23.9	196	35.1
Aged 22 to 24	262	18.1	132	19.6	130	16.7
Aged 25 to 29	269	10.4	124	10.3	145	10.5
Aged 30 to 34	149	5.5	37	3.1	112	7.5
Aged 35 to 44	225	4.8	73	3.5	152	5.9
Aged 45 to 54	72	2.4	28	2.1	43	2.6
Aged 55 or older	24	0.5	6	0.3	18	0.6

Source: Bureau of the Census, School Enrollment—Social and Economic Characteristics of Students: October 1993, *Current Population Reports, P20-479, 1994*

Black Families With Children in College, 1993

(total number of black families, number with children aged 18 to 24, and number and percent with children aged 18 to 24 attending college full-time as of October 1993, by household income in 1992; numbers in thousands)

	total	with children aged 18-24	with one or more children attending college full-time		
			number	percent of total families	percent of families with children 18-24
Total families	7,860	1,598	453	5.8%	28.3%
Under $20,000	4,045	711	125	3.1	17.6
$20,000 to $29,999	1,120	251	78	7.0	31.1
$30,000 to $39,999	859	196	81	9.4	41.3
$40,000 to $49,999	428	107	38	8.9	35.5
$50,000 to $74,999	512	131	57	11.1	43.5
$75,000 or more	244	61	34	13.9	55.7

Source: Bureau of the Census, School Enrollment—Social and Economic Characteristics of Students: October 1993, *Current Population Reports, P20-479, 1994*

College Enrollment of Blacks by Age, 1993

(number of blacks enrolled in college by age and attendance status, October 1993; numbers in thousands)

	total	undergraduate total	two-year college			four-year college			graduate		
			total	full-time	part-time	total	full-time	part-time	total	full-time	part-time
Total enrolled, aged 15 or older	1,545	1,363	530	308	222	833	659	174	182	48	134
Aged 15 to 17	13	12	1	1	-	11	11	-	-	-	-
Aged 18 and 19	311	311	113	90	24	198	185	13	-	-	-
Aged 20 and 21	297	294	78	62	16	216	204	12	4	4	-
Aged 22 to 24	253	238	63	34	29	175	145	30	15	9	6
Aged 25 to 29	245	201	104	44	60	97	46	51	44	17	27
Aged 30 to 34	141	108	62	32	31	46	28	18	33	2	31
Aged 35 to 39	119	90	57	34	22	33	16	17	30	6	24
Aged 40 to 44	82	49	20	-	20	29	14	15	33	8	25
Aged 45 to 49	47	31	16	11	5	15	5	10	16	-	16
Aged 50 to 54	15	12	8	8	-	4	2	2	3	-	3
Aged 55 to 59	9	5	-	-	-	5	3	2	4	2	2
Aged 60 to 64	12	12	7	7	-	5	-	5	-	-	-
Aged 65 or older	-	-	-	-	-	-	-	-	-	-	-

Note: (-) means insufficient data
Source: Bureau of the Census, School Enrollment—Social and Economic Characteristics of Students: October 1993, Current Population Reports, P20-479, 1994

Bachelor's, Master's, and Doctoral Degrees
Earned by Non-Hispanic Blacks by Field of Study, 1992-93

(number and percent of bachelor's, master's, and doctoral degrees earned by non-Hispanic blacks, by field of study, 1992-93)

	bachelor's		master's		doctoral	
	number	*percent*	*number*	*percent*	*number*	*percent*
Total degrees	77,872	6.7%	19,780	5.4%	1,352	3.2%
Agriculture and natural resources	435	2.6	93	2.3	13	1.1
Architecture and related programs	293	3.2	145	3.8	11	7.4
Area, ethnic, and cultural studies	530	9.7	131	8.6	11	6.2
Biological/life sciences	2,784	5.9	141	3.0	63	1.4
Business, management, and admin. services	19,187	7.5	4,474	5.0	29	2.2
Communications	4,164	7.7	273	5.7	21	7.2
Communications technologies	93	11.2	25	5.5	-	-
Computer and information sciences	2,261	9.3	324	3.2	6	0.7
Construction trades	7	10.1	-	-	-	-
Education	5,590	5.2	6,725	7.0	552	7.9
Engineering	2,630	4.2	600	2.2	42	0.7
Engineering related technologies	1,068	6.7	40	3.6	1	5.0
English language and literature	3,065	5.5	269	3.5	32	2.4
Foreign languages and literature	477	3.3	44	1.4	8	1.0
Health professions and related sciences	4,744	7.1	1,301	5.1	66	3.7
Home economics	945	6.3	153	6.2	16	4.6
Law and legal studies	192	9.3	41	1.9	1	1.2
Liberal arts and sciences	2,725	8.1	106	4.4	9	11.1
Library science	4	4.8	187	3.8	6	7.8
Mathematics	978	6.6	105	2.6	8	0.7
Mechanics and repairers	6	5.7	-	-	-	-
Multi/interdisciplinary studies	1,495	6.2	96	3.8	1	0.5
Parks, recreation, leisure and fitness	447	4.5	80	5.6	3	2.8
Philosophy and religion	333	4.3	57	4.0	17	3.8
Physical sciences	850	4.8	112	2.1	37	0.8
Precision production trades	34	8.8	-	-	-	-
Protective services	3,099	14.8	214	15.8	2	6.3
Psychology	4,727	7.1	578	5.3	134	3.7
Public administration and services	2,506	14.9	2,271	11.0	47	10.2
R.O.T.C. and military sciences	-	-	6	5.6	-	-
Social sciences and history	9,964	7.3	645	4.8	91	2.6
Theological studies/religious vocations	151	2.8	227	4.6	102	7.2
Transportation and material moving	163	4.1	22	4.4	-	-
Visual and performing arts	1,925	4.0	295	3.1	23	2.6

Source: National Center for Education Statistics, Digest of Education Statistics 1995, *NCES 95-029, 1995*

First-Professional Degrees Earned by Non-Hispanic Blacks by Field of Study, 1992-93

(number and percent of first-professional degrees earned by blacks, by field of study, 1992-93)

	number	percent
Total degrees	4,100	5.5%
Dentistry (D.D.S. or D.M.D.)	159	4.4
Medicine (M.D.)	900	5.8
Optometry (O.D.)	24	2.1
Osteopathic medicine (D.O.)	45	2.8
Pharmacy (Pharm. D.)	109	5.7
Podiatry (Pod. D. or D.P. or D.P.M.)	42	8.8
Veterinary medicine (D.V.M.)	51	2.5
Chiropractic medicine (D.C. or D.C.M.)	38	1.4
Law (L.L.B. or J.D.)	2,284	5.7
Theology (M.Div., M.H.L., B.D., or Ord.)	447	8.2
Other	1	1.6

Source: National Center for Education Statistics, Digest of Education Statistics 1995, *NCES 95-029, 1995*

Blacks:
Health

A 56 percent majority of blacks say they are in excellent or very good health, compared with 66 percent of the total population. Only 15 percent of blacks say they are in fair or poor health, slightly greater than the 10.5 percent of the total population who feel this way.

Death rates for blacks due to heart disease and cancer are well above average. While the suicide rate for blacks is below average, the homicide rate is nearly four times greater than that for the population as a whole.

Disability rates among blacks are about average, with 20 percent of blacks disabled in 1991-92, versus 19 percent of the total population. Blacks contact a doctor an average of 5.7 times a year, less than the 7.2 times the average American contacts a physician. One reason blacks are less likely to contact a doctor is that they are less likely to have health insurance. Fully 20.5 percent of blacks had no health insurance in 1993, versus 15 percent of the total population.

Black life expectancy is well below that of the average American. At birth, black males can expect to live to age 65, or nearly eight years less than the average American male. Black females can expect to live to age 74.5, or five years less than the average female.

Health Status of Blacks by Age, 1993

(percent distribution of self-assessed or parent-assessed health status of blacks, by age, 1993)

	total	excellent	very good	good	fair	poor
Total	100.0%	30.1%	26.3%	28.2%	11.3%	4.1%
Under age 5	100.0	42.1	28.4	23.5	5.5	0.5
Aged 5 to 17	100.0	40.4	29.1	25.5	4.3	0.7
Aged 18 to 24	100.0	35.7	27.8	29.0	6.5	1.0
Aged 25 to 44	100.0	29.3	28.4	29.4	10.2	2.7
Aged 45 to 64	100.0	16.0	20.6	31.5	21.7	10.2
Aged 65 or older	100.0	9.3	17.3	29.6	27.6	16.2

Source: National Center for Health Statistics, Current Estimates From the National Health Interview Survey, *1993, Series 10, No. 190, 1994*

Health Indicators for Blacks, 1992

(selected indicators of total and black health status, and index of black health indicators to total, 1992 except where otherwise noted)

	total population indicator	black indicator	index
Infant mortality rate (deaths < age 1 per 1,000 live births, 1991)	8.6	16.6	193
Total deaths per 100,000 population	504.5	767.5	152
Motor vehicle crash deaths per 100,000 population	15.8	16.3	103
Work-related injury deaths per 100,000 people aged 16 or older, 1993	3.2	2.9	91
Suicides per 100,000 population	11.1	6.9	62
Homicides per 100,000 population	10.5	39.4	375
Lung cancer deaths per 100,000 population	39.3	49.8	127
Female breast cancer deaths per 100,000 women	21.9	27.0	123
Cardiovascular disease deaths per 100,000 population	180.4	265.3	147
Heart disease deaths per 100,000 population	144.3	205.4	142
Stroke deaths per 100,000 population	26.2	45.0	172
Reported incidence of AIDS per 100,000 population, 1993*	31.2	104.2	334
Reported incidence of tuberculosis per 100,000 population, 1993*	9.8	29.1	297
Reported incidence of syphilis per 100,000 population, 1993*	10.4	76.5	736
Prevalence of low birth weight, as percent of total live births	7.1	13.3	187
Births to girls aged 10 to 17, as percent of total live births	4.9	10.3	210
Percent of mothers without care, first trimester of pregnancy	22.3	36.1	162
Percent < age 18 living in poverty, 1993	22.7	46.1	203
Percent living in counties exceeding U.S. air quality standards, 1993	23.5	24.8	106

* Data are for the non-Hispanic population.
Note: The index is calculated by dividing the black figure by the total figure for each indicator and multiplying by 100. For example, the index of 193 indicates that the black infant mortality rate is 93 percent above the rate for all infants.
Source: National Center for Health Statistics, Health Status Indicators: Differentials by Race and Hispanic Origin, *Healthy People 2000, No. 10, 1995*

Acute Health Conditions Among Blacks by Age, 1993

(number of acute conditions affecting blacks and rate per 100 blacks in specified age groups, by type of acute condition, 1993; numbers in thousands)

	total		under age 18		aged 18 to 44		aged 45 or older	
	number	rate	number	rate	number	rate	number	rate
Total acute conditions	52,441	163.7	23,913	221.9	19,751	146.9	8,777	112.4
Infective and								
parasitic diseases	5,859	18.3	3,662	34.0	1,663	12.4	534	6.8
Common childhood								
diseases	1,185	3.7	1,185	11.0	-	-	-	-
Intestinal virus	1,277	4.0	514	4.8	504	3.7	259	3.3
Viral infections	1,765	5.5	888	8.2	714	5.3	163	2.1
Other	1,633	5.1	1,076	10.0	445	3.3	112	1.4
Respiratory conditions	23,308	72.8	10,554	97.9	8,410	62.6	4,343	55.6
Common cold	9,474	29.6	5,315	49.3	2,887	21.5	1,273	16.3
Other acute upper								
respiratory infections	2,285	7.1	719	6.7	1,097	8.2	469	6.0
Influenza	9,567	29.9	3,255	30.2	4,057	30.2	2,255	28.9
Acute bronchitis	704	2.2	335	3.1	229	1.7	141	1.8
Pneumonia	593	1.9	533	4.9	60	0.4	-	-
Other respiratory								
conditions	685	2.1	398	3.7	81	0.6	206	2.6
Digestive system								
conditions	2,721	8.5	1,233	11.4	1,088	8.1	400	5.1
Dental conditions	416	1.3	247	2.3	169	1.3	-	-
Indigestion, nausea,								
and vomiting	1,146	3.6	538	5.0	493	3.7	114	1.5
Other digestive								
conditions	1,159	3.6	448	4.2	426	3.2	285	3.6
Injuries	7,497	23.4	2,187	20.3	3,992	29.7	1,318	16.9
Fractures and dislocations	736	2.3	168	1.6	367	2.7	202	2.6
Sprains and strains	1,789	5.6	349	3.2	1,262	9.4	178	2.3
Open wounds								
and lacerations	962	3.0	412	3.8	343	2.6	207	2.7
Contusions and								
superficial injuries	2,089	6.5	592	5.5	1,106	8.2	391	5.0
Other current injuries	1,920	6.0	667	6.2	913	6.8	340	4.4

(continued)

(continued from previous page)

	total		under age 18		aged 18 to 44		aged 45 or older	
	number	*rate*	*number*	*rate*	*number*	*rate*	*number*	*rate*
Selected other								
acute conditions	10,027	31.3	5,256	48.8	3,501	26.0	1,270	16.3
Eye conditions	471	1.5	410	3.8	25	0.2	36	0.5
Acute ear infections	3,054	9.5	2,581	23.9	330	2.5	143	1.8
Other ear conditions	344	1.1	187	1.7	157	1.2	-	-
Acute urinary conditions	1,001	3.1	235	2.2	366	2.7	401	5.1
Disorders of menstruation	173	0.5	75	0.7	98	0.7	-	-
Other disorders of female genital tract	226	0.7	-	-	226	1.7	-	-
Delivery and other conditions of pregnancy	445	1.4	81	0.8	363	2.7	-	-
Skin conditions	1,097	3.4	439	4.1	498	3.7	161	2.1
Acute musculoskeletal conditions	1,799	5.6	199	1.8	1,118	8.3	482	6.2
Headache, excluding migraine	643	2.0	339	3.1	257	1.9	48	0.6
Fever, unspecified	774	2.4	711	6.6	63	0.5	-	-
All other								
acute conditions	3,030	9.5	1,020	9.5	1,097	8.2	912	11.7

Note: The acute conditions shown here are those that caused people to restrict their activity for at least half a day, or that caused people to contact a physician about the illness or injury. (-) means number in sample is too small to make a reliable estimate.
Source: National Center for Health Statistics, Current Estimates From the National Health Interview Survey, 1993, Series 10, No. 190, 1994

Chronic Health Conditions Among Blacks by Age, 1993

(number of chronic conditions affecting blacks and rate per 1,000 blacks in specified age group, by type of chronic condition, 1993; numbers in thousands)

	total		under age 45		aged 45 to 64		aged 65 to 74		aged 75 or older	
	number	rate	number	rate	number	rate	number	rate	number	rate
Selected skin and musculoskeletal conditions										
Arthritis	3,606	112.6	470	19.4	1,496	291.3	1,066	636.8	574	574.6
Gout	374	11.7	42	1.7	118	23.0	156	93.2	58	58.1
Intervertebral disc disorders	467	14.6	208	8.6	233	45.4	26	15.5	-	-
Bone spur or tendinitis	151	4.7	18	0.7	102	19.9	12	7.2	19	19.0
Disorders of bone or cartilage	68	2.1	34	1.4	24	4.7	5	3.0	5	5.0
Trouble with bunions	309	9.6	36	1.5	164	31.9	49	29.3	60	60.1
Bursitis	420	13.1	125	5.2	214	41.7	34	20.3	47	47.0
Sebaceous skin cyst	178	5.6	89	3.7	85	16.5	-	-	4	4.0
Trouble with acne	779	24.3	738	30.5	41	8.0	-	-	-	-
Psoriasis	60	1.9	3	0.1	38	7.4	19	11.4	-	-
Dermatitis	1,042	32.5	859	35.5	124	24.1	46	27.5	13	13.0
Trouble with dry (itching) skin	492	15.4	290	12.0	99	19.3	70	41.8	33	33.0
Trouble with ingrown nails	726	22.7	325	13.4	249	48.5	66	39.4	86	86.1
Trouble with corns and calluses	935	29.2	395	16.3	260	50.6	198	118.3	82	82.1
Impairments										
Visual impairment	1,023	31.9	393	16.2	376	73.2	165	98.6	89	89.1
Color blindness	186	5.8	97	4.0	35	6.8	54	32.3	-	-
Cataracts	693	21.6	70	2.9	188	36.6	165	98.6	270	270.3
Glaucoma	442	13.8	40	1.7	173	33.7	108	64.5	121	121.1
Hearing impairment	1,626	50.8	642	26.5	478	93.1	254	151.7	252	252.3
Tinnitus	661	20.6	277	11.4	290	56.5	65	38.8	29	29.0
Speech impairment	796	24.9	664	27.4	99	19.3	27	16.1	6	6.0
Absence of extremities	226	7.1	15	0.6	162	31.5	39	23.3	10	10.0
Paralysis of extremities	351	11.0	148	6.1	105	20.4	28	16.7	70	70.1
Deformity or orthopedic impairment	3,399	106.1	1,899	78.4	878	171.0	431	257.5	191	191.2

(continued)

(continued from previous page)

	total		under age 45		aged 45 to 64		aged 65 to 74		aged 75 or older	
	number	*rate*	*number*	*rate*	*number*	*rate*	*number*	*rate*	*number*	*rate*
Selected digestive conditions										
Ulcer	708	22.1	441	18.2	165	32.1	68	40.6	34	34.0
Hernia of abdominal cavity	293	9.1	73	3.0	106	20.6	33	19.7	81	81.1
Gastritis or duodenitis	506	15.8	233	9.6	173	33.7	87	52.0	13	13.0
Frequent indigestion	673	21.0	375	15.5	218	42.4	73	43.6	7	7.0
Enteritis or colitis	102	3.2	102	4.2	-	-	-	-	-	-
Spastic colon	29	0.9	15	0.6	10	1.9	-	-	4	4.0
Diverticula of intestines	46	1.4	3	0.1	26	5.1	17	10.2	-	-
Frequent constipation	690	21.5	257	10.6	225	43.8	106	63.3	102	102.1
Selected conditions of the genitourinary, nervous, endocrine, metabolic, or blood systems										
Goiter or other disorders of the thyroid	354	11.1	152	6.3	79	15.4	45	26.9	78	78.1
Diabetes	1,315	41.1	304	12.6	578	112.5	292	174.4	141	141.1
Anemias	803	25.1	657	27.1	105	20.4	22	13.1	19	19.0
Epilepsy	250	7.8	153	6.3	85	16.5	12	7.2	-	-
Migraine	1,083	33.8	755	31.2	267	52.0	45	26.9	16	16.0
Neuralgia or neuritis	65	2.0	17	0.7	-	-	28	16.7	20	20.0
Kidney trouble	440	13.7	257	10.6	104	20.2	52	31.1	27	27.0
Bladder disorders	273	8.5	184	7.6	68	13.2	11	6.6	10	10.0
Diseases of prostate	140	4.4	9	0.4	62	12.1	35	20.9	34	34.0
Diseases of female genital organs	633	19.8	493	20.4	140	27.3	-	-	-	-
Selected circulatory conditions										
Rheumatic fever	109	3.4	57	2.4	36	7.0	16	9.6	-	-
Heart disease	2,156	67.3	886	36.6	691	134.5	364	217.4	215	215.2
Ischemic heart disease	588	18.4	142	5.9	280	54.5	118	70.5	48	48.0
Heart rhythm disorders	941	29.4	571	23.6	196	38.2	121	72.3	53	53.1
Other diseases of the heart, excl. hypertension	627	19.6	173	7.1	215	41.9	125	74.7	114	114.1
High blood pressure (hypertension)	3,999	124.8	1,222	50.5	1,707	332.4	590	352.4	480	480.5
Cerebrovascular disease	365	11.4	42	1.7	150	29.2	69	41.2	104	104.1
Hardening of the arteries	93	2.9	5	0.2	25	4.9	30	17.9	33	33.0

(continued)

(continued from previous page)

	total		under age 45		aged 45 to 64		aged 65 to 74		aged 75 or older	
	number	*rate*	*number*	*rate*	*number*	*rate*	*number*	*rate*	*number*	*rate*
Varicose veins of										
lower extremities	499	15.6	154	6.4	294	57.2	10	6.0	41	41.0
Hemorrhoids	656	20.5	333	13.7	209	40.7	57	34.1	57	57.1
Selected respiratory conditions										
Chronic bronchitis	1,432	44.7	968	40.0	324	63.1	125	74.7	15	15.0
Asthma	1,967	61.4	1,554	64.2	315	61.3	26	15.5	72	72.1
Hay fever	2,200	68.7	1,616	66.7	448	87.2	103	61.5	33	33.0
Chronic sinusitis	4,043	126.2	2,610	107.8	1,027	200.0	299	178.6	107	107.1
Deviated nasal septum	35	1.1	35	1.4	-	-	-	-	-	-
Chronic disease of										
tonsils or adenoids	294	9.2	253	10.4	32	6.2	9	5.4	-	-
Emphysema	180	5.6	12	0.5	70	13.6	63	37.6	35	35.0

Note: Chronic conditions are those that last at least three months or belong to a group of conditions that are considered to be chronic regardless of when they began. (-) means number in sample is too small to make a reliable estimate.
Source: National Center for Health Statistics, Current Estimates From the National Health Interview Survey, 1993, *Series 10, No. 190, 1994*

Blacks With Disabilities, 1991-92

(total number of blacks, number and percent with a disability, and number and percent with a severe disability, by selected characteristics, 1991-92; numbers in thousands)

	total	with a disability		with a severe disability	
		number	percent	number	percent
Total persons	31,420	6,277	20.0%	3,836	12.2%
AGE					
Under age 6	3,703	126	3.4	16	0.4
Aged 6 to 14	5,165	302	5.9	44	0.8
Aged 15 to 17	1,700	184	10.9	94	5.5
Aged 18 to 24	3,416	384	11.2	156	4.6
Aged 25 to 34	5,475	910	16.6	548	10.0
Aged 35 to 44	4,457	879	19.7	523	11.7
Aged 45 to 54	2,734	867	31.7	528	19.3
Aged 55 to 64	2,033	897	44.1	667	32.8
Aged 65 to 74	1,584	822	51.9	537	33.9
Aged 75 or older	1,152	905	78.5	723	62.8
HOUSEHOLD TYPE					
Family householder or spouse	11,042	2,883	26.1	1,784	16.2
With children under age 18	6,303	1,178	18.7	624	9.9
Married, spouse present	7,165	1,648	23.0	974	13.6
With children under age 18	3,903	584	15.0	297	7.6
No spouse present	3,877	1,234	31.8	810	20.9
With children under age 18	2,400	594	24.8	327	13.6
Nonfamily householder	3,336	1,381	41.4	926	27.8
Living alone	2,961	1,301	43.9	875	29.6
REGION					
Northeast	5,650	962	17.0	600	10.6
Midwest	5,564	1,249	22.4	776	14.0
South	17,390	3,556	20.5	2,151	12.4
West	2,815	510	18.1	308	10.9

Source: Bureau of the Census, Americans With Disabilities: 1991-92, *Current Population Reports, P70-33, 1993*

Physician Contacts by Blacks, 1993

(total number of physician contacts by blacks and number per person per year by age and type of contact, by age, 1993)

	total contacts	telephone	office	hospital	other
Total contacts (in thousands)	182,686	14,497	84,129	38,014	44,735
Under age 18	38,154	3,137	19,269	7,590	7,949
Aged 18 to 44	67,547	5,923	32,677	16,052	12,319
Aged 45 to 64	44,646	3,901	20,366	8,357	11,638
Aged 65 or older	32,339	1,535	11,817	6,015	12,828
Contacts per person	5.7	0.5	2.6	1.2	1.4
Under age 18	3.5	0.3	1.8	0.7	0.7
Aged 18 to 44	5.0	0.4	2.4	1.2	0.9
Aged 45 to 64	8.7	0.8	4.0	1.6	2.3
Aged 65 or older	12.1	0.6	4.4	2.3	4.8

Source: National Center for Health Statistics, Current Estimates From the National Health Interview Survey, 1993, *Series 10, No. 190, 1994*

Health Insurance Coverage of Blacks by Age, 1993

(number and percent distribution of blacks by age and health insurance coverage status, 1993; numbers in thousands)

		covered by private or government health insurance							
		private health insurance			government health insurance				
	total persons	total	total	group health	total	Medicaid	Medicare	Champus	not covered
Number									
Total	33,040	26,279	16,590	13,693	12,588	9,283	3,072	1,331	6,761
Under 18	11,257	9,501	5,120	4,039	5,572	5,229	11	412	1,756
18 to 24	3,680	2,655	1,725	1,155	1,143	1,000	41	156	1,025
25 to 34	5,479	3,923	2,702	2,383	1,427	1,163	120	232	1,556
35 to 44	5,031	3,657	2,940	2,751	848	627	127	166	1,374
45 to 54	3,048	2,453	1,969	1,799	638	419	172	138	595
55 to 64	2,034	1,648	1,184	1,022	611	343	263	139	386
65 or older	2,510	2,442	950	545	2,349	501	2,337	88	68
Percent									
Total	100.0%	79.5%	50.2%	41.4%	38.1%	28.1%	9.3%	4.0%	20.5%
Under 18	100.0	84.4	45.5	35.9	49.5	46.5	0.1	3.7	15.6
18 to 24	100.0	72.1	46.9	31.4	31.1	27.2	1.1	4.2	27.9
25 to 34	100.0	71.6	49.3	43.5	26.0	21.2	2.2	4.2	28.4
35 to 44	100.0	72.7	58.4	54.7	16.8	12.5	2.5	3.3	27.3
45 to 54	100.0	80.5	64.6	59.0	20.9	13.7	5.6	4.5	19.5
55 to 64	100.0	81.0	58.2	50.2	30.0	16.9	13.0	6.8	19.0
65 or older	100.0	97.3	37.9	21.7	93.6	20.0	93.1	3.5	2.7

Source: Bureau of the Census, unpublished tables from the 1994 Current Population Survey

Leading Causes of Death Among Blacks, 1993

(number of deaths among blacks, and number and percent of deaths accounted for by ten leading causes of death, 1993)

		number	percent
	All causes	282,151	100.0%
1.	Diseases of heart	79,011	28.0
2.	Malignant neoplasms	59,873	21.2
3.	Cerebrovascular diseases	17,557	6.2
4.	Human immunodeficiency virus	13,319	4.7
5.	Homicide and legal intervention	12,937	4.6
6.	Accidents and adverse effects	12,707	4.5
7.	Diabetes mellitus	9,380	3.3
8.	Pneumonia and influenza	7,724	2.7
9.	Chronic obstructive pulmonary diseases and allied conditions	6,435	2.3
10.	Certain conditions originating in perinatal period	5891	2.1
	All other causes	57,317	20.3

Source: National Center for Health Statistics, Advance Report of Final Mortality Statistics, 1993, *Vol. 44, No. 7 Supplement, 1996*

Life Expectancy of Blacks at Birth and Age 65, 1995 to 2020

(average number of years of life remaining at birth and at age 65 for black males and females, 1995-2050; difference between black life expectancy and total life expectancy for males and females at birth and at age 65, 1995 and 2020)

	life expectancy (years)	
	males	females
AT BIRTH		
1995	64.8	74.5
2000	64.6	74.7
2005	64.5	75.0
2010	65.1	75.5
2015	65.8	76.0
2020	66.5	76.5
Life exp. of blacks minus		
life exp. of total Americans		
1995	-7.7	-4.8
2020	-9.0	-5.0
AT AGE 65		
1995	13.6	17.6
2000	13.8	17.8
2005	14.0	18.0
2010	14.3	18.3
2015	14.6	18.5
2020	14.8	18.8
Life exp. of blacks minus		
life exp. of total Americans		
1995	-1.9	-1.6
2020	-2.8	-1.8

Source: Bureau of the Census, Population Projections of the United States, by Age, Sex, Race, and Hispanic Origin: 1995 to 2050, *Current Population Reports, P25-1130, 1996*

Blacks:
Households and Living Arrangements

Black householders are somewhat younger than householders in the nation as a whole. Only 15 percent are aged 65 or older, versus 21 percent of total householders. Forty-nine percent of black householders are aged 25 to 44, versus 43 percent of the total.

Female-headed families are the dominant household type among blacks, accounting for 34 percent of all black households. Only 33 percent of black households are married couples. Nuclear families—married couples with children—represent just 17 percent of black households, while female-headed families with children are a larger 23 percent.

Only 37 percent of black children live with both parents, while 59 percent live with their mother only. Among black children under age 6, fully 47 percent live with a never-married mother.

Thirty-eight percent of black women are currently married, versus 56 percent of women in the nation as a whole. The proportion of black women who are married is above 50 percent only among those aged 40 to 64. In contrast, among all women a majority of those aged 25 to 74 are married.

Black Households by Age of Householder, 1994

(number and percent distribution of black households by age of householder, 1994, numbers in thousands)

	number	percent
Total households	11,281	100.0%
Under age 25	773	6.9
Aged 25 to 29	1,198	10.6
Aged 30 to 34	1,546	13.7
Aged 35 to 39	1,504	13.3
Aged 40 to 44	1,322	11.7
Aged 45 to 49	1,058	9.4
Aged 50 to 54	798	7.1
Aged 55 to 59	688	6.1
Aged 60 to 64	626	5.5
Aged 65 to 69	579	5.1
Aged 70 to 74	492	4.4
Aged 75 or older	696	6.2

Source: Bureau of the Census, Household and Family Characteristics: March 1994, *Current Population Reports, P20-483, 1995*

Black Households by Household Type, 1994

(number and percent distribution of black households by type of household, 1994; numbers in thousands)

	number	percent
Total households	11,281	100.0%
Family households	7,989	70.8
Married-couple families	3,714	32.9
With children <18	1,924	17.1
Without children <18	1,790	15.9
Female householder,		
no spouse present	3,825	33.9
With children <18	2,630	23.3
Without children <18	1,194	10.6
Male householder,		
no spouse present	450	4.0
Nonfamily households	3,292	29.2
Female householder	1,840	16.3
Living alone	1,657	14.7
Male householder	1,452	12.9
Living alone	1,147	10.2

Source: Bureau of the Census, Household and Family Characteristics: March 1994, *Current Population Reports, P20-483, 1995*

Black Households by Type and Age of Householder, 1994

(number and percent distribution of black households by age of householder and household type, 1994; numbers in thousands)

	total	family households				nonfamily households	
		total	married couples	female householder, no spouse present	male householder, no spouse no present	female householder	male householder
Total, number	11,281	7,989	3,714	3,825	450	1,840	1,452
Under 20	91	65	1	58	6	18	7
20 to 24	682	510	117	359	33	84	88
25 to 29	1,198	882	317	498	67	158	158
30 to 34	1,546	1,181	433	657	91	137	228
35 to 39	1,504	1,178	465	643	70	115	211
40 to 44	1,322	1,006	520	440	45	151	166
45 to 49	1,058	782	427	324	31	138	138
50 to 54	798	597	356	209	33	122	78
55 to 59	688	476	284	176	16	134	79
60 to 64	626	368	233	125	9	168	91
65 to 74	1,071	613	374	208	31	337	122
75 to 84	553	290	172	105	13	191	73
85 or older	143	41	14	22	5	88	14
Total, percent	100.0%	70.8%	32.9%	33.9%	4.0%	16.3%	12.9%
Under 20	100.0	71.4	1.1	63.7	6.6	19.8	7.7
20 to 24	100.0	74.8	17.2	52.6	4.8	12.3	12.9
25 to 29	100.0	73.6	26.5	41.6	5.6	13.2	13.2
30 to 34	100.0	76.4	28.0	42.5	5.9	8.9	14.7
35 to 39	100.0	78.3	30.9	42.8	4.7	7.6	14.0
40 to 44	100.0	76.1	39.3	33.3	3.4	11.4	12.6
45 to 49	100.0	73.9	40.4	30.6	2.9	13.0	13.0
50 to 54	100.0	74.8	44.6	26.2	4.1	15.3	9.8
55 to 59	100.0	69.2	41.3	25.6	2.3	19.5	11.5
60 to 64	100.0	58.8	37.2	20.0	1.4	26.8	14.5
65 to 74	100.0	57.2	34.9	19.4	2.9	31.5	11.4
75 to 84	100.0	52.4	31.1	19.0	2.4	34.5	13.2
85 or older	100.0	28.7	9.8	15.4	3.5	61.5	9.8

Source: Bureau of the Census, Household and Family Characteristics: March 1994, *Current Population Reports, P20-483, 1995*

Black Households by Size, 1994

(number and percent distribution of black households by size, 1994; numbers in thousands)

	number	percent
Total households	11,281	100.0%
One person	2,804	24.9
Two persons	2,918	25.9
Three persons	2,256	20.0
Four persons	1,760	15.6
Five persons	867	7.7
Six persons	363	3.2
Seven or more persons	312	2.8

Source: Bureau of the Census, Household and Family Characteristics: March 1994, *Current Population Reports, P20-483, 1995*

Black Married Couples by Age of Householder and Presence of Children, 1994

(number and percent of black married couples, by presence and number of own children under age 18 at home and by age of householder, 1994; numbers in thousands)

	total	< age 20	20-24	25-29	30-34	35-39	40-44	45-54	55-64	65+
Number	3,714	1	117	317	433	465	520	783	517	560
Without children <18	1,790	-	45	74	65	67	144	412	437	546
With children <18	1,924	1	73	243	368	397	376	371	81	14
One	771	1	36	93	85	120	139	241	48	8
Two	696	-	22	92	179	157	141	77	25	3
Three or more	458	-	15	58	104	121	96	53	8	3
Percent	100.0%	100.0%	100.0%	100.0%	100.0%	100.0%	100.0%	100.0%	100.0%	100.0%
Without children <18	48.2	-	38.5	23.3	15.0	14.4	27.7	52.6	84.5	97.5
With children <18	51.8	-	62.4	76.7	85.0	85.4	72.3	47.4	15.7	2.5
One	20.8	-	30.8	29.3	19.6	25.8	26.7	30.8	9.3	1.4
Two	18.7	-	18.8	29.0	41.3	33.8	27.1	9.8	4.8	0.5
Three or more	12.3	-	12.8	18.3	24.0	26.0	18.5	6.8	1.5	0.5

Note: (-) means number in sample is too small to make a reliable estimate.
Source: Bureau of the Census, Household and Family Characteristics: March 1994, *Current Population Reports, P20-483, 1995*

Black Female-Headed Families by Age of Householder and Presence of Children, 1994

(number and percent of black female-headed families, by presence and number of own children under age 18 at home and by age of householder, 1994; numbers in thousands)

	total	< age 20	20-24	25-29	30-34	35-39	40-44	45-54	55-64	65+
Number	3,825	58	359	498	657	643	440	533	301	335
Without children <18	1,194	2	23	20	24	69	125	332	272	327
With children <18	2,630	56	336	478	633	574	315	201	29	8
One	1,068	29	154	133	184	234	157	152	19	6
Two	871	19	105	153	232	200	117	33	10	1
Three or more	691	8	76	192	217	140	42	17	-	-
Percent	100.0%	100.0%	100.0%	100.0%	100.0%	100.0%	100.0%	100.0%	100.0%	100.0%
Without children <18	31.2	3.4	6.4	4.0	3.7	10.7	28.4	62.3	90.4	97.6
With children <18	68.8	96.6	93.6	96.0	96.3	89.3	71.6	37.7	9.6	2.4
One	27.9	50.0	42.9	26.7	28.0	36.4	35.7	28.5	6.3	1.8
Two	22.8	32.8	29.2	30.7	35.3	31.1	26.6	6.2	3.3	0.3
Three or more	18.1	13.8	21.2	38.6	33.0	21.8	9.5	3.2	-	-

Note: (-) means number in sample is too small to make a reliable estimate.
Source: Bureau of the Census, Household and Family Characteristics: March 1994, *Current Population Reports, P20-483, 1995*

Black Single-Person Households by Age of Householder, 1994

(number and percent distribution of black single-person households and single-person households as a percent of total black households, by age of householder, 1994; numbers in thousands)

	number	percent	percent of total black households
Total households	2,804	100.0%	24.9%
Under age 25	109	3.9	14.1
Aged 25 to 29	232	8.3	19.4
Aged 30 to 34	285	10.2	18.4
Aged 35 to 39	278	9.9	18.5
Aged 40 to 44	279	10.0	21.1
Aged 45 to 54	408	14.6	22.0
Aged 55 to 64	431	15.4	32.8
Aged 65 to 74	428	15.3	40.0
Aged 75 or older	355	12.7	51.0
Median age (years)	49.6	-	-

Source: Bureau of the Census, Household and Family Characteristics: March 1994, *Current Population Reports, P20-483, 1995*

Living Arrangements of Black Children by Age, 1994

(number and percent distribution of black children by living arrangement, marital status of parent, and age of child, 1994; numbers in thousands)

	total	under age 6	6 to 11	12 to 17
Number with one or both parents	10,106	3,657	3,353	3,097
Living with both parents	3,722	1,183	1,289	1,250
Living with mother only	5,967	2,298	1,922	1,746
Divorced	1,138	216	391	532
Married, spouse absent	1,356	391	463	502
Widowed	151	25	36	89
Never married	3,321	1,667	1,032	623
Living with father only	417	176	141	101
Divorced	154	69	40	44
Married, spouse absent	70	16	33	20
Widowed	19	-	9	10
Never married	175	91	59	26
Percent with one or both parents	100.0%	100.0%	100.0%	100.0%
Living with both parents	36.8	32.3	38.4	40.4
Living with mother only	59.0	62.8	57.3	56.4
Divorced	11.3	5.9	11.7	17.2
Married, spouse absent	13.4	10.7	13.8	16.2
Widowed	1.5	0.7	1.1	2.9
Never married	32.9	45.6	30.8	20.1
Living with father only	4.1	4.8	4.2	3.3
Divorced	1.5	1.9	1.2	1.4
Married, spouse absent	0.7	0.4	1.0	0.6
Widowed	0.2	-	0.3	0.3
Never married	1.7	2.5	1.8	0.8

Note: (-) means number in sample is too small to make a reliable estimate.
Source: Bureau of the Census, Marital Status and Living Arrangements: March 1993, Current Population Reports, P20-484, 1996

Living Arrangements of Black Women by Age, 1994

(number and percent distribution of black women aged 18 or older by living arrangement and age, 1994; numbers in thousands)

	total	18 to 19	20 to 24	25 to 29	30 to 34	35 to 39	40 to 44	45 to 54	55 to 64	65 to 74	75 or older
Number	12,025	553	1,419	1,446	1,535	1,468	1,251	1,670	1,151	937	595
Family householder or spouse	7,434	63	528	858	1,129	1,142	957	1,250	761	512	234
Child of householder	1,634	397	592	258	159	112	45	49	14	6	3
Other member of family household	740	60	144	101	62	48	48	69	55	75	76
Nonfamily householder	1,837	15	84	158	137	115	151	260	302	337	279
Other member of nonfamily household	367	18	69	68	43	51	47	42	19	7	3
Group quarters*	13	-	2	3	5	-	3	-	-	-	-
Percent	100.0%	100.0%	100.0%	100.0%	100.0%	100.0%	100.0%	100.0%	100.0%	100.0%	100.0%
Family householder or spouse	61.8	11.4	37.2	59.3	73.6	77.8	76.5	74.9	66.1	54.6	39.3
Child of householder	13.6	71.8	41.7	17.8	10.4	7.6	3.6	2.9	1.2	0.6	0.5
Other member of family household	6.2	10.8	10.1	7.0	4.0	3.3	3.8	4.1	4.8	8.0	12.8
Nonfamily householder	15.3	2.7	5.9	10.9	8.9	7.8	12.1	15.6	26.2	36.0	46.9
Other member of nonfamily household	3.1	3.3	4.9	4.7	2.8	3.5	3.8	2.5	1.7	0.7	0.5
Group quarters*	0.1	-	0.1	0.2	0.3	-	0.2	-	-	-	-

* The Current Population Survey does not include people living in institutions such as prisons, the military, or college dormitories. It defines people living in group quarters as those in noninstitutional living arrangements that are not conventional housing units, such as rooming houses, staff quarters at a hospital, or halfway houses.
Note: (-) means number in sample is too small to make a reliable estimate.
Source: Bureau of the Census, Marital Status and Living Arrangements: March 1994, Current Population Reports, P20-484, 1996

Living Arrangements of Black Men by Age, 1994

(number and percent distribution of black men aged 18 or older by living arrangement and age, 1994; numbers in thousands)

	total	18 to 19	20 to 24	25 to 29	30 to 34	35 to 39	40 to 44	45 to 54	55 to 64	65 to 74	75 or older
Number	9,758	491	1,216	1,172	1,327	1,243	1,069	1,379	883	620	358
Family householder or spouse	4,195	8	143	351	524	552	588	820	554	434	219
Child of householder	2,306	363	745	397	301	247	115	126	8	-	5
Other member of family household	891	95	138	102	113	81	88	116	83	35	44
Nonfamily householder	1,452	7	88	158	228	211	166	216	169	122	87
Other member of nonfamily household	889	15	98	164	161	140	110	100	69	29	3
Group quarters*	25	3	4	-	-	12	2	1	2	-	-
Percent	100.0%	100.0%	100.0%	100.0%	100.0%	100.0%	100.0%	100.0%	100.0%	100.0%	100.0%
Family householder or spouse	43.0	1.6	11.8	29.9	39.5	44.4	55.0	59.5	62.7	70.0	61.2
Child of householder	23.6	73.9	61.3	33.9	22.7	19.9	10.8	9.1	0.9	-	1.4
Other member of family household	9.1	19.3	11.3	8.7	8.5	6.5	8.2	8.4	9.4	5.6	12.3
Nonfamily householder	14.9	1.4	7.2	13.5	17.2	17.0	15.5	15.7	19.1	19.7	24.3
Other member of nonfamily household	9.1	3.1	8.1	14.0	12.1	11.3	10.3	7.3	7.8	4.7	0.8
Group quarters*	0.3	0.6	0.3	-	-	1.0	0.2	0.1	0.2	-	-

* The Current Population Survey does not include people living in institutions such as prisons, the military, or college dormitories. It defines people living in group quarters as those in noninstitutional living arrangements that are not conventional housing units, such as rooming houses, staff quarters at a hospital, or halfway houses.
Note: (–) means number in sample is too small to make a reliable estimate.
Source: Bureau of the Census, Marital Status and Living Arrangements: March 1994, Current Population Reports, P20-484 1996

Marital Status of Black Women by Age, 1994

(number and percent distribution of black women aged 15 or older by age and marital status, 1994; numbers in thousands)

	total	never married	married	widowed	divorced
Total, number	12,872	5,190	4,863	1,322	1,497
Under age 20	1,400	1,381	17	2	-
Aged 20 to 24	1,419	1,148	247	3	21
Aged 25 to 29	1,446	877	508	-	61
Aged 30 to 34	1,535	655	665	12	203
Aged 35 to 39	1,468	456	721	27	264
Aged 40 to 44	1,251	271	682	35	263
Aged 45 to 54	1,670	230	952	129	359
Aged 55 to 64	1,151	95	597	273	186
Aged 65 to 74	937	57	350	414	116
Aged 75 to 84	449	11	112	306	20
Aged 85 or older	146	9	14	119	4
Total, percent	100.0%	40.3%	37.8%	10.3%	11.6%
Under age 20	100.0	98.6	1.2	0.1	-
Aged 20 to 24	100.0	80.9	17.4	0.2	1.5
Aged 25 to 29	100.0	60.7	35.1	-	4.2
Aged 30 to 34	100.0	42.7	43.3	0.8	13.2
Aged 35 to 39	100.0	31.1	49.1	1.8	18.0
Aged 40 to 44	100.0	21.7	54.5	2.8	21.0
Aged 45 to 54	100.0	13.8	57.0	7.7	21.5
Aged 55 to 64	100.0	8.3	51.9	23.7	16.2
Aged 65 to 74	100.0	6.1	37.4	44.2	12.4
Aged 75 to 84	100.0	2.4	24.9	68.2	4.5
Aged 85 or older	100.0	6.2	9.6	81.5	2.7

Note: (-) means number in sample is too small to make a reliable estimate.
Source: Bureau of the Census, Marital Status and Living Arrangements: March 1993, *Current Population Reports, P20-484, 1996*

Marital Status of Black Men by Age, 1994

(number and percent distribution of black men aged 15 or older by age and marital status, 1994; numbers in thousands)

	total	never married	married	widowed	divorced
Total, number	10,639	5,007	4,486	295	851
Under age 20	1,372	1,356	16	-	-
Aged 20 to 24	1,216	1,071	132	3	10
Aged 25 to 29	1,172	773	356	-	43
Aged 30 to 34	1,327	682	545	-	100
Aged 35 to 39	1,243	468	632	8	135
Aged 40 to 44	1,069	259	661	7	142
Aged 45 to 54	1,379	236	865	33	245
Aged 55 to 64	883	106	605	67	105
Aged 65 to 74	620	38	453	71	58
Aged 75 to 84	73	10	(26)	76	13
Aged 85 or older	57	7	20	30	-
Total, percent	100.0%	47.1%	42.2%	2.8%	8.0%
Under age 20	100.0	98.8	1.2	-	-
Aged 20 to 24	100.0	88.1	10.9	0.2	0.8
Aged 25 to 29	100.0	66.0	30.4	-	3.7
Aged 30 to 34	100.0	51.4	41.1	-	7.5
Aged 35 to 39	100.0	37.7	50.8	0.6	10.9
Aged 40 to 44	100.0	24.2	61.8	0.7	13.3
Aged 45 to 54	100.0	17.1	62.7	2.4	17.8
Aged 55 to 64	100.0	12.0	68.5	7.6	11.9
Aged 65 to 74	100.0	6.1	73.1	11.5	9.4
Aged 75 to 84	100.0	13.7	-35.6	104.1	17.8
Aged 85 or older	100.0	12.3	35.1	52.6	-

Note: (-) means number in sample is too small to make a reliable estimate.
Source: Bureau of the Census, Marital Status and Living Arrangements: March 1994, Current Population Reports, P20-484, 1996

Blacks:
Housing

Forty-three percent of the nation's 10 million black householders own their home. This compares with a homeownership rate of 64 percent for all Americans. The median value of the homes owned by blacks was $50,700 in 1990, versus a median of $78,300 for the average American home.

Among the 50 metropolitan areas with the most black households, New York has the largest number—over 750,000 in 1990. Blacks account for the largest share of households—37 percent—in Jacksonville, Florida.

Most black householders are satisfied with their homes. On a scale of one to ten, 65 percent of blacks rate their homes an eight or higher. Even among black renters, 56 percent rate their homes an eight or more. Few blacks think their neighborhood has a crime problem—only 11 percent of homeowners and 18 percent of renters say crime is a problem in their area. Fully 55 percent of black householders say their neighborhood has no problems.

Nineteen percent of blacks moved between 1993 and 1994, versus 16 percent of the total population. The most common reason for moving among black movers is to establish their own household.

Black homeowners paid a median of $29,300 for their homes and most paid for the downpayment with savings. Nineteen percent of black homeowners had their roof repaired within the past two years, the most common home repair not only for black homeowners, but for homeowners in the nation as a whole.

Characteristics of Black Households
by Metropolitan Status, 1990

(number of black households, percent of total households that are black, percent of black house-holds that are owner-occupied, and median value of owner-occupied houses, by metropolitan status, 1990; numbers in thousands)

	number	black share of total households	owner-occupied percent	owner-occupied median value
Black households	9,976	10.8%	43.4%	$50,700
Inside metropolitan areas	8,456	11.9	40.6	55,500
Central cities	5,925	19.9	36.6	47,800
Suburbs*	2,531	6.1	50.0	72,900
Outside metropolitan areas	1,520	7.4	58.9	34,400

* The suburbs are the portion of a metropolitan area that is outside the central city.
Source: Bureau of the Census, Housing in Metropolitan Areas—Black Households, *Statistical Brief, SB/95-5, 1995*

Black Homeownership in the 50 Metropolitan Areas
With the Most Black Households, 1990

*(number of black households, percent of total households that are black, percent of black house-
holds that are owner occupied, and median value of owner-occupied houses, in the total U.S. and
in the 50 metropolitan areas with the most black households, ranked alphabetically, 1990; numbers
in thousands)*

	number	black share of total households	owner-occupied percent	owner-occupied median value
Total U.S. black households	9,976	10.8%	43.4%	$50,700
Atlanta, GA	254	24.0	40.4	66,700
Augusta, GA	40	28.2	51.7	47,700
Baltimore, MD	207	23.5	39.4	57,100
Baton Rouge, LA	49	26.1	52.8	45,900
Birmingham, AL	85	24.6	53.3	38,900
Boston, MA	71	6.5	24.7	160,200
Buffalo, NY	43	11.3	34.2	38,500
Charleston, SC	47	26.7	57.1	52,800
Charlotte-Gastonia-Rock Hill, NC-SC	78	17.6	43.8	49,900
Chicago, IL	440	19.8	37.1	64,100
Cincinnati, OH	71	13.0	33.1	54,400
Cleveland, OH	132	18.5	42.2	45,500
Columbia, SC	42	26.0	50.3	53,200
Columbus, OH	58	11.1	38.9	50,400
Dallas, TX	140	14.7	37.9	57,000
Dayton-Springfield, OH	46	12.6	47.3	42,100
Detroit, MI	329	20.3	48.7	29,200
Fort Lauderdale-Hollywood-Pompano Beach, FL	59	11.1	44.9	67,300
Fort Worth-Arlington, TX	49	9.9	43.9	47,600
Gary-Hammond, IN	40	18.7	50.8	34,200
Greensboro-Winston-Salem-High Point, NC	66	17.7	41.3	53,700
Houston, TX	209	17.6	43.1	43,200
Indianapolis, IN	62	12.9	42.5	41,000
Jackson, MS	62	18.0	50.2	41,500
Jacksonville, FL	52	36.9	54.0	42,100
Kansas City, MO-KS	71	11.7	46.7	37,600
Los Angeles-Long Beach, CA	353	11.8	36.5	143,500
Louisville, KY-IN	46	12.4	42.7	34,800

(continued)

(continued from previous page)

	number	black share of total households	owner-occupied	
			percent	median value
Memphis, TN	129	36.0%	47.9%	$44,500
Miami-Hialeah, FL	120	17.4	43.7	62,800
Milwaukee, WI	62	11.5	30.3	40,600
Mobile, AL	42	24.3	54.8	38,500
Nashville, TN	54	14.3	41.7	57,100
Nassau-Suffolk, NY	52	6.0	61.5	152,600
New Orleans, LA	141	30.9	40.9	56,300
New York, NY	762	23.4	20.8	159,900
Newark, NJ	141	21.6	30.9	132,400
Norfolk-Virginia Beach-Newport News, VA	132	26.7	42.3	66,300
Oakland, CA	111	14.3	36.7	138,100
Orlando, FL	41	10.3	46.0	59,400
Philadelphia, PA-NJ	316	17.8	55.5	36,200
Pittsburgh, PA	64	7.7	38.9	36,200
Raleigh-Durham, NC	65	22.8	41.4	63,400
Richmond-Petersburg, VA	89	26.8	49.0	57,300
Riverside-San Bernardino, CA	54	6.2	45.5	127,900
San Diego, CA	50	5.7	28.4	129,700
San Francisco, CA	44	6.9	31.5	223,200
St. Louis, MO-IL	144	15.6	45.3	43,800
Tampa-St. Petersburg-Clearwater, FL	63	7.2	45.4	47,000
Washington, DC-MD-VA	371	25.4	41.1	111,700

Source: Bureau of the Census, Housing in Metropolitan Areas—Black Households, *Statistical Brief, SB/95-5, 1995*

Characteristics of Housing Units Occupied by Blacks, 1993

(number and percent distribution of housing units occupied by blacks, by selected housing characteristics and homeownership status, 1993; numbers in thousands except medians)

	total		owner-occupied		renter-occupied	
	number	percent	number	percent	number	percent
Total occupied						
housing units	11,128	100.0%	4,788	100.0%	6,340	100.0%
Region						
Northeast	1,990	17.9	678	14.2	1,313	20.7
Midwest	2,249	20.2	927	19.4	1,323	20.9
South	5,902	53.0	2,842	59.4	3,059	48.2
West	987	8.9	341	7.1	645	10.2
Units in structure						
1, detached	5,232	47.0	3,875	80.9	1,358	21.4
1, attached	1,015	9.1	421	8.8	594	9.4
2 to 4	1,627	14.6	151	3.2	1,476	23.3
5 to 9	953	8.6	25	0.5	928	14.6
10 to 19	762	6.8	20	0.4	741	11.7
20 to 49	532	4.8	13	0.3	519	8.2
50 or more	671	6.0	32	0.7	639	10.1
Mobile home or trailer	337	3.0	252	5.3	85	1.3
Median number of						
rooms in unit	5	-	6	-	4	-
Median square footage						
of unit	1,426	-	1,546	-	1,142	-
Number of complete bathrooms						
None	120	1.1	38	0.8	82	1.3
One	6,895	62.0	1,984	41.4	4,912	77.5
One and one-half	1,778	16.0	1,106	23.1	672	10.6
Two or more	2,335	21.0	1,661	34.7	674	10.6
Primary heating fuel						
Total with						
heating fuel	11,004	98.9	4,757	99.4	6,247	98.5
Electricity	2,922	26.3	958	20.0	1,964	31.0
Piped gas	5,945	53.4	2,832	59.1	3,113	49.1
Bottled gas	362	3.3	270	5.6	91	1.4

(continued)

(continued from previous page)

	total		owner-occupied		renter-occupied	
	number	*percent*	*number*	*percent*	*number*	*percent*
Fuel oil	1,242	11.2%	393	8.2%	849	13.4%
Kerosene or other liquid fuel	174	1.6	101	2.1	73	1.2
Coal or coke	21	0.2	9	0.2	12	0.2
Wood	297	2.7	193	4.0	105	1.7
Solar energy	-	-	-	-	-	-
Other	42	0.4	3	0.1	40	0.6
Selected equipment						
Dishwasher	3,019	27.1	1,536	32.1	1,483	23.4
Washing machine	6,716	60.4	4,175	87.2	2,542	40.1
Clothes dryer	5,127	46.1	3,394	70.9	1,733	27.3
Disposal in kitchen sink	3,169	28.5	1,216	25.4	1,954	30.8
Central air conditioning	3,841	34.5	1,866	39.0	1,974	31.1
Porch, deck, balcony, or patio	7,497	67.4	3,730	77.9	3,767	59.4
Telephone	9,525	85.6	4,515	94.3	5,010	79.0
Usable fireplace	1,804	16.2	1,289	26.9	515	8.1
Garage or carport	3,641	32.7	2,594	54.2	1,047	16.5
Cars and trucks available						
No cars, trucks, or vans	3,114	28.0	579	12.1	2,536	40.0
1 car, with or without trucks or vans	5,078	45.6	2,231	46.6	2,848	44.9
2 or more cars	2,611	23.5	1,806	37.7	804	12.7
Overall opinion of housing unit						
1 (worst)	168	1.5	13	0.3	155	2.4
2	87	0.8	14	0.3	72	1.1
3	140	1.3	30	0.6	110	1.7
4	202	1.8	20	0.4	182	2.9
5	1,004	9.0	277	5.8	727	11.5
6	753	6.8	228	4.8	525	8.3
7	1,392	12.5	474	9.9	917	14.5
8	2,580	23.2	1,187	24.8	1,393	22.0
9	1,480	13.3	719	15.0	761	12.0
10 (best)	3,200	28.8	1,781	37.2	1,419	22.4

Note: (-) means not applicable or number in sample is too small to make a reliable estimate.
Source: Bureau of the Census, American Housing Survey for the United States in 1993, Current Housing Reports, H150/93, 1995

Neighborhood Characteristics of Black Housing Units, 1993

(number and percent distribution of housing units occupied by blacks, by selected characteristics of neighborhoods and homeownership status, 1993; numbers in thousands)

	total		owner-occupied		renter-occupied	
	number	*percent*	*number*	*percent*	*number*	*percent*
Total occupied						
housing units	11,128	100.0%	4,788	100.0%	6,340	100.0%
Overall opinion of neighborhood						
1 (worst)	560	5.0	112	2.3	448	7.1
2	201	1.8	61	1.3	140	2.2
3	292	2.6	58	1.2	234	3.7
4	360	3.2	107	2.2	253	4.0
5	1,172	10.5	410	8.6	761	12.0
6	707	6.4	259	5.4	448	7.1
7	1,347	12.1	577	12.1	770	12.1
8	2,181	19.6	1,022	21.3	1,158	18.3
9	1,209	10.9	576	12.0	633	10.0
10 (best)	2,924	26.3	1,528	31.9	1,397	22.0
Neighborhood problems						
No problems	6,151	55.3	2,765	57.7	3,386	53.4
With problems*	4,763	42.8	1,929	40.3	2,835	44.7
Crime	1,659	14.9	513	10.7	1,147	18.1
Noise	1,120	10.1	386	8.1	735	11.6
Traffic	598	5.4	248	5.2	350	5.5
Litter or housing deterioration	640	5.8	305	6.4	336	5.3
Poor city or county services	250	2.2	127	2.7	124	2.0
Undesirable commercial, institutional, industrial	152	1.4	50	1.0	102	1.6
People	1,712	15.4	558	11.7	1,154	18.2
Other	1,125	10.1	570	11.9	555	8.8
Not reported	116	1.0	45	0.9	70	1.1

* Figures will not add to total because more than one problem could be cited.
Source: Bureau of the Census, American Housing Survey for the United States in 1993, *Current Housing Reports, H150/93, 1995*

Geographical Mobility of the Black Population by Age, 1993-94

(total number of blacks aged 1 or older, and percent nonmovers and movers between March 1993 and March 1994, by age of person and type of move; numbers in thousands)

	total	same house (non-movers)	different house in the U.S. total	same county	different county total	same state	different state total	same region	different region	movers from abroad
Total, 1 or older	32,485	80.4%	19.2%	13.4%	5.9%	3.1%	2.8%	1.5%	1.3%	0.4%
Aged 1 to 4	2,803	75.2	24.3	17.8	6.5	3.1	3.3	1.3	2.0	0.5
Aged 5 to 9	3,119	78.2	21.4	15.6	5.8	3.0	2.8	1.5	1.3	0.4
Aged 10 to 14	3,058	83.7	15.7	11.1	4.5	2.8	1.8	1.3	0.5	0.6
Aged 15 to 19	2,768	80.7	18.9	12.8	6.2	3.1	3.0	1.5	1.6	0.4
Aged 15 to 17	1,724	82.0	17.6	11.4	6.3	2.7	3.5	1.8	1.8	0.3
Aged 18 and 19	1,044	78.4	21.1	15.0	6.0	3.8	2.2	1.1	1.1	0.5
Aged 20 to 24	2,636	68.2	31.1	20.9	10.2	5.7	4.6	2.2	2.4	0.7
Aged 25 to 29	2,617	71.2	28.5	19.3	9.2	4.8	4.4	2.6	1.8	0.3
Aged 30 to 34	2,862	73.4	25.8	18.0	7.8	3.4	4.4	2.5	1.9	0.8
Aged 35 to 39	2,710	78.7	21.2	15.4	5.9	3.0	2.9	1.3	1.6	0.1
Aged 40 to 44	2,320	84.5	14.8	9.2	5.6	3.9	1.7	1.3	0.5	0.7
Aged 45 to 49	1,748	87.0	13.0	9.7	3.3	1.7	1.5	0.7	0.9	0.1
Aged 50 to 54	1,300	89.4	10.3	7.3	3.0	0.6	2.5	1.4	1.0	0.4
Aged 55 to 59	1,079	92.1	7.7	3.4	4.3	2.2	2.0	1.1	0.9	0.2
Aged 60 to 64	955	91.0	9.0	6.5	2.4	1.0	1.4	0.9	0.4	0.1
Aged 60 and 61	419	93.3	6.7	6.0	0.7	-	0.7	0.7	-	0.2
Aged 62 to 64	536	89.2	10.8	6.9	3.7	1.9	1.9	1.3	0.7	-
Aged 65 to 69	855	95.0	5.0	2.5	2.6	1.4	1.2	1.2	-	-
Aged 70 to 74	703	93.2	6.8	4.6	2.1	1.1	1.1	0.3	0.7	-
Aged 75 to 79	476	93.9	6.1	5.9	0.2	-	0.2	0.2	-	-
Aged 80 to 84	274	93.1	6.9	2.9	4.0	2.6	1.5	0.7	0.7	-
Aged 85 or older	202	96.5	3.5	2.5	1.5	-	1.5	-	1.5	-
Median age	28.6	30.1	24.7	24.5	25.3	24.8	25.9	26.8	24.7	22.7

Note: (-) means number in sample is too small to make a reliable estimate.
Source: Bureau of the Census, Geographical Mobility: March 1993 to March 1994, Current Population Reports, P20-485, 1995

Reasons for Moving Among Black Movers, 1993

(number and percent distribution of black households moving in the previous 12 months by reason for move and for choosing new neighborhood and house, and by comparison with previous home and neighborhood, by homeownership status, 1993; numbers in thousands)

	total		owner-occupied		renter-occupied	
	number	percent	number	percent	number	percent
Total households moving in past 12 months	2,208	100.0%	259	100.0%	1,949	100.0%
Reasons for leaving previous unit*						
Private displacement	117	5.3	17	6.6	100	5.1
Government displacement	40	1.8	5	1.9	35	1.8
Disaster loss	20	0.9	5	1.9	16	0.8
New job or job transfer	154	7.0	7	2.7	147	7.5
To be closer to work, school, other	136	6.2	10	3.9	126	6.5
Other, financial/employment related	101	4.6	7	2.7	95	4.9
To establish own household	459	20.8	38	14.7	420	21.5
Needed larger house or apartment	396	17.9	50	19.3	346	17.8
Married	26	1.2	8	3.1	19	1.0
Widowed, divorced, or separated	82	3.7	5	1.9	78	4.0
Other, family/person related	184	8.3	19	7.3	165	8.5
Wanted better home	295	13.4	32	12.4	263	13.5
Change from owner to renter	19	0.9	-	0.0	19	1.0
Change from renter to owner	86	3.9	86	33.2	-	0.0
Wanted lower rent or maintenance	152	6.9	3	1.2	150	7.7
Choice of present neighborhood*						
Convenient to job	408	18.5	39	15.1	370	19.0
Convenient to friends or relatives	420	19.0	28	10.8	392	20.1
Convenient to leisure activities	46	2.1	12	4.6	34	1.7
Convenient to public transportation	110	5.0	8	3.1	102	5.2
Good schools	161	7.3	45	17.4	116	6.0
Other public services	46	2.1	11	4.2	36	1.8
Looks/design of neighborhood	348	15.8	62	23.9	285	14.6
House was most important consideration	475	21.5	92	35.5	384	19.7
Neighborhood search						
Looked at just this neighborhood	877	39.7	66	25.5	811	41.6
Looked at other neighborhoods	1,261	57.1	179	69.1	1,083	55.6

(continued)

(continued from previous page)

	total		owner-occupied		renter-occupied	
	number	*percent*	*number*	*percent*	*number*	*percent*
Choice of present home*						
Financial reasons	874	39.6%	140	54.1%	734	37.7%
Room layout/design	407	18.4	76	29.3	331	17.0
Kitchen	40	1.8	18	6.9	22	1.1
Size	346	15.7	49	18.9	298	15.3
Exterior appearance	135	6.1	46	17.8	90	4.6
Yard/trees/view	99	4.5	24	9.3	75	3.8
Quality of construction	81	3.7	40	15.4	41	2.1
Only one available	333	15.1	10	3.9	323	16.6
Other reasons	636	28.8	48	18.5	588	30.2
Comparison to previous home						
Better home	1,099	49.8	178	68.7	921	47.3
Worse home	375	17.0	15	5.8	360	18.5
About the same	655	29.7	52	20.1	603	30.9
Comparison to previous neighborhood						
Better neighborhood	783	35.5	118	45.6	665	34.1
Worse neighborhood	326	14.8	17	6.6	309	15.9
About the same	843	38.2	108	41.7	735	37.7
Same neighborhood	180	8.2	4	1.5	176	9.0

* Figures may not add to total because more than one category may apply and unreported reasons are not shown.
Source: Bureau of the Census, American Housing Survey for the United States in 1993, *Current Housing Reports, H150/93, 1995*

Housing Value and Purchase Price for Black Homeowners, 1993

(number and percent distribution of black homeowners by value of home, purchase price, and major source of downpayment, 1993; numbers in thousands)

	number	percent
Total homeowners	4,788	100.0%
Value of home		
Under $50,000	2,008	41.9
$50,000 to $79,999	1,224	25.6
$80,000 to $99,999	533	11.1
$100,000 to $149,999	589	12.3
$150,000 to $199,999	264	5.5
$200,000 to $299,999	128	2.7
$300,000 or more	41	0.9
Median	$58,372	-
Purchase price*		
Home purchased or built	4,395	91.8
Under $50,000	2,619	54.7
$50,000 to $79,999	612	12.8
$80,000 to $99,999	227	4.7
$100,000 to $149,999	177	3.7
$150,000 to $199,999	50	1.0
$200,000 to $299,999	40	0.8
$300,000 or more	18	0.4
Median purchase price	$29,003	-
Received as inheritance or gift	213	4.4
Major source of downpayment*		
Sale of previous home	463	9.7
Savings or cash on hand	2,759	57.6
Sale of other investment	14	0.3
Borrowing, other than mortgage on this property	193	4.0
Inheritance or gift	74	1.5
Land where building built used for financing	30	0.6
Other	231	4.8
No downpayment	453	9.5

* Figures may not add to total because "not reported" is not shown.
Source: Bureau of the Census, American Housing Survey for the United States in 1993, Current Housing Reports, H150/93, 1995

Repairs, Improvements, and Alterations by Black Homeowners, 1993

(number and percent of black homeowners performing selected repairs, improvements, and alterations to their homes in the past two years; among those doing work, percent who had most of it done by others; among those doing work, percent spending $500 or more, 1993; numbers in thousands)

	number	percent having work done	percent having most work done by others	percent spending $500 or more
Total homeowners	4,788	-	-	-
Roof replaced (all or part)	904	18.9%	78.5%	68.5%
Additions built	170	3.6	77.1	71.2
Kitchen remodeled or added	389	8.1	61.7	66.1
Bathroom remodeled or added	452	9.4	52.0	53.3
Siding replaced or added	221	4.6	76.5	52.0
Storm doors/windows bought and installed	604	12.6	71.4	49.3
Major equipment replaced or added	375	7.8	86.7	66.1
Insulation added	235	4.9	58.3	17.0

Source: Bureau of the Census, American Housing Survey for the United States in 1993, *Current Housing Reports, H150/93, 1995*

Blacks:
Income

The median income of black households fell by a scant 0.7 percent between 1990 and 1994, to $21,027 after adjusting for inflation. All racial and ethnic groups lost ground during those years, but the decline for black households was smaller than that for any other group.

While black household income grew relative to the incomes of other racial and ethnic groups, it stood at just 65 percent of the median for all households in 1994. The fact that married couples—typically the most affluent household type—are just 33 percent of all black households accounts in large part for the lower household incomes of blacks. Black married couples had a median income of $40,432 in 1994, while black female-headed families (who are as numerous as couples) had a median income of just $14,650.

For black men and women, incomes peak in the 45-to-54 age group. Black men aged 45 to 54 who work full-time had a median income of $31,310 in 1994, while black women in this age group who work full-time had a median income of $23,233. The earnings of blacks rise steadily with education. Black men with at least a bachelor's degree who work full-time had median earnings of $36,072, while similarly educated black women earned $31,890.

Black families are more likely to be poor than the average American family, but black poverty rates dropped sharply between 1990 and 1994. Overall, 31 percent of blacks were poor in 1994, with poverty the highest (44 percent) among blacks under age 18.

Median Income of Black Households, 1980 to 1994

(median income of black households, and ratio of black to total median income, 1980-1994; percent change in income and ratio, selected years; in 1994 dollars)

	median income	ratio black/total
1994	$21,027	0.65
1993	20,033	0.63
1992	19,811	0.61
1991	20,464	0.62
1990	21,177	0.62
1989	21,612	0.63
1988	20,554	0.60
1987	20,445	0.60
1986	20,391	0.61
1985	20,411	0.63
1984	19,215	0.60
1983	18,559	0.59
1982	18,553	0.59
1981	18,601	0.59
1980	19,383	0.61
Percent change		
1990-1994	-0.7%	4.5%
1980-1994	8.5	7.2

Note: The ratio is calculated by dividing the median income of black households by the median for total households.
Source: Bureau of the Census, unpublished tables from the 1995 Current Population Survey

Income Distribution of Black Households by Age of Householder, 1994

(number and percent distribution of black households by income and age of householder, 1994; households in thousands as of 1995)

	total	< 25	25-34	35-44	45-54	55-64	65+
Total	11,655	833	2,674	2,950	2,046	1,325	1,825
Under $10,000	3,066	361	684	606	303	380	733
$10,000 to $19,999	2,548	227	632	548	369	232	542
$20,000 to $29,999	1,831	109	502	490	297	205	227
$30,000 to $39,999	1,236	69	272	376	245	129	146
$40,000 to $49,999	982	26	233	288	238	126	69
$50,000 to $59,999	656	27	138	222	175	63	32
$60,000 to $69,999	458	3	108	153	123	52	20
$70,000 to $79,999	269	3	26	105	76	40	19
$80,000 to $89,999	175	3	24	40	72	26	9
$90,000 to $99,999	136	6	19	41	38	23	9
$100,000 or more	299	-	35	82	112	50	21
Median income	$21,207	$11,765	$20,348	$25,943	$31,432	$22,577	$12,510
Percent distribution	100.0%	100.0%	100.0%	100.0%	100.0%	100.0%	100.0%
Under $10,000	26.3	43.3	25.6	20.5	14.8	28.7	40.2
$10,000 to $19,999	21.9	27.3	23.6	18.6	18.0	17.5	29.7
$20,000 to $29,999	15.7	13.1	18.8	16.6	14.5	15.5	12.4
$30,000 to $39,999	10.6	8.3	10.2	12.7	12.0	9.7	8.0
$40,000 to $49,999	8.4	3.1	8.7	9.8	11.6	9.5	3.8
$50,000 to $59,999	5.6	3.2	5.2	7.5	8.6	4.8	1.8
$60,000 to $69,999	3.9	0.4	4.0	5.2	6.0	3.9	1.1
$70,000 to $79,999	2.3	0.4	1.0	3.6	3.7	3.0	1.0
$80,000 to $89,999	1.5	0.4	0.9	1.4	3.5	2.0	0.5
$90,000 to $99,999	1.2	0.7	0.7	1.4	1.9	1.7	0.5
$100,000 or more	2.6	-	1.3	2.8	5.5	3.8	1.2

Note: (-) means number in sample is too small to make a reliable estimate.
Source: Bureau of the Census, unpublished tables from the 1995 Current Population Survey

Income Distribution of Black Households by Household Type, 1994

(number and percent distribution of black households by income and type of household, 1994; households in thousands as of 1995)

	total households	family households				total	nonfamily households			
		total	married couples	female hh no spouse present	male hh no spouse present		female householder		male householder	
							total	living alone	total	living alone
Total	11,655	8,093	3,842	3,716	536	3,562	1,909	1,728	1,653	1,381
Under $10,000	3,066	1,621	196	1,317	109	1,445	925	895	521	498
$10,000 to $19,999	2,548	1,673	543	1,012	118	876	460	416	415	342
$20,000 to $29,999	1,831	1,269	619	533	117	560	264	228	296	239
$30,000 to $39,999	1,236	985	539	378	67	251	97	76	154	121
$40,000 to $49,999	982	779	528	208	44	203	75	54	128	96
$50,000 to $59,999	656	567	424	107	37	89	34	24	55	37
$60,000 to $69,999	458	402	326	61	15	57	20	11	37	22
$70,000 to $79,999	269	247	197	45	5	22	12	12	10	6
$80,000 to $89,999	175	160	149	11	-	14	6	5	8	5
$90,000 to $99,999	136	122	93	21	9	13	6	2	7	2
$100,000 or more	299	267	228	22	17	32	11	7	21	15
Median income	$21,027	$25,475	$40,432	$14,650	$23,073	$13,320	$10,458	$9,621	$16,868	$15,223

(continued)

(continued from previous page)

	total households	family households				nonfamily households					
		total	married couples	female hh no spouse present	male hh no spouse present	total	female householder		male householder		
							total	living alone	total	living alone
Percent distribution	100.0%	100.0%	100.0%	100.0%	100.0%	100.0%	100.0%	100.0%	100.0%	100.0%
Under $10,000	26.3	20.0	5.1	35.4	20.3	40.6	48.5	51.8	31.5	36.1
$10,000 to $19,999	21.9	20.7	14.1	27.2	22.0	24.6	24.1	24.1	25.1	24.8
$20,000 to $29,999	15.7	15.7	16.1	14.3	21.8	15.7	13.8	13.2	17.9	17.3
$30,000 to $39,999	10.6	12.2	14.0	10.2	12.5	7.0	5.1	4.4	9.3	8.8
$40,000 to $49,999	8.4	9.6	13.7	5.6	8.2	5.7	3.9	3.1	7.7	7.0
$50,000 to $59,999	5.6	7.0	11.0	2.9	6.9	2.5	1.8	1.4	3.3	2.7
$60,000 to $69,999	3.9	5.0	8.5	1.6	2.8	1.6	1.0	0.6	2.2	1.6
$70,000 to $79,999	2.3	3.1	5.1	1.2	0.9	0.6	0.6	0.7	0.6	0.4
$80,000 to $89,999	1.5	2.0	3.9	0.3	-	0.4	0.3	0.3	0.5	0.4
$90,000 to $99,999	1.2	1.5	2.4	0.6	1.7	0.4	0.3	0.1	0.4	0.1
$100,000 or more	2.6	3.3	5.9	0.6	3.2	0.9	0.6	0.4	1.3	1.1

Note: (-) means number in sample is too small to make a reliable estimate.
Source: Bureau of the Census, unpublished tables from the 1995 Current Population Survey

Income Distribution of Black Men by Age, 1994

(number and percent distribution of black men aged 15 or older by income and age, 1994; men in thousands as of 1995)

	total	< 25	25-34	35-44	45-54	55-64	65+
TOTAL	10,825	2,624	2,477	2,388	1,441	896	999
Without income	1,625	1,068	219	180	66	61	31
With income	9,199	1,556	2,259	2,209	1,374	834	968
Under $10,000	3,218	1,075	590	554	284	240	474
$10,000 to $19,999	2,426	371	688	523	301	200	343
$20,000 to $29,999	1,561	87	573	444	230	149	76
$30,000 to $39,999	883	19	225	317	216	74	33
$40,000 to $49,999	467	3	78	175	131	65	15
$50,000 to $74,999	466	-	87	136	156	78	9
$75,000 to $99,999	97	-	7	29	32	19	10
$100,000 or more	80	-	12	29	25	8	6
Median income							
Total men	$14,982	$ 5,819	$17,383	$20,439	$24,639	$18,546	$10,190
Year-round, full-time workers	24,405	12,483	22,411	26,859	31,310	28,813	25,606
PERCENT DISTRIB.	100.0%	100.0%	100.0%	100.0%	100.0%	100.0%	100.0%
Without income	15.0	40.7	8.8	7.5	4.6	6.8	3.1
With income	85.0	59.3	91.2	92.5	95.4	93.1	96.9
Under $10,000	29.7	41.0	23.8	23.2	19.7	26.8	47.4
$10,000 to $19,999	22.4	14.1	27.8	21.9	20.9	22.3	34.3
$20,000 to $29,999	14.4	3.3	23.1	18.6	16.0	16.6	7.6
$30,000 to $39,999	8.2	0.7	9.1	13.3	15.0	8.3	3.3
$40,000 to $49,999	4.3	0.1	3.1	7.3	9.1	7.3	1.5
$50,000 to $74,999	4.3	-	3.5	5.7	10.8	8.7	0.9
$75,000 to $99,999	0.9	-	0.3	1.2	2.2	2.1	1.0
$100,000 or more	0.7	-	0.5	1.2	1.7	0.9	0.6

Note: (-) means number in sample is too small to make a reliable estimate.
Source: Bureau of the Census, unpublished tables from the 1995 Current Population Survey

Income Distribution of Black Women by Age, 1994

(number and percent distribution of black women aged 15 or older by income and age, 1994; women in thousands as of 1995)

	total	< 25	25-34	35-44	45-54	55-64	65+
TOTAL	13,097	2,841	2,969	2,801	1,754	1,174	1,558
Without income	1,647	927	203	171	158	121	67
With income	11,450	1,914	2,765	2,631	1,596	1,053	1,491
Under $10,000	5,511	1,460	1,058	868	488	517	1,121
$10,000 to $19,999	2,992	346	913	751	458	256	271
$20,000 to $29,999	1,518	82	462	484	297	128	66
$30,000 to $39,999	742	12	208	276	150	80	17
$40,000 to $49,999	344	6	71	137	98	26	4
$50,000 to $74,999	256	6	39	86	78	41	6
$75,000 to $99,999	43	3	6	14	13	1	6
$100,000 or more	44	-	9	15	15	5	-
Median income							
Total women	$10,544	$4,930	$13,083	$15,486	$16,075	$10,295	$6,986
Year-round, full-time workers	20,628	15,035	19,603	22,007	23,233	20,502	-
PERCENT DISTRIB.	100.0%	100.0%	100.0%	100.0%	100.0%	100.0%	100.0%
Without income	12.6	32.6	6.8	6.1	9.0	10.3	4.3
With income	87.4	67.4	93.1	93.9	91.0	89.7	95.7
Under $10,000	42.1	51.4	35.6	31.0	27.8	44.0	72.0
$10,000 to $19,999	22.8	12.2	30.8	26.8	26.1	21.8	17.4
$20,000 to $29,999	11.6	2.9	15.6	17.3	16.9	10.9	4.2
$30,000 to $39,999	5.7	0.4	7.0	9.9	8.6	6.8	1.1
$40,000 to $49,999	2.6	0.2	2.4	4.9	5.6	2.2	0.3
$50,000 to $74,999	2.0	0.2	1.3	3.1	4.4	3.5	0.4
$75,000 to $99,999	0.3	0.1	0.2	0.5	0.7	0.1	0.4
$100,000 or more	0.3	-	0.3	0.5	0.9	0.4	-

Note: (-) means number in sample is too small to make a reliable estimate.
Source: Bureau of the Census, unpublished tables from the 1995 Current Population Survey

Median Earnings of Black Men and Women
Who Work Full-Time, 1980 to 1994

(median earnings of black men and women aged 15 or older who work year-round, full-time; ratio of black to total median earnings, and ratio of black female to black male median earnings, 1980-1994; percent change in earnings and ratios for selected years; in 1994 dollars)

	black men		black women		
	median earnings	ratio black/total	median earnings	ratio black/total	ratio black female/male
1994	$23,742	0.77	$19,910	0.90	0.84
1993	23,608	0.76	20,323	0.91	0.86
1992	23,658	0.74	20,877	0.92	0.88
1991	24,020	0.75	20,369	0.91	0.85
1990	23,941	0.76	20,455	0.91	0.85
1989	24,412	0.75	20,783	0.93	0.85
1988	25,520	0.76	20,718	0.94	0.81
1987	24,947	0.74	20,548	0.93	0.82
1986	24,798	0.73	19,923	0.91	0.80
1985	24,074	0.72	19,707	0.92	0.82
1984	23,729	0.72	19,570	0.93	0.82
1983	24,035	0.74	18,882	0.91	0.79
1982	24,033	0.74	18,807	0.93	0.78
1981	24,224	0.73	18,421	0.93	0.76
1980	24,394	0.73	19,217	0.95	0.79
Percent change					
1990-1994	-0.8%	0.9%	-2.7%	-1.5%	-1.8%
1980-1994	-2.7	5.7	3.6	-5.9	6.5

Note: The black/total ratios are calculated by dividing the median earnings of black men and women by the median for total men and women. The female/male ratio is calculated by dividing the median earnings of black women by the median earnings of black men.
Source: Bureau of the Census, unpublished tables from the 1995 Current Population Survey

Median Earnings of Black Men and Women by Education, 1994

(median earnings of black men and women aged 25 or older by work experience and educational attainment, 1994)

	men		women	
	total	year-round full-time workers	total	year-round full-time workers
Total	$21,224	$25,349	$16,110	$20,611
Less than 9th grade	14,346	16,643	8,039	12,231
9th to 12th grade, no diploma	14,799	21,403	9,351	14,444
High school graduate	18,926	22,028	14,093	17,754
Some college, no degree	21,808	25,949	17,114	20,928
Associate's degree	30,128	31,702	17,573	21,492
Bachelor's degree or more	32,911	36,072	30,346	31,890
Bachelor's degree	30,602	32,314	26,787	30,549
Master's degree	41,596	48,608	34,991	40,104
Professional degree	-	-	-	-
Doctoral degree	-	-	-	-

Note: (-) means number in sample is too small to make a reliable estimate.
Source: Bureau of the Census, unpublished tables from the 1995 Current Population Survey

Black Families Below the Poverty Level, 1980 to 1994

(total number of black families, and number and percent below poverty level by type of family and presence of children under age 18, 1980-94; percent change in numbers and rates for selected years; families in thousands as of March the following year)

	total families			married couples			female hh, no spouse present		
		in poverty			in poverty			in poverty	
	total	number	percent	total	number	percent	total	number	percent
With & without children <18									
1994	8,093	2,212	27.3%	3,842	336	8.7%	3,716	1,715	46.2%
1993	7,993	2,499	31.3	3,715	458	12.3	3,828	1,906	49.9
1992	7,982	2,484	31.1	3,777	490	13.0	3,738	1,878	50.2
1991	7,716	2,343	30.4	3,631	399	11.0	3,582	1,834	51.2
1990	7,471	2,193	29.3	3,569	448	12.6	3,430	1,648	48.1
1989	7,470	2,077	27.8	3,750	443	11.8	3,275	1,524	46.5
1988	7,409	2,069	28.2	3,722	421	11.3	3,223	1,579	49.0
1987	7,202	2,117	29.4	3,681	439	11.9	3,089	1,577	51.1
1986	7,096	1,967	28.0	3,742	403	10.8	2,967	1,488	50.1
1985	6,921	1,963	28.7	3,680	447	12.2	2,874	1,452	50.5
1984	6,778	2,094	30.9	3,469	479	13.8	2,964	1,533	51.7
1983	6,681	2,161	32.3	3,454	535	15.5	2,871	1,541	53.7
1982	6,530	2,158	33.0	3,486	543	15.6	2,734	1,535	56.2
1981	6,413	1,972	30.8	3,535	543	15.4	2,605	1,377	52.9
1980	6,317	1,826	28.9	3,392	474	14.0	2,634	1,301	49.4
Percent change									
1990-1994	8.3%	0.9%	-6.8%	7.6%	-25.0%	-31.0%	8.3%	4.1%	-4.0%
1980-1994	28.1	21.1	-5.5	13.3	-29.1	-37.9	41.1	31.8	-6.5

(continued)

(continued from previous page)

	total families			married couples			female hh, no spouse present		
		in poverty			in poverty			in poverty	
	total	number	percent	total	number	percent	total	number	percent
With children <18									
1994	5,439	1,954	35.9%	2,147	245	11.4%	2,951	1,591	53.9%
1993	5,525	2,171	39.3	2,147	298	13.9	3,084	1,780	57.7
1992	5,448	2,132	39.1	2,229	343	15.4	2,971	1,706	57.4
1991	5,143	2,016	39.2	2,129	263	12.4	2,771	1,676	60.5
1990	5,069	1,887	37.2	2,104	301	14.3	2,698	1,513	56.1
1989	5,031	1,783	35.4	2,179	291	13.3	2,624	1,415	53.9
1988	5,010	1,802	36.0	2,181	272	12.5	2,583	1,452	56.2
1987	4,880	1,788	36.6	2,205	290	13.2	2,453	1,437	58.6
1986	4,806	1,699	35.4	2,236	257	11.5	2,386	1,384	58.0
1985	4,636	1,670	36.0	2,185	281	12.9	2,269	1,336	58.9
1984	4,512	1,758	39.0	2,001	331	16.6	2,335	1,364	58.4
1983	4,482	1,789	39.9	2,052	369	18.0	2,244	1,362	60.7
1982	4,470	1,819	40.7	2,093	360	17.2	2,199	1,401	63.7
1981	4,455	1,652	37.1	2,202	357	16.2	2,118	1,261	59.5
1980	4,465	1,583	35.5	2,154	333	15.5	2,171	1,217	56.0
Percent change									
1990-1994	7.3%	3.6%	-3.5%	2.0%	-18.6%	-20.3%	9.4%	5.2%	-3.9%
1980-1994	21.8	23.4	1.1	-0.3	-26.4	-26.5	35.9	30.7	-3.8

Source: Bureau of the Census, unpublished tables from the 1995 Current Population Survey

Blacks in Poverty by Age and Sex, 1994

(total number of blacks, and number and percent below poverty level by age and sex, 1994; persons in thousands as of 1995)

	total	in poverty	
		number	percent
Total	33,353	10,196	30.6%
Under age 18	11,211	4,906	43.8
Aged 18 to 24	3,685	1,068	29.0
Aged 25 to 34	5,446	1,347	24.7
Aged 35 to 44	5,190	1,135	21.9
Aged 45 to 54	3,195	537	16.8
Aged 55 to 59	1,128	239	21.2
Aged 60 to 64	942	264	28.0
Aged 65 to 74	1,542	401	26.0
Aged 75 or older	1,015	299	29.4
Female, total	17,754	5,980	33.7
Under age 18	5,533	2,449	44.3
Aged 18 to 24	1,965	722	36.8
Aged 25 to 34	2,969	957	32.2
Aged 35 to 44	2,801	692	24.7
Aged 45 to 54	1,754	317	18.1
Aged 55 to 59	645	177	27.4
Aged 60 to 64	529	171	32.4
Aged 65 to 74	895	266	29.7
Aged 75 or older	662	228	34.4
Male, total	15,599	4,216	27.0
Under age 18	5,678	2,457	43.3
Aged 18 to 24	1,720	346	20.1
Aged 25 to 34	2,477	389	15.7
Aged 35 to 44	2,388	443	18.5
Aged 45 to 54	1,441	221	15.3
Aged 55 to 59	483	62	12.9
Aged 60 to 64	413	92	22.4
Aged 65 to 74	646	135	20.8
Aged 75 or older	353	71	20.1

Source: Bureau of the Census, unpublished tables from the 1995 Current Population Survey

Blacks:
Labor Force

Sixty-four percent of blacks aged 16 or older are in the labor force, including 69 percent of black men and 60 percent of black women. Black men are less likely to be in the labor force than are men nationally, who have a labor force participation rate of 75 percent. The labor force paticipation rate of black women is close to that for all women.

Only 35 percent of black households have two or more earners, well below the 45 percent of all U.S. households with two earners. Behind this lower figure is the fact that relatively few black households are headed by married couples. Among black couples, fully 56 percent are dual earners, slightly greater than the 55 percent of total couples that are dual earners. Fewer than 18 percent of black couples are traditional—meaning only the husband works. Among all married couples, 22 percent are traditional.

Twenty percent of blacks are employed in managerial or professional specialty occupations, below the 28 percent of all workers employed in these occupations. Conversely, 22 percent of blacks are employed in service occupations, compared with just 14 percent of all workers. Blacks account for 11 percent of all employed Americans, but for 17 percent of social, recreation, and religious workers and for 28 percent of bus drivers. Twenty percent of employed blacks are union members, versus 15 percent of all workers.

Between 1994 and 2005, the number of black workers will grow by 15 percent. Blacks will account for 11 percent of the labor force in 2005.

Employment Status of Blacks by Age and Sex, 1995

(employment status of the civilian noninstitutional black population aged 16 or older, by age and sex, 1995; numbers in thousands)

	civilian labor force						not in labor force	
	total	percent of population	employed	percent of labor force	unem- ployed	percent of labor force	total	percent of population
Total persons	14,817	63.7%	13,279	89.6%	1,538	10.4%	8,429	36.3%
Aged 16 to 19	911	39.9	586	64.3	325	35.7	1,372	60.1
Aged 20 to 24	1,754	68.7	1,443	82.3	311	17.7	800	31.3
Aged 25 to 34	4,267	80.0	3,844	90.1	423	9.9	1,070	20.0
Aged 35 to 44	4,165	80.4	3,861	92.7	303	7.3	1,013	19.6
Aged 45 to 54	2,404	74.1	2,288	95.2	116	4.8	840	25.9
Aged 55 to 64	1,046	50.3	1,004	96.0	42	4.0	1,034	49.7
Aged 65 or older	271	10.5	253	93.4	18	6.7	2,300	89.5
Total men	7,183	69.0	6,422	89.4	762	10.6	3,228	31.0
Aged 16 to 19	453	40.1	285	62.9	168	37.1	677	59.9
Aged 20 to 24	866	74.6	714	82.4	153	17.7	295	25.4
Aged 25 to 34	2,089	87.5	1,895	90.7	195	9.3	299	12.5
Aged 35 to 44	1,987	84.1	1,836	92.4	150	7.5	375	15.9
Aged 45 to 54	1,148	78.5	1,085	94.5	63	5.5	314	21.5
Aged 55 to 64	490	54.4	468	95.5	21	4.3	411	45.6
Aged 65 or older	150	14.9	138	92.0	11	7.6	857	85.1
Total women	7,634	59.5	6,857	89.8	777	10.2	5,201	40.5
Aged 16 to 19	458	39.8	301	65.7	157	34.3	695	60.3
Aged 20 to 24	887	63.7	729	82.2	158	17.8	505	36.3
Aged 25 to 34	2,177	73.9	1,949	89.5	228	10.5	771	26.2
Aged 35 to 44	2,178	77.3	2,025	93.0	153	7.0	638	22.7
Aged 45 to 54	1,256	70.5	1,202	95.7	53	4.2	527	29.6
Aged 55 to 64	556	47.2	536	96.4	20	3.6	623	52.8
Aged 65 or older	121	7.7	114	94.2	7	5.6	1,443	92.3

Note: The civilian labor force equals the number employed plus the number unemployed. The civilian population equals the number in the labor force plus the number not in the labor force.
Source: Bureau of Labor Statistics, Employment and Earnings, January 1996

Black Households by Number of Earners, 1994

(number and percent distribution of black households, by number of earners, 1994; numbers in thousands)

	number	percent
Total households	11,281	100.0%
No earners	2,831	25.1
One earner	4,513	40.0
Two or more earners	3,938	34.9
Two earners	3,072	27.2
Three earners	706	6.3
Four or more earners	160	1.4

Source: Bureau of the Census, Income, Poverty, and Valuation of Noncash Benefits: 1993, *Current Population Reports, P60-188, 1995*

Labor Force Status of Black Married Couples, 1994

(number and percent distribution of black married couples by age of householder and labor force status of husband and wife, 1994; numbers in thousands)

	total married couples	husband and/or wife in labor force			neither husband nor wife in labor force
		husband and wife	husband only	wife only	
Total, number	3,714	2,083	650	357	623
Under age 20	1	1	-	-	-
Aged 20 to 24	117	68	36	9	5
Aged 25 to 29	317	208	63	31	15
Aged 30 to 34	433	333	80	16	3
Aged 35 to 39	465	337	89	18	21
Aged 40 to 44	520	406	72	31	12
Aged 45 to 49	427	296	69	33	29
Aged 50 to 54	356	225	83	37	12
Aged 55 to 59	284	124	61	41	58
Aged 60 to 64	233	57	45	61	71
Aged 65 to 74	374	22	46	63	243
Aged 75 to 84	172	6	8	18	140
Aged 85 or older	14	-	-	-	14
Total, percent	100.0%	56.1%	17.5%	9.6%	16.8%
Under age 20	100.0	100.0	-	-	-
Aged 20 to 24	100.0	58.1	30.8	7.7	4.3
Aged 25 to 29	100.0	65.6	19.9	9.8	4.7
Aged 30 to 34	100.0	76.9	18.5	3.7	0.7
Aged 35 to 39	100.0	72.5	19.1	3.9	4.5
Aged 40 to 44	100.0	78.1	13.8	6.0	2.3
Aged 45 to 49	100.0	69.3	16.2	7.7	6.8
Aged 50 to 54	100.0	63.2	23.3	10.4	3.4
Aged 55 to 59	100.0	43.7	21.5	14.4	20.4
Aged 60 to 64	100.0	24.5	19.3	26.2	30.5
Aged 65 to 74	100.0	5.9	12.3	16.8	65.0
Aged 75 to 84	100.0	3.5	4.7	10.5	81.4
Aged 85 or older	100.0	-	-	-	100.0

Note: (-) means number in sample is too small to make a reliable estimate.
Source: Bureau of the Census, Household and Family Characteristics: March 1994, *Current Population Reports, P20-483, 1995*

Occupations of Blacks by Sex, 1995

(number and percent distribution of employed blacks aged 16 or older in the civilian labor force, by occupation and sex, 1995; numbers in thousands)

	total	*men*	*women*
Total employed, number	13,279	6,422	6,857
Total employed, percent	100.0%	100.0%	100.0%
Managerial and professional specialty	20.0	17.7	22.1
Executive, administrative, and managerial	9.3	9.2	9.4
Professional specialty	10.7	8.6	12.7
Technical, sales, and administrative support	28.7	17.7	39.0
Technicians and related support	2.8	2.3	3.4
Sales occupations	8.9	7.0	10.7
Administrative support, including clerical	16.9	8.4	25.0
Service occupations	21.7	17.8	25.4
Private household	1.0	0.1	1.9
Protective service	3.1	4.7	1.5
Service, except private household and protective	17.6	12.9	22.0
Precision production, craft, and repair	8.1	14.3	2.3
Operators, fabricators, and laborers	20.4	30.3	11.1
Machine operators, assemblers, and inspectors	9.2	10.4	8.0
Transportation and material moving occupations	5.7	10.5	1.2
Handlers, equipment cleaners, helpers, and laborers	5.5	9.4	1.9
Farming, forestry, and fishing	1.2	2.2	0.2

Source: Bureau of Labor Statistics, Employment and Earnings, *January 1996*

Black Workers by Detailed Occupation, 1995

(total number of employed persons aged 16 or older in the civilian labor force; number and percent distribution of employed blacks; and black share of total employed, by selected occupation, 1995; numbers in thousands)

	total	black number	black percent	black share of total employed
Total employed	124,900	13,279	100.0%	10.6%
Managerial and professional specialty	35,318	2,656	20.0	7.5
Executive, administrative, and managerial	17,186	1,235	9.3	7.2
Officials and administrators, public admin.	618	84	0.6	13.6
Financial managers	605	38	0.3	6.3
Personnel and labor relations managers	125	20	0.1	15.8
Purchasing managers	135	9	0.1	6.6
Managers, marketing, advertising, and public relations	663	15	0.1	2.2
Administrators, education and related fields	701	79	0.6	11.2
Managers, medicine and health	653	59	0.4	9.0
Managers, food serving and lodging establishments	1,276	117	0.9	9.2
Managers, property and real estate	522	35	0.3	6.8
Professional specialty	18,132	1,421	10.7	7.8
Architects	163	4	-	2.5
Engineers	1,934	91	0.7	4.7
Mathematical and computer scientists	1,195	86	0.6	7.2
Natural scientists	519	20	0.2	3.9
Physicians	693	34	0.3	4.9
Dentists	155	3	-	1.9
Registered nurses	1,977	166	1.3	8.4
Pharmacists	170	7	0.1	4.3
Dietitians	94	17	0.1	18.4
Therapists	466	43	0.3	9.2
Teachers, college and university	846	52	0.4	6.2
Teachers, except college and university	4,507	419	3.2	9.3
Librarians, archivists, and curators	211	16	0.1	7.5
Economists	148	7	0.1	5.0
Psychologists	260	27	0.2	10.2
Social, recreation, and religious workers	1,303	219	1.6	16.8
Lawyers and judges	926	33	0.3	3.6
Writers, artists, entertainers, and athletes	2,054	127	1.0	6.2

(continued)

(continued from previous page)

		black		
	total	*number*	*percent*	*share of total employed*
Technical, sales, administrative support	37,417	3,811	28.7%	10.2%
Technicians and related support	3,909	372	2.8	9.7
Health technologists and technicians	1,648	213	1.6	12.9
Engineering and related technologists and technicians	880	70	0.5	8.0
Science technicians	276	25	0.2	8.9
Technicians, except health, engineering, and science	1,106	70	0.5	6.3
Airplane pilots and navigators	114	1	-	1.2
Computer programmers	553	36	0.3	6.5
Legal assistants	285	19	0.1	6.8
Sales occupations	15,119	1,182	8.9	7.8
Supervisors and proprietors	4,480	251	1.9	5.6
Sales representatives, finance and business services	2,399	132	1.0	5.5
Sales representatives, commodities, except retail	1,529	41	0.3	2.7
Sales workers, retail and personal services	6,613	754	5.7	11.4
Administrative support, including clerical	18,389	2,244	16.9	12.2
Supervisors	712	104	0.8	14.6
Computer equipment operators	491	76	0.6	15.5
Secretaries, stenographers, and typists	4,106	411	3.1	10.0
Information clerks	1,872	187	1.4	10.0
Records processing occupations, except financial	959	148	1.1	15.4
Financial records processing	2,255	138	1.0	6.1
Mail and message distributiong	1,006	205	1.5	20.4
Miscellaneous administrative support	3,441	485	3.7	14.1
Service occupations	16,930	2,882	21.7	17.0
Private household	821	133	1.0	16.7
Protective	2,237	412	3.1	18.2
Firefighting and fire prevention	249	38	0.3	15.1
Police and detectives	949	160	1.2	16.9
Guards	846	183	1.4	21.6
Service occupations, ex. private hh and protect. serv.	13,872	2,337	17.6	16.8
Food preparation and service occupations	5,800	673	5.1	11.6

(continued)

(continued from previous page)

| | total | black | | |
		number	percent	share of total employed
Health service occupations	2,315	639	4.8%	27.6%
Cleaning and building service occupations	2,946	645	4.9	21.9
Personal service occupations	2,810	379	2.9	13.5
Precision production, craft, and repair	13,524	1,076	8.1	7.9
Mechanics and repairers	4,423	367	2.8	8.3
Construction trades	5,098	362	2.7	7.1
Extractive occupations	136	4	-	2.6
Precision production occupations	3,867	340	2.6	8.8
Operators, fabricators, and laborers	18,068	2,709	20.4	15.0
Machine operators, assemblers, inspectors	7,907	1,222	9.2	15.4
Transportation and material moving occupations	5,171	757	5.7	14.7
Motor vehicle operators	3,904	593	4.5	15.2
Truck drivers	2,861	360	2.7	12.6
Bus drivers	526	147	1.1	27.9
Taxicab drivers and chauffeurs	213	49	0.4	22.8
Material moving equipment operators	1,098	145	1.1	13.2
Handlers, equipment cleaners, helpers, and laborers	4,990	730	5.5	14.7
Farming, forestry, and fishing	3,642	159	1.2	4.2

Note: Numbers will not add to total because not all occupations are shown. (-) means is less than 0.05.
Source: Bureau of Labor Statistics, Employment and Earnings, *January 1996*

Black Workers by Industry, 1995

(total number of employed persons aged 16 or older in the civilian labor force; number and percent distribution of employed blacks, and black share of total employed, by selected industry, 1995; numbers in thousands)

	total	black number	black percent	black share of total employed
Total employed	124,900	13,279	100.0%	10.6%
Agriculture	3,440	100	0.8	2.9
Mining	627	24	0.2	3.8
Construction	7,668	506	3.8	6.6
Manufacturing	20,493	2,123	16.0	10.4
Durable goods	12,015	1,021	7.7	8.5
Nondurable goods	8,478	1,102	8.3	13.0
Transportation, communications, and other public utilities	8,709	1,261	9.5	14.5
Transportation	5,589	889	6.7	15.9
Communications	1,607	198	1.5	12.3
Utilities and sanitary services	1,512	174	1.3	11.5
Wholesale and retail trade	26,071	2,233	16.8	8.6
Wholesale trade	4,986	314	2.4	6.3
Retail trade	21,086	1,919	14.5	9.1
Finance, insurance, and real estate	7,983	742	5.6	9.3
Services	43,953	5,264	39.6	12.0
Private households	971	178	1.3	18.3
Other service industries	42,982	5,086	38.3	11.8
Business, automobile, and repair services	7,526	850	6.4	11.3
Personal services, except private household	3,404	446	3.4	13.1
Entertainment and recreation services	2,238	181	1.4	8.1
Professional and related services	29,661	3,602	27.1	12.1
Hospitals	4,961	804	6.1	16.2
Health services, except hospitals	5,967	806	6.1	13.5
Educational services	9,894	1,108	8.3	11.2
Social services	2,979	521	3.9	17.5
Other professional services	5,860	363	2.7	6.2
Forestry and fisheries	152	7	0.1	4.8
Public administration	5,957	1,007	7.6	16.9

Note: Numbers of employed blacks may not add to total due to rounding.
Source: Bureau of Labor Statistics, Employment and Earnings, *January 1996*

Union Membership of Blacks, 1995

(number of employed black wage and salary workers aged 16 or older, number and percent who are represented by unions or are union members, and median weekly earnings by union membership status; by sex, 1995; numbers in thousands)

	total	men	women
Total employed	12,644	6,005	6,639
Represented by unions*	2,819	1,460	1,358
Percent of employed	22.3%	24.3%	20.5%
Members of unions**	2,519	1,353	1,167
Percent of employed	19.9%	22.5%	17.6%
Median weekly earnings, total*	$383	$411	$355
Represented by unions*	500	526	468
Members of unions**	503	526	473
Non-union	348	374	325

* Members of a labor union or an employee association similar to a union as well as workers who report no union affiliation but whose jobs are covered by a union or an employee association contract.
** Members of a labor union or an employee association similar to a union.
*** Full-time wage and salary workers.
Source: Bureau of Labor Statistics, Employment and Earnings, *January 1996*

Black Labor Force Projections by Sex, 1994 to 2005

(number of blacks aged 16 or older in the civilian labor force in 1994 and 2005, labor force participation rate of blacks in 1994 and 2005, and black share of total labor force in 1994 and 2005; percent change in number and percentage point change in share; by sex; numbers in thousands)

	1994	2005	percent change 1994-2005
Number in labor force			
Total	14,502	16,619	14.6%
Men	7,089	7,904	11.5
Women	7,413	8,714	17.5
			percentage point change 1994-2005
Labor force participation rate			
Total	63.4%	61.9%	-1.5
Men	69.1	65.8	-3.3
Women	58.7	58.8	0.1
Percent of labor force			
Total	11.1	11.3	0.2
Men	10.0	10.3	0.3
Women	12.3	12.4	0.1

Source: Bureau of Labor Statistics, Monthly Labor Review, *November 1995*

Blacks:
Population

The black population is projected to grow from 34 million in 1996 to more than 45 million by 2020, when blacks will account for 14 percent of the total U.S. population. Blacks will remain the largest minority in the U.S. for about another ten years. Sometime between 2005 and 2010, Hispanics will surpass blacks and become the dominant minority in the U.S.

Blacks account for a larger share of children and young adults than of older Americans because black fertility and mortality is greater than that of the white majority population. While only 7.6 percent of people aged 85 or older are black, fully 16 percent of children under age 5 are black.

More than half of blacks live in the South, where they account for 19 percent of the population. In Mississippi, 36 percent of the population is black, as is over 30 percent of the population in Louisiana and South Carolina. No single state is home to more than 10 percent of the black population.

Among metropolitan areas, New York has the largest number of blacks, with over 3.4 million in 1990. Blacks account for 18 percent of the population in the greater New York metropolitan area. Overall, there are 51 metropolitan areas with more than 100,000 blacks. Among them, the black share of the population is highest in Jackson, Mississippi, at 42.5 percent.

Nearly 659,000 babies were born to black mothers in 1993, or 16.5 percent of all babies born that year. Fully 69 percent of black babies are born to unmarried mothers, the highest proportion among all racial and ethnic groups. Blacks accounted for 48 percent of all births in Mississippi in 1993 and for at least one-third of births in Alabama, Georgia, Louisiana, Maryland, and South Carolina.

Blacks by Age, 1990 to 2020

(number of blacks by age, selected years 1990-2020; percent change 1990-2000 and 2000-2010; numbers in thousands)

	1990	1996	2000	2010	2020	percent change 1990-2000	2000-2010
Total							
persons	30,620	33,611	35,454	40,109	45,075	15.8%	13.1%
Under 5	2,981	3,097	3,127	3,454	3,818	4.9	10.5
5 to 9	2,713	3,094	3,158	3,296	3,717	16.4	4.4
10 to 14	2,650	2,906	3,175	3,338	3,677	19.8	5.1
15 to 19	2,709	2,892	3,032	3,494	3,639	11.9	15.2
20 to 24	2,652	2,578	2,742	3,245	3,399	3.4	18.3
25 to 29	2,774	2,601	2,551	2,830	3,242	-8.0	10.9
30 to 34	2,729	2,812	2,621	2,659	3,126	-4.0	1.4
35 to 39	2,377	2,831	2,868	2,605	2,879	20.7	-9.2
40 to 44	1,912	2,477	2,781	2,632	2,673	45.4	-5.4
45 to 49	1,419	1,998	2,307	2,735	2,493	62.6	18.6
50 to 54	1,184	1,412	1,804	2,591	2,466	52.4	43.6
55 to 59	1,043	1,163	1,325	2,150	2,565	27.0	62.3
60 to 64	974	995	1,081	1,651	2,399	11.0	52.7
65 to 69	863	925	933	1,200	1,966	8.1	28.6
70 to 74	643	703	742	833	1,289	15.4	12.3
75 to 79	485	525	554	606	788	14.2	9.4
80 to 84	290	320	336	395	455	15.9	17.6
85 or older	224	284	317	396	482	41.5	24.9
18 to 24	3,808	3,703	3,974	4,747	4,888	4.4	19.5
18 or older	20,724	22,749	24,186	27,957	31,679	16.7	15.6
65 or older	2,505	2,756	2,883	3,430	4,981	15.1	19.0

Source: Bureau of the Census, Population Projections of the United States, by Age, Sex, Race, and Hispanic Origin: 1995 to 2050, *Current Population Reports, P25-1130, 1996; and* U.S. Population Estimates, by Age, Sex, Race, and Hispanic Origin: 1980 to 1991, *Current Population Reports, P25-1095, 1993*

Black Share of the Total Population by Age, 1990 to 2020

(blacks as a percent of the total population by age, selected years 1990-2020)

	1990	1996	2000	2010	2020
Total persons	12.3%	12.7%	12.9%	13.5%	14.0%
Under age 5	15.8	16.0	16.5	17.3	17.4
Aged 5 to 9	15.0	15.8	15.9	16.9	17.2
Aged 10 to 14	15.4	15.2	15.8	16.5	17.2
Aged 15 to 19	15.3	15.6	15.3	16.0	17.0
Aged 20 to 24	13.9	14.8	15.0	15.4	16.0
Aged 25 to 29	13.1	13.7	14.4	14.4	15.0
Aged 30 to 34	12.5	13.2	13.4	14.3	14.6
Aged 35 to 39	11.9	12.6	12.9	14.1	14.0
Aged 40 to 44	10.7	11.9	12.4	13.2	14.0
Aged 45 to 49	10.3	10.8	11.6	12.5	13.6
Aged 50 to 54	10.4	10.1	10.5	12.0	12.7
Aged 55 to 59	10.0	10.2	10.0	11.3	12.1
Aged 60 to 64	9.2	9.9	10.1	10.2	11.7
Aged 65 to 69	8.6	9.4	9.9	9.9	11.2
Aged 70 to 74	8.0	8.0	8.5	9.3	9.3
Aged 75 to 79	7.9	7.6	7.5	8.5	8.4
Aged 80 to 84	7.4	7.0	6.9	7.1	7.7
Aged 85 or older	7.3	7.6	7.4	7.0	7.5
Aged 18 to 24	14.2	15.0	15.1	15.8	16.3
Aged 18 or older	11.2	11.6	11.9	12.4	12.9
Aged 65 or older	8.0	8.1	8.3	8.7	9.4

Source: Bureau of the Census, Population Projections of the United States, by Age, Sex, Race, and Hispanic Origin: 1995 to 2050, *Current Population Reports, P25-1130, 1996; and* U.S. Population Estimates, by Age, Sex, Race, and Hispanic Origin: 1980 to 1991, *Current Population Reports, P25-1095, 1993*

Non-Hispanic Blacks by Age, 1990 to 2020

(number of non-Hispanic blacks by age, selected years 1990-2020; percent change 1990-2000 and 2000-2010; numbers in thousands)

	1990	1996	2000	2010	2020	percent change 1990-2000	percent change 2000-2010
Total							
persons	29,400	31,999	33,568	37,466	41,538	14.2%	11.6%
Under 5	2,841	2,915	2,929	3,187	3,466	3.1	8.8
5 to 9	2,597	2,928	2,966	3,054	3,391	14.2	3.0
10 to 14	2,544	2,763	2,997	3,104	3,370	17.8	3.6
15 to 19	2,600	2,755	2,872	3,252	3,342	10.5	13.2
20 to 24	2,524	2,449	2,592	3,023	3,121	2.7	16.6
25 to 29	2,642	2,455	2,405	2,635	2,973	-9.0	9.6
30 to 34	2,610	2,658	2,458	2,476	2,875	-5.8	0.7
35 to 39	2,281	2,693	2,706	2,428	2,655	18.6	-10.3
40 to 44	1,839	2,365	2,641	2,448	2,469	43.6	-7.3
45 to 49	1,368	1,914	2,199	2,563	2,307	60.7	16.6
50 to 54	1,144	1,353	1,723	2,446	2,279	50.6	42.0
55 to 59	1,010	1,116	1,267	2,036	2,388	25.4	60.7
60 to 64	947	958	1,034	1,565	2,249	9.2	51.4
65 to 69	842	893	894	1,135	1,845	6.2	27.0
70 to 74	630	682	714	786	1,206	13.3	10.1
75 to 79	476	511	536	573	732	12.6	6.9
80 to 84	285	312	327	375	420	14.7	14.7
85 or older	221	279	310	381	449	40.3	22.9
18 to 24	3,632	3,520	3,749	4,354	4,459	3.2	16.1
18 or older	19,927	21,709	22,963	26,201	29,306	15.2	14.1
65 or older	2,454	2,677	2,781	3,249	4,651	13.3	16.8

Note: Hispanics may be of any race and most are white. For a breakdown of the Hispanic composition of racial groups and the racial composition of Hispanics, see the introduction to this book.
Source: Bureau of the Census, Population Projections of the United States, by Age, Sex, Race, and Hispanic Origin: 1995 to 2050, *Current Population Reports, P25-1130, 1996; and* U.S. Population Estimates, by Age, Sex, Race, and Hispanic Origin: 1980 to 1991, *Current Population Reports, P25-1095, 1993*

Blacks by Age and Sex, 1996

(number of blacks by age and sex, and sex ratio by age, 1996; numbers in thousands)

	total	male	female	sex ratio*
Total persons	33,611	15,939	17,672	90
Under age 5	3,097	1,571	1,526	103
Aged 5 to 9	3,094	1,569	1,524	103
Aged 10 to 14	2,906	1,475	1,431	103
Aged 15 to 19	2,892	1,466	1,426	103
Aged 20 to 24	2,578	1,270	1,308	97
Aged 25 to 29	2,601	1,242	1,360	91
Aged 30 to 34	2,812	1,320	1,492	88
Aged 35 to 39	2,831	1,328	1,503	88
Aged 40 to 44	2,477	1,151	1,327	87
Aged 45 to 49	1,998	912	1,086	84
Aged 50 to 54	1,412	633	779	81
Aged 55 to 59	1,163	509	653	78
Aged 60 to 64	995	426	569	75
Aged 65 to 69	925	395	530	75
Aged 70 to 74	703	284	419	68
Aged 75 to 79	525	201	324	62
Aged 80 to 84	320	108	212	51
Aged 85 or older	284	81	203	40
Aged 18 to 24	3,703	1,821	1,856	98
Aged 18 or older	22,749	10,424	12,325	85
Aged 65 or older	2,756	1,068	1,688	63

* The sex ratio is the number of males per 100 females.
Source: Bureau of the Census, Population Projections of the United States, by Age, Sex, Race, and Hispanic Origin: 1995 to 2050, Current Population Reports, P25-1130, 1996

Blacks by Region and Division, 1990 to 2020

(number and percent distribution of blacks and black share of the total population by region and division, selected years 1990-2020; percent change in number and percentage point change in distribution and share, 1990-2000 and 2000-2010; numbers in thousands)

	1990	1995	2000	2010	2020	percent change 1990-2000	percent change 2000-2010
Number							
UNITED STATES	30,483	33,117	35,469	40,224	45,408	16.4%	13.4%
Northeast	5,905	6,263	6,567	7,266	8,041	11.2	10.6
New England	667	692	716	809	920	7.3	13.0
Middle Atlantic	5,237	5,572	5,851	6,457	7,121	11.7	10.4
Midwest	5,750	6,250	6,689	7,526	8,448	16.3	12.5
East North Central	4,847	5,277	5,654	6,379	7,182	16.6	12.8
West North Central	904	973	1,036	1,148	1,267	14.6	10.8
South	15,903	17,377	18,706	21,296	24,074	17.6	13.8
South Atlantic	8,963	9,961	10,866	12,615	14,470	21.2	16.1
East South Central	2,980	3,165	3,331	3,634	3,962	11.8	9.1
West South Central	3,960	4,252	4,510	5,047	5,641	13.9	11.9
West	2,925	3,227	3,506	4,136	4,845	19.9	18.0
Mountain	384	436	484	554	624	26.0	14.5
Pacific	2,541	2,791	3,023	3,582	4,221	19.0	18.5

	1990	1995	2000	2010	2020	percentage point change 1990-2000	percentage point change 2000-2010
Percent distribution							
UNITED STATES	100.0%	100.0%	100.0%	100.0%	100.0%	-	-
Northeast	19.4	18.9	18.5	18.1	17.7	-0.9	-0.4
New England	2.2	2.1	2.0	2.0	2.0	-0.2	0.0
Middle Atlantic	17.2	16.8	16.5	16.1	15.7	-0.7	-0.4
Midwest	18.9	18.9	18.9	18.7	18.6	0.0	-0.2
East North Central	15.9	15.9	15.9	15.9	15.8	0.0	0.0
West North Central	3.0	2.9	2.9	2.9	2.8	-0.1	0.0
South	52.2	52.5	52.7	52.9	53.0	0.6	0.2
South Atlantic	29.4	30.1	30.6	31.4	31.9	1.2	0.8
East South Central	9.8	9.6	9.4	9.0	8.7	-0.4	-0.4
West South Central	13.0	12.8	12.7	12.5	12.4	-0.3	-0.2
West	9.6	9.7	9.9	10.3	10.7	0.3	0.4
Mountain	1.3	1.3	1.4	1.4	1.4	0.1	0.0
Pacific	8.3	8.4	8.5	8.9	9.3	0.2	0.4

(continued)

(continued from previous page)

	1990	1995	2000	2010	2020	percentage point change	
						1990-2000	2000-2010
Percent share							
UNITED STATES	12.3%	12.6%	12.8%	13.4%	13.9%	0.5	0.6
Northeast	11.6	12.2	12.7	13.6	14.5	1.1	0.9
New England	5.1	5.2	5.4	5.9	6.3	0.3	0.5
Middle Atlantic	13.9	14.6	15.1	16.3	17.4	1.2	1.2
Midwest	9.6	10.1	10.5	11.3	12.2	0.9	0.8
East North Central	11.5	12.1	12.6	13.8	15.0	1.1	1.2
West North Central	5.1	5.3	5.4	5.7	6.0	0.3	0.3
South	18.6	18.9	19.2	19.8	20.5	0.6	0.6
South Atlantic	20.6	21.2	21.7	22.8	23.9	1.1	1.1
East South Central	19.6	19.8	19.9	20.3	20.8	0.3	0.4
West South Central	14.8	14.8	14.8	14.8	14.9	0.0	0.0
West	5.5	5.5	5.5	5.6	5.8	0.0	0.1
Mountain	2.8	2.8	2.9	2.9	3.0	0.1	0.0
Pacific	6.5	6.5	6.5	6.6	6.7	0.0	0.1

Note: The 1990 population figures are for April 1, 1990. Projections of total blacks for 2000, 2010, and 2020 are different from those at the beginning of the population section because they are from an earlier report for states and regions.
Source: Bureau of the Census, Population Projections for States, by Age, Sex, Race, and Hispanic Origin: 1993 to 2020, *Current Population Reports, P25-1111, 1994*

Blacks by State, 1995 to 2020

(number of blacks by state, selected years 1995-2020; percent change 1995-2020; numbers in thousands)

	1995	2000	2010	2020	percent change 1995-2020
United States	33,118	35,469	40,224	45,408	37.1%
Alabama	1,083	1,139	1,243	1,359	25.5
Alaska	26	28	29	31	19.2
Arizona	123	131	143	157	27.6
Arkansas	386	395	412	434	12.4
California	2,512	2,719	3,245	3,849	53.2
Colorado	156	174	200	224	43.6
Connecticut	293	304	347	400	36.5
Delaware	132	149	181	215	62.9
District of Columbia	369	349	365	404	9.5
Florida	2,073	2,351	2,906	3,482	68.0
Georgia	1,955	2,139	2,485	2,851	45.8
Hawaii	36	42	50	58	61.1
Idaho	5	6	8	9	80.0
Illinois	1,843	1,957	2,181	2,434	32.1
Indiana	476	514	582	652	37.0
Iowa	57	65	78	91	59.6
Kansas	159	174	198	221	39.0
Kentucky	286	307	345	387	35.3
Louisiana	1,371	1,427	1,550	1,690	23.3
Maine	5	5	5	6	20.0
Maryland	1,368	1,514	1,776	2,052	50.0
Massachusetts	340	352	393	441	29.7
Michigan	1,417	1,520	1,737	1,988	40.3
Minnesota	104	111	122	132	26.9
Mississippi	952	980	1,032	1,091	14.6
Missouri	581	609	664	727	25.1
Montana	2	2	3	3	50.0
Nebraska	64	69	76	84	31.3
Nevada	100	118	144	166	66.0
New Hampshire	7	8	10	12	71.4
New Jersey	1,156	1,242	1,434	1,645	42.3
New Mexico	32	33	35	39	21.9
New York	3,249	3,391	3,705	4,039	24.3

(continued)

(continued from previous page)

	1995	2000	2010	2020	percent change 1995-2020
North Carolina	1,594	1,715	1,916	2,122	33.1%
North Dakota	4	4	5	6	50.0
Ohio	1,253	1,335	1,483	1,643	31.1
Oklahoma	244	251	269	292	19.7
Oregon	54	60	70	81	50.0
Pennsylvania	1,167	1,219	1,318	1,438	23.2
Rhode Island	44	46	51	57	29.5
South Carolina	1,131	1,207	1,344	1,486	31.4
South Dakota	3	4	4	5	66.7
Tennessee	845	905	1,014	1,125	33.1
Texas	2,251	2,436	2,817	3,225	43.3
Utah	14	16	18	19	35.7
Vermont	2	3	4	4	100.0
Virginia	1,284	1,391	1,592	1,808	40.8
Washington	164	174	187	203	23.8
West Virginia	54	53	50	50	-7.4
Wisconsin	288	327	396	465	61.5
Wyoming	4	5	5	6	50.0

Note: Projections of total blacks for 2000, 2010, and 2020 are different from those at the beginning of the population section because they are from an earlier report for states and regions.
Source: Bureau of the Census, Population Projections for States, by Age, Sex, Race, and Hispanic Origin: 1993 to 2020, *Current Population Reports, P25-1111, 1994*

Distribution of Blacks by State, 1995 to 2020

(percent distribution of blacks by state, selected years 1995-2020)

	1995	2000	2010	2020
United States	100.0%	100.0%	100.0%	100.0%
Alabama	3.3	3.2	3.1	3.0
Alaska	0.1	0.1	0.1	0.1
Arizona	0.4	0.4	0.4	0.3
Arkansas	1.2	1.1	1.0	1.0
California	7.6	7.7	8.1	8.5
Colorado	0.5	0.5	0.5	0.5
Connecticut	0.9	0.9	0.9	0.9
Delaware	0.4	0.4	0.4	0.5
District of Columbia	1.1	1.0	0.9	0.9
Florida	6.3	6.6	7.2	7.7
Georgia	5.9	6.0	6.2	6.3
Hawaii	0.1	0.1	0.1	0.1
Idaho	0.0	0.0	0.0	0.0
Illinois	5.6	5.5	5.4	5.4
Indiana	1.4	1.4	1.4	1.4
Iowa	0.2	0.2	0.2	0.2
Kansas	0.5	0.5	0.5	0.5
Kentucky	0.9	0.9	0.9	0.9
Louisiana	4.1	4.0	3.9	3.7
Maine	0.0	0.0	0.0	0.0
Maryland	4.1	4.3	4.4	4.5
Massachusetts	1.0	1.0	1.0	1.0
Michigan	4.3	4.3	4.3	4.4
Minnesota	0.3	0.3	0.3	0.3
Mississippi	2.9	2.8	2.6	2.4
Missouri	1.8	1.7	1.7	1.6
Montana	0.0	0.0	0.0	0.0
Nebraska	0.2	0.2	0.2	0.2
Nevada	0.3	0.3	0.4	0.4
New Hampshire	0.0	0.0	0.0	0.0
New Jersey	3.5	3.5	3.6	3.6
New Mexico	0.1	0.1	0.1	0.1
New York	9.8	9.6	9.2	8.9

(continued)

(continued from previous page)

	1995	2000	2010	2020
North Carolina	4.8%	4.8%	4.8%	4.7%
North Dakota	0.0	0.0	0.0	0.0
Ohio	3.8	3.8	3.7	3.6
Oklahoma	0.7	0.7	0.7	0.6
Oregon	0.2	0.2	0.2	0.2
Pennsylvania	3.5	3.4	3.3	3.2
Rhode Island	0.1	0.1	0.1	0.1
South Carolina	3.4	3.4	3.3	3.3
South Dakota	0.0	0.0	0.0	0.0
Tennessee	2.6	2.6	2.5	2.5
Texas	6.8	6.9	7.0	7.1
Utah	0.0	0.0	0.0	0.0
Vermont	0.0	0.0	0.0	0.0
Virginia	3.9	3.9	4.0	4.0
Washington	0.5	0.5	0.5	0.4
West Virginia	0.2	0.1	0.1	0.1
Wisconsin	0.9	0.9	1.0	1.0
Wyoming	0.0	0.0	0.0	0.0

Source: Bureau of the Census, Population Projections for States, by Age, Sex, Race, and Hispanic Origin: 1993 to 2020, *Current Population Reports, P25-1111, 1994*

Black Share of State Populations, 1995 to 2020

(blacks as a percent of state populations, selected years 1995-2020; percentage point change in share, 1995-2020)

	1995	2000	2010	2020	percentage point change 1995-2020
United States	12.6%	12.8%	13.4%	13.9%	1.3
Alabama	25.3	25.4	25.6	26.0	0.7
Alaska	4.1	4.0	3.7	3.6	-0.5
Arizona	3.0	3.0	2.8	2.7	-0.3
Arkansas	15.6	15.3	14.8	14.4	-1.2
California	7.8	7.8	7.9	8.0	0.2
Colorado	4.2	4.3	4.5	4.6	0.4
Connecticut	8.9	9.3	10.2	11.1	2.2
Delaware	18.4	19.6	22.2	24.7	6.3
District of Columbia	66.0	65.0	63.3	63.5	-2.5
Florida	14.6	15.4	16.7	17.9	3.3
Georgia	27.5	28.0	29.1	30.2	2.7
Hawaii	2.9	3.2	3.2	3.2	0.3
Idaho	0.4	0.5	0.6	0.6	0.2
Illinois	15.5	16.1	17.2	18.4	2.9
Indiana	8.2	8.5	9.3	10.0	1.8
Iowa	2.0	2.2	2.6	3.0	1.0
Kansas	6.1	6.4	6.8	7.1	1.0
Kentucky	7.4	7.7	8.3	9.0	1.6
Louisiana	31.5	31.9	32.2	32.5	1.0
Maine	0.4	0.4	0.4	0.4	0.0
Maryland	26.9	28.4	30.7	32.6	5.7
Massachusetts	5.7	5.9	6.4	6.9	1.2
Michigan	14.8	15.6	17.3	19.2	4.4
Minnesota	2.3	2.3	2.4	2.4	0.1
Mississippi	35.7	35.6	35.4	35.2	-0.5
Missouri	11.0	11.2	11.5	11.9	0.9
Montana	0.2	0.2	0.3	0.3	0.1
Nebraska	3.9	4.0	4.2	4.5	0.6
Nevada	6.8	7.0	7.4	7.7	0.9
New Hampshire	0.6	0.7	0.8	0.9	0.3
New Jersey	14.6	15.3	16.7	18.2	3.6
New Mexico	1.9	1.8	1.7	1.7	-0.2
New York	17.9	18.6	20.0	21.1	3.2

(continued)

(continued from previous page)

	1995	2000	2010	2020	percentage point change 1995-2020
North Carolina	22.3%	22.5%	23.0%	23.5%	1.2
North Dakota	0.6	0.6	0.7	0.8	0.2
Ohio	11.2	11.7	12.7	13.8	2.6
Oklahoma	7.5	7.4	7.3	7.3	-0.2
Oregon	1.7	1.8	1.8	1.9	0.2
Pennsylvania	9.6	9.9	10.6	11.4	1.8
Rhode Island	4.4	4.6	4.9	5.2	0.8
South Carolina	30.3	30.7	31.2	31.7	1.4
South Dakota	0.4	0.5	0.5	0.6	0.2
Tennessee	16.2	16.3	16.9	17.5	1.3
Texas	12.1	12.2	12.3	12.6	0.5
Utah	0.7	0.7	0.7	0.7	0.0
Vermont	0.3	0.5	0.6	0.6	0.3
Virginia	19.3	19.7	20.6	21.6	2.3
Washington	3.0	2.9	2.7	2.6	-0.4
West Virginia	3.0	2.9	2.7	2.7	-0.3
Wisconsin	5.6	6.1	7.0	8.0	2.4
Wyoming	0.8	1.0	0.8	0.9	0.1

Source: Bureau of the Census, Population Projections for States, by Age, Sex, Race, and Hispanic Origin: 1993 to 2020, *Current Population Reports, P25-1111, 1994*

Metropolitan Areas With the Most Blacks, 1990

(metropolitan areas with at least 100,000 blacks ranked by size of black population; number of blacks and black share of total metropolitan population, 1990; numbers in thousands)

		number	percent
1.	New York-Northern New Jersey-Long Island, NY-NJ-CT-PA	3,439	17.8%
2.	Washington-Baltimore, DC-MD-VA-WV	1,696	25.2
3.	Chicago-Gary-Kenosha, IL-IN-WI	1,564	19.0
4.	Los Angeles-Riverside-Orange County, CA	1,230	8.5
5.	Philadelphia-Wilmington-Atlantic City, PA-NJ-DE-MD	1,083	18.4
6.	Detroit-Ann Arbor-Flint, MI	1,061	20.5
7.	Atlanta, GA	747	25.2
8.	Houston-Galveston-Brazoria, TX	668	17.9
9.	Miami-Fort Lauderdale, FL	591	18.5
10.	Dallas-Fort Worth, TX	566	14.0
11.	San Francisco-Oakland-San Jose, CA	538	8.6
12.	New Orleans, LA	447	34.8
13.	Cleveland-Akron, OH	445	15.6
14.	St. Louis, MO-IL	424	17.0
15.	Memphis, TN-AR-MS	410	40.7
16.	Norfolk-Virginia Beach-Newport News, VA-NC	409	28.3
17.	Boston-Brockton-Nashua, MA-NH-ME-CT	261	4.8
18.	Richmond-Petersburg, VA	252	29.2
19.	Birmingham, AL	241	28.7
20.	Charlotte-Gastonia-Rock Hill, NC-SC	232	19.9
21.	Milwaukee-Racine, WI	214	13.3
22.	Raleigh-Durham-Chapel Hill, NC	207	24.2
23.	Cincinnati-Hamilton, OH-KY-IN	204	11.2
24.	Greensboro-Winston-Salem-High Point, NC	203	19.3
25.	Kansas City, MO-KS	201	12.7
26.	Tampa-St. Petersburg-Clearwater, FL	186	9.0
27.	Indianapolis, IN	182	13.2
28.	Jacksonville, FL	181	20.0
29.	Pittsburgh, PA	180	7.5
30.	Jackson, MS	168	42.5
31.	Columbus, OH	163	12.1
32.	San Diego, CA	159	6.4
33.	Charleston-North Charleston, SC	153	30.2
34.	Nashville, TN	152	15.5

(continued)

(continued from previous page)

	number	percent
35. Orlando, FL	147	12.0%
36. Greenville-Spartansburg-Anderson, SC	145	17.4
37. Baton Rouge, LA	143	30.5
38. Columbia, SC	138	30.4
39. Seattle-Tacoma-Bremerton, WA	133	4.5
40. Mobile, AL	131	27.4
41. Shreveport-Bossier City, LA	130	34.6
42. Dayton-Springfield, OH	126	13.3
43. Augusta-Aiken, GA-SC	125	31.6
44. Louisville, KY-IN	122	12.9
45. Buffalo-Niagara Falls, NY	122	10.3
46. West Palm Beach-Boca Raton, FL	108	12.5
47. Montgomery, AL	105	36.0
48. Sacramento-Yolo, CA	102	6.9
49. Little Rock-North Little Rock, AR	102	19.9
50. Macon, GA	102	35.0
51. Oklahoma City, OK	101	10.5

Source: Bureau of the Census, Statistical Abstract of the United States 1993

Black Births by Age of Mother, 1993

(number and percent distribution of births to black women, by age of mother, 1993)

	number	percent
Total births	658,875	100.0%
Under age 15	6,417	1.0
Aged 15 to 19	143,153	21.7
Aged 20 to 24	208,149	31.6
Aged 25 to 29	151,566	23.0
Aged 30 to 34	100,966	15.3
Aged 35 to 39	41,348	6.3
Aged 40 or older	7,276	1.1

Source: National Center for Health Statistics, Advance Report of Final Natality Statistics, 1993, *Vol. 44, No. 3 Supplement, 1995*

Births to Unmarried Black Women by Age, 1993

(number and percent of births to unmarried black women, by age of mother; 1993)

	number	percent of total births in age group
Total births to unmarried women	452,476	68.7%
Under age 15	6,293	98.1
Aged 15 to 19	133,031	92.9
Aged 20 to 24	159,598	76.7
Aged 25 to 29	84,604	55.8
Aged 30 to 34	47,330	46.9
Aged 35 to 39	18,526	44.8
Aged 40 or older	3,094	42.5

Source: National Center for Health Statistics, Advance Report of Final Natality Statistics, 1993, *Vol. 44, No. 3 Supplement, 1995*

Black Births by State, 1993

(number and percent distribution of black births by state, and black births as a percent of total births by state, 1993)

	number	percent	percent of total births
United States	658,875	100.0%	16.5%
Alabama	21,116	3.2	34.2
Alaska	585	0.1	5.3
Arizona	2,403	0.4	3.5
Arkansas	7,848	1.2	22.9
California	44,973	6.8	7.7
Colorado	2,939	0.4	5.4
Connecticut	5,960	0.9	12.8
Delaware	2,411	0.4	22.8
District of Columbia	8,500	1.3	80.0
Florida	44,483	6.8	23.1
Georgia	39,873	6.1	36.0
Hawaii	624	0.1	3.2
Idaho	46	0.0	0.3
Illinois	42,900	6.5	22.5
Indiana	9,374	1.4	11.2
Iowa	1,092	0.2	2.9
Kansas	3,238	0.5	8.7
Kentucky	4,840	0.7	9.1
Louisiana	26,698	4.1	38.5
Maine	57	0.0	0.4
Maryland	24,658	3.7	32.9
Massachusetts	8,356	1.3	9.9
Michigan	28,312	4.3	20.2
Minnesota	2,828	0.4	4.4
Mississippi	20,421	3.1	48.4
Missouri	13,007	2.0	17.3
Montana	48	0.0	0.4
Nebraska	1,260	0.2	5.4
Nevada	1,997	0.3	8.9
New Hampshire	109	0.0	0.7
New Jersey	23,128	3.5	19.7
New Mexico	561	0.1	2.0
New York	60,083	9.1	21.3

(continued)

(continued from previous page)

	number	percent	percent of total births
North Carolina	29,487	4.5%	29.1%
North Dakota	89	0.0	1.0
Ohio	25,458	3.9	16.0
Oklahoma	4,944	0.8	10.7
Oregon	893	0.1	2.1
Pennsylvania	24,411	3.7	15.2
Rhode Island	1,151	0.2	8.2
South Carolina	20,520	3.1	38.1
South Dakota	77	0.0	0.7
Tennessee	17,578	2.7	24.1
Texas	41,694	6.3	12.9
Utah	278	0.0	0.7
Vermont	29	0.0	0.4
Virginia	23,334	3.5	24.6
Washington	3,145	0.5	4.0
West Virginia	818	0.1	3.8
Wisconsin	7,180	1.1	10.3
Wyoming	61	0.0	0.9

Source: National Center for Health Statistics, Advance Report of Final Natality Statistics, 1993, Vol. 44, No. 3 Supplement, 1995

Projections of Black Births, 1995 to 2020

(number of black births and black births as a percent of total births, 1995-2020; numbers in thousands)

	number	black share of total births
1995	669	17.0%
1996	671	17.1
1997	674	17.3
1998	677	17.4
1999	681	17.5
2000	685	17.6
2001	690	17.7
2002	695	17.7
2003	702	17.8
2004	709	17.9
2005	718	17.9
2006	728	18.0
2007	738	18.0
2008	748	18.1
2009	758	18.1
2010	767	18.1
2011	776	18.1
2012	783	18.1
2013	791	18.1
2014	797	18.1
2015	804	18.1
2016	810	18.1
2017	816	18.1
2018	822	18.1
2019	828	18.2
2020	834	18.2

Source: Bureau of the Census, Population Projections of the United States, by Age, Sex, Race, and Hispanic Origin: 1995 to 2050, *Current Population Reports, P25-1130, 1996*

Blacks:
Wealth and Spending

Blacks have very little wealth compared with the average American household. The median net worth of black households amounted to just $4,418 in 1993, far below the $37,587 net worth of the average household. The net worth of blacks is below average in part because blacks are less likely to own a home than the average householder, and homes comprise the largest share of Americans' net worth. Only 45 percent of black householders own their homes, versus 64 percent of householders in the nation as a whole.

Fully 26 percent of black households have zero or negative net worth (their debts exceed their assets). Among all households, 11.5 percent have zero or negative net worth. Eight percent of black households have net worth in excess of $100,000, versus 29 percent of total households.

Black households spent an average of $22,418 in 1994, according to the Consumer Expenditure Survey—71 percent as much as the average American household. On many items, however, blacks spend more than the average household. These include fish and seafood, fresh fruit juices, baby food, telephone services, soaps and detergents, men's suits and sportcoats, and color-TV consoles.

Distribution of Net Worth Among Black Households, 1993

(number and percent distribution of black households by net worth, 1993; numbers in thousands)

	number	percent
Total households	11,248	100.0%
Zero or negative net worth	2,879	25.6
$1 to $4,999	2,598	23.1
$5,000 to $9,999	810	7.2
$10,000 to $24,999	1,350	12.0
$25,000 to $49,999	1,361	12.1
$50,000 to $99,999	1,350	12.0
$100,000 to $249,999	720	6.4
$250,000 to $499,999	146	1.3
$500,000 or more	45	0.4
Median net worth	$4,418	-

Source: Bureau of the Census, Internet web site, http://www.census.gov

Asset Ownership and Value of Assets for Black Households, 1993

(percent of black households owning assets and median value of asset among owners, 1993)

	percent owning	median value
Interest-earning assets at financial institutions*	45.5%	$799
Other interest-earning assets**	1.8	3,500
Regular checking accounts	29.6	390
Stocks and mutual fund shares	6.2	3,900
Own business or profession	3.3	2,500
Motor vehicles	64.5	3,242
Own home	45.0	28,796
Rental property	4.3	19,000
Other real estate	3.7	8,000
U.S. savings bonds	10.3	450
IRA or KEOGH accounts	6.3	4,700

* Includes passbook savings accounts, money market deposit accounts, certificates of deposit, and interest-earning checking accounts.
** Includes money market funds, U.S. government securities, municipal and corporate bonds, and other interest-earning assets.
Source: Bureau of the Census, Internet web site: http://www.census.gov

Average and Indexed Spending of Black Households, 1994

(average annual expenditures of total and black consumer units, and indexed expenditures of black consumer units, 1994)

	average spending of total consumer units	black consumer units	
		average spending	indexed spending*
No. of consumer units (in thousands)	102,210	11,470	-
Average before-tax income	$36,838.00	$25,250.00	69
Total average annual spending	31,750.63	22,418.00	71
FOOD	$4,410.52	$3,389.94	77
Food at home	2,712.05	2,390.00	88
Cereals and bakery products	428.68	342.97	80
Cereals and cereal products	161.74	154.93	96
Flour	7.60	11.94	157
Prepared flour mixes	12.79	13.75	108
Ready-to-eat and cooked cereals	98.27	87.62	89
Rice	15.43	18.79	122
Pasta, cornmeal, other cereal products	27.65	22.83	83
Bakery products	266.93	188.04	70
Bread	76.22	65.12	85
White bread	37.65	38.66	103
Bread, other than white	38.57	26.46	69
Crackers and cookies	62.56	45.01	72
Cookies	42.97	33.33	78
Crackers	19.59	11.68	60
Frozen and refrigerated bakery products	21.56	14.84	69
Other bakery products	106.59	63.07	59
Biscuits and rolls	35.96	19.53	54
Cakes and cupcakes	31.19	21.85	70
Bread and cracker products	4.72	1.97	42
Sweetrolls, coffee cakes, doughnuts	21.92	12.88	59
Pies, tarts, turnovers	12.80	6.85	54
Meats, poultry, fish, and eggs	732.45	857.65	117
Beef	226.76	250.47	110
Ground beef	88.45	93.70	106
Roast	39.41	47.20	120
Chuck roast	12.26	14.96	122
Round roast	14.84	14.52	98
Other roast	12.31	17.72	144
Steak	84.75	90.61	107
Round steak	16.00	17.43	109

(continued)

(continued from previous page)

	average spending of total consumer units	black consumer units	
		average spending	indexed spending*
Sirloin steak	$24.44	$22.28	91
Other steak	44.31	50.90	115
Other beef	14.15	18.97	134
Pork	155.74	216.10	139
Bacon	22.78	34.78	153
Pork chops	39.32	60.08	153
Ham	36.88	32.97	89
Ham, not canned	34.16	31.77	93
Canned ham	2.72	1.20	44
Sausage	22.82	37.86	166
Other pork	33.93	50.42	149
Other meats	93.95	87.95	94
Frankfurters	18.76	19.58	104
Lunch meats (cold cuts)	65.66	56.04	85
Bologna, liverwurst, salami	23.73	24.29	102
Other lunch meats	41.93	31.75	76
Lamb, organ meats and others	9.53	12.34	129
Lamb and organ meats	9.35	12.20	130
Mutton, goat, and game	0.18	0.14	78
Poultry	136.58	163.58	120
Fresh and frozen chickens	107.89	138.97	129
Fresh and frozen whole chicken	29.56	44.47	150
Fresh and frozen chicken parts	78.33	94.51	121
Other poultry	28.69	24.61	86
Fish and seafood	89.43	105.26	118
Canned fish and seafood	15.03	12.03	80
Fresh fish and shellfish	51.26	72.15	141
Frozen fish and shellfish	23.15	21.08	91
Eggs	30.00	34.27	114
Dairy products	288.92	192.67	67
Fresh milk and cream	127.13	93.82	74
Fresh milk, all types	118.94	88.79	75
Cream	8.19	5.03	61
Other dairy products	161.79	98.85	61
Butter	11.65	10.20	88
Cheese	81.83	44.65	55
Ice cream and related products	47.64	31.98	67
Miscellaneous dairy products	20.66	12.03	58
Fruits and vegetables	436.57	369.99	85
Fresh fruits	133.02	98.31	74
Apples	25.37	19.39	76

(continued)

(continued from previous page)

	average spending of total consumer units	black consumer units	
		average spending	indexed spending*
Bananas	$29.66	$23.37	79
Oranges	16.36	16.33	100
Citrus fruits, excluding oranges	10.96	7.37	67
Other fresh fruits	50.67	31.85	63
Fresh vegetables	134.89	107.75	80
Potatoes	28.01	27.51	98
Lettuce	17.38	10.90	63
Tomatoes	21.01	15.47	74
Other fresh vegetables	68.50	53.87	79
Processed fruits	93.08	90.33	97
Frozen fruits and fruit juices	16.28	12.94	79
Frozen orange juice	9.49	7.61	80
Frozen fruits	1.60	1.57	98
Frozen fruit juices	5.19	3.77	73
Canned fruit	14.23	8.33	59
Dried fruit	5.89	4.81	82
Fresh fruit juices	17.90	22.64	126
Canned and bottled fruit juices	38.78	41.61	107
Processed vegetables	75.57	73.59	97
Frozen vegetables	24.83	21.78	88
Canned and dried vegetables and juices	50.74	51.81	102
Canned beans	10.44	11.67	112
Canned corn	6.81	8.58	126
Other canned and dried vegetables	27.05	25.57	95
Frozen vegetable juices	0.23	0.45	196
Fresh and canned vegetable juices	6.21	5.54	89
Other food at home	825.43	626.73	76
Sugar and other sweets	105.25	87.41	83
Candy and chewing gum	62.32	39.66	64
Sugar	18.31	27.08	148
Artificial sweeteners	3.39	2.90	86
Jams, preserves, other sweets	21.23	17.77	84
Fats and oils	79.25	70.56	89
Margarine	14.16	10.68	75
Fats and oils	23.09	28.67	124
Salad dressings	23.75	17.48	74
Nondairy cream and imitation milk	6.56	4.06	62
Peanut butter	11.70	9.65	82
Miscellaneous foods	361.62	268.49	74
Frozen prepared foods	66.14	37.10	56
Frozen meals	21.43	11.25	52
Other frozen prepared foods	44.71	25.84	58

(continued)

(continued from previous page)

	average spending of total consumer units	black consumer units	
		average spending	indexed spending*
Canned and packaged soups	$29.55	$20.48	69
Potato chips, nuts, and other snacks	74.07	42.16	57
Potato chips and other snacks	58.18	33.95	58
Nuts	15.89	8.20	52
Condiments and seasonings	79.74	67.28	84
Salt, spices, and other seasonings	19.30	25.53	132
Olives, pickles, relishes	10.16	6.07	60
Sauces and gravies	36.43	27.83	76
Baking needs and misc. products	13.85	7.86	57
Other canned/packaged prepared foods	112.12	101.47	91
Prepared salads	10.97	6.94	63
Prepared desserts	7.99	3.76	47
Baby food	28.11	42.10	150
Miscellaneous prepared foods	65.05	48.67	75
Nonalcoholic beverages	232.89	186.51	80
Cola	89.45	68.89	77
Other carbonated drinks	38.89	31.48	81
Coffee	43.01	23.07	54
Roasted coffee	29.13	15.06	52
Instant and freeze-dried coffee	13.88	8.01	58
Noncarb. fruit flavored drinks, incl. nonfrozen lemonade	21.86	28.26	129
Tea	16.25	12.48	77
Nonalcoholic beer	0.66	0.54	82
Other nonalcoholic beverages	22.77	21.79	96
Food prepared by cu on out-of-town trips	46.41	13.76	30
Food away from home	**1,698.46**	**999.94**	**59**
Meals at restaurants, carryouts, other	1,306.21	834.03	64
Lunch	451.76	323.33	72
Dinner	651.79	392.27	60
Snacks and nonalcoholic beverages	101.72	56.36	55
Breakfast and brunch	100.95	62.07	61
Board (including at school)	50.72	20.28	40
Catered affairs	56.09	19.60	35
Food on out-of-town trips	207.89	59.19	28
School lunches	53.76	45.98	86
Meals as pay	23.79	20.86	88
ALCOHOLIC BEVERAGES	**$278.03**	**$149.49**	**54**
At home	**165.13**	**121.15**	**73**
Beer and ale	99.68	75.98	76

(continued)

(continued from previous page)

	average spending of total consumer units	black consumer units	
		average spending	indexed spending*
Whiskey	$13.68	$9.99	73
Wine	36.41	17.74	49
Other alcoholic beverages	15.35	17.43	114
Away from home	**112.91**	**28.34**	**25**
Beer and ale	38.56	7.88	20
Wine	15.79	4.90	31
Other alcoholic beverages	27.96	8.78	31
Alcoholic beverages purchased on trips	30.61	6.78	22
HOUSING	**$10,106.32**	**$7,672.68**	**76**
Shelter	**5,686.26**	**4,261.48**	**75**
Owned dwellings**	3,491.71	1,694.88	49
Mortgage interest and charges	1,918.71	958.57	50
Mortgage interest	1,822.54	927.90	51
Interest paid, home equity loan	44.51	22.63	51
Interest paid, home equity line of credit	51.11	7.49	15
Prepayment penalty charges	0.55	0.56	102
Property taxes	921.61	407.69	44
Maintenance, repairs, insurance, and other expenses	651.39	328.61	50
Homeowners and related insurance	207.71	105.82	51
Fire and extended coverage	5.95	4.59	77
Homeowners insurance	201.76	101.23	50
Ground rent	37.79	2.78	7
Maintenance and repair services	313.66	190.64	61
Painting and papering	44.00	13.55	31
Plumbing and water heating	36.33	24.51	67
Heat, air conditioning, electrical work	55.27	24.34	44
Roofing and gutters	50.96	44.33	87
Other repair and maintenance services	108.66	82.72	76
Repair and replacement of hard surface flooring	16.78	0.50	3
Repair of built-in appliances	1.67	0.69	41
Maintenance and repair materials	71.89	21.76	30
Paint, wallpaper, and supplies	18.40	7.84	43
Tools and equipment for painting and wallpapering	1.98	0.84	42
Plumbing supplies and equipment	8.59	2.48	29
Electrical supplies, heating/ cooling equipment	5.12	1.60	31

(continued)

(continued from previous page)

	average spending of total consumer units	black consumer units	
		average spending	indexed spending*
Material for hard surface flooring, repair and replacement	$5.01	$0.77	15
Material and equipment for roofing and gutters	5.36	2.14	40
Plaster, paneling, siding, windows, doors, screens, awnings	11.75	1.09	9
Patio, walk, fence, driveway, masonry, brick, stucco materials	0.47	0.03	6
Material for landscape maintenance	1.47	0.01	1
Miscellaneous supplies and equipment	13.73	4.96	36
Material for insulation, other maintenance and repair	9.37	4.94	53
Material to finish basement, remodel rooms, etc. (owner)	4.37	0.02	0
Property management and security	20.16	7.54	37
Property management	12.17	5.29	43
Management and upkeep services for security	7.99	2.25	28
Parking	0.18	0.07	39
Rented dwellings	1,799.39	2,442.57	136
Rent	1,728.66	2,382.48	138
Rent as pay	42.90	40.39	94
Maintenance, repairs, insurance, and other expenses	27.84	19.70	71
Tenant's insurance	8.99	12.91	144
Maintenance and repair services	10.13	3.61	36
Repair or maintenance services	9.07	3.56	39
Repair and replacement of hard surface flooring	0.94	-	-
Repair of built-in appliances	0.12	0.05	42
Maintenance and repair materials	8.72	3.17	36
Paint, wallpaper, and supplies	1.85	1.29	70
Tools and equipment for painting and wallpapering	0.20	0.14	70
Plaster, paneling, roofing, gutters, etc.	1.13	-	-
Patio, walk, fence, driveway, masonry, brick, stucco materials	0.08	-	-
Plumbing supplies and equipment	0.69	0.90	130
Electrical supplies, heating/ cooling equipment	1.14	0.01	1
Miscellaneous supplies and equipment	2.90	0.56	19
Material for insulation, other maintenance and repair	0.99	0.47	47

(continued)

(continued from previous page)

	average spending of total consumer units	black consumer units	
		average spending	indexed spending*
Material for additions, finishing basements, remodeling rooms	$1.40	$0.09	6
Construction materials for jobs not started	0.51	-	-
Material for hard surface flooring	0.46	0.27	59
Material for landscape maintenance	0.26	-	-
Other lodging	395.16	124.03	31
Owned vacation homes	117.35	35.23	30
Mortgage interest and charges	41.73	28.80	69
Mortgage interest	38.43	28.80	75
Interest paid, home equity loan	0.49	-	-
Interest paid, home equity line of credit	2.81	-	-
Property taxes	49.87	5.14	10
Maintenance, insurance, and other expenses	25.75	1.29	5
Homeowners and related insurance	7.33	0.54	7
Homeowners insurance	7.04	0.54	8
Fire and extended coverage	0.29	-	-
Ground rent	3.27	-	-
Maintenance and repair services	10.66	0.27	3
Maintenance and repair materials	1.24	0.26	21
Property management and security	3.20	0.12	4
Property management	2.30	0.12	5
Management and upkeep services for security	0.90	-	-
Parking	0.05	0.10	200
Housing while attending school	60.57	27.10	45
Lodging on out-of-town trips	217.24	61.70	28
Utilities, fuels, and public services	**2,188.56**	**2,181.71**	**100**
Natural gas	282.73	347.42	123
Electricity	861.50	829.80	96
Fuel oil and other fuels	97.97	31.09	32
Fuel oil	59.72	15.44	26
Coal	1.46	-	-
Bottled/tank gas	30.20	12.07	40
Wood and other fuels	6.59	3.58	54
Telephone services	689.82	756.48	110
Telephone services in home city, excl. mobile car phones	676.16	746.16	110
Telephone services for mobile car phones	13.66	10.31	75
Water and other public services	256.53	216.92	85

(continued)

(continued from previous page)

	average spending of total consumer units	black consumer units	
		average spending	indexed spending*
Water and sewerage maintenance	$183.05	$163.80	89
Trash and garbage collection	72.27	53.12	74
Septic tank cleaning	1.22	-	-
Household services	**490.15**	**266.53**	**54**
Personal services	229.80	192.39	84
Babysitting and child care in own home	47.24	28.44	60
Babysitting and child care in someone else's home	32.71	34.69	106
Care for elderly, invalids, handicapped, etc.	19.25	2.07	11
Day care centers, nursery and preschools	130.60	127.19	97
Other household services	260.35	74.13	28
Housekeeping services	85.14	8.31	10
Gardening, lawn care service	69.26	23.15	33
Water softening service	2.68	0.23	9
Household laundry and dry cleaning (nonclothing), not coin-operated	1.80	1.76	98
Coin-operated household laundry and dry cleaning (nonclothing)	5.34	10.25	192
Termite/pest control maintenance	6.84	1.87	27
Other home services	19.44	3.63	19
Termite/pest control products	0.27	0.05	19
Moving, storage, and freight express	26.91	11.66	43
Appliance repair, including service center	14.21	8.28	58
Reupholstering and furniture repair	10.19	1.12	11
Repairs/rentals of lawn, garden equipment, hand or power tools, other hh equip.	8.09	1.43	18
Appliance rental	1.57	0.22	14
Rental of office equipment for nonbusiness use	0.27	0.50	185
Repair of miscellaneous household equip. and furnishings	6.91	1.12	16
Repair of computer systems for nonbusiness use	1.42	0.55	39
Housekeeping supplies	**393.32**	**270.96**	**69**
Laundry and cleaning supplies	109.37	101.61	93
Soaps and detergents	62.00	70.24	113
Other laundry cleaning products	47.37	31.37	66
Other household products	173.91	115.00	66
Cleansing and toilet tissue, paper towels and napkins	55.89	47.44	85

(continued)

	average spending of total consumer units	black consumer units	
		average spending	indexed spending*
Miscellaneous household products	$73.73	$41.55	56
Lawn and garden supplies	44.29	26.01	59
Postage and stationery	110.05	54.35	49
Stationery, stationery supplies, giftwrap	58.09	22.00	38
Postage	51.96	32.36	62
Household furnishings and equipment	**1,348.04**	**692.00**	**51**
Household textiles	99.52	52.20	52
Bathroom linens	12.63	5.19	41
Bedroom linens	48.69	30.97	64
Kitchen and dining room linens	6.87	1.76	26
Curtains and draperies	18.55	9.80	53
Slipcovers, decorative pillows	1.93	1.49	77
Sewing materials for household items	9.84	2.24	23
Other linens	0.99	0.76	77
Furniture	318.43	198.26	62
Mattress and springs	41.64	26.71	64
Other bedroom furniture	51.84	38.84	75
Sofas	78.50	50.68	65
Living room chairs	33.00	18.83	57
Living room tables	14.61	8.75	60
Kitchen and dining room furniture	48.70	34.94	72
Infants' furniture	6.12	4.42	72
Outdoor furniture	11.11	1.50	14
Wall units, cabinets and other furniture	32.92	13.59	41
Floor coverings	119.76	52.65	44
Major appliances	148.95	94.24	63
Dishwashers (built-in), garbage disposals, range hoods (renter)	0.68	0.14	21
Dishwashers (built-in), garbage disposals, range hoods (owner)	10.34	2.64	26
Refrigerators and freezers (renter)	6.92	10.83	157
Refrigerators and freezers (owner)	39.28	21.85	56
Washing machines (renter)	5.98	8.14	136
Washing machines (owner)	14.04	4.15	30
Clothes dryers (renter)	3.98	3.81	96
Clothes dryers (owner)	8.96	3.21	36
Cooking stoves, ovens (renter)	2.29	2.37	103
Cooking stoves, ovens (owner)	21.32	11.64	55
Microwave ovens (renter)	3.13	4.12	132
Microwave ovens (owner)	6.15	2.68	44
Portable dishwasher (renter)	0.06	-	-

(continued)

(continued from previous page)

	average spending of total consumer units	black consumer units	
		average spending	indexed spending*
Portable dishwasher (owner)	$0.66	-	-
Window air conditioners (renter)	2.63	$4.09	156
Window air conditioners (owner)	4.49	1.56	35
Electric floor cleaning equipment	13.44	9.15	68
Sewing machines	3.21	1.31	41
Miscellaneous household appliances	1.40	2.55	182
Small appliances, misc. housewares	80.76	40.75	50
Housewares	57.18	24.70	43
Plastic dinnerware	1.50	0.74	49
China and other dinnerware	10.72	5.24	49
Flatware	4.95	1.71	35
Glassware	8.07	3.64	45
Silver serving pieces	1.67	0.73	44
Other serving pieces	1.60	0.51	32
Nonelectric cookware	14.19	6.64	47
Tableware, nonelectric kitchenware	14.48	5.50	38
Small appliances	23.57	16.05	68
Small electric kitchen appliances	17.27	10.09	58
Portable heating and cooling equipment	6.30	5.95	94
Miscellaneous household equipment	580.63	253.89	44
Window coverings	13.52	2.83	21
Infants' equipment	6.78	2.69	40
Laundry and cleaning equipment	10.48	8.80	84
Outdoor equipment	5.20	0.91	18
Clocks	4.76	1.98	42
Lamps and lighting fixtures	34.97	8.41	24
Other household decorative items	125.25	55.84	45
Telephones and accessories	38.87	13.94	36
Lawn and garden equipment	48.56	29.45	61
Power tools	13.16	2.68	20
Small miscellaneous furnishings	1.95	0.28	14
Hand tools	10.48	1.52	15
Indoor plants and fresh flowers	49.35	10.91	22
Closet and storage items	7.85	4.48	57
Rental of furniture	4.12	4.57	111
Luggage	7.70	6.50	84
Computers and computer hardware, nonbusiness use	112.01	48.66	43
Computer software and accessories, nonbusiness use	19.31	8.94	46
Telephone answering devices	3.87	2.84	73

(continued)

(continued from previous page)

	average spending of total consumer units	black consumer units	
		average spending	indexed spending*
Calculators	$2.18	$2.17	100
Business equipment for home use	4.93	5.30	108
Other hardware	20.66	7.38	36
Smoke alarms (owner)	0.81	0.18	22
Smoke alarms (renter)	0.15	0.17	113
Other household appliances (renter)	6.25	1.75	28
Other household appliances (owner)	1.33	2.75	207
Misc. household equipment and parts	26.12	17.99	69
APPAREL AND SERVICES	**$1,644.03**	**$1,592.06**	**97**
Men and boys	**394.67**	**365.82**	**93**
Men, aged 16 or older	304.52	271.45	89
Suits	31.94	31.43	98
Sportcoats and tailored jackets	12.96	5.53	43
Coats and jackets	26.57	37.23	140
Underwear	11.96	16.02	134
Hosiery	9.55	7.31	77
Nightwear	2.61	0.16	6
Accessories	27.69	25.13	91
Sweaters and vests	14.33	8.97	63
Active sportswear	11.70	7.06	60
Shirts	75.18	67.54	90
Pants	60.44	49.53	82
Shorts and shorts sets	14.22	11.68	82
Uniforms	3.36	3.70	110
Costumes	2.03	0.17	8
Boys, aged 2 to 15	90.15	94.37	105
Coats and jackets	6.28	0.81	13
Sweaters	2.60	5.09	196
Shirts	20.60	18.60	90
Underwear	4.04	2.38	59
Nightwear	1.78	2.46	138
Hosiery	3.23	3.27	101
Accessories	6.93	7.99	115
Suits, sportcoats, and vests	5.02	17.62	351
Pants	21.03	20.51	98
Shorts and shorts sets	9.66	4.08	42
Uniforms and active sportswear	7.63	9.72	127
Costumes	1.35	1.84	136
Women and girls	**651.83**	**612.37**	**94**
Women, aged 16 or older	552.01	493.58	89

(continued)

(continued from previous page)

	average spending of total consumer units	black consumer units	
		average spending	indexed spending*
Coats and jackets	$51.10	$66.53	130
Dresses	76.08	104.73	138
Sportcoats and tailored jackets	4.47	4.24	95
Sweaters and vests	35.23	10.11	29
Shirts, blouses, and tops	92.00	53.70	58
Skirts	22.91	19.22	84
Pants	57.78	32.07	56
Shorts and shorts sets	24.25	19.50	80
Active sportswear	23.62	21.89	93
Sleepwear	25.57	24.40	95
Undergarments	27.72	25.55	92
Hosiery	24.60	31.17	127
Suits	36.11	41.21	114
Accessories	47.23	38.10	81
Uniforms	1.34	-	-
Costumes	2.00	1.18	59
Girls, aged 2 to 15	99.81	118.78	119
Coats and jackets	7.75	10.22	132
Dresses and suits	13.82	18.26	132
Shirts, blouses, and sweaters	23.96	20.09	84
Skirts and pants	16.29	22.35	137
Shorts and shorts sets	9.02	13.60	151
Active sportswear	7.15	3.49	49
Underwear and sleepwear	7.59	9.68	128
Hosiery	5.17	8.57	166
Accessories	4.08	6.34	155
Uniforms	1.95	2.82	145
Costumes	3.06	3.35	109
Children under age 2	**79.85**	**81.32**	**102**
Coats, jackets, and snowsuits	2.72	4.83	178
Dress and outerwear	21.37	19.05	89
Underwear	46.65	46.03	99
Nightwear and loungewear	3.84	3.62	94
Accessories	5.26	7.79	148
Footwear	**253.65**	**278.47**	**110**
Men's	80.57	80.37	100
Boys'	33.02	56.00	170
Women's	114.13	112.11	98
Girls'	25.93	29.98	116
Other apparel products and services	**264.03**	**254.08**	**96**
Material for making clothes	6.85	5.12	75

(continued)

(continued from previous page)

	average spending of total consumer units	black consumer units	
		average spending	indexed spending*
Sewing patterns and notions	$2.32	$1.33	57
Watches	23.41	24.42	104
Jewelry	103.30	67.16	65
Shoe repair and other shoe services	2.97	2.20	74
Coin-operated apparel laundry and dry cleaning	36.01	70.72	196
Alteration, repair, and tailoring of apparel and accessories	6.73	3.55	53
Clothing rental	3.70	1.54	42
Watch and jewelry repair services	5.51	2.92	53
Apparel laundry, dry cleaning, not coin-operated	72.44	75.03	104
Clothing storage	0.81	0.09	11
TRANSPORTATION	**$6,044.16**	**$4,271.10**	**71**
Vehicle purchases (net outlay)	**2,724.66**	**2,014.43**	**74**
Cars and trucks, new	1,390.51	896.98	65
New cars	749.71	695.79	93
New trucks	640.80	201.19	31
Cars and trucks, used	1,289.97	1,117.35	87
Used cars	863.70	992.66	115
Used trucks	426.27	124.69	29
Other vehicles	44.18	0.10	0
Gasoline and motor oil	**985.91**	**712.59**	**72**
Gasoline	878.15	665.45	76
Diesel fuel	9.23	4.19	45
Gasoline on out-of-town trips	86.21	35.56	41
Gasohol	0.15	-	-
Motor oil	11.31	7.03	62
Motor oil on out-of-town trips	0.87	0.36	41
Other vehicle expenses	**1,952.54**	**1,282.88**	**66**
Vehicle finance charges	235.30	172.63	73
Automobile finance charges	137.45	140.50	102
Truck finance charges	86.14	30.59	36
Motorcycle and plane finance charges	0.97	0.47	48
Other vehicle finance charges	10.74	1.07	10
Maintenance and repairs	680.27	479.89	71
Coolant, additives, brake, transmission fluids	6.11	5.21	85
Tires	86.89	52.22	60

(continued)

(continued from previous page)

	average spending of total consumer units	black consumer units	
		average spending	indexed spending*
Parts, equipment, and accessories	$112.58	$68.74	61
Vehicle audio equipment, excluding labor	5.11	0.29	6
Vehicle products	4.78	1.54	32
Misc. auto repair, servicing	33.27	11.57	35
Body work and painting	34.63	17.97	52
Clutch, transmission repair	44.21	41.19	93
Drive shaft and rear-end repair	5.69	4.55	80
Brake work	42.05	36.82	88
Repair to steering or front-end	17.98	10.87	60
Repair to engine cooling system	22.08	13.44	61
Motor tune-up	41.69	32.31	78
Lube, oil change, and oil filters	38.53	23.05	60
Front-end alignment, wheel balance and rotation	9.54	4.60	48
Shock absorber replacement	6.59	2.90	44
Brake adjustment	3.69	3.35	91
Gas tank repair, replacement	2.23	4.61	207
Repair tires and other repair work	26.87	25.15	94
Vehicle air conditioning repair	15.00	6.92	46
Exhaust system repair	19.74	13.62	69
Electrical system repair	30.22	30.47	101
Motor repair, replacement	65.90	64.02	97
Auto repair service policy	4.87	4.49	92
Vehicle insurance	689.64	467.90	68
Vehicle rental, leases, licenses, and other charges	347.34	162.45	47
Leased and rented vehicles	200.82	80.42	40
Rented vehicles	37.56	29.51	79
Auto rental	5.99	10.76	180
Auto rental, out-of-town trips	24.44	15.09	62
Truck rental	1.54	0.99	64
Truck rental, out-of-town trips	4.32	2.67	62
Leased vehicles	163.26	50.91	31
Car lease payments	109.24	44.27	41
Cash downpayment (car lease)	13.22	6.64	50
Termination fee (car lease)	0.37	-	-
Truck lease payments	36.55	-	-
Cash downpayment (truck lease)	3.86	-	-
Termination fee (truck lease)	0.03	-	-
State and local registration	79.21	37.27	47
Driver's license	6.96	3.72	53
Vehicle inspection	8.36	5.37	64

(continued)

(continued from previous page)

	average spending of total consumer units	black consumer units	
		average spending	indexed spending*
Parking fees	$25.59	$22.61	88
Parking fees in home city, excluding residence	22.49	21.66	96
Parking fees, out-of-town trips	3.10	0.95	31
Tolls	9.34	1.84	20
Tolls on out-of-town trips	4.63	1.54	33
Towing charges	4.96	5.87	118
Automobile service clubs	7.47	3.82	51
Public transportation	381.05	261.21	69
Airline fares	249.48	87.22	35
Intercity bus fares	11.34	8.93	79
Intracity mass transit fares	47.65	124.12	260
Local trans. on out-of-town trips	10.35	3.07	30
Taxi fares on trips	6.08	1.81	30
Taxi fares	7.70	16.21	211
Intercity train fares	16.24	6.88	42
Ship fares	31.13	10.96	35
School bus	1.07	2.01	188
HEALTH CARE	**$1,754.74**	**$923.24**	**53**
Health insurance	**814.95**	**476.20**	**58**
Commercial health insurance	262.44	171.92	66
Blue Cross/Blue Shield	160.50	64.44	40
Health maintenance plans (HMOs)	122.81	78.31	64
Medicare payments	153.65	124.07	81
Commercial Medicare supplements/ other health insurance	115.55	37.47	32
Medical services	**571.04**	**223.11**	**39**
Physician's services	163.63	78.82	48
Dental services	188.04	75.26	40
Eye care services	29.51	13.47	46
Services by professionals other than physicians	31.92	4.90	15
Lab tests, x-rays	24.95	7.66	31
Hospital room	47.81	12.09	25
Hospital services other than room	59.54	24.07	40
Care in convalescent or nursing home	13.49	0.66	5
Repair of medical equipment	0.03	-	-
Other medical care services	12.12	6.18	51
Drugs	**285.78**	**168.35**	**59**
Non-prescription drugs	76.19	48.97	64

(continued)

(continued from previous page)

	average spending of total consumer units	black consumer units	
		average spending	indexed spending*
Prescription drugs	$209.58	$119.38	57
Medical supplies	**82.98**	**55.57**	**67**
Eyeglasses and contact lenses	50.99	30.57	60
Hearing aids	0.73	-	-
Topicals and dressings	22.94	19.32	84
Medical equipment for general use	2.53	1.41	56
Supportive/convalescent medical equipment	3.83	3.36	88
Rental of medical equipment	0.68	0.17	25
Rental of supportive, convalescent medical equipment	1.28	0.75	59
ENTERTAINMENT	**$1,566.93**	**$767.50**	**49**
Fees and admissions	**439.11**	**144.59**	**33**
Recreation expenses, out-of-town trips	20.93	6.44	31
Social, recreation, civic club membership	84.23	21.06	25
Fees for participant sports	73.54	17.64	24
Participant sports, out-of-town trips	26.99	5.35	20
Movie, theater, opera, ballet	76.23	40.47	53
Movie, other admissions, out-of-town trips	36.38	9.77	27
Admission to sporting events	32.42	15.11	47
Admission to sports events, out-of-town trips	12.13	3.26	27
Fees for recreational lessons	55.31	19.05	34
Other entertainment services, out-of-town trips	20.93	6.44	31
Television, radio, and sound equipment	**533.16**	**433.03**	**81**
Televisions	370.56	334.37	90
Community antenna or cable TV	209.60	203.96	97
Black and white TV	1.79	0.57	32
Color TV, console	24.03	29.44	123
Color TV, portable/table model	53.02	44.52	84
VCRs and video disc players	32.24	19.21	60
Video cassettes, tapes, and discs	21.90	11.13	51
Video game hardware and software	19.21	20.71	108
Repair of TV, radio, sound equipment	8.43	4.16	49
Rental of televisions	0.33	0.67	203
Radios and sound equipment	162.60	98.66	61
Radios	9.21	2.07	22
Tape recorders and players	6.05	2.91	48
Sound components, component systems	30.28	26.58	88
Miscellaneous sound equipment	1.18	0.15	13

(continued)

(continued from previous page)

	average spending of total consumer units	black consumer units	
		average spending	indexed spending*
Sound equipment accessories	$4.75	$3.38	71
Compact disc, tape, record, and			
video mail order clubs	12.08	5.45	45
Records, CDs, audio tapes, needles	36.16	23.30	64
Rental of VCR, radio, sound equipment	0.36	0.16	44
Musical instruments and accessories	17.02	6.56	39
Rental and repair of musical instruments	1.92	0.93	48
Rental of video cassettes, tapes,			
films, and discs	43.58	27.18	62
Pets, toys, and playground equipment	**288.73**	**127.98**	**44**
Pets	165.03	47.16	29
Pet food	75.80	23.85	31
Pet purchase, supplies, and medicines	26.15	11.92	46
Pet services	15.53	3.79	24
Veterinary services	47.56	7.60	16
Toys, games, hobbies, and tricycles	121.11	80.82	67
Playground equipment	2.59	0.01	0
Other entertainment equipment,			
supplies, and services	**305.92**	**61.89**	**20**
Unmotored recreational vehicles	27.76	-	-
Boats without motor and boat trailer	5.13	-	-
Trailers and other attachable campers	22.63	-	-
Motorized recreational vehicles	81.56	-	-
Motorized campers	16.55	-	-
Other motorized recreational vehicles	22.84	-	-
Boats with motor	42.17	-	-
Rental of recreational vehicles	2.33	0.18	8
Outboard motors	1.79	-	-
Docking and landing fees	5.59	1.37	25
Sports, recreation, exercise equipment	107.91	27.18	1
Athletic gear, game tables, and			
exercise equipment	51.01	14.09	28
Bicycles	13.36	7.65	57
Camping equipment	3.23	0.04	1
Hunting and fishing equipment	18.99	3.30	17
Winter sports equipment	5.08	0.64	13
Water sports equipment	6.03	-	-
Other sports equipment	8.44	1.12	13
Rental and repair of sports equipment	1.77	0.33	19

(continued)

(continued from previous page)

	average spending of total consumer units	black consumer units	
		average spending	indexed spending*
Photographic equipment, supplies, and services	$70.55	$30.64	43
Film	19.61	9.44	48
Other photographic supplies	0.36	0.63	175
Film processing	27.15	11.16	41
Repair and rental of photographic equip.	0.32	0.04	13
Photographic equipment	12.50	3.37	27
Photographer fees	10.60	6.00	57
Fireworks	1.58	-	-
Souvenirs	0.51	-	-
Visual goods	1.77	-	-
Pinball and electronic video games	4.58	2.52	55
PERSONAL CARE PRODUCTS AND SERVICES	**$396.66**	**$359.66**	**91**
Personal care products	**219.22**	**187.79**	**86**
Hair care products	46.35	44.49	96
Nonelectric articles for the hair	6.36	4.60	72
Wigs and hairpieces	0.83	2.06	248
Oral hygiene products, articles	23.10	18.80	81
Shaving needs	12.07	10.65	88
Cosmetics, perfume, and bath preparation	99.46	79.01	79
Deodorant, feminine hygiene products, and misc.	26.87	25.28	94
Electric personal care appliances	4.18	2.91	70
Personal care services	**177.45**	**171.86**	**97**
Personal care services/female	87.44	80.09	92
Personal care services/male	89.89	91.75	102
Repair of personal care appliances	0.12	0.03	25
READING	**$164.80**	**$77.43**	**47**
Newspapers, subscription	52.48	23.36	45
Newspapers, non-subscription	17.83	16.28	91
Magazines, subscription	24.59	9.85	40
Magazines, non-subscription	12.19	6.92	57
Newsletters	0.11	-	-
Books purchased through book clubs	10.51	4.36	41
Books not purchased through book clubs	45.85	16.27	35
Encyclopedia and other reference book sets	1.23	0.40	33

(continued)

	average spending of total consumer units	black consumer units	
		average spending	indexed spending*
EDUCATION	**$459.88**	**$258.50**	**56**
College tuition	271.59	114.56	42
Elementary/high school tuition	64.79	52.00	80
Other school tuition	14.46	6.84	47
Other school expenses, including rentals	18.85	11.35	60
School books, supplies, equipment for college	38.29	30.23	79
School books, supplies, equipment for elementary/high school	9.51	10.49	110
School books, supplies, equipment for day care, nursery, other	3.34	2.40	72
School supplies, etc., unspecified	39.04	30.63	78
TOBACCO PRODUCTS AND SMOKING SUPPLIES	**$258.55**	**$202.22**	**78**
Cigarettes	236.05	191.06	81
Other tobacco products	21.06	10.73	51
Smoking accessories	1.44	0.43	30
MISCELLANEOUS EXPENSES	**$748.51**	**$428.12**	**57**
Miscellaneous fees, pari-mutuel losses	44.69	36.35	81
Legal fees	112.87	36.29	32
Funeral expenses	85.75	42.88	50
Safe deposit box rental	5.69	1.73	30
Checking accounts, other bank service charges	26.49	20.48	77
Cemetery lots, vaults, maintenance fees	18.48	7.04	38
Accounting fees	43.06	10.31	24
Miscellaneous personal services	22.50	15.99	71
Finance charges, excl. mortgage, vehicles	205.23	147.09	72
Occupational expenses	84.96	58.51	69
Expenses for other properties	93.52	48.08	51
Interest paid, home equity line of credit (other property)	0.42	-	-
Credit card memberships	4.87	3.38	70
CASH CONTRIBUTIONS	**$960.31**	**$493.54**	**51**
Cash contributions to non-cu member, incl. students, alimony, child support	265.01	158.36	60
Gifts of cash, stocks, and bonds to non-cu member	206.25	28.24	14
Contributions to charities	90.33	24.40	27
Contributions to church	363.85	275.40	76
Contributions to educational organizations	21.24	3.22	15

(continued)

(continued from previous page)

	average spending of total consumer units	black consumer units	
		average spending	indexed spending*
Contributions to political organizations	$7.17	$1.25	17
Other contributions	6.45	2.66	41
PERSONAL INSURANCE			
AND PENSIONS	**$2,957.19**	**$1,832.80**	**62**
Life and other personal insurances			
except health	**397.69**	**320.65**	**81**
Life, endowment, annuity,			
other personal insurance	380.59	315.90	83
Other nonhealth insurance	17.11	4.74	28
Pensions and Social Security	**2,559.49**	**1,512.15**	**59**
Deductions for government retirement	70.79	54.73	77
Deductions for railroad retirement	4.53	1.36	30
Deductions for private pensions	273.66	119.93	44
Non-payroll deposit to retirement plans	298.11	91.61	31
Deductions for Social Security	1,912.40	1,244.52	65
GIFTS*	**$1,007.51**	**$499.52**	**50**
Food	**84.05**	**34.12**	**41**
Cakes and cupcakes	2.44	0.94	39
Candy and chewing gum	9.86	3.09	31
Potato chips and other snacks	2.04	0.54	26
Board (including at school)	27.35	14.94	55
Catered affairs	18.48	1.56	8
Housing	**262.20**	**114.46**	**44**
Housekeeping supplies	37.84	16.59	44
Other household products	8.28	6.18	75
Miscellaneous household products	4.99	1.57	31
Lawn and garden supplies	2.14	3.64	170
Postage and stationery	27.69	9.03	33
Stationery, stationery supplies, giftwraps	22.27	7.71	35
Postage	5.42	1.32	24
Household textiles	15.73	6.28	40
Bathroom linens	2.56	0.75	29
Bedroom linens	10.39	5.10	49
Appliances and misc. housewares	26.36	10.94	42
Major appliances	5.46	4.98	91
Small appliances and misc. housewares	20.90	5.96	29
China and other dinnerware	3.43	0.69	20
Glassware	4.29	0.04	1
Nonelectric cookware	2.54	3.40	134

(continued)

(continued from previous page)

	average spending of total consumer units	black consumer units	
		average spending	indexed spending*
Tableware, nonelectric kitchenware	$3.07	$0.04	1
Small electric kitchen appliances	3.79	1.31	35
Miscellaneous household equipment	65.40	13.04	20
Lamps and lighting fixtures	3.66	0.77	21
Other household decorative items	24.59	0.19	1
Lawn and garden equipment	2.30	-	-
Indoor plants and flowers	16.77	2.99	18
Computers and computer hardware, nonbusiness use	5.60	3.71	66
Other housing	116.87	67.61	58
Repair or maintenance services	5.00	0.39	8
Housing while attending school	36.93	19.55	53
Lodging on out-of-town trips	2.49	0.69	28
Electricity (renter)	9.95	7.96	80
Telephone services in home city, excl. mobile car phone	12.04	5.51	46
Day-care centers, nursery, preschools	12.40	16.19	131
Housekeeping services	5.52	1.55	28
Gardening, lawn care services	2.48	1.31	53
Moving, storage, freight express	2.29	0.08	3
Sofas	2.72	2.76	101
Kitchen, dining room furniture	2.26	2.64	117
Infants' furniture	2.18	1.01	46
Apparel and services	**246.23**	**153.13**	**62**
Males, aged 2 or older	64.05	31.47	49
Men's coats and jackets	4.46	-	-
Men's accessories	5.71	8.20	144
Men's sweaters and vests	3.26	0.94	29
Men's active sportswear	2.24	0.94	42
Men's shirts	15.44	5.07	33
Men's pants	5.72	-	-
Boys' shirts	4.95	4.03	81
Boys' accessories	2.02	0.50	25
Boys' pants	3.73	3.06	82
Boys' shorts and short sets	2.07	0.15	7
Females, aged 2 or older	93.94	70.56	75
Women's coats and jackets	10.55	5.75	55
Women's dresses	9.92	24.69	249
Women's vests and sweaters	6.44	0.23	4
Women's shirts, tops, blouses	14.50	3.13	22
Women's pants	5.12	0.49	10

(continued)

(continued from previous page)

	average spending of total consumer units	black consumer units	
		average spending	indexed spending*
Women's active sportswear	$3.30	$0.71	22
Women's sleepwear	5.85	4.36	75
Women's undergarments	2.30	1.48	64
Women's suits	2.42	4.49	186
Women's accessories	10.27	3.74	36
Girls' dresses and suits	3.23	2.29	71
Girls' shirts, blouses, sweaters	6.04	4.20	70
Girls' skirts and pants	2.23	1.37	61
Children under age 2	34.90	27.32	78
Infant dresses, outerwear	13.81	10.85	79
Infant underwear	14.38	10.22	71
Infant nightwear, loungewear	2.50	2.19	88
Infant accessories	2.78	2.25	81
Other apparel products and services	53.33	23.79	45
Jewelry and watches	25.94	4.29	17
Watches	3.40	2.61	77
Jewelry	22.54	1.68	7
All other apparel products and services	27.40	19.50	71
Men's footwear	8.18	0.16	2
Boys' footwear	4.83	13.44	278
Women's footwear	7.59	0.77	10
Girls' footwear	4.94	3.64	74
Transportation	**56.11**	**66.76**	**119**
New cars	7.43	51.23	690
Used cars	11.40	-	-
Gasoline on out-of-town trips	13.14	4.06	31
Airline fares	9.19	3.54	39
Ship fares	4.74	1.52	32
Health care	**34.69**	**5.59**	**16**
Physicians' services	2.66	1.33	50
Dental services	3.43	0.79	23
Hospital room	3.66	-	-
Hospital service other than room	3.68	0.04	1
Care in convalescent or nursing home	11.30	0.27	2
Prescription drugs	2.28	1.12	49
Entertainment	**83.57**	**37.55**	**45**
Toys, games, hobbies, tricycles	32.48	14.63	45
Other entertainment	51.08	22.92	45
Movie, other admission, out-of-town trips	7.27	2.31	32

(continued)

(continued from previous page)

	average spending of total consumer units	black consumer units	
		average spending	indexed spending*
Admission to sports events, out-of-town trips	$2.42	$0.77	32
Fees for recreational lessons	4.96	3.46	70
Community antenna or cable TV	2.81	0.35	12
Color TV, portable/table model	2.01	2.08	103
VCRs, video disc players	2.67	0.58	22
Video game hardware and software	2.00	1.83	92
Radios	4.70	0.56	12
Sound components and component systems	2.05	0.67	33
Veterinary services	3.48	0.83	24
Athletic gear, game tables, and exercise equipment	3.46	0.86	25
Education	**114.09**	**37.09**	**33**
College tuition	86.94	25.58	29
Elementary, high school tuition	6.43	-	-
Other schools' tuition	3.09	-	-
Other school expenses including rentals	4.72	5.13	109
School books, supplies, equipment for college	6.56	4.73	72
School supplies, etc., unspecified	5.32	0.63	12
All other gifts	**126.58**	**50.83**	**40**

The index compares the spending of the average black consumer unit with the spending of the average consumer unit by dividing black spending by average spending in each category and multiplying by 100. An index of 100 means that black spending in that category equals average spending. An index of 132 means that black spending is 32 percent above average, while an index of 75 means that black spending is 25 percent below average.
**This figure does not include the amount paid for mortgage principal, which is considered an asset.*
***Expenditures on gifts are also included in the preceding product and service categories. Food spending, for example, includes the amount spent on food gifts. Only gift categories with average spending of $2.00 or more by the average consumer unit are shown.*
Note: The Bureau of Labor Statistics uses consumer units rather than households as the sampling unit in the Consumer Expenditure Survey. For the definition of consumer unit, see the Glossary. Expenditures listed for items in a given category may not add to the total for that category because the listing is incomplete. (-) means number in sample is too small to make a reliable estimate.
Source: Bureau of Labor Statistics, unpublished tables from the 1994 Consumer Expenditure Survey

3

Hispanics

■ The Hispanic population is projected to grow from 28 million in 1996 to more than 52 million by 2020. Hispanics will become the largest minority in 2009, when they begin to outnumber blacks.

■ Hispanics lag far behind the total population in educational attainment. In large part this is due to the fact that many are immigrants who came to the United States as adults with few years of schooling.

■ Hispanics are more likely to be without health insurance than any other racial or ethnic group. In 1993, 32 percent did not have health insurance, double the proportion uninsured among the total population.

■ The married-couple share of Hispanic households varies widely by Hispanic ethnicity. Married couples account for fully 60 percent of Mexican-American households versus just 38 percent of Puerto Rican households.

■ Eighteen percent of Hispanic households do not have a telephone, versus just 8 percent of households in the nation as a whole. Among Puerto Ricans, 24 percent have no telephone in their home.

■ The median income of Hispanic households fell by 7.5 percent between 1990 and 1994, the sharpest income decline among all racial and ethnic groups.

■ Hispanic households spend more than the average household on a number of items, including meats, fruits and vegetables, baby food, and hair care products.

Hispanics:
Education

Hispanics lag far behind the total population in educational attainment. This is largely due to the fact that many are immigrants who came to the United States as adults with few years of schooling. Overall, only 53 percent of Hispanics had a high school diploma in 1994, versus 81 percent of the total population. The proportion of Hispanics who are high school graduates ranges from 47 percent of Mexican Americans to 68 percent of "other" Hispanics.

Only 9 percent of Hispanics have a college degree, versus 22 percent of the total population. Among Hispanic families with children aged 18 to 24, 26 percent have at least one child in college full-time. Over half of those with incomes of $50,000 or more have a child in college full-time.

Hispanics earned over 45,000 bachelor's degrees in 1992-93, or 4 percent of all bachelor's degrees awarded that year. This is far below the Hispanic share of the population because so many Hispanics never graduate from high school. Hispanics earned 11 percent of bachelor's degrees in foreign languages and literature in 1992-93. At the first-professional degree level, they earned 6 percent of degrees in podiatry.

Educational Attainment of Hispanics by Ethnicity, 1994

(number of Hispanics aged 25 or older by educational attainment and ethnicity, and percent with a high school and/or college degree, 1994; numbers in thousands)

	total		Mexican		Puerto Rican		Cuban		Central & S. Amer.		other Hispanic	
	number	percent	number	percent	number	percent	number	percent	number	percent	number	percent
Total, aged 25 or older	13,714	100.0%	8,181	100.0%	1,465	100.0%	833	100.0%	2,083	100.0%	1,151	100.0%
Not a high school graduate	6,404	46.7	4,357	53.3	595	40.6	299	35.9	784	37.6	368	32.0
High school graduate or more	7,310	53.3	3,824	46.7	871	59.5	534	64.1	1,300	62.4	782	67.9
Some college or associate's degree	2,472	18.0	1,332	16.3	264	18.0	181	21.7	444	21.3	250	21.7
Bachelor's degree or more	1,252	9.1	516	6.3	143	9.8	135	16.2	265	12.7	193	16.8

Source: Bureau of the Census, Internet web site, http://www.census.gov

Educational Attainment of Hispanics by Sex, 1980 to 1993

(percent of Hispanics aged 25 or older who are high school or college graduates, by sex, 1980-93)

	total	*men*	*women*
High school graduates			
1993	53.1%	52.9%	53.2%
1990	50.8	50.3	51.3
1985	47.9	48.5	47.4
1980	45.3	46.4	44.1
College graduates			
1993	9.0	9.5	8.5
1990	9.2	9.8	8.7
1985	8.5	9.7	7.3
1980	7.9	9.7	6.2

Source: Bureau of the Census, Educational Attainment in the United States: March 1993 and 1992, *Current Population Reports, P20-476, 1994*

Educational Attainment of Hispanics by Age and Sex, 1993

(percent of Hispanics aged 25 or older who are high school or college graduates, by age and sex, 1993)

	total	men	women
HIGH SCHOOL GRADUATES			
Total, aged 25 or older	53.1%	52.9%	53.2%
Aged 25 to 29	60.9	58.3	64.0
Aged 30 to 34	59.8	56.3	63.4
Aged 35 to 39	59.1	59.6	58.6
Aged 40 to 44	57.4	56.1	58.7
Aged 45 to 49	54.9	55.2	54.6
Aged 50 to 54	50.8	50.7	50.9
Aged 55 to 59	44.5	45.2	44.0
Aged 60 to 64	34.1	41.2	28.4
Aged 65 to 69	33.2	31.9	34.1
Aged 70 to 74	28.8	29.8	28.0
Aged 75 or older	17.1	15.2	18.3
COLLEGE GRADUATES			
Total, aged 25 or older	9.0	9.5	8.5
Aged 25 to 29	8.3	7.1	9.8
Aged 30 to 34	9.8	9.1	10.5
Aged 35 to 39	11.3	12.3	10.4
Aged 40 to 44	8.9	8.2	9.5
Aged 45 to 49	10.4	12.5	8.2
Aged 50 to 54	9.4	11.0	7.7
Aged 55 to 59	8.2	12.6	5.0
Aged 60 to 64	4.7	6.3	3.4
Aged 65 to 69	8.1	8.2	8.1
Aged 70 to 74	5.6	8.0	3.7
Aged 75 or older	4.6	6.1	3.6

Source: Bureau of the Census, Educational Attainment in the United States: March 1993 and 1992, *Current Population Reports, P20-476, 1994*

Educational Attainment of Hispanics by Age and Region, 1993

(percent of Hispanics aged 25 or older who are high school or college graduates, by age and region, 1993)

	Northeast	Midwest	South	West
HIGH SCHOOL GRADUATES				
Total, aged 25 or older	58.0%	53.8%	54.8%	50.0%
Aged 25 to 34	70.1	61.8	63.5	55.2
Aged 35 to 44	61.6	58.7	66.1	52.7
Aged 45 to 54	56.5	50.8	54.2	51.1
Aged 55 to 64	39.7	-	38.8	41.9
Aged 65 or older	27.5	-	27.9	24.2
COLLEGE GRADUATES				
Total, aged 25 or older	9.3	9.6	12.0	6.7
Aged 25 to 34	11.5	11.7	11.6	6.3
Aged 35 to 44	9.7	10.4	14.6	7.9
Aged 45 to 54	7.9	9.6	13.7	7.5
Aged 55 to 64	6.1	-	8.0	6.3
Aged 65 or older	6.3	-	9.2	2.9

Note: (-) means number in sample is too small to make a reliable estimate.
Source: Bureau of the Census, Educational Attainment in the United States: March 1993 and 1992, *Current Population Reports, P20-476, 1994*

Educational Attainment of Hispanics by State, 1990

(percent of Hispanics aged 25 or older who are high school or college graduates, by state, 1990)

	high school graduate or more	college graduate		high school graduate or more	college graduate
United States	49.8%	9.2%	Missouri	71.0%	18.0%
Alabama	73.8	20.1	Montana	66.4	10.9
Alaska	80.4	14.6	Nebraska	60.0	9.4
Arizona	51.7	6.9	Nevada	53.7	7.0
Arkansas	59.1	11.1	New Hampshire	78.2	25.5
California	45.0	7.1	New Jersey	53.9	10.8
Colorado	58.3	8.6	New Mexico	59.6	8.7
Connecticut	53.5	12.1	New York	50.4	9.3
Delaware	60.1	16.5	North Carolina	71.0	17.9
District of Columbia	52.6	24.0	North Dakota	75.2	15.9
Florida	57.2	14.2	Ohio	63.3	14.2
Georgia	66.2	20.5	Oklahoma	55.9	10.5
Hawaii	73.9	10.3	Oregon	53.0	10.1
Idaho	43.4	6.6	Pennsylvania	52.2	11.8
Illinois	45.0	8.0	Rhode Island	46.8	8.9
Indiana	62.6	10.8	South Carolina	71.8	19.8
Iowa	64.2	13.7	South Dakota	71.3	13.4
Kansas	58.1	10.1	Tennessee	71.5	21.9
Kentucky	74.0	18.9	Texas	44.6	7.3
Louisiana	67.6	16.6	Utah	61.0	9.1
Maine	83.8	23.6	Vermont	84.7	28.2
Maryland	70.3	25.2	Virginia	70.5	22.4
Massachusetts	52.0	13.6	Washington	56.7	11.0
Michigan	60.9	11.6	West Virginia	70.3	17.6
Minnesota	71.1	17.2	Wisconsin	54.1	10.0
Mississippi	67.7	17.1	Wyoming	59.3	4.8

Source: National Center for Education Statistics, Digest of Education Statistics 1993, *NCES 93-292, 1993*

School Enrollment of Hispanics by Age, Sex, and Ethnicity, 1993

(number and percent of Hispanics and Mexican Hispanics aged 3 or older enrolled in school as of October 1993, by age and sex; numbers in thousands)

	total		male		female	
	number	*percent*	*number*	*percent*	*number*	*percent*
TOTAL HISPANICS						
Total, aged 3 or older	6,839	31.6%	3,414	31.5%	3,425	31.6%
Aged 3 and 4	275	26.8	149	27.0	126	26.7
Aged 5 and 6	844	93.8	387	93.6	457	93.9
Aged 7 to 9	1,352	99.6	705	99.8	647	99.4
Aged 10 to 13	1,639	99.2	829	98.8	810	99.6
Aged 14 and 15	793	97.6	395	96.9	398	98.2
Aged 16 and 17	727	88.3	399	89.1	328	87.4
Aged 18 and 19	355	50.0	155	47.7	200	51.9
Aged 20 and 21	260	31.8	130	31.6	130	32.0
Aged 22 to 24	170	13.7	79	12.8	91	14.5
Aged 25 to 29	159	7.7	60	5.5	100	10.2
Aged 30 to 34	116	5.1	69	5.4	47	4.8
Aged 35 to 44	99	2.9	36	2.2	63	3.5
Aged 45 to 54	47	2.4	18	1.8	30	2.9
Aged 55 or older	4	0.1	4	0.3	-	-
MEXICAN						
Total, aged 3 or older	4,681	33.4	2,326	32.4	2,355	34.4
Aged 3 and 4	192	27.3	109	29.1	83	25.2
Aged 5 and 6	613	94.7	287	94.1	326	95.2
Aged 7 to 9	960	99.6	481	100.0	479	99.2
Aged 10 to 13	1,174	98.9	610	98.5	563	99.4
Aged 14 and 15	524	96.8	258	95.4	266	98.3
Aged 16 and 17	509	86.2	255	85.8	255	86.5
Aged 18 and 19	234	48.2	96	44.9	138	50.8
Aged 20 and 21	167	31.0	88	31.6	79	30.4
Aged 22 to 24	91	10.6	41	9.5	50	11.8
Aged 25 to 29	69	5.2	27	3.7	42	6.8
Aged 30 to 34	62	4.2	36	4.2	26	4.2
Aged 35 to 44	57	2.6	26	2.3	31	2.8
Aged 45 to 54	28	2.5	11	1.9	17	3.0
Aged 55 or older	1	0.1	1	0.2	-	-

Note: (-) means number in sample is too small to make a reliable estimate.
Source: Bureau of the Census, School Enrollment—Social and Economic Characteristics of Students: October 1993, *Current Population Reports, P20-479, 1994*

Hispanic Families With Children in College, 1993

(total number of Hispanic families, number with children aged 18 to 24, and number and percent with children aged 18 to 24 attending college full-time as of October 1993, by household income in 1992; numbers in thousands)

	total	with children aged 18-24	with one or more children attending college full-time		
			number	percent of total families	percent of families with children 18-24
Total families	5,529	1,164	306	5.5%	26.3%
Under $20,000	2,709	541	102	3.8	18.9
$20,000 to $29,999	974	219	61	6.3	27.9
$30,000 to $39,999	620	144	45	7.3	31.3
$40,000 to $49,999	363	64	18	5.0	28.1
$50,000 to $74,999	417	91	45	10.8	49.5
$75,000 or more	182	35	18	9.9	51.4

Source: Bureau of the Census, School Enrollment—Social and Economic Characteristics of Students: October 1993, *Current Population Reports, P20-479, 1994*

College Enrollment of Hispanics by Age, 1993

(number of Hispanics enrolled in college, by age and attendance status, October 1993; numbers in thousands)

	total	undergraduate							graduate		
		total	two-year college			four-year college			total	full-time	part-time
			total	full-time	part-time	total	full-time	part-time			
Total enrolled, aged 15 or older	995	897	446	251	196	451	314	137	98	42	56
Aged 15 to 17	15	15	6	2	4	9	9	-	-	-	-
Aged 18 and 19	195	194	113	80	34	81	71	10	-	-	-
Aged 20 and 21	241	239	107	61	47	132	116	16	2	2	-
Aged 22 to 24	166	157	64	47	17	93	68	25	10	8	2
Aged 25 to 29	149	123	67	24	44	56	27	28	26	13	13
Aged 30 to 34	100	73	40	22	18	33	10	23	27	13	14
Aged 35 to 39	50	34	21	10	11	13	2	11	16	3	13
Aged 40 to 44	31	18	11	5	6	7	5	2	13	4	10
Aged 45 to 49	29	27	9	-	9	18	4	15	2	-	2
Aged 50 to 54	15	14	5	1	4	9	2	7	1	-	1
Aged 55 to 59	-	-	-	-	-	-	-	-	-	-	-
Aged 60 to 64	1	-	-	-	-	-	-	-	1	-	1
Aged 65 or older	3	3	3	-	3	-	-	-	-	-	-

Note: (-) means insufficient data
Source: Bureau of the Census, School Enrollment—Social and Economic Characteristics of Students: October 1993, Current Population Reports, P20-479, 1994

Bachelor's, Master's, and Doctoral Degrees
Earned by Hispanics by Field of Study, 1992-93

(number and percent of bachelor's, master's, and doctoral degrees earned by Hispanics, by field of study, 1992-93)

	bachelor's		master's		doctoral	
	number	percent	number	percent	number	percent
Total degrees	45,376	3.9%	10,665	2.9%	827	2.0%
Agriculture and natural resources	325	1.9	85	2.1	20	1.7
Architecture and related programs	461	5.0	148	3.9	5	3.4
Area, ethnic, and cultural studies	437	8.0	77	5.1	5	2.8
Biological/life sciences	1,855	3.9	140	2.9	84	1.9
Business, management, and admin. services	9,588	3.7	2,241	2.5	10	0.7
Communications	1,883	3.5	122	2.6	8	2.7
Communications technologies	26	3.1	10	2.2	-	-
Computer and information sciences	860	3.6	167	1.6	7	0.9
Construction trades	1	1.4	-	-	-	-
Education	2,973	2.8	3,181	3.3	185	2.6
Engineering	2,312	3.7	618	2.2	51	0.9
Engineering related technologies	622	3.9	17	1.5	1	5.0
English language and literature	1,756	3.1	174	2.2	22	1.6
Foreign languages and literature	1,647	11.4	262	8.2	65	7.8
Health professions and related sciences	2,009	3.0	638	2.5	26	1.5
Home economics	400	2.6	105	4.2	3	0.9
Law and legal studies	100	4.9	84	3.8	-	-
Liberal arts and sciences	1,892	5.7	50	2.1	1	1.2
Library science	2	2.4	118	2.4	2	2.6
Mathematics	437	3.0	69	1.7	8	0.7
Mechanics and repairers	5	4.8	-	-	-	-
Multi/interdisciplinary studies	1,556	6.5	65	2.6	4	2.0
Parks, recreation, leisure and fitness	285	2.9	25	1.7	-	-
Philosophy and religion	244	3.1	26	1.8	5	1.1
Physical sciences	438	2.5	107	2.0	68	1.5
Precision production trades	4	1.0	-	-	-	-
Protective services	1,265	6.1	45	3.3	-	-
Psychology	3,175	4.8	425	3.9	125	3.4
Public administration and services	886	5.3	890	4.3	9	2.0
R.O.T.C. and military sciences	-	-	3	2.8	-	-
Social sciences and history	6,067	4.5	396	2.9	85	2.5
Theological studies/religious vocations	111	2.0	123	2.5	12	0.8
Transportation and material moving	136	3.5	19	3.8	-	-
Visual and performing arts	1,618	3.4	235	2.5	16	1.8

Source: National Center for Education Statistics, Digest of Education Statistics 1995, *NCES 95-029, 1995*

First-Professional Degrees Earned by Hispanics by Field of Study, 1992-93

(number and percent of first-professional degrees earned by Hispanics, by field of study, 1992-93)

	number	percent
Total	2,984	4.0%
Dentistry (D.D.S. or D.M.D.)	212	5.9
Medicine (M.D.)	610	3.9
Optometry (O.D.)	31	2.7
Osteopathic medicine (D.O.)	69	4.2
Pharmacy (Pharm. D.)	56	2.9
Podiatry (Pod. D. or D.P. or D.P.M.)	30	6.3
Veterinary medicine (D.V.M.)	60	2.9
Chiropractic medicine (D.C. or D.C.M.)	113	4.0
Law (L.L.B. or J.D.)	1,665	4.1
Theology (M.Div., M.H.L., B.D., or Ord.)	137	2.5
Other	1	1.6

Source: National Center for Education Statistics, Digest of Education Statistics 1995, *NCES 95-029, 1995*

Hispanics:
Health

Hispanics fare better than the total population on some health measures and worse on others. Hispanics are less likely to die of cancer or heart disease than the average American, but their homicide rate is 68 percent above average. Infant mortality is below average, but the incidence of AIDS and tuberculosis is above average.

Hispanics are more likely to be without health insurance than any other racial or ethnic group. In 1993, 32 percent did not have health insurance, double the proportion who are uninsured among the total population.

The leading cause of death among Hispanics is heart disease, which is also true for the population as a whole. But heart disease accounts for only 24 percent of all Hispanic deaths, versus 33 percent of deaths for the total population.

Hispanic life expectancy exceeds that of the average American. At birth, Hispanic males can expect to live to age 75, or 2 years longer than the average American male. Hispanic females can expect to live to age 82, or 3 years longer than the average female.

Health Indicators for Hispanics, 1992

(selected indicators of total and Hispanic health status, and index of Hispanic health indicators to total, 1992 except where otherwise noted)

	total population indicator	Hispanic indicator	index
Infant mortality rate (deaths < age 1 per 1,000 live births, 1991)	8.6	7.1	83
Total deaths per 100,000 population	504.5	380.6	75
Motor vehicle crash deaths per 100,000 population	15.8	16.3	103
Work-related injury deaths per 100,000 people aged 16 or older, 1993	3.2	3.5	203
Suicides per 100,000 population	11.1	7.2	65
Homicides per 100,000 population	10.5	17.6	168
Lung cancer deaths per 100,000 population	39.3	14.5	37
Female breast cancer deaths per 100,000 women	21.9	13.0	59
Cardiovascular disease deaths per 100,000 population	180.4	120.5	67
Heart disease deaths per 100,000 population	144.3	94.8	66
Stroke deaths per 100,000 population	26.2	19.3	74
Reported incidence of AIDS per 100,000 population, 1993	31.2	52.6	169
Reported incidence of tuberculosis per 100,000 population, 1993	9.8	20.6	210
Reported incidence of syphilis per 100,000 population, 1993	10.4	6.0	58
Prevalence of low birth weight, as percent of total live births	7.1	6.1	86
Births to girls aged 10 to 17, as percent of total live births	4.9	7.1	145
Percent of mothers without care, first trimester of pregnancy	22.3	35.8	161
Percent < age 18 living in poverty, 1993	22.7	40.9	180
Percent living in counties exceeding U.S. air quality standards, 1993	23.5	42.3	180

Note: The index is calculated by dividing the Hispanic figure by the total figure for each indicator and multiplying by 100. For example, the index of 83 indicates that the Hispanic infant mortality rate is 17 percent below the rate for all infants.
Source: National Center for Health Statistics, Health Status Indicators: Differentials by Race and Hispanic Origin, *Healthy People 2000, No. 10, 1995*

Hispanics With Disabilities, 1991-92

(total number of Hispanics, number and percent with a disability, and number and percent with a severe disability, by selected characteristics, 1991-92; numbers in thousands)

	total	with a disability		with a severe disability	
		number	*percent*	*number*	*percent*
Total persons	21,905	3,343	15.3%	1,838	8.4%
AGE					
Under age 6	2,818	52	1.8	5	0.2
Aged 6 to 14	3,688	151	4.1	22	0.6
Aged 15 to 17	1,230	104	8.5	28	2.3
Aged 18 to 24	2,553	219	8.6	78	3.1
Aged 25 to 34	4,367	481	11.0	241	5.5
Aged 35 to 44	3,047	542	17.8	286	9.4
Aged 45 to 54	1,810	496	27.4	261	14.4
Aged 55 to 64	1,158	554	47.9	390	33.7
Aged 65 to 74	803	417	51.9	261	32.5
Aged 75 or older	430	328	76.2	267	62.2
HOUSEHOLD TYPE					
Family householder or spouse	8,614	1,869	21.7	1,039	12.1
With children under age 18	5,494	897	16.3	448	8.2
Married, spouse present	6,937	1,405	20.3	760	11.0
With children under age 18	4,495	665	14.8	324	7.2
No spouse present	1,677	464	27.7	279	16.7
With children under age 18	999	232	23.2	124	12.4
Nonfamily householder	1,476	500	33.8	335	22.7
Living alone	1,262	469	37.2	323	25.6
REGION					
Northeast	3,448	548	15.9	386	11.2
Midwest	1,698	296	17.5	161	9.5
South	8,163	1,357	16.6	738	9.0
West	8,595	1,142	13.3	554	6.4

Source: Bureau of the Census, Household Economic Studies, *Current Population Reports, P70-33, 1993*

Health Insurance Coverage of Hispanics by Age, 1993

(number and percent distribution of Hispanics, by age and health insurance coverage status, 1993; numbers in thousands)

| | total persons | covered by private or government health insurance | | | | | | | not covered |
| | | private health insurance | | | government health insurance | | | | |
		total	total	group health	total	Medicaid	Medicare	Champus	
Number									
Total	26,646	18,235	12,021	9,981	7,873	6,328	1,613	530	8,411
Under 18	9,549	7,093	3,996	3,262	3,891	3,739	11	162	2,456
18 to 24	3,383	1,849	1,355	993	590	499	29	78	1,534
25 to 34	5,046	3,070	2,319	2,072	861	756	55	82	1,976
35 to 44	3,700	2,430	1,954	1,782	569	466	62	68	1,270
45 to 54	2,213	1,521	1,212	1,048	365	283	75	48	692
55 to 64	1,366	959	695	582	337	205	132	49	406
65 or older	1,390	1,313	490	241	1,259	380	1,250	42	77
Percent									
Total	100.0%	68.4%	45.1%	37.5%	29.5%	23.7%	6.1%	2.0%	31.6%
Under 18	100.0	74.3	41.8	34.2	40.7	39.2	0.1	1.7	25.7
18 to 24	100.0	54.7	40.1	29.3	17.4	14.7	0.9	2.3	45.3
25 to 34	100.0	60.8	46.0	41.1	17.1	15.0	1.1	1.6	39.2
35 to 44	100.0	65.7	52.8	48.2	15.4	12.6	1.7	1.8	34.3
45 to 54	100.0	68.7	54.8	47.4	16.5	12.8	3.4	2.2	31.3
55 to 64	100.0	70.3	50.9	42.7	24.7	15.0	9.7	3.6	29.7
65 or older	100.0	94.5	35.2	17.3	90.6	27.3	89.9	3.0	5.5

Source: Bureau of the Census, unpublished tables from the 1994 Current Population Survey

Leading Causes of Death Among Hispanics, 1993

(total number of deaths among Hispanics, and number and percent accounted for by ten leading causes of death, 1993)

		number	percent
	All causes	86,935	100.0%
1.	Diseases of heart	20,794	23.9
2.	Malignant neoplasms	15,740	18.1
3.	Accidents and adverse effects	7,564	8.7
4.	Human immunodeficiency virus infection	4,829	5.6
5.	Cerebrovascular diseases	4,316	5.0
6.	Homicide and legal intervention	4,283	4.9
7.	Diabetes mellitus	3,343	3.8
8.	Pneumonia and influenza	2,683	3.1
9.	Chronic liver disease and cirrhosis	2,554	2.9
10.	Chronic obstructive pulmonary diseases	2,050	2.4
	All other causes	18,779	21.6

Source: National Center for Health Statistics, Advance Report of Final Mortality Statistics, 1993, *Vol. 44, No. 7 Supplement, 1996*

Life Expectancy of Hispanics at Birth and Age 65, 1995-2020

(average number of years of life remaining at birth and at age 65 for Hispanic males and females, 1995-2020; difference between Hispanic life expectancy and total life expectancy for males and females at birth and at age 65, 1995 and 2020)

	life expectancy (years)	
	males	*females*
AT BIRTH		
1995	74.9	82.2
2000	75.2	82.8
2005	75.5	83.3
2010	76.4	84.0
2015	77.4	84.7
2020	78.3	85.4
Life exp. of Hispanics minus life exp. of total Americans		
1995	2.4	2.9
2020	2.8	3.9
AT AGE 65		
1995	18.5	21.8
2000	19.1	22.4
2005	19.8	23.0
2010	20.4	23.5
2015	21.0	24.0
2020	21.6	24.5
Life exp. of Hispanics minus life exp. of total Americans		
1995	3.0	2.6
2020	4.0	3.9

Source: Bureau of the Census, Population Projections of the United States, by Age, Sex, Race, and Hispanic Origin: 1995 to 2050, *Current Population Reports, P25-1130, 1996*

Hispanics:

Households and
Living Arrangements

Largely because of immigration, Hispanic householders are much younger than householders in the nation as a whole. Only 11 percent are aged 65 or older, versus 21 percent of total householders. Fully 54 percent are aged 25 to 44, versus 43 percent of total householders.

Married couples represent 55 percent of Hispanic households, equal to the married-couple share of total households. But couples with children account for 35 percent of Hispanic households, versus a much smaller 26 percent of total households. The married-couple share of households varies widely by Hispanic ethnicity, accounting for fully 60 percent of Mexican-American households versus just 38 percent of Puerto Rican households. Overall, two out of three Hispanic children live with both parents, while 29 percent live with their mother only.

The marital status of Hispanic men and women is similar to that of the population as a whole, with over half of men and women currently married.

Hispanic Households by Age of Householder, 1994

(number and percent distribution of Hispanic households by age of householder, 1994; numbers in thousands)

	number	percent
Total households	7,362	100.0%
Under age 25	592	8.0
Aged 25 to 29	934	12.7
Aged 30 to 34	1,191	16.2
Aged 35 to 39	983	13.4
Aged 40 to 44	873	11.9
Aged 45 to 49	698	9.5
Aged 50 to 54	523	7.1
Aged 55 to 59	406	5.5
Aged 60 to 64	363	4.9
Aged 65 to 69	285	3.9
Aged 70 to 74	240	3.3
Aged 75 or older	274	3.7

Source: Bureau of the Census, Household and Family Characteristics: March 1994, *Current Population Reports, P20-483, 1995*

Hispanic Households by Household Type, 1994

(number and percent distribution of Hispanic households by type of household, 1994; numbers in thousands)

	number	percent
Total households	7,362	100.0%
Family households	5,940	80.7
Married-couple families	4,033	54.8
With children <18	2,609	35.4
Without children <18	1,423	19.3
Female householder,		
no spouse present	1,498	20.3
With children <18	1,006	13.7
Without children <18	492	6.7
Male householder,		
no spouse present	410	5.6
Nonfamily households	1,423	19.3
Female householder	676	9.2
Living alone	552	7.5
Male householder	747	10.1
Living alone	511	6.9

Source: Bureau of the Census, Household and Family Characteristics: March 1994, *Current Population Reports, P20-483, 1995*

Hispanic Households by Type and Age of Householder, 1994

(number and percent distribution of Hispanic households by age of householder and household type, 1994; numbers in thousands)

		family households				nonfamily households	
	total	total	married couples	female householder, no spouse present	male householder, no spouse present	female householder	male householder
Total, number	7,362	5,940	4,033	1,498	410	676	747
Under 20	46	36	11	19	6	5	6
20 to 24	546	400	215	119	66	59	87
25 to 29	934	753	489	195	69	63	118
30 to 34	1,191	1,020	698	257	65	52	119
35 to 39	983	867	591	225	51	29	87
40 to 44	873	762	554	168	39	46	65
45 to 49	698	590	408	141	42	46	61
50 to 54	523	435	304	113	17	42	47
55 to 59	406	319	219	90	10	40	47
60 to 64	363	270	199	57	13	76	18
65 to 74	525	337	243	73	21	125	62
75 to 84	206	119	84	27	8	68	19
85 or older	68	32	17	13	2	26	10
Total, percent	100.0%	80.7%	54.8%	20.3%	5.6%	9.2%	10.1%
Under 20	100.0	78.3	23.9	41.3	13.0	10.9	13.0
20 to 24	100.0	73.3	39.4	21.8	12.1	10.8	15.9
25 to 29	100.0	80.6	52.4	20.9	7.4	6.7	12.6
30 to 34	100.0	85.6	58.6	21.6	5.5	4.4	10.0
35 to 39	100.0	88.2	60.1	22.9	5.2	3.0	8.9
40 to 44	100.0	87.3	63.5	19.2	4.5	5.3	7.4
45 to 49	100.0	84.5	58.5	20.2	6.0	6.6	8.7
50 to 54	100.0	83.2	58.1	21.6	3.3	8.0	9.0
55 to 59	100.0	78.6	53.9	22.2	2.5	9.9	11.6
60 to 64	100.0	74.4	54.8	15.7	3.6	20.9	5.0
65 to 74	100.0	64.2	46.3	13.9	4.0	23.8	11.8
75 to 84	100.0	57.8	40.8	13.1	3.9	33.0	9.2
85 or older	100.0	47.1	25.0	19.1	2.9	38.2	14.7

Source: Bureau of the Census, Household and Family Characteristics: March 1994, *Current Population Reports, P20-483, 1995*

Hispanic Households by Household Type and Ethnicity, 1994

(number and percent distribution of Hispanic households by type of household and ethnicity of householder, 1994; numbers in thousands)

	total	Mexican	Puerto Rican	Cuban	Central & S. Amer.	other Hispanic
Total, number	7,362	4,280	933	437	1,033	679
Family households	5,940	3,584	692	326	843	495
Married-couple families	4,031	2,571	357	237	558	309
Female householder, no spouse present	1,499	727	301	79	231	161
Male householder, no spouse present	410	287	34	10	55	25
Nonfamily households	1,423	696	241	111	190	184
Female householder	677	307	126	68	76	100
Male householder	746	389	115	43	114	84
Total, percent	100.0%	100.0%	100.0%	100.0%	100.0%	100.0%
Family households	80.7	83.8	74.1	74.6	81.6	72.8
Married-couple families	54.8	60.1	38.3	54.2	54.0	45.5
Female householder, no spouse present	20.4	17.0	32.2	18.2	22.3	23.7
Male householder, no spouse present	5.6	6.7	3.6	2.2	5.3	3.7
Nonfamily households	19.3	16.3	25.9	25.4	18.4	27.2
Female householder	9.2	7.2	13.5	15.6	7.3	14.8
Male householder	10.1	9.1	12.3	9.8	11.1	12.4

Source: Bureau of the Census, Internet web site, http://www.census.gov

Hispanic Households by Size, 1994

(number and percent distribution of Hispanic households by size, 1994; numbers in thousands)

	number	percent
Total households	7,362	100.0%
One person	1,063	14.4
Two persons	1,671	22.7
Three persons	1,406	19.1
Four persons	1,410	19.2
Five persons	960	13.0
Six persons	420	5.7
Seven or more persons	433	5.9

Source: Bureau of the Census, Household and Family Characteristics: March 1994, *Current Population Reports, P20-483, 1995*

Hispanic Married Couples by Age of Householder and Presence of Children, 1994

(number and percent of Hispanic married couples by presence and number of own children under age 18 at home and by age of householder, 1994; numbers in thousands)

	total	< age 20	20-24	25-29	30-34	35-39	40-44	45-54	55-64	65+
Number	4,033	11	215	489	698	591	554	712	419	344
Without children <18	1,423	2	78	99	97	77	92	300	339	340
With children <18	2,609	8	137	390	602	513	463	412	79	4
One	821	1	80	140	143	83	128	191	53	3
Two	966	5	52	160	253	210	129	138	16	1
Three or more	822	2	5	89	205	220	205	83	11	-
Percent	100.0%	100.0%	100.0%	100.0%	100.0%	100.0%	100.0%	100.0%	100.0%	100.0%
Without children <18	35.3	18.2	36.3	20.2	13.9	13.0	16.6	42.1	80.9	98.8
With children <18	64.7	72.7	63.7	79.8	86.2	86.8	83.6	57.9	18.9	1.2
One	20.4	9.1	37.2	28.6	20.5	14.0	23.1	26.8	12.6	0.9
Two	24.0	45.5	24.2	32.7	36.2	35.5	23.3	19.4	3.8	0.3
Three or more	20.4	18.2	2.3	18.2	29.4	37.2	37.0	11.7	2.6	-

Note: (-) means number in sample is too small to make a reliable estimate.
Source: Bureau of the Census, Household and Family Characteristics: March 1994, *Current Population Reports, P20-483, 1995*

Hispanic Female-Headed Families by Age of Householder and Presence of Children, 1994

(number and percent of Hispanic female-headed families by presence and number of own children under age 18 at home and by age of householder, 1994; numbers in thousands)

	total	< age 20	20-24	25-29	30-34	35-39	40-44	45-54	55-64	65+
Number	1,498	19	119	195	257	225	168	254	147	113
Without children <18	492	2	20	12	6	12	44	149	133	113
With children <18	1,006	17	99	183	251	213	124	105	14	-
One	383	16	46	62	65	65	52	67	9	-
Two	339	1	36	63	102	69	41	22	4	-
Three or more	284	-	17	57	83	79	31	15	-	-
Percent	100.0%	100.0%	100.0%	100.0%	100.0%	100.0%	100.0%	100.0%	100.0%	100.0%
Without children <18	32.8	10.5	16.8	6.2	2.3	5.3	26.2	58.7	90.5	100.0
With children <18	67.2	89.5	83.2	93.8	97.7	94.7	73.8	41.3	9.5	-
One	25.6	84.2	38.7	31.8	25.3	28.9	31.0	26.4	6.1	-
Two	22.6	5.3	30.3	32.3	39.7	30.7	24.4	8.7	2.7	-
Three or more	19.0	-	14.3	29.2	32.3	35.1	18.5	5.9	-	-

Note: (-) means number in sample is too small to make a reliable estimate.
Source: Bureau of the Census, Household and Family Characteristics: March 1994, *Current Population Reports, P20-483, 1995*

Hispanic Single-Person Households by Age of Householder, 1994

(number and percent distribution of Hispanic single-person households and single-person households as a percent of total Hispanic households, by age of householder, 1994; numbers in thousands)

	number	percent	percent of total Hispanic households
Total households	1,063	100.0%	14.4%
Under age 25	68	6.4	11.5
Aged 25 to 29	90	8.5	9.6
Aged 30 to 34	105	9.9	8.8
Aged 35 to 39	88	8.3	9.0
Aged 40 to 44	89	8.4	10.2
Aged 45 to 54	152	14.3	12.4
Aged 55 to 64	168	15.8	21.8
Aged 65 to 74	182	17.1	34.7
Aged 75 or older	123	11.6	44.9
Median age (years)	50.9	-	-

Source: Bureau of the Census, Household and Family Characteristics: March 1994, *Current Population Reports, P20-483, 1995*

Living Arrangements of Hispanic Children by Age, 1994

(number and percent distribution of Hispanic children by living arrangement, marital status of parent, and age of child, 1994; numbers in thousands)

	total	under age 6	6 to 11	12 to 17
Number with one or both parents	9,041	3,571	2,944	2,526
Living with both parents	6,022	2,356	1,973	1,692
Living with mother only	2,646	1,045	861	740
Divorced	581	123	233	225
Married, spouse absent	832	288	266	278
Widowed	151	25	46	80
Never married	1,083	609	316	157
Living with father only	373	170	110	93
Divorced	108	22	42	44
Married, spouse absent	79	23	23	33
Widowed	16	-	10	6
Never married	169	124	36	10
Percent with one or both parents	100.0%	100.0%	100.0%	100.0%
Living with both parents	66.6	66.0	67.0	67.0
Living with mother only	29.3	29.3	29.2	29.3
Divorced	6.4	3.4	7.9	8.9
Married, spouse absent	9.2	8.1	9.0	11.0
Widowed	1.7	0.7	1.6	3.2
Never married	12.0	17.1	10.7	6.2
Living with father only	4.1	4.8	3.7	3.7
Divorced	1.2	0.6	1.4	1.7
Married, spouse absent	0.9	0.6	0.8	1.3
Widowed	0.2	-	0.3	0.2
Never married	1.9	3.5	1.2	0.4

Note: (-) means number in sample is too small to make a reliable estimate.
Source: Bureau of the Census, Marital Status and Living Arrangements: March 1994, Current Population Reports, P20-484, 1996

Living Arrangements of Hispanic Women by Age, 1994

(number and percent distribution of Hispanic women aged 18 or older by living arrangement and age, 1994; numbers in thousands)

	total	18 to 19	20 to 24	25 to 29	30 to 34	35 to 39	40 to 44	45 to 54	55 to 64	65 to 74	75 or older
Number	8,499	453	1,184	1,174	1,173	1,010	858	1,106	759	514	268
Family householder or spouse	5,653	73	452	771	948	853	727	904	539	294	91
Child of householder	944	282	390	133	52	32	23	18	11	-	6
Other member of family household	858	64	168	146	77	58	30	75	79	88	73
Nonfamily householder	676	5	59	63	52	29	46	88	115	125	93
Other member of nonfamily household	356	29	110	58	44	36	32	21	14	7	5
Group quarters*	12	-	5	3	-	2	-	-	1	-	-
Percent	100.0%	100.0%	100.0%	100.0%	100.0%	100.0%	100.0%	100.0%	100.0%	100.0%	100.0%
Family householder or spouse	66.5	16.1	38.2	65.7	80.8	84.5	84.7	81.7	71.0	57.2	34.0
Child of householder	11.1	62.3	32.9	11.3	4.4	3.2	2.7	1.6	1.4	-	2.2
Other member of family household	10.1	14.1	14.2	12.4	6.6	5.7	3.5	6.8	10.4	17.1	27.2
Nonfamily householder	8.0	1.1	5.0	5.4	4.4	2.9	5.4	8.0	15.2	24.3	34.7
Other member of nonfamily household	4.2	6.4	9.3	4.9	3.8	3.6	3.7	1.9	1.8	1.4	1.9
Group quarters*	0.1	-	0.4	0.3	-	0.2	-	-	0.1	-	-

* The Current Population Survey does not include people living in institutions such as prisons, the military, or college dormitories. It defines people living in group quarters as those in noninstitutional living arrangements that are not conventional housing units, such as rooming houses, staff quarters at a hospital, or halfway houses.

Note: (-) means number in sample is too small to make a reliable estimate.

Source: Bureau of the Census, Marital Status and Living Arrangements: March 1994, Current Population Reports, P20-484, 1996

Living Arrangements of Hispanic Men by Age, 1994

(number and percent distribution of Hispanic men aged 18 or older by living arrangement and age, 1994; numbers in thousands)

	total	18 to 19	20 to 24	25 to 29	30 to 34	35 to 39	40 to 44	45 to 54	55 to 64	65 to 74	75 or older
Number	8,598	445	1,301	1,435	1,263	1,011	821	1,107	607	414	193
Family householder or spouse	4,427	14	262	563	749	633	579	795	438	275	118
Child of householder	1,432	307	551	240	129	86	42	54	14	7	2
Other member of family household	1,079	74	221	273	126	97	51	69	67	65	39
Nonfamily householder	747	6	87	118	119	87	65	108	65	62	29
Other member of nonfamily household	900	44	174	241	138	106	84	80	23	4	5
Group quarters*	13	-	6	-	2	2	-	1	-	1	-
Percent	100.0%	100.0%	100.0%	100.0%	100.0%	100.0%	100.0%	100.0%	100.0%	100.0%	100.0%
Family householder or spouse	51.5	3.1	20.1	39.2	59.3	62.6	70.5	71.8	72.2	66.4	61.1
Child of householder	16.7	69.0	42.4	16.7	10.2	8.5	5.1	4.9	2.3	1.7	1.0
Other member of family household	12.5	16.6	17.0	19.0	10.0	9.6	6.2	6.2	11.0	15.7	20.2
Nonfamily householder	8.7	1.3	6.7	8.2	9.4	8.6	7.9	9.8	10.7	15.0	15.0
Other member of nonfamily household	10.5	9.9	13.4	16.8	10.9	10.5	10.2	7.2	3.8	1.0	2.6
Group quarters*	0.2	-	0.5	-	0.2	0.2	-	0.1	-	0.2	-

* The Current Population Survey does not include people living in institutions such as prisons, the military, or college dormitories. It defines people living in group quarters as those in noninstitutional living arrangements that are not conventional housing units, such as rooming houses, staff quarters at a hospital, or halfway houses.

Note: (-) means number in sample is too small to make a reliable estimate.

Source: Bureau of the Census, Marital Status and Living Arrangements: March 1994, Current Population Reports, P20-484, 1996

Marital Status of Hispanic Women by Age, 1994

(number and percent distribution of Hispanic women aged 15 or older by age and marital status, 1994; numbers in thousands)

	total	never married	married	widowed	divorced
Total, number	9,146	2,680	5,145	582	739
Under age 20	1,100	978	121	-	1
Aged 20 to 24	1,184	679	481	3	21
Aged 25 to 29	1,174	371	747	1	55
Aged 30 to 34	1,173	248	829	10	86
Aged 35 to 39	1,010	128	739	18	125
Aged 40 to 44	858	82	643	23	110
Aged 45 to 54	1,106	86	794	58	168
Aged 55 to 64	759	46	462	147	104
Aged 65 to 74	514	31	268	161	54
Aged 75 to 84	192	18	55	109	10
Aged 85 or older	76	11	7	52	6
Total, percent	100.0%	29.3%	56.3%	6.4%	8.1%
Under age 20	100.0	88.9	11.0	-	0.1
Aged 20 to 24	100.0	57.3	40.6	0.3	1.8
Aged 25 to 29	100.0	31.6	63.6	0.1	4.7
Aged 30 to 34	100.0	21.1	70.7	0.9	7.3
Aged 35 to 39	100.0	12.7	73.2	1.8	12.4
Aged 40 to 44	100.0	9.6	74.9	2.7	12.8
Aged 45 to 54	100.0	7.8	71.8	5.2	15.2
Aged 55 to 64	100.0	6.1	60.9	19.4	13.7
Aged 65 to 74	100.0	6.0	52.1	31.3	10.5
Aged 75 to 84	100.0	9.4	28.6	56.8	5.2
Aged 85 or older	100.0	14.5	9.2	68.4	7.9

Note: (-) means number in sample is too small to make a reliable estimate.
Source: Bureau of the Census, Marital Status and Living Arrangements: March 1994, *Current Population Reports, P20-484, 1996*

Marital Status of Hispanic Men by Age, 1994

(number and percent distribution of Hispanic men aged 15 or older by age and marital status, 1994; numbers in thousands)

	total	never married	married	widowed	divorced
Total, number	9,312	3,737	4,863	172	540
Under age 20	1,159	1,116	36	-	7
Aged 20 to 24	1,301	1,013	284	-	4
Aged 25 to 29	1,435	727	654	2	52
Aged 30 to 34	1,263	349	836	-	78
Aged 35 to 39	1,011	209	698	2	102
Aged 40 to 44	821	113	631	3	74
Aged 45 to 54	1,107	123	843	23	118
Aged 55 to 64	607	49	467	34	57
Aged 65 to 74	414	23	295	59	37
Aged 75 to 84	142	4	94	34	10
Aged 85 or older	51	12	23	16	-
Total, percent	100.0%	40.1%	52.2%	1.8%	5.8%
Under age 20	100.0	96.3	3.1	-	-
Aged 20 to 24	100.0	77.9	21.8	-	0.3
Aged 25 to 29	100.0	50.7	45.6	0.1	3.6
Aged 30 to 34	100.0	27.6	66.2	-	6.2
Aged 35 to 39	100.0	20.7	69.0	0.2	10.1
Aged 40 to 44	100.0	13.8	76.9	0.4	9.0
Aged 45 to 54	100.0	11.1	76.2	2.1	10.7
Aged 55 to 64	100.0	8.1	76.9	5.6	9.4
Aged 65 to 74	100.0	5.6	71.3	14.3	8.9
Aged 75 to 84	100.0	2.8	66.2	23.9	7.0
Aged 85 or older	100.0	23.5	45.1	31.4	-

Note: (-) means number in sample is too small to make a reliable estimate.
Source: Bureau of the Census, Marital Status and Living Arrangements: March 1994, *Current Population Reports, P20-484, 1996*

Hispanics:

Housing

Forty-two percent of the nation's 6 million Hispanic householders own their home. This compares with a homeownership rate of 64 percent for all Americans. Fifty-three percent of Cubans own their home, versus 24 percent of Puerto Ricans. The median value of the homes owned by Hispanics was $77,200 in 1990, about the same as the $78,300 median value of the average American home.

Among the 50 metropolitan areas with the most Hispanic households, Los Angeles has the largest number—784,000 in 1990. Hispanics account for the largest share of households—fully 91 percent—in Laredo, Texas.

Most Hispanic householders are satisfied with their homes. On a scale of one to ten, 65 percent of Hispanics rate their homes an eight or higher. Even among Hispanic renters, 55 percent rate their homes an eight or more. Few Hispanics think their neighborhood has a crime problem—only 7 percent of homeowners and 15 percent of renters say crime is a problem in their area. Fully 59 percent of Hispanic householders say their neighborhood has no problems.

Eighteen percent of Hispanic households do not have a telephone in their home, versus just 8 percent of households in the nation as a whole. Among Puerto Ricans, 24 percent have no telephone in their home.

Characteristics of Hispanic Households
by Metropolitan Status, 1990

(number of Hispanic households, percent of total households that are Hispanic, percent of Hispanic households that are owner occupied, and median value of owner-occupied Hispanic households, by metropolitan status, 1990; numbers in thousands)

	number	Hispanic share of total households	owner-occupied percent	owner-occupied median value
Hispanic households	6,002	6.5%	42.4%	$77,200
Inside metropolitan areas	5,428	7.6	40.8	84,600
Central cities	3,197	10.7	33.3	66,300
Suburbs*	2,231	5.4	51.4	107,100
Outside metropolitan areas	574	2.8	58.1	39,900

* The suburbs are the portion of a metropolitan area that is outside the central city.
Source: Bureau of the Census, Housing in Metropolitan Areas—Hispanic Origin Households, *Statistical Brief, SB/95-4, 1995*

Hispanic Homeownership in the 50 Metropolitan Areas With the Most Hispanic Households, 1990

(number of Hispanic households, percent of total households that are Hispanic, percent of Hispanic households that are owner occupied, and median value of owner-occupied Hispanic households, in the U.S. and in the 50 metropolitan areas with the most Hispanic households, ranked alphabetically, 1990; numbers in thousands)

	number	Hispanic share of total households	owner-occupied percent	owner-occupied median value
Total Hispanic households	6,002	6.5%	42.4%	$77,200
Albuquerque, NM	58	31.1	59.7	69,500
Anaheim-Santa Ana, CA	121	14.7	39.2	201,200
Austin, TX	47	15.6	39.6	56,300
Bakersfield, CA	36	19.6	43.9	64,600
Bergen-Passaic, NJ	41	8.9	31.5	195,500
Boston, MA	37	3.4	19.1	176,100
Brownsville-Harlingen, TX	53	71.7	60.9	33,500
Chicago, IL	189	8.5	36.7	84,500
Corpus Christi, TX	51	43.4	57.2	40,500
Dallas, TX	95	9.9	38.2	58,100
Denver, CO	66	10.1	47.6	70,500
Detroit, MI	25	1.6	58.8	52,300
El Paso, TX	108	60.3	58.2	50,500
Fort Lauderdale-Hollywood-Pompano Beach, FL	35	6.7	54.2	85,000
Fort Worth-Arlington, TX	40	8.1	45.6	50,100
Fresno, CA	59	26.8	40.8	64,900
Houston, TX	187	15.7	39.3	44,200
Jersey City, NJ	60	28.7	20.0	164,500
Laredo, TX	31	90.9	61.3	47,800
Las Cruces, NM	21	47.2	66.0	52,200
Las Vegas, NV	24	8.4	39.0	81,700
Los Angeles-Long Beach, CA	784	26.2	35.1	172,800
McAllen-Edinburg-Mission, TX	79	76.3	68.1	31,200
Miami-Hialeah, FL	320	46.2	48.2	86,700
Middlesex-Somerset-Hunterdon, NJ	20	5.4	40.5	162,100
Modesto, CA	19	15.5	49.0	104,000
Nassau-Suffolk, NY	40	4.7	56.4	164,400
New Orleans, LA	18	3.9	50.9	67,800
New York, NY	584	17.9	12.1	183,300

(continued)

(continued from previous page)

	number	Hispanic share of total households	owner-occupied	
			percent	median value
Newark, NJ	55	8.5%	30.2%	$165,400
Oakland, CA	76	9.8	48.9	183,700
Orlando, FL	29	7.3	51.4	79,300
Oxnard-Ventura, CA	39	17.8	47.4	203,100
Philadelphia, PA-NJ	48	2.7	47.1	43,300
Phoenix, AZ	90	11.2	49.1	62,100
Riverside-San Bernardino, CA	164	18.9	55.0	117,800
Sacramento, CA	49	8.8	47.5	110,300
Salinas-Seaside-Monterey, CA	26	23.0	35.9	140,500
Salt Lake City-Ogden, UT	17	5.0	49.7	57,300
San Antonio, TX	178	39.6	56.5	42,200
San Diego, CA	125	14.0	37.9	148,500
San Francisco, CA	65	10.0	34.1	277,300
San Jose, CA	78	14.9	45.1	226,300
Santa Barbara-Santa Maria-Lompoc, CA	23	18.1	38.6	170,000
Stockton, CA	28	17.7	44.5	93,800
Tampa-St. Petersburg-Clearwater, FL	47	5.4	59.8	66,200
Tucson, AZ	47	18.0	55.7	58,600
Visalia-Tulare-Porterville, CA	28	28.5	46.1	58,400
Washington, DC-MD-VA	62	4.2	37.5	159,100
West Palm Beach-Boca Raton-Delray Beach, FL	20	5.4	52.8	80,900

Source: Bureau of the Census, Housing in Metropolitan Areas—Hispanic Households, *Statistical Brief, SB/95-4, 1995*

Characteristics of Housing Units Occupied by Hispanics, 1993

(number and percent distribution of housing units occupied by Hispanics, by selected housing characteristics and homeownership status, 1993; numbers in thousands except for medians)

	total		owner-occupied		renter-occupied	
	number	*percent*	*number*	*percent*	*number*	*percent*
Total occupied housing units	6,614	100.0%	2,788	100.0%	3,826	100.0%
Region						
Northeast	1,133	17.1	214	7.7	919	24.0
Midwest	474	7.2	192	6.9	282	7.4
South	2,197	33.2	1,123	40.3	1,075	28.1
West	2,810	42.5	1,260	45.2	1,550	40.5
Units in structure						
1, detached	3,107	47.0	2,291	82.2	816	21.3
1, attached	383	5.8	116	4.2	267	7.0
2 to 4	964	14.6	105	3.8	858	22.4
5 to 9	557	8.4	24	0.9	533	13.9
10 to 19	505	7.6	16	0.6	489	12.8
20 to 49	473	7.2	22	0.8	451	11.8
50 or more	363	5.5	24	0.9	339	8.9
Mobile home or trailer	261	3.9	190	6.8	72	1.9
Median number of rooms in unit	5	-	6	-	4	-
Median square footage of unit	1,384	-	1,472	-	1,142	-
Number of complete bathrooms						
None	52	0.8	7	0.3	46	1.2
One	4,085	61.8	1,104	39.6	2,981	77.9
One and one-half	665	10.1	393	14.1	272	7.1
Two or more	1,811	27.4	1,284	46.1	527	13.8
Heating fuel						
Total with heating fuel	6,364	96.2	2,718	97.5	3,646	95.3
Electricity	1,858	28.1	733	26.3	1,125	29.4
Piped gas	3,452	52.2	1,651	59.2	1,801	47.1
Bottled gas	114	1.7	67	2.4	46	1.2
Fuel oil	645	9.8	93	3.3	551	14.4

(continued)

(continued from previous page)

	total		owner-occupied		renter-occupied	
	number	*percent*	*number*	*percent*	*number*	*percent*
Kerosene or other liquid fuel	39	0.6%	19	0.7%	20	0.5%
Coal or coke	2	0.0	2	0.1	-	-
Wood	219	3.3	132	4.7	87	2.3
Solar energy	1	0.0	1	0.0	-	-
Other	35	0.5	19	0.7	16	0.4
Selected equipment						
Dishwasher	2,246	34.0	1,216	43.6	1,031	26.9
Washing machine	3,986	60.3	2,501	89.7	1,485	38.8
Clothes dryer	2,928	44.3	2,014	72.2	914	23.9
Disposal in kitchen sink	2,677	40.5	1,232	44.2	1,445	37.8
Central air conditioning	2,376	35.9	1,259	45.2	1,117	29.2
Porch, deck, balcony, or patio	4,220	63.8	2,224	79.8	1,996	52.2
Telephone	5,777	87.3	2,623	94.1	3,154	82.4
Usable fireplace	1,252	18.9	894	32.1	357	9.3
Garage or carport	3,219	48.7	2,013	72.2	1,206	31.5
Cars and trucks available						
No cars, trucks, or vans	1,155	17.5	139	5.0	1,016	26.6
1 car, with or without						
trucks or vans	3,071	46.4	1,288	46.2	1,783	46.6
2 or more cars	1,840	27.8	1,104	39.6	737	19.3
Overall opinion of housing unit						
1 (worst)	101	1.5	9	0.3	92	2.4
2	45	0.7	2	0.1	43	1.1
3	82	1.2	23	0.8	59	1.5
4	118	1.8	29	1.0	89	2.3
5	651	9.8	163	5.8	488	12.8
6	454	6.9	131	4.7	323	8.4
7	802	12.1	254	9.1	548	14.3
8	1,397	21.1	570	20.4	827	21.6
9	888	13.4	450	16.1	439	11.5
10 (best)	1,982	30.0	1,143	41.0	839	21.9

Note: (-) means not applicable or number in sample is too small to make a reliable estimate.
Source: Bureau of the Census, American Housing Survey for the United States in 1993, *Current Housing Reports, H150/93, 1995*

Characteristics of Hispanic Households by Ethnicity, 1993

(percent of Hispanic households by homeownership status and telephone availability, by ethnicity, 1994)

	total Hispanic	Mexican	Puerto Rican	Cuban	Central & South Am.	other Hispanic
Homeownership status	100.0%	100.0%	100.0%	100.0%	100.0%	100.0%
Own or buying home	41.6	46.9	24.0	52.7	27.8	45.5
Renting	58.5	53.1	76.0	47.3	72.2	54.5
Availability of telephone	100.0	100.0	100.0	100.0	100.0	100.0
Telephone in household	81.6	80.8	75.8	93.3	83.8	83.8
Telephone available to household	3.7	3.8	4.6	2.0	3.6	3.1
Telephone not available	14.7	15.3	19.7	4.7	12.6	13.1

Source: Bureau of the Census, Internet web site, http://www.census.gov

Neighborhood Characteristics of Hispanic Housing Units, 1993

(number and percent distribution of housing units occupied by Hispanics, by selected characteristics of neighborhoods and homeownership status, 1993; numbers in thousands)

	total		owner-occupied		renter-occupied	
	number	*percent*	*number*	*percent*	*number*	*percent*
Total occupied housing units	6,614	100.0%	2,788	100.0%	3,826	100.0%
Overall opinion of neighborhood						
1 (worst)	221	3.3	42	1.5	179	4.7
2	103	1.6	14	0.5	89	2.3
3	159	2.4	41	1.5	118	3.1
4	151	2.3	44	1.6	107	2.8
5	695	10.5	216	7.7	479	12.5
6	387	5.9	123	4.4	264	6.9
7	761	11.5	304	10.9	457	11.9
8	1,257	19.0	521	18.7	735	19.2
9	814	12.3	398	14.3	416	10.9
10 (best)	1,942	29.4	1,053	37.8	889	23.2
Neighborhood problems						
No problems	3,888	58.8	1,712	61.4	2,175	56.8
With problems*	2,593	39.2	1,033	37.1	1,560	40.8
Crime	790	11.9	201	7.2	589	15.4
Noise	738	11.2	212	7.6	527	13.8
Traffic	460	7.0	183	6.6	277	7.2
Litter or housing deterioration	302	4.6	121	4.3	181	4.7
Poor city or county services	116	1.8	48	1.7	68	1.8
Undesirable commercial, institutional, industrial	73	1.1	38	1.4	35	0.9
People	1,008	15.2	390	14.0	618	16.2
Other	607	9.2	303	10.9	304	7.9
Not reported	21	0.3	15	0.5	6	0.2

* Figures will not add to total because more than one problem could be cited.
Source: Bureau of the Census, American Housing Survey for the United States in 1993, *Current Housing Reports, H150/93, 1995*

Geographical Mobility of the Hispanic Population by Age, 1993-94

(total number of Hispanics aged 1 or older, number and percent of those who moved between March 1993 and March 1994, by age of person and type of move; numbers in thousands)

			different house in the U.S.							
					different county					
							different state			
		same house (non-		same		same		same	different	movers from
	total	movers)	total	county	total	state	total	region	region	abroad
Total, 1 or older	25,999	77.6%	20.7%	16.2%	4.5%	2.7%	1.9%	1.0%	0.9%	1.7%
Aged 1 to 4	2,496	74.0	24.4	19.4	5.0	3.3	1.8	1.0	0.7	1.6
Aged 5 to 9	2,621	79.7	19.4	14.4	5.0	3.1	1.9	1.4	0.4	1.0
Aged 10 to 14	2,426	84.7	14.7	12.1	2.6	1.5	1.0	0.3	0.7	0.7
Aged 15 to 19	2,257	76.3	21.8	16.9	4.9	2.3	2.5	1.3	1.2	2.0
Aged 15 to 17	1,360	78.8	19.6	15.5	4.0	1.8	2.2	1.0	1.2	1.6
Aged 18 and 19	897	72.4	25.1	19.1	6.0	3.0	3.1	1.7	1.3	2.6
Aged 20 to 24	2,485	62.6	34.2	25.4	8.8	5.4	3.4	1.4	2.0	3.3
Aged 25 to 29	2,609	64.1	32.3	25.5	6.8	3.8	3.0	1.8	1.2	3.6
Aged 30 to 34	2,436	74.2	24.1	18.7	5.4	3.6	1.8	1.1	0.7	1.8
Aged 35 to 39	2,021	79.9	18.2	14.0	4.2	2.2	2.0	0.8	1.2	1.9
Aged 40 to 44	1,679	83.8	14.9	12.2	2.6	1.3	1.4	0.4	1.0	1.3
Aged 45 to 49	1,278	82.6	15.8	13.4	2.4	1.5	0.9	0.6	0.3	1.5
Aged 50 to 54	935	88.1	11.2	9.5	1.7	1.3	0.5	0.1	0.4	0.5
Aged 55 to 59	747	90.0	9.5	7.1	2.4	1.2	1.2	0.5	0.5	0.4
Aged 60 to 64	619	91.9	7.3	5.5	1.8	1.1	0.8	0.8	-	0.8
Aged 60 and 61	228	96.1	3.9	3.9	0.4	0.4	-	-	-	-
Aged 62 to 64	391	89.8	9.2	6.4	2.8	1.5	1.3	1.3	-	1.3
Aged 65 to 69	519	92.3	6.9	5.8	1.2	0.4	0.8	0.8	-	1.0
Aged 70 to 74	409	92.9	7.1	5.9	1.2	1.0	0.5	0.2	0.2	-
Aged 75 to 79	194	94.3	5.7	5.2	1.0	0.5	0.5	-	-	-
Aged 80 to 84	141	92.2	7.1	6.4	0.7	0.7	-	-	-	-
Aged 85 or older	127	89.8	7.9	7.1	0.8	-	0.8	0.8	0.8	2.4
Median age	26.4	27.5	24.3	24.5	23.7	23.5	24.0	24.0	23.9	25.8

Note: (-) means number in sample is too small to make a reliable estimate.
Source: Bureau of the Census, Geographical Mobility: March 1993 to March 1994, *Current Population Reports, P20-485, 1995*

Reasons for Moving Among Hispanic Movers, 1993

(number and percent distribution of Hispanic households moving in the previous 12 months by reason for move and for choosing new neighborhood and house, and by comparison with previous home and neighborhood, by homeownership status, 1993; numbers in thousands)

	total		owner-occupied		renter-occupied	
	number	*percent*	*number*	*percent*	*number*	*percent*
Total households moving in past 12 months	1,673	100.0%	300	100.0%	1,373	100.0%
Reasons for leaving previous unit*						
Private displacement	105	6.3	25	8.3	80	5.8
Government displacement	20	1.2	-	0.0	20	1.5
Disaster loss	33	2.0	6	2.0	27	2.0
New job or job transfer	107	6.4	6	2.0	102	7.4
To be closer to work, school, other	130	7.8	3	1.0	127	9.2
Other, financial/employment related	107	6.4	12	4.0	95	6.9
To establish own household	211	12.6	27	9.0	184	13.4
Needed larger house or apartment	315	18.8	49	16.3	266	19.4
Married	35	2.1	6	2.0	30	2.2
Widowed, divorced, or separated	69	4.1	8	2.7	61	4.4
Other, family/person related	173	10.3	16	5.3	157	11.4
Wanted better home	231	13.8	50	16.7	181	13.2
Change from owner to renter	6	0.4	-	0.0	6	0.4
Change from renter to owner	129	7.7	129	43.0	-	0.0
Wanted lower rent or maintenance	127	7.6	3	1.0	124	9.0
Choice of present neighborhood*						
Convenient to job	345	20.6	66	22.0	279	20.3
Convenient to friends or relatives	318	19.0	50	16.7	268	19.5
Convenient to leisure activities	42	2.5	16	5.3	26	1.9
Convenient to public transportation	69	4.1	7	2.3	62	4.5
Good schools	132	7.9	19	6.3	112	8.2
Other public services	49	2.9	15	5.0	34	2.5
Looks/design of neighborhood	331	19.8	82	27.3	249	18.1
House was most important consideration	346	20.7	75	25.0	271	19.7
Neighborhood search						
Looked at just this neighborhood	829	49.6	92	30.7	737	53.7
Looked at other neighborhoods	796	47.6	188	62.7	608	44.3
Choice of present home*						
Financial reasons	727	43.5	150	50.0	577	42.0
Room layout/design	276	16.5	64	21.3	213	15.5

(continued)

(continued from previous page)

	total		owner-occupied		renter-occupied	
	number	percent	number	percent	number	percent
Kitchen	14	0.8%	-	0.0%	14	1.0%
Size	322	19.2	63	21.0	259	18.9
Exterior appearance	115	6.9	23	7.7	92	6.7
Yard/trees/view	84	5.0	24	8.0	60	4.4
Quality of construction	50	3.0	11	3.7	39	2.8
Only one available	225	13.4	5	1.7	220	16.0
Other reasons	465	27.8	86	28.7	379	27.6
Comparison to previous home						
Better home	876	52.4	207	69.0	669	48.7
Worse home	254	15.2	18	6.0	236	17.2
About the same	495	29.6	58	19.3	437	31.8
Comparison to previous neighborhood						
Better neighborhood	724	43.3	143	47.7	580	42.2
Worse neighborhood	221	13.2	25	8.3	195	14.2
About the same	546	32.6	99	33.0	446	32.5
Same neighborhood	131	7.8	15	5.0	117	8.5

* Figures may not add to total because more than one category may apply and unreported reasons are not shown.
Source: Bureau of the Census, American Housing Survey for the United States in 1993, Current Housing Reports, H150/93, 1995

Housing Value and Purchase Price for Hispanic Homeowners, 1993

(number and percent distribution of Hispanic homeowners by value of home, purchase price, and major source of downpayment, 1993; numbers in thousands)

	number	percent
Total homeowners	2,788	100.0%
Value of home		
Under $50,000	756	27.1
$50,000 to $79,999	575	20.6
$80,000 to $99,999	306	11.0
$100,000 to $149,999	444	15.9
$150,000 to $199,999	326	11.7
$200,000 to $299,999	274	9.8
$300,000 or more	105	3.8
Median	$84,022	-
Purchase price*		
Home purchased or built	2,633	94.4
Under $50,000	1,214	43.5
$50,000 to $79,999	442	15.9
$80,000 to $99,999	188	6.7
$100,000 to $149,999	232	8.3
$150,000 to $199,999	164	5.9
$200,000 to $299,999	77	2.8
$300,000 or more	22	0.8
Median purchase price	$47,645	-
Received as inheritance or gift	65	2.3
Major source of downpayment*		
Sale of previous home	489	17.5
Savings or cash on hand	1,576	56.5
Sale of other investment	19	0.7
Borrowing, other than mortgage on this property	105	3.8
Inheritance or gift	54	1.9
Land where building built used for financing	4	0.1
Other	116	4.2
No downpayment	180	6.5

* Figures may not add to total because not reported is not shown.
Source: Bureau of the Census, American Housing Survey for the United States in 1993, Current Housing Reports, H150/93, 1995

Repairs, Improvements, and Alterations
by Hispanic Homeowners, 1993

(number and percent of Hispanic homeowners performing selected repairs, improvements, and alterations to their homes in the past two years; among those doing work, percent who had most of it done by others; and percent spending $500 or more, 1993; numbers in thousands)

	number	*percent having work done*	*percent having most work done by others*	*percent spending $500 or more*
Total homeowners	2,788	-	-	-
Roof replaced (all or part)	575	20.6%	65.4%	74.1%
Additions built	125	4.5	51.2	88.0
Kitchen remodeled or added	240	8.6	47.9	67.5
Bathroom remodeled or added	363	13.0	38.8	58.4
Siding replaced or added	134	4.8	52.2	50.7
Storm doors/windows bought and installed	237	8.5	46.4	40.5
Major equipment replaced or added	227	8.1	67.0	67.8
Insulation added	212	7.6	44.3	31.6

Source: Bureau of the Census, American Housing Survey for the United States in 1993, *Current Housing Reports, H150/93, 1995*

Hispanics:
Income

The median income of Hispanic households fell by 7.5 percent between 1990 and 1994, after adjusting for inflation, to $23,421. This was a sharpest income decline among racial and ethnic groups. Consequently, Hispanic median household income fell relative to the median income of total households, from 75 to 73 percent.

Household income was greatest for Central and South American Hispanics in 1993, at $25,126. It was lowest for Puerto Ricans, at $18,541. As with other racial and ethnic groups, household income peaks in the 45-to-54 age group, which had a median income of $29,208 in 1994. By household type, median income is greatest for married couples, at $29,915.

Hispanic men who worked full-time had a median income of $20,525 in 1994, while women who worked full-time had a median income of $18,418. By ethnicity, earnings are greatest for Cuban men. Fully 20 percent of Cuban men who worked full-time earned over $50,000 in 1993. Between 1990 and 1994, the median income of Hispanic men who worked full-time fell by 6 percent after adjusting for inflation, while the median income of Hispanic women who worked full-time fell by 1 percent. Hispanic men and women earn less than the average worker because many Hispanics are recent immigrants and because the educational level of Hispanics is much lower than that of the average American.

Hispanic and black families are about equally likely to be poor, but Hispanic married couples have a much higher poverty rate (20 percent) than do black couples (9 percent).

Median Income of Hispanic Households, 1980 to 1994

(median income of Hispanic households, and ratio of Hispanic to total median income, 1980-1994; percent change in income and ratio, selected years; in 1994 dollars)

	median income	ratio Hispanic/total
1994	$23,421	0.73
1993	23,472	0.73
1992	23,869	0.74
1991	24,690	0.75
1990	25,320	0.75
1989	26,199	0.76
1988	25,505	0.75
1987	25,225	0.74
1986	24,815	0.74
1985	24,055	0.74
1984	24,237	0.76
1983	23,501	0.75
1982	23,529	0.75
1981	25,166	0.80
1980	24,582	0.77
Percent change		
1990-1994	-7.5%	-2.7%
1980-1994	-4.7	-5.8

Note: The ratio is calculated by dividing the median income of Hispanic households by the median for total households.
Source: Bureau of the Census, unpublished tables from the 1995 Current Population Survey

Income Distribution of Hispanic Households by Ethnicity, 1993

(number and percent distribution of Hispanic households by income and ethnicity of householder, 1993; households in thousands as of 1994)

	total	Mexican	Puerto Rican	Cuban	Central & South Am.	other Hispanic
Total	7,362	4,280	933	437	1,033	679
Under $10,000	1,476	753	303	99	177	145
$10,000 to $24,999	2,496	1,555	254	129	337	222
$25,000 to $49,999	2,197	1,316	244	112	349	176
$50,000 or more	1,193	656	132	98	170	136
Median income	$22,879	$23,992	$18,541	$23,881	$25,126	$23,300
Percent distribution	100.0%	100.0%	100.0%	100.0%	100.0%	100.0%
Under $10,000	20.1	17.6	32.5	22.5	17.1	21.4
$10,000 to $24,999	33.9	36.3	27.2	29.4	32.6	32.6
$25,000 to $49,999	29.8	30.7	26.1	25.5	33.8	26.0
$50,000 or more	16.2	15.3	14.1	22.5	16.5	20.0

Source: Bureau of the Census, Internet web site, http://www.census.gov

Income Distribution of Hispanic Households by Age of Householder, 1994

(number and percent distribution of Hispanic households by income and age of householder, 1994; households in thousands as of 1995)

	total	< 25	25-34	35-44	45-54	55-64	65+
Total	7,735	674	2,237	1,950	1,232	755	889
Under $10,000	1,586	202	397	289	176	176	348
$10,000 to $19,999	1,752	190	547	387	228	146	253
$20,000 to $29,999	1,403	146	429	333	229	129	138
$30,000 to $39,999	990	55	329	288	162	84	74
$40,000 to $49,999	641	30	191	193	137	63	27
$50,000 to $59,999	431	21	103	154	86	51	18
$60,000 to $69,999	315	9	103	100	64	30	9
$70,000 to $79,999	195	6	47	75	50	16	2
$80,000 to $89,999	128	6	29	50	25	16	2
$90,000 to $99,999	78	1	19	19	26	8	3
$100,000 or more	215	8	44	63	48	37	15
Median income	$23,421	$16,713	$23,780	$28,225	$29,208	$24,536	$13,121
Percent distribution	100.0%	100.0%	100.0%	100.0%	100.0%	100.0%	100.0%
Under $10,000	20.5	30.0	17.7	14.8	14.3	23.3	39.1
$10,000 to $19,999	22.7	28.2	24.5	19.8	18.5	19.3	28.5
$20,000 to $29,999	18.1	21.7	19.2	17.1	18.6	17.1	15.5
$30,000 to $39,999	12.8	8.2	14.7	14.8	13.1	11.1	8.3
$40,000 to $49,999	8.3	4.5	8.5	9.9	11.1	8.3	3.0
$50,000 to $59,999	5.6	3.1	4.6	7.9	7.0	6.8	2.0
$60,000 to $69,999	4.1	1.3	4.6	5.1	5.2	4.0	1.0
$70,000 to $79,999	2.5	0.9	2.1	3.8	4.1	2.1	0.2
$80,000 to $89,999	1.7	0.9	1.3	2.6	2.0	2.1	0.2
$90,000 to $99,999	1.0	0.1	0.8	1.0	2.1	1.1	0.3
$100,000 or more	2.8	1.2	2.0	3.2	3.9	4.9	1.7

Source: Bureau of the Census, unpublished tables from the 1995 Current Population Survey

Income Distribution of Hispanic Households by Household Type, 1994

(number and percent distribution of Hispanic households by income and type of household, 1994; households in thousands as of 1995)

| | total households | family households | | | | nonfamily households | | | | |
| | | total | married couples | female hh, no spouse present | male hh, no spouse present | total | female householder | | male householder | |
							total	living alone	total	living alone
Total	7,735	6,200	4,235	1,485	479	1,535	745	615	790	541
Under $10,000	1,586	1,038	401	565	73	548	382	366	166	147
$10,000 to $19,999	1,752	1,409	900	397	111	343	140	121	202	149
$20,000 to $29,999	1,403	1,147	821	223	103	257	118	76	139	99
$30,000 to $39,999	990	839	637	129	73	152	43	23	109	68
$40,000 to $49,999	641	557	427	79	50	84	22	15	62	26
$50,000 to $59,999	431	380	321	30	28	50	21	10	30	13
$60,000 to $69,999	315	281	245	19	16	34	6	-	28	14
$70,000 to $79,999	195	181	155	17	8	14	5	2	10	5
$80,000 to $89,999	128	114	93	10	11	14	1	-	13	7
$90,000 to $99,999	78	70	64	4	2	8	2	-	6	6
$100,000 or more	215	185	168	11	6	30	5	3	26	7
Median income	$23,421	$25,210	$29,915	$13,200	$25,596	$15,789	$9,757	$8,382	$21,712	$17,474

(continued)

(continued from previous page)

Percent distribution	total households	family households				nonfamily households				
		total	married couples	female hh, no spouse present	male hh, no spouse present	total	female householder		male householder	
							total	living alone	total	living alone
	100.0%	100.0%	100.0%	100.0%	100.0%	100.0%	100.0%	100.0%	100.0%	100.0%
Under $10,000	20.5	16.7	9.5	38.0	15.2	35.7	51.3	59.5	21.0	27.2
$10,000 to $19,999	22.7	22.7	21.3	26.7	23.2	22.3	18.8	19.7	25.6	27.5
$20,000 to $29,999	18.1	18.5	19.4	15.0	21.5	16.7	15.8	12.4	17.6	18.3
$30,000 to $39,999	12.8	13.5	15.0	8.7	15.2	9.9	5.8	3.7	13.8	12.6
$40,000 to $49,999	8.3	9.0	10.1	5.3	10.4	5.5	3.0	2.4	7.8	4.8
$50,000 to $59,999	5.6	6.1	7.6	2.0	5.8	3.3	2.8	1.6	3.8	2.4
$60,000 to $69,999	4.1	4.5	5.8	1.3	3.3	2.2	0.8	-	3.5	2.6
$70,000 to $79,999	2.5	2.9	3.7	1.1	1.7	0.9	0.7	0.3	1.3	0.9
$80,000 to $89,999	1.7	1.8	2.2	0.7	2.3	0.9	0.1	-	1.6	1.3
$90,000 to $99,999	1.0	1.1	1.5	0.3	0.4	0.5	0.3	-	0.8	1.1
$100,000 or more	2.8	3.0	4.0	0.7	1.3	2.0	0.7	0.5	3.3	1.3

Note: (-) means number in sample is too small to make a reliable estimate.
Source: Bureau of the Census, unpublished tables from the 1995 Current Population Survey

Income Distribution of Hispanic Men by Age, 1994

(number and percent distribution of Hispanic men aged 15 or older by income and age, 1994; men in thousands as of 1995)

	total	< 25	25-34	35-44	45-54	55-64	65+
TOTAL	9,555	2,553	2,771	1,900	1,093	603	634
Without income	1,180	866	129	83	39	31	32
With income	8,375	1,687	2,643	1,817	1,054	572	602
Under $10,000	2,766	967	670	397	245	178	309
$10,000 to $19,999	2,680	552	981	500	287	154	205
$20,000 to $29,999	1,455	130	559	381	233	97	56
$30,000 to $39,999	663	17	225	228	116	64	13
$40,000 to $49,999	345	6	103	131	74	25	8
$50,000 to $74,999	294	11	65	117	68	28	6
$75,000 to $99,999	93	2	19	37	18	12	4
$100,000 or more	78	-	21	27	13	14	4
Median income							
Total men	$14,500	$8,351	$15,948	$20,182	$19,746	$16,455	$9,830
Year-round, full-time workers	20,525	13,285	19,732	24,091	24,375	25,922	-
PERCENT DISTRIB.	100.0%	100.0%	100.0%	100.0%	100.0%	100.0%	100.0%
Without income	12.3	33.9	4.7	4.4	3.6	5.1	5.0
With income	87.7	66.1	95.4	95.6	96.4	94.9	95.0
Under $10,000	28.9	37.9	24.2	20.9	22.4	29.5	48.7
$10,000 to $19,999	28.0	21.6	35.4	26.3	26.3	25.5	32.3
$20,000 to $29,999	15.2	5.1	20.2	20.1	21.3	16.1	8.8
$30,000 to $39,999	6.9	0.7	8.1	12.0	10.6	10.6	2.1
$40,000 to $49,999	3.6	0.2	3.7	6.9	6.8	4.1	1.3
$50,000 to $74,999	3.1	0.4	2.3	6.2	6.2	4.6	0.9
$75,000 to $99,999	1.0	0.1	0.7	1.9	1.6	2.0	0.6
$100,000 or more	0.8	-	0.8	1.4	1.2	2.3	0.6

Note: (-) means number in sample is too small to make a reliable estimate.
Source: Bureau of the Census, unpublished tables from the 1995 Current Population Survey

Income Distribution of Hispanic Women by Age, 1994

(number and percent distribution of Hispanic women aged 15 or older by income and age, 1994; women in thousands as of 1995)

	total	< 25	25-34	35-44	45-54	55-64	65+
TOTAL	9,433	2,264	2,444	1,961	1,178	791	794
Without income	2,135	932	529	254	209	147	64
With income	7,298	1,333	1,916	1,707	968	644	730
Under $10,000	4,077	995	909	736	431	400	605
$10,000 to $19,999	1,790	270	543	467	280	141	88
$20,000 to $29,999	818	46	277	264	144	59	26
$30,000 to $39,999	337	13	120	119	60	17	8
$40,000 to $49,999	151	1	31	68	34	17	-
$50,000 to $74,999	89	3	21	40	16	8	1
$75,000 to $99,999	13	1	6	6	-	-	-
$100,000 or more	24	2	9	8	5	-	1
Median income							
Total women	$8,613	$5,498	$10,570	$11,655	$11,177	$7,390	$6,409
Year-round, full-time workers	18,418	12,179	18,983	20,763	20,007	18,285	-
PERCENT DISTRIB.	100.0%	100.0%	100.0%	100.0%	100.0%	100.0%	100.0%
Without income	22.6	41.2	21.6	13.0	17.7	18.6	8.1
With income	77.4	58.9	78.4	87.0	82.2	81.4	91.9
Under $10,000	43.2	43.9	37.2	37.5	36.6	50.6	76.2
$10,000 to $19,999	19.0	11.9	22.2	23.8	23.8	17.8	11.1
$20,000 to $29,999	8.7	2.0	11.3	13.5	12.2	7.5	3.3
$30,000 to $39,999	3.6	0.6	4.9	6.1	5.1	2.1	1.0
$40,000 to $49,999	1.6	0.0	1.3	3.5	2.9	2.1	-
$50,000 to $74,999	0.9	0.1	0.9	2.0	1.4	1.0	0.1
$75,000 to $99,999	0.1	0.0	0.2	0.3	-	-	-
$100,000 or more	0.3	0.1	0.4	0.4	0.4	-	0.1

Note: (-) means number in sample is too small to make a reliable estimate.
Source: Bureau of the Census, unpublished tables from the 1995 Current Population Survey

Median Earnings of Hispanic Men and Women Who Work Full-Time, 1980 to 1994

(median earnings of Hispanic men and women aged 15 or older who work year-round, full-time; ratio of Hispanic to total median earnings, and ratio of Hispanic female to Hispanic male median earnings, 1980-1994; percent change in earnings and ratios for selected years; in 1994 dollars)

| | Hispanic men | | Hispanic women | | |
	median earnings	ratio Hispanic/total	median earnings	ratio Hispanic/total	ratio Hispanic female/male
1994	$20,314	0.66	$17,569	0.79	0.86
1993	20,665	0.66	17,187	0.77	0.83
1992	20,641	0.65	18,048	0.80	0.87
1991	21,513	0.67	17,675	0.79	0.82
1990	21,698	0.69	17,770	0.79	0.82
1989	21,941	0.67	18,719	0.83	0.85
1988	22,363	0.67	18,597	0.84	0.83
1987	22,744	0.67	18,949	0.86	0.83
1986	22,737	0.67	18,709	0.85	0.82
1985	23,485	0.70	17,996	0.84	0.77
1984	24,163	0.73	17,894	0.85	0.74
1983	24,059	0.74	17,355	0.84	0.72
1982	23,845	0.73	17,226	0.85	0.72
1981	24,212	0.73	17,647	0.89	0.73
1980	24,414	0.73	17,429	0.86	0.71
Percent change					
1990-1994	-6.4%	-4.8%	-1.1%	0.1%	5.6%
1980-1994	-16.8	-9.6	0.8	-8.5	21.1

Note: The Hispanic/total ratios are calculated by dividing the median earnings of Hispanic men and women by the median for total men and women. The female/male ratio is calculated by dividing the median earnings of Hispanic women by the median earnings of Hispanic men.
Source: Bureau of the Census, unpublished tables from the 1995 Current Population Survey

Earnings of Hispanic Men by Ethnicity, 1993

(number and percent distribution of Hispanic men aged 15 or older by earnings and ethnicity, and number and percent distribution of Hispanic men who work year-round, full-time by earnings and ethnicity, 1993; men in thousands as of 1994)

	total	Mexican	Puerto Rican	Cuban	Central & South Am.	other Hispanic
TOTAL MEN						
Total	7,107	4,660	546	296	1,100	506
Loss or < $10,000	2,273	1,590	133	67	346	136
$10,000 to $24,999	3,054	2,021	223	116	496	197
$25,000 to $49,999	1,425	858	156	71	206	133
$50,000 or more	355	192	33	41	51	38
Percent distribution	100.0%	100.0%	100.0%	100.0%	100.0%	100.0%
Loss or < $10,000	32.0	34.1	24.4	22.6	31.5	27.0
$10,000 to $24,999	43.0	43.4	40.9	39.4	45.1	39.1
$25,000 to $49,999	20.1	18.4	28.6	24.2	18.8	26.4
$50,000 or more	5.0	4.1	6.1	13.9	4.6	7.6
YEAR-ROUND, FULL-TIME WORKERS						
Total	4,462	2,852	384	208	691	328
Loss or < $10,000	492	346	26	10	87	24
$10,000 to $24,999	2,370	1,554	179	99	384	155
$25,000 to $49,999	1,267	770	145	58	179	115
$50,000 or more	332	182	33	41	42	34
Percent distribution	100.0%	100.0%	100.0%	100.0%	100.0%	100.0%
Loss or < $10,000	11.0	12.1	6.8	4.8	12.5	7.2
$10,000 to $24,999	53.1	54.5	46.6	47.5	55.5	47.3
$25,000 to $49,999	28.4	27.0	37.9	27.9	25.9	35.0
$50,000 or more	7.4	6.4	8.6	19.8	6.1	10.4

Source: Bureau of the Census, Internet web site, http://www.census.gov

Earnings of Hispanic Women by Ethnicity, 1993

(number and percent distribution of Hispanic women aged 15 or older by earnings and ethnicity, and number and percent distribution of Hispanic women who work year-round, full-time by earnings and ethnicity, 1993; women in thousands as of 1994)

	total	Mexican	Puerto Rican	Cuban	Central & South Am.	other Hispanic
TOTAL WOMEN						
Total	4,808	2,867	476	243	787	434
Loss or < $10,000	2,269	1,436	170	90	376	196
$10,000 to $24,999	1,857	1,107	198	102	299	151
$25,000 to $49,999	608	283	98	48	102	77
$50,000 or more	75	41	10	3	10	10
Percent distribution	100.0%	100.0%	100.0%	100.0%	100.0%	100.0%
Loss or < $10,000	47.2	50.1	35.8	36.9	47.8	45.1
$10,000 to $24,999	38.6	38.6	41.5	42.0	38.0	34.7
$25,000 to $49,999	12.6	9.9	20.5	19.7	13.0	17.7
$50,000 or more	1.6	1.4	2.2	1.4	1.2	2.4
YEAR-ROUND, FULL-TIME WORKERS						
Total	2,439	1,380	249	159	424	226
Loss or < $10,000	419	256	21	21	85	37
$10,000 to $24,999	1,396	827	130	87	240	111
$25,000 to $49,999	559	261	91	47	90	70
$50,000 or more	65	37	8	3	10	8
Percent distribution	100.0%	100.0%	100.0%	100.0%	100.0%	100.0%
Loss or < $10,000	17.2	18.5	8.4	13.3	20.0	16.2
$10,000 to $24,999	57.2	59.9	52.1	54.8	56.5	49.3
$25,000 to $49,999	22.9	18.9	36.3	29.7	21.2	31.0
$50,000 or more	2.7	2.7	3.1	2.1	2.2	3.5

Source: Bureau of the Census, Internet web site, http://www.census.gov

Median Earnings of Hispanic Men and Women by Education, 1994

(median earnings of Hispanic men and women aged 25 or older by work experience and educational attainment, 1994)

	men		women	
	total	year-round full-time workers	total	year-round full-time workers
Total	$18,001	$21,724	$12,415	$18,864
Less than 9th grade	13,152	16,013	7,899	11,661
9th to 12th grade, no diploma	14,145	17,870	9,104	12,486
High school graduate	19,945	22,268	13,096	17,956
Some college, no degree	25,056	27,678	18,076	22,592
Associate degree	26,284	31,218	19,857	25,122
Bachelor's degree or more	32,349	37,887	26,189	30,726
Bachelor's degree	30,251	34,097	23,997	27,630
Master's degree	34,036	43,888	34,327	-
Professional degree	-	-	-	-
Doctoral degree	-	-	-	-

Note: (-) means number in sample is too small to make a reliable estimate.
Source: Bureau of the Census, unpublished tables from the 1995 Current Population Survey

Hispanic Families Below the Poverty Level, 1980 to 1994

(total number of Hispanic families, and number and percent below poverty level by type of family and presence of children under age 18, 1980-94; percent change in numbers and rates for selected years; families in thousands as of March the following year)

	total families			married couples			female hh, no spouse present		
		in poverty			in poverty			in poverty	
	total	number	percent	total	number	percent	total	number	percent
With and without children <18									
1994	6,202	1,724	27.8%	4,236	827	19.5%	1,485	773	52.1%
1993	5,946	1,625	27.3	4,038	770	19.1	1,498	772	51.6
1992	5,733	1,529	26.7	3,940	743	18.8	1,348	664	49.3
1991	5,177	1,372	26.5	3,532	674	19.1	1,261	627	49.7
1990	4,981	1,244	25.0	3,454	605	17.5	1,186	573	48.3
1989	4,840	1,133	23.4	3,395	549	16.2	1,116	530	47.5
1988	4,823	1,141	23.7	3,398	547	16.1	1,112	546	49.1
1987	4,576	1,168	25.5	3,196	556	17.4	1,082	565	52.2
1986	4,403	1,085	24.7	3,118	518	16.6	1,032	528	51.2
1985	4,206	1,074	25.5	2,962	505	17.0	980	521	53.1
1984	3,939	991	25.2	2,824	469	16.6	905	483	53.4
1983	3,788	961	25.9	2,752	437	17.7	860	454	52.8
1982	3,369	916	27.2	2,448	465	19.0	767	425	55.4
1981	3,305	792	24.0	2,414	366	15.1	750	399	53.2
1980	3,235	751	23.2	2,365	363	15.3	706	362	51.3
Percent change									
1990-1994	24.5%	38.6%	11.2%	22.6%	36.7%	11.4%	25.2%	34.9%	7.9%
1980-1994	91.7	129.6	19.8	79.1	127.8	27.5	110.3	113.5	1.6

(continued)

(continued from previous page)

	total families			married couples			female hh, no spouse present		
		in poverty			in poverty			in poverty	
	total	number	percent	total	number	percent	total	number	percent
With children <18									
1994	4,377	1,497	34.2%	2,923	698	23.9%	1,182	700	59.2%
1993	4,153	1,424	34.3	2,747	652	23.7	1,167	706	60.5
1992	3,962	1,302	32.9	2,692	615	22.9	1,037	598	57.7
1991	3,621	1,219	33.7	2,445	575	23.5	972	584	60.1
1990	3,497	1,065	31.0	2,405	501	20.8	921	536	58.2
1989	3,314	986	29.8	2,309	453	19.6	848	491	57.9
1988	3,325	988	29.7	2,339	445	19.0	861	510	59.2
1987	3,201	1,022	31.9	2,197	460	20.9	865	527	60.9
1986	3,080	949	30.8	-	-	-	822	489	59.5
1985	2,973	955	32.1	-	-	-	771	493	64.0
1984	2,789	872	31.3	-	-	-	711	447	62.8
1983	2,697	867	21.1	-	-	-	660	418	63.4
1982	2,458	802	32.6	-	-	-	613	391	63.8
1981	2,428	692	28.5	-	-	-	622	374	60.0
1980	2,409	655	27.2	-	-	-	-	-	-
Percent change									
1990-1994	25.2%	40.6%	10.3%	21.5%	39.3%	14.9%	28.3%	30.6%	1.7%
1980-1994	81.7	128.5	25.7	-	-	-	-	-	-

Note: (-) means data not available.
Source: Bureau of the Census, unpublished tables from the 1995 Current Population Survey

Hispanics in Poverty by Age and Sex, 1994

(total number of Hispanics, and number and percent below poverty level by age and sex, 1994; persons in thousands as of 1995)

	total	in poverty number	in poverty percent
Total	27,442	8,416	30.7%
Under age 18	9,822	4,075	41.5
Aged 18 to 24	3,448	1,042	30.2
Aged 25 to 34	5,216	1,333	25.6
Aged 35 to 44	3,861	889	23.0
Aged 45 to 54	2,271	438	19.3
Aged 55 to 59	734	170	23.2
Aged 60 to 64	661	146	22.0
Aged 65 to 74	959	214	22.3
Aged 75 or older	469	109	23.2
Female, total	13,564	4,527	33.4
Under age 18	4,766	2,019	42.4
Aged 18 to 24	1,629	586	36.0
Aged 25 to 34	2,444	729	29.8
Aged 35 to 44	1,961	522	26.6
Aged 45 to 54	1,178	255	21.7
Aged 55 to 59	417	106	25.4
Aged 60 to 64	374	86	22.9
Aged 65 to 74	513	139	27.1
Aged 75 or older	280	86	30.7
Male, total	13,878	3,889	28.0
Under age 18	5,056	2,056	40.7
Aged 18 to 24	1,819	456	25.0
Aged 25 to 34	2,771	605	21.8
Aged 35 to 44	1,900	367	19.3
Aged 45 to 54	1,093	183	16.8
Aged 55 to 59	316	64	20.3
Aged 60 to 64	287	60	20.9
Aged 65 to 74	446	75	16.7
Aged 75 or older	189	23	12.1

Source: Bureau of the Census, unpublished tables from the 1995 Current Population Survey

Hispanics:
Labor Force

Two out of three Hispanics aged 16 or older are in the labor force, including 79 percent of Hispanic men and 53 percent of Hispanic women. This compares with participation rates of 75 percent for all men and 59 percent for all women. Labor force participation rates peak at 66 percent for Hispanic women in the 35-to-44 age group, far below the 77 percent peak among all women in this age group. Among Hispanic ethnic groups, labor force participation rates are highest for Mexican Americans.

Forty-seven percent of Hispanic households have two or more earners, slightly greater than the 45 percent of all U.S. households with two earners. Nevertheless, among Hispanic married couples, only 48 percent are dual earners, less than the 55 percent share among all married couples. The husband, but not the wife, is in the labor force in 35 percent of Hispanic couples, versus 22 percent of all couples.

Only 14 percent of Hispanics are employed in managerial or professional specialty occupations, versus 28 percent of all workers. Conversely, 23 percent of Hispanics are operators, fabricators, or laborers, versus 14.5 percent of all workers. Hispanics account for 9 percent of employed Americans, but for 25 percent of private household workers.

Between 1994 and 2005, the number of Hispanic workers will grow by 36 percent. Hispanics will account for 11 percent of the labor force in 2005.

Employment Status of Hispanics by Age and Sex, 1995

(employment status of the civilian noninstitutional Hispanic population aged 16 or older by age and sex, 1995; numbers in thousands)

	civilian labor force						not in labor force	
	total	percent of population	employed	percent of labor force	unem-ployed	percent of labor force	total	percent of population
Total persons	12,267	65.8%	11,127	90.7%	1,140	9.3%	6,362	34.2%
Aged 16 to 19	850	45.4	645	75.9	205	24.1	1,022	54.6
Aged 20 to 24	1,818	71.9	1,609	88.5	209	11.5	710	28.1
Aged 25 to 34	3,943	78.1	3,618	91.8	325	8.2	1,108	21.9
Aged 35 to 44	3,113	78.5	2,889	92.8	224	7.2	852	21.5
Aged 45 to 54	1,671	72.8	1,565	93.7	106	6.4	623	27.2
Aged 55 to 64	720	48.6	666	92.5	54	7.5	762	51.4
Aged 65 or older	152	10.5	135	88.8	16	10.6	1,285	89.4
Total men	7,376	79.1	6,725	91.2	651	8.8	1,952	20.9
Aged 16 to 19	479	50.2	358	74.7	121	25.3	475	49.8
Aged 20 to 24	1,153	86.2	1,030	89.3	123	10.6	185	13.8
Aged 25 to 34	2,469	92.9	2,284	92.5	185	7.5	188	7.1
Aged 35 to 44	1,795	91.3	1,675	93.3	120	6.7	171	8.7
Aged 45 to 54	965	85.6	908	94.1	57	5.9	162	14.4
Aged 55 to 64	417	62.4	384	92.1	33	7.9	251	37.6
Aged 65 or older	98	15.8	85	86.7	13	12.9	521	84.2
Total women	4,891	52.6	4,403	90.0	488	10.0	4,409	47.4
Aged 16 to 19	371	40.4	287	77.4	84	22.6	547	59.6
Aged 20 to 24	666	55.9	579	86.9	86	13.0	525	44.1
Aged 25 to 34	1,473	61.6	1,334	90.6	140	9.5	920	38.4
Aged 35 to 44	1,318	65.9	1,213	92.0	104	7.9	681	34.1
Aged 45 to 54	706	60.5	657	93.1	50	7.0	461	39.5
Aged 55 to 64	303	37.2	282	93.1	21	6.8	511	62.8
Aged 65 or older	53	6.6	50	94.3	3	6.4	765	93.5

Note: The civilian labor force equals the number employed plus the number unemployed. The civilian population equals the number in the labor force plus the number not in the labor force.
Source: Bureau of Labor Statistics, Employment and Earnings, *January 1996*

Employment Status of Hispanics by Sex and Ethnicity, 1995

(employment status of the civilian noninstitutional Hispanic population aged 16 or older by sex and ethnicity, 1995; numbers in thousands)

	civilian labor force						not in labor force	
	total	percent of population	employed	percent of labor force	unem-ployed	percent of labor force	total	percent of population
Total Hispanic men	7,376	79.1%	6,725	91.2%	651	8.8%	1,952	20.9%
Mexican	4,862	80.9	4,427	91.1	436	9.0	1,147	19.1
Puerto Rican	605	70.6	535	88.4	69	11.4	252	29.4
Cuban	350	69.9	324	92.6	27	7.6	151	30.1
Total Hispanic women	4,891	52.6	4,403	90.0	488	10.0	4,409	47.4
Mexican	2,903	51.8	2,589	89.2	314	10.8	2,697	48.2
Puerto Rican	493	47.4	439	89.0	54	11.0	546	52.6
Cuban	263	50.8	244	92.8	18	7.0	255	49.2

Note: The civilian labor force equals the number employed plus the number unemployed. The civilian population equals the number in the labor force plus the number not in the labor force.
Source: Bureau of Labor Statistics, Employment and Earnings, *January 1996*

Hispanic Households by Number of Earners, 1994

(number and percent distribution of Hispanic households, by number of earners, 1994; numbers in thousands)

	number	percent
Total households	7,362	100.0%
No earners	1,255	17.0
One earner	2,648	36.0
Two or more earners	3,460	47.0
Two earners	2,499	33.9
Three earners	646	8.8
Four or more earners	315	4.3

Source: Bureau of the Census, Income, Poverty, and Valuation of Noncash Benefits: 1993, *Current Population Reports, P60-188, 1995*

Labor Force Status of Hispanic Married Couples, 1994

(number and percent distribution of Hispanic married couples, by age of householder and labor force status of husband and wife, 1994; numbers in thousands)

| | total married couples | husband and/or wife in labor force | | | neither husband nor wife in labor force |
		husband and wife	husband only	wife only	
Total, number	4,033	1,942	1,405	187	499
Under age 20	11	4	5	-	2
Aged 20 to 24	215	118	88	7	2
Aged 25 to 29	489	242	223	7	17
Aged 30 to 34	698	398	260	15	25
Aged 35 to 39	591	319	239	12	20
Aged 40 to 44	554	328	176	22	28
Aged 45 to 49	408	215	135	29	28
Aged 50 to 54	304	162	104	13	25
Aged 55 to 59	219	97	72	18	32
Aged 60 to 64	199	36	60	36	67
Aged 65 to 74	243	17	37	22	166
Aged 75 to 84	84	3	4	5	72
Aged 85 or older	17	2	-	1	13
Total, percent	100.0%	48.2%	34.8%	4.6%	12.4%
Under age 20	100.0	36.4	45.5	-	18.2
Aged 20 to 24	100.0	54.9	40.9	3.3	0.9
Aged 25 to 29	100.0	49.5	45.6	1.4	3.5
Aged 30 to 34	100.0	57.0	37.2	2.1	3.6
Aged 35 to 39	100.0	54.0	40.4	2.0	3.4
Aged 40 to 44	100.0	59.2	31.8	4.0	5.1
Aged 45 to 49	100.0	52.7	33.1	7.1	6.9
Aged 50 to 54	100.0	53.3	34.2	4.3	8.2
Aged 55 to 59	100.0	44.3	32.9	8.2	14.6
Aged 60 to 64	100.0	18.1	30.2	18.1	33.7
Aged 65 to 74	100.0	7.0	15.2	9.1	68.3
Aged 75 to 84	100.0	3.6	4.8	6.0	85.7
Aged 85 or older	100.0	11.8	-	5.9	76.5

Note: (-) means number in sample is too small to make a reliable estimate.
Source: Bureau of the Census, Household and Family Characteristics: March 1994, *Current Population Reports, P20-483, 1995*

Occupations of Hispanics by Ethnicity, 1995

(number and percent distribution of employed Hispanics aged 16 or older in the civilian labor force, by occupation and ethnicity, 1995; numbers in thousands)

	total	Mexican	Puerto Rican	Cuban
Total employed, number	11,127	7,016	974	568
Total employed, percent	100.0%	100.0%	100.0%	100.0%
Managerial and professional specialty	13.9	11.7	19.6	22.0
Executive, administrative, and managerial	7.4	6.4	8.5	10.9
Professional specialty	6.5	5.3	11.0	11.1
Technical, sales, and administrative support	24.4	21.7	29.8	37.5
Technicians and related support	2.2	1.9	2.6	4.8
Sales occupations	9.4	8.1	10.5	14.3
Administrative support, including clerical	12.9	11.7	16.8	18.7
Service occupations	19.7	19.5	17.4	14.1
Private household	1.8	1.7	0.2	0.5
Protective service	1.5	1.3	3.2	1.9
Service, except private household and protective	16.4	16.5	14.0	11.6
Precision production, craft, and repair	12.9	13.5	10.8	10.4
Operators, fabricators, and laborers	23.2	25.4	21.0	14.3
Machine operators, assemblers, and inspectors	11.2	12.3	10.5	5.5
Transportation and material moving occupations	4.6	4.7	4.7	4.8
Handlers, equipment cleaners, helpers, and laborers	7.3	8.4	5.9	3.9
Farming, forestry, and fishing	5.9	8.3	1.4	1.8

Note: Numbers by ethnicity will not add to total because not all ethnicities are shown.
Source: Bureau of Labor Statistics, Employment and Earnings, *January 1996*

Hispanic Workers by Detailed Occupation, 1995

(total number of employed persons aged 16 or older in the civilian labor force; number and percent distribution of employed Hispanics; and Hispanic share of total employed, by selected occupation, 1995; numbers in thousands)

		Hispanic		
	total	number	percent	share of total employed
Total employed	124,900	11,127	100.0%	8.9%
Managerial and professional specialty	35,318	1,548	13.9	4.4
Executive, administrative, and managerial	17,186	821	7.4	4.8
Officials and administrators, public admin.	618	29	0.3	4.7
Financial managers	605	34	0.3	5.7
Personnel and labor relations managers	125	4	-	3.4
Purchasing managers	135	4	-	3.1
Managers, marketing, advertising, and public relations	663	22	0.2	3.3
Administrators, education and related fields	701	33	0.3	4.7
Managers, medicine and health	653	33	0.3	5.1
Managers, food serving and lodging establishments	1,276	100	0.9	7.8
Managers, property and real estate	522	37	0.3	7.1
Professional specialty	18,132	727	6.5	4.0
Architects	163	9	0.1	5.8
Engineers	1,934	64	0.6	3.3
Mathematical and computer scientists	1,195	33	0.3	2.8
Natural scientists	519	13	0.1	2.6
Physicians	693	30	0.3	4.3
Dentists	155	4	-	2.6
Registered nurses	1,977	51	0.5	2.6
Pharmacists	170	3	-	1.8
Dietitians	94	7	0.1	7.5
Therapists	466	21	0.2	4.6
Teachers, college and university	846	30	0.3	3.6
Teachers, except college and university	4,507	198	1.8	4.4
Librarians, archivists, and curators	211	5	-	2.3
Economists	148	12	0.1	7.9
Psychologists	260	9	0.1	3.4
Social, recreation, and religious workers	1,303	83	0.7	6.4
Lawyers and judges	926	29	0.3	3.1
Writers, artists, entertainers, and athletes	2,054	99	0.9	4.8

continued

(continued from previous page)

	total	Hispanic number	percent	share of total employed
Technical, sales, administrative support	37,417	2,719	24.4%	7.3%
Technicians and related support	3,909	240	2.2	6.1
Health technologists and technicians	1,648	109	1.0	6.6
Engineering and related technologists and technicians	880	55	0.5	6.2
Science technicians	276	20	0.2	7.3
Technicians, except health, engineering, and science	1,106	58	0.5	5.2
Airplane pilots and navigators	114	4	-	3.9
Computer programmers	553	27	0.2	4.8
Legal assistants	285	20	0.2	6.9
Sales occupations	15,119	1,048	9.4	6.9
Supervisors and proprietors	4,480	251	2.3	5.6
Sales representatives, finance and business services	2,399	122	1.1	5.1
Sales representatives, commodities, except retail	1,529	75	0.7	4.9
Sales workers, retail and personal services	6,613	589	5.3	8.9
Administrative support, including clerical	18,389	1,431	12.9	7.8
Supervisors	712	45	0.4	6.3
Computer equipment operators	491	44	0.4	8.9
Secretaries, stenographers, and typists	4,106	271	2.4	6.6
Information clerks	1,872	150	1.3	8.0
Records processing occupations, except financial	959	74	0.7	7.7
Financial records processing	2,255	120	1.1	5.3
Mail and message distributing	1,006	88	0.8	8.7
Miscellaneous administrative support	3,441	330	3.0	9.6
Service occupations	16,930	2,195	19.7	13.0
Private household	821	204	1.8	24.8
Protective	2,237	166	1.5	7.4
Firefighting and fire prevention	249	13	0.1	5.1
Police and detectives	949	70	0.6	7.4
Guards	846	73	0.7	8.6
Service occupations, ex. private hh and protect. serv.	13,872	1,825	16.4	13.2
Food preparation and service occupations	5,800	824	7.4	14.2

continued

(continued from previous page)

	total	Hispanic number	percent	share of total employed
Health service occupations	2,315	194	1.7%	8.4%
Cleaning and building service occupations	2,946	560	5.0	19.0
Personal service occupations	2,810	247	2.2	8.8
Precision production, craft, and repair	13,524	1,430	12.9	10.6
Mechanics and repairers	4,423	367	3.3	8.3
Construction trades	5,098	581	5.2	11.4
Extractive occupations	136	11	0.1	7.8
Precision production occupations	3,867	476	4.3	12.3
Operators, fabricators, and laborers	18,068	2,577	23.2	14.3
Machine operators, assemblers, and inspectors	7,907	1,250	11.2	15.8
Transportation and material moving occupations	5,171	512	4.6	9.9
Motor vehicle operators	3,904	394	3.5	10.1
Truck drivers	2,861	298	2.7	10.4
Bus drivers	526	42	0.4	8.0
Taxicab drivers and chauffeurs	213	26	0.2	12.3
Material moving equipment operators	1,098	112	1.0	10.2
Handlers, equipment cleaners, helpers, and laborers	4,990	816	7.3	16.4
Farming, forestry, and fishing	3,642	658	5.9	18.1

Note: Numbers will not add to total because not all occupations are shown. (-) means less than 0.5.
Source: Bureau of Labor Statistics, Employment and Earnings, *January 1996*

Hispanic Workers by Industry, 1995

(total number of employed persons aged 16 or older in the civilian labor force; number and percent distribution of employed Hispanics, and Hispanic share of total employed, by selected industry, 1995; numbers in thousands)

	total	Hispanic number	Hispanic percent	Hispanic share of total employed
Total employed	124,900	11,127	100.0%	8.9%
Agriculture	3,440	602	5.4	17.5
Mining	627	36	0.3	5.8
Construction	7,668	797	7.2	10.4
Manufacturing	20,493	2,091	18.8	10.2
Durable goods	12,015	1,057	9.5	8.8
Nondurable goods	8,478	1,034	9.3	12.2
Transportation, communications, and other public utilities	8,709	669	6.0	7.7
Transportation	5,589	464	4.2	8.3
Communications	1,607	96	0.9	6.0
Utilities and sanitary services	1,512	109	1.0	7.2
Wholesale and retail trade	26,071	2,550	22.9	9.8
Wholesale trade	4,986	484	4.3	9.7
Retail trade	21,086	2,066	18.6	9.8
Finance, insurance, and real estate	7,983	535	4.8	6.7
Services	43,953	3,479	31.3	7.9
Private households	971	225	2.0	23.2
Other service industries	42,982	3,254	29.2	7.6
Business, automobile, and repair services	7,526	768	6.9	10.2
Personal services, except private household	3,404	446	4.0	13.1
Entertainment and recreation services	2,238	177	1.6	7.9
Professional and related services	29,661	1,850	16.6	6.2
Hospitals	4,961	298	2.7	6.0
Health services, except hospitals	5,967	406	3.6	6.8
Educational services	9,894	653	5.9	6.6
Social services	2,979	229	2.1	7.7
Other professional services	5,860	264	2.4	4.5
Forestry and fisheries	152	13	0.1	8.6
Public administration	5,957	363	3.3	6.1

Note: numbers of employed Hispanics may not add to total due to rounding.
Source: Bureau of Labor Statistics, Employment and Earnings, *January 1996*

Union Membership of Hispanics, 1995

(number of employed Hispanic wage and salary workers aged 16 or older, number and percent who are represented by unions or are union members, and median weekly earnings by union membership status; by sex, 1995; numbers in thousands)

	total	men	women
Total employed	10,401	6,223	4,178
Represented by unions*	1,535	969	565
Percent of employed	14.8%	15.6%	13.5%
Members of unions**	1,357	871	486
Percent of employed	13.0%	14.0%	11.6%
Median weekly earnings, total*	$329	$350	$305
Represented by unions*	493	523	419
Members of unions**	499	528	423
Non-union	311	321	291

* Members of a labor union or an employee association similar to a union as well as workers who report no union affiliation but whose jobs are covered by a union or an employee association contract.
** Members of a labor union or an employee association similar to a union.
*** Full-time wage and salary workers.
Source: Bureau of Labor Statistics, Employment and Earnings, *January 1996*

Hispanic Labor Force Projections by Sex, 1994 to 2005

(number of Hispanics aged 16 or older in the civilian labor force in 1994 and 2005, labor force participation rate of Hispanics in 1994 and 2005, and Hispanic share of total labor force in 1994 and 2005; by sex; percent change in number and percentage point change in share; numbers in thousands)

	1994	2005	percent change 1994-2005
Number in labor force			
Total	11,975	16,330	36.4%
Men	7,210	9,492	31.6
Women	4,765	6,838	43.5

			percentage point change 1994-2005
Labor force participation rate			
Total	66.1%	64.7%	-1.4
Men	79.2	76.1	-3.1
Women	52.9	53.6	0.7
Percent of labor force			
Total	9.1	11.1	2.0
Men	10.2	12.4	2.2
Women	7.9	9.7	1.8

Source: Bureau of Labor Statistics, Monthly Labor Review, *November 1995*

Hispanics:
Population

The Hispanic population is projected to grow from 28 million in 1996 to more than 52 million by 2020, when Hispanics will account for 16 percent of the total U.S. population. Although the Hispanic population is growing faster than the black population, the number of Hispanics will not surpass the number of blacks in the U.S. for another decade. But by 2020, Hispanics will outnumber blacks by over 7 million.

Sixteen percent of children under age 5 are Hispanic, versus only 4 percent of people aged 85 or older. Hispanics account for a much larger share of children and young adults than of older people because Hispanic fertility is higher than that of most other racial and ethnic groups.

Among Hispanics, the three largest ethnic groups are Mexican (64 percent), Puerto Rican (10 percent), and Cuban (4 percent). Among Cuban Americans, fully 72 percent are foreign born. In contrast, only 33 percent of Mexican Americans are foreign born, despite the fact that Mexico accounts for a large share of immigrants to the U.S. Only 39 percent of Hispanics aged 5 or older do not speak English fluently.

More than half of Mexican Americans live in the West, while 69 percent of Puerto Ricans live in the Northeast, and 71 percent of Cubans live in the South. Hispanics account for 26 percent of California's population, with Los Angeles home to more Hispanics than any other metropolitan area. One-third of the population of Los Angeles is Hispanic.

Over 654,000 babies were born to Hispanic mothers in 1993, or 16 percent of all births. This proportion should rise to 24 percent by 2020. Hispanics accounted for 45 percent of all births in California in 1993 and for 41 percent of births in Texas.

Hispanics by Age, 1990 to 2020

(number of Hispanics by age, selected years 1990-2020; percent change 1990-2000 and 2000-2010; numbers in thousands)

	1990	1996	2000	2010	2020	percent change 1990-2000	percent change 2000-2010
Total							
persons	22,554	27,804	31,366	41,139	52,652	39.1%	31.2%
Under 5	2,495	3,144	3,203	4,080	5,185	28.4	27.4
5 to 9	2,193	2,811	3,298	3,742	4,839	50.4	13.5
10 to 14	2,008	2,499	2,906	3,627	4,529	44.7	24.8
15 to 19	2,078	2,385	2,732	3,893	4,362	31.5	42.5
20 to 24	2,329	2,335	2,574	3,499	4,231	10.5	35.9
25 to 29	2,352	2,517	2,510	3,154	4,250	6.7	25.7
30 to 34	2,071	2,580	2,671	2,905	3,796	29.0	8.8
35 to 39	1,666	2,263	2,618	2,760	3,411	57.1	5.4
40 to 44	1,301	1,824	2,218	2,802	3,044	70.5	26.3
45 to 49	947	1,406	1,727	2,640	2,787	82.4	52.9
50 to 54	757	1,014	1,322	2,193	2,762	74.6	65.9
55 to 59	638	793	962	1,709	2,599	50.8	77.7
60 to 64	556	652	755	1,288	2,123	35.8	70.6
65 to 69	437	565	618	922	1,629	41.4	49.2
70 to 74	289	424	502	684	1,175	73.7	36.3
75 to 79	214	276	362	521	795	69.2	43.9
80 to 84	131	175	206	374	531	57.3	81.6
85 or older	94	141	183	345	605	94.7	88.5
18 to 24	3,218	3,275	3,678	5,101	5,981	14.3	38.7
18 or older	14,669	17,905	20,332	27,398	35,488	38.6	34.8
65 or older	1,165	1,580	1,872	2,847	4,735	60.7	52.1

Source: Bureau of the Census, Population Projections of the United States, by Age, Sex, Race, and Hispanic Origin: 1995 to 2050, *Current Population Reports, P25-1130, 1996; and* U.S. Population Estimates, by Age, Sex, Race, and Hispanic Origin: 1980 to 1991, *Current Population Reports, P25-1095, 1993*

Hispanic Share of the Total Population by Age, 1990 to 2020

(Hispanics as a percent of the total U.S. population by age, selected years 1990-2020)

	1990	*1996*	*2000*	*2010*	*2020*
Total persons	9.0%	10.5%	11.4%	13.8%	16.3%
Under age 5	13.2	16.2	16.9	20.4	23.6
Aged 5 to 9	12.1	14.4	16.6	19.2	22.5
Aged 10 to 14	11.7	13.1	14.5	17.9	21.2
Aged 15 to 19	11.7	12.8	13.8	17.9	20.4
Aged 20 to 24	12.2	13.4	14.1	16.6	19.9
Aged 25 to 29	11.1	13.2	14.2	16.0	19.7
Aged 30 to 34	9.5	12.1	13.7	15.6	17.8
Aged 35 to 39	8.3	10.0	11.8	14.9	16.6
Aged 40 to 44	7.3	8.8	9.9	14.0	16.0
Aged 45 to 49	6.9	7.6	8.7	12.1	15.2
Aged 50 to 54	6.7	7.3	7.7	10.1	14.3
Aged 55 to 59	6.1	7.0	7.2	9.0	12.3
Aged 60 to 64	5.2	6.5	7.1	7.9	10.3
Aged 65 to 69	4.3	5.7	6.6	7.6	9.3
Aged 70 to 74	3.6	4.8	5.8	7.6	8.5
Aged 75 to 79	3.5	4.0	4.9	7.3	8.4
Aged 80 to 84	3.3	3.8	4.2	6.7	8.9
Aged 85 or older	3.1	3.8	4.3	6.1	9.4
Aged 18 to 24	12.0	13.3	14.0	16.9	20.0
Aged 18 or older	7.9	9.1	10.0	12.2	14.5
Aged 65 or older	3.7	4.7	5.4	7.2	8.9

Source: Bureau of the Census, Population Projections of the United States, by Age, Sex, Race, and Hispanic Origin: 1995 to 2050, *Current Population Reports, P25-1130, 1996; and* U.S. Population Estimates, by Age, Sex, Race, and Hispanic Origin: 1980 to 1991, *Current Population Reports, P25-1095, 1993*

Hispanics by Age and Sex, 1996

(number of Hispanics by age and sex, and sex ratio by age, 1996; numbers in thousands)

	total	male	female	sex ratio*
Total persons	27,804	14,063	13,741	102
Under age 5	3,144	1,608	1,536	105
Aged 5 to 9	2,811	1,438	1,374	105
Aged 10 to 14	2,499	1,276	1,223	104
Aged 15 to 19	2,385	1,224	1,162	105
Aged 20 to 24	2,335	1,217	1,118	109
Aged 25 to 29	2,517	1,346	1,171	115
Aged 30 to 34	2,580	1,358	1,222	111
Aged 35 to 39	2,263	1,168	1,095	107
Aged 40 to 44	1,824	918	906	101
Aged 45 to 49	1,406	691	715	97
Aged 50 to 54	1,014	487	527	92
Aged 55 to 59	793	374	419	89
Aged 60 to 64	652	301	351	86
Aged 65 to 69	565	252	312	81
Aged 70 to 74	424	184	239	77
Aged 75 to 79	276	112	164	68
Aged 80 to 84	175	64	111	58
Aged 85 or older	141	45	96	47
Aged 18 to 24	3,275	1,700	1,578	108
Aged 18 or older	17,905	9,000	8,906	101
Aged 65 or older	1,580	658	923	71

* The sex ratio is the number of males per 100 females.
Source: *Bureau of the Census*, Population Projections of the United States, by Age, Sex, Race, and Hispanic Origin: 1995 to 2050, *Current Population Reports, P25-1130, 1996*

Hispanics by Age and Ethnicity, 1994

(number and percent of Hispanics by age and ethnicity, and median age by ethnicity, 1994; numbers in thousands)

	total	Mexican	Puerto Rican	Cuban	Central & South American	other Hispanic
Total, number	26,646	17,090	2,776	1,111	3,725	1,944
Under age 5	3,145	2,222	303	49	406	165
Aged 5 to 9	2,621	1,857	287	57	283	138
Aged 10 to 14	2,426	1,641	282	65	286	151
Aged 15 to 19	2,254	1,514	253	42	296	149
Aged 20 to 24	2,485	1,674	186	64	371	191
Aged 25 to 29	2,609	1,675	233	70	460	171
Aged 30 to 34	2,436	1,545	258	81	373	180
Aged 35 to 39	2,021	1,229	209	83	328	171
Aged 40 to 44	1,679	1,043	180	77	254	125
Aged 45 to 49	1,278	726	163	78	213	97
Aged 50 to 54	935	517	117	78	132	90
Aged 55 to 59	747	406	91	81	84	84
Aged 60 to 64	619	325	72	75	92	55
Aged 65 to 69	519	295	42	70	45	67
Aged 70 to 74	409	195	50	61	52	51
Aged 75 to 79	194	87	19	35	24	29
Aged 80 to 84	141	74	16	19	16	16
Aged 85 or older	127	64	15	24	10	14
Median age (years)	26	24	27	43	27	30

(continued)

(continued from previous page)

	total	Mexican	Puerto Rican	Cuban	Central & South American	other Hispanic
Total, percent	100.0%	64.1%	10.4%	4.2%	14.0%	7.3%
Under age 5	100.0	70.7	9.6	1.6	12.9	5.2
Aged 5 to 9	100.0	70.9	11.0	2.2	10.8	5.3
Aged 10 to 14	100.0	67.6	11.6	2.7	11.8	6.2
Aged 15 to 19	100.0	67.2	11.2	1.9	13.1	6.6
Aged 20 to 24	100.0	67.4	7.5	2.6	14.9	7.7
Aged 25 to 29	100.0	64.2	8.9	2.7	17.6	6.6
Aged 30 to 34	100.0	63.4	10.6	3.3	15.3	7.4
Aged 35 to 39	100.0	60.8	10.3	4.1	16.2	8.5
Aged 40 to 44	100.0	62.1	10.7	4.6	15.1	7.4
Aged 45 to 49	100.0	56.8	12.8	6.1	16.7	7.6
Aged 50 to 54	100.0	55.3	12.5	8.3	14.1	9.6
Aged 55 to 59	100.0	54.4	12.2	10.8	11.2	11.2
Aged 60 to 64	100.0	52.5	11.6	12.1	14.9	8.9
Aged 65 to 69	100.0	56.8	8.1	13.5	8.7	12.9
Aged 70 to 74	100.0	47.7	12.2	14.9	12.7	12.5
Aged 75 to 79	100.0	44.8	9.8	18.0	12.4	14.9
Aged 80 to 84	100.0	52.5	11.3	13.5	11.3	11.3
Aged 85 or older	100.0	50.4	11.8	18.9	7.9	11.0

Source: Bureau of the Census, Internet web site, http://www.census.gov

Hispanics by Age and Foreign-Born Status, 1990

(total number of Hispanics, and number and percent who are foreign born, by age; 1990; numbers in thousands)

	total	foreign born	
		number	percent
Total persons	21,900	7,842	35.8%
Under age 5	2,330	148	6.4
Aged 5 to 9	2,174	248	11.4
Aged 10 to 14	1,988	352	17.7
Aged 15 to 19	1,982	594	30.0
Aged 20 to 24	2,199	1,000	45.5
Aged 25 to 34	4,380	2,178	49.7
Aged 35 to 44	2,919	1,433	49.1
Aged 45 to 54	1,706	851	49.9
Aged 55 to 64	1,166	522	44.8
Aged 65 to 74	671	300	44.7
Aged 75 to 84	304	163	53.8
Aged 85 or older	82	52	63.2
Aged 18 or older	14,263	6,791	47.6
Aged 65 or older	1,056	515	48.8

Note: The 1990 population figures are from the April 1, 1990, census sample.
Source: Bureau of the Census, Persons of Hispanic Origin in the United States, *1990 Census of Population, CP-3-3, 1990*

Hispanics by Ethnicity and Foreign-Born Status, 1990

(total number of Hispanics, and number and percent who are foreign-born, by age and ethnicity, 1990; for the three largest Hispanic ethnic groups and other Hispanics, 1990; numbers in thousands)

| | Mexican | | | Puerto Rican* | | | Cuban | | | other Hispanic | | |
	total	foreign born number	percent	total	foreign born number	percent	total	foreign born number	percent	total	foreign born number	percent
Total persons	13,393	4,460	33.3%	2,652	33	1.2%	1,053	755	71.7%	4,802	2,594	54.0%
Under age 5	1,566	107	6.8	281	1	0.3	58	2	3.2	425	38	9.0
Aged 5 to 9	1,466	160	10.9	266	1	0.4	51	3	5.7	391	84	21.5
Aged 10 to 14	1,304	207	15.9	261	1	0.5	50	12	23.5	374	132	35.2
Aged 15 to 19	1,290	394	30.5	238	2	0.9	58	20	34.5	396	179	45.1
Aged 20 to 24	1,405	680	48.4	252	4	1.5	68	32	47.0	473	285	60.2
Aged 25 to 34	2,646	1,299	49.1	502	9	1.8	184	138	75.1	1,048	732	69.8
Aged 35 to 44	1,682	777	46.2	362	6	1.7	139	123	88.4	735	527	71.7
Aged 45 to 54	904	405	44.8	228	4	1.7	139	132	94.6	434	310	71.3
Aged 55 to 64	606	215	35.5	147	2	1.6	140	134	95.8	273	171	62.7
Aged 65 to 74	339	120	35.4	75	1	1.9	98	94	95.9	159	85	53.6
Aged 75 to 84	145	70	48.7	31	1	2.5	55	53	95.9	73	40	54.0
Aged 85 or older	41	26	62.7	7	-	3.5	14	13	95.2	20	13	63.1
Aged 18 or older	8,310	3,793	45.6	1,705	29	1.7	861	727	84.4	3,386	2,243	66.2
Aged 65 or older	524	216	41.2	113	2	2.2	167	160	95.8	252	137	54.4

* People born in Puerto Rico are not considered foreign born.
Note: The 1990 population figures are from the April 1, 1990, census sample.
Source: Bureau of the Census, Persons of Hispanic Origin in the United States, 1990 Census of Population, CP-3-3, 1990

Hispanics by Age, Ethnicity, and Ability to Speak English, 1990

(number and percent of Hispanics aged 5 or older who do not speak English "very well," by age and ethnicity, for three largest Hispanic ethnic groups and other Hispanics, 1990; numbers in thousands)

	total		Mexican		Puerto Rican		Cuban		other Hispanic	
	number	*percent*	*number*	*percent*	*number*	*percent*	*number*	*percent*	*number*	*percent*
Total, aged 5 or older	7,717	39.4%	4,605	38.9%	794	33.5%	484	48.6%	1,833	41.9%
Aged 5 to 17	1,450	27.3	988	28.1	169	25.5	25	19.0	267	27.0
Aged 18 to 64	5,645	42.7	3,325	42.7	554	34.8	321	46.2	1,446	46.1
Aged 65 to 74	378	56.4	179	52.7	47	62.3	79	81.1	73	46.2
Aged 75 or older	243	63.0	113	61.3	24	63.7	58	85.0	47	50.0

Source: Bureau of the Census, Persons of Hispanic Origin in the United States, 1990 Census of Population, CP-3-3, 1990

Hispanic Immigrants by Country of Birth, 1994

(total number of immigrants and number of Hispanic immigrants for countries sending at least 1,000 immigrants to the U.S., Hispanic immigrants as a percent of total immigrants by country of birth, 1994)

	number	percent
Total immigrants	804,416	100.0%
TOTAL HISPANIC IMMIGRANTS	303,485	37.7
Mexico	111,398	13.8
Caribbean	104,804	13.0
Dominican Republic	51,189	6.4
Cuba	14,727	1.8
Jamaica	14,349	1.8
Haiti	13,333	1.7
Trinidad & Tobago	6,292	0.8
Central America	39,908	5.0
El Salvador	17,644	2.2
Guatemala	7,389	0.9
Honduras	5,265	0.7
Nicaragua	5,255	0.7
Panama	2,378	0.3
Costa Rica	1,205	0.1
South America	47,377	5.9
Colombia	10,847	1.3
Peru	9,177	1.1
Guyana	7,662	1.0
Ecuador	5,906	0.7
Brazil	4,491	0.6
Venezuela	2,427	0.3
Argentina	2,318	0.3
Chile	1,640	0.2
Bolivia	1,404	0.2

Note: Numbers may not add to total because not all countries are shown.
Source: U.S. Immigration and Naturalization Service, Statistical Yearbook of the Immigration and Naturalization Service, *1995*

Characteristics of Mexican and Cuban Foreign-Born Population, 1994

(number and percent distribution of the Hispanic foreign-born population by age, sex, education, region of residence, and metropolitan status, and selected countries of origin, 1994; numbers in thousands)

	Mexico		Cuba	
	number	percent	number	percent
Total foreign born	6,264	100.0%	805	100.0%
Age				
Under age 5	136	2.2	3	0.4
Aged 5 to 15	650	10.4	10	1.2
Aged 16 or 17	169	2.7	5	0.6
Aged 18 to 24	1,087	17.4	27	3.4
Aged 25 to 29	1,026	16.4	34	4.2
Aged 30 to 34	851	13.6	66	8.2
Aged 35 to 44	1,159	18.5	139	17.3
Aged 45 to 64	900	14.4	318	39.5
Aged 65 or older	287	4.6	203	25.2
Sex				
Male	3,404	54.3	382	47.5
Female	2,860	45.7	423	52.5
Education, aged 25 or older				
Not a high school graduate	3,006	71.2	277	36.4
High school graduate or some college	1,026	24.3	336	44.2
Bachelor's degree	136	3.2	82	10.8
Graduate degree	54	1.3	64	8.4
Region				
Northeast	124	2.0	110	13.7
Midwest	610	9.7	19	2.4
South	1,603	25.6	620	77.0
West	3,927	62.7	56	7.0
Metropolitan status				
Metropolitan, total	5,670	90.5	799	99.3
Central city	3,053	48.7	353	43.9
Suburbs*	2,617	41.8	446	55.4
Nonmetropolitan	593	9.5	6	0.7

* The suburbs are the portion of a metropolitan area that is outside the central city.
Source: Bureau of the Census, Internet web site, http://www.census.gov

Hispanics by Region, Division, and Ethnicity, 1990

(number and percent distribution of Hispanics, and Hispanic share of the total population, by region, division, and ethnicity, 1990; numbers in thousands)

	total	Mexican	Puerto Rican	Cuban	other Hispanic
Number					
UNITED STATES	22,354	13,496	2,728	1,044	5,086
Northeast	3,754	175	1,872	184	1,524
New England	568	29	316	16	207
Middle Atlantic	3,186	146	1,556	167	1,317
Midwest	1,727	1,153	258	37	279
East North Central	1,438	944	244	30	220
West North Central	289	209	14	6	60
South	6,767	4,344	406	735	1,282
South Atlantic	2,133	315	338	702	778
East South Central	95	39	13	5	39
West South Central	4,539	3,990	55	28	466
West	10,106	7,824	192	88	2,002
Mountain	1,992	1,440	26	12	514
Pacific	8,114	6,384	166	76	1,488
Percent distribution					
UNITED STATES	100.0%	100.0%	100.0%	100.0%	100.0%
Northeast	16.8	1.3	68.6	17.6	30.0
New England	2.5	0.2	11.6	1.6	4.1
Middle Atlantic	14.3	1.1	57.0	16.0	25.9
Midwest	7.7	8.5	9.4	3.5	5.5
East North Central	6.4	7.0	8.9	2.9	4.3
West North Central	1.3	1.5	0.5	0.6	1.2
South	30.3	32.2	14.9	70.5	25.2
South Atlantic	9.5	2.3	12.4	67.3	15.3
East South Central	0.4	0.3	0.5	0.5	0.8
West South Central	20.3	29.6	2.0	2.7	9.2
West	45.2	58.0	7.0	8.5	39.4
Mountain	8.9	10.7	1.0	1.1	10.1
Pacific	36.3	47.3	6.1	7.3	29.2

(continued)

(continued from previous page)

	total	Mexican	Puerto Rican	Cuban	other Hispanic
Percent share					
UNITED STATES	9.0%	5.4%	1.1%	0.4%	2.0%
Northeast	7.4	0.3	3.7	0.4	3.0
New England	4.3	0.2	2.4	0.1	1.6
Middle Atlantic	8.5	0.4	4.1	0.4	3.5
Midwest	2.9	1.9	0.4	0.1	0.5
East North Central	3.4	2.2	0.6	0.1	0.5
West North Central	1.6	1.2	0.1	0.0	0.3
South	7.9	5.1	0.5	0.9	1.5
South Atlantic	4.9	0.7	0.8	1.6	1.8
East South Central	0.6	0.3	0.1	0.0	0.3
West South Central	17.0	14.9	0.2	0.1	1.7
West	19.1	14.8	0.4	0.2	3.8
Mountain	14.6	10.5	0.2	0.1	3.8
Pacific	20.7	16.3	0.4	0.2	3.8

Note: The 1990 population figures are for April 1, 1990.
Source: Bureau of the Census, General Population Characteristics, *1990 Census of Population, CP-1-1, 1992*

Hispanics by Region and Division, 1990 to 2020

(number and percent distribution of Hispanics and Hispanic share of the total population by region and division, selected years 1990-2020; percent change in number and percentage point change in distribution and share, 1990-2000 and 2000-2010; numbers in thousands)

	1990	1995	2000	2010	2020	percent change 1990-2000	2000-2010
Number							
UNITED STATES	22,354	26,798	31,166	40,525	51,217	39.4%	30.0%
Northeast	3,754	4,251	4,691	5,559	6,474	25.0	18.5
New England	568	684	797	1,035	1,283	40.3	29.9
Middle Atlantic	3,186	3,567	3,895	4,524	5,191	22.3	16.1
Midwest	1,727	2,102	2,478	3,284	4,204	43.5	32.5
East North Central	1,438	1,737	2,037	2,685	3,424	41.7	31.8
West North Central	289	365	441	600	780	52.6	36.1
South	6,767	8,260	9,752	12,943	16,568	44.1	32.7
South Atlantic	2,133	2,645	3,165	4,315	5,596	48.4	36.3
East South Central	95	113	132	176	224	38.9	33.3
West South Central	4,539	5,502	6,455	8,452	10,748	42.2	30.9
West	10,106	12,185	14,244	18,739	23,972	40.9	31.6
Mountain	1,992	2,471	2,946	3,954	5,130	47.9	34.2
Pacific	8,114	9,714	11,298	14,785	18,842	39.2	30.9

	1990	1995	2000	2010	2020	percentage point change 1990-2000	2000-2010
Percent distribution							
UNITED STATES	100.0%	100.0%	100.0%	100.0%	100.0%	-	-
Northeast	16.8	15.9	15.1	13.7	12.6	-1.7	-1.4
New England	2.5	2.6	2.6	2.6	2.5	0.1	0.0
Middle Atlantic	14.3	13.3	12.5	11.2	10.1	-1.8	-1.3
Midwest	7.7	7.8	8.0	8.1	8.2	0.3	0.1
East North Central	6.4	6.5	6.5	6.6	6.7	0.1	0.1
West North Central	1.3	1.4	1.4	1.5	1.5	0.1	0.1
South	30.3	30.8	31.3	31.9	32.3	1.0	0.6
South Atlantic	9.5	9.9	10.2	10.6	10.9	0.7	0.4
East South Central	0.4	0.4	0.4	0.4	0.4	0.0	0.0
West South Central	20.3	20.5	20.7	20.9	21.0	0.4	0.2
West	45.2	45.5	45.7	46.2	46.8	0.5	0.5
Mountain	8.9	9.2	9.5	9.8	10.0	0.6	0.3
Pacific	36.3	36.2	36.3	36.5	36.8	0.0	0.2

(continued)

(continued from previous page)

	1990	1995	2000	2010	2020	percentage point change 1990-2000	2000-2010
Percent share							
UNITED STATES	9.0%	10.2%	11.3%	13.5%	15.7%	2.3	2.2
Northeast	7.4	8.3	9.0	10.4	11.7	1.6	1.4
New England	4.3	5.2	6.0	7.5	8.8	1.7	1.5
Middle Atlantic	8.5	9.3	10.1	11.4	12.7	1.6	1.3
Midwest	2.9	3.4	3.9	5.0	6.1	1.0	1.1
East North Central	3.4	4.0	4.5	5.8	7.2	1.1	1.3
West North Central	1.6	2.0	2.3	3.0	3.7	0.7	0.7
South	7.9	9.0	10.0	12.1	14.1	2.1	2.1
South Atlantic	4.9	5.6	6.3	7.8	9.2	1.4	1.5
East South Central	0.6	0.7	0.8	1.0	1.2	0.2	0.2
West South Central	17.0	19.2	21.2	24.8	28.4	4.2	3.6
West	19.1	20.9	22.5	25.5	28.5	3.4	3.0
Mountain	14.6	16.1	17.4	20.7	24.3	2.8	3.3
Pacific	20.7	22.6	24.4	27.2	29.9	3.7	2.8

Note: The 1990 population figures are for April 1, 1990. Projections of total Hispanics for 2000, 2010, and 2020 are different from those at the beginning of the population section because they are from an earlier report for states and regions.
Source: Bureau of the Census, Population Projections for States, by Age, Sex, Race, and Hispanic Origin: 1993 to 2020, *Current Population Reports, P25-1111, 1994*

Hispanics by State and Ethnicity, 1990

(number of Hispanics, by state and ethnicity, 1990; numbers in thousands)

	total	Mexican	Puerto Rican	Cuban	other Hispanic
United States	22,354	13,496	2,728	1,044	5,086
Alabama	25	10	4	1	10
Alaska	18	9	2	-	6
Arizona	688	616	8	2	62
Arkansas	20	12	1	-	6
California	7,688	6,119	126	72	1,371
Colorado	424	282	7	2	133
Connecticut	213	8	147	6	51
Delaware	16	3	8	1	4
District of Columbia	33	3	2	1	26
Florida	1,574	161	247	674	492
Georgia	109	49	17	8	34
Hawaii	81	14	26	1	41
Idaho	53	43	1	-	9
Illinois	904	624	146	18	116
Indiana	99	67	14	2	16
Iowa	33	24	1	-	7
Kansas	94	76	4	1	13
Kentucky	22	9	4	1	9
Louisiana	93	23	6	9	55
Maine	7	2	1	-	3
Maryland	125	18	18	6	83
Massachusetts	288	13	151	8	116
Michigan	202	138	19	5	40
Minnesota	54	35	3	2	14
Mississippi	16	7	1	-	7
Missouri	62	38	4	2	17
Montana	12	8	-	-	3
Nebraska	37	30	1	-	6
Nevada	124	85	4	6	29
New Hampshire	11	2	3	1	5
New Jersey	740	29	320	85	306
New Mexico	579	329	3	1	247
New York	2,214	93	1,087	74	960

(continued)

(continued from previous page)

	total	Mexican	Puerto Rican	Cuban	other Hispanic
North Carolina	77	33	15	4	26
North Dakota	5	3	-	-	1
Ohio	140	58	46	4	32
Oklahoma	86	63	5	1	17
Oregon	113	86	3	1	23
Pennsylvania	232	24	149	7	52
Rhode Island	46	2	13	1	29
South Carolina	31	11	6	2	11
South Dakota	5	3	-	-	1
Tennessee	33	14	4	2	13
Texas	4,340	3,891	43	18	388
Utah	85	57	2	-	25
Vermont	4	1	1	-	2
Virginia	160	33	24	6	97
Washington	215	156	9	2	47
West Virginia	8	3	1	-	5
Wisconsin	93	58	19	2	15
Wyoming	26	19	-	-	7

Note: The 1990 population figures are for April 1, 1990.
Source: Bureau of the Census, Internet web site, http://www.census.gov

Distribution of Hispanics by State and Ethnicity, 1990

(percent distribution of Hispanics by state and ethnicity, 1990)

	total	Mexican	Puerto Rican	Cuban	other Hispanic
United States	100.0%	100.0%	100.0%	100.0%	100.0%
Alabama	0.1	0.1	0.1	0.1	0.2
Alaska	0.1	0.1	0.1	0.0	0.1
Arizona	3.1	4.6	0.3	0.2	1.2
Arkansas	0.1	0.1	0.0	0.0	0.1
California	34.4	45.3	4.6	6.9	26.9
Colorado	1.9	2.1	0.3	0.2	2.6
Connecticut	1.0	0.1	5.4	0.6	1.0
Delaware	0.1	0.0	0.3	0.1	0.1
District of Columbia	0.1	0.0	0.1	0.1	0.5
Florida	7.0	1.2	9.1	64.6	9.7
Georgia	0.5	0.4	0.6	0.7	0.7
Hawaii	0.4	0.1	0.9	0.1	0.8
Idaho	0.2	0.3	0.0	0.0	0.2
Illinois	4.0	4.6	5.4	1.7	2.3
Indiana	0.4	0.5	0.5	0.2	0.3
Iowa	0.1	0.2	0.0	0.0	0.1
Kansas	0.4	0.6	0.1	0.1	0.3
Kentucky	0.1	0.1	0.1	0.1	0.2
Louisiana	0.4	0.2	0.2	0.8	1.1
Maine	0.0	0.0	0.0	0.0	0.1
Maryland	0.6	0.1	0.6	0.6	1.6
Massachusetts	1.3	0.1	5.5	0.8	2.3
Michigan	0.9	1.0	0.7	0.5	0.8
Minnesota	0.2	0.3	0.1	0.1	0.3
Mississippi	0.1	0.0	0.0	0.0	0.1
Missouri	0.3	0.3	0.1	0.2	0.3
Montana	0.1	0.1	0.0	0.0	0.1
Nebraska	0.2	0.2	0.0	0.0	0.1
Nevada	0.6	0.6	0.2	0.6	0.6
New Hampshire	0.1	0.0	0.1	0.1	0.1
New Jersey	3.3	0.2	11.7	8.2	6.0
New Mexico	2.6	2.4	0.1	0.1	4.9
New York	9.9	0.7	39.8	7.1	18.9

(continued)

(continued from previous page)

	total	Mexican	Puerto Rican	Cuban	other Hispanic
North Carolina	0.3%	0.2%	0.5%	0.4%	0.5%
North Dakota	0.0	0.0	0.0	0.0	0.0
Ohio	0.6	0.4	1.7	0.3	0.6
Oklahoma	0.4	0.5	0.2	0.1	0.3
Oregon	0.5	0.6	0.1	0.1	0.5
Pennsylvania	1.0	0.2	5.5	0.7	1.0
Rhode Island	0.2	0.0	0.5	0.1	0.6
South Carolina	0.1	0.1	0.2	0.2	0.2
South Dakota	0.0	0.0	0.0	0.0	0.0
Tennessee	0.1	0.1	0.2	0.2	0.2
Texas	19.4	28.8	1.6	1.7	7.6
Utah	0.4	0.4	0.1	0.0	0.5
Vermont	0.0	0.0	0.0	0.0	0.0
Virginia	0.7	0.2	0.9	0.6	1.9
Washington	1.0	1.2	0.3	0.2	0.9
West Virginia	0.0	0.0	0.0	0.0	0.1
Wisconsin	0.4	0.4	0.7	0.2	0.3
Wyoming	0.1	0.1	0.0	0.0	0.1

Source: Bureau of the Census, Internet web site, http://www.census.gov

Hispanic Share of the Total Population by State and Ethnicity, 1990

(Hispanics as a percent of state populations, by ethnicity, 1990)

	total	Mexican	Puerto Rican	Cuban	other
United States	9.0%	5.4%	1.1%	0.4%	2.0%
Alabama	0.6	0.2	0.1	0.0	0.3
Alaska	3.2	1.7	0.4	0.1	1.1
Arizona	18.8	16.8	0.2	0.1	1.7
Arkansas	0.8	0.5	0.1	0.0	0.2
California	25.8	20.6	0.4	0.2	4.6
Colorado	12.9	8.6	0.2	0.1	4.0
Connecticut	6.5	0.3	4.5	0.2	1.6
Delaware	2.4	0.5	1.2	0.1	0.6
District of Columbia	5.4	0.5	0.4	0.2	4.3
Florida	12.2	1.2	1.9	5.2	3.8
Georgia	1.7	0.8	0.3	0.1	0.5
Hawaii	7.3	1.3	2.3	0.1	3.7
Idaho	5.3	4.3	0.1	0.0	0.9
Illinois	7.9	5.5	1.3	0.2	1.0
Indiana	1.8	1.2	0.3	0.0	0.3
Iowa	1.2	0.9	0.0	0.0	0.2
Kansas	3.8	3.1	0.1	0.1	0.5
Kentucky	0.6	0.2	0.1	0.0	0.2
Louisiana	2.2	0.6	0.1	0.2	1.3
Maine	0.6	0.2	0.1	0.0	0.3
Maryland	2.6	0.4	0.4	0.1	1.7
Massachusetts	4.8	0.2	2.5	0.1	1.9
Michigan	2.2	1.5	0.2	0.1	0.4
Minnesota	1.2	0.8	0.1	0.0	0.3
Mississippi	0.6	0.3	0.1	0.0	0.3
Missouri	1.2	0.7	0.1	0.0	0.3
Montana	1.5	1.0	0.1	0.0	0.4
Nebraska	2.3	1.9	0.1	0.0	0.4
Nevada	10.4	7.1	0.4	0.5	2.4
New Hampshire	1.0	0.2	0.3	0.1	0.5
New Jersey	9.6	0.4	4.1	1.1	4.0
New Mexico	38.2	21.7	0.2	0.1	16.3
New York	12.3	0.5	6.0	0.4	5.3

(continued)

(continued from previous page)

	total	Mexican	Puerto Rican	Cuban	other
North Carolina	1.2%	0.5%	0.2%	0.1%	0.4%
North Dakota	0.7	0.5	0.1	0.0	0.2
Ohio	1.3	0.5	0.4	0.0	0.3
Oklahoma	2.7	2.0	0.1	0.0	0.5
Oregon	4.0	3.0	0.1	0.0	0.8
Pennsylvania	2.0	0.2	1.3	0.1	0.4
Rhode Island	4.6	0.2	1.3	0.1	2.9
South Carolina	0.9	0.3	0.2	0.0	0.3
South Dakota	0.8	0.5	0.1	0.0	0.2
Tennessee	0.7	0.3	0.1	0.0	0.3
Texas	25.5	22.9	0.3	0.1	2.3
Utah	4.9	3.3	0.1	0.0	1.5
Vermont	0.7	0.1	0.1	0.0	0.4
Virginia	2.6	0.5	0.4	0.1	1.6
Washington	4.4	3.2	0.2	0.0	1.0
West Virginia	0.5	0.2	0.1	0.0	0.3
Wisconsin	1.9	1.2	0.4	0.0	0.3
Wyoming	5.7	4.1	0.1	0.0	1.5

Source: Bureau of the Census, Internet web site, http://www.census.gov

Hispanics by State, 1995 to 2020

(number of Hispanics by state, selected years 1995-2020; percent change 1995-2020; numbers in thousands)

	1995	2000	2010	2020	percent change 1995-2020
United States	26,798	31,166	40,525	51,217	91.1%
Alabama	29	35	49	63	117.2
Alaska	22	26	33	42	90.9
Arizona	853	1,019	1,382	1,810	112.2
Arkansas	27	33	44	57	111.1
California	9,143	10,584	13,775	17,489	91.3
Colorado	511	595	771	975	90.8
Connecticut	258	300	383	467	81.0
Delaware	22	28	39	51	131.8
District of Columbia	30	29	32	39	30.0
Florida	1,948	2,333	3,202	4,173	114.2
Georgia	144	176	237	304	111.1
Hawaii	106	131	186	249	134.9
Idaho	74	95	138	187	152.7
Illinois	1,086	1,264	1,643	2,076	91.2
Indiana	122	145	197	257	110.7
Iowa	45	56	75	97	115.6
Kansas	116	139	190	246	112.1
Kentucky	23	26	34	43	87.0
Louisiana	109	124	154	188	72.5
Maine	9	11	15	20	122.2
Maryland	158	188	248	313	98.1
Massachusetts	342	394	510	632	84.8
Michigan	242	283	375	481	98.8
Minnesota	68	83	116	153	125.0
Mississippi	18	20	26	32	77.8
Missouri	71	82	108	137	93.0
Montana	15	17	22	28	86.7
Nebraska	53	67	93	122	130.2
Nevada	195	264	402	559	186.7
New Hampshire	13	16	24	31	138.5
New Jersey	898	1,037	1,287	1,539	71.4
New Mexico	686	792	1,024	1,295	88.8
New York	2,372	2,498	2,750	3,031	27.8

(continued)

(continued from previous page)

	1995	2000	2010	2020	percent change 1995-2020
North Carolina	100	123	167	216	116.0%
North Dakota	5	6	8	10	100.0
Ohio	170	201	268	344	102.4
Oklahoma	106	124	160	201	89.6
Oregon	151	189	265	355	135.1
Pennsylvania	297	359	487	620	108.8
Rhode Island	58	70	95	123	112.1
South Carolina	40	49	67	86	115.0
South Dakota	7	9	11	14	100.0
Tennessee	42	51	67	86	104.8
Texas	5,260	6,173	8,094	10,302	95.9
Utah	106	127	170	220	107.5
Vermont	4	5	8	10	150.0
Virginia	193	228	308	392	103.1
Washington	291	368	526	707	143.0
West Virginia	10	12	16	20	100.0
Wisconsin	118	144	200	266	125.4
Wyoming	31	36	45	56	80.6

Note: Projections of total Hispanics for 2000, 2010, and 2020 are different from those at the beginning of the population section because they are from an earlier report for states and regions.
Source: Bureau of the Census, Population Projections for States, by Age, Sex, Race, and Hispanic Origin: 1993 to 2020, *Current Population Reports, P25-1111, 1994*

Distribution of Hispanics by State, 1995 to 2020

(percent distribution of Hispanics by state, selected years 1995-2020)

	1995	2000	2010	2020
United States	100.0%	100.0%	100.0%	100.0%
Alabama	0.1	0.1	0.1	0.1
Alaska	0.1	0.1	0.1	0.1
Arizona	3.2	3.3	3.4	3.5
Arkansas	0.1	0.1	0.1	0.1
California	34.1	34.0	34.0	34.1
Colorado	1.9	1.9	1.9	1.9
Connecticut	1.0	1.0	0.9	0.9
Delaware	0.1	0.1	0.1	0.1
District of Columbia	0.1	0.1	0.1	0.1
Florida	7.3	7.5	7.9	8.1
Georgia	0.5	0.6	0.6	0.6
Hawaii	0.4	0.4	0.5	0.5
Idaho	0.3	0.3	0.3	0.4
Illinois	4.1	4.1	4.1	4.1
Indiana	0.5	0.5	0.5	0.5
Iowa	0.2	0.2	0.2	0.2
Kansas	0.4	0.4	0.5	0.5
Kentucky	0.1	0.1	0.1	0.1
Louisiana	0.4	0.4	0.4	0.4
Maine	0.0	0.0	0.0	0.0
Maryland	0.6	0.6	0.6	0.6
Massachusetts	1.3	1.3	1.3	1.2
Michigan	0.9	0.9	0.9	0.9
Minnesota	0.3	0.3	0.3	0.3
Mississippi	0.1	0.1	0.1	0.1
Missouri	0.3	0.3	0.3	0.3
Montana	0.1	0.1	0.1	0.1
Nebraska	0.2	0.2	0.2	0.2
Nevada	0.7	0.8	1.0	1.1
New Hampshire	0.0	0.1	0.1	0.1
New Jersey	3.4	3.3	3.2	3.0
New Mexico	2.6	2.5	2.5	2.5
New York	8.9	8.0	6.8	5.9

(continued)

(continued from previous page)

	1995	2000	2010	2020
North Carolina	0.4%	0.4%	0.4%	0.4%
North Dakota	0.0	0.0	0.0	0.0
Ohio	0.6	0.6	0.7	0.7
Oklahoma	0.4	0.4	0.4	0.4
Oregon	0.6	0.6	0.7	0.7
Pennsylvania	1.1	1.2	1.2	1.2
Rhode Island	0.2	0.2	0.2	0.2
South Carolina	0.1	0.2	0.2	0.2
South Dakota	0.0	0.0	0.0	0.0
Tennessee	0.2	0.2	0.2	0.2
Texas	19.6	19.8	20.0	20.1
Utah	0.4	0.4	0.4	0.4
Vermont	0.0	0.0	0.0	0.0
Virginia	0.7	0.7	0.8	0.8
Washington	1.1	1.2	1.3	1.4
West Virginia	0.0	0.0	0.0	0.0
Wisconsin	0.4	0.5	0.5	0.5
Wyoming	0.1	0.1	0.1	0.1

Source: Bureau of the Census, Population Projections for States, by Age, Sex, Race, and Hispanic Origin: 1993 to 2020, *Current Population Reports, P25-1111, 1994*

Hispanic Share of State Populations, 1995 to 2020

(Hispanics as a percent of state populations, selected years 1995-2020; percentage point change in share, 1995-2020)

	1995	2000	2010	2020	percentage point change 1995-2020
United States	10.2%	11.3%	13.5%	15.7%	5.5
Alabama	0.7	0.8	1.0	1.2	0.5
Alaska	3.5	3.7	4.2	4.8	1.4
Arizona	20.9	23.0	27.2	31.7	10.7
Arkansas	1.1	1.3	1.6	1.9	0.8
California	28.2	30.3	33.5	36.5	8.3
Colorado	13.8	14.7	17.2	20.0	6.2
Connecticut	7.9	9.2	11.2	12.9	5.0
Delaware	3.1	3.7	4.8	5.9	2.8
District of Columbia	5.4	5.4	5.5	6.1	0.8
Florida	13.7	15.2	18.4	21.5	7.7
Georgia	2.0	2.3	2.8	3.2	1.2
Hawaii	8.7	9.9	12.0	13.7	5.0
Idaho	6.4	7.4	9.5	11.7	5.3
Illinois	9.2	10.4	13.0	15.7	6.5
Indiana	2.1	2.4	3.1	4.0	1.9
Iowa	1.6	1.9	2.5	3.2	1.6
Kansas	4.5	5.1	6.5	7.9	3.4
Kentucky	0.6	0.7	0.8	1.0	0.4
Louisiana	2.5	2.8	3.2	3.6	1.1
Maine	0.7	0.9	1.1	1.4	0.7
Maryland	3.1	3.5	4.3	5.0	1.9
Massachusetts	5.7	6.6	8.4	9.9	4.2
Michigan	2.5	2.9	3.7	4.6	2.1
Minnesota	1.5	1.7	2.3	2.8	1.3
Mississippi	0.7	0.7	0.9	1.0	0.4
Missouri	1.3	1.5	1.9	2.2	0.9
Montana	1.7	1.8	2.2	2.6	0.9
Nebraska	3.2	3.9	5.2	6.5	3.2
Nevada	13.2	15.6	20.8	26.1	12.9
New Hampshire	1.1	1.4	1.9	2.2	1.1
New Jersey	11.3	12.7	15.0	17.0	5.7
New Mexico	40.9	43.4	49.2	55.4	14.5
New York	13.0	13.7	14.8	15.9	2.8

(continued)

(continued from previous page)

	1995	2000	2010	2020	percentage point change 1995-2020
North Carolina	1.4%	1.6%	2.0%	2.4%	1.0
North Dakota	0.8	0.9	1.2	1.4	0.6
Ohio	1.5	1.8	2.3	2.9	1.4
Oklahoma	3.2	3.7	4.3	5.0	1.8
Oregon	4.8	5.6	6.8	8.1	3.3
Pennsylvania	2.4	2.9	3.9	4.9	2.5
Rhode Island	5.8	7.0	9.2	11.3	5.5
South Carolina	1.1	1.2	1.6	1.8	0.8
South Dakota	1.0	1.2	1.3	1.6	0.7
Tennessee	0.8	0.9	1.1	1.3	0.5
Texas	28.3	30.8	35.4	40.3	12.0
Utah	5.5	5.9	6.9	8.0	2.6
Vermont	0.7	0.8	1.3	1.5	0.8
Virginia	2.9	3.2	4.0	4.7	1.8
Washington	5.3	6.1	7.5	8.9	3.6
West Virginia	0.5	0.7	0.9	1.1	0.5
Wisconsin	2.3	2.7	3.6	4.6	2.3
Wyoming	6.4	6.9	7.6	8.5	2.1

Source: Bureau of the Census, Population Projections for States, by Age, Sex, Race, and Hispanic Origin: 1993 to 2020, *Current Population Reports, P25-1111, 1994*

Metropolitan Areas With the Most Hispanics, 1990

(metropolitan areas with at least 100,000 Hispanics ranked by size of Hispanic population; number of Hispanics and Hispanic share of the total metropolitan population, 1990; numbers in thousands)

		number	percent
1.	Los Angeles-Riverside-Orange County, CA	4,779	32.9%
2.	New York-Northern New Jersey-Long Island, NY-NJ-CT-PA	2,843	14.7
3.	Miami-Fort Lauderdale, FL	1,062	33.3
4.	San Francisco-Oakland-San Jose, CA	970	15.5
5.	Chicago-Gary-Kenosha, IL-IN-WI	898	10.9
6.	Houston-Galveston-Brazoria, TX	773	20.7
7.	San Antonio, TX	628	47.4
8.	Dallas-Fort Worth, TX	526	13.0
9.	San Diego, CA	511	20.4
10.	El Paso, TX	412	69.6
11.	Phoenix-Mesa, AZ	380	17.0
12.	McAllen-Edinburg-Mission, TX	327	85.2
13.	Fresno, CA	267	35.3
14.	Washington-Baltimore, DC-MD-VA-WV	259	3.9
15.	Denver-Boulder-Greeley, CO	254	12.8
16.	Boston-Brockton-Nashua, MA-NH-ME-CT	239	4.4
17.	Philadelphia-Wilmington-Atlantic City, PA-NJ-DE-MD	224	3.8
18.	Albuquerque, NM	218	37.1
19.	Brownsville-Harlingen-San Benito, TX	213	81.9
20.	Corpus Christi, TX	182	52.0
21.	Austin-San Marcos, TX	177	20.9
22.	Sacramento-Yolo, CA	172	11.6
23.	Tucson, AZ	163	24.5
24.	Bakersfield, CA	152	28.0
25.	Tampa-St. Petersburg-Clearwater, FL	139	6.7
26.	Laredo, TX	125	93.9
27.	Visalia-Tulare-Porterville, CA	121	38.8
28.	Salinas, CA	120	33.6
29.	Stockton-Lodi, CA	113	23.4
30.	Detroit-Ann Arbor-Flint, MI	105	2.0
31.	Orlando, FL	101	8.2

Source: Bureau of the Census, Statistical Abstract of the United States 1993

Hispanic Births by Age of Mother, 1993

(number and percent distribution of births to Hispanic women, by age of mother, 1993)

	number	percent
Total births	654,418	100.0%
Under age 15	2,950	0.5
Aged 15 to 19	110,695	16.9
Aged 20 to 24	204,875	31.3
Aged 25 to 29	176,057	26.9
Aged 30 to 34	108,531	16.6
Aged 35 to 39	42,788	6.5
Aged 40 or older	8,522	1.3

Source: National Center for Health Statistics, Advance Report of Final Natality Statistics, 1993, *Vol. 44, No. 3 Supplement, 1995*

Births to Unmarried Hispanic Women by Age, 1993

(number and percent of births to unmarried Hispanic women, by age of mother; 1993)

	number	percent of total births in age group
Total births to unmarried women	261,586	40.0%
Under age 15	2,358	79.9
Aged 15 to 19	69,523	62.8
Aged 20 to 24	88,946	43.4
Aged 25 to 29	55,826	31.7
Aged 30 to 34	29,862	27.5
Aged 35 to 39	12,389	29.0
Aged 40 or older	2,682	31.5

Source: National Center for Health Statistics, Advance Report of Final Natality Statistics, 1993, *Vol. 44, No. 3 Supplement, 1995*

Hispanic Births by Age and Ethnicity of Mother, 1993

(number and percent distribution of births to Hispanic women, by age and ethnicity of mother, 1993)

	total	Mexican	Puerto Rican	Cuban	Central & S. American	other Hispanic
Total, number	654,418	443,733	58,102	11,916	92,371	48,296
Under age 15	2,950	2,008	405	16	217	304
Aged 15 to 19	110,695	78,587	12,566	790	8,924	9,828
Aged 20 to 24	204,875	146,264	18,532	2,219	23,350	14,510
Aged 25 to 29	176,057	117,489	14,388	3,935	28,182	12,063
Aged 30 to 34	108,531	67,721	8,460	3,565	20,800	7,985
Aged 35 to 39	42,788	26,315	3,121	1,198	9,083	3,071
Aged 40 or older	8,522	5,349	630	193	1,815	535
Total, percent	100.0%	67.8%	8.9%	1.8%	14.1%	7.4%
Under age 15	100.0	68.1	13.7	0.5	7.4	10.3
Aged 15 to 19	100.0	71.0	11.4	0.7	8.1	8.9
Aged 20 to 24	100.0	71.4	9.0	1.1	11.4	7.1
Aged 25 to 29	100.0	66.7	8.2	2.2	16.0	6.9
Aged 30 to 34	100.0	62.4	7.8	3.3	19.2	7.4
Aged 35 to 39	100.0	61.5	7.3	2.8	21.2	7.2
Aged 40 or older	100.0	62.8	7.4	2.3	21.3	6.3

Source: National Center for Health Statistics, Advance Report of Final Natality Statistics, 1993, *Vol. 44, No. 3 Supplement, 1995*

Hispanic Births by State and Ethnicity, 1993

(number of Hispanic births, by state and ethnicity of mother, 1993)

	total	Mexican	Puerto Rican	Cuban	Central & S. American	other Hispanic
United States	654,418	443,733	58,102	11,916	92,371	48,296
Alabama	509	288	87	15	81	38
Alaska	439	221	45	8	79	86
Arizona	22,579	21,693	149	39	423	275
Arkansas	579	473	23	5	42	36
California	262,313	221,905	2,162	864	29,739	7,643
Colorado	10,268	5,823	139	35	204	4,067
Connecticut	5,381	188	3,929	43	874	347
Delaware	472	190	187	9	60	26
District of Columbia	930	44	8	3	830	45
Florida	31,550	5,758	5,327	7,976	10,409	2,080
Georgia	3,467	2,328	313	90	520	216
Hawaii	2,192	394	662	12	61	1,063
Idaho	1,850	1,555	17	8	35	235
Illinois	28,610	22,028	3,228	223	1,540	1,591
Indiana	2,131	1,608	260	18	87	158
Iowa	967	804	23	6	52	82
Kansas	2,417	2,040	65	12	94	206
Kentucky	401	205	51	12	26	107
Louisiana	1,001	282	80	55	292	292
Maine	107	26	8	-	8	65
Maryland	2,996	534	271	71	1,878	242
Massachusetts	8,252	226	4,484	100	3,141	301
Michigan	4,389	2,824	369	48	210	938
Minnesota	1,560	1,158	80	15	108	199
Mississippi	141	68	14	8	7	44
Missouri	1,150	855	71	19	114	91
Montana	190	146	1	1	4	38
Nebraska	1,261	964	23	5	65	204
Nevada	4,413	3,563	91	80	423	256
New Hampshire	190	43	55	3	23	66
New Jersey	17,650	1,563	8,259	941	5,884	1,003
New Mexico	13,054	3,945	43	48	69	8,949
New York	51,847	5,221	19,197	515	23,534	3,380

(continued)

(continued from previous page)

	total	Mexican	Puerto Rican	Cuban	Central & S. American	other Hispanic
North Carolina	2,560	1,695	308	37	370	150
North Dakota	122	69	1	1	14	37
Ohio	2,655	1,191	1,019	46	139	260
Oklahoma	2,133	1,638	122	15	15	343
Oregon	4,002	3,660	42	14	151	135
Pennsylvania	6,302	582	4,101	100	625	894
Rhode Island	1,594	94	546	12	826	116
South Carolina	617	293	118	11	58	137
South Dakota	122	84	12	3	14	9
Tennessee	694	407	75	22	65	125
Texas	131,293	114,250	814	243	5,885	10,101
Utah	2,456	1,707	64	11	370	304
Vermont	25	6	6	3	4	6
Virginia	4,135	763	461	69	2,486	356
Washington	7,708	6,503	188	24	217	776
West Virginia	81	25	10	-	9	37
Wisconsin	2,175	1,397	485	16	205	72
Wyoming	488	406	9	2	2	69

Source: National Center for Health Statistics, Advance Report of Final Natality Statistics, 1993, *Vol. 44, No. 3 Supplement, 1995*

Distribution of Hispanic Births by State and Ethnicity, 1993

(percent distribution of Hispanic births, by state and ethnicity of mother, 1993)

	total	Mexican	Puerto Rican	Cuban	Central & S. American	other Hispanic
United States	100.0%	100.0%	100.0%	100.0%	100.0%	100.0%
Alabama	0.1	0.1	0.1	0.1	0.1	0.1
Alaska	0.1	0.0	0.1	0.1	0.1	0.2
Arizona	3.5	4.9	0.3	0.3	0.5	0.6
Arkansas	0.1	0.1	0.0	0.0	0.0	0.1
California	40.1	50.0	3.7	7.3	32.2	15.8
Colorado	1.6	1.3	0.2	0.3	0.2	8.4
Connecticut	0.8	0.0	6.8	0.4	0.9	0.7
Delaware	0.1	0.0	0.3	0.1	0.1	0.1
District of Columbia	0.1	0.0	0.0	0.0	0.9	0.1
Florida	4.8	1.3	9.2	66.9	11.3	4.3
Georgia	0.5	0.5	0.5	0.8	0.6	0.4
Hawaii	0.3	0.1	1.1	0.1	0.1	2.2
Idaho	0.3	0.4	0.0	0.1	0.0	0.5
Illinois	4.4	5.0	5.6	1.9	1.7	3.3
Indiana	0.3	0.4	0.4	0.2	0.1	0.3
Iowa	0.1	0.2	0.0	0.1	0.1	0.2
Kansas	0.4	0.5	0.1	0.1	0.1	0.4
Kentucky	0.1	0.0	0.1	0.1	0.0	0.2
Louisiana	0.2	0.1	0.1	0.5	0.3	0.6
Maine	0.0	0.0	0.0	-	0.0	0.1
Maryland	0.5	0.1	0.5	0.6	2.0	0.5
Massachusetts	1.3	0.1	7.7	0.8	3.4	0.6
Michigan	0.7	0.6	0.6	0.4	0.2	1.9
Minnesota	0.2	0.3	0.1	0.1	0.1	0.4
Mississippi	0.0	0.0	0.0	0.1	0.0	0.1
Missouri	0.2	0.2	0.1	0.2	0.1	0.2
Montana	0.0	0.0	0.0	0.0	0.0	0.1
Nebraska	0.2	0.2	0.0	0.0	0.1	0.4
Nevada	0.7	0.8	0.2	0.7	0.5	0.5
New Hampshire	0.0	0.0	0.1	0.0	0.0	0.1
New Jersey	2.7	0.4	14.2	7.9	6.4	2.1
New Mexico	2.0	0.9	0.1	0.4	0.1	18.5
New York	7.9	1.2	33.0	4.3	25.5	7.0

(continued)

(continued from previous page)

	total	Mexican	Puerto Rican	Cuban	Central & S. American	other Hispanic
North Carolina	0.4%	0.4%	0.5%	0.3%	0.4%	0.3%
North Dakota	0.0	0.0	0.0	0.0	0.0	0.1
Ohio	0.4	0.3	1.8	0.4	0.2	0.5
Oklahoma	0.3	0.4	0.2	0.1	0.0	0.7
Oregon	0.6	0.8	0.1	0.1	0.2	0.3
Pennsylvania	1.0	0.1	7.1	0.8	0.7	1.9
Rhode Island	0.2	0.0	0.9	0.1	0.9	0.2
South Carolina	0.1	0.1	0.2	0.1	0.1	0.3
South Dakota	0.0	0.0	0.0	0.0	0.0	0.0
Tennessee	0.1	0.1	0.1	0.2	0.1	0.3
Texas	20.1	25.7	1.4	2.0	6.4	20.9
Utah	0.4	0.4	0.1	0.1	0.4	0.6
Vermont	0.0	0.0	0.0	0.0	0.0	0.0
Virginia	0.6	0.2	0.8	0.6	2.7	0.7
Washington	1.2	1.5	0.3	0.2	0.2	1.6
West Virginia	0.0	0.0	0.0	-	0.0	0.1
Wisconsin	0.3	0.3	0.8	0.1	0.2	0.1
Wyoming	0.1	0.1	0.0	0.0	0.0	0.1

Source: National Center for Health Statistics, Advance Report of Final Natality Statistics, 1993, *Vol. 44, No. 3 Supplement, 1995*

Hispanic Share of Births by State and Ethnicity, 1993

(Hispanic births as a percent of total births, by state and ethnicity of mother, 1993)

	total Hispanic	Mexican	Puerto Rican	Cuban	Central & South American	other Hispanic
United States	16.4%	11.1%	1.5%	0.3%	2.3%	1.2%
Alabama	0.8	0.5	0.1	0.0	0.1	0.1
Alaska	4.0	2.0	0.4	0.1	0.7	0.8
Arizona	32.7	31.4	0.2	0.1	0.6	0.4
Arkansas	1.7	1.4	0.1	0.0	0.1	0.1
California	44.8	37.9	0.4	0.1	5.1	1.3
Colorado	19.0	10.8	0.3	0.1	0.4	7.5
Connecticut	11.5	0.4	8.4	0.1	1.9	0.7
Delaware	4.5	1.8	1.8	0.1	0.6	0.2
District of Columbia	8.7	0.4	0.1	0.0	7.8	0.4
Florida	16.4	3.0	2.8	4.1	5.4	1.1
Georgia	3.1	2.1	0.3	0.1	0.5	0.2
Hawaii	11.2	2.0	3.4	0.1	0.3	5.4
Idaho	10.6	8.9	0.1	0.0	0.2	1.3
Illinois	15.0	11.5	1.7	0.1	0.8	0.8
Indiana	2.5	1.9	0.3	0.0	0.1	0.2
Iowa	2.6	2.1	0.1	0.0	0.1	0.2
Kansas	6.5	5.5	0.2	0.0	0.3	0.6
Kentucky	0.8	0.4	0.1	0.0	0.0	0.2
Louisiana	1.4	0.4	0.1	0.1	0.4	0.4
Maine	0.7	0.2	0.1	-	0.1	0.4
Maryland	4.0	0.7	0.4	0.1	2.5	0.3
Massachusetts	9.7	0.3	5.3	0.1	3.7	0.4
Michigan	3.1	2.0	0.3	0.0	0.2	0.7
Minnesota	2.4	1.8	0.1	0.0	0.2	0.3
Mississippi	0.3	0.2	0.0	0.0	0.0	0.1
Missouri	1.5	1.1	0.1	0.0	0.2	0.1
Montana	1.7	1.3	0.0	0.0	0.0	0.3
Nebraska	5.4	4.2	0.1	0.0	0.3	0.9
Nevada	19.7	15.9	0.4	0.4	1.9	1.1
New Hampshire	1.2	0.3	0.4	0.0	0.1	0.4
New Jersey	15.0	1.3	7.0	0.8	5.0	0.9
New Mexico	46.9	14.2	0.2	0.2	0.2	32.1
New York	18.4	1.8	6.8	0.2	8.3	1.2

(continued)

(continued from previous page)

	total Hispanic	Mexican	Puerto Rican	Cuban	Central & South American	other Hispanic
North Carolina	2.5%	1.7%	0.3%	0.0%	0.4%	0.1%
North Dakota	1.4	0.8	0.0	0.0	0.2	0.4
Ohio	1.7	0.8	0.6	0.0	0.1	0.2
Oklahoma	4.6	3.5	0.3	0.0	0.0	0.7
Oregon	9.6	8.8	0.1	0.0	0.4	0.3
Pennsylvania	3.9	0.4	2.6	0.1	0.4	0.6
Rhode Island	11.4	0.7	3.9	0.1	5.9	0.8
South Carolina	1.1	0.5	0.2	0.0	0.1	0.3
South Dakota	1.1	0.8	0.1	0.0	0.1	0.1
Tennessee	1.0	0.6	0.1	0.0	0.1	0.2
Texas	40.8	35.5	0.3	0.1	1.8	3.1
Utah	6.6	4.6	0.2	0.0	1.0	0.8
Vermont	0.3	0.1	0.1	0.0	0.1	0.1
Virginia	4.4	0.8	0.5	0.1	2.6	0.4
Washington	9.8	8.3	0.2	0.0	0.3	1.0
West Virginia	0.4	0.1	0.0	-	0.0	0.2
Wisconsin	3.1	2.0	0.7	0.0	0.3	0.1
Wyoming	7.4	6.2	0.1	0.0	0.0	1.1

Source: National Center for Health Statistics, Advance Report of Final Natality Statistics, 1993, *Vol. 44, No. 3, Supplement, 1995*

Projections of Hispanic Births, 1995 to 2020

(number of Hispanic births, and Hispanic births as a percent of total births, 1995-2020; numbers in thousands)

	number	Hispanic share of total births
1995	614	15.6%
1996	627	16.0
1997	640	16.4
1998	654	16.8
1999	668	17.1
2000	683	17.5
2001	699	17.9
2002	715	18.2
2003	732	18.6
2004	750	18.9
2005	769	19.2
2006	790	19.5
2007	813	19.9
2008	837	20.2
2009	863	20.6
2010	888	20.9
2011	913	21.3
2012	936	21.6
2013	959	21.9
2014	980	22.2
2015	1,001	22.5
2016	1,021	22.8
2017	1,041	23.1
2018	1,060	23.4
2019	1,079	23.7
2020	1,099	24.0

Source: Bureau of the Census, Population Projections of the United States, by Age, Sex, Race, and Hispanic Origin: 1995 to 2050, *Current Population Reports, P25-1130, 1996*

Hispanics:
Wealth and Spending

Hispanics have very little wealth compared with the average American household. The median net worth of Hispanic households amounted to just $4,656 in 1993, far below the $37,587 net worth of the average household. The net worth of Hispanics is below average in part because Hispanics are less likely to own a home than the average householder, and homes comprise the largest share of Americans' net worth. Only 41 percent of Hispanic householders own their homes versus 64 percent of householders in the nation as a whole.

Fully 24 percent of Hispanic households have zero or negative net worth (their debts exceed their assets). Among all households, 11.5 percent have zero or negative net worth. Eleven percent of Hispanic households have net worth in excess of $100,000, versus 29 percent of total households.

Hispanic households spent an average of $26,437 in 1994, according to the Consumer Expenditure Survey—83 percent as much as the average American household. On many items, however, Hispanics spend more than the average household. These items include meats, fruits and vegetables, baby food, soaps and detergents, children's clothes, photographer fees, and hair-care products.

Distribution of Net Worth Among Hispanic Households, 1993

(number and percent distribution of Hispanic households, by net worth, 1993; numbers in thousands)

	number	percent
Total households	7,403	100.0%
Zero or negative net worth	1,799	24.3
$1 to $4,999	1,873	25.3
$5,000 to $9,999	577	7.8
$10,000 to $24,999	725	9.8
$25,000 to $49,999	777	10.5
$50,000 to $99,999	851	11.5
$100,000 to $249,999	548	7.4
$250,000 to $499,999	163	2.2
$500,000 or more	74	1.0
Median net worth	$4,656	-

Source: Bureau of the Census, Internet web site, http://www.census.gov

Asset Ownership and Value of Assets for Hispanic Households, 1993

(percent of Hispanic households owning assets and median value of asset among owners, 1993)

	percent owning	median value
Interest-earning assets at financial institutions*	50.7%	$1,098
Other interest-earning assets**	2.1	-
Regular checking accounts	33.1	375
Stocks and mutual fund shares	6.1	2,365
Own business or profession	6.1	200
Motor vehicles	74.4	3,333
Own home	41.1	36,069
Rental property	5.4	13,000
Other real estate	5.1	13,000
U.S. savings bonds	8.0	525
IRA or KEOGH accounts	7.8	7,000

Includes passbook savings accounts, money market deposit accounts, certificates of deposit, and interest-earning checking accounts.
**Includes money market funds, U.S. government securities, municipal and corporate bonds, and other interest-earning assets.*
Note: (-) means number in sample is too small to make a reliable estimate.
Source: Bureau of the Census, Internet web site, http://www.census.gov

Average and Indexed Spending of Hispanic Households, 1994

(average annual expenditures of total and Hispanic consumer units, and indexed expenditures of Hispanic consumer units, 1994)

	average spending of total consumer units	Hispanic consumer units	
		average spending	indexed spending*
No. of consumer units (in thousands)	102,210	7,730	-
Average before-tax income	$36,838.00	$26,821.00	73
Total average annual spending	31,750.63	26,437.49	83
FOOD	**$4,410.52**	**$4,495.88**	**102**
Food at home	2,712.05	3,322.31	123
Cereals and bakery products	428.68	480.09	112
Cereals and cereal products	161.74	228.38	141
Flour	7.60	20.39	268
Prepared flour mixes	12.79	14.39	113
Ready-to-eat and cooked cereals	98.27	117.22	119
Rice	15.43	38.36	249
Pasta, cornmeal, other cereal products	27.65	38.02	138
Bakery products	266.93	251.71	94
Bread	76.22	89.95	118
White bread	37.65	45.95	122
Bread, other than white	38.57	43.90	114
Crackers and cookies	62.56	54.79	88
Cookies	42.97	42.37	99
Crackers	19.59	12.42	63
Frozen and refrigerated bakery products	21.56	15.02	70
Other bakery products	106.59	92.06	86
Biscuits and rolls	35.96	26.50	74
Cakes and cupcakes	31.19	31.35	101
Bread and cracker products	4.72	2.41	51
Sweetrolls, coffee cakes, doughnuts	21.92	22.44	102
Pies, tarts, turnovers	12.80	9.37	73
Meats, poultry, fish, and eggs	732.45	1,027.96	140
Beef	226.76	364.23	161
Ground beef	88.45	132.97	150
Roast	39.41	53.06	135
Chuck roast	12.26	15.46	126
Round roast	14.84	23.07	155
Other roast	12.31	14.53	118
Steak	84.75	148.70	175
Round steak	16.00	42.22	264

(continued)

(continued from previous page)

	average spending of total consumer units	Hispanic consumer units	
		average spending	indexed spending*
Sirloin steak	$24.44	$43.00	176
Other steak	44.31	63.47	143
Other beef	14.15	29.51	209
Pork	155.74	199.58	128
Bacon	22.78	25.55	112
Pork chops	39.32	53.70	137
Ham	36.88	42.86	116
Ham, not canned	34.16	39.10	114
Canned ham	2.72	3.76	138
Sausage	22.82	24.06	105
Other pork	33.93	53.40	157
Other meats	93.95	114.07	121
Frankfurters	18.76	24.42	130
Lunch meats (cold cuts)	65.66	67.88	103
Bologna, liverwurst, salami	23.73	33.36	141
Other lunch meats	41.93	34.52	82
Lamb, organ meats, and others	9.53	21.77	228
Lamb and organ meats	9.35	21.25	227
Mutton, goat, and game	0.18	0.53	294
Poultry	136.58	180.34	132
Fresh and frozen chickens	107.89	162.48	151
Fresh and frozen whole chicken	29.56	51.70	175
Fresh and frozen chicken parts	78.33	110.78	141
Other poultry	28.69	17.86	62
Fish and seafood	89.43	105.88	118
Canned fish and seafood	15.03	16.51	110
Fresh fish and shellfish	51.26	72.83	142
Frozen fish and shellfish	23.15	16.54	71
Eggs	30.00	63.86	213
Dairy products	288.92	340.78	118
Fresh milk and cream	127.13	182.70	144
Fresh milk, all types	118.94	174.78	147
Cream	8.19	7.92	97
Other dairy products	161.79	158.08	98
Butter	11.65	14.84	127
Cheese	81.83	85.59	105
Ice cream and related products	47.64	38.71	81
Miscellaneous dairy products	20.66	18.94	92
Fruits and vegetables	436.57	568.05	130
Fresh fruits	133.02	183.96	138
Apples	25.37	30.74	121

(continued)

(continued from previous page)

	average spending of total consumer units	Hispanic consumer units	
		average spending	indexed spending*
Bananas	$29.66	$48.63	164
Oranges	16.36	23.98	147
Citrus fruits, excluding oranges	10.96	17.48	159
Other fresh fruits	50.67	63.13	125
Fresh vegetables	134.89	190.19	141
Potatoes	28.01	33.54	120
Lettuce	17.38	23.96	138
Tomatoes	21.01	42.30	201
Other fresh vegetables	68.50	90.40	132
Processed fruits	93.08	111.13	119
Frozen fruits and fruit juices	16.28	17.51	108
Frozen orange juice	9.49	10.43	110
Frozen fruits	1.60	1.33	83
Frozen fruit juices	5.19	5.75	111
Canned fruit	14.23	11.06	78
Dried fruit	5.89	5.15	87
Fresh fruit juices	17.90	23.99	134
Canned and bottled fruit juices	38.78	53.42	138
Processed vegetables	75.57	82.76	110
Frozen vegetables	24.83	17.99	72
Canned and dried vegetables and juices	50.74	64.78	128
Canned beans	10.44	12.00	115
Canned corn	6.81	7.88	116
Other canned and dried vegetables	27.05	38.13	141
Frozen vegetable juices	0.23	0.10	43
Fresh and canned vegetable juices	6.21	6.66	107
Other food at home	825.43	905.43	110
Sugar and other sweets	105.25	116.24	110
Candy and chewing gum	62.32	58.05	93
Sugar	18.31	30.47	166
Artificial sweeteners	3.39	4.50	133
Jams, preserves, other sweets	21.23	23.21	109
Fats and oils	79.25	107.17	135
Margarine	14.16	11.02	78
Fats and oils	23.09	55.39	240
Salad dressings	23.75	25.26	106
Nondairy cream and imitation milk	6.56	4.71	72
Peanut butter	11.70	10.80	92
Miscellaneous foods	361.62	389.48	108
Frozen prepared foods	66.14	40.21	61
Frozen meals	21.43	11.10	52
Other frozen prepared foods	44.71	29.12	65

(continued)

(continued from previous page)

	average spending of total consumer units	Hispanic consumer units	
		average spending	indexed spending*
Canned and packaged soups	$29.55	$27.68	94
Potato chips, nuts, and other snacks	74.07	57.30	77
Potato chips and other snacks	58.18	43.68	75
Nuts	15.89	13.62	86
Condiments and seasonings	79.74	77.99	98
Salt, spices and other seasonings	19.30	24.50	127
Olives, pickles, relishes	10.16	6.32	62
Sauces and gravies	36.43	36.40	100
Baking needs and misc. products	13.85	10.77	78
Other canned/packaged prepared foods	112.12	186.29	166
Prepared salads	10.97	5.12	47
Prepared desserts	7.99	7.49	94
Baby food	28.11	54.59	194
Miscellaneous prepared foods	65.05	119.10	183
Nonalcoholic beverages	232.89	266.99	115
Cola	89.45	101.19	113
Other carbonated drinks	38.89	41.75	107
Coffee	43.01	44.48	103
Roasted coffee	29.13	25.66	88
Instant and freeze-dried coffee	13.88	18.83	136
Noncarb. fruit flavored drinks incl. non-frozen lemonade	21.86	35.82	164
Tea	16.25	14.53	89
Nonalcoholic beer	0.66	-	-
Other nonalcoholic beverages	22.77	29.21	128
Food prepared by cu on out-of-town trips	46.41	25.55	55
Food away from home	**1,698.46**	**1,173.57**	**69**
Meals at restaurants, carry-outs, other	1,306.21	1,000.31	77
Lunch	451.76	384.34	85
Dinner	651.79	460.72	71
Snacks and nonalcoholic beverages	101.72	71.71	70
Breakfast and brunch	100.95	83.53	83
Board (including at school)	50.72	9.17	18
Catered affairs	56.09	13.25	24
Food on out-of-town trips	207.89	82.65	40
School lunches	53.76	48.64	90
Meals as pay	23.79	19.55	82
ALCOHOLIC BEVERAGES	**$278.03**	**$210.75**	**76**
At home	**165.13**	**150.36**	**91**
Beer and ale	99.68	124.58	125

(continued)

(continued from previous page)

	average spending of total consumer units	Hispanic consumer units	
		average spending	indexed spending*
Whiskey	$13.68	$4.51	33
Wine	36.41	15.65	43
Other alcoholic beverages	15.35	5.63	37
Away from home	**112.91**	**60.39**	**53**
Beer and ale	38.56	20.28	53
Wine	15.79	11.97	76
Other alcoholic beverages	27.96	15.40	55
Alcoholic beverages purchased on trips	30.61	12.74	42
HOUSING	**$10,106.32**	**$8,938.33**	**88**
Shelter	**5,686.26**	**5,314.04**	**93**
Owned dwellings**	3,491.71	2,312.05	66
Mortgage interest and charges	1,918.71	1,557.12	81
Mortgage interest	1,822.54	1,488.31	82
Interest paid, home equity loan	44.51	30.97	70
Interest paid, home equity line of credit	51.11	37.84	74
Prepayment penalty charges	0.55	-	-
Property taxes	921.61	449.58	49
Maintenance, repairs, insurance, and other expenses	651.39	305.36	47
Homeowners and related insurance	207.71	124.58	60
Fire and extended coverage	5.95	1.11	19
Homeowners insurance	201.76	123.47	61
Ground rent	37.79	36.37	96
Maintenance and repair services	313.66	81.92	26
Painting and papering	44.00	10.10	23
Plumbing and water heating	36.33	13.12	36
Heat, air conditioning, electrical work	55.27	15.32	28
Roofing and gutters	50.96	15.75	31
Other repair and maintenance services	108.66	16.37	15
Repair and replacement of hard surface flooring	16.78	10.70	64
Repair of built-in appliances	1.67	0.57	34
Maintenance and repair materials	71.89	49.38	69
Paint, wallpaper, and supplies	18.40	15.68	85
Tools and equipment for painting and wallpapering	1.98	1.68	85
Plumbing supplies and equipment	8.59	4.47	52
Electrical supplies, heating/ cooling equipment	5.12	2.71	53
Material for hard surface flooring, repair and replacement	5.01	12.02	240

(continued)

(continued from previous page)

	average spending of total consumer units	Hispanic consumer units	
		average spending	indexed spending*
Material and equipment for roofing and gutters	$5.36	$2.50	47
Plaster, paneling, siding, windows, doors, screens, awnings	11.75	4.17	35
Patio, walk, fence, driveway, masonry, brick, stucco materials	0.47	0.45	96
Material for landscape maintenance	1.47	1.14	78
Miscellaneous supplies and equipment	13.73	4.56	33
Material for insulation, other maintenance and repair	9.37	3.55	38
Material to finish basement, remodel rooms, etc. (owner)	4.37	1.00	23
Property management and security	20.16	12.94	64
Property management	12.17	7.70	63
Management and upkeep services for security	7.99	5.24	66
Parking	0.18	0.17	94
Rented dwellings	1,799.39	2,873.39	160
Rent	1,728.66	2,773.85	160
Rent as pay	42.90	78.91	184
Maintenance, repairs, insurance, and other expenses	27.84	20.63	74
Tenant's insurance	8.99	4.20	47
Maintenance and repair services	10.13	8.35	82
Repair or maintenance services	9.07	7.09	78
Repair and replacement of hard surface flooring	0.94	0.61	65
Repair of built-in appliances	0.12	0.66	550
Maintenance and repair materials	8.72	8.08	93
Paint, wallpaper, and supplies	1.85	4.14	224
Tools and equipment for painting and wallpapering	0.20	0.44	220
Plaster, paneling, roofing, gutters, etc.	1.13	1.39	123
Patio, walk, fence, driveway, masonry, brick, stucco materials	0.08	0.01	13
Plumbing supplies and equipment	0.69	0.22	32
Electrical supplies, heating/ cooling equipment	1.14	0.02	2
Miscellaneous supplies and equipment	2.90	0.21	7
Material for insulation, other maintenance and repair	0.99	0.21	21

(continued)

(continued from previous page)

	average spending of total consumer units	Hispanic consumer units	
		average spending	indexed spending*
Material for additions, finishing basements, remodeling rooms	$1.40	-	-
Construction materials for jobs not started	0.51	-	-
Material for hard surface flooring	0.46	$1.48	322
Material for landscape maintenance	0.26	0.16	62
Other lodging	395.16	128.59	33
Owned vacation homes	117.35	46.58	40
Mortgage interest and charges	41.73	13.63	33
Mortgage interest	38.43	13.16	34
Interest paid, home equity loan	0.49	0.47	96
Interest paid, home equity line of credit	2.81	-	-
Property taxes	49.87	27.48	55
Maintenance, insurance, and other expenses	25.75	5.47	21
Homeowners and related insurance	7.33	1.63	22
Homeowners insurance	7.04	1.26	18
Fire and extended coverage	0.29	0.37	128
Ground rent	3.27	-	-
Maintenance and repair services	10.66	3.84	36
Maintenance and repair materials	1.24	-	-
Property management and security	3.20	-	-
Property management	2.30	-	-
Management and upkeep services for security	0.90	-	-
Parking	0.05	-	-
Housing while attending school	60.57	8.88	15
Lodging on out-of-town trips	217.24	73.13	34
Utilities, fuels, and public services	**2,188.56**	**1,962.16**	**90**
Natural gas	282.73	220.08	78
Electricity	861.50	713.69	83
Fuel oil and other fuels	97.97	18.62	19
Fuel oil	59.72	11.48	19
Coal	1.46	-	-
Bottled/tank gas	30.20	5.96	20
Wood and other fuels	6.59	1.17	18
Telephone services	689.82	792.60	115
Telephone services in home city, excl. mobile car phones	676.16	782.04	116
Telephone services for mobile car phones	13.66	10.56	77
Water and other public services	256.53	217.18	85

(continued)

(continued from previous page)

	average spending of total consumer units	Hispanic consumer units	
		average spending	indexed spending*
Water and sewerage maintenance	$183.05	$152.94	84
Trash and garbage collection	72.27	63.90	88
Septic tank cleaning	1.22	0.33	27
Household services	**490.15**	**353.61**	**72**
Personal services	229.80	203.49	89
Babysitting and child care in own home	47.24	43.63	92
Babysitting and child care in someone else's home	32.71	69.16	211
Care for elderly, invalids, handicapped, etc.	19.25	1.36	7
Day care centers, nursery and preschools	130.60	89.33	68
Other household expenses	260.35	150.12	58
Housekeeping services	85.14	64.61	76
Gardening, lawn care service	69.26	31.87	46
Water softening service	2.68	1.36	51
Household laundry and dry cleaning (nonclothing), not coin-operated	1.80	0.74	41
Coin-operated household laundry and dry cleaning (nonclothing)	5.34	12.74	239
Termite/pest control maintenance	6.84	6.96	102
Other home services	19.44	9.66	50
Termite/pest control products	0.27	0.25	93
Moving, storage, and freight express	26.91	8.10	30
Appliance repair, including service center	14.21	7.83	55
Reupholstering and furniture repair	10.19	2.53	25
Repairs/rentals of lawn, garden equipment, hand or power tools, other hh equip.	8.09	0.65	8
Appliance rental	1.57	2.25	143
Rental of office equipment for nonbusiness use	0.27	0.15	56
Repair of miscellaneous household equip. and furnishings	6.91	0.19	3
Repair of computer systems for nonbusiness use	1.42	0.24	17
Housekeeping supplies	**393.32**	**357.80**	**91**
Laundry and cleaning supplies	109.37	140.50	128
Soaps and detergents	62.00	91.78	148
Other laundry cleaning products	47.37	48.72	103
Other household products	173.91	170.87	98
Cleansing and toilet tissue, paper towels and napkins	55.89	70.50	126

(continued)

(continued from previous page)

	average spending of total consumer units	Hispanic consumer units	
		average spending	indexed spending*
Miscellaneous household products	$73.73	$56.13	76
Lawn and garden supplies	44.29	44.24	100
Postage and stationery	110.05	46.43	42
Stationery, stationery supplies, giftwrap	58.09	25.40	44
Postage	51.96	21.03	40
Household furnishings and equipment	**1,348.04**	**950.72**	**71**
Household textiles	99.52	93.51	94
Bathroom linens	12.63	8.69	69
Bedroom linens	48.69	62.07	127
Kitchen and dining room linens	6.87	6.57	96
Curtains and draperies	18.55	8.23	44
Slipcovers, decorative pillows	1.93	2.68	139
Sewing materials for household items	9.84	4.48	46
Other linens	0.99	0.78	79
Furniture	318.43	286.63	90
Mattress and springs	41.64	38.32	92
Other bedroom furniture	51.84	52.30	101
Sofas	78.50	75.40	96
Living room chairs	33.00	16.72	51
Living room tables	14.61	17.67	121
Kitchen and dining room furniture	48.70	43.51	89
Infants' furniture	6.12	6.15	100
Outdoor furniture	11.11	7.74	70
Wall units, cabinets and other furniture	32.92	28.81	88
Floor coverings	119.76	17.19	14
Major appliances	148.95	127.30	85
Dishwashers (built-in), garbage disposals, range hoods (renter)	0.68	0.66	97
Dishwashers (built-in), garbage disposals, range hoods (owner)	10.34	0.45	4
Refrigerators and freezers (renter)	6.92	10.97	159
Refrigerators and freezers (owner)	39.28	34.05	87
Washing machines (renter)	5.98	11.95	200
Washing machines (owner)	14.04	14.27	102
Clothes dryers (renter)	3.98	1.73	43
Clothes dryers (owner)	8.96	13.14	147
Cooking stoves, ovens (renter)	2.29	4.68	204
Cooking stoves, ovens (owner)	21.32	9.99	47
Microwave ovens (renter)	3.13	3.84	123
Microwave ovens (owner)	6.15	3.95	64
Portable dishwasher (renter)	0.06	-	-

(continued)

(continued from previous page)

	average spending of total consumer units	Hispanic consumer units	
		average spending	indexed spending*
Portable dishwasher (owner)	$0.66	-	-
Window air conditioners (renter)	2.63	$3.69	140
Window air conditioners (owner)	4.49	2.70	60
Electric floor cleaning equipment	13.44	7.42	55
Sewing machines	3.21	3.16	98
Miscellaneous household appliances	1.40	0.66	47
Small appliances, misc. housewares	80.76	62.71	78
Housewares	57.18	44.81	78
Plastic dinnerware	1.50	2.14	143
China and other dinnerware	10.72	7.18	67
Flatware	4.95	3.23	65
Glassware	8.07	9.98	124
Silver serving pieces	1.67	0.21	13
Other serving pieces	1.60	0.95	59
Nonelectric cookware	14.19	6.85	48
Tableware, nonelectric kitchenware	14.48	14.26	98
Small appliances	23.57	17.90	76
Small electric kitchen appliances	17.27	13.72	79
Portable heating and cooling equipment	6.30	4.18	66
Miscellaneous household equipment	580.63	363.38	63
Window coverings	13.52	9.53	70
Infants' equipment	6.78	11.19	165
Laundry and cleaning equipment	10.48	11.49	110
Outdoor equipment	5.20	2.49	48
Clocks	4.76	1.37	29
Lamps and lighting fixtures	34.97	16.82	48
Other household decorative items	125.25	111.92	89
Telephones and accessories	38.87	9.69	25
Lawn and garden equipment	48.56	14.38	30
Power tools	13.16	5.61	43
Small miscellaneous furnishings	1.95	-	-
Hand tools	10.48	33.91	324
Indoor plants and fresh flowers	49.35	33.69	68
Closet and storage items	7.85	1.51	19
Rental of furniture	4.12	7.01	170
Luggage	7.70	3.58	46
Computers and computer hardware, nonbusiness use	112.01	37.24	33
Computer software and accessories, nonbusiness use	19.31	6.58	34
Telephone answering devices	3.87	1.56	40

(continued)

(continued from previous page)

	average spending of total consumer units	Hispanic consumer units	
		average spending	indexed spending*
Calculators	$2.18	$1.30	60
Business equipment for home use	4.93	2.76	56
Other hardware	20.66	21.97	106
Smoke alarms (owner)	0.81	0.07	9
Smoke alarms (renter)	0.15	0.12	80
Other household appliances (renter)	6.25	2.18	35
Other household appliances (owner)	1.33	2.66	200
Misc. household equipment and parts	26.12	12.76	49
APPAREL AND SERVICES	**$1,644.03**	**$1,887.58**	**115**
Men and boys	**394.67**	**558.25**	**141**
Men, aged 16 or older	304.52	376.20	124
Suits	31.94	14.46	45
Sportcoats and tailored jackets	12.96	8.03	62
Coats and jackets	26.57	40.14	151
Underwear	11.96	18.85	158
Hosiery	9.55	17.55	184
Nightwear	2.61	4.49	172
Accessories	27.69	32.11	116
Sweaters and vests	14.33	10.87	76
Active sportswear	11.70	5.42	46
Shirts	75.18	86.62	115
Pants	60.44	120.81	200
Shorts and shorts sets	14.22	13.06	92
Uniforms	3.36	3.10	92
Costumes	2.03	0.67	33
Boys, aged 2 to 15	90.15	182.05	202
Coats and jackets	6.28	7.42	118
Sweaters	2.60	3.84	148
Shirts	20.60	54.41	264
Underwear	4.04	9.64	239
Nightwear	1.78	2.28	128
Hosiery	3.23	9.61	298
Accessories	6.93	11.29	163
Suits, sportcoats, and vests	5.02	5.06	101
Pants	21.03	51.16	243
Shorts and shorts sets	9.66	18.41	191
Uniforms and active sportswear	7.63	7.44	98
Costumes	1.35	1.49	110
Women and girls	**651.83**	**529.78**	**81**
Women, aged 16 or older	552.01	401.70	73

(continued)

(continued from previous page)

	average spending of total consumer units	Hispanic consumer units	
		average spending	indexed spending*
Coats and jackets	$51.10	$47.26	92
Dresses	76.08	84.02	110
Sportcoats and tailored jackets	4.47	-	-
Sweaters and vests	35.23	8.25	23
Shirts, blouses, and tops	92.00	59.77	65
Skirts	22.91	15.77	69
Pants	57.78	51.90	90
Shorts and shorts sets	24.25	11.98	49
Active sportswear	23.62	6.31	27
Sleepwear	25.57	19.23	75
Undergarments	27.72	20.75	75
Hosiery	24.60	17.87	73
Suits	36.11	14.97	41
Accessories	47.23	38.65	82
Uniforms	1.34	4.51	337
Costumes	2.00	0.47	24
Girls, aged 2 to 15	99.81	128.07	128
Coats and jackets	7.75	7.63	98
Dresses and suits	13.82	16.03	116
Shirts, blouses, and sweaters	23.96	40.94	171
Skirts and pants	16.29	19.44	119
Shorts and shorts sets	9.02	10.65	118
Active sportswear	7.15	2.78	39
Underwear and sleepwear	7.59	8.22	108
Hosiery	5.17	9.24	179
Accessories	4.08	7.47	183
Uniforms	1.95	3.13	161
Costumes	3.06	2.53	83
Children under age 2	**79.85**	**144.95**	**182**
Coats, jackets, and snowsuits	2.72	3.63	133
Dress and outerwear	21.37	27.74	130
Underwear	46.65	99.00	212
Nightwear and loungewear	3.84	5.49	143
Accessories	5.26	9.08	173
Footwear	**253.65**	**405.54**	**160**
Men's	80.57	132.86	165
Boys'	33.02	63.30	192
Women's	114.13	154.11	135
Girls'	25.93	55.28	213
Other apparel products and services	**264.03**	**249.06**	**94**
Material for making clothes	6.85	5.48	80

(continued)

(continued from previous page)

	average spending of total consumer units	Hispanic consumer units	
		average spending	indexed spending*
Sewing patterns and notions	$2.32	$1.83	79
Watches	23.41	15.61	67
Jewelry	103.30	76.47	74
Shoe repair and other shoe services	2.97	1.10	37
Coin-operated apparel laundry and dry cleaning	36.01	92.40	257
Alteration, repair, and tailoring of apparel and accessories	6.73	3.74	56
Clothing rental	3.70	5.24	142
Watch and jewelry repair services	5.51	2.63	48
Apparel laundry, dry cleaning, not coin-operated	72.44	44.37	61
Clothing storage	0.81	0.19	23
TRANSPORTATION	**$6,044.16**	**$4,846.73**	**80**
Vehicle purchases (net outlay)	**2,724.66**	**2,161.50**	**79**
Cars and trucks, new	1,390.51	868.25	62
New cars	749.71	223.71	30
New trucks	640.80	644.54	101
Cars and trucks, used	1,289.97	1,293.25	100
Used cars	863.70	925.83	107
Used trucks	426.27	367.42	86
Other vehicles	44.18	-	-
Gasoline and motor oil	**985.91**	**905.78**	**92**
Gasoline	878.15	845.00	96
Diesel fuel	9.23	4.55	49
Gasoline on out-of-town trips	86.21	40.98	48
Gasohol	0.15	0.67	447
Motor oil	11.31	14.16	125
Motor oil on out-of-town trips	0.87	0.41	47
Other vehicle expenses	**1,952.54**	**1,480.70**	**76**
Vehicle finance charges	235.30	179.24	76
Automobile finance charges	137.45	109.06	79
Truck finance charges	86.14	64.76	75
Motorcycle and plane finance charges	0.97	0.27	28
Other vehicle finance charges	10.74	5.14	48
Maintenance and repairs	680.27	536.43	79
Coolant, additives, brake, transmission fluids	6.11	6.66	109
Tires	86.89	76.89	88

(continued)

(continued from previous page)

	average spending of total consumer units	Hispanic consumer units	
		average spending	indexed spending*
Parts, equipment, and accessories	$112.58	$45.20	40
Vehicle audio equipment, excluding labor	5.11	5.30	104
Vehicle products	4.78	3.52	74
Misc. auto repair, servicing	33.27	17.63	53
Body work and painting	34.63	32.39	94
Clutch, transmission repair	44.21	46.45	105
Drive shaft and rear-end repair	5.69	6.75	119
Brake work	42.05	29.30	70
Repair to steering or front-end	17.98	20.32	113
Repair to engine cooling system	22.08	20.36	92
Motor tune-up	41.69	37.61	90
Lube, oil change, and oil filters	38.53	25.47	66
Front-end alignment, wheel balance and rotation	9.54	3.70	39
Shock absorber replacement	6.59	5.97	91
Brake adjustment	3.69	3.36	91
Gas tank repair, replacement	2.23	-	-
Repair tires and other repair work	26.87	22.43	83
Vehicle air-conditioning repair	15.00	8.68	58
Exhaust system repair	19.74	7.05	36
Electrical system repair	30.22	25.54	85
Motor repair, replacement	65.90	83.04	126
Auto repair service policy	4.87	2.79	57
Vehicle insurance	689.64	520.64	75
Vehicle rental, leases, licenses, and other charges	347.34	244.39	70
Leased and rented vehicles	200.82	107.60	54
Rented vehicles	37.56	20.65	55
Auto rental	5.99	3.77	63
Auto rental, out-of-town trips	24.44	13.83	57
Truck rental	1.54	0.97	63
Truck rental, out-of-town trips	4.32	2.08	48
Leased vehicles	163.26	86.95	53
Car lease payments	109.24	53.14	49
Cash downpayment (car lease)	13.22	14.77	112
Termination fee (car lease)	0.37	-	-
Truck lease payments	36.55	15.68	43
Cash downpayment (truck lease)	3.86	3.37	87
Termination fee (truck lease)	0.03	-	-
State and local registration	79.21	81.79	103
Drivers' license	6.96	4.44	64
Vehicle inspection	8.36	9.52	114

(continued)

(continued from previous page)

	average spending of total consumer units	Hispanic consumer units	
		average spending	indexed spending*
Parking fees	$25.59	$19.22	75
Parking fees in home city, excluding residence	22.49	18.15	81
Parking fees, out-of-town trips	3.10	1.07	35
Tolls	9.34	10.96	117
Tolls on out-of-town trips	4.63	2.15	46
Towing charges	4.96	4.20	85
Automobile service clubs	7.47	4.52	61
Public transportation	381.05	298.76	78
Airline fares	249.48	153.03	61
Intercity bus fares	11.34	9.51	84
Intracity mass transit fares	47.65	103.06	216
Local trans. on out-of-town trips	10.35	3.92	38
Taxi fares on trips	6.08	2.30	38
Taxi fares	7.70	7.64	99
Intercity train fares	16.24	5.34	33
Ship fares	31.13	10.63	34
School bus	1.07	3.34	312
HEALTH CARE	**$1,754.74**	**$1,061.00**	**60**
Health insurance	**814.95**	**476.74**	**58**
Commercial health insurance	262.44	110.16	42
Blue Cross/Blue Shield	160.50	68.41	43
Health maintenance plans (HMOs)	122.81	146.37	119
Medicare payments	153.65	84.77	55
Commercial Medicare supplements/ other health insurance	115.55	67.02	58
Medical services	**571.04**	**397.29**	**70**
Physician's services	163.63	112.33	69
Dental services	188.04	135.24	72
Eye-care services	29.51	24.44	83
Services by professionals other than physicians	31.92	20.26	63
Lab tests, x-rays	24.95	19.64	79
Hospital room	47.81	33.26	70
Hospital services other than room	59.54	47.90	80
Care in convalescent or nursing home	13.49	0.14	1
Repair of medical equipment	0.03	-	-
Other medical care services	12.12	4.07	34
Drugs	**285.78**	**148.11**	**52**
Non-prescription drugs	76.19	66.91	88

(continued)

(continued from previous page)

	average spending of total consumer units	Hispanic consumer units	
		average spending	indexed spending*
Prescription drugs	$209.58	$81.20	39
Medical supplies	**82.98**	**38.86**	**47**
Eyeglasses and contact lenses	50.99	24.35	48
Hearing aids	0.73	-	-
Topicals and dressings	22.94	13.36	58
Medical equipment for general use	2.53	0.28	11
Supportive/convalescent medical equipment	3.83	0.69	18
Rental of medical equipment	0.68	0.01	1
Rental of supportive, convalescent medical equipment	1.28	0.18	14
ENTERTAINMENT	**$1,566.93**	**$937.28**	**60**
Fees and admissions	**439.11**	**194.13**	**44**
Recreation expenses, out-of-town trips	20.93	10.92	52
Social, recreation, civic club membership	84.23	25.07	30
Fees for participant sports	73.54	31.93	43
Participant sports, out-of-town trips	26.99	8.53	32
Movie, theater, opera, ballet	76.23	52.72	69
Movie, other admissions, out-of-town trips	36.38	15.34	42
Admission to sporting events	32.42	13.24	41
Admission to sports events, out-of-town trips	12.13	5.11	42
Fees for recreational lessons	55.31	20.35	37
Other entertainment services, out-of-town trips	20.93	10.92	52
Television, radio, and sound equipment	**533.16**	**461.14**	**86**
Televisions	370.56	321.08	87
Community antenna or cable TV	209.60	166.05	79
Black and white TV	1.79	-	-
Color TV, console	24.03	20.41	85
Color TV, portable/table model	53.02	67.17	127
VCRs and video disc players	32.24	26.59	82
Video cassettes, tapes, and discs	21.90	14.60	67
Video game hardware and software	19.21	14.54	76
Repair of TV, radio, and sound equipment	8.43	10.24	121
Rental of televisions	0.33	1.50	455
Radios and sound equipment	162.60	140.06	86
Radios	9.21	11.18	121
Tape recorders and players	6.05	-	-
Sound components, component systems	30.28	21.91	72
Miscellaneous sound equipment	1.18	0.04	3

(continued)

(continued from previous page)

	average spending of total consumer units	Hispanic consumer units	
		average spending	indexed spending*
Sound equipment accessories	$4.75	$5.61	118
Compact disc, tape, record, and video mail-order clubs	12.08	10.38	86
Records, CDs, audio tapes, needles	36.16	31.51	87
Rental of VCR, radio, sound equipment	0.36	0.06	17
Musical instruments and accessories	17.02	11.62	68
Rental and repair of musical instruments	1.92	1.68	88
Rental of video cassettes, tapes, films, and discs	43.58	46.07	106
Pets, toys, and playground equipment	**288.73**	**171.05**	**59**
Pets	165.03	81.93	50
Pet food	75.80	45.26	60
Pet purchase, supplies, and medicines	26.15	19.32	74
Pet services	15.53	3.46	22
Veterinary services	47.56	13.89	29
Toys, games, hobbies, and tricycles	121.11	86.49	71
Playground equipment	2.59	2.63	102
Other entertainment equipment, supplies, and services	**305.92**	**110.96**	**36**
Unmotored recreational vehicles	27.76	1.33	5
Boats without motor and boat trailer	5.13	-	-
Trailers and other attachable campers	22.63	1.33	6
Motorized recreational vehicles	81.56	12.21	15
Motorized campers	16.55	-	-
Other motorized recreational vehicles	22.84	12.21	53
Boats with motor	42.17	-	-
Rental of recreational vehicles	2.33	-	-
Outboard motors	1.79	-	-
Docking and landing fees	5.59	-	-
Sports, recreation, exercise equipment	107.91	43.61	40
Athletic gear, game tables, and exercise equipment	51.01	23.94	47
Bicycles	13.36	6.83	51
Camping equipment	3.23	1.82	56
Hunting and fishing equipment	18.99	3.13	16
Winter sports equipment	5.08	2.48	49
Water sports equipment	6.03	3.00	50
Other sports equipment	8.44	2.25	27
Rental and repair of sports equipment	1.77	0.17	10

(continued)

	average spending of total consumer units	Hispanic consumer units	
		average spending	indexed spending*
Photographic equipment, supplies, and services	$70.55	$49.74	71
Film	19.61	11.80	60
Other photographic supplies	0.36	0.23	64
Film processing	27.15	16.03	59
Repair and rental of photographic equip.	0.32	0.11	34
Photographic equipment	12.50	6.54	52
Photographer fees	10.60	15.04	142
Fireworks	1.58	-	-
Souvenirs	0.51	-	-
Visual goods	1.77	1.17	66
Pinball and electronic video games	4.58	2.90	63
PERSONAL CARE PRODUCTS AND SERVICES	**$396.66**	**$453.73**	**114**
Personal care products	**219.22**	**308.10**	**141**
Hair care products	46.35	57.57	124
Nonelectric articles for the hair	6.36	10.55	166
Wigs and hairpieces	0.83	0.11	13
Oral hygiene products, articles	23.10	25.20	109
Shaving needs	12.07	16.82	139
Cosmetics, perfume, and bath preparation	99.46	169.78	171
Deodorant, feminine hygiene products, and misc.	26.87	25.53	95
Electric personal care appliances	4.18	2.56	61
Personal care services	**177.45**	**145.63**	**82**
Personal care services/female	87.44	41.18	47
Personal care services/male	89.89	104.45	116
Repair of personal care appliances	0.12	-	-
READING	**$164.80**	**$75.61**	**46**
Newspapers, subscription	52.48	20.35	39
Newspapers, non-subscription	17.83	12.89	72
Magazines, subscription	24.59	9.26	38
Magazines, non-subscription	12.19	7.07	58
Newsletters	0.11	-	-
Books purchased through book clubs	10.51	5.93	56
Books not purchased through book clubs	45.85	19.68	43
Encyclopedia and other reference book sets	1.23	0.44	36

(continued)

(continued from previous page)

	average spending of total consumer units	Hispanic consumer units	
		average spending	indexed spending*
EDUCATION	**$459.88**	**$334.75**	**73**
College tuition	271.59	169.24	62
Elementary/high school tuition	64.79	72.17	111
Other school tuition	14.46	4.03	28
Other school expenses, including rentals	18.85	7.24	38
School books, supplies, equipment for college	38.29	33.85	88
School books, supplies, equipment for elementary/high school	9.51	11.06	116
School books, supplies, equipment for day care, nursery, other	3.34	2.04	61
School supplies, etc., unspecified	39.04	35.13	90
TOBACCO PRODUCTS AND SMOKING SUPPLIES	**$258.55**	**$137.13**	**53**
Cigarettes	236.05	128.54	54
Other tobacco products	21.06	7.33	35
Smoking accessories	1.44	1.26	88
MISCELLANEOUS EXPENSES	**$748.51**	**$578.74**	**77**
Miscellaneous fees, pari-mutuel losses	44.69	22.94	51
Legal fees	112.87	84.32	75
Funeral expenses	85.75	47.98	56
Safe deposit box rental	5.69	2.37	42
Checking accounts, other bank service charges	26.49	26.17	99
Cemetery lots, vaults, and maintenance fees	18.48	19.63	106
Accounting fees	43.06	22.93	53
Miscellaneous personal services	22.50	17.04	76
Finance charges, excl. mortgage, vehicles	205.23	231.08	113
Occupational expenses	84.96	56.63	67
Expenses for other properties	93.52	44.58	48
Interest paid, home equity line of credit (other property)	0.42	-	-
Credit card memberships	4.87	3.08	63
CASH CONTRIBUTIONS	**$960.31**	**$453.38**	**47**
Cash contributions to non-cu member, incl. students, alimony, child support	265.01	194.13	73
Gifts of cash, stocks, and bonds to non-cu member	206.25	108.08	52
Contributions to charities	90.33	22.15	25
Contributions to church	363.85	118.63	33
Contributions to educational organizations	21.24	8.33	39

(continued)

(continued from previous page)

	average spending of total consumer units	Hispanic consumer units	
		average spending	indexed spending*
Contributions to political organizations	$7.17	$1.03	14
Other contributions	6.45	1.04	16
PERSONAL INSURANCE AND PENSIONS	**$2,957.19**	**$2,026.58**	**69**
Life and other personal insurances except health	**397.69**	**191.92**	**48**
Life, endowment, annuity, other personal insurance	380.59	181.30	48
Other nonhealth insurance	17.11	10.62	62
Pensions and Social Security	**2,559.49**	**1,834.66**	**72**
Deductions for government retirement	70.79	48.71	69
Deductions for railroad retirement	4.53	10.70	236
Deductions for private pensions	273.66	128.29	47
Non-payroll deposit to retirement plans	298.11	66.89	22
Deductions for Social Security	1,912.40	1,580.06	83
GIFTS*	**$1,007.51**	**$595.06**	**59**
Food	**84.05**	**39.65**	**47**
Cakes and cupcakes	2.44	3.54	145
Candy and chewing gum	9.86	9.15	93
Potato chips and other snacks	2.04	0.76	37
Board (including at school)	27.35	2.78	10
Catered affairs	18.48	1.77	10
Housing	**262.20**	**114.56**	**44**
Housekeeping supplies	37.84	5.03	13
Other household products	8.28	1.02	12
Miscellaneous household products	4.99	0.41	8
Lawn and garden supplies	2.14	-	-
Postage and stationery	27.69	3.77	14
Stationery, stationery supplies, giftwraps	22.27	3.33	15
Postage	5.42	0.44	8
Household textiles	15.73	3.89	25
Bathroom linens	2.56	0.46	18
Bedroom linens	10.39	2.98	29
Appliances and misc. housewares	26.36	26.05	99
Major appliances	5.46	8.45	155
Small appliances and misc. housewares	20.90	17.60	84
China and other dinnerware	3.43	1.74	51
Glassware	4.29	6.73	157
Nonelectric cookware	2.54	0.09	4

(continued)

(continued from previous page)

	average spending of total consumer units	Hispanic consumer units	
		average spending	indexed spending*
Tableware, nonelectric kitchenware	$3.07	$6.29	205
Small electric kitchen appliances	3.79	2.36	62
Miscellaneous household equipment	65.40	32.21	49
Lamps and lighting fixtures	3.66	3.59	98
Other household decorative items	24.59	12.38	50
Lawn and garden equipment	2.30	-	-
Indoor plants and flowers	16.77	8.21	49
Computers and computer hardware, nonbusiness use	5.60	-	-
Other housing	116.87	47.38	41
Repair or maintenance services	5.00	0.86	17
Housing while attending school	36.93	6.02	16
Lodging on out-of-town trips	2.49	0.05	2
Electricity (renter)	9.95	4.52	45
Telephone services in home city, excl. mobile car phone	12.04	8.57	71
Day-care centers, nursery, preschools	12.40	8.92	72
Housekeeping services	5.52	0.16	3
Gardening, lawn-care services	2.48	-	-
Moving, storage, freight express	2.29	0.45	20
Sofas	2.72	0.15	6
Kitchen, dining room furniture	2.26	2.52	112
Infants' furniture	2.18	1.98	91
Apparel and services	**246.23**	**270.24**	**110**
Males, aged 2 or older	64.05	102.74	160
Men's coats and jackets	4.46	19.73	442
Men's accessories	5.71	8.83	155
Men's sweaters and vests	3.26	0.89	27
Men's active sportswear	2.24	0.81	36
Men's shirts	15.44	22.16	144
Men's pants	5.72	17.18	300
Boys' shirts	4.95	3.90	79
Boys' accessories	2.02	0.90	45
Boys' pants	3.73	2.50	67
Boys' shorts and short sets	2.07	3.83	185
Females, aged 2 or older	93.94	64.80	69
Women's coats and jackets	10.55	1.98	19
Women's dresses	9.92	2.06	21
Women's vests and sweaters	6.44	2.01	31
Women's shirts, tops, blouses	14.50	15.72	108
Women's pants	5.12	4.60	90

(continued)

(continued from previous page)

	average spending of total consumer units	Hispanic consumer units	
		average spending	indexed spending*
Women's active sportswear	$3.30	$2.26	68
Women's sleepwear	5.85	4.40	75
Women's undergarments	2.30	1.15	50
Women's suits	2.42	1.32	55
Women's accessories	10.27	8.27	81
Girls' dresses and suits	3.23	1.76	54
Girls' shirts, blouses, sweaters	6.04	8.26	137
Girls' skirts and pants	2.23	1.75	78
Children under age 2	34.90	42.16	121
Infant dresses, outerwear	13.81	12.30	89
Infant underwear	14.38	21.21	147
Infant nightwear, loungewear	2.50	3.36	134
Infant accessories	2.78	3.65	131
Other apparel products and services	53.33	60.54	114
Jewelry and watches	25.94	10.97	42
Watches	3.40	2.30	68
Jewelry	22.54	8.67	38
All other apparel products and services	27.40	49.57	181
Men's footwear	8.18	18.35	224
Boys' footwear	4.83	6.22	129
Women's footwear	7.59	16.98	224
Girls' footwear	4.94	7.77	157
Transportation	**56.11**	**20.62**	**37**
New cars	7.43	-	-
Used cars	11.40	-	-
Gasoline on out-of-town trips	13.14	4.35	33
Airline fares	9.19	5.04	55
Ship fares	4.74	4.51	95
Health care	**34.69**	**23.69**	**68**
Physicians services	2.66	2.08	78
Dental services	3.43	6.67	194
Hospital room	3.66	5.75	157
Hospital service other than room	3.68	5.62	153
Care in convalescent or nursing home	11.30	-	-
Prescription drugs	2.28	0.40	18
Entertainment	**83.57**	**37.73**	**45**
Toys, games, hobbies, tricycles	32.48	24.57	76
Other entertainment	51.08	13.16	26
Movie, other admission, out-of-town trips	7.27	1.80	25

(continued)

(continued from previous page)

	average spending of total consumer units	Hispanic consumer units	
		average spending	indexed spending*
Admission to sports events,			
out-of-town trips	$2.42	$0.60	25
Fees for recreational lessons	4.96	1.59	32
Community antenna or cable TV	2.81	1.78	63
Color TV, portable/table model	2.01	4.77	237
VCRs, video disc players	2.67	-	-
Video game hardware and software	2.00	0.69	35
Radios	4.70	-	-
Sound components and component systems	2.05	0.59	29
Veterinary services	3.48	0.12	3
Athletic gear, game tables, and			
exercise equipment	3.46	0.24	7
Education	**114.09**	**17.02**	**15**
College tuition	86.94	10.48	12
Elementary, high school tuition	6.43	-	-
Other school tuition	3.09	-	-
Other school expenses including rentals	4.72	0.05	1
School books, supplies, equipment for college	6.56	3.70	56
School supplies, etc., unspecified	5.32	2.02	38
All other gifts	**126.58**	**71.55**	**57**

* The index compares the spending of the average Hispanic consumer unit with the spending of the average consumer unit by dividing Hispanic spending by average spending in each category and multiplying by 100. An index of 100 means that Hispanic spending in that category equals average spending. An index of 132 means that Hispanic spending is 32 percent above average, while an index of 75 means that Hispanic spending is 25 percent below average.
** This figure does not include the amount paid for mortgage principal, which is considered an asset.
*** Expenditures on gifts are also included in the preceding product and service categories. Food spending, for example, includes the amount spent on food gifts. Only gift categories with average spending of $2.00 or more by the average consumer unit are shown.
Note: The Bureau of Labor Statistics uses consumer units rather than households as the sampling unit in the Consumer Expenditure Survey. For the definition of consumer unit, see the Glossary. Expenditures listed for items in a given category may not add to the total for that category because the listing is incomplete. (-) means number in sample is too small to make a reliable estimate.
Source: Bureau of Labor Statistics, unpublished tables from the 1994 Consumer Expenditure Survey

Native Americans

■ Numbering 2.3 million, Native Americans are the smallest racial minority in the U.S., accounting for just 0.9 percent of all Americans. The largest tribe is the Cherokee, accounting for 19 percent of all Native Americans.

■ While most Native Americans are high school graduates, their educational attainment, which varies greatly by tribe, is far below that of the average American.

■ On many measures, the health of Native Americans is better than that of the average American. They are less likely to die from lung cancer, breast cancer, or cardiovascular diseases, and AIDS is relatively rare among this population segment.

■ Native American households are far more likely than American households overall to include children. Consequently, household size is larger for Native American households than for the average household.

■ Fully 30 percent of Native Americans are poor, with poverty greatest among those under age 18. Poverty rates vary greatly by tribe, however.

■ More than 40 percent of Native American workers can be found in three occupations: precision production, craft, and repair; administrative support; and service occupations.

Note: There are no spending or wealth data for Native Americans.

Native Americans:

Education

While most Native Americans are high school graduates, their educational attainment is far below that of the average American. In 1990, 66 percent of Native Americans were high school graduates, versus nearly 80 percent of the total population. Only 9 percent were college graduates, far below the 22 percent of the total population. But the educational attainment of Native Americans varies greatly by tribe. The Osage, for example, are more likely to be high school graduates than the average American.

Over 100,000 Native Americans were enrolled in college in 1993, accounting for just under 1 percent of total college enrollment. Among Native Americans in college, women greatly outnumber men. Native Americans earned 5,671 bachelor's degrees in 1992-93, just 0.5 percent of all bachelor's degrees awarded that year.

Educational Attainment of Native Americans by Sex, 1990

(number and percent distribution of Native Americans aged 25 or older, by educational attainment and sex, 1990; numbers in thousands)

	total		men		women	
	number	*percent*	*number*	*percent*	*number*	*percent*
Total, aged 25 or older	1,041	100.0%	498	100.0%	543	100.0%
Not a high school graduate	358	34.4	170	34.2	188	34.6
High school graduate or more	683	65.6	328	65.8	356	65.4
Some college or associate's degree	284	27.3	134	26.9	151	27.7
Bachelor's degree or more	97	9.4	50	10.1	47	8.7

Source: Bureau of the Census, Characteristics of American Indians by Tribe and Language, *1990 Census of Population, CP-3-7, 1994*

Educational Attainment of Native Americans by Tribe, 1990

(percent of Native Americans aged 25 or older who are high school or college graduates, by 25 largest tribes, 1990)

	high school graduates	college graduates
Total, aged 25 or older	65.6%	9.4%
Cherokee	68.2	11.1
Navajo	51.0	4.5
Sioux	69.7	8.9
Chippewa	69.7	8.2
Choctaw	70.3	13.3
Pueblo	71.5	7.3
Apache	63.8	6.9
Iroquois	71.9	11.3
Lumbee	51.6	9.4
Creek	73.2	12.7
Blackfoot	71.4	9.5
Canadian and Latin American	59.0	10.5
Chickasaw	74.2	14.6
Tohono O'Odham	53.4	1.2
Potawatomi	76.5	14.4
Seminole	70.5	11.1
Pima	47.5	2.8
Tlingit	73.3	6.7
Alaskan Athabaskans	65.1	5.1
Cheyenne	69.5	6.9
Comanche	74.2	14.2
Paiute	66.2	5.4
Osage	86.7	22.1
Puget Sound Salish	69.1	7.7
Yaqui	48.5	4.3

Source: Bureau of the Census, Characteristics of American Indians by Tribe and Language, *1990 Census of Population, CP-3-7, 1994*

Educational Attainment of Native Americans by State, 1990

(percent of Native Americans aged 25 or older who are high school or college graduates, by state, 1990)

	high school graduates	college graduates		high school graduates	college graduates
United States	65.5%	9.3%	Missouri	65.1%	11.0%
Alabama	64.9	11.6	Montana	68.1	7.9
Alaska	63.1	4.1	Nebraska	69.0	8.8
Arizona	52.1	4.6	Nevada	69.8	8.0
Arkansas	65.4	9.8	New Hampshire	65.9	16.0
California	71.4	11.1	New Jersey	66.9	14.8
Colorado	73.9	12.1	New Mexico	58.2	5.8
Connecticut	68.9	12.5	New York	65.2	13.4
Delaware	62.0	10.2	North Carolina	51.5	7.9
District of Columbia	66.3	17.7	North Dakota	64.3	8.3
Florida	68.2	11.5	Ohio	65.3	8.3
Georgia	71.6	12.5	Oklahoma	68.1	10.8
Hawaii	84.4	17.7	Oregon	71.0	8.3
Idaho	68.1	7.2	Pennsylvania	67.8	12.0
Illinois	71.4	13.4	Rhode Island	64.5	8.3
Indiana	65.0	8.4	South Carolina	62.5	10.9
Iowa	67.6	9.7	South Dakota	62.5	6.8
Kansas	75.4	10.8	Tennessee	63.1	10.5
Kentucky	59.8	8.0	Texas	70.9	13.9
Louisiana	49.1	5.5	Utah	59.3	6.4
Maine	69.9	7.7	Vermont	66.8	11.1
Maryland	73.4	19.7	Virginia	70.7	14.7
Massachusetts	71.1	14.9	Washington	72.3	9.1
Michigan	67.8	7.6	West Virginia	57.9	6.5
Minnesota	68.2	7.7	Wisconsin	66.8	5.5
Mississippi	57.4	8.1	Wyoming	68.2	6.2

Source: National Center for Education Statistics, Digest of Education Statistics 1993, *NCES 93-292, 1993*

School Enrollment of Native Americans by Age, 1990

(number and percent of Native Americans aged 3 or older enrolled in school as of April 1990, by age; numbers in thousands)

	number	percent
Total, aged 3 or older	612	33.5%
Aged 3 and 4	18	24.6
Aged 5 to 14	343	92.6
Aged 15 to 19	130	75.1
Aged 20 to 24	38	23.1
Aged 25 to 34	42	12.0
Aged 35 or older	39	5.7

Source: U.S. Bureau of the Census, Characteristics of American Indians by Tribe and Language, *1990 Census of Population, 1990 CP-3-7, 1994*

College Enrollment of Native Americans by Sex, 1993

(number of Native Americans enrolled in institutions of higher education by level of study and sex, and Native American enrollment as a percent of total enrollment, fall 1993; numbers in thousands)

	total		men		women	
	number	percent of total enrollment	number	percent of total men enrolled	number	percent of total women enrolled
Total enrolled	122	0.9%	51	0.8%	71	0.9%
Undergraduate	113	0.9	47	0.9	66	1.0
Graduate	7	0.4	3	0.4	4	0.5
First-professional	2	0.5	1	0.5	1	0.6

Source: National Center for Education Statistics, Digest of Education Statistics 1995, *NCES 95-029, 1995*

Bachelor's, Master's, and Doctoral Degrees Earned by Native Americans by Field of Study, 1992-93

(number and percent of bachelor's, master's, and doctoral degrees earned by Native Americans, by field of study, 1992-93)

	bachelor's		master's		doctoral	
	number	percent	number	percent	number	percent
Total degrees	5,671	0.5%	1,407	0.4%	106	0.3%
Agriculture and natural resources	90	0.5	10	0.3	-	-
Architecture and related programs	35	0.4	12	0.3	-	-
Area, ethnic, and cultural studies	51	0.9	10	0.7	1	0.6
Biological/life sciences	215	0.5	27	0.6	5	0.1
Business, management, and admin. services	1,051	0.4	269	0.3	3	0.2
Communications	201	0.4	10	0.2	3	1.0
Communications technologies	10	1.2	1	0.2	-	-
Computer and information sciences	83	0.3	15	0.1	1	0.1
Construction trades	1	1.4	-	-	-	-
Education	644	0.6	459	0.5	35	0.5
Engineering	180	0.3	53	0.2	2	0.0
Engineering related technologies	103	0.6	8	0.7	-	-
English language and literature	235	0.4	37	0.5	7	0.5
Foreign languages and literature	53	0.4	6	0.2	3	0.4
Health professions and related sciences	348	0.5	120	0.5	4	0.2
Home economics	59	0.4	9	0.4	-	-
Law and legal studies	12	0.6	5	0.2	1	1.2
Liberal arts and sciences	258	0.8	7	0.3	1	1.2
Library science	1	1.2	16	0.3	-	-
Mathematics	56	0.4	8	0.2	-	-
Mechanics and repairers	-	-	-	-	-	-
Multi/interdisciplinary studies	117	0.5	14	0.6	-	-
Parks, recreation, leisure and fitness	36	0.4	4	0.3	-	-
Philosophy and religion	46	0.6	5	0.4	-	-
Physical sciences	93	0.5	13	0.2	4	0.1
Precision production trades	2	0.5	-	-	-	-
Protective services	130	0.6	6	0.4	-	-
Psychology	344	0.5	61	0.6	22	0.6
Public administration and services	187	1.1	92	0.4	2	0.4
R.O.T.C. and military sciences	-	-	1	0.9	-	-
Social sciences and history	772	0.6	72	0.5	7	0.2
Theological studies/religious vocations	27	0.5	9	0.2	4	0.3
Transportation and material moving	18	0.5	1	0.2	-	-
Visual and performing arts	213	0.4	47	0.5	1	0.1

Source: National Center for Education Statistics, Digest of Education Statistics 1995, *NCES 95-029, 1995*

First-Professional Degrees Earned by Native Americans by Field of Study, 1992-93

(number and percent of first-professional degrees earned by Native Americans, by field of study, 1992-93)

	number	percent
Total degrees	368	0.5%
Dentistry (D.D.S. or D.M.D.)	10	0.3
Medicine (M.D.)	73	0.5
Optometry (O.D.)	3	0.3
Osteopathic medicine (D.O.)	9	0.6
Pharmacy (Pharm. D.)	7	0.4
Podiatry (Pod. D. or D.P. or D.P.M.)	1	0.2
Veterinary medicine (D.V.M.)	12	0.6
Chiropractic medicine (D.C. or D.C.M.)	23	0.8
Law (L.L.B. or J.D.)	213	0.5
Theology (M.Div., M.H.L., B.D., or Ord.)	15	0.3
Other	2	3.1

Source: National Center for Education Statistics, Digest of Education Statistics 1995, *NCES 95-029, 1995*

Native Americans:

Health

On many measures, the health of Native Americans is better than that of the average American. They are less likely to die from lung cancer, breast cancer, or cardiovascular diseases, and AIDS is relatively rare among this population segment.

But Native Americans are more likely to die in motor vehicle accidents than the average American. They also have an above-average incidence of tuberculosis. Teen births are common among Native Americans, with 8 percent of all births occurring to girls aged 17 or younger—63 percent higher than the proportion for the total population. Because many Native Americans are nonmetropolitan residents, only 18 percent live in counties with polluted air.

Because cancer and heart disease are less likely among Native Americans than the total population, their life expectancy at age 65 exceeds that of the average American. Native American men aged 65 can expect to live 18 more years, two years longer than the average 65-year-old man. Native American women aged 65 can expect to live 22 more years, three years longer than the average American woman.

Health Indicators for Native Americans, 1992

(selected indicators of total and Native American health status, and index of Native American health indicators to total, 1992 except where otherwise noted)

	total population indicator	Native American indicator	index
Infant mortality rate (deaths < age 1 per 1,000 live births, 1991)	8.6	11.3	131
Total deaths per 100,000 population	504.5	453.1	90
Motor vehicle crash deaths per 100,000 population	15.8	32.0	203
Work-related injury deaths per 100,000 people aged 16 or older, 1993	3.2	3.2	100
Suicides per 100,000 population	11.1	11.0	99
Homicides per 100,000 population	10.5	10.5	100
Lung cancer deaths per 100,000 population	39.3	22.2	56
Female breast cancer deaths per 100,000 women	21.9	11.0	50
Cardiovascular disease deaths per 100,000 population	180.4	132.8	74
Heart disease deaths per 100,000 population	144.3	107.1	74
Stroke deaths per 100,000 population	26.2	19.1	73
Reported incidence of AIDS per 100,000 population, 1993*	31.2	11.9	38
Reported incidence of tuberculosis per 100,000 population, 1993*	9.8	14.6	149
Reported incidence of syphilis per 100,000 population, 1993*	10.4	1.7	16
Prevalence of low birth weight, as percent of total live births	7.1	6.2	87
Births to girls aged 10 to 17, as percent of total live births	4.9	8.0	163
Percent of mothers without care, first trimester of pregnancy	22.3	37.9	170
Percent < age 18 living in poverty, 1993	22.7	-	-
Percent living in counties exceeding U.S. air quality standards, 1993	23.5	17.6	75

* Data are for the non-Hispanic population.
Note: The index is calculated by dividing the Native American figure by the total figure for each indicator and multiplying by 100. For example, the index of 131 indicates that the Native American infant mortality rate is 31 percent above the rate for all infants.
Source: National Center for Health Statistics, Health Status Indicators: Differentials by Race and Hispanic Origin, Healthy People 2000, No. 10, 1995

Disability Status of Native Americans, 1990

(number and percent of Native Americans who are disabled, by age and type of disability, 1990; numbers in thousands)

	number	percent
Persons aged 16 to 64	1,190	100.0%
With a work disability	164	13.8
In labor force	61	37.3
No work disability	1,026	86.2
In labor force	749	73.0
Persons aged 65 to 74	71	100.0
With a mobility or self-care limitation	16	22.2
Persons aged 75 or older	39	100.0
With a mobility or self-care limitation	15	37.9

Source: Bureau of the Census, Characteristics of American Indians by Tribe and Language, *1990 Census of Population, CP-3-7, 1994*

Life Expectancy of Native Americans at Birth and Age 65, 1995 to 2020

(average number of years of life remaining at birth and at age 65 for Native American males and females, 1995-2020; difference between Native American life expectancy and total life expectancy for males and females at birth and at age 65, 1995 and 2020)

	life expectancy (years)	
	males	*females*
AT BIRTH		
1995	72.0	80.4
2000	72.6	80.9
2005	73.1	81.4
2010	73.8	81.9
2015	74.4	82.3
2020	75.1	82.8
Life exp. of Native Americans		
minus life exp. of total Americans		
1995	-0.5	1.1
2020	-0.4	1.3
AT AGE 65		
1995	17.9	22.4
2000	18.2	22.7
2005	18.6	23.0
2010	18.9	23.2
2015	19.3	23.5
2020	19.7	23.8
Life exp. of Native Americans		
minus life exp. of total Americans		
1995	2.4	3.2
2020	2.1	3.2

Source: Bureau of the Census, Population Projections of the United States, by Age, Sex, Race, and Hispanic Origin: 1995 to 2050, *Current Population Reports, P25-1130, 1996*

Native Americans:
Households and Living Arrangements

There are important differences between the households of Native Americans and those of the total population. Native American households are far more likely than households overall to include children. In 1990, 45 percent of Native American households included children under age 18 compared with 35 percent of total households.

Married couples head a smaller share of Native American households—49 percent—than total households (55 percent). Female-headed families, in contrast, account for a significant 20 percent of Native American households, versus just 13 percent of total households.

Because there are more children in Native American households, household size is larger than for overall households. Fifty-five percent of Native American households and 44 percent of total households are home to three or more people.

Native American Households by Household Type, 1990

(number and percent distribution of Native American households, by type of household, 1990; numbers in thousands)

	number	percent
Total households	605	100.0%
Family households	449	74.3
With own children under age 18	272	45.0
Without own children under age 18	177	29.3
Married couples	296	48.9
With own children under age 18	172	28.5
Without own children under age 18	123	20.4
Female householder, no spouse present	118	19.5
With own children under age 18	78	13.0
Without own children under age 18	39	6.5
Male householder, no spouse present	36	5.9
Nonfamily households	156	25.7
Living alone	122	20.1

Source: Bureau of the Census, Characteristics of American Indians by Tribe and Language, *1990 Census of Population, CP-3-7, 1994*

Native American Households by Size, 1990

(number and percent distribution of Native American households, by size, 1990; numbers in thousands)

	number	percent
Total households	605	100.0%
One person	122	20.1
Two persons	153	25.2
Three persons	113	18.7
Four persons	101	16.7
Five persons	61	10.1
Six persons	30	4.9
Seven or more persons	25	4.2

Source: Bureau of the Census, Characteristics of American Indians by Tribe and Language, 1990 Census of Population, CP-3-7, 1994

Marital Status of Native Americans by Sex, 1990

(number and percent distribution of Native Americans aged 15 or older, by sex and marital status, 1990; numbers in thousands)

	number	percent
Women, aged 15 or older	706	100.0%
Never married	199	28.2
Married	325	46.0
Separated	29	4.1
Widowed	61	8.6
Divorced	93	13.1
Men, aged 15 or older	672	100.0
Never married	248	37.0
Married	318	47.3
Separated	20	2.9
Widowed	15	2.3
Divorced	71	10.6

Source: Bureau of the Census, Characteristics of American Indians by Tribe and Language, *1990 Census of Population, CP-3-7, 1994*

Native Americans:
Housing

Most Native Americans own their homes, with a homeownership rate of 53 percent. The majority of their homes are detached, single-family houses. Utility gas is the most common house heating fuel among both homeowners and renters, but over 18 percent of homeowners use wood.

Native American homeowners are more likely than any other racial or ethnic group to lack complete plumbing in their homes, with 8 percent not having hot or cold piped water, a flush toilet, or a bathtub/shower. Most Native Americans have at least one vehicle available to them and most homeowners have at least two.

Characteristics of Housing Units
Occupied by Native Americans, 1990

(number and percent distribution of housing units occupied by Native Americans, by selected housing characteristics and homeownership status, 1990; numbers in thousands except medians)

	total		owner		renter	
	number	*percent*	*number*	*percent*	*number*	*percent*
Total occupied housing units	599	100.0%	317	52.9%	282	47.1%
Median number of persons in unit	2.77	-	2.91	-	2.61	-
Median number of rooms in unit	4.7	-	5.2	-	4.1	-
Plumbing facilities						
Complete plumbing	567	94.7	292	92.2	275	97.6
Lack complete plumbing	32	5.3	25	7.8	7	2.4
Primary house heating fuel						
Utility gas	258	43.0	125	39.5	132	46.9
Electricity	145	24.2	58	18.4	87	30.8
Wood	75	12.5	59	18.5	16	5.7
Bottled tank or LP gas	69	11.5	46	14.5	23	8.3
Fuel oil, kerosene, etc.	41	6.8	23	7.3	18	6.4
Other	11	1.9	6	1.8	6	1.9
Vehicles available						
None	97	16.1	30	9.4	67	23.8
One	222	37.0	94	29.7	128	45.2
Two	187	31.2	120	37.8	67	23.9
Three or more	94	15.6	73	23.1	20	7.2

Source: Bureau of the Census, Characteristics of American Indians by Tribe and Language, *1990 Census of Population, CP-3-7, 1994*

Number of Units in Structures Occupied by Native Americans, 1990

(number and percent distribution of housing units in structures occupied by Native Americans, 1990; numbers in thousands)

	number	percent
Total occupied housing units	599	100.0%
Units in structure		
1, detached	347	57.9
1, attached	24	4.1
2 to 4	59	9.8
5 to 9	28	4.6
10 to 19	25	4.2
20 to 49	19	3.1
50 or more	14	2.3
Mobile home or trailer	75	12.4
Other	9	1.5

Source: Bureau of the Census, Internet web site, http://www.census.gov

Native Americans:
Income

The latest available income statistics for Native Americans are from the 1990 census, reporting income for 1989. According to the 1990 census, the median income of Native American households is far below the national median, $19,900 versus $30,056 in 1989. Just 1 percent of Native American households had a median income of $100,000 or more. Median household income varies by tribe, however, ranging from $29,211 for those in the Osage tribe to just $11,402 for the Tohono O'Odham.

The many female-headed households account for the low incomes of Native American households. Nearly half of Native American female-headed families have incomes under $10,000. In contrast, most Native American married couples have incomes of $25,000 or more.

Fully 30 percent of Native Americans are poor, with poverty greatest among those under age 18. Overall, 51 percent of female-headed Native American families are poor, versus just 17 percent of married couples. Poverty rates vary greatly by tribe, however. Over 50 percent of the Tohono O'Odham and Pima are poor, versus only 15 percent of Tlingit families.

Income Distribution of Native American Households, 1989

(number and percent distribution of Native American households, by income, 1989; households in thousands as of 1990)

	number	percent
Total households	605	100.0%
Under $10,000	165	27.4
$10,000 to $14,999	73	12.1
$15,000 to $24,999	123	20.3
$25,000 to $34,999	88	14.6
$35,000 to $49,999	81	13.4
$50,000 to $74,999	52	8.7
$75,000 to $99,999	14	2.3
$100,000 or more	8	1.4
Median income	$19,900	-

Source: Bureau of the Census, Characteristics of American Indians by Tribe and Language, *1990 Census of Population, CP-3-7, 1994*

Household Income of Native Americans by Tribe, 1989

(median household income of Native Americans, by 25 largest tribes, 1989)

	median income
Total	$19,900
Cherokee	21,922
Navajo	12,817
Sioux	15,611
Chippewa	18,801
Choctaw	21,640
Pueblo	19,097
Apache	18,484
Iroquois	23,460
Lumbee	21,708
Creek	21,913
Blackfoot	20,860
Canadian and Latin American	24,502
Chickasaw	23,325
Tohono O'Odham	11,402
Potawatomi	23,722
Seminole	21,633
Pima	12,063
Tlingit	28,703
Alaskan Athabaskans	17,348
Cheyenne	16,371
Comanche	22,958
Paiute	19,154
Osage	29,211
Puget Sound Salish	19,191
Yaqui	18,667

Source: Bureau of the Census, Characteristics of American Indians by Tribe and Language, *1990 Census of Population, CP-3-7, 1994*

Income Distribution of Native American Families by Family Type, 1989

(number and percent distribution of Native American families, by income and type of family, 1989; families in thousands as of 1990)

	number	percent
Total families	449	100.0%
Under $10,000	107	23.8
$10,000 to $14,999	53	11.9
$15,000 to $24,999	92	20.4
$25,000 to $34,999	69	15.3
$35,000 to $49,999	66	14.7
$50,000 to $74,999	44	9.8
$75,000 to $99,999	12	2.6
$100,000 or more	7	1.5
Median family income	$21,619	-
Married couples	296	100.0
Under $15,000	69	23.4
$15,000 to $24,999	61	20.6
$25,000 to $34,999	53	18.0
$35,000 to $49,999	56	18.9
$50,000 to $74,999	40	13.4
$75,000 or more	17	5.7
Female householders, no spouse present	118	100.0
Under $10,000	56	47.7
$10,000 to $14,999	18	15.3
$15,000 to $24,999	23	19.2
$25,000 to $49,999	17	14.8
$50,000 or more	3	3.0

Source: Bureau of the Census, Characteristics of American Indians by Tribe and Language, *1990 Census of Population, CP-3-7, 1994*

Incomes of Native Americans by Sex, 1989

(number and median income of Native Americans aged 15 or older with income, percent who are full-time workers, and median income of full-time workers, 1989; persons with income in thousands as of 1990)

	men	women
Total persons with income, aged 15 or older	581	564
Median income	$12,226	$7,327
Percent year-round, full-time workers	41.5%	30.1%
Median income of year-round, full-time workers	$22,005	$16,613

Source: Bureau of the Census, Characteristics of American Indians by Tribe and Language, *1990 Census of Population, CP-3-7, 1994*

Poverty Status of Native Americans, 1989

(number of Native American families and persons, and number and percent below poverty level by type of family and age of person, 1989; families and persons in thousands as of 1990)

	total	in poverty	
		number	percent
Total families	449	122	27.2%
Married couples	296	50	17.0
Female householders, no spouse present	118	60	50.8
Total persons	1,937	585	30.2
Under age 18	662	253	38.2
Aged 65 or older	114	33	28.5

Source: Bureau of the Census, Characteristics of American Indians by Tribe and Language, *1990 Census of Population, CP-3-7, 1994*

Native Americans in Poverty by Tribe, 1989

(number and percent of Native American families and persons below poverty level, by 25 largest tribes, 1989; families and persons in thousands as of 1990)

	families		persons	
	number	*percent*	*number*	*percent*
Total in poverty	122	27.2%	585	31.2%
Cherokee	19	19.4	79	22.0
Navajo	21	47.3	108	48.8
Sioux	9	39.4	46	44.4
Chippewa	8	31.2	35	34.3
Choctaw	4	19.9	19	23.0
Pueblo	4	31.2	18	33.2
Apache	4	31.8	19	37.5
Iroquois	2	17.3	10	20.1
Lumbee	3	20.2	11	22.1
Creek	2	19.0	11	23.4
Blackfoot	3	27.6	11	30.9
Canadian and Latin American	1	19.9	6	23.1
Chickasaw	1	17.0	5	21.4
Tohono O'Odham	2	54.1	9	55.8
Potawatomi	1	17.3	3	21.1
Seminole	1	22.6	4	27.6
Pima	2	53.6	8	53.3
Tlingit	-	14.9	2	15.8
Alaskan Athabaskans	1	28.6	4	28.1
Cheyenne	1	35.8	5	42.3
Comanche	1	20.9	3	27.5
Paiute	1	27.2	3	28.9
Osage	-	16.4	2	15.9
Puget Sound Salish	1	28.8	3	30.0
Yaqui	1	37.0	4	40.9

Note: (-) means fewer than 500.
Source: Bureau of the Census, Characteristics of American Indians by Tribe and Language, 1990 Census of Population, CP-3-7, 1994

Native Americans:
Labor Force

Over half of Native American families have two or more workers. Among married couples, 53 percent are dual earners, while 26 percent are traditional single earners—the husband works while the wife stays home.

More than 40 percent of Native American workers can be found in three occupations: precision production, craft, and repair (14 percent); administrative support (14.8 percent); and service occupations (16 percent). Just 9 percent of Native Americans are executives, administrators, or managers. By industry, Native Americans are most heavily represented in mining and public administration. They account for 1 percent of total employment in each of these industries.

Native American Families by Number of Workers, 1990

(number and percent distribution of Native American families by number of workers and type of family, 1990; numbers in thousands)

	total		married couples		female householders, no spouse present	
	number	percent	number	percent	number	percent
Total families	449	100.0%	296	100.0%	118	100.0%
No workers	66	14.6	29	9.8	31	26.6
One worker	149	33.2	73	24.8	56	47.9
Two or more workers	234	52.2	193	65.4	30	25.5

Source: Bureau of the Census, Characteristics of American Indians by Tribe and Language, 1990 Census of Population, CP-3-7, 1994

Labor Force Status of Native American Husbands and Wives, 1990

(number and percent distribution of Native American married couples by labor force status of husbands and wives, 1990; numbers in thousands)

	total		wife in labor force		wife not in labor force	
	number	percent	number	percent	number	percent
Total married couples	296	100.0%	175	59.4%	120	40.6%
Husband in labor force	233	78.8	155	52.5	78	26.3
Husband not in labor force	63	21.2	20	6.9	42	14.3

Source: Bureau of the Census, Characteristics of American Indians by Tribe and Language, 1990 Census of Population, CP-3-7, 1994

Native Americans by Occupation, 1990

(number and percent distribution of employed Native Americans aged 16 or older by occupation, and Native Americans as a percent of total employed workers by occupation, 1990; numbers in thousands)

	number	percent	share of total workers
Total employed, aged 16 or older	706	100.0%	0.6%
Executive, administrative, and managerial	61	8.6	0.4
Professional specialty	68	9.7	0.4
Technicians and related support	23	3.2	0.5
Sales	61	8.7	0.4
Administrative support, including clerical	104	14.8	0.6
Private household	4	0.5	0.6
Protective service	17	2.4	0.9
Service occ., except protective and household	109	15.5	0.9
Farming, forestry, and fishing	24	3.4	0.8
Precision production, craft, and repair	97	13.8	0.7
Machine operators, assemblers, and inspectors	59	8.4	0.7
Transportation and material moving	38	5.4	0.8
Handlers, equip. cleaners, helpers, and laborers	40	5.7	0.9

Source: Bureau of the Census, Characteristics of American Indians by Tribe and Language, *1990 Census of Population, CP-3-7, 1994*

Native Americans by Industry, 1990

(total number and percent distribution of employed Native Americans aged 16 or older by industry, and Native Americans as a percent of total employed workers by industry, 1990; numbers in thousands)

	number	percent	share of total workers
Total employed, aged 16 or older	706	100.0%	0.6%
Agriculture, forestry, and fisheries	25	3.5	0.8
Mining	8	1.1	1.1
Construction	60	8.5	0.8
Manufacturing	115	16.3	0.6
Durable goods	44	6.2	0.4
Nondurable goods	71	10.1	0.9
Transportation	30	4.3	0.6
Communication and other public utilities	19	2.6	0.6
Wholesale trade	23	3.2	0.5
Retail trade	115	16.3	0.6
Finance, insurance, and real estate	28	4.0	0.4
Business and repair services	33	4.6	0.6
Personal, entertainment, and recreation services	39	5.5	0.7
Professional and related services	156	22.0	0.6
Health services	57	8.0	0.6
Educational services	56	8.0	0.6
Public administration	56	7.9	1.0

Source: Bureau of the Census, Characteristics of American Indians by Tribe and Language, *1990 Census of Population, CP-3-7, 1994*

Native Americans:
Population

Numbering 2.3 million, Native Americans are the smallest racial minority in the U.S., accounting for just 0.9 percent of all Americans. This proportion is expected to rise to 1.0 percent by 2020. The largest tribe is the Cherokee, accounting for 19 percent of all Native Americans.

Nearly half of Native Americans live in the West, with another 30 percent in the South. Each of three states is home to more than 10 percent of the nation's Native Americans: Arizona (10 percent), California (12 percent), and Oklahoma (13 percent). Native Americans account for 16 percent of Alaska's population, the largest share among the 50 states.

Native Americans account for only 0.9 percent of all U.S. births, but for 22 percent of births in Alaska, 11 percent in Montana, 14 percent in New Mexico, and 16 percent in South Dakota.

Native Americans by Age, 1990 to 2020

(number of Native Americans by age, selected years 1990-2020; percent change 1990-2000 and 2000-2010; numbers in thousands)

	1990	1996	2000	2010	2020	percent change 1990-2000	percent change 2000-2010
Total persons	2,075	2,273	2,402	2,754	3,129	15.8%	14.7%
Under 5	223	207	210	245	266	-5.8	16.7
5 to 9	210	227	215	235	269	2.4	9.3
10 to 14	199	237	253	244	285	27.1	-3.6
15 to 19	190	209	235	242	265	23.7	3.0
20 to 24	179	181	194	248	240	8.4	27.8
25 to 29	187	183	184	228	236	-1.6	23.9
30 to 34	181	183	177	192	246	-2.2	8.5
35 to 39	158	179	181	178	221	14.6	-1.7
40 to 44	133	160	173	171	186	30.1	-1.2
45 to 49	100	130	146	168	166	46.0	15.1
50 to 54	79	97	117	154	152	48.1	31.6
55 to 59	64	74	86	126	146	34.4	46.5
60 to 64	53	59	66	99	131	24.5	50.0
65 to 69	44	48	52	70	104	18.2	34.6
70 to 74	30	38	41	52	78	36.7	26.8
75 to 79	22	26	32	38	53	45.5	18.8
80 to 84	12	17	19	27	35	58.3	42.1
85 or older	9	16	22	36	51	144.4	63.6
18 to 24	255	259	282	343	340	10.6	21.6
18 or older	1,330	1,469	1,578	1,882	2,145	18.6	19.3
65 or older	117	146	165	223	321	41.0	35.2

Source: Bureau of the Census, Population Projections of the United States, by Age, Sex, Race, and Hispanic Origin: 1995 to 2050, *Current Population Reports, P25-1130, 1996; and* U.S. Population Estimates, by Age, Sex, Race, and Hispanic Origin: 1980 to 1991, *Current Population Reports, P25-1095, 1993*

Native American Share of the Total Population by Age, 1990 to 2020

(Native Americans as a percent of total population by age, selected years 1990-2020)

	1990	1996	2000	2010	2020
Total persons	0.8%	0.9%	0.9%	0.9%	1.0%
Under age 5	1.2	1.1	1.1	1.2	1.2
Aged 5 to 9	1.2	1.2	1.1	1.2	1.2
Aged 10 to 14	1.2	1.2	1.3	1.2	1.3
Aged 15 to 19	1.1	1.1	1.2	1.1	1.2
Aged 20 to 24	0.9	1.0	1.1	1.2	1.1
Aged 25 to 29	0.9	1.0	1.0	1.2	1.1
Aged 30 to 34	0.8	0.9	0.9	1.0	1.2
Aged 35 to 39	0.8	0.8	0.8	1.0	1.1
Aged 40 to 44	0.7	0.8	0.8	0.9	1.0
Aged 45 to 49	0.7	0.7	0.7	0.8	0.9
Aged 50 to 54	0.7	0.7	0.7	0.7	0.8
Aged 55 to 59	0.6	0.7	0.6	0.7	0.7
Aged 60 to 64	0.5	0.6	0.6	0.6	0.6
Aged 65 to 69	0.4	0.5	0.6	0.6	0.6
Aged 70 to 74	0.4	0.4	0.5	0.6	0.6
Aged 75 to 79	0.4	0.4	0.4	0.5	0.6
Aged 80 to 84	0.3	0.4	0.4	0.5	0.6
Aged 85 or older	0.3	0.4	0.5	0.6	0.8
Aged 18 to 24	1.0	1.1	1.1	1.1	1.1
Aged 18 or older	0.7	0.7	0.8	0.8	0.9
Aged 65 or older	0.4	0.4	0.5	0.6	0.6

Source: Bureau of the Census, Population Projections of the United States, by Age, Sex, Race, and Hispanic Origin: 1995 to 2050, *Current Population Reports, P25-1130, 1996; and* U.S. Population Estimates, by Age, Sex, Race, and Hispanic Origin: 1980 to 1991, *Current Population Reports, P25-1095, 1993*

Non-Hispanic Native Americans by Age, 1990 to 2020

(number of non-Hispanic Native Americans by age, selected years 1990-2020; percent change 1990-2000 and 2000-2010; numbers in thousands)

	1990	1996	2000	2010	2020	percent change 1990-2000	percent change 2000-2010
Total persons	1,806	1,956	2,054	2,320	2,601	13.7%	13.0%
Under 5	189	176	180	206	222	-4.8	14.4
5 to 9	179	191	182	199	224	1.7	9.3
10 to 14	172	200	212	207	236	23.3	-2.4
15 to 19	164	178	197	202	221	20.1	2.5
20 to 24	151	154	164	204	200	8.6	24.4
25 to 29	160	154	156	189	194	-2.5	21.2
30 to 34	156	154	147	160	199	-5.8	8.8
35 to 39	138	154	152	149	181	10.1	-2.0
40 to 44	118	139	149	141	154	26.3	-5.4
45 to 49	90	115	127	141	138	41.1	11.0
50 to 54	72	87	104	131	125	44.4	26.0
55 to 59	58	67	77	109	122	32.8	41.6
60 to 64	49	54	59	86	110	20.4	45.8
65 to 69	40	43	46	61	89	15.0	32.6
70 to 74	28	35	36	45	67	28.6	25.0
75 to 79	20	24	28	33	45	40.0	17.9
80 to 84	12	16	18	23	30	50.0	27.8
85 or older	9	15	21	34	45	133.3	61.9
18 to 24	217	218	238	282	282	9.7	18.5
18 or older	1,168	1,275	1,358	1,584	1,781	16.3	16.6
65 or older	109	133	149	197	275	36.7	32.2

Note: Hispanics may be of any race and most are white. For a breakdown of the Hispanic composition of racial groups and the racial composition of Hispanics, see the introduction to this book.
Source: Bureau of the Census, Population Projections of the United States, by Age, Sex, Race, and Hispanic Origin: 1995 to 2050, *Current Population Reports, P25-1130, 1996; and* U.S. Population Estimates, by Age, Sex, Race, and Hispanic Origin: 1980 to 1991, *Current Population Reports, P25-1095, 1993*

Native Americans by Sex, 1996

(number of Native Americans by age and sex, and sex ratio by age, 1996; numbers in thousands)

	total	male	female	sex ratio*
Total persons	2,273	1,124	1,149	98
Under age 5	207	105	102	103
Aged 5 to 9	227	116	111	105
Aged 10 to 14	237	120	117	103
Aged 15 to 19	209	105	104	101
Aged 20 to 24	181	92	89	103
Aged 25 to 29	183	95	88	108
Aged 30 to 34	183	92	91	101
Aged 35 to 39	179	89	91	98
Aged 40 to 44	160	77	82	94
Aged 45 to 49	130	63	67	94
Aged 50 to 54	97	46	51	90
Aged 55 to 59	74	35	39	90
Aged 60 to 64	59	28	32	88
Aged 65 to 69	48	22	27	81
Aged 70 to 74	38	17	22	77
Aged 75 to 79	26	11	16	69
Aged 80 to 84	17	7	11	64
Aged 85 or older	16	5	11	45
Aged 18 to 24	259	129	125	103
Aged 18 or older	1,469	716	753	95
Aged 65 or older	146	61	85	72

* The sex ratio is the number of males per 100 females.
Source: Bureau of the Census, Population Projections of the United States, by Age, Sex, Race, and Hispanic Origin: 1995 to 2050, Current Population Reports, P25-1130, 1996

Native Americans by Tribe, 1990 and 1980

(number and percent distribution of Native Americans by tribe for 25 largest tribes, 1990 and 1980; change in number and percent change 1980-90; numbers in thousands)

	1990		1980		change, 1980-90	
	number	percent	number	percent	number	percent
Total persons	1,937	100.0%	1,479	100.0%	459	31.0%
Cherokee	369	19.0	232	15.7	137	59.0
Navajo	225	11.6	159	10.7	67	42.0
Sioux	107	5.5	79	5.3	29	36.5
Chippewa	106	5.5	74	5.0	32	44.0
Choctaw	86	4.5	50	3.4	36	71.7
Pueblo	55	2.9	43	2.9	13	30.0
Apache	53	2.8	36	2.4	17	48.7
Iroquois	53	2.7	38	2.6	14	37.5
Lumbee	51	2.6	29	1.9	22	77.7
Creek	46	2.4	28	1.9	18	62.2
Blackfoot	38	2.0	22	1.5	16	73.0
Canadian and Latin American	27	1.4	8	0.5	19	248.3
Chickasaw	22	1.1	10	0.7	11	108.6
Tohono O'Odham	17	0.9	13	0.9	4	26.9
Potawatomi	17	0.9	10	0.7	7	72.1
Seminole	16	0.8	10	0.7	5	50.2
Pima	15	0.8	12	0.8	3	28.6
Tlingit	14	0.7	10	0.6	5	51.6
Alaskan Athabaskans	14	0.7	10	0.7	4	40.1
Cheyenne	12	0.6	10	0.7	2	19.1
Comanche	11	0.6	9	0.6	2	26.6
Paiute	11	0.6	10	0.6	2	19.4
Osage	10	0.5	7	0.5	4	51.5
Puget Sound Salish	10	0.5	7	0.4	4	57.5
Yaqui	10	0.5	5	0.4	5	89.3

Note: Total excludes Eskimos and Aleuts. Numbers by tribe will not sum to total because not all tribes are shown.
Source: U.S. Bureau of the Census, Internet web site, http://www.census.gov

Native Americans by Tribe and Ability to Speak English, 1990

(number of Native Americans aged 5 or older, and percent who do not speak English "very well,"
for 25 largest tribes, 1990; numbers in thousands)

	number	percent who do not speak English "very well"
Total persons, aged 5 or older	1,750	8.9%
Cherokee	346	1.9
Navajo	195	33.4
Sioux	94	4.6
Chippewa	95	1.6
Choctaw	79	5.1
Pueblo	50	23.0
Apache	48	15.6
Iroquois	48	2.2
Lumbee	47	1.2
Creek	42	3.1
Blackfoot	35	1.7
Canadian and Latin American	25	23.8
Chickasaw	20	1.5
Tohono O'Odham	15	26.1
Potawatomi	15	1.0
Seminole	14	6.3
Pima	13	11.8
Tlingit	13	2.4
Alaskan Athabaskans	13	5.8
Cheyenne	10	6.2
Comanche	10	2.2
Paiute	10	4.9
Osage	9	0.9
Puget Sound Salish	9	0.8
Yaqui	9	30.6

Note: Numbers by tribe will not sum to total because not all tribes are shown.
Source: Bureau of the Census, Characteristics of American Indians by Tribe and Language, *1990 Census of Population, CP-3-7, 1994*

Native Americans by Region and Tribe, 1990

(number and percent distribution of Native Americans by 25 largest tribes and region, 1990; numbers in thousands)

	number	percent total	Northeast	Midwest	South	West
Total persons	1,937	100.0%	6.3%	17.9%	30.2%	45.6%
Cherokee	369	100.0	4.8	15.5	55.0	24.8
Navajo	225	100.0	0.5	1.2	2.2	96.1
Sioux	107	100.0	2.3	64.7	7.3	25.6
Chippewa	106	100.0	1.4	77.5	4.7	16.4
Choctaw	86	100.0	0.9	4.7	76.1	18.4
Pueblo	55	100.0	1.1	1.7	4.6	92.5
Apache	53	100.0	3.0	7.1	15.2	74.7
Iroquois	53	100.0	44.8	25.4	16.3	13.6
Lumbee	51	100.0	1.0	2.7	94.7	1.6
Creek	46	100.0	1.4	5.1	80.6	12.9
Blackfoot	38	100.0	11.2	16.5	15.0	57.3
Canadian and Latin American	27	100.0	15.8	14.3	18.9	51.0
Chickasaw	22	100.0	0.7	3.7	75.1	20.4
Tohono O'Odham	17	100.0	0.4	1.1	1.1	97.4
Potawatomi	17	100.0	1.5	39.7	37.6	21.2
Seminole	16	100.0	6.3	7.0	69.2	17.5
Pima	15	100.0	0.3	1.0	2.0	96.7
Tlingit	14	100.0	1.0	1.9	2.0	95.2
Alaskan Athabaskans	14	100.0	1.3	2.5	2.6	93.6
Cheyenne	12	100.0	2.2	10.1	29.3	58.5
Comanche	11	100.0	2.3	8.2	66.1	23.3
Paiute	11	100.0	0.5	1.9	2.4	95.2
Osage	10	100.0	1.0	10.6	62.5	25.9
Puget Sound Salish	10	100.0	0.7	1.7	2.8	94.7
Yaqui	10	100.0	0.2	1.3	2.4	96.1

Note: Total excludes Eskimos and Aleuts. Numbers by tribe will not sum to total because not all tribes are shown.
Source: Bureau of the Census, Characteristics of American Indians by Tribe and Language, *1990 Census of Population, CP-3-7, 1994*

Native Americans by Region and Division, 1990 to 2020

(number and percent distribution of Native Americans and Native American share of the total population by region and division, selected years 1990-2020; percent change in number and percentage point change in distribution and share, 1990-2000 and 2000-2010; numbers in thousands)

	1990	1995	2000	2010	2020	percent change 1990-2000	percent change 2000-2010
Number							
UNITED STATES	2,065	2,226	2,379	2,719	3,090	15.2%	14.3%
Northeast	132	118	108	99	96	-18.2	-8.3
New England	34	32	31	32	33	-8.8	3.2
Middle Atlantic	98	86	77	67	63	-21.4	-13.0
Midwest	348	382	412	461	511	18.4	11.9
East North Central	156	164	170	174	178	9.0	2.4
West North Central	192	217	241	287	333	25.5	19.1
South	578	605	628	676	725	8.7	7.6
South Atlantic	175	185	193	208	221	10.3	7.8
East South Central	41	43	45	45	47	9.8	0.0
West South Central	362	376	390	423	457	7.7	8.5
West	1,007	1,122	1,232	1,483	1,758	22.3	20.4
Mountain	502	589	668	817	976	33.1	22.3
Pacific	505	533	564	666	782	11.7	18.1

	1990	1995	2000	2010	2020	percentage point change 1990-2000	percentage point change 2000-2010
Percent distribution							
UNITED STATES	100.0%	100.0%	100.0%	100.0%	100.0%	-	-
Northeast	6.4	5.3	4.5	3.6	3.1	-1.9	-0.9
New England	1.7	1.4	1.3	1.2	1.1	-0.4	-0.1
Middle Atlantic	4.7	3.9	3.2	2.5	2.0	-1.5	-0.8
Midwest	17.2	17.2	17.3	17.0	16.5	0.1	-0.3
East North Central	7.7	7.4	7.1	6.4	5.8	-0.6	-0.7
West North Central	9.6	9.7	10.1	10.6	10.8	0.5	0.5
South	28.7	27.2	26.4	24.9	23.5	-2.3	-1.5
South Atlantic	8.8	8.3	8.1	7.6	7.2	-0.7	-0.5
East South Central	2.1	1.9	1.9	1.7	1.5	-0.2	-0.2
West South Central	17.8	16.9	16.4	15.6	14.8	-1.4	-0.8
West	47.6	50.4	51.8	54.5	56.9	4.2	2.7
Mountain	24.5	26.5	28.1	30.0	31.6	3.6	1.9
Pacific	23.1	23.9	23.7	24.5	25.3	0.6	0.8

(continued)

(continued from previous page)

	1990	1995	2000	2010	2020	percentage point change 1990-2000	2000-2010
Percent share							
UNITED STATES	0.8%	0.8%	0.9%	0.9%	0.9%	0.1	0.0
Northeast	0.3	0.2	0.2	0.2	0.2	-0.1	0.0
New England	0.3	0.2	0.2	0.2	0.2	-0.1	0.0
Middle Atlantic	0.3	0.2	0.2	0.2	0.2	-0.1	-0.1
Midwest	0.6	0.6	0.6	0.7	0.7	0.0	0.1
East North Central	0.4	0.4	0.4	0.4	0.4	0.0	0.0
West North Central	1.1	1.2	1.3	1.4	1.6	0.2	0.1
South	0.7	0.7	0.6	0.6	0.6	-0.1	0.0
South Atlantic	0.4	0.4	0.4	0.4	0.4	0.0	0.0
East South Central	0.3	0.3	0.3	0.3	0.2	0.0	0.0
West South Central	1.4	1.3	1.3	1.2	1.2	-0.1	-0.1
West	1.9	1.9	1.9	2.0	2.1	0.0	0.1
Mountain	3.7	3.8	4.0	4.3	4.6	0.3	0.3
Pacific	1.3	1.2	1.2	1.2	1.2	-0.1	0.0

Note: The total for April 1, 1990 and has been adjusted for those who reported "other" race in the 1990 census. Projections of total Native Americans for 2000, 2010, and 2020 are different from those at the beginning of the population section because they are from an earlier report for states and regions.
Source: Bureau of the Census, Population Projections for States, by Age, Sex, Race, and Hispanic Origin:1993 to 2020, *Current Population Reports, P25-1111, 1994*

Native American Births by State, 1993

(number and percent distribution of Native American births by state, and Native American births as a percent of total births by state, 1993)

	number	percent	Native American share of total births
United States	38,732	100.0%	1.0%
Alabama	107	0.3	0.2
Alaska	2,460	6.4	22.2
Arizona	5,784	14.9	8.4
Arkansas	197	0.5	0.6
California	3,336	8.6	0.6
Colorado	533	1.4	1.0
Connecticut	106	0.3	0.2
Delaware	21	0.1	0.2
District of Columbia	10	0.0	0.1
Florida	442	1.1	0.2
Georgia	111	0.3	0.1
Hawaii	189	0.5	1.0
Idaho	286	0.7	1.6
Illinois	231	0.6	0.1
Indiana	90	0.2	0.1
Iowa	175	0.5	0.5
Kansas	353	0.9	0.9
Kentucky	55	0.1	0.1
Louisiana	257	0.7	0.4
Maine	91	0.2	0.6
Maryland	221	0.6	0.3
Massachusetts	111	0.3	0.1
Michigan	762	2.0	0.5
Minnesota	1,139	2.9	1.8
Mississippi	183	0.5	0.4
Missouri	229	0.6	0.3
Montana	1,246	3.2	11.0
Nebraska	371	1.0	1.6
Nevada	367	0.9	1.6
New Hampshire	25	0.1	0.2
New Jersey	385	1.0	0.3
New Mexico	3,872	10.0	13.9
New York	939	2.4	0.3

(continued)

(continued from previous page)

	number	percent	Native American share of total births
North Carolina	1,466	3.8%	1.4%
North Dakota	763	2.0	8.8
Ohio	216	0.6	0.1
Oklahoma	4,430	11.4	9.6
Oregon	574	1.5	1.4
Pennsylvania	179	0.5	0.1
Rhode Island	132	0.3	0.9
South Carolina	105	0.3	0.2
South Dakota	1,721	4.4	16.1
Tennessee	126	0.3	0.2
Texas	700	1.8	0.2
Utah	676	1.7	1.8
Vermont	11	0.0	0.1
Virginia	134	0.3	0.1
Washington	1,697	4.4	2.2
West Virginia	15	0.0	0.1
Wisconsin	866	2.2	1.2
Wyoming	237	0.6	3.6

Source: National Center for Health Statistics, Advance Report of Final Natality Statistics, *1993, Vol. 44, No. 3 Supplement, 1995*

Native Americans by State, 1995 to 2020

(number of Native Americans by state, selected years 1995-2020; percent change 1995 to 2020; numbers in thousands)

	1995	2000	2010	2020	percent change 1995-2020
United States	2,226	2,379	2,719	3,090	38.8%
Alabama	18	18	19	20	11.1
Alaska	102	116	150	189	85.3
Arizona	251	285	348	415	65.3
Arkansas	15	17	18	20	33.3
California	277	276	314	362	30.7
Colorado	34	36	38	41	20.6
Connecticut	7	6	6	6	-14.3
Delaware	3	3	3	3	0.0
District of Columbia	1	1	1	1	0.0
Florida	38	40	42	44	15.8
Georgia	13	12	12	12	-7.7
Hawaii	7	8	10	12	71.4
Idaho	18	21	24	27	50.0
Illinois	23	22	21	21	-8.7
Indiana	14	15	15	14	0.0
Iowa	8	8	8	8	0.0
Kansas	27	29	33	36	33.3
Kentucky	6	6	6	6	0.0
Louisiana	19	19	20	21	10.5
Maine	6	6	6	6	0.0
Maryland	13	13	14	14	7.7
Massachusetts	11	10	10	10	-9.1
Michigan	61	63	64	66	8.2
Minnesota	58	64	74	84	44.8
Mississippi	9	10	10	10	11.1
Missouri	20	20	21	22	10.0
Montana	55	62	74	86	56.4
Nebraska	14	15	16	18	28.6
Nevada	27	31	36	39	44.4
New Hampshire	2	3	3	4	100.0
New Jersey	14	13	11	11	-21.4
New Mexico	159	181	231	288	81.1
New York	57	50	43	39	-31.6

(continued)

(continued from previous page)

	1995	2000	2010	2020	percent change 1995-2020
North Carolina	90	98	109	118	31.1%
North Dakota	28	31	37	44	57.1
Ohio	22	22	22	21	-4.5
Oklahoma	276	290	320	349	26.4
Oregon	47	52	60	68	44.7
Pennsylvania	15	14	13	13	-13.3
Rhode Island	4	4	4	5	25.0
South Carolina	9	9	9	10	11.1
South Dakota	62	74	97	122	96.8
Tennessee	11	11	11	11	0.0
Texas	67	65	65	68	1.5
Utah	33	39	50	59	78.8
Vermont	2	2	2	3	50.0
Virginia	15	15	15	15	0.0
Washington	101	112	131	151	49.5
West Virginia	3	3	3	3	0.0
Wisconsin	45	48	52	55	22.2
Wyoming	12	14	17	21	75.0

Note: Projections of total Native Americans for 2000, 2010, and 2020 are different from those at the beginning of the population section because they are from an earlier report for states and regions.
Source: Bureau of the Census, Population Projections for States, by Age, Sex, Race, and Hispanic Origin: 1993 to 2020, *Current Population Reports, P25-1111, 1994*

Distribution of Native Americans by State, 1995 to 2020

(percent distribution of Native Americans by state, selected years 1995-2020)

	1995	*2000*	*2010*	*2020*
United States	100.0%	100.0%	100.0%	100.0%
Alabama	0.8	0.8	0.7	0.6
Alaska	4.6	4.9	5.5	6.1
Arizona	11.3	12.0	12.8	13.4
Arkansas	0.7	0.7	0.7	0.6
California	12.4	11.6	11.5	11.7
Colorado	1.5	1.5	1.4	1.3
Connecticut	0.3	0.3	0.2	0.2
Delaware	0.1	0.1	0.1	0.1
District of Columbia	0.0	0.0	0.0	0.0
Florida	1.7	1.7	1.5	1.4
Georgia	0.6	0.5	0.4	0.4
Hawaii	0.3	0.3	0.4	0.4
Idaho	0.8	0.9	0.9	0.9
Illinois	1.0	0.9	0.8	0.7
Indiana	0.6	0.6	0.6	0.5
Iowa	0.4	0.3	0.3	0.3
Kansas	1.2	1.2	1.2	1.2
Kentucky	0.3	0.3	0.2	0.2
Louisiana	0.9	0.8	0.7	0.7
Maine	0.3	0.3	0.2	0.2
Maryland	0.6	0.5	0.5	0.5
Massachusetts	0.5	0.4	0.4	0.3
Michigan	2.7	2.6	2.4	2.1
Minnesota	2.6	2.7	2.7	2.7
Mississippi	0.4	0.4	0.4	0.3
Missouri	0.9	0.8	0.8	0.7
Montana	2.5	2.6	2.7	2.8
Nebraska	0.6	0.6	0.6	0.6
Nevada	1.2	1.3	1.3	1.3
New Hampshire	0.1	0.1	0.1	0.1
New Jersey	0.6	0.5	0.4	0.4
New Mexico	7.1	7.6	8.5	9.3
New York	2.6	2.1	1.6	1.3

(continued)

(continued from previous page)

	1995	2000	2010	2020
North Carolina	4.0%	4.1%	4.0%	3.8%
North Dakota	1.3	1.3	1.4	1.4
Ohio	1.0	0.9	0.8	0.7
Oklahoma	12.4	12.2	11.8	11.3
Oregon	2.1	2.2	2.2	2.2
Pennsylvania	0.7	0.6	0.5	0.4
Rhode Island	0.2	0.2	0.1	0.2
South Carolina	0.4	0.4	0.3	0.3
South Dakota	2.8	3.1	3.6	3.9
Tennessee	0.5	0.5	0.4	0.4
Texas	3.0	2.7	2.4	2.2
Utah	1.5	1.6	1.8	1.9
Vermont	0.1	0.1	0.1	0.1
Virginia	0.7	0.6	0.6	0.5
Washington	4.5	4.7	4.8	4.9
West Virginia	0.1	0.1	0.1	0.1
Wisconsin	2.0	2.0	1.9	1.8
Wyoming	0.5	0.6	0.6	0.7

Source: Bureau of the Census, Population Projections for States, by Age, Sex, Race, and Hispanic Origin: 1993 to 2020, *Current Population Reports, P25-1111, 1994*

Native American Share of State Populations, 1995 to 2020

(Native Americans as a percent of state populations, selected years 1995-2020; percentage point change, 1995-2020)

	1995	2000	2010	2020	percentage point change 1995-2020
United States	0.8%	0.9%	0.9%	0.9%	0.1
Alabama	0.4	0.4	0.4	0.4	0.0
Alaska	16.1	16.6	19.2	21.8	5.7
Arizona	6.2	6.4	6.9	7.3	1.1
Arkansas	0.6	0.7	0.6	0.7	0.1
California	0.9	0.8	0.8	0.8	-0.1
Colorado	0.9	0.9	0.8	0.8	-0.1
Connecticut	0.2	0.2	0.2	0.2	0.0
Delaware	0.4	0.4	0.4	0.3	-0.1
District of Columbia	0.2	0.2	0.2	0.2	0.0
Florida	0.3	0.3	0.2	0.2	-0.1
Georgia	0.2	0.2	0.1	0.1	-0.1
Hawaii	0.6	0.6	0.6	0.7	0.1
Idaho	1.6	1.6	1.7	1.7	0.1
Illinois	0.2	0.2	0.2	0.2	0.0
Indiana	0.2	0.2	0.2	0.2	0.0
Iowa	0.3	0.3	0.3	0.3	0.0
Kansas	1.0	1.1	1.1	1.2	0.2
Kentucky	0.2	0.2	0.1	0.1	-0.1
Louisiana	0.4	0.4	0.4	0.4	0.0
Maine	0.5	0.5	0.5	0.4	-0.1
Maryland	0.3	0.2	0.2	0.2	-0.1
Massachusetts	0.2	0.2	0.2	0.2	0.0
Michigan	0.6	0.6	0.6	0.6	0.0
Minnesota	1.3	1.3	1.4	1.5	0.2
Mississippi	0.3	0.4	0.3	0.3	0.0
Missouri	0.4	0.4	0.4	0.4	0.0
Montana	6.4	6.7	7.4	8.0	1.6
Nebraska	0.9	0.9	0.9	1.0	0.1
Nevada	1.8	1.8	1.9	1.8	0.0
New Hampshire	0.2	0.3	0.2	0.3	0.1
New Jersey	0.2	0.2	0.1	0.1	-0.1
New Mexico	9.5	9.9	11.1	12.3	2.8
New York	0.3	0.3	0.2	0.2	-0.1

(continued)

(continued from previous page)

	1995	2000	2010	2020	percentage point change 1995-2020
North Carolina	1.3%	1.3%	1.3%	1.3%	0.0
North Dakota	4.4	4.8	5.5	6.1	1.7
Ohio	0.2	0.2	0.2	0.2	0.0
Oklahoma	8.4	8.6	8.7	8.7	0.3
Oregon	1.5	1.5	1.5	1.6	0.1
Pennsylvania	0.1	0.1	0.1	0.1	0.0
Rhode Island	0.4	0.4	0.4	0.5	0.1
South Carolina	0.2	0.2	0.2	0.2	0.0
South Dakota	8.4	9.6	11.9	14.1	5.7
Tennessee	0.2	0.2	0.2	0.2	0.0
Texas	0.4	0.3	0.3	0.3	-0.1
Utah	1.7	1.8	2.0	2.1	0.4
Vermont	0.3	0.3	0.3	0.5	0.2
Virginia	0.2	0.2	0.2	0.2	0.0
Washington	1.8	1.8	1.9	1.9	0.1
West Virginia	0.2	0.2	0.2	0.2	0.0
Wisconsin	0.9	0.9	0.9	0.9	0.0
Wyoming	2.5	2.7	2.9	3.2	0.7

Source: Bureau of the Census, Population Projections for States, by Age, Sex, Race, and Hispanic Origin: 1993 to 2020, *Current Population Reports, P25-1111, 1994*

Metropolitan Areas With the Most Native Americans, 1990

(ten metropolitan areas with the most Native Americans ranked by size of Native American population; number of Native Americans and Native American share of the total metropolitan population, 1990; numbers in thousands)

		number	percent
1.	Los Angeles-Riverside-Orange County, CA	87	0.6%
2.	Phoenix-Mesa, AZ	49	2.2
3.	New York-Northern New Jersey-Long Island, NY-NJ-CT-PA	48	0.2
4.	Tulsa, OK	48	6.8
5.	Oklahoma City, OK	46	4.8
6.	San Francisco-Oakland-San Jose, CA	41	0.7
7.	Seattle-Tacoma-Bremerton, WA	38	1.3
8.	Albuquerque, NM	30	5.1
9.	Minneapolis-St. Paul, MN	24	1.0
10.	Detroit-Ann Arbor-Flint, MI	21	0.4

Source: Bureau of the Census, Statistical Abstract of the United States 1993

Native American Births by Age of Mother, 1993

(number and percent distribution of births to Native American women, by age of mother, 1993)

	number	percent
Total births	38,732	100.0%
Under age 15	157	0.4
Aged 15 to 19	7,714	19.9
Aged 20 to 24	12,608	32.6
Aged 25 to 29	9,472	24.5
Aged 30 to 34	5,910	15.3
Aged 35 to 39	2,409	6.2
Aged 40 or older	462	1.2

Source: National Center for Health Statistics, Advance Report of Final Natality Statistics, 1993, *Vol. 44, No. 3 Supplement, 1995*

Native American Births by State, 1993

(number and percent distribution of Native American births by state, and Native American births as a percent of total births by state, 1993)

	number	percent	Native American share of total births
United States	38,732	100.0%	1.0%
Alabama	107	0.3	0.2
Alaska	2,460	6.4	22.2
Arizona	5,784	14.9	8.4
Arkansas	197	0.5	0.6
California	3,336	8.6	0.6
Colorado	533	1.4	1.0
Connecticut	106	0.3	0.2
Delaware	21	0.1	0.2
District of Columbia	10	0.0	0.1
Florida	442	1.1	0.2
Georgia	111	0.3	0.1
Hawaii	189	0.5	1.0
Idaho	286	0.7	1.6
Illinois	231	0.6	0.1
Indiana	90	0.2	0.1
Iowa	175	0.5	0.5
Kansas	353	0.9	0.9
Kentucky	55	0.1	0.1
Louisiana	257	0.7	0.4
Maine	91	0.2	0.6
Maryland	221	0.6	0.3
Massachusetts	111	0.3	0.1
Michigan	762	2.0	0.5
Minnesota	1,139	2.9	1.8
Mississippi	183	0.5	0.4
Missouri	229	0.6	0.3
Montana	1,246	3.2	11.0
Nebraska	371	1.0	1.6
Nevada	367	0.9	1.6
New Hampshire	25	0.1	0.2
New Jersey	385	1.0	0.3
New Mexico	3,872	10.0	13.9
New York	939	2.4	0.3

(continued)

(continued from previous page)

	number	percent	Native American share of total births
North Carolina	1,466	3.8%	1.4%
North Dakota	763	2.0	8.8
Ohio	216	0.6	0.1
Oklahoma	4,430	11.4	9.6
Oregon	574	1.5	1.4
Pennsylvania	179	0.5	0.1
Rhode Island	132	0.3	0.9
South Carolina	105	0.3	0.2
South Dakota	1,721	4.4	16.1
Tennessee	126	0.3	0.2
Texas	700	1.8	0.2
Utah	676	1.7	1.8
Vermont	11	0.0	0.1
Virginia	134	0.3	0.1
Washington	1,697	4.4	2.2
West Virginia	15	0.0	0.1
Wisconsin	866	2.2	1.2
Wyoming	237	0.6	3.6

Source: National Center for Health Statistics, Advance Report of Final Natality Statistics, 1993, *Vol. 44, No. 3 Supplement, 1995*

Projections of Native American Births, 1995 to 2020

(number of Native American births, and Native American births as a percent of total births, 1995-2020; numbers in thousands)

	number	Native American share of total births
1995	34	0.9%
1996	34	0.9
1997	34	0.9
1998	34	0.9
1999	35	0.9
2000	35	0.9
2001	36	0.9
2002	36	0.9
2003	37	0.9
2004	38	1.0
2005	38	0.9
2006	39	1.0
2007	39	1.0
2008	40	1.0
2009	41	1.0
2010	41	1.0
2011	41	1.0
2012	42	1.0
2013	42	1.0
2014	42	1.0
2015	42	0.9
2016	43	1.0
2017	43	1.0
2018	43	0.9
2019	44	1.0
2020	44	1.0

Source: Bureau of the Census, Population Projections of the United States, by Age, Sex, Race, and Hispanic Origin: 1995 to 2050, *Current Population Reports, P25-1130, 1996*

5

Whites

■ The white population is projected to grow from 220 million in 1996 to nearly 255 million by 2020, when whites will account for 78 percent of the total U.S. population.

■ Eighty-two percent of whites are high school graduates and 23 percent have graduated from college. For the total population, the proportions are 81 and 22 percent, respectively.

■ Two out of three whites report being in excellent or very good health, while just 10 percent say their health is only fair or poor.

■ Fifty-eight percent of white households are married couples and 27 percent are nuclear families, about the same as for households in the nation as a whole. Female-headed families with children account for just 6 percent of white households.

■ Among white households, median income peaks at $50,019 for household-ers aged 45 to 54. By household type, white married couples have the highest incomes—$45,555 in 1994

■ The nation's white households spent an average of $32,935 in 1994 and their net worth was $45,740.

Whites:
Education

Educational attainment among whites closely matches that of the total population, since the great majority of Americans are white. Overall, 82 percent of whites are high school graduates and 23 percent have graduated from college. For the total population, the proportions are 81 percent and 22 percent, respectively.

Among white families with children aged 18 to 24, 42 percent have at least one child in college full-time—far higher than the proportion of black or Hispanic families with a child in college. Among white families with dependents in the 18-to-24 age group and incomes of $75,000 or more, 64 percent have a child in college full-time.

Non-Hispanic whites earned 82 percent of all bachelor's degrees, 76 percent of all master's degrees, and 64 percent of doctorates in 1992-93. Together, minorities (blacks, Hispanics, Asians, and Native Americans) earned just 9 percent of all doctorates, while nonresident aliens earned 27 percent.

White High School and College Graduates, 1980 to 1993

(percent of whites aged 25 or older who are high school or college graduates, by sex, 1980-93)

	total	men	women
High school graduates			
1993	81.5%	81.8%	81.3%
1990	79.1	79.1	79.0
1985	75.5	76.0	75.1
1980	70.5	71.0	70.1
College graduates			
1993	22.6	25.7	19.7
1990	22.0	25.3	19.0
1985	20.0	24.0	16.3
1980	17.8	22.1	14.0

Source: Bureau of the Census, Educational Attainment in the United States: March 1993 and 1992, *Current Population Reports, P20-476, 1994*

Educational Attainment of Whites by Sex, 1993

(number and percent distribution of whites aged 25 or older, by educational attainment and sex, 1993; numbers in thousands)

	total		men		women	
	number	percent	number	percent	number	percent
Total, aged 25 or older	139,019	100.0%	66,797	100.0%	72,222	100.0%
Not a high school graduate	25,666	18.5	12,150	18.2	13,516	18.7
High school graduate or more	113,353	81.5	54,647	81.8	58,706	81.3
Some college or associate's degree	32,428	23.3	15,358	23.0	17,070	23.6
Bachelor's degree or more	31,385	22.6	17,173	25.7	14,213	19.7

Source: Bureau of the Census, Educational Attainment in the United States: March 1993 and 1992, *Current Population Reports, P20-476, 1994*

Educational Attainment of Whites by Age and Sex, 1993

(percent of whites aged 25 or older who are high school or college graduates, by sex and age, 1993)

	total	men	women
HIGH SCHOOL GRADUATES			
Total, aged 25 or older	81.5%	81.8%	81.3%
Aged 25 to 29	87.3	86.1	88.5
Aged 30 to 34	87.7	86.5	88.8
Aged 35 to 39	89.2	88.8	89.6
Aged 40 to 44	89.9	90.0	89.8
Aged 45 to 49	88.1	88.2	87.9
Aged 50 to 54	84.2	84.1	84.3
Aged 55 to 59	78.3	78.3	78.4
Aged 60 to 64	74.5	74.2	74.8
Aged 65 to 69	70.4	68.3	72.0
Aged 70 to 74	67.8	67.8	67.8
Aged 75 or older	54.8	55.0	54.7
COLLEGE GRADUATES			
Total, aged 25 or older	22.6	25.7	19.7
Aged 25 to 29	24.7	24.4	25.1
Aged 30 to 34	24.8	25.7	23.9
Aged 35 to 39	26.2	26.9	25.6
Aged 40 to 44	29.5	32.6	26.3
Aged 45 to 49	27.9	32.2	23.6
Aged 50 to 54	23.6	27.4	20.0
Aged 55 to 59	20.6	26.9	14.8
Aged 60 to 64	18.2	22.9	13.8
Aged 65 to 69	14.9	19.7	11.1
Aged 70 to 74	12.6	17.8	8.5
Aged 75 or older	10.6	13.7	8.7

Source: Bureau of the Census, Educational Attainment in the United States: March 1993 and 1992, *Current Population Reports, P20-476, 1994*

Educational Attainment of Whites by Age and Region, 1993

(percent of whites aged 25 or older who are high school or college graduates, by age and region, 1993)

	Northeast	Midwest	South	West
HIGH SCHOOL GRADUATES				
Total, aged 25 or older	82.4%	83.3%	78.8%	82.7%
Aged 25 to 34	90.5	90.8	85.9	83.2
Aged 35 to 44	91.3	92.7	87.8	86.9
Aged 45 to 54	86.5	89.5	83.4	87.3
Aged 55 to 64	78.0	77.2	71.6	81.5
Aged 65 or older	62.7	60.2	60.2	72.6
COLLEGE GRADUATES				
Total, aged 25 or older	24.8	20.5	21.4	24.5
Aged 25 to 34	29.6	24.8	23.6	22.0
Aged 35 to 44	31.2	25.4	26.9	28.4
Aged 45 to 54	28.5	24.0	23.8	29.0
Aged 55 to 64	19.8	15.8	18.1	25.6
Aged 65 or older	12.4	8.6	12.4	17.4

Source: Bureau of the Census, Educational Attainment in the United States: March 1993 and 1992, *Current Population Reports, P20-476, 1994*

Educational Attainment of Whites by State, 1990

(percent of whites aged 25 or older who are high school or college graduates, by state, 1990)

	high school graduate or more	college graduate		high school graduate or more	college graduate
United States	77.9%	21.5%	Missouri	74.9%	18.3%
Alabama	70.3	17.3	Montana	81.7	20.3
Alaska	91.1	26.8	Nebraska	82.4	19.2
Arizona	82.4	22.2	Nevada	80.9	15.9
Arkansas	68.6	14.1	New Hampshire	82.2	24.2
California	81.1	25.4	New Jersey	78.6	25.8
Colorado	86.1	28.3	New Mexico	78.6	23.4
Connecticut	80.9	28.5	New York	78.5	25.3
Delaware	80.3	23.0	North Carolina	73.1	19.3
District of Columbia	93.1	69.0	North Dakota	76.9	18.3
Florida	77.0	19.3	Ohio	76.9	17.6
Georgia	74.9	21.8	Oklahoma	75.7	18.7
Hawaii	89.3	30.2	Oregon	82.3	20.8
Idaho	80.9	18.0	Pennsylvania	75.9	18.5
Illinois	79.1	22.4	Rhode Island	73.0	21.8
Indiana	76.5	17.6	South Carolina	73.6	19.8
Iowa	80.3	16.7	South Dakota	77.8	17.6
Kansas	82.4	21.7	Tennessee	68.2	16.7
Kentucky	64.7	13.9	Texas	76.2	22.6
Louisiana	74.2	18.7	Utah	86.2	22.7
Maine	78.9	18.8	Vermont	80.8	24.2
Maryland	80.8	28.9	Virginia	78.3	27.0
Massachusetts	81.2	27.7	Washington	85.0	23.3
Michigan	78.6	18.1	West Virginia	66.0	12.2
Minnesota	82.8	21.9	Wisconsin	79.6	18.1
Mississippi	71.7	17.2	Wyoming	83.9	19.3

Source: National Center for Education Statistics, Digest of Education Statistics 1993, *NCES 93-292, 1993*

School Enrollment of Whites by Age and Sex, 1993

(number and percent of whites aged 3 or older enrolled in school as of October 1993, by age and sex; numbers in thousands)

	total		male		female	
	number	*percent*	*number*	*percent*	*number*	*percent*
Total, aged 3 or older	52,152	25.7%	26,229	26.4%	25,923	24.9%
Aged 3 and 4	2,581	40.8	1,350	41.7	1,231	39.9
Aged 5 and 6	5,784	95.5	2,955	95.2	2,830	95.8
Aged 7 to 9	8,911	99.5	4,573	99.5	4,338	99.5
Aged 10 to 13	11,828	99.5	6,065	99.5	5,762	99.5
Aged 14 and 15	5,572	98.9	2,859	99.0	2,714	98.9
Aged 16 and 17	5,060	94.1	2,619	95.1	2,442	93.0
Aged 18 and 19	3,242	61.7	1,601	60.6	1,642	62.9
Aged 20 and 21	2,295	44.0	1,152	44.8	1,143	43.3
Aged 22 to 24	2,091	23.3	1,101	24.9	990	21.8
Aged 25 to 29	1,537	9.8	716	9.1	821	10.4
Aged 30 to 34	1,083	5.9	484	5.2	599	6.5
Aged 35 to 44	1,431	4.2	526	3.1	905	5.3
Aged 45 to 54	600	2.4	181	1.5	419	3.3
Aged 55 or older	136	0.3	47	0.2	89	0.4

Source: Bureau of the Census, School Enrollment—Social and Economic Characteristics of Students: October 1993, *Current Population Reports, P20-479, 1994*

White Families With Children in College, 1993

(total number of white families, number with children aged 18 to 24, and number and percent with children aged 18 to 24 attending college full-time as of October 1993, by household income in 1992; numbers in thousands)

	total	with children aged 18-24	with one or more children attending college full-time		
			number	percent of total families	percent of families with children 18-24
Total families	58,111	8,296	3,513	6.0%	42.3%
Under $20,000	13,905	1,526	304	2.2	19.9
$20,000 to $29,999	9,324	1,108	351	3.8	31.7
$30,000 to $39,999	8,866	1,216	473	5.3	38.9
$40,000 to $49,999	6,250	983	472	7.6	48.0
$50,000 to $74,999	9,190	1,632	885	9.6	54.2
$75,000 or more	6,303	1,222	782	12.4	64.0

Source: Bureau of the Census, School Enrollment—Social and Economic Characteristics of Students: October 1993, *Current Population Reports, P20-479, 1994*

College Enrollment of Whites by Age, 1993

(number of whites enrolled in college by age and attendance status, October 1993; numbers in thousands)

	total	undergraduate total	two-year college total	two-year full-time	two-year part-time	four-year college total	four-year full-time	four-year part-time	graduate total	graduate full-time	graduate part-time
Total enrolled, aged 15 or older	11,434	9,421	3,431	1,814	1,617	5,990	4,631	1,358	2,013	829	1,183
Aged 15 to 17	98	98	32	16	16	66	60	6	-	-	-
Aged 18 and 19	2,456	2,453	891	712	179	1,562	1,494	68	3	3	-
Aged 20 and 21	2,243	2,234	560	377	183	1,674	1,564	111	9	6	3
Aged 22 to 24	2,064	1,610	503	254	250	1,107	853	254	454	305	148
Aged 25 to 29	1,490	982	418	151	267	564	315	249	508	263	245
Aged 30 to 34	1,015	690	332	115	217	358	138	220	326	115	211
Aged 35 to 39	795	568	308	94	214	260	104	156	227	71	155
Aged 40 to 44	572	370	168	42	127	202	52	150	201	30	172
Aged 45 to 49	392	235	123	40	83	112	28	84	157	17	139
Aged 50 to 54	190	108	49	13	36	59	14	45	82	10	72
Aged 55 to 59	55	34	18	2	16	16	7	9	21	2	18
Aged 60 to 64	15	3	2	-	2	1	-	1	13	6	7
Aged 65 or older	50	37	26	-	26	11	2	8	13	-	13

Note: (–) means number in sample is too small to make a reliable estimate.
Source: Bureau of the Census, School Enrollment—Social and Economic Characteristics of Students: October 1993, Current Population Reports, P20-479, 1994

Bachelor's, Master's, and Doctoral Degrees
Earned by Non-Hispanic Whites by Field of Study, 1992-93

(number and percent of bachelor's, master's, and doctoral degrees earned by non-Hispanic whites, by field of study, 1992-93)

	bachelor's		master's		doctoral	
	number	percent	number	percent	number	percent
Total degrees	947,309	81.7%	278,829	75.6%	26,700	63.5%
Agriculture and natural resources	15,152	90.3	2,743	69.2	564	48.1
Architecture and related programs	7,289	79.5	2,586	67.9	61	41.2
Area, ethnic, and cultural studies	3,864	70.5	1,040	68.3	114	64.0
Biological/life sciences	35,766	76.0	3,281	69.0	2,810	63.4
Business, management, and admin. services	205,083	79.8	66,535	74.2	815	60.5
Communications	45,480	84.4	3,461	72.8	196	66.9
Communications technologies	666	80.0	307	67.5	5	62.5
Computer and information sciences	16,502	68.2	4,700	46.2	383	47.6
Construction trades	58	84.1	-	-	-	-
Education	96,857	89.9	81,290	84.7	5,497	78.2
Engineering	45,803	73.9	14,827	53.7	2,210	38.0
Engineering related technologies	12,929	81.3	824	74.9	9	45.0
English language and literature	48,957	87.2	6,732	86.4	1,094	81.6
Foreign languages and literature	11,240	78.1	2,060	64.4	488	58.8
Health professions and related sciences	56,464	84.2	21,328	82.9	1,205	68.2
Home economics	13,019	86.2	1,935	78.1	255	73.9
Law and legal studies	1,678	81.6	1,188	54.1	11	12.8
Liberal arts and sciences	26,965	80.6	2,076	85.9	65	80.2
Library science	74	89.2	4,154	85.3	46	59.7
Mathematics	11,867	80.1	2,530	62.2	484	40.7
Mechanics and repairers	76	72.4	-	-	-	-
Multi/interdisciplinary studies	19,207	80.2	2,100	84.1	140	71.4
Parks, recreation, leisure and fitness	8,885	90.1	1,227	85.6	77	71.3
Philosophy and religion	6,693	86.0	1,170	82.1	340	75.9
Physical sciences	14,275	81.4	3,262	60.8	2,405	54.7
Precision production trades	331	85.3	2	100.0	-	-
Protective services	15,952	76.3	1,024	75.5	22	68.8
Psychology	55,057	82.5	9,357	85.4	3,125	85.6
Public administration and services	12,716	75.8	16,130	78.2	318	69.3
R.O.T.C. and military sciences	11	100.0	93	86.1	-	-
Social sciences and history	109,942	81.0	9,474	70.3	2,201	63.6
Theological studies/religious vocations	4,841	89.1	3,836	77.0	1,065	75.2
Transportation and material moving	3,482	88.6	439	88.7	-	-
Visual and performing arts	40,128	84.0	7,118	75.4	695	78.8

Source: National Center for Education Statistics, Digest of Education Statistics 1995, *NCES 95-029, 1995*

First-Professional Degrees Earned by
Non-Hispanic Whites by Field of Study, 1992-93

(number and percent of first-professional degrees earned by non-Hispanic whites, by field of study, 1992-93)

	number	percent
Total	60,830	81.1%
Dentistry (D.D.S. or D.M.D.)	2,451	68.0
Medicine (M.D.)	11,729	75.5
Optometry (O.D.)	903	78.7
Osteopathic medicine (D.O.)	1,359	83.5
Pharmacy (Pharm. D.)	1,263	66.3
Podiatry (Pod. D. or D.P. or D.P.M.)	350	73.5
Veterinary medicine (D.V.M.)	1,888	91.8
Chiropractic medicine (D.C. or D.C.M.)	2,383	85.1
Law (L.L.B. or J.D.)	34,267	85.0
Theology (M.Div., M.H.L., B.D., or Ord.)	4,189	76.9
Other	48	75.0

Source: National Center for Education Statistics, Digest of Education Statistics 1995, NCES 95-029, 1995

Whites:
Health

Two out of three whites report being in excellent or very good health, while just 10 percent say their health is only fair or poor. Because whites comprise the majority of the American population, these proportions closely match those of the total population.

Health indicators for whites are close to the average on most measures, with a few exceptions. The incidence of AIDS, tuberculosis, and syphilis is much lower among whites than for the total population. The suicide rate among whites is slightly higher than average.

Twenty percent of whites are disabled, about average for the population as a whole. Only 14 percent of whites lack health insurance.

Heart disease is the leading cause of death among all whites. White life expectancy is slightly above average. At birth, non-Hispanic white males can expect to live about one year longer than the average American male, while non-Hispanic white females can expect to live 0.7 year longer than the average female.

Health Status of Whites by Age, 1993

(percent distribution of self-assessed or parent-assessed health status of whites, by age, 1993)

	total	excellent	very good	good	fair	poor
Total	100.0%	38.8%	28.6%	22.9%	7.2%	2.6%
Under age 5	100.0	55.1	26.8	15.3	2.5	0.3
Aged 5 to 17	100.0	53.6	27.3	16.7	2.1	0.3
Aged 18 to 24	100.0	42.5	31.8	21.4	3.5	0.7
Aged 25 to 44	100.0	40.2	31.6	21.6	5.2	1.4
Aged 45 to 64	100.0	29.9	27.8	27.0	10.7	4.6
Aged 65 or older	100.0	17.1	23.1	33.3	18.6	7.9

Source: National Center for Health Statistics, Current Estimates From the National Health Interview Survey, 1993, *Series 10, No. 190, 1994*

Health Indicators for Whites, 1992

(selected indicators of total and white health status, and index of white health indicators to total, 1992 except where otherwise noted)

	total population indicator	white indicator	index
Infant mortality rate (deaths < age 1 per 1,000 live births, 1991)	8.6	7.1	83
Total deaths per 100,000 population	504.5	477.5	95
Motor vehicle crash deaths per 100,000 population	15.8	15.9	101
Work-related injury deaths per 100,000 people aged 16 or older, 1993	3.2	3.1	97
Suicides per 100,000 population	11.1	11.8	106
Homicides per 100,000 population	10.5	6.1	58
Lung cancer deaths per 100,000 population	39.3	38.8	99
Female breast cancer deaths per 100,000 women	21.9	21.7	99
Cardiovascular disease deaths per 100,000 population	180.4	172.8	96
Heart disease deaths per 100,000 population	144.3	139.2	96
Stroke deaths per 100,000 population	26.2	24.2	92
Reported incidence of AIDS per 100,000 population, 1993*	31.2	17.9	57
Reported incidence of tuberculosis per 100,000 population, 1993*	9.8	3.6	37
Reported incidence of syphilis per 100,000 population, 1993*	10.4	1.2	12
Prevalence of low birth weight, as percent of total live births	7.1	5.8	82
Births to girls aged 10 to 17, as percent of total live births	4.9	3.9	80
Percent of mothers without care, first trimester of pregnancy	22.3	19.2	86
Percent < age 18 living in poverty, 1993	22.7	17.8	78
Percent living in counties exceeding U.S. air quality standards, 1993	23.5	23.1	98

* Data are for the non-Hispanic population.
Note: The index is calculated by dividing the white figure by the total figure for each indicator and multiplying by 100. For example, the index of 83 indicates that the white infant mortality rate is 17 percent below the rate for all infants.
Source: National Center for Health Statistics, Health Status Indicators: Differentials by Race and Hispanic Origin, *Healthy People 2000, No. 10, 1995*

Acute Health Conditions Among Whites by Age, 1993

(number of acute conditions affecting whites and rate per 100 whites in specified age group, by type of acute condition, 1993; numbers in thousands)

	total		under age 18		aged 18 to 44		aged 45 or older	
	number	*rate*	*number*	*rate*	*number*	*rate*	*number*	*rate*
Total acute conditions	415,189	196.5	172,689	322.4	156,640	180.1	85,859	121.3
Infective and								
parasitic diseases	47,106	22.3	25,979	48.5	13,516	15.5	7,611	10.8
Common childhood								
diseases	3,444	1.6	3,198	6.0	246	0.3	-	-
Intestinal virus	9,977	4.7	4,936	9.2	3,561	4.1	1,479	2.1
Viral infections	16,006	7.6	7,788	14.5	4,642	5.3	3,575	5.1
Other	17,679	8.4	10,056	18.8	5,066	5.8	2,557	3.6
Respiratory conditions	219,654	103.9	88,233	164.7	88,898	102.2	42,523	60.1
Common cold	56,136	26.6	25,353	47.3	20,437	23.5	10,345	14.6
Other acute upper								
respiratory infections	25,986	12.3	12,235	22.8	8,630	9.9	5,120	7.2
Influenza	117,915	55.8	43,195	80.6	52,984	60.9	21,735	30.7
Acute bronchitis	11,286	5.3	4,458	8.3	4,328	5.0	2,500	3.5
Pneumonia	4,120	1.9	1,421	2.7	1,334	1.5	1,365	1.9
Other respiratory								
conditions	4,211	2.0	1,570	2.9	1,184	1.4	1,457	2.1
Digestive system								
conditions	13,062	6.2	4,685	8.7	5,437	6.2	2,940	4.2
Dental conditions	2,838	1.3	1,042	1.9	1,482	1.7	314	0.4
Indigestion, nausea,								
and vomiting	5,972	2.8	2,612	4.9	2,349	2.7	1,012	1.4
Other digestive								
conditions	4,252	2.0	1,031	1.9	1,606	1.8	1,614	2.3
Injuries	52,912	25.0	14,745	27.5	24,128	27.7	14,039	19.8
Fractures and dislocations	6,982	3.3	1,547	2.9	3,418	3.9	2,018	2.9
Sprains and strains	12,015	5.7	2,174	4.1	6,375	7.3	3,465	4.9
Open wounds								
and lacerations	11,234	5.3	4,361	8.1	4,633	5.3	2,240	3.2
Contusions and								
superficial injuries	9,705	4.6	3,443	6.4	3,952	4.5	2,311	3.3
Other current injuries	12,976	6.1	3,221	6.0	5,750	6.6	4,006	5.7

(continued)

(continued from previous page)

	total		under age 18		aged 18 to 44		aged 45 or older	
	number	*rate*	*number*	*rate*	*number*	*rate*	*number*	*rate*
Selected other								
acute conditions	61,717	29.2	32,913	61.5	17,711	20.4	11,094	15.7
Eye conditions	2,566	1.2	1,104	2.1	612	0.7	850	1.2
Acute ear infections	24,064	11.4	19,202	35.9	3,003	3.5	1,859	2.6
Other ear conditions	3,051	1.4	1,774	3.3	666	0.8	610	0.9
Acute urinary conditions	6,076	2.9	990	1.8	2,502	2.9	2,584	3.7
Disorders of menstruation	569	0.3	162	0.3	207	0.2	200	0.3
Other disorders of female genital tract	1,465	0.7	201	0.4	1,146	1.3	118	0.2
Delivery and other conditions of pregnancy	3,295	1.6	104	0.2	3,191	3.7	-	-
Skin conditions	5,106	2.4	3,072	5.7	1,308	1.5	727	1.0
Acute musculoskeletal conditions	7,638	3.6	904	1.7	3,381	3.9	3,353	4.7
Headache, excluding migraine	3,203	1.5	1,541	2.9	1,194	1.4	469	0.7
Fever, unspecified	4,685	2.2	3,860	7.2	501	0.6	324	0.5
All other								
acute conditions	20,738	9.8	6,133	11.5	6,952	8.0	7,653	10.8

Note: The acute conditions shown here are those that caused people to restrict their activity for at least half a day or that caused people to contact a physician about the illness or injury. (-) means number in sample is too small to make a reliable estimate.
Source: National Center for Health Statistics, Current Estimates From the National Health Interview Survey, 1993, *Series 10, No. 190, 1994*

Chronic Health Conditions Among Whites by Age, 1993

(number of chronic conditions affecting whites and rate per 1,000 white persons in specified age group, by type of chronic condition, 1993; numbers in thousands)

	total number	total rate	under age 45 number	under age 45 rate	aged 45 to 64 number	aged 45 to 64 rate	aged 65 to 74 number	aged 65 to 74 rate	aged 75 or older number	aged 75 or older rate
Selected skin and musculoskeletal conditions										
Arthritis	28,230	133.6	4,785	34.0	9,907	231.3	7,410	448.5	6,128	536.2
Gout	1,744	8.3	336	2.4	708	16.5	510	30.9	190	16.6
Intervertebral disc disorders	5,529	26.2	2,471	17.6	2,015	47.0	704	42.6	339	29.7
Bone spur or tendinitis	2,206	10.4	785	5.6	845	19.7	473	28.6	103	9.0
Disorders of bone or cartilage	1,520	7.2	465	3.3	489	11.4	255	15.4	311	27.2
Trouble with bunions	2,591	12.3	825	5.9	808	18.9	562	34.0	396	34.6
Bursitis	3,883	18.4	1,229	8.7	1,747	40.8	549	33.2	358	31.3
Sebaceous skin cyst	1,329	6.3	705	5.0	456	10.6	87	5.3	81	7.1
Trouble with acne	4,675	22.1	4,311	30.7	313	7.3	41	2.5	10	0.9
Psoriasis	2,360	11.2	1,338	9.5	705	16.5	174	10.5	143	12.5
Dermatitis	8,344	39.5	5,633	40.1	1,712	40.0	616	37.3	383	33.5
Trouble with dry (itching) skin	4,362	20.6	2,248	16.0	1,045	24.4	744	45.0	325	28.4
Trouble with ingrown nails	5,329	25.2	2,605	18.5	1,330	31.1	621	37.6	773	67.6
Trouble with corns and calluses	4,084	19.3	1,589	11.3	1,381	32.2	544	32.9	570	49.9
Impairments										
Visual impairment	8,164	38.6	3,393	24.1	2,074	48.4	1,040	62.9	1,657	145.0
Color blindness	2,933	13.9	1,670	11.9	724	16.9	212	12.8	327	28.6
Cataracts	5,299	25.1	261	1.9	788	18.4	1,945	117.7	2,305	201.7
Glaucoma	2,307	10.9	127	0.9	593	13.8	645	39.0	942	82.4
Hearing impairment	22,079	104.5	6,314	44.9	6,568	153.4	4,499	272.3	4,698	411.1
Tinnitus	8,064	38.2	2,441	17.4	2,656	62.0	1,818	110.0	1,149	100.5
Speech impairment	2,252	10.7	1,605	11.4	291	6.8	185	11.2	171	15.0
Absence of extremities	1,320	6.2	432	3.1	386	9.0	260	15.7	242	21.2
Paralysis of extremities	1,367	6.5	421	3.0	337	7.9	392	23.7	217	19.0
Deformity or orthopedic impairment	27,095	128.2	14,622	104.0	7,558	176.5	2,606	157.7	2,309	202.0

(continued)

(continued from previous page)

	total		under age 45		aged 45 to 64		aged 65 to 74		aged 75 or older	
	number	rate	number	rate	number	rate	number	rate	number	rate
Selected digestive conditions										
Ulcer	3,712	17.6	1,698	12.1	1,010	23.6	592	35.8	412	36.0
Hernia of abdominal cavity	4,508	21.3	962	6.8	1,435	33.5	1,191	72.1	920	80.5
Gastritis or duodenitis	2,820	13.3	1,173	8.3	868	20.3	491	29.7	288	25.2
Frequent indigestion	5,408	25.6	2,667	19.0	1,502	35.1	621	37.6	618	54.1
Enteritis or colitis	2,532	12.0	1,103	7.8	827	19.3	333	20.2	269	23.5
Spastic colon	1,759	8.3	770	5.5	625	14.6	246	14.9	118	10.3
Diverticula of intestines	1,963	9.3	120	0.9	418	9.8	782	47.3	643	56.3
Frequent constipation	3,678	17.4	1,167	8.3	955	22.3	585	35.4	971	85.0
Selected conditions of the genitourinary, nervous, endocrine, metabolic, or blood systems										
Goiter or other disorders of the thyroid	3,708	17.5	1,436	10.2	1,189	27.8	652	39.5	431	37.7
Diabetes	6,301	29.8	1,151	8.2	2,413	56.3	1,576	95.4	1,161	101.6
Anemias	2,952	14.0	1,788	12.7	534	12.5	320	19.4	310	27.1
Epilepsy	1,093	5.2	753	5.4	189	4.4	100	6.1	51	4.5
Migraine	9,554	45.2	6,362	45.3	2,649	61.9	329	19.9	214	18.7
Neuralgia or neuritis	569	2.7	90	0.6	216	5.0	107	6.5	156	13.6
Kidney trouble	3,259	15.4	1,633	11.6	895	20.9	373	22.6	358	31.3
Bladder disorders	3,637	17.2	1,459	10.4	980	22.9	522	31.6	676	59.1
Diseases of prostate	1,852	8.8	158	1.1	618	14.4	467	28.3	609	53.3
Diseases of female genital organs	4,521	21.4	2,995	21.3	1,175	27.4	174	10.5	177	15.5
Selected circulatory conditions										
Rheumatic fever	1,874	8.9	827	5.9	656	15.3	264	16.0	127	11.1
Heart disease	18,629	88.1	4,709	33.5	5,108	119.3	4,699	284.4	4,113	359.9
Ischemic heart disease	6,404	30.3	478	3.4	1,947	45.5	2,260	136.8	1,719	150.4
Heart rhythm disorders	7,945	37.6	3,220	22.9	1,936	45.2	1,577	95.4	1,212	106.0
Other diseases of heart, excl. hypertension	4,280	20.3	1,010	7.2	1,224	28.6	863	52.2	1,183	103.5
High blood pressure (hypertension)	22,783	107.8	4,499	32.0	8,726	203.7	5,627	340.6	3,931	343.9
Cerebrovascular disease	2,863	13.5	148	1.1	745	17.4	772	46.7	1,198	104.8

(continued)

(continued from previous page)

	total		under age 45		aged 45 to 64		aged 65 to 74		aged 75 or older	
	number	*rate*	*number*	*rate*	*number*	*rate*	*number*	*rate*	*number*	*rate*
Hardening of the arteries	1,634	7.7	47	0.3	322	7.5	627	37.9	638	55.8
Varicose veins of lower extremities	6,981	33.0	2,437	17.3	2,354	55.0	1,279	77.4	911	79.7
Hemorrhoids	9,182	43.4	4,014	28.6	3,006	70.2	1,315	79.6	847	74.1
Selected respiratory conditions										
Chronic bronchitis	12,143	57.5	7,693	54.7	2,660	62.1	1,167	70.6	623	54.5
Asthma	10,616	50.2	7,338	52.2	1,904	44.5	925	56.0	449	39.3
Hay fever	20,534	97.2	13,827	98.4	4,584	107.0	1,391	84.2	732	64.0
Chronic sinusitis	32,048	151.6	19,800	140.9	8,004	186.9	2,856	172.9	1,388	121.4
Deviated nasal septum	1,702	8.1	961	6.8	480	11.2	181	11.0	80	7.0
Chronic disease of tonsils or adenoids	2,413	11.4	2,310	16.4	59	1.4	44	2.7	-	0.0
Emphysema	1,730	8.2	212	1.5	684	16.0	446	27.0	388	33.9

Note: Chronic conditions are those that last at least three months or belong to a group of conditions that are considered to be chronic regardless of when they began. (-) means number in sample is too small to make a reliable estimate.
Source: National Center for Health Statistics, Current Estimates From the National Health Interview Survey, 1993, *Series 10, No. 190, 1994*

Whites With Disabilities, 1991-92

(total numbers of whites, number and percent with a disability, and number and percent with a severe disability, by selected characteristics, 1991-92; numbers in thousands)

	total	number	percent	number	percent
		with a disability		**with a severe disability**	
Total persons	210,873	41,521	19.7%	19,736	9.4%
AGE					
Under age 6	18,561	701	3.8	94	0.5
Aged 6 to 14	26,143	1,702	6.5	357	1.4
Aged 15 to 17	7,886	702	8.9	207	2.6
Aged 18 to 24	20,195	2,084	10.3	653	3.2
Aged 25 to 34	35,750	4,313	12.1	1,494	4.2
Aged 35 to 44	33,510	5,627	16.8	2,030	6.1
Aged 45 to 54	23,086	5,184	22.5	2,239	9.7
Aged 55 to 64	18,346	6,650	36.3	3,663	20.0
Aged 65 to 74	16,396	7,207	44.0	4,015	24.5
Aged 75 or older	11,000	7,352	66.8	4,984	45.3
HOUSEHOLD TYPE					
Family householder or spouse	104,124	23,932	23.0	10,952	10.5
With children under age 18	47,574	6,951	14.6	2,344	4.9
Married, spouse present	93,903	20,902	22.3	9,375	10.0
With children under age 18	42,379	5,701	13.5	1,797	4.2
No spouse present	10,221	3,030	29.7	1,578	15.4
With children under age 18	5,195	1,250	24.1	547	10.5
Nonfamily householder	24,974	8,855	35.5	5,108	20.5
Living alone	21,816	8,368	38.4	4,962	22.8
REGION					
Northeast	43,650	7,948	18.2	4,271	9.8
Midwest	57,287	10,946	19.1	4,639	8.1
South	65,405	14,003	21.4	7,008	10.7
West	44,530	8,624	19.4	3,818	8.6

Source: Bureau of the Census, Americans With Disabilities: 1991-92, *Current Population Reports, P70-33, 1993*

Physician Contacts by Whites, 1993

(total number of physician contacts by whites and number per person per year, by age and place of contact, 1993)

	total places	telephone	office	hospital	other
Total contacts (in thousands)	1,313,638	166,812	748,298	155,270	233,605
Under age 18	265,837	39,083	162,393	29,656	32,883
Aged 18 to 44	448,696	60,624	257,330	53,569	73,091
Aged 45 to 64	299,277	43,937	170,659	37,388	45,728
Aged 65 or older	299,828	23,168	157,917	34,656	81,902
Contacts per person	6.2	0.8	3.5	0.7	1.1
Under age 18	5.0	0.7	3.0	0.6	0.6
Aged 18 to 44	5.2	0.7	3.0	0.6	0.8
Aged 45 to 64	7.0	1.0	4.0	0.9	1.1
Aged 65 or older	10.7	0.8	5.6	1.2	2.9

Source: National Center for Health Statistics, Current Estimates From the National Health Interview Survey, 1993, *Series 10, No. 190, 1994*

Health Insurance Coverage of Whites by Age, 1993

(number and percent distribution of whites, by age and health insurance coverage status, 1993; numbers in thousands)

| | total persons | covered by private or government health insurance | | | | | | | not covered |
| | | total | private health insurance | | government health insurance | | | | |
			total	group health	total	Medicaid	Medicare	Champus	
Number									
Total	215,221	184,732	158,586	128,855	53,222	20,642	29,297	7,689	30,489
Under 18	54,961	47,741	39,646	33,889	12,045	10,533	33	1,715	7,219
18 to 24	20,500	15,159	13,272	9,578	2,747	1,835	103	901	5,342
25 to 34	34,302	27,384	24,600	21,926	3,636	2,611	368	887	6,918
35 to 44	34,600	29,335	27,203	24,228	3,025	1,797	474	995	5,265
45 to 54	25,230	21,977	20,491	18,110	2,443	1,022	622	1,047	3,253
55 to 64	18,048	15,808	14,319	11,895	2,773	817	1,231	1,050	2,240
65 or older	27,580	27,329	19,054	9,229	26,552	2,027	26,467	1,094	252
Percent									
Total	100.0%	85.8%	73.7%	59.9%	24.7%	9.6%	13.6%	3.6%	14.2%
Under 18	100.0	86.9	72.1	61.7	21.9	19.2	0.1	3.1	13.1
18 to 24	100.0	73.9	64.7	46.7	13.4	8.9	0.5	4.4	26.1
25 to 34	100.0	79.8	71.7	63.9	10.6	7.6	1.1	2.6	20.2
35 to 44	100.0	84.8	78.6	70.0	8.7	5.2	1.4	2.9	15.2
45 to 54	100.0	87.1	81.2	71.8	9.7	4.1	2.5	4.1	12.9
55 to 64	100.0	87.6	79.3	65.9	15.4	4.5	6.8	5.8	12.4
65 or older	100.0	99.1	69.1	33.5	96.3	7.3	96.0	4.0	0.9

Source: Bureau of the Census, unpublished tables from the 1994 Current Population Survey

Leading Causes of Death Among Whites, 1993

(number of deaths among whites, and number and percent accounted for by ten leading causes of death, 1993)

		number	percent
	All causes	1,951,437	100.0%
1.	Diseases of heart	655,365	33.6
2.	Malignant neoplasms	461,904	23.7
3.	Cerebrovascular diseases	129,992	6.7
4.	Chronic obstructive pulmonary diseases and allied conditions	93,615	4.8
5.	Accidents and adverse effects	75,218	3.9
6.	Pneumonia and influenza	73,720	3.8
7.	Diabetes mellitus	43,461	2.2
8.	Suicide	28,035	1.4
9.	Human immunodeficiency virus infection	23,586	1.2
10.	Chronic liver disease and cirrhosis	21,348	1.1
	All other causes	345,193	17.7

Source: National Center for Health Statistics, Advance Report of Final Mortality Statistics, 1993, *Vol. 44, No. 7 Supplement, 1996*

Life Expectancy of Whites and Non-Hispanic Whites at Birth and Age 65, 1995-2020

(average number of years of life remaining at birth and at age 65 for white and non-Hispanic white males and females, 1995-2050; difference between white and non-Hispanic white life expectancy and total life expectancy for males and females at birth and at age 65, 1995 and 2020)

| | life expectancy (years) | | | |
| | white | | non-Hispanic white | |
	males	females	males	females
AT BIRTH				
1995	73.6	80.1	73.6	80.0
2000	74.2	80.5	74.3	80.5
2005	74.7	81.0	74.9	81.0
2010	75.5	81.6	75.7	81.5
2015	76.3	82.1	76.4	81.9
2020	77.1	82.6	77.2	82.4
Life exp. of white or non-Hispanic white minus				
life exp. of total Americans				
1995	1.1	0.8	1.1	0.7
2020	1.6	1.1	1.7	0.9
AT AGE 65				
1995	15.7	19.4	15.6	19.3
2000	16.2	19.7	16.1	19.6
2005	16.8	20.0	16.7	19.9
2010	17.3	20.4	17.1	20.2
2015	17.8	20.8	17.5	20.5
2020	18.3	21.1	18.0	20.8
Life exp. of white or non-Hispanic white minus				
life exp. of total Americans				
1995	0.2	0.2	0.1	0.1
2020	0.7	0.5	0.4	0.2

Note: Hispanics may be of any race and most are white. For a breakdown of the Hispanic composition of racial groups and the racial composition of Hispanics, see the tables in the introduction to this book.
Source: Bureau of the Census, Population Projections of the United States, by Age, Sex, Race, and Hispanic Origin: 1995 to 2050, *Current Population Reports, P25-1130, 1996*

Whites:
Households and Living Arrangements

Because whites make up the majority of the American population, the household composition and living arrangements of the white population mirror those of the total. Twenty-three percent of white householders are aged 65 or older, versus 21 percent of the total. Forty-two percent of white householders are aged 25 to 44, versus 43 percent of total householders.

Fifty-eight percent of white households are married couples, and 27 percent are nuclear families, about the same as for households in the nation as a whole. Female-headed families with children account for just 6 percent of white households.

Seventy-nine percent of white children live with both parents, while 18 percent live with their mother only. Nearly half of white men aged 20 to 24 still live with their parents, versus 37 percent of white women in this age group. Overall, 59 percent of white women and 61 percent of white men aged 15 or older are married.

White Households by Age of Householder, 1994

(number and percent distribution of white households, by age of householder, 1994; numbers in thousands)

	number	percent
Total households	82,387	100.0%
Under age 25	4,227	5.1
Aged 25 to 29	6,885	8.4
Aged 30 to 34	9,158	11.1
Aged 35 to 39	9,770	11.9
Aged 40 to 44	8,748	10.6
Aged 45 to 49	7,799	9.5
Aged 50 to 54	6,525	7.9
Aged 55 to 59	5,368	6.5
Aged 60 to 64	5,205	6.3
Aged 65 to 69	5,329	6.5
Aged 70 to 74	5,018	6.1
Aged 75 or older	8,355	10.1

Source: Bureau of the Census, Household and Family Characteristics: March 1994, *Current Population Reports, P20-483, 1995*

White Households by Household Type, 1994

(number and percent distribution of white households, by type of household, 1994; numbers in thousands)

	number	percent
Total households	82,387	100.0%
Family households	57,870	70.2
Married-couple families	47,443	57.6
With children <18	21,884	26.6
Without children <18	25,559	31.0
Female householder,		
no spouse present	8,130	9.9
With children <18	4,748	5.8
Without children <18	3,381	4.1
Male householder,		
no spouse present	2,297	2.8
Nonfamily households	24,518	29.8
Female householder	13,916	16.9
Living alone	12,180	14.8
Male householder	10,602	12.9
Living alone	8,023	9.7

Source: Bureau of the Census, Household and Family Characteristics: March 1994, *Current Population Reports, P20-483, 1995*

White Households by Type and Age of Householder, 1994

(number and percent distribution of white households, by age of householder and household type, 1994; numbers in thousands)

	total	family households				nonfamily households	
		total	married couples	female householder, no spouse present	male householder, no spouse present	female householder	male householder
Total, number	82,387	57,870	47,443	8,130	2,297	13,916	10,602
Under 20	421	218	73	123	22	123	80
20 to 24	3,806	2,080	1,320	538	222	761	966
25 to 29	6,885	4,573	3,524	786	263	902	1,410
30 to 34	9,158	6,906	5,606	1,035	265	842	1,411
35 to 39	9,770	7,804	6,309	1,196	299	705	1,261
40 to 44	8,748	7,025	5,744	980	301	690	1,033
45 to 49	7,799	6,195	5,107	876	212	785	818
50 to 54	6,525	5,154	4,409	581	164	716	655
55 to 59	5,368	4,094	3,504	466	123	730	544
60 to 64	5,205	3,768	3,331	333	104	958	480
65 to 74	10,347	6,473	5,572	714	186	2,882	992
75 to 84	6,488	2,968	2,486	374	109	2,814	706
85 or older	1,867	612	457	128	28	1,007	248
Total, percent	100.0%	70.2%	57.6%	9.9%	2.8%	16.9%	12.9%
Under 20	100.0	51.8	17.3	29.2	5.2	29.2	19.0
20 to 24	100.0	54.7	34.7	14.1	5.8	20.0	25.4
25 to 29	100.0	66.4	51.2	11.4	3.8	13.1	20.5
30 to 34	100.0	75.4	61.2	11.3	2.9	9.2	15.4
35 to 39	100.0	79.9	64.6	12.2	3.1	7.2	12.9
40 to 44	100.0	80.3	65.7	11.2	3.4	7.9	11.8
45 to 49	100.0	79.4	65.5	11.2	2.7	10.1	10.5
50 to 54	100.0	79.0	67.6	8.9	2.5	11.0	10.0
55 to 59	100.0	76.3	65.3	8.7	2.3	13.6	10.1
60 to 64	100.0	72.4	64.0	6.4	2.0	18.4	9.2
65 to 74	100.0	62.6	53.9	6.9	1.8	27.9	9.6
75 to 84	100.0	45.7	38.3	5.8	1.7	43.4	10.9
85 or older	100.0	32.8	24.5	6.9	1.5	53.9	13.3

Source: Bureau of the Census, Household and Family Characteristics: March 1994, *Current Population Reports, P20-483, 1995*

White Households by Size, 1994

(number and percent distribution of white households, by size, 1994; numbers in thousands)

	number	percent
Total households	82,387	100.0%
One person	20,202	24.5
Two persons	27,472	33.3
Three persons	13,982	17.0
Four persons	12,612	15.3
Five persons	5,512	6.7
Six persons	1,656	2.0
Seven or more persons	951	1.2

Source: Bureau of the Census, Household and Family Characteristics: March 1994, *Current Population Reports, P20-483, 1995*

White Married Couples by Age of Householder and Presence of Children, 1994

(number and percent of white married couples, by presence and number of own children under age 18 at home and by age of householder, 1994; numbers in thousands)

	total	< age 20	20-24	25-29	30-34	35-39	40-44	45-54	55-64	65+
Number	47,443	73	1320	3,524	5,606	6,309	5,744	9,517	6,836	8,515
Without children <18	25,559	42	580	1,210	1,170	959	1,337	5,528	6,324	8,410
With children <18	21,884	31	740	2,315	4,436	5,350	4,407	3,988	512	106
One	8,240	18	441	1,028	1,353	1,290	1,418	2,258	354	78
Two	8,981	11	240	921	2,017	2,493	1,929	1,234	114	20
Three or more	4,663	2	59	365	1,065	1,567	1,060	495	43	7
Percent	100.0%	100.0%	100.0%	100.0%	100.0%	100.0%	100.0%	100.0%	100.0%	100.0%
Without children <18	53.9	57.5	43.9	34.3	20.9	15.2	23.3	58.1	92.5	98.8
With children <18	46.1	42.5	56.1	65.7	79.1	84.8	76.7	41.9	7.5	1.2
One	17.4	24.7	33.4	29.2	24.1	20.4	24.7	23.7	5.2	0.9
Two	18.9	15.1	18.2	26.1	36.0	39.5	33.6	13.0	1.7	0.2
Three or more	9.8	2.7	4.5	10.4	19.0	24.8	18.5	5.2	0.6	0.1

Source: Bureau of the Census, Household and Family Characteristics: March 1994, *Current Population Reports, P20-483, 1995*

White Female-Headed Families by Age of Householder and Presence of Children, 1994

(number and percent of white female-headed families, by presence and number of own children under age 18 at home and by age of householder, 1994; numbers in thousands)

	total	< age 20	20-24	25-29	30-34	35-39	40-44	45-54	55-64	65+
Number	8,130	123	538	786	1,035	1,196	980	1,457	799	1,216
Without children <18	3,381	32	75	54	48	86	209	907	758	1,211
With children <18	4,748	91	462	732	987	1,110	771	549	41	6
One	2,362	68	270	315	397	463	423	383	38	6
Two	1,586	23	148	266	376	402	235	133	2	-
Three or more	800	-	44	151	214	244	113	32	-	-
Percent	100.0%	100.0%	100.0%	100.0%	100.0%	100.0%	100.0%	100.0%	100.0%	100.0%
Without children <18	41.6	26.0	13.9	6.9	4.6	7.2	21.3	62.3	94.9	99.6
With children <18	58.4	74.0	85.9	93.1	95.4	92.8	78.7	37.7	5.1	0.5
One	29.1	55.3	50.2	40.1	38.4	38.7	43.2	26.3	4.8	0.5
Two	19.5	18.7	27.5	33.8	36.3	33.6	24.0	9.1	0.3	-
Three or more	9.8	-	8.2	19.2	20.7	20.4	11.5	2.2	-	-

Note: (-) means number in sample is too small to make a reliable estimate.
Source: Bureau of the Census, Household and Family Characteristics: March 1994, *Current Population Reports, P20-483, 1995*

White Single-Person Households by Age of Householder, 1994

(number and percent distribution of white single-person households and single-person households as a percent of total white households, by age of householder, 1994; numbers in thousands)

	number	percent	percent of total white households
Total households	20,202	100.0%	24.5%
Under age 25	940	4.7	22.2
Aged 25 to 29	1,417	7.0	20.6
Aged 30 to 34	1,618	8.0	17.7
Aged 35 to 39	1,521	7.5	15.6
Aged 40 to 44	1,330	6.6	15.2
Aged 45 to 54	2,520	12.5	17.6
Aged 55 to 64	2,469	12.2	23.4
Aged 65 to 74	3,706	18.3	35.8
Aged 75 or older	4,681	23.2	56.0
Median age (years)	58.3	-	-

Source: Bureau of the Census, Household and Family Characteristics: March 1994, *Current Population Reports, P20-483, 1995*

Living Arrangements of White Children by Age, 1994

(number and percent distribution of white children by living arrangement, marital status of parent, and age of child, 1994; numbers in thousands)

	total	under age 6	6 to 11	12 to 17
Number with one or both parents	53,200	18,660	17,853	16,687
Living with both parents	41,766	14,754	14,073	12,939
Living with mother only	9,724	3,328	3,265	3,131
Divorced	4,466	928	1,659	1,879
Married, spouse absent	2,343	791	824	728
Widowed	503	72	157	273
Never married	2,412	1,538	624	250
Living with father only	1,710	578	515	617
Divorced	874	194	278	402
Married, spouse absent	313	63	101	149
Widowed	88	6	41	41
Never married	435	315	94	26
Percent with one or both parents	100.0%	100.0%	100.0%	100.0%
Living with both parents	78.5	79.1	78.8	77.5
Living with mother only	18.3	17.8	18.3	18.8
Divorced	8.4	5.0	9.3	11.3
Married, spouse absent	4.4	4.2	4.6	4.4
Widowed	0.9	0.4	0.9	1.6
Never married	4.5	8.2	3.5	1.5
Living with father only	3.2	3.1	2.9	3.7
Divorced	1.6	1.0	1.6	2.4
Married, spouse absent	0.6	0.3	0.6	0.9
Widowed	0.2	0.0	0.2	0.2
Never married	0.8	1.7	0.5	0.2

Source: Bureau of the Census, Marital Status and Living Arrangements: March 1994, *Current Population Reports, P20-484, 1996*

Living Arrangements of White Women by Age, 1994

(number and percent distribution of white women aged 18 or older by living arrangement and age, 1994; numbers in thousands)

	total	18 to 19	20 to 24	25 to 29	30 to 34	35 to 39	40 to 44	45 to 54	55 to 64	65 to 74	75 or older
Number	82,622	2,743	7,416	7,920	9,131	9,040	8,205	12,756	9,300	8,966	7,146
Family householder or spouse	55,408	267	2,633	5,151	7,168	7,606	6,907	10,511	7,179	5,591	2,396
Child of householder	6,879	1,933	2,724	899	461	299	205	220	77	30	33
Other member of family household	3,307	199	502	364	249	205	141	240	232	402	772
Nonfamily householder	13,914	121	761	902	842	705	690	1,501	1,688	2,882	3,821
Other member of nonfamily household	3,034	220	773	596	409	220	262	282	115	50	107
Group quarters*	80	3	23	8	2	5	-	2	9	11	17
Percent	100.0%	100.0%	100.0%	100.0%	100.0%	100.0%	100.0%	100.0%	100.0%	100.0%	100.0%
Family householder or spouse	67.1	9.7	35.5	65.0	78.5	84.1	84.2	82.4	77.2	62.4	33.5
Child of householder	8.3	70.5	36.7	11.4	5.0	3.3	2.5	1.7	0.8	0.3	0.5
Other member of family household	4.0	7.3	6.8	4.6	2.7	2.3	1.7	1.9	2.5	4.5	10.8
Nonfamily householder	16.8	4.4	10.3	11.4	9.2	7.8	8.4	11.8	18.2	32.1	53.5
Other member of nonfamily household	3.7	8.0	10.4	7.5	4.5	2.4	3.2	2.2	1.2	0.6	1.5
Group quarters*	0.1	0.1	0.3	0.1	0.0	0.1	-	0.0	0.1	0.1	0.2

* The Current Population Survey does not include people living in institutions such as prisons, the military, or college dormitories. It defines people living in group quarters as those in noninstitutional living arrangements that are not conventional housing units, such as rooming houses, staff quarters at a hospital, or halfway houses.

Note: (-) means number in sample is too small to make a reliable estimate.

Source: Bureau of the Census, Marital Status and Living Arrangements: March 1994, Current Population Reports, P20-484, 1996

Living Arrangements of White Men by Age, 1994

(number and percent distribution of white men aged 18 or older by living arrangement and age, 1994; numbers in thousands)

	total	18 to 19	20 to 24	25 to 29	30 to 34	35 to 39	40 to 44	45 to 54	55 to 64	65 to 74	75 or older
Number	77,639	2,816	7,525	8,047	9,204	9,152	8,203	12,474	8,748	7,116	4,353
Family householder or spouse	49,688	56	1,445	3,719	5,852	6,510	6,050	9,953	7,120	5,766	3,217
Child of householder	10,198	2,330	3,755	1,451	965	639	495	382	151	16	15
Other member of family household	2,769	202	517	506	340	234	163	215	233	223	133
Nonfamily householder	10,602	80	966	1,410	1,411	1,261	1,033	1,473	1,024	992	954
Other member of nonfamily household	4,314	145	821	949	633	504	462	440	217	115	28
Group quarters*	68	3	21	12	3	4	-	11	3	4	6
Percent	100.0%	100.0%	100.0%	100.0%	100.0%	100.0%	100.0%	100.0%	100.0%	100.0%	100.0%
Family householder or spouse	64.0	2.0	19.2	46.2	63.6	71.1	73.8	79.8	81.4	81.0	73.9
Child of householder	13.1	82.7	49.9	18.0	10.5	7.0	6.0	3.1	1.7	0.2	-
Other member of family household	3.6	7.2	6.9	6.3	3.7	2.6	2.0	1.7	2.7	3.1	3.1
Nonfamily householder	13.7	2.8	12.8	17.5	15.3	13.8	12.6	11.8	11.7	13.9	21.9
Other member of nonfamily household	5.6	5.1	10.9	11.8	6.9	5.5	5.6	3.5	2.5	1.6	0.6
Group quarters*	0.1	0.1	0.3	0.1	0.0	0.0	-	0.1	0.0	0.1	0.1

* The Current Population Survey does not include people living in institutions such as prisons, the military, or college dormitories. It defines people living in group quarters as those in noninstitutional living arrangements that are not conventional housing units, such as rooming houses, staff quarters at a hospital, or halfway houses.

Note: (-) means number in sample is too small to make a reliable estimate.

Source: Bureau of the Census, Marital Status and Living Arrangements: March 1994, Current Population Reports, P20-484, 1996

Marital Status of White Women by Age, 1994

(number and percent distribution of white women aged 15 or older by age and marital status, 1994; numbers in thousands)

	total	never married	married	widowed	divorced
Total, number	86,765	18,235	50,765	9424	8341
Under age 20	6,916	6,541	344	1	30
Aged 20 to 24	7,416	4,669	2,538	8	201
Aged 25 to 29	7,920	2,415	4,881	29	595
Aged 30 to 34	9,131	1,475	6,626	66	964
Aged 35 to 39	9,040	897	6,808	98	1237
Aged 40 to 44	8,205	602	6,321	102	1180
Aged 45 to 54	12,756	624	9,553	522	2057
Aged 55 to 64	9,300	337	6,638	1177	1148
Aged 65 to 74	8,966	313	5,053	2947	653
Aged 75 to 84	5,407	220	1,761	3201	225
Aged 85 or older	1,739	143	275	1271	50
Total, percent	100.0%	21.0%	58.5%	10.9%	9.6%
Under age 20	100.0	94.6	5.0	0.0	0.4
Aged 20 to 24	100.0	63.0	34.2	0.1	2.7
Aged 25 to 29	100.0	30.5	61.6	0.4	7.5
Aged 30 to 34	100.0	16.2	72.6	0.7	10.6
Aged 35 to 39	100.0	9.9	75.3	1.1	13.7
Aged 40 to 44	100.0	7.3	77.0	1.2	14.4
Aged 45 to 54	100.0	4.9	74.9	4.1	16.1
Aged 55 to 64	100.0	3.6	71.4	12.7	12.3
Aged 65 to 74	100.0	3.5	56.4	32.9	7.3
Aged 75 to 84	100.0	4.1	32.6	59.2	4.2
Aged 85 or older	100.0	8.2	15.8	73.1	2.9

Source: Bureau of the Census, Marital Status and Living Arrangements: March 1994, *Current Population Reports, P20-484, 1996*

Marital Status of White Men by Age, 1994

(number and percent distribution of white men aged 15 or older by age and marital status, 1994; numbers in thousands)

	total	never married	married	widowed	divorced
Total, number	82,026	23,704	50,226	1,878	6,218
Under age 20	7,203	7,095	97	2	9
Aged 20 to 24	7,525	5,977	1,467	2	79
Aged 25 to 29	8,047	3,823	3,853	9	362
Aged 30 to 34	9,204	2,442	6,019	6	737
Aged 35 to 39	9,152	1,538	6,588	23	1,003
Aged 40 to 44	8,203	970	6,109	24	1,100
Aged 45 to 54	12,474	912	9,980	101	1,481
Aged 55 to 64	8,748	423	7,173	253	899
Aged 65 to 74	7,116	339	5,755	607	415
Aged 75 to 84	3,513	135	2,668	590	120
Aged 85 or older	840	50	515	260	15
Total, percent	100.0%	28.9%	61.2%	2.3%	7.6%
Under age 20	100.0	98.5	1.3	0.0	0.1
Aged 20 to 24	100.0	79.4	19.5	0.0	1.0
Aged 25 to 29	100.0	47.5	47.9	0.1	4.5
Aged 30 to 34	100.0	26.5	65.4	0.1	8.0
Aged 35 to 39	100.0	16.8	72.0	0.3	11.0
Aged 40 to 44	100.0	11.8	74.5	0.3	13.4
Aged 45 to 54	100.0	7.3	80.0	0.8	11.9
Aged 55 to 64	100.0	4.8	82.0	2.9	10.3
Aged 65 to 74	100.0	4.8	80.9	8.5	5.8
Aged 75 to 84	100.0	3.8	75.9	16.8	3.4
Aged 85 or older	100.0	6.0	61.3	31.0	1.8

Source: Bureau of the Census, Marital Status and Living Arrangements: March 1994, *Current Population Reports, P20-484, 1996*

Whites:

Housing

Sixty-eight percent of the nation's white householders own their homes, which had a median value of $80,200 in 1990. This compares with a median value of $78,300 for the average homeowner.

The white share of households is lowest in the nation's central cities and highest in nonmetropolitan areas. Non-Hispanic whites account for only 66 percent of households in central cities, but for 88 percent of households in nonmetropolitan areas. Among the 50 metropolitan areas with the most non-Hispanic white households, non-Hispanic whites account for the largest share of households (over 93 percent) in Albany-Schenectady-Troy, New York, and Minneapolis, Minnesota. Non-Hispanic whites account for the smallest share of households in Los Angeles (53 percent) and New York (56 percent).

Sixteen percent of whites moved between 1993 and 1994, the same mobility rate as for the nation as a whole. Those aged 20 to 24 are most likely to move, while mobility rates are lowest for people in their 70s.

Characteristics of White Households
by Metropolitan Status, 1990

(number of white households, percent of total households that are white, percent of white households that are owner occupied, and median value of owner-occupied white households, by metropolitan status, 1990; numbers in thousands)

	number	white share of total households	owner-occupied percent	owner-occupied median value
White households	76,880	83.6%	68.2%	$80,200
Inside metropolitan areas	58,334	81.9	66.3	91,700
Central cities	21,323	71.6	54.3	75,800
Suburbs*	37,011	89.2	73.3	99,400
Outside metropolitan areas	18,546	89.7	74.0	51,400

* The suburbs are the portion of a metropolitan area that is outside the central city.
Source: Bureau of the Census, unpublished tables from the 1990 census

Characteristics of Non-Hispanic White Households
by Metropolitan Status, 1990

(number of non-Hispanic white households, percent of total households that are non-Hispanic white, percent of non-Hispanic white households that are owner occupied, and median value of owner-occupied non-Hispanic white households, by metropolitan status, 1990; numbers in thousands)

	number	non-Hispanic white share of total households	owner-occupied percent	owner-occupied median value
Non-Hispanic white households	73,634	80.0%	69.1%	$80,300
Inside metropolitan areas	55,417	77.8	67.4	91,900
Central cities	19,719	66.2	55.5	76,200
Suburbs*	35,698	86.0	73.9	99,200
Outside metropolitan areas	18,217	88.1	74.2	51,600

* The suburbs are the portion of a metropolitan area that is outside the central city.
Note: Hispanics may be of any race and most are white. For a breakdown of the Hispanic composition of racial groups or the racial composition of Hispanics, see the tables in the introduction to this book.
Source: Bureau of the Census, unpublished tables from the 1990 census

White Homeownership in the 50 Metropolitan Areas
With the Most White Households, 1990

(number of white households, percent of total households that are white, percent of white house-holds that are owner occupied, and median value of owner-occupied white households, in the total U.S. and in the 50 metropolitan areas with the most white households, ranked alphabetically, 1990; numbers in thousands)

	number	white share of total households	owner-occupied percent	owner-occupied median value
Total white households	76,880	83.6%	68.2%	$80,200
Anaheim-Santa Ana, CA	700	84.6	62.4	255,700
Atlanta, GA	781	73.9	70.0	94,000
Baltimore, MD	657	74.6	71.6	109,900
Bergen-Passaic, NJ	397	85.5	68.5	215,400
Boston, MA	965	89.3	59.4	186,600
Buffalo, NY	326	86.6	68.3	75,200
Charlotte-Gastonia-Rock Hill, NC-SC	358	81.2	72.1	76,100
Chicago, IL	1,614	72.7	66.3	118,900
Cincinnati, OH	472	86.1	67.8	72,000
Cleveland, OH	568	79.8	71.3	77,500
Columbus, OH	458	87.3	63.2	73,700
Dallas, TX	739	77.4	60.1	86,700
Denver, CO	570	87.7	64.3	88,100
Detroit, MI	1,259	77.8	75.7	74,200
Fort Lauderdale-Hollywood-Pompano Beach, FL	459	86.8	71.4	94,400
Fort Worth-Arlington, TX	414	83.7	63.6	74,500
Houston, TX	844	71.2	59.9	70,100
Indianapolis, IN	413	86.1	67.2	69,300
Kansas City, MO-KS	518	86.1	68.3	68,700
Los Angeles-Long Beach, CA	1,941	64.9	53.7	246,600
Louisville, KY-IN	320	86.9	71.2	58,300
Miami-Hialeah, FL	534	77.1	57.5	91,900
Middlesex-Somerset-Hunterdon, NJ	321	88.0	73.8	173,500
Milwaukee, WI	462	86.0	64.1	78,400
Minneapolis-St. Paul, MN-WI	880	94.1	70.8	87,600
Monmouth-Ocean, NJ	339	92.7	79.5	151,300
Nashville, TN	318	84.6	67.1	78,200
Nassau-Suffolk, NY	779	91.0	82.1	188,800
New York, NY	2,053	63.1	41.1	222,400

(continued)

(continued from previous page)

	number	white share of total households	owner-occupied percent	owner-occupied median value
Newark, NJ	478	73.3%	68.9%	$196,400
Norfolk-Virginia Beach-Newport News, VA	349	70.8	65.3	90,600
Oakland, CA	554	71.1	64.0	234,400
Orlando, FL	346	86.1	64.3	85,300
Philadelphia, PA-NJ	1,405	79.0	73.6	112,400
Phoenix, AZ	716	88.7	65.7	86,000
Pittsburgh, PA	750	91.5	72.1	55,700
Portland, OR	452	92.8	62.1	72,700
Riverside-San Bernardino, CA	696	80.2	68.5	135,400
Rochester, NY	335	89.3	71.4	86,500
Sacramento, CA	463	83.1	61.8	139,600
Salt Lake City-Ogden, UT	327	94.1	68.8	71,300
San Antonio, TX	354	78.4	61.9	61,500
San Diego, CA	725	81.7	57.4	192,900
San Francisco, CA	477	74.2	50.4	348,200
San Jose, CA	395	76.0	61.8	297,100
Seattle, WA	703	89.3	62.2	138,000
St. Louis, MO-IL	770	83.3	73.1	72,600
Tampa-St. Petersburg-Clearwater, FL	790	90.9	71.6	72,700
West Palm Beach-Boca Raton-Delray Beach, FL	1,006	68.9	68.5	180,500
Washington, DC-MD-VA	326	89.2	75.5	103,200

Source: Bureau of the Census, unpublished tables from the 1990 census

Non-Hispanic White Homeownership in the 50 Metropolitan Areas With the Most Non-Hispanic White Households, 1990

(number of non-Hispanic white households, percent of total households that are non-Hispanic white, percent of non-Hispanic white households that are owner occupied, and median value of owner-occupied non-Hispanic white households, in the U.S. and in the 50 metropolitan areas with the most non-Hispanic white households, ranked alphabetically, 1990; numbers in thousands)

	number	percent of total households	owner-occupied percent	owner-occupied median value
Total non-Hispanic white households	73,634	80.0%	69.1%	$80,300
Albany-Schenectady-Troy, NY	314	93.6	66.3	99,300
Anaheim-Santa Ana, CA	627	75.8	64.8	260,100
Atlanta, GA	771	73.0	70.3	94,000
Baltimore, MD	651	74.0	71.7	109,900
Bergen-Passaic, NJ	374	80.6	70.3	215,800
Boston, MA	947	87.6	60.0	186,600
Buffalo, NY	323	85.7	68.6	75,200
Charlotte-Gastonia-Rock Hill, NC-SC	356	80.7	72.2	76,100
Chicago, IL	1,529	68.8	67.6	119,700
Cincinnati, OH	471	85.8	67.8	72,000
Cleveland, OH	563	79.1	71.4	77,600
Columbus, OH	456	86.9	63.2	73,700
Dallas, TX	698	73.1	61.2	87,700
Dayton-Springfield, OH	313	85.9	68.6	66,700
Denver, CO	533	82.1	65.1	89,000
Detroit, MI	1,245	76.9	75.8	74,300
Fort Lauderdale-Hollywood-Pompano Beach, FL	431	81.5	72.3	95,100
Fort Worth-Arlington, TX	396	80.0	64.2	75,100
Houston, TX	755	63.6	62.0	72,300
Indianapolis, IN	411	85.6	67.2	69,300
Kansas City, MO-KS	512	84.9	68.4	68,800
Los Angeles-Long Beach, CA	1,585	53.0	56.6	262,400
Louisville, KY-IN	318	86.5	71.2	58,200
Miami-Hialeah, FL	309	84.8	74.8	98,100
Milwaukee, WI	456	84.7	64.4	78,600
Minneapolis-St. Paul, MN-WI	874	93.5	70.9	87,700
Monmouth-Ocean, NJ	332	90.9	79.9	151,300
Nashville, TN	316	84.2	67.2	78,200

(continued)

(continued from previous page)

	number	percent of total households	owner-occupied percent	owner-occupied median value
Nassau-Suffolk, NY	750	87.6%	82.9%	$189,400
New York, NY	1,813	55.7	44.2	223,700
Newark, NJ	445	68.2	71.3	197,100
Norfolk-Virginia Beach-Newport News, VA	345	69.8	65.5	90,600
Oakland, CA	515	66.0	64.6	237,400
Orlando, FL	325	81.0	64.9	85,600
Philadelphia, PA-NJ	1,387	78.0	73.8	112,700
Phoenix, AZ	673	83.4	66.5	87,000
Pittsburgh, PA	747	91.1	72.1	55,700
Portland, OR	446	91.5	62.4	72,800
Riverside-San Bernardino, CA	619	71.4	69.7	137,000
Rochester, NY	331	88.3	71.7	86,500
Sacramento, CA	438	78.7	62.3	140,500
Salt Lake City-Ogden, UT	318	91.6	69.2	71,600
San Diego, CA	664	74.8	58.7	195,300
San Francisco, CA	438	68.2	51.5	353,100
San Jose, CA	354	68.1	63.3	304,400
Seattle, WA	694	88.2	62.4	138,000
St. Louis, MO-IL	764	82.6	73.2	72,600
Tampa-St. Petersburg-Clearwater, FL	753	86.6	72.0	73,000
Washington, DC-MD-VA	972	66.6	69.3	180,700
West Palm Beach-Boca Raton-Delray Beach, FL	311	85.2	76.4	104,700

Note: Hispanics may be of any race and most are white. For a breakdown of the Hispanic composition of racial groups or the racial composition of Hispanics, see the tables in the introduction to this book.
Source: Bureau of the Census, unpublished tables from the 1990 census

Geographical Mobility of the White Population by Age, 1993 to 1994

(total number of whites aged 1 or older, number and percent of those who moved between March 1993 and March 1994, by age of person and type of move; numbers in thousands)

	total	same house (non-movers)	different house in the U.S.								movers from abroad
			total	same county	different county						
					total	same state	different state				
							total	same region	different region		
Total, 1 or older	212,024	84.0%	15.6%	9.8%	5.8%	3.2%	2.5%	1.4%	1.2%	0.4%
Aged 1 to 4	12,857	78.9	20.8	13.8	7.0	3.7	3.3	1.8	1.5	0.4
Aged 5 to 9	15,246	84.0	15.7	10.2	5.5	3.1	2.4	1.4	1.0	0.3
Aged 10 to 14	15,143	87.6	12.2	8.2	4.0	2.2	1.8	0.9	0.9	0.2
Aged 15 to 19	14,085	83.3	16.1	10.2	5.9	3.1	2.8	1.5	1.3	0.6
Aged 15 to 17	8,526	86.7	12.9	7.9	5.0	2.5	2.5	1.5	1.0	0.4
Aged 18 and 19	5,559	78.1	21.0	13.8	7.3	4.0	3.3	1.5	1.7	0.8
Aged 20 to 24	14,941	63.9	35.1	22.2	12.9	7.8	5.1	2.6	2.5	1.0
Aged 25 to 29	15,963	69.4	29.7	18.9	10.9	6.2	4.6	2.5	2.2	0.8
Aged 30 to 34	18,336	78.1	21.4	13.7	7.7	4.8	3.0	1.5	1.5	0.5
Aged 35 to 39	18,190	84.3	15.4	9.7	5.8	2.9	2.9	1.5	1.4	0.3
Aged 40 to 44	16,408	87.1	12.6	7.7	4.9	2.9	2.0	1.1	0.9	0.3
Aged 45 to 49	14,073	89.0	10.6	6.4	4.2	1.9	2.2	1.1	1.1	0.4
Aged 50 to 54	11,157	91.0	8.8	5.1	3.7	2.1	1.5	0.9	0.6	0.2
Aged 55 to 59	9,252	93.2	6.7	3.8	2.9	1.3	1.5	0.7	0.8	0.1
Aged 60 to 64	8,794	94.2	5.7	3.4	2.3	1.4	1.0	0.6	0.4	0.1
Aged 60 and 61	3,470	94.5	5.4	3.0	2.4	1.7	0.7	0.5	0.3	0.1
Aged 62 to 64	5,324	94.0	5.9	3.7	2.2	1.1	1.1	0.7	0.4	0.1
Aged 65 to 69	8,491	93.6	6.3	3.3	3.1	1.5	1.6	1.1	0.5	0.1
Aged 70 to 74	7,588	95.1	4.9	3.0	1.9	0.9	1.0	0.6	0.4	0.0
Aged 75 to 79	5,380	95.6	4.3	2.5	1.9	0.8	1.0	0.8	0.2	0.1
Aged 80 to 84	3,540	94.7	5.2	3.0	2.1	1.0	1.1	0.6	0.5	0.2
Aged 85 or older	2,579	94.2	5.8	3.5	2.3	1.1	1.2	0.5	0.8	0.0
Median age	34.9	37.0	27.2	26.8	27.9	27.6	28.3	28.4	28.2	26.6

Source: Bureau of the Census, Geographical Mobility: March 1993 to March 1994, *Current Population Reports, P20-485, 1995*

Whites:
Income

The median income of white households fell by nearly 4 percent between 1990 and 1994, to $34,028, after adjusting for inflation. But after removing Hispanics (who may be of any race) from the white statistics, the median income of non-Hispanic whites fell by a smaller 3 percent during those years. The median income of all white households is slightly greater than that of the average household, while the median income of non-Hispanic white households is slightly greater than that of all whites.

Among white households, median income peaks at $50,019 for householders aged 45 to 54. By household type, white married couples have the highest incomes—a median of $45,555 in 1994.

White men who work full-time earned a median of $33,300 in 1994, while white women earned $23,770. The median earnings of white women stood at 71 percent of the median earnings of white men in 1994.

White poverty rates were higher in 1994 than they were in 1990, but only 9 percent of white families were poor. Overall, about 12 percent of whites are poor, including 17 percent of children under age 18.

Median Income of White and Non-Hispanic White Households, 1980 to 1994

(median income of white and non-Hispanic white households, ratio of white and non-Hispanic white to total median income, and ratio of non-Hispanic white to white median income; percent change in incomes and ratios, selected years; in 1994 dollars)

| | white | | non-Hispanic white | | |
	median income	ratio white/total	median income	ratio non-Hispanic white/total	ratio non-Hispanic white/white
1994	$34,028	1.05	$35,126	1.09	1.03
1993	33,804	1.06	35,048	1.09	1.04
1992	34,023	1.05	35,164	1.09	1.03
1991	34,350	1.05	35,171	1.07	1.02
1990	35,413	1.04	36,222	1.07	1.02
1989	36,340	1.05	37,122	1.07	1.02
1988	36,055	1.06	37,049	1.09	1.03
1987	35,821	1.05	36,806	1.08	1.03
1986	35,394	1.05	36,198	1.08	1.02
1985	34,306	1.05	35,078	1.08	1.02
1984	33,729	1.05	34,430	1.08	1.02
1983	32,787	1.05	33,427	1.07	1.02
1982	32,736	1.05	33,285	1.06	1.02
1981	33,148	1.06	33,627	1.07	1.01
1980	33,645	1.06	34,241	1.07	1.02
Percent change					
1990-1994	-3.9%	1.1%	-3.0%	2.0%	0.9%
1980-1994	1.1	0.0	2.6	1.4	1.4

Note: The white and non-Hispanic white/total ratios are calculated by dividing the median income of white and non-Hispanic white households by the median for total households and multiplying by 100. The non-Hispanic white/white ratio is calculated by dividing the median income of non-Hispanic white households by the median for white households. Hispanics may be of any race and most are white. For a breakdown of the Hispanic composition of racial groups and the racial composition of Hispanics, see the tables in the introduction to this book.
Source: U.S. Bureau of the Census, unpublished tables from the 1995 Current Population Survey

Income Distribution of White Households by Age of Householder, 1994

(number and percent distribution of white households by income and age of householder, 1994; households in thousands as of 1995)

	total	< 25	25-34	35-44	45-54	55-64	65+
Total	83,737	4,365	15,845	18,978	14,796	10,574	19,179
Under $10,000	9,824	840	1,352	1,265	963	1,221	4,183
$10,000 to $19,999	14,210	1,247	2,284	1,838	1,323	1,442	6,075
$20,000 to $29,999	12,867	1,027	2,755	2,455	1,574	1,588	3,469
$30,000 to $39,999	11,269	583	2,680	2,782	1,776	1,392	2,056
$40,000 to $49,999	8,776	307	2,131	2,427	1,758	1,137	1,015
$50,000 to $59,999	6,993	150	1,588	2,121	1,423	939	771
$60,000 to $69,999	5,455	82	1,070	1,720	1,443	718	422
$70,000 to $79,999	3,939	56	707	1,268	1,095	527	286
$80,000 to $89,999	2,528	24	392	767	848	293	204
$90,000 to $99,999	1,867	6	272	508	607	307	167
$100,000 or more	6,007	44	610	1,826	1,985	1,009	531
Median income	$34,028	$20,769	$35,518	$44,397	$50,019	$36,817	$18,670
Percent distribution	100.0%	100.0%	100.0%	100.0%	100.0%	100.0%	100.0%
Under $10,000	11.7	19.2	8.5	6.7	6.5	11.5	21.8
$10,000 to $19,999	17.0	28.6	14.4	9.7	8.9	13.6	31.7
$20,000 to $29,999	15.4	23.5	17.4	12.9	10.6	15.0	18.1
$30,000 to $39,999	13.5	13.4	16.9	14.7	12.0	13.2	10.7
$40,000 to $49,999	10.5	7.0	13.4	12.8	11.9	10.8	5.3
$50,000 to $59,999	8.4	3.4	10.0	11.2	9.6	8.9	4.0
$60,000 to $69,999	6.5	1.9	6.8	9.1	9.8	6.8	2.2
$70,000 to $79,999	4.7	1.3	4.5	6.7	7.4	5.0	1.5
$80,000 to $89,999	3.0	0.5	2.5	4.0	5.7	2.8	1.1
$90,000 to $99,999	2.2	0.1	1.7	2.7	4.1	2.9	0.9
$100,000 or more	7.2	1.0	3.8	9.6	13.4	9.5	2.8

Source: Bureau of the Census, unpublished tables from the 1995 Current Population Survey

Income Distribution of White Households by Household Type, 1994

(number and percent distribution of white households, by income and type of household, 1994; households in thousands as of 1995)

	total households	family households				nonfamily households				
		total	married couples	female hh, no spouse present	male hh, no spouse present	total	female householder total	female householder living alone	male householder total	male householder living alone
Total	83,737	58,437	47,899	8,031	2,507	25,300	14,207	12,547	11,093	8,453
Under $10,000	9,824	3,697	1,752	1,723	222	6,128	4,405	4,327	1,723	1,583
$10,000 to $19,999	14,210	7,577	5,254	1,853	471	6,633	4,119	3,866	2,514	2,196
$20,000 to $29,999	12,867	8,506	6,583	1,462	461	4,362	2,241	1,954	2,121	1,675
$30,000 to $39,999	11,269	8,330	6,765	1,181	384	2,940	1,393	1,123	1,547	1,168
$40,000 to $49,999	8,776	7,032	6,005	721	306	1,744	767	561	977	615
$50,000 to $59,999	6,993	5,831	5,188	431	213	1,161	473	313	689	416
$60,000 to $69,999	5,455	4,729	4,327	257	144	726	268	134	457	262
$70,000 to $79,999	3,939	3,448	3,174	154	120	503	185	99	307	147
$80,000 to $89,999	2,528	2,229	2,082	83	63	300	108	39	192	97
$90,000 to $99,999	1,867	1,707	1,616	60	32	160	45	14	115	59
$100,000 or more	6,007	5,352	5,153	108	91	655	202	115	452	236
Median income	$34,028	$41,334	$45,555	$22,605	$32,227	$19,783	$15,521	$13,912	$25,756	$22,153

(continued)

(continued from previous page)

Percent distribution	total households	family households				total	nonfamily households			
		total	married couples	female hh, no spouse present	male hh, no spouse present		female householder		male householder	
							total	living alone	total	living alone
Percent distribution	100.0%	100.0%	100.0%	100.0%	100.0%	100.0%	100.0%	100.0%	100.0%	100.0%
Under $10,000	11.7	6.3	3.7	21.5	8.9	24.2	31.0	34.5	15.5	18.7
$10,000 to $19,999	17.0	13.0	11.0	23.1	18.8	26.2	29.0	30.8	22.7	26.0
$20,000 to $29,999	15.4	14.6	13.7	18.2	18.4	17.2	15.8	15.6	19.1	19.8
$30,000 to $39,999	13.5	14.3	14.1	14.7	15.3	11.6	9.8	9.0	13.9	13.8
$40,000 to $49,999	10.5	12.0	12.5	9.0	12.2	6.9	5.4	4.5	8.8	7.3
$50,000 to $59,999	8.4	10.0	10.8	5.4	8.5	4.6	3.3	2.5	6.2	4.9
$60,000 to $69,999	6.5	8.1	9.0	3.2	5.7	2.9	1.9	1.1	4.1	3.1
$70,000 to $79,999	4.7	5.9	6.6	1.9	4.8	2.0	1.3	0.8	2.8	1.7
$80,000 to $89,999	3.0	3.8	4.3	1.0	2.5	1.2	0.8	0.3	1.7	1.1
$90,000 to $99,999	2.2	2.9	3.4	0.7	1.3	0.6	0.3	0.1	1.0	0.7
$100,000 or more	7.2	9.2	10.8	1.3	3.6	2.6	1.4	0.9	4.1	2.8

Source: Bureau of the Census, unpublished tables from the 1995 Current Population Survey

Income Distribution of White Men by Age, 1994

(number and percent distribution of white men aged 15 or older by income and age, 1994; men in thousands as of 1995)

	total	< 25	25-34	35-44	45-54	55-64	65+
TOTAL	82,566	14,681	16,952	17,630	12,908	8,712	11,683
Without income	4,347	3,157	331	354	221	168	116
With income	78,220	11,524	16,621	17,276	12,687	8,544	11,568
Under $10,000	16,452	6,865	2,425	1,936	1,285	1,329	2,613
$10,000 to $19,999	18,013	3,130	4,184	2,714	1,639	1,669	4,677
$20,000 to $29,999	13,895	1,069	4,140	3,213	2,029	1,470	1,972
$30,000 to $39,999	10,236	272	2,703	3,095	2,075	1,237	854
$40,000 to $49,999	6,666	93	1,469	2,225	1,665	761	453
$50,000 to $74,999	7,832	60	1,189	2,465	2,375	1,158	586
$75,000 to $99,999	2,438	13	311	762	747	421	183
$100,000 or more	2,688	22	200	866	873	499	228
Median income							
Total men	$22,669	$7,208	$23,697	$31,994	$36,117	$28,384	$15,934
Year-round, full-time workers	32,440	16,222	27,117	36,431	41,189	39,060	36,484
PERCENT DISTRIB.	100.0%	100.0%	100.0%	100.0%	100.0%	100.0%	100.0%
Without income	5.3	21.5	2.0	2.0	1.7	1.9	1.0
With income	94.7	78.5	98.0	98.0	98.3	98.1	99.0
Under $10,000	19.9	46.8	14.3	11.0	10.0	15.3	22.4
$10,000 to $19,999	21.8	21.3	24.7	15.4	12.7	19.2	40.0
$20,000 to $29,999	16.8	7.3	24.4	18.2	15.7	16.9	16.9
$30,000 to $39,999	12.4	1.9	15.9	17.6	16.1	14.2	7.3
$40,000 to $49,999	8.1	0.6	8.7	12.6	12.9	8.7	3.9
$50,000 to $74,999	9.5	0.4	7.0	14.0	18.4	13.3	5.0
$75,000 to $99,999	3.0	0.1	1.8	4.3	5.8	4.8	1.6
$100,000 or more	3.3	0.1	1.2	4.9	6.8	5.7	2.0

Source: Bureau of the Census, unpublished tables from the 1995 Current Population Survey

Income Distribution of White Women by Age, 1994

(number and percent distribution of white women aged 15 or older by income and age, 1994; women in thousands as of 1995)

	total	< 25	25-34	35-44	45-54	55-64	65+
TOTAL	87,484	14,257	16,787	17,569	13,246	9,323	16,302
Without income	7,439	3,437	1,253	974	799	684	292
With income	80,045	10,820	15,534	16,595	12,447	8,639	16,010
Under $10,000	35,523	7,591	5,369	5,667	3,991	4,060	8,846
$10,000 to $19,999	20,336	2,297	4,324	3,883	2,957	2,089	4,787
$20,000 to $29,999	11,570	721	3,143	3,040	2,192	1,155	1,319
$30,000 to $39,999	6,232	125	1,547	1,869	1,527	617	548
$40,000 to $49,999	3,001	36	615	991	833	341	184
$50,000 to $74,999	2,414	28	407	804	679	273	224
$75,000 to $99,999	473	8	58	170	133	53	50
$100,000 or more	493	14	69	171	135	50	54
Median income							
Total women	$11,630	$5,631	$15,327	$16,413	$17,354	$10,946	$9,226
Year-round, full-time workers	23,894	15,039	23,079	26,396	26,334	23,543	24,919
PERCENT DISTRIB.	100.0%	100.0%	100.0%	100.0%	100.0%	100.0%	100.0%
Without income	8.5	24.1	7.5	5.5	6.0	7.3	1.8
With income	91.5	75.9	92.5	94.5	94.0	92.7	98.2
Under $10,000	40.6	53.2	32.0	32.3	30.1	43.5	54.3
$10,000 to $19,999	23.2	16.1	25.8	22.1	22.3	22.4	29.4
$20,000 to $29,999	13.2	5.1	18.7	17.3	16.5	12.4	8.1
$30,000 to $39,999	7.1	0.9	9.2	10.6	11.5	6.6	3.4
$40,000 to $49,999	3.4	0.3	3.7	5.6	6.3	3.7	1.1
$50,000 to $74,999	2.8	0.2	2.4	4.6	5.1	2.9	1.4
$75,000 to $99,999	0.5	0.1	0.3	1.0	1.0	0.6	0.3
$100,000 or more	0.6	0.1	0.4	1.0	1.0	0.5	0.3

Source: Bureau of the Census, unpublished tables from the 1995 Current Population Survey

Median Earnings of White Men and Women
Who Work Full-Time, 1980 to 1994

(median earnings of white men and women who work year-round, full-time; ratio of white to total median earnings, and ratio of white female to white male median earnings, 1980-1994; percent change in earnings and ratios for selected years; in 1994 dollars)

	white men		white women		
	median earnings	ratio white/total	median earnings	ratio white/total	ratio white female/male
1994	$31,598	1.02	$22,623	1.02	0.72
1993	31,885	1.02	22,587	1.01	0.71
1992	32,593	1.02	22,810	1.01	0.70
1991	32,933	1.03	22,626	1.01	0.69
1990	32,748	1.04	22,732	1.01	0.69
1989	34,111	1.04	22,615	1.01	0.66
1988	34,110	1.02	22,323	1.01	0.65
1987	34,609	1.02	22,276	1.01	0.64
1986	35,058	1.03	22,206	1.01	0.63
1985	34,518	1.04	21,756	1.01	0.63
1984	34,179	1.03	21,259	1.01	0.62
1983	33,355	1.02	20,930	1.01	0.63
1982	33,488	1.02	20,401	1.01	0.61
1981	34,058	1.02	19,916	1.01	0.58
1980	34,497	1.03	20,307	1.01	0.59
Percent change					
1990-1994	-3.5%	-1.9%	-0.5%	0.7%	3.1%
1980-1994	-8.4	-0.5	11.4	1.2	21.6

Note: The white/total ratios are calculated by dividing the median earnings of white men and women by the median for total men and women. The female/male ratio is calculated by dividing the median earnings of white women by the median earnings of white men.
Source: U.S. Bureau of the Census, unpublished tables from the 1995 Current Population Survey

Median Earnings of White Men and Women by Education, 1994

(median earnings of white men and women aged 25 or older by work experience and educational attainment, 1994)

	men		women	
	total	year-round full-time workers	total	year-round full-time workers
Total	$29,209	$33,300	$16,935	$23,770
Less than 9th grade	13,746	17,308	7,780	11,982
9th to 12th grade, no diploma	17,378	21,832	9,468	14,700
High school graduate	25,515	28,550	14,065	19,918
Some college, no degree	27,894	31,882	15,970	22,392
Associate's degree	31,339	35,414	20,363	25,527
Bachelor's degree or more	42,392	47,963	27,454	33,593
Bachelor's degree	40,225	43,056	24,991	30,731
Master's degree	46,617	51,608	32,814	37,457
Professional degree	65,053	72,922	37,777	48,556
Doctoral degree	57,315	60,080	38,486	45,956

Source: U.S. Bureau of the Census, unpublished tables from the 1995 Current Population Survey

White Families Below the Poverty Level, 1980 to 1994

(total number of white families, and number and percent below poverty level by type of family and presence of children under age 18, 1980-94; percent change in numbers and rates for selected years; families in thousands as of March the following year)

	total families			married couples			female hh, no spouse present		
		in poverty			in poverty			in poverty	
	total	number	percent	total	number	percent	total	number	percent
With and without children <18									
1994	58,444	5,312	9.1%	47,905	2,629	5.5%	8,031	2,329	29.0%
1993	57,881	5,452	9.4	47,452	2,757	5.8	8,131	2,376	29.2
1992	57,669	5,255	9.1	47,383	2,677	5.7	7,868	2,245	28.5
1991	57,224	5,022	8.8	47,124	2,573	5.5	7,726	2,192	28.4
1990	56,803	4,622	8.1	47,014	2,386	5.1	7,512	2,010	26.8
1989	56,590	4,409	7.8	46,981	2,329	5.0	7,306	1,858	25.4
1988	56,492	4,471	7.9	46,877	2,294	4.9	7,342	1,945	26.5
1987	56,086	4,567	8.1	46,510	2,382	5.1	7,297	1,961	26.9
1986	55,676	4,811	8.6	46,410	2,591	5.6	7,227	2,041	28.2
1985	54,991	4,983	9.1	45,924	2,815	6.1	7,111	1,950	27.4
1984	54,400	4,925	9.1	45,643	2,858	6.3	6,941	1,878	27.1
1983	53,890	5,220	9.7	45,470	3,125	6.9	6,796	1,926	28.3
1982	53,407	5,118	9.6	42,252	3,104	6.9	6,507	1,813	27.9
1981	53,269	4,670	8.8	45,007	2,712	6.0	6,620	1,814	27.4
1980	52,710	4,195	8.0	44,860	2,437	5.4	6,266	1,609	25.7
Percent change									
1990-1994	2.9%	14.9%	12.3%	1.9%	10.2%	7.8%	6.9%	15.9%	8.2%
1980-1994	10.9	26.6	13.8	6.8	7.9	1.9	28.2	44.7	12.8

(continued)

(continued from previous page)

	total families			married couples			female hh, no spouse present		
		in poverty			in poverty			in poverty	
	total	number	percent	total	number	percent	total	number	percent
With children <18									
1994	29,548	4,025	13.6%	22,839 ·	1,706	7.5%	5,390	2,064	38.3%
1993	29,234	4,226	14.5	22,670	1,868	8.2	5,361	2,123	39.6
1992	28,790	4,020	14.0	22,440	1,753	7.8	5,099	2,021	39.6
1991	28,368	3,880	13.7	22,213	1,715	7.7	4,967	1,969	39.6
1990	28,117	3,553	12.6	22,289	1,572	7.1	4,786	1,814	37.9
1989	27,977	3,290	11.8	22,271	1,457	6.5	4,627	1,671	36.1
1988	27,999	3,321	11.9	22,435	1,434	6.4	4,553	1,740	38.2
1987	27,930	3,433	12.3	22,336	1,538	6.9	4,548	1,742	38.3
1986	27,929	3,637	13.0	22,466	1,692	7.5	4,552	1,812	39.8
1985	27,795	3,695	13.3	22,399	1,827	8.2	4,470	1,730	38.7
1984	27,380	3,679	13.4	22,181	1,879	8.5	4,337	1,682	38.8
1983	27,303	3,859	14.1	22,361	2,060	9.2	4,210	1,676	39.8
1982	27,118	3,709	13.7	22,390	2,005	9.0	4,037	1,584	39.3
1981	27,223	3,362	12.4	22,334	1,723	7.7	4,237	1,564	36.9
1980	27,416	3,078	11.2	22,793	1,544	6.8	3,995	1,433	35.9
Percent change									
1990-1994	5.1%	13.3%	7.9%	2.5%	8.5%	5.6%	12.6%	13.8%	1.1%
1980-1994	7.8	30.8	21.4	0.2	10.5	10.3	34.9	44.0	6.7

Source: Bureau of the Census, unpublished tables from the 1995 Current Population Survey

Whites in Poverty by Age and Sex, 1994

(total number of whites, and number and percent below poverty level by age and sex, 1994; persons in thousands as of 1995)

	total	in poverty	
		number	percent
Total	216,460	25,379	11.7%
Under age 18	55,186	9,346	16.9
Aged 18 to 24	20,161	3,157	15.7
Aged 25 to 34	33,739	3,686	10.9
Aged 35 to 44	35,199	3,022	8.6
Aged 45 to 54	26,154	1,675	6.4
Aged 55 to 59	9,337	827	8.9
Aged 60 to 64	8,698	819	9.4
Aged 65 to 74	16,201	1,370	8.5
Aged 75 or older	11,785	1,476	12.5
Female, total	110,073	14,460	13.1
Under age 18	26,854	4,656	17.3
Aged 18 to 24	9,992	1,935	19.4
Aged 25 to 34	16,787	2,174	13.0
Aged 35 to 44	17,569	1,681	9.6
Aged 45 to 54	13,246	940	7.1
Aged 55 to 59	4,821	470	9.7
Aged 60 to 64	4,502	444	9.9
Aged 65 to 74	8,953	981	11.0
Aged 75 or older	7,349	1,179	16.0
Male, total	106,387	10,919	10.3
Under age 18	28,332	4,690	16.6
Aged 18 to 24	10,169	1,222	12.0
Aged 25 to 34	16,952	1,512	8.9
Aged 35 to 44	17,630	1,342	7.6
Aged 45 to 54	12,908	735	5.7
Aged 55 to 59	4,516	357	7.9
Aged 60 to 64	4,196	375	8.9
Aged 65 to 74	7,248	389	5.4
Aged 75 or older	4,436	297	6.7

Source: Bureau of the Census, unpublished tables from the 1995 Current Population Survey

Whites:
Labor Force

Sixty-seven percent of whites aged 16 or older are in the labor force, including 76 percent of white men and 59 percent of white women. Because whites comprise the great majority of the population, their labor force participation rates closely match those for the total population.

Forty-six percent of white households have two or more earners. Among white couples, 55 percent are dual earners, while 22 percent are traditional—meaning only the husband works.

Twenty-nine percent of whites are employed in managerial or professional specialty occupations. White men are more likely than women to be executives, administrators, or managers. White women are more likely than men to be employed in professional specialty occupations, which include teaching and nursing. Only 14 percent of white workers are union members, including 17 percent of men and 11 percent of women.

Between 1994 and 2005, the number of white workers will grow by 11 percent, while the number of non-Hispanic white workers will increase by just 8 percent. In the year 2005, non-Hispanic whites will account for just 74 percent of all workers, down from 77 percent in 1994.

Employment Status of Whites by Age and Sex, 1995

(employment status of the civilian noninstitutional white population aged 16 or older by age and sex, 1995; numbers in thousands)

			civilian labor force				not in labor force	
	total	percent of population	employed	percent of labor force	unem- ployed	percent of labor force	total	percent of population
Total persons	111,950	67.1%	106,490	95.1%	5,459	4.9%	54,965	32.9%
Aged 16 to 19	6,545	57.1	5,593	85.5	952	14.5	4,923	42.9
Aged 20 to 24	11,266	78.7	10,400	92.3	866	7.7	3,047	21.3
Aged 25 to 34	28,325	84.9	27,014	95.4	1,311	4.6	5,030	15.1
Aged 35 to 44	30,112	85.5	28,951	96.1	1,161	3.9	5,110	14.5
Aged 45 to 54	21,804	82.5	21,127	96.9	676	3.1	4,614	17.5
Aged 55 to 64	10,432	58.0	10,070	96.5	362	3.5	7,554	42.0
Aged 65 or older	3,466	12.3	3,335	96.2	131	3.8	24,686	87.7
Total men	61,146	75.7	58,146	95.1	2,999	4.9	19,587	24.3
Aged 16 to 19	3,427	58.5	2,892	84.4	535	15.6	2,427	41.5
Aged 20 to 24	6,096	85.1	5,613	92.1	483	7.9	1,067	14.9
Aged 25 to 34	15,669	94.1	14,958	95.5	711	4.5	984	5.9
Aged 35 to 44	16,414	93.4	15,793	96.2	621	3.8	1,153	6.6
Aged 45 to 54	11,730	90.0	11,359	96.8	371	3.2	1,298	10.0
Aged 55 to 64	5,809	67.1	5,609	96.6	200	3.4	2,843	32.9
Aged 65 or older	2,000	16.9	1,921	96.1	79	4.0	9,815	83.1
Total women	50,804	59.0	48,344	95.2	2,460	4.8	35,377	41.0
Aged 16 to 19	3,118	55.5	2,701	86.6	418	13.4	2,496	44.5
Aged 20 to 24	5,170	72.3	4,787	92.6	384	7.4	1,979	27.7
Aged 25 to 34	12,656	75.8	12,056	95.3	600	4.7	4,046	24.2
Aged 35 to 44	13,697	77.6	13,157	96.1	540	3.9	3,957	22.4
Aged 45 to 54	10,074	75.2	9,768	97.0	306	3.0	3,316	24.8
Aged 55 to 64	4,622	49.5	4,461	96.5	162	3.5	4,711	50.5
Aged 65 or older	1,466	9.0	1,415	96.5	52	3.5	14,871	91.0

Note: The civilian labor force equals the number employed plus the number unemployed. The civilian population equals the number in the labor force plus the number not in the labor force.
Source: Bureau of Labor Statistics, Employment and Earnings, *January 1996*

White Households by Number of Earners, 1994

(number and percent distribution of white households, by number of earners, 1994; numbers in thousands)

	number	percent
Total households	82,387	100.0%
No earners	17,745	21.5
One earner	26,711	32.4
Two or more earners	37,931	46.0
Two earners	29,645	36.0
Three earners	6,164	7.5
Four or more earners	2,121	2.6

Source: Bureau of the Census, Income, Poverty, and Valuation of Noncash Benefits: 1993, *Current Population Reports, P60-188, 1995*

Labor Force Status of White Married Couples, 1994

(number and percent distribution of white married couples, by age of householder and labor force status of husband and wife, 1994; numbers in thousands)

	total married couples	husband and/or wife in labor force			neither husband nor wife in labor force
		husband and wife	husband only	wife only	
Total, number	47,443	26,057	10,496	2,604	8,286
Under age 20	73	43	26	-	3
Aged 20 to 24	1,320	876	400	24	19
Aged 25 to 29	3,524	2,498	931	64	31
Aged 30 to 34	5,606	3,911	1,479	118	97
Aged 35 to 39	6,309	4,353	1,739	131	86
Aged 40 to 44	5,744	4,247	1,233	154	110
Aged 45 to 49	5,107	3,697	1,079	199	132
Aged 50 to 54	4,409	2,961	1,016	247	186
Aged 55 to 59	3,504	1,847	942	344	370
Aged 60 to 64	3,331	976	762	557	1,037
Aged 65 to 74	5,572	559	703	643	3,668
Aged 75 to 84	2,486	64	159	104	2,159
Aged 85 or older	457	25	26	18	387
Total, percent	100.0%	54.9%	22.1%	5.5%	17.5%
Under age 20	100.0	58.9	35.6	-	4.1
Aged 20 to 24	100.0	66.4	30.3	1.8	1.4
Aged 25 to 29	100.0	70.9	26.4	1.8	0.9
Aged 30 to 34	100.0	69.8	26.4	2.1	1.7
Aged 35 to 39	100.0	69.0	27.6	2.1	1.4
Aged 40 to 44	100.0	73.9	21.5	2.7	1.9
Aged 45 to 49	100.0	72.4	21.1	3.9	2.6
Aged 50 to 54	100.0	67.2	23.0	5.6	4.2
Aged 55 to 59	100.0	52.7	26.9	9.8	10.6
Aged 60 to 64	100.0	29.3	22.9	16.7	31.1
Aged 65 to 74	100.0	10.0	12.6	11.5	65.8
Aged 75 to 84	100.0	2.6	6.4	4.2	86.8
Aged 85 or older	100.0	5.5	5.7	3.9	84.7

Note: (-) means number in sample is too small to make a reliable estimate.
Source: Bureau of the Census, Household and Family Characteristics: March 1994, *Current Population Reports, P20-483, 1995*

Occupations of Whites by Sex, 1995

(number and percent distribution of employed whites aged 16 or older in the civilian labor force, by occupation and sex, 1995; numbers in thousands)

	total	men	women
Total employed, number	106,490	58,146	48,344
Total employed, percent	100.0%	100.0%	100.0%
Managerial and professional specialty	29.4	28.4	30.6
Executive, administrative, and managerial	14.5	15.4	13.3
Professional specialty	15.0	13.0	17.3
Technical, sales, and administrative support	30.2	20.0	42.5
Technicians and related support	3.2	2.9	3.5
Sales occupations	12.6	11.9	13.4
Administrative support, including clerical	14.5	5.2	25.7
Service occupations	12.4	9.0	16.5
Private household	0.6	-	1.3
Protective service	1.7	2.6	0.5
Service, except private household and protective	10.1	6.3	14.7
Precision production, craft, and repair	11.2	18.9	2.0
Operators, fabricators, and laborers	13.6	19.2	6.9
Machine operators, assemblers, and inspectors	5.8	6.9	4.5
Transportation and material moving occupations	4.0	6.6	0.8
Handlers, equipment cleaners, helpers, and laborers	3.8	5.6	1.6
Farming, forestry, and fishing	3.1	4.6	1.4

Note: (-) means less than 0.05 percent.
Source: Bureau of Labor Statistics, Employment and Earnings, *January 1996*

Union Membership of Whites, 1995

(number of employed white wage and salary workers aged 16 or older, number and percent who are represented by unions or are union members, and median weekly earnings by union membership status; by sex, 1995; numbers in thousands)

	total	men	women
Total employed	92,760	49,162	43,598
Represented by unions*	14,747	8,960	5,787
Percent of employed	15.9%	18.2%	13.3%
Members of unions**	13,149	8,178	4,971
Percent of employed	14.2%	16.6%	11.4%
Median weekly earnings, total***	$494	$566	$415
Represented by unions*	616	658	546
Members of unions**	621	661	551
Non-union	466	526	395

* Members of a labor union or an employee association similar to a union as well as workers who report no union affiliation but whose jobs are covered by a union or an employee association contract.
** Members of a labor union or an employee association similar to a union.
*** Full-time wage and salary workers.
Source: Bureau of Labor Statistics, Employment and Earnings, *January 1996*

White and Non-Hispanic White Labor Force Projections by Sex, 1994 to 2005

(number of whites and non-Hispanic whites aged 16 or older in the civilian labor force in 1994 and 2005, labor force participation rate of whites and non-Hispanic whites in 1994 and 2005, and white and non-Hispanic white share of total labor force in 1994 and 2005; by sex; percent change in number and percentage point change in share; numbers in thousands)

	whites			non-Hispanic whites		
	1994	2005	percent change 1992-2005	1994	2005	percent change 1992-2005
Number in labor force						
Total	111,082	122,855	10.6%	100,462	108,345	7.8%
Men	60,727	64,884	6.8	54,306	56,429	3.9
Women	50,356	57,971	15.1	46,157	51,916	12.5
						percentage point change 1994-2005
Labor force participation rate						
Total	67.1%	67.7%	0.6%	67.2%	68.6%	1.4
Men	75.9	73.9	-2.0	75.5	73.6	-1.9
Women	58.9	62.6	3.7	59.5	63.8	4.3
Percent of labor force						
Total	84.8	83.5	-1.3	76.7	73.7	-3.0
Men	85.8	84.4	-1.4	76.7	73.4	-3.3
Women	83.6	82.5	-1.1	76.6	73.9	-2.7

Note: Hispanics may be of any race and most are white. For a breakdown of the Hispanic composition of racial groups and the racial composition of Hispanics, see the tables in the introduction to this book.
Source: Bureau of Labor Statistics, Monthly Labor Review, *November 1995*

Whites:
Population

The white population is projected to grow from 220 million in 1996 to nearly 255 million by 2020, when whites will account for 79 percent of the total U.S. population. A growing share of the white population is Hispanic, however. The non-Hispanic white population will account for just 64 percent of the total population in 2020.

Non-Hispanic whites account for a smaller share of children and young adults than of older Americans because Hispanic fertility is much higher than that of non-Hispanics. Just 64 percent of Americans under age 5 are non-Hispanic whites, versus 87 percent of those aged 85 or older. While there are 96 non-Hispanic whites for every 100 whites among people aged 75 or older, the ratio falls to 81 among children under age 5.

Because whites comprise the great majority of the American population, the regional distribution of whites is similar to that of the population as a whole. Twelve percent of whites live in California, the most populous state. The white share of the population is smallest in Hawaii, at 41 percent, because the majority of Hawaii's population is Asian. The white share of the population is greatest in Maine, at 98.5 percent.

While 79 percent of all births in 1993 were to white women, many of these white women were Hispanic. Only 62 percent of births in 1993 were to non-Hispanic white mothers. Non-Hispanic white women accounted for fewer than half of births in California, Hawaii, New Mexico, and Texas in 1993. By 2020, only 52 percent of births nationwide will be to non-Hispanic whites.

Whites and Non-Hispanic Whites by Age, 1996

(number of whites and non-Hispanic whites, and ratio of non-Hispanic whites to whites, by age, 1996; numbers in thousands)

	white	non-Hispanic white	ratio*
Total persons	219,641	194,353	88
Under age 5	15,249	12,378	81
Aged 5 to 9	15,463	12,913	84
Aged 10 to 14	15,157	12,894	85
Aged 15 to 19	14,744	12,576	85
Aged 20 to 24	13,867	11,738	85
Aged 25 to 29	15,370	13,089	85
Aged 30 to 34	17,483	15,140	87
Aged 35 to 39	18,650	16,598	89
Aged 40 to 44	17,350	15,699	90
Aged 45 to 49	15,633	14,356	92
Aged 50 to 54	11,948	11,025	92
Aged 55 to 59	9,765	9,041	93
Aged 60 to 64	8,654	8,059	93
Aged 65 to 69	8,669	8,151	94
Aged 70 to 74	7,860	7,469	95
Aged 75 to 79	6,207	5,952	96
Aged 80 to 84	4,162	3,999	96
Aged 85 or older	3,407	3,274	96
Aged 18 to 24	19,649	16,663	85
Aged 18 or older	164,807	148,515	90
Aged 65 or older	30,306	28,847	95

* The ratio is the number of non-Hispanic whites per 100 whites.
Note: Hispanics may be of any race and most are white. For a breakdown of the Hispanic composition of racial groups and the racial composition of Hispanics, see the tables in the introduction to this book.
Source: Bureau of the Census, Population Projections of the United States, by Age, Sex, Race, and Hispanic Origin: 1993 to 2050, *Current Population Reports, P25-1104, 1993*

Whites by Age, 1990 to 2020

(number of whites by age, selected years 1990-2020; percent change 1990-2000 and 2000-2010; numbers in thousands)

	1990	1996	2000	2010	2020	percent change 1990-2000	2000-2010
Total							
persons	209,150	219,641	225,532	239,588	254,887	7.8%	6.2%
Under 5	15,014	15,249	14,724	15,142	16,419	-1.9	2.8
5 to 9	14,522	15,463	15,622	14,813	16,122	7.6	-5.2
10 to 14	13,767	15,157	15,728	15,416	15,848	14.2	-2.0
15 to 19	14,229	14,744	15,658	16,799	15,958	10.0	7.3
20 to 24	15,630	13,867	14,511	16,499	16,186	-7.2	13.7
25 to 29	17,541	15,370	14,092	15,488	16,576	-19.7	9.9
30 to 34	18,243	17,483	15,745	14,611	16,542	-13.7	-7.2
35 to 39	16,753	18,650	18,156	14,605	16,016	8.4	-19.6
40 to 44	15,157	17,350	18,606	16,041	14,921	22.8	-13.8
45 to 49	11,887	15,633	16,574	17,916	14,479	39.4	8.1
50 to 54	9,786	11,948	14,674	17,995	15,591	49.9	22.6
55 to 59	9,110	9,765	11,449	16,013	17,411	25.7	39.9
60 to 64	9,368	8,654	9,151	13,833	17,107	-2.3	51.2
65 to 69	8,989	8,669	8,135	10,385	14,711	-9.5	27.7
70 to 74	7,224	7,860	7,711	7,716	11,906	6.7	0.1
75 to 79	5,556	6,207	6,670	6,232	8,210	20.1	-6.6
80 to 84	3,587	4,162	4,461	4,975	5,209	24.4	11.5
85 or older	2,787	3,407	3,866	5,108	5,677	38.7	32.1
18 to 24	21,827	19,649	20,852	23,489	22,665	-4.5	12.6
18 or older	157,814	164,807	170,142	184,407	197,021	7.8	8.4
65 or older	28,142	30,306	30,843	34,416	45,712	9.6	11.6

Source: Bureau of the Census, Population Projections of the United States, by Age, Sex, Race, and Hispanic Origin: 1995 to 2050, *Current Population Reports, P25-1130, 1996; and* U.S. Population Estimates, by Age, Sex, Race, and Hispanic Origin: 1980 to 1991, *Current Population Reports, P25-1095, 1993*

Non-Hispanic Whites by Age, 1990 to 2020

(number of non-Hispanic whites by age, selected years 1990-2020; percent change 1990-2000 and 2000-2010; numbers in thousands)

	1990	1996	2000	2010	2020	percent change 1990-2000	2000-2010
Total							
persons	188,559	194,353	197,061	202,390	207,393	4.5%	2.7%
Under 5	12,744	12,378	11,807	11,445	11,724	-7.4	-3.1
5 to 9	12,523	12,913	12,615	11,422	11,748	0.7	-9.5
10 to 14	11,934	12,894	13,109	12,135	11,770	9.8	-7.4
15 to 19	12,330	12,576	13,184	13,270	12,026	6.9	0.7
20 to 24	13,506	11,738	12,171	13,345	12,360	-9.9	9.6
25 to 29	15,398	13,089	11,816	12,643	12,734	-23.3	7.0
30 to 34	16,361	15,140	13,328	11,988	13,134	-18.5	-10.1
35 to 39	15,241	16,598	15,783	12,114	12,949	3.6	-23.2
40 to 44	13,973	15,699	16,599	13,514	12,181	18.8	-18.6
45 to 49	11,023	14,356	15,012	15,528	11,967	36.2	3.4
50 to 54	9,092	11,025	13,473	16,013	13,102	48.2	18.9
55 to 59	8,522	9,041	10,574	14,469	15,060	24.1	36.8
60 to 64	8,853	8,059	8,465	12,668	15,192	-4.4	49.7
65 to 69	8,583	8,151	7,574	9,554	13,249	-11.8	26.1
70 to 74	6,956	7,469	7,251	7,099	10,849	4.2	-2.1
75 to 79	5,356	5,952	6,336	5,761	7,495	18.3	-9.1
80 to 84	3,464	3,999	4,271	4,633	4,729	23.3	8.5
85 or older	2,698	3,274	3,694	4,788	5,123	36.9	29.6
18 to 24	18,892	16,663	17,509	18,880	17,261	-7.3	7.8
18 or older	144,413	148,515	151,685	159,652	165,025	5.0	5.3
65 or older	27,057	28,847	29,126	31,835	41,445	7.6	9.3

Note: Hispanics may be of any race and most are white. For a breakdown of the Hispanic composition of racial groups and the racial composition of Hispanics, see the tables in the introduction to this book.
Source: Bureau of the Census, Population Projections of the United States, by Age, Sex, Race, and Hispanic Origin: 1995 to 2050, *Current Population Reports, P25-1130, 1996; and* U.S. Population Estimates, by Age, Sex, Race, and Hispanic Origin: 1980 to 1991, *Current Population Reports, P25-1095, 1993*

White Share of the Total Population by Age, 1990 to 2020

(whites as a percent of the total population by age, selected years 1990-2020)

	1990	1996	2000	2010	2020
Total persons	83.9%	82.8%	82.1%	80.5%	79.0%
Under age 5	79.5	78.6	77.5	75.7	74.7
Aged 5 to 9	80.4	79.1	78.4	76.0	74.8
Aged 10 to 14	80.1	79.4	78.4	76.2	74.3
Aged 15 to 19	80.1	79.4	79.0	77.1	74.7
Aged 20 to 24	81.7	79.9	79.5	78.1	76.0
Aged 25 to 29	82.6	80.9	79.5	78.6	76.9
Aged 30 to 34	83.3	81.8	80.7	78.6	77.4
Aged 35 to 39	83.9	82.8	81.9	78.8	78.0
Aged 40 to 44	85.2	83.5	82.8	80.3	78.2
Aged 45 to 49	86.0	84.9	83.7	81.9	78.8
Aged 50 to 54	86.1	85.8	85.2	83.0	80.5
Aged 55 to 59	87.0	86.0	86.0	84.0	82.3
Aged 60 to 64	88.2	86.5	85.9	85.3	83.2
Aged 65 to 69	89.2	87.6	86.5	85.7	83.9
Aged 70 to 74	90.1	89.4	88.4	86.3	85.9
Aged 75 to 79	90.4	90.3	90.0	87.5	87.0
Aged 80 to 84	91.2	91.2	91.0	89.5	87.7
Aged 85 or older	91.4	91.0	90.8	90.1	87.9
Aged 18 to 24	81.4	79.8	79.4	77.9	75.8
Aged 18 or older	85.2	84.1	83.5	81.9	80.4
Aged 65 or older	90.1	89.5	88.9	87.3	85.9

Source: Bureau of the Census, Population Projections of the United States, by Age, Sex, Race, and Hispanic Origin: 1995 to 2050, *Current Population Reports, P25-1130, 1996; and* U.S. Population Estimates, by Age, Sex, Race, and Hispanic Origin: 1980 to 1991, *Current Population Reports, P25-1095, 1993*

Non-Hispanic White Share of the Total Population by Age, 1990 to 2020

(non-Hispanic whites as a percent of the total population by age, selected years 1990-2020)

	1990	1996	2000	2010	2020
Total persons	75.6%	73.3%	71.8%	68.0%	64.3%
Under age 5	67.5	63.8	62.2	57.2	53.3
Aged 5 to 9	69.3	66.0	63.3	58.6	54.5
Aged 10 to 14	69.4	67.5	65.4	60.0	55.2
Aged 15 to 19	69.4	67.7	66.5	60.9	56.3
Aged 20 to 24	70.6	67.6	66.7	63.1	58.0
Aged 25 to 29	72.5	68.9	66.7	64.1	59.0
Aged 30 to 34	74.7	70.8	68.3	64.5	61.5
Aged 35 to 39	76.3	73.7	71.2	65.4	63.1
Aged 40 to 44	78.5	75.6	73.8	67.6	63.8
Aged 45 to 49	79.8	77.9	75.8	71.0	65.1
Aged 50 to 54	80.0	79.2	78.2	73.9	67.7
Aged 55 to 59	81.4	79.6	79.5	75.9	71.2
Aged 60 to 64	83.4	80.6	79.5	78.1	73.9
Aged 65 to 69	85.2	82.4	80.5	78.9	75.6
Aged 70 to 74	86.7	84.9	83.1	79.4	78.3
Aged 75 to 79	87.2	86.6	85.4	80.9	79.4
Aged 80 to 84	88.1	87.6	87.2	83.4	79.6
Aged 85 or older	88.5	87.4	86.7	84.4	79.3
Aged 18 to 24	70.4	67.7	66.7	62.6	57.7
Aged 18 or older	78.0	75.8	74.4	70.9	67.3
Aged 65 or older	86.7	85.2	83.9	80.8	77.9

Note: Hispanics may be of any race and most are white. For a breakdown of the Hispanic composition of racial groups and the racial composition of Hispanics, see the tables in the introduction to this book.
Source: Bureau of the Census, Population Projections of the United States, by Age, Sex, Race, and Hispanic Origin: 1995 to 2050, *Current Population Reports, P25-1130, 1996; and* U.S. Population Estimates, by Age, Sex, Race, and Hispanic Origin: 1980 to 1991, *Current Population Reports, P25-1095, 1993*

Whites by Age and Sex, 1996

(number of whites by age and sex, and sex ratio by age, 1996; numbers in thousands)

	total	male	female	sex ratio*
Total persons	219,641	107,769	111,872	96
Under age 5	15,249	7,817	7,432	105
Aged 5 to 9	15,463	7,932	7,531	105
Aged 10 to 14	15,157	7,781	7,377	105
Aged 15 to 19	14,744	7,582	7,162	106
Aged 20 to 24	13,867	7,091	6,777	105
Aged 25 to 29	15,370	7,769	7,601	102
Aged 30 to 34	17,483	8,807	8,676	102
Aged 35 to 39	18,650	9,385	9,266	101
Aged 40 to 44	17,350	8,673	8,676	100
Aged 45 to 49	15,633	7,759	7,874	99
Aged 50 to 54	11,948	5,864	6,084	96
Aged 55 to 59	9,765	4,738	5,026	94
Aged 60 to 64	8,654	4,127	4,528	91
Aged 65 to 69	8,669	3,981	4,688	85
Aged 70 to 74	7,860	3,439	4,421	78
Aged 75 to 79	6,207	2,557	3,650	70
Aged 80 to 84	4,162	1,518	2,644	57
Aged 85 or older	3,407	948	2,459	39
Aged 18 to 24	19,649	9,955	9,595	104
Aged 18 or older	164,807	79,520	85,188	93
Aged 65 or older	30,306	12,444	17,862	70

* The sex ratio is the number of males per 100 females.
Source: Bureau of the Census, Population Projections of the United States, by Age, Sex, Race, and Hispanic Origin: 1995 to 2050, *Current Population Reports, P25-1130, 1996*

Non-Hispanic Whites by Age and Sex, 1996

(number of non-Hispanic whites by age and sex, and sex ratio by age, 1996; numbers in thousands)

	total	male	female	sex ratio*
Total persons	194,353	94,964	99,389	96
Under age 5	12,378	6,349	6,029	105
Aged 5 to 9	12,913	6,629	6,284	105
Aged 10 to 14	12,894	6,625	6,269	106
Aged 15 to 19	12,576	6,470	6,106	106
Aged 20 to 24	11,738	5,978	5,760	104
Aged 25 to 29	13,089	6,547	6,542	100
Aged 30 to 34	15,140	7,572	7,569	100
Aged 35 to 39	16,598	8,324	8,274	101
Aged 40 to 44	15,699	7,842	7,857	100
Aged 45 to 49	14,356	7,130	7,225	99
Aged 50 to 54	11,025	5,420	5,605	97
Aged 55 to 59	9,041	4,396	4,645	95
Aged 60 to 64	8,059	3,850	4,208	91
Aged 65 to 69	8,151	3,749	4,403	85
Aged 70 to 74	7,469	3,267	4,202	78
Aged 75 to 79	5,952	2,453	3,499	70
Aged 80 to 84	3,999	1,459	2,540	57
Aged 85 or older	3,274	905	2,369	38
Aged 18 to 24	16,663	8,502	8,161	104
Aged 18 or older	148,515	71,416	77,099	93
Aged 65 or older	28,847	11,833	17,014	70

* The sex ratio is the number of males per 100 females.
Note: Hispanics may be of any race and most are white. For a breakdown of the Hispanic composition of racial groups and the racial composition of Hispanics, see the tables in the introduction to this book.
Source: Bureau of the Census, Population Projections of the United States, by Age, Sex, Race, and Hispanic Origin: 1995 to 2050, Current Population Reports, P25-1130, 1996

Whites by Region and Division, 1990 to 2020

(number and percent distribution of whites and white share of the total population by region and division, selected years 1990-2020; percent change in number and percentage point change in distribution and share, 1990-2000 and 2000-2010; numbers in thousands)

	1990	1995	2000	2010	2020	percent change 1990-2000	percent change 2000-2010
Number							
UNITED STATES	208,704	218,334	226,267	240,297	254,791	8.4%	6.2%
Northeast	43,411	43,381	43,219	43,268	43,843	-0.4	0.1
New England	12,269	12,183	12,121	12,408	12,893	-1.2	2.4
Middle Atlantic	31,141	31,198	31,098	30,860	30,950	-0.1	-0.8
Midwest	52,789	54,305	55,391	56,443	57,551	4.9	1.9
East North Central	36,423	37,392	38,005	38,351	38,702	4.3	0.9
West North Central	16,366	16,913	17,386	18,092	18,849	6.2	4.1
South	67,820	72,123	75,812	82,388	88,736	11.8	8.7
South Atlantic	33,789	35,963	37,770	40,807	43,707	11.8	8.0
East South Central	12,070	12,690	13,232	14,042	14,782	9.6	6.1
West South Central	21,960	23,470	24,810	27,539	30,247	13.0	11.0
West	44,684	48,525	51,845	58,198	64,662	16.0	12.3
Mountain	12,547	14,004	15,247	16,974	18,529	21.5	11.3
Pacific	32,137	34,521	36,598	41,224	46,133	13.9	12.6

	1990	1995	2000	2010	2020	percentage point change 1990-2000	percentage point change 2000-2010
Percent distribution							
UNITED STATES	100.0%	100.0%	100.0%	100.0%	100.0%	-	-
Northeast	20.8	19.9	19.1	18.0	17.2	-1.7	-1.1
New England	5.9	5.6	5.4	5.2	5.1	-0.5	-0.2
Middle Atlantic	14.9	14.3	13.7	12.8	12.1	-1.2	-0.9
Midwest	25.3	24.9	24.5	23.5	22.6	-0.8	1.0
East North Central	17.5	17.1	16.8	16.0	15.2	-0.7	-0.8
West North Central	7.8	7.7	7.7	7.5	7.4	-0.1	-0.2
South	32.5	33.0	33.5	34.3	34.8	1.0	0.8
South Atlantic	16.2	16.5	16.7	17.0	17.2	0.5	0.7
East South Central	5.8	5.8	5.8	5.8	5.8	0.0	0.0
West South Central	10.5	10.7	11.0	11.5	11.9	0.5	0.5
West	21.4	22.2	22.9	24.2	25.4	1.5	1.3
Mountain	6.0	6.4	6.7	7.1	7.3	0.7	0.4
Pacific	15.4	15.8	16.2	17.2	18.1	0.8	1.0

(continued)

(continued from previous page)

	1990	1995	2000	2010	2020	percentage point change 1990-2000	2000-2010
Percent share							
UNITED STATES	83.9%	82.9%	81.9%	80.0%	78.2%	-2.0	-1.9
Northeast	85.4	84.3	83.3	81.2	79.2	-2.1	-2.1
New England	92.9	92.3	91.7	90.2	88.8	-1.2	-1.5
Middle Atlantic	82.8	81.6	80.4	78.0	75.8	-2.4	-2.4
Midwest	88.5	87.6	86.8	85.1	83.4	-1.7	-1.7
East North Central	86.7	85.7	84.8	82.9	81.0	-1.9	-1.9
West North Central	92.7	92.0	91.4	90.1	89.0	-1.3	-1.3
South	79.4	78.6	78.0	76.7	75.5	-1.4	-1.3
South Atlantic	77.6	76.5	75.5	73.8	72.1	-2.1	-1.7
East South Central	79.5	79.2	78.9	78.3	77.5	-0.6	-0.6
West South Central	82.2	81.8	81.4	80.7	80.0	-0.8	-0.7
West	84.7	83.3	81.9	79.3	76.9	-2.8	-2.6
Mountain	91.9	91.0	90.3	88.9	87.6	-1.6	-1.4
Pacific	82.1	80.5	78.9	75.9	73.3	-3.2	-3.0

Note: The 1990 population figures are for April 1, 1990. Projections of total whites for 2000, 2010, and 2020 are different from those at the beginning of the population section because they are from an earlier report for states and regions.
Source: Bureau of the Census, Population Projections for States, by Age, Sex, Race, and Hispanic Origin: 1993 to 2020, *Current Population Reports, P25-1111, 1994*

Whites by State, 1995 to 2020

(number of whites by state, selected years 1995-2020, and percent change 1995-2020; numbers in thousands)

	1995	2000	2010	2020	percent change 1995-2020
United States	218,334	226,267	240,297	254,791	16.7%
Alabama	3,140	3,284	3,529	3,766	19.9
Alaska	477	516	543	565	18.4
Arizona	3,606	3,894	4,379	4,854	34.6
Arkansas	2,047	2,139	2,311	2,496	21.9
California	25,701	26,987	30,357	34,058	32.5
Colorado	3,431	3,733	4,090	4,390	28.0
Connecticut	2,915	2,891	2,960	3,081	5.7
Delaware	570	589	603	616	8.1
District of Columbia	178	176	195	210	18.0
Florida	11,867	12,619	13,981	15,338	29.2
Georgia	5,025	5,346	5,857	6,306	25.5
Hawaii	499	596	745	870	74.3
Idaho	1,118	1,242	1,392	1,524	36.3
Illinois	9,603	9,713	9,801	9,944	3.6
Indiana	5,275	5,444	5,587	5,691	7.9
Iowa	2,763	2,816	2,841	2,873	4.0
Kansas	2,365	2,450	2,588	2,735	15.6
Kentucky	3,535	3,646	3,769	3,869	9.4
Louisiana	2,909	2,953	3,119	3,320	14.1
Maine	1,217	1,220	1,283	1,368	12.4
Maryland	3,500	3,546	3,631	3,749	7.1
Massachusetts	5,445	5,373	5,387	5,501	1.0
Michigan	7,958	8,000	7,979	7,990	0.4
Minnesota	4,344	4,498	4,699	4,889	12.5
Mississippi	1,688	1,738	1,845	1,957	15.9
Missouri	4,629	4,737	4,970	5,234	13.1
Montana	798	847	908	968	21.3
Nebraska	1,550	1,598	1,669	1,744	12.5
Nevada	1,281	1,443	1,609	1,743	36.1
New Hampshire	1,109	1,137	1,236	1,338	20.6
New Jersey	6,405	6,445	6,526	6,659	4.0
New Mexico	1,460	1,574	1,760	1,934	32.5
New York	14,025	13,819	13,542	13,487	-3.8

(continued)

(continued from previous page)

	1995	2000	2010	2020	percent change 1995-2020
North Carolina	5,378	5,682	6,125	6,517	21.2%
North Dakota	600	601	622	653	8.8
Ohio	9,806	9,943	9,948	9,944	1.4
Oklahoma	2,699	2,770	2,979	3,218	19.2
Oregon	2,929	3,139	3,508	3,893	32.9
Pennsylvania	10,768	10,834	10,792	10,804	0.3
Rhode Island	927	917	933	966	4.2
South Carolina	2,561	2,677	2,902	3,115	21.6
South Dakota	663	685	702	722	8.9
Tennessee	4,327	4,563	4,899	5,189	19.9
Texas	15,814	16,948	19,130	21,213	34.1
Utah	1,843	2,017	2,272	2,500	35.6
Vermont	570	582	609	639	12.1
Virginia	5,127	5,367	5,743	6,084	18.7
Washington	4,915	5,360	6,071	6,747	37.3
West Virginia	1,756	1,770	1,768	1,771	0.9
Wisconsin	4,750	4,906	5,035	5,133	8.1
Wyoming	467	498	564	618	32.3

Note: Projections of total whites for 2000, 2010, and 2020 are different from those at the beginning of the population section because they are from an earlier report for states and regions.
Source: Bureau of the Census, Population Projections for States, by Age, Sex, Race, and Hispanic Origin: 1993

Distribution of Whites by State, 1995 to 2020

(percent distribution of whites by state, selected years 1995-2020)

	1995	*2000*	*2010*	*2020*
United States	100.0%	100.0%	100.0%	100.0%
Alabama	1.4	1.5	1.5	1.5
Alaska	0.2	0.2	0.2	0.2
Arizona	1.7	1.7	1.8	1.9
Arkansas	0.9	0.9	1.0	1.0
California	11.8	11.9	12.6	13.4
Colorado	1.6	1.6	1.7	1.7
Connecticut	1.3	1.3	1.2	1.2
Delaware	0.3	0.3	0.3	0.2
District of Columbia	0.1	0.1	0.1	0.1
Florida	5.4	5.6	5.8	6.0
Georgia	2.3	2.4	2.4	2.5
Hawaii	0.2	0.3	0.3	0.3
Idaho	0.5	0.5	0.6	0.6
Illinois	4.4	4.3	4.1	3.9
Indiana	2.4	2.4	2.3	2.2
Iowa	1.3	1.2	1.2	1.1
Kansas	1.1	1.1	1.1	1.1
Kentucky	1.6	1.6	1.6	1.5
Louisiana	1.3	1.3	1.3	1.3
Maine	0.6	0.5	0.5	0.5
Maryland	1.6	1.6	1.5	1.5
Massachusetts	2.5	2.4	2.2	2.2
Michigan	3.6	3.5	3.3	3.1
Minnesota	2.0	2.0	2.0	1.9
Mississippi	0.8	0.8	0.8	0.8
Missouri	2.1	2.1	2.1	2.1
Montana	0.4	0.4	0.4	0.4
Nebraska	0.7	0.7	0.7	0.7
Nevada	0.6	0.6	0.7	0.7
New Hampshire	0.5	0.5	0.5	0.5
New Jersey	2.9	2.8	2.7	2.6
New Mexico	0.7	0.7	0.7	0.8
New York	6.4	6.1	5.6	5.3

(continued)

(continued from previous page)

	1995	2000	2010	2020
North Carolina	2.5%	2.5%	2.5%	2.6%
North Dakota	0.3	0.3	0.3	0.3
Ohio	4.5	4.4	4.1	3.9
Oklahoma	1.2	1.2	1.2	1.3
Oregon	1.3	1.4	1.5	1.5
Pennsylvania	4.9	4.8	4.5	4.2
Rhode Island	0.4	0.4	0.4	0.4
South Carolina	1.2	1.2	1.2	1.2
South Dakota	0.3	0.3	0.3	0.3
Tennessee	2.0	2.0	2.0	2.0
Texas	7.2	7.5	8.0	8.3
Utah	0.8	0.9	0.9	1.0
Vermont	0.3	0.3	0.3	0.3
Virginia	2.3	2.4	2.4	2.4
Washington	2.3	2.4	2.5	2.6
West Virginia	0.8	0.8	0.7	0.7
Wisconsin	2.2	2.2	2.1	2.0
Wyoming	0.2	0.2	0.2	0.2

Source: Bureau of the Census, Population Projections for States, by Age, Sex, Race, and Hispanic Origin: 1993 to 2020, *Current Population Reports, P25-1111, 1994*

White Share of State Populations, 1995 to 2020

(whites as a percent of state populations, selected years 1995-2020; percentage point change in share, 1995-2020)

	1995	2000	2010	2020	percentage point change 1995-2020
United States	82.9%	81.9%	80.0%	78.2%	-4.7
Alabama	73.5	73.2	72.7	72.0	-1.5
Alaska	75.2	73.8	69.5	65.2	-10.0
Arizona	88.6	87.8	86.3	85.0	-3.6
Arkansas	82.9	83.0	83.1	83.1	0.2
California	79.3	77.4	73.9	71.0	-8.3
Colorado	92.5	92.0	91.0	90.1	-2.4
Connecticut	89.0	88.4	86.8	85.2	-3.8
Delaware	79.4	77.6	74.0	70.7	-8.7
District of Columbia	31.8	32.8	33.8	33.0	1.2
Florida	83.5	82.4	80.5	78.9	-4.6
Georgia	70.8	70.0	68.5	66.9	-3.9
Hawaii	40.9	44.9	48.0	47.9	7.0
Idaho	96.7	96.3	95.7	95.3	-1.4
Illinois	81.0	79.8	77.5	75.2	-5.8
Indiana	90.6	90.1	88.9	87.7	-2.9
Iowa	96.6	96.1	95.3	94.6	-2.0
Kansas	90.9	90.0	88.6	87.4	-3.5
Kentucky	91.8	91.4	90.6	89.7	-2.1
Louisiana	66.7	65.9	64.9	63.9	-2.8
Maine	98.5	98.4	98.0	97.7	-0.8
Maryland	68.9	66.6	62.8	59.6	-9.3
Massachusetts	91.1	90.3	88.4	86.5	-4.6
Michigan	83.1	82.0	79.5	77.0	-6.1
Minnesota	94.0	93.2	91.7	90.1	-3.9
Mississippi	63.3	63.2	63.2	63.1	-0.2
Missouri	87.6	87.1	86.3	85.5	-2.1
Montana	92.6	92.1	91.2	90.4	-2.2
Nebraska	94.3	93.8	93.1	92.5	-1.8
Nevada	86.7	85.3	83.2	81.3	-5.4
New Hampshire	98.0	97.6	96.6	95.6	-2.4
New Jersey	80.8	79.2	76.2	73.5	-7.3
New Mexico	87.1	86.3	84.5	82.7	-4.4
New York	77.2	75.8	73.0	70.6	-6.6

(continued)

(continued from previous page)

	1995	2000	2010	2020	percentage point change 1995-2020
North Carolina	75.2%	74.6%	73.4%	72.3%	-2.9
North Dakota	94.2	93.5	92.0	90.8	-3.4
Ohio	87.5	86.8	85.3	83.8	-3.7
Oklahoma	82.5	81.9	80.9	80.0	-2.5
Oregon	93.3	92.2	90.5	89.1	-4.2
Pennsylvania	88.7	88.1	86.8	85.4	-3.3
Rhode Island	92.6	91.9	90.2	88.6	-4.0
South Carolina	68.6	68.1	67.3	66.5	-2.1
South Dakota	90.2	89.0	86.1	83.7	-6.5
Tennessee	82.8	82.4	81.6	80.6	-2.2
Texas	85.1	84.6	83.7	82.9	-2.2
Utah	94.8	93.9	92.3	90.9	-3.9
Vermont	98.4	98.3	97.8	97.1	-1.3
Virginia	77.1	76.1	74.3	72.5	-4.6
Washington	89.4	88.3	86.4	84.8	-4.6
West Virginia	96.3	96.2	96.0	95.6	-0.7
Wisconsin	92.1	91.2	89.4	87.8	-4.3
Wyoming	95.9	95.4	94.6	93.9	-2.0

Source: Bureau of the Census, Population Projections for States, by Age, Sex, Race, and Hispanic Origin: 1993 to 2020, *Current Population Reports, P25-1111, 1994*

White and Non-Hispanic White Births by Age of Mother, 1993

(number and percent distribution of births to white and non-Hispanic white women, by age of mother, 1993)

	white		non-Hispanic white	
	number	*percent*	*number*	*percent*
Total births	3,149,833	100.0%	2,472,031	100.0%
Under age 15	5,755	0.2	2,867	0.1
Aged 15 to 19	341,817	10.9	231,038	9.3
Aged 20 to 24	790,154	25.1	581,946	23.5
Aged 25 to 29	920,772	29.2	738,136	29.9
Aged 30 to 34	749,446	23.8	632,562	25.6
Aged 35 to 39	292,693	9.3	245,717	9.9
Aged 40 or older	49,196	1.6	39,765	1.6

Note: Hispanics may be of any race and most are white. For a breakdown of the Hispanic composition of racial groups and the racial composition of Hispanics, see the tables in the introduction to this book.
Source: National Center for Health Statistics, Advance Report of Final Natality Statistics, 1993, *Vol. 44, No. 3 Supplement, 1995*

Births to Unmarried White Women by Age, 1993

(number and percent of births to unmarried white women, by age of mother; 1993)

	number	percent of total births in age group
Total births to unmarried women	742,129	23.6%
Under age 15	4,868	84.6
Aged 15 to 19	213,080	62.3
Aged 20 to 24	263,538	33.4
Aged 25 to 29	139,905	15.2
Aged 30 to 34	79,136	10.6
Aged 35 to 39	34,283	11.7
Aged 40 or older	7,319	14.9

Source: National Center for Health Statistics, Advance Report of Final Natality Statistics, 1993, *Vol. 44, No. 3 Supplement, 1995*

White and Non-Hispanic White Births by State, 1993

(number and percent distribution of white and non-Hispanic white births by state; white and non-Hispanic white births as a percent of total births by state, and ratio of non-Hispanic white to white births, 1993)

	white			non-Hispanic white			ratio of non-Hispanic white to white births*
	number	percent	percent of total births	number	percent	percent of total births	
United States	3,149,833	100.0%	78.7%	2,472,031	100.0%	61.8%	78
Alabama	39,990	1.3	64.8	39,508	1.6	64.0	99
Alaska	7,508	0.2	67.8	7,106	0.3	64.2	95
Arizona	59,701	1.9	86.5	36,517	1.5	52.9	61
Arkansas	25,986	0.8	75.8	25,403	1.0	74.1	98
California	478,472	15.2	81.7	213,326	8.6	36.4	45
Colorado	49,256	1.6	91.2	39,156	1.6	72.5	79
Connecticut	39,539	1.3	84.7	32,664	1.3	69.9	83
Delaware	7,943	0.3	75.2	7,510	0.3	71.1	95
District of Columbia	1,595	0.1	15.0	1,355	0.1	12.7	85
Florida	144,486	4.6	75.0	114,016	4.6	59.2	79
Georgia	68,759	2.2	62.2	65,281	2.6	59.0	95
Hawaii	5,594	0.2	28.6	4,858	0.2	24.8	87
Idaho	16,891	0.5	96.9	15,044	0.6	86.3	89
Illinois	142,175	4.5	74.5	113,842	4.6	59.7	80
Indiana	73,713	2.3	87.8	71,507	2.9	85.2	97
Iowa	35,972	1.1	95.1	35,004	1.4	92.5	97
Kansas	33,035	1.0	88.3	30,262	1.2	80.9	92
Kentucky	47,674	1.5	90.0	47,266	1.9	89.2	99
Louisiana	38,528	1.2	55.5	37,658	1.5	54.3	98
Maine	14,779	0.5	98.1	14,340	0.6	95.2	97
Maryland	46,812	1.5	62.4	44,519	1.8	59.4	95
Massachusetts	72,845	2.3	86.0	65,659	2.7	77.5	90
Michigan	109,182	3.5	78.1	99,426	4.0	71.1	91
Minnesota	58,302	1.9	90.2	50,870	2.1	78.7	87
Mississippi	21,258	0.7	50.4	21,091	0.9	50.0	99
Missouri	61,045	1.9	81.1	59,912	2.4	79.6	98
Montana	9,986	0.3	87.9	9,445	0.4	83.1	95
Nebraska	21,233	0.7	91.4	19,621	0.8	84.5	92
Nevada	19,075	0.6	85.1	14,739	0.6	65.8	77
New Hampshire	15,149	0.5	98.1	12,795	0.5	82.9	84
New Jersey	88,852	2.8	75.5	72,747	2.9	61.8	82

(continued)

(continued from previous page)

| | white | | | non-Hispanic white | | | ratio of non-Hispanic white to white births* |
	number	percent	percent of total births	number	percent	percent of total births	
New Mexico	23,082	0.7%	82.9%	10,155	0.4%	36.5%	44
New York	208,093	6.6	73.7	147,516	6.0	52.2	71
North Carolina	68,998	2.2	68.1	66,506	2.7	65.6	96
North Dakota	7,742	0.2	89.1	7,544	0.3	86.8	97
Ohio	131,439	4.2	82.8	128,656	5.2	81.0	98
Oklahoma	36,135	1.1	78.1	34,074	1.4	73.7	94
Oregon	38,703	1.2	93.1	34,726	1.4	83.5	90
Pennsylvania	133,063	4.2	82.8	126,991	5.1	79.0	95
Rhode Island	12,204	0.4	87.3	9,624	0.4	68.9	79
South Carolina	32,690	1.0	60.7	32,116	1.3	59.7	98
South Dakota	8,827	0.3	82.3	8,721	0.4	81.4	99
Tennessee	54,609	1.7	74.8	53,896	2.2	73.8	99
Texas	272,211	8.6	84.5	141,086	5.7	43.8	52
Utah	35,198	1.1	94.8	32,834	1.3	88.4	93
Vermont	7,346	0.2	98.5	6,940	0.3	93.1	94
Virginia	68,345	2.2	72.0	64,359	2.6	67.8	94
Washington	68,921	2.2	87.6	59,636	2.4	75.8	87
West Virginia	20,834	0.7	95.6	20,771	0.8	95.3	100
Wisconsin	59,868	1.9	85.8	57,720	2.3	82.7	96
Wyoming	6,190	0.2	94.4	5,713	0.2	87.2	92

* Ratio is the number of non-Hispanic white births per 100 white births.
Note: Hispanics may be of any race and most are white. For a breakdown of the Hispanic composition of racial groups and the racial composition of Hispanics, see the tables in the introduction to this book.
Source: National Center for Health Statistics, Advance Report of Final Natality Statistics, 1993, Vol. 44, No. 3 Supplement, 1995

Projections of White and Non-Hispanic White Births, 1995 to 2020

(number of white and non-Hispanic white births, and white and non-Hispanic white births as a percent of total births, 1995-2020; numbers in thousands)

	white		non-Hispanic white	
	number	share of total births	number	share of total births
1995	3,071	77.9%	2,511	63.7%
1996	3,045	77.7	2,473	63.1
1997	3,022	77.3	2,440	62.5
1998	3,005	77.1	2,410	61.8
1999	2,993	76.8	2,385	61.2
2000	2,986	76.6	2,365	60.7
2001	2,983	76.4	2,348	60.1
2002	2,985	76.1	2,336	59.6
2003	2,993	76.0	2,329	59.1
2004	3,006	75.8	2,326	58.6
2005	3,025	75.6	2,328	58.2
2006	3,050	75.5	2,334	57.7
2007	3,080	75.3	2,344	57.3
2008	3,114	75.2	2,356	56.9
2009	3,149	75.1	2,368	56.5
2010	3,184	75.0	2,380	56.1
2011	3,217	75.0	2,391	55.7
2012	3,247	74.9	2,400	55.4
2013	3,274	74.8	2,406	55.0
2014	3,299	74.7	2,411	54.6
2015	3,320	74.6	2,414	54.2
2016	3,338	74.5	2,414	53.9
2017	3,353	74.4	2,411	53.5
2018	3,365	74.2	2,407	53.1
2019	3,376	74.1	2,400	52.7
2020	3,384	73.9	2,391	52.2

Note: Hispanics may be of any race and most are white. For a breakdown of the Hispanic composition of racial groups and the racial composition of Hispanics, see the tables in the introduction to this book.
Source: Bureau of the Census, Population Projections of the United States, by Age, Sex, Race, and Hispanic Origin: 1995 to 2050, *Current Population Reports, P25-1130, 1995*

Whites:
Wealth and Spending

The net worth of whites, at $45,740 in 1993, exceeds the $37,587 net worth of the average household. In part, this is because whites are more likely to own their homes than is the average householder. Sixty-seven percent of whites own their homes, versus 64 percent of householders in the nation as a whole. Homes comprise the largest share of Americans' net worth.

Only 10 percent of white households have zero or negative net worth (their debts exceed their assets), slightly lower than the 11.5 percent of total households with zero or negative net worth. Fully 31 percent of white households have net worth in excess of $100,000, versus 29 percent of total households.

The nation's 90.7 million white households spent an average of $32,935 in 1994, according to the Consumer Expenditure Survey—4 percent more than the average American household. Because whites comprise the majority of the population, white spending is close to the average on most items.

Distribution of Net Worth Among White Households, 1993

(number and percent distribution of white households by net worth, 1993; numbers in thousands)

	number	percent
Total households	$82,190	100.0%
Zero or negative net worth	8,055	9.8
$1 to $4,999	10,274	12.5
$5,000 to $9,999	5,096	6.2
$10,000 to $24,999	8,794	10.7
$25,000 to $49,999	10,109	12.3
$50,000 to $99,999	14,054	17.1
$100,000 to $249,999	16,438	20.0
$250,000 to $499,999	6,246	7.6
$500,000 or more	3,205	3.9
Median net worth	$45,740	-

Source: Bureau of the Census, Internet web site, http://www.census.gov

Asset Ownership and Value of Assets for White Households, 1993

(percent of white households owning assets and median value of asset among owners, 1993)

	percent owning	median value
Interest-earning assets at financial institutions*	74.6%	$3,199
Other interest-earning assets**	9.6	13,648
Regular checking accounts	48.2	499
Stocks and mutual fund shares	23.0	7,100
Own business or profession	11.8	7,000
Motor vehicles	88.7	5,472
Own home	67.3	49,500
Rental property	8.9	29,300
Other real estate	10.2	19,415
U.S. savings bonds	19.8	775
IRA or KEOGH accounts	25.5	13,999

Includes passbook savings accounts, money market deposit accounts, certificates of deposit, and interest-earning checking accounts.
**Includes money market funds, U.S. government securities, municipal and corporate bonds, and other interest-earning assets.*
Source: Bureau of the Census, Internet web site, http://www.census.gov

Average and Indexed Spending of White Households, 1994

(average annual expenditures of total and white consumer units, and indexed expenditures of white consumer units, 1994; figures for whites are for white and other races, which includes a small number of Asian and Pacific Islanders and Native Americans)

	average spending of total consumer units	white consumer units	
		average spending	indexed spending*
No. of consumer units (in thousands)	102,210	90,740	–
Average before-tax income	$36,838.00	$38,212.00	104
Total average annual spending	31,750.63	32,934.93	104
FOOD	**$4,410.52**	**$4,541.71**	**103**
Food at home	**2,712.05**	**2,753.59**	**102**
Cereals and bakery products	428.68	439.76	103
Cereals and cereal products	161.74	162.63	101
Flour	7.60	7.04	93
Prepared flour mixes	12.79	12.67	99
Ready-to-eat and cooked cereals	98.27	99.65	101
Rice	15.43	14.99	97
Pasta, cornmeal, other cereal products	27.65	28.28	102
Bakery products	266.93	277.13	104
Bread	76.22	77.65	102
White bread	37.65	37.52	100
Bread, other than white	38.57	40.13	104
Crackers and cookies	62.56	64.82	104
Cookies	42.97	44.21	103
Crackers	19.59	20.61	105
Frozen and refrigerated bakery products	21.56	22.43	104
Other bakery products	106.59	112.22	105
Biscuits and rolls	35.96	38.08	106
Cakes and cupcakes	31.19	32.40	104
Bread and cracker products	4.72	5.08	108
Sweetrolls, coffee cakes, doughnuts	21.92	23.09	105
Pies, tarts, turnovers	12.80	13.57	106
Meats, poultry, fish, and eggs	732.45	716.27	98
Beef	226.76	223.69	99
Ground beef	88.45	87.77	99
Roast	39.41	38.40	97
Chuck roast	12.26	11.91	97
Round roast	14.84	14.88	100
Other roast	12.31	11.61	94
Steak	84.75	83.99	99
Round steak	16.00	15.82	99

(continued)

(continued from previous page)

	average spending of total consumer units	white consumer units	
		average spending	indexed spending*
Sirloin steak	$24.44	$24.72	101
Other steak	44.31	43.45	98
Other beef	14.15	13.53	96
Pork	155.74	147.93	95
Bacon	22.78	21.23	93
Pork chops	39.32	36.64	93
Ham	36.88	37.39	101
Ham, not canned	34.16	34.47	101
Canned ham	2.72	2.92	107
Sausage	22.82	20.88	91
Other pork	33.93	31.79	94
Other meats	93.95	94.72	101
Frankfurters	18.76	18.65	99
Lunch meats (cold cuts)	65.66	66.90	102
Bologna, liverwurst, salami	23.73	23.65	100
Other lunchmeats	41.93	43.25	103
Lamb, organ meats and others	9.53	9.17	96
Lamb and organ meats	9.35	8.98	96
Mutton, goat and game	0.18	0.19	106
Poultry	136.58	133.09	97
Fresh and frozen chickens	107.89	103.88	96
Fresh and frozen whole chicken	29.56	27.63	93
Fresh and frozen chicken parts	78.33	76.24	97
Other poultry	28.69	29.22	102
Fish and seafood	89.43	87.38	98
Canned fish and seafood	15.03	15.41	103
Fresh fish and shellfish	51.26	48.55	95
Frozen fish and shellfish	23.15	23.41	101
Eggs	30.00	29.45	98
Dairy products	288.92	301.36	104
Fresh milk and cream	127.13	131.44	103
Fresh milk, all types	118.94	122.84	103
Cream	8.19	8.60	105
Other dairy products	161.79	169.92	105
Butter	11.65	11.84	102
Cheese	81.83	86.64	106
Ice cream and related products	47.64	49.66	104
Miscellaneous dairy products	20.66	21.78	105
Fruits and vegetables	436.57	445.18	102
Fresh fruits	133.02	137.51	103
Apples	25.37	26.14	103

(continued)

(continued from previous page)

	average spending of total consumer units	white consumer units	
		average spending	indexed spending*
Bananas	$29.66	$30.47	103
Oranges	16.36	16.36	100
Citrus fruits, excl. oranges	10.96	11.43	104
Other fresh fruits	50.67	53.10	105
Fresh vegetables	134.89	138.40	103
Potatoes	28.01	28.07	100
Lettuce	17.38	18.21	105
Tomatoes	21.01	21.73	103
Other fresh vegetables	68.50	70.39	103
Processed fruits	93.08	93.44	100
Frozen fruits and fruit juices	16.28	16.71	103
Frozen orange juice	9.49	9.73	103
Frozen fruits	1.60	1.60	100
Frozen fruit juices	5.19	5.38	104
Canned fruit	14.23	15.00	105
Dried fruit	5.89	6.03	102
Fresh fruit juices	17.90	17.28	97
Canned and bottled fruit juices	38.78	38.41	99
Processed vegetables	75.57	75.83	100
Frozen vegetables	24.83	25.23	102
Canned and dried vegetables and juices	50.74	50.60	100
Canned beans	10.44	10.28	98
Canned corn	6.81	6.58	97
Other canned and dried vegetables	27.05	27.24	101
Frozen vegetable juices	0.23	0.20	87
Fresh and canned vegetable juices	6.21	6.30	101
Other food at home	825.43	851.02	103
Sugar and other sweets	105.25	107.56	102
Candy and chewing gum	62.32	65.25	105
Sugar	18.31	17.17	94
Artificial sweeteners	3.39	3.46	102
Jams, preserves, other sweets	21.23	21.68	102
Fats and oils	79.25	80.38	101
Margarine	14.16	14.61	103
Fats and oils	23.09	22.37	97
Salad dressings	23.75	24.56	103
Nondairy cream and imitation milk	6.56	6.89	105
Peanut butter	11.70	11.96	102
Miscellaneous foods	361.62	373.66	103
Frozen prepared foods	66.14	69.90	106
Frozen meals	21.43	22.75	106
Other frozen prepared foods	44.71	47.15	105

(continued)

(continued from previous page)

	average spending of total consumer units	white consumer units	
		average spending	indexed spending*
Canned and packaged soups	$29.55	$30.72	104
Potato chips, nuts, and other snacks	74.07	78.19	106
Potato chips and other snacks	58.18	61.31	105
Nuts	15.89	16.88	106
Condiments and seasonings	79.74	81.35	102
Salt, spices, and other seasonings	19.30	18.50	96
Olives, pickles, relishes	10.16	10.69	105
Sauces and gravies	36.43	37.54	103
Baking needs and misc. products	13.85	14.62	106
Other canned/packaged prepared foods	112.12	113.50	101
Prepared salads	10.97	11.50	105
Prepared desserts	7.99	8.54	107
Baby food	28.11	26.30	94
Miscellaneous prepared foods	65.05	67.17	103
Nonalcoholic beverages	232.89	238.89	103
Cola	89.45	92.11	103
Other carbonated drinks	38.89	39.85	102
Coffee	43.01	45.59	106
Roasted coffee	29.13	30.95	106
Instant and freeze-dried coffee	13.88	14.64	105
Noncarb. fruit-flavored drinks, incl. non-frozen lemonade	21.86	21.03	96
Tea	16.25	16.73	103
Nonalcoholic beer	0.66	0.68	103
Other nonalcoholic beverages	22.77	22.90	101
Food prepared by cu on out-of-town trips	46.41	50.54	109
Food away from home	**1,698.46**	**1,788.12**	**105**
Meals at restaurants, carry-outs, other	1,306.21	1,367.26	105
Lunch	451.76	468.36	104
Dinner	651.79	685.34	105
Snacks and nonalcoholic beverages	101.72	107.58	106
Breakfast and brunch	100.95	105.98	105
Board (including at school)	50.72	54.56	108
Catered affairs	56.09	60.71	108
Food on out-of-town trips	207.89	226.69	109
School lunches	53.76	54.74	102
Meals as pay	23.79	24.16	102
ALCOHOLIC BEVERAGES	**$278.03**	**$294.58**	**106**
At home	**165.13**	**170.81**	**103**
Beer and ale	99.68	102.75	103

(continued)

(continued from previous page)

	average spending of total consumer units	white consumer units	
		average spending	indexed spending*
Whiskey	$13.68	$14.16	104
Wine	36.41	38.82	107
Other alcoholic beverages	15.35	15.08	98
Away from home	**112.91**	**123.77**	**110**
Beer and ale	38.56	42.52	110
Wine	15.79	17.20	109
Other alcoholic beverages	27.96	30.44	109
Alcoholic beverages purchased on trips	30.61	33.62	110
HOUSING	**$10,106.32**	**$10,415.20**	**103**
Shelter	**5,686.26**	**5,866.35**	**103**
Owned dwellings**	3,491.71	3,718.83	107
Mortgage interest and charges	1,918.71	2,040.07	106
Mortgage interest	1,822.54	1,935.63	106
Interest paid, home equity loan	44.51	47.28	106
Interest paid, home equity line of credit	51.11	56.62	111
Prepayment penalty charges	0.55	0.54	98
Property taxes	921.61	986.57	107
Maintenance, repairs, insurance, and other expenses	651.39	692.19	106
Homeowners and related insurance	207.71	220.59	106
Fire and extended coverage	5.95	6.12	103
Homeowners insurance	201.76	214.47	106
Ground rent	37.79	42.22	112
Maintenance and repair services	313.66	329.21	105
Painting and papering	44.00	47.85	109
Plumbing and water heating	36.33	37.82	104
Heat, air conditioning, electrical work	55.27	59.18	107
Roofing and gutters	50.96	51.79	102
Other repair, maintenance services	108.66	111.93	103
Repair and replacement of hard surface flooring	16.78	18.84	112
Repair of built-in appliances	1.67	1.79	107
Maintenance and repair materials	71.89	78.23	109
Paint, wallpaper, and supplies	18.40	19.74	107
Tools and equipment for painting and wallpapering	1.98	2.12	107
Plumbing supplies and equipment	8.59	9.37	109
Electrical supplies, heating/cooling equipment	5.12	5.57	109

(continued)

(continued from previous page)

	average spending of total consumer units	white consumer units	
		average spending	indexed spending*
Material for hard surface flooring, repair and replacement	$5.01	$5.55	111
Material and equipment for roofing and gutters	5.36	5.76	107
Plaster, paneling, siding, windows, doors, screens, awnings	11.75	13.10	111
Patio, walk, fence, driveway, masonry, brick, stucco materials	0.47	0.53	113
Material for landscape maintenance	1.47	1.66	113
Miscellaneous supplies and equipment	13.73	14.84	108
Material for insulation, other maintenance and repair	9.37	9.93	106
Material to finish basement, remodel rooms, etc. (owner)	4.37	4.91	112
Property management and security	20.16	21.75	108
Property management	12.17	13.04	107
Management and upkeep services for security	7.99	8.71	109
Parking	0.18	0.19	106
Rented dwellings	1,799.39	1,718.09	95
Rent	1,728.66	1,646.01	95
Rent as pay	42.90	43.21	101
Maintenance, repairs, insurance, and other expenses	27.84	28.86	104
Tenant's insurance	8.99	8.50	95
Maintenance and repair services	10.13	10.95	108
Repair or maintenance services	9.07	9.77	108
Repair and replacement of hard surface flooring	0.94	1.06	113
Repair of built-in appliances	0.12	0.12	100
Maintenance and repair materials	8.72	9.42	108
Paint, wallpaper, and supplies	1.85	1.93	104
Tools and equipment for painting and wallpapering	0.20	0.21	105
Plaster, paneling, roofing, gutters, etc.	1.13	1.27	112
Patio, walk, fence, driveway, masonry, brick, stucco materials	0.08	0.09	113
Plumbing supplies and equipment	0.69	0.66	96
Electrical supplies, heating/ cooling equipment	1.14	1.29	113
Miscellaneous supplies and equipment	2.90	3.20	110
Material for insulation, other maintenance and repair	0.99	1.05	106

(continued)

(continued from previous page)

	average spending of total consumer units	white consumer units	
		average spending	indexed spending*
Material for additions, finishing basements, remodeling rooms	$1.40	$1.57	112
Construction materials for jobs not started	0.51	0.58	114
Material for hard surface flooring	0.46	0.49	107
Material for landscape maintenance	0.26	0.29	112
Other lodging	395.16	429.43	109
Owned vacation homes	117.35	127.73	109
Mortgage interest and charges	41.73	43.37	104
Mortgage interest	38.43	39.65	103
Interest paid, home equity loan	0.49	0.55	112
Interest paid, home equity line of credit	2.81	3.17	113
Property taxes	49.87	55.53	111
Maintenance, insurance, and other expenses	25.75	28.84	112
Homeowners and related insurance	7.33	8.18	112
Homeowners insurance	7.04	7.86	112
Fire and extended coverage	0.29	0.32	110
Ground rent	3.27	3.68	113
Maintenance and repair services	10.66	11.98	112
Maintenance and repair materials	1.24	1.36	110
Property management and security	3.20	3.59	112
Property management	2.30	2.58	112
Management and upkeep services for security	0.90	1.01	112
Parking	0.05	0.04	80
Housing while attending school	60.57	64.80	107
Lodging on out-of-town trips	217.24	236.90	109
Utilities, fuels, and public services	**2,188.56**	**2,189.42**	**100**
Natural gas	282.73	274.56	97
Electricity	861.50	865.50	100
Fuel oil and other fuels	97.97	106.43	109
Fuel oil	59.72	65.32	109
Coal	1.46	1.65	113
Bottled/tank gas	30.20	32.49	108
Wood and other fuels	6.59	6.97	106
Telephone services	689.82	681.39	99
Telephone services in home city, excl. mobile car phones	676.16	667.31	99
Telephone services for mobile car phones	13.66	14.08	103
Water and other public services	256.53	261.54	102

(continued)

(continued from previous page)

	average spending of total consumer units	white consumer units	
		average spending	indexed spending*
Water and sewerage maintenance	$183.05	$185.48	101
Trash and garbage collection	72.27	74.69	103
Septic tank cleaning	1.22	1.37	112
Household operations	**490.15**	**518.43**	**106**
Personal services	229.80	234.52	102
Babysitting and child care in own home	47.24	49.61	105
Babysitting and child care in someone else's home	32.71	32.46	99
Care for elderly, invalids, handicapped, etc.	19.25	21.42	111
Day care centers, nursery and preschools	130.60	131.03	100
Other household expenses	260.35	283.91	109
Housekeeping services	85.14	94.85	111
Gardening, lawn care service	69.26	75.09	108
Water softening service	2.68	2.99	112
Household laundry and drycleaning (nonclothing), not coin-operated	1.80	1.81	101
Coin-operated household laundry and dry cleaning (nonclothing)	5.34	4.71	88
Termite/pest control maintenance	6.84	7.47	109
Other home services	19.44	21.44	110
Termite/pest control products	0.27	0.29	107
Moving, storage, and freight express	26.91	28.84	107
Appliance repair, including service center	14.21	14.96	105
Reupholstering and furniture repair	10.19	11.34	111
Repairs/rentals of lawn, garden equipment, hand or power tools, other hh equip.	8.09	8.94	111
Appliance rental	1.57	1.74	111
Rental of office equipment for nonbusiness use	0.27	0.24	89
Repair of miscellaneous household equip. and furnishings	6.91	7.66	111
Repair of computer systems for nonbusiness use	1.42	1.53	108
Housekeeping supplies	**393.32**	**409.14**	**104**
Laundry and cleaning supplies	109.37	110.37	101
Soaps and detergents	62.00	60.94	98
Other laundry cleaning products	47.37	49.43	104
Other household products	173.91	181.52	104
Cleansing and toilet tissue, paper towels and napkins	55.89	56.98	102

(continued)

(continued from previous page)

	average spending of total consumer units	white consumer units	
		average spending	indexed spending*
Miscellaneous household products	$73.73	$77.89	106
Lawn and garden supplies	44.29	46.65	105
Postage and stationery	110.05	117.25	107
Stationery, stationery supplies, giftwrap	58.09	62.76	108
Postage	51.96	54.49	105
Household furnishings and equipment	**1,348.04**	**1,431.85**	**106**
Household textiles	99.52	105.60	106
Bathroom linens	12.63	13.60	108
Bedroom linens	48.69	50.99	105
Kitchen and dining room linens	6.87	7.53	110
Curtains and draperies	18.55	19.66	106
Slipcovers, decorative pillows	1.93	1.99	103
Sewing materials for household items	9.84	10.82	110
Other linens	0.99	1.02	103
Furniture	318.43	333.62	105
Mattress and springs	41.64	43.52	105
Other bedroom furniture	51.84	53.48	103
Sofas	78.50	82.01	104
Living room chairs	33.00	34.79	105
Living room tables	14.61	15.36	105
Kitchen and dining room furniture	48.70	50.44	104
Infants' furniture	6.12	6.34	104
Outdoor furniture	11.11	12.32	111
Wall units, cabinets and other furniture	32.92	35.36	107
Floor coverings	119.76	128.39	107
Major appliances	148.95	155.86	105
Dishwashers (built-in), garbage disposals, range hoods (renter)	0.68	0.74	109
Dishwashers (built-in), garbage disposals, range hoods (owner)	10.34	11.31	109
Refrigerators and freezers (renter)	6.92	6.42	93
Refrigerators and freezers (owner)	39.28	41.49	106
Washing machines (renter)	5.98	5.71	95
Washing machines (owner)	14.04	15.29	109
Clothes dryers (renter)	3.98	4.00	101
Clothes dryers (owner)	8.96	9.68	108
Cooking stoves, ovens (renter)	2.29	2.28	100
Cooking stoves, ovens (owner)	21.32	22.54	106
Microwave ovens (renter)	3.13	3.00	96
Microwave ovens (owner)	6.15	6.59	107
Portable dishwasher (renter)	0.06	0.07	117

(continued)

(continued from previous page)

	average spending of total consumer units	white consumer units	
		average spending	indexed spending*
Portable dishwasher (owner)	$0.66	$0.75	114
Window air conditioners (renter)	2.63	2.44	93
Window air conditioners (owner)	4.49	4.86	108
Electric floor cleaning equipment	13.44	13.98	104
Sewing machines	3.21	3.45	107
Miscellaneous household appliances	1.40	1.25	89
Small appliances, misc. housewares	80.76	85.88	106
Housewares	57.18	61.35	107
Plastic dinnerware	1.50	1.59	106
China and other dinnerware	10.72	11.41	106
Flatware	4.95	5.36	108
Glassware	8.07	8.64	107
Silver serving pieces	1.67	1.80	108
Other serving pieces	1.60	1.74	109
Nonelectric cookware	14.19	15.16	107
Tableware, nonelectric kitchenware	14.48	15.65	108
Small appliances	23.57	24.53	104
Small electric kitchen appliances	17.27	18.18	105
Portable heating and cooling equipment	6.30	6.35	101
Miscellaneous household equipment	580.63	622.50	107
Window coverings	13.52	14.88	110
Infants' equipment	6.78	7.31	108
Laundry and cleaning equipment	10.48	10.70	102
Outdoor equipment	5.20	5.74	110
Clocks	4.76	5.11	107
Lamps and lighting fixtures	34.97	38.40	110
Other household decorative items	125.25	134.23	107
Telephones and accessories	38.87	42.09	108
Lawn and garden equipment	48.56	50.98	105
Power tools	13.16	14.48	110
Small miscellaneous furnishings	1.95	2.16	111
Hand tools	10.48	11.64	111
Indoor plants and fresh flowers	49.35	54.32	110
Closet and storage items	7.85	8.29	106
Rental of furniture	4.12	4.07	99
Luggage	7.70	7.85	102
Computers and computer hardware, nonbusiness use	112.01	120.02	107
Computer software and accessories, nonbusiness use	19.31	20.63	107
Telephone answering devices	3.87	4.00	103

(continued)

(continued from previous page)

	average spending of total consumer units	white consumer units	
		average spending	indexed spending*
Calculators	$2.18	$2.18	100
Business equipment for home use	4.93	4.89	99
Other hardware	20.66	22.37	108
Smoke alarms (owner)	0.81	0.89	110
Smoke alarms (renter)	0.15	0.14	93
Other household appliances (renter)	6.25	6.82	109
Other household appliances (owner)	1.33	1.16	87
Misc. household equipment and parts	26.12	27.18	104
APPAREL AND SERVICES	**$1,644.03**	**$1,650.77**	**100**
Men and boys	**394.67**	**398.36**	**101**
Men, aged 16 or older	304.52	308.74	101
Suits	31.94	32.00	100
Sportcoats and tailored jackets	12.96	13.90	107
Coats and jackets	26.57	25.19	95
Underwear	11.96	11.44	96
Hosiery	9.55	9.84	103
Nightwear	2.61	2.93	112
Accessories	27.69	28.02	101
Sweaters and vests	14.33	15.01	105
Active sportswear	11.70	12.28	105
Shirts	75.18	76.16	101
Pants	60.44	61.84	102
Shorts and shorts sets	14.22	14.55	102
Uniforms	3.36	3.32	99
Costumes	2.03	2.26	111
Boys, aged 2 to 15	90.15	89.62	99
Coats and jackets	6.28	6.98	111
Sweaters	2.60	2.29	88
Shirts	20.60	20.86	101
Underwear	4.04	4.25	105
Nightwear	1.78	1.70	96
Hosiery	3.23	3.23	100
Accessories	6.93	6.79	98
Suits, sportcoats, and vests	5.02	3.39	68
Pants	21.03	21.10	100
Shorts and shorts sets	9.66	10.38	107
Uniforms and active sportswear	7.63	7.36	96
Costumes	1.35	1.29	96
Women and girls	**651.83**	**657.02**	**101**
Women, aged 16 or older	552.01	559.60	101

(continued)

(continued from previous page)

	average spending of total consumer units	white consumer units	
		average spending	indexed spending*
Coats and jackets	$51.10	$49.11	96
Dresses	76.08	72.37	95
Sportcoats and tailored jackets	4.47	4.50	101
Sweaters and vests	35.23	38.48	109
Shirts, blouses, and tops	92.00	96.96	105
Skirts	22.91	23.39	102
Pants	57.78	61.10	106
Shorts and shorts sets	24.25	24.87	103
Active sportswear	23.62	23.84	101
Sleepwear	25.57	25.72	101
Undergarments	27.72	28.00	101
Hosiery	24.60	23.77	97
Suits	36.11	35.47	98
Accessories	47.23	48.41	102
Uniforms	1.34	1.52	113
Costumes	2.00	2.11	106
Girls, aged 2 to 15	99.81	97.42	98
Coats and jackets	7.75	7.44	96
Dresses and suits	13.82	13.25	96
Shirts, blouses, and sweaters	23.96	24.46	102
Skirts and pants	16.29	15.52	95
Shorts and shorts sets	9.02	8.44	94
Active sportswear	7.15	7.62	107
Underwear and sleepwear	7.59	7.32	96
Hosiery	5.17	4.73	91
Accessories	4.08	3.78	93
Uniforms	1.95	1.84	94
Costumes	3.06	3.02	99
Children under age 2	**79.85**	**79.66**	**100**
Coats, jackets, and snowsuits	2.72	2.46	90
Dress and outerwear	21.37	21.67	101
Underwear	46.65	46.73	100
Nightwear and loungewear	3.84	3.87	101
Accessories	5.26	4.94	94
Footwear	**253.65**	**250.44**	**99**
Men's	80.57	80.60	100
Boys'	33.02	30.05	91
Women's	114.13	114.39	100
Girls'	25.93	25.40	98
Other apparel products and services	**264.03**	**265.29**	**100**
Material for making clothes	6.85	7.06	103

(continued)

(continued from previous page)

	average spending of total consumer units	white consumer units	
		average spending	indexed spending*
Sewing patterns and notions	$2.32	$2.44	105
Watches	23.41	23.28	99
Jewelry	103.30	107.87	104
Shoe repair and other shoe services	2.97	3.06	103
Coin-operated apparel laundry and dry cleaning	36.01	31.62	88
Alteration, repair, and tailoring of apparel and accessories	6.73	7.13	106
Clothing rental	3.70	3.97	107
Watch and jewelry repair services	5.51	5.83	106
Apparel laundry, dry cleaning, not coin-operated	72.44	72.11	100
Clothing storage	0.81	0.91	112
TRANSPORTATION	**$6,044.16**	**$6,268.49**	**104**
Vehicle purchases (net outlay)	**2,724.66**	**2,814.43**	**103**
Cars and trucks, new	1,390.51	1,452.90	104
New cars	749.71	756.53	101
New trucks	640.80	696.37	109
Cars and trucks, used	1,289.97	1,311.79	102
Used cars	863.70	847.40	98
Used trucks	426.27	464.39	109
Other vehicles	44.18	49.75	113
Gasoline and motor oil	**985.91**	**1,020.46**	**104**
Gasoline	878.15	905.03	103
Diesel fuel	9.23	9.86	107
Gasoline on out-of-town trips	86.21	92.61	107
Gasohol	0.15	0.17	113
Motor oil	11.31	11.85	105
Motor oil on out-of-town trips	0.87	0.94	108
Other vehicle expenses	**1,952.54**	**2,037.40**	**104**
Vehicle finance charges	235.30	243.22	103
Automobile finance charges	137.45	137.07	100
Truck finance charges	86.14	93.16	108
Motorcycle and plane finance charges	0.97	1.03	106
Other vehicle finance charges	10.74	11.96	111
Maintenance and repairs	680.27	705.79	104
Coolant, additives, brake, transmission fluids	6.11	6.23	102
Tires	86.89	91.28	105

(continued)

(continued from previous page)

	average spending of total consumer units	white consumer units	
		average spending	indexed spending*
Parts, equipment, and accessories	$112.58	$118.24	105
Vehicle audio equipment, excluding labor	5.11	5.72	112
Vehicle products	4.78	5.20	109
Misc. auto repair, servicing	33.27	36.07	108
Body work and painting	34.63	36.74	106
Clutch, transmission repair	44.21	44.59	101
Drive shaft and rear-end repair	5.69	5.84	103
Brake work	42.05	42.71	102
Repair to steering or front-end	17.98	18.88	105
Repair to engine cooling system	22.08	23.18	105
Motor tune-up	41.69	42.87	103
Lube, oil change, and oil filters	38.53	40.49	105
Front-end alignment, wheel balance and rotation	9.54	10.17	107
Shock absorber replacement	6.59	7.05	107
Brake adjustment	3.69	3.73	101
Gas tank repair, replacement	2.23	1.92	86
Repair tires and other repair work	26.87	27.09	101
Vehicle air conditioning repair	15.00	16.03	107
Exhaust system repair	19.74	20.51	104
Electrical system repair	30.22	30.19	100
Motor repair, replacement	65.90	66.13	100
Auto repair service policy	4.87	4.92	101
Vehicle insurance	689.64	717.67	104
Vehicle rental, leases, licenses, and other charges	347.34	370.73	107
Leased and rented vehicles	200.82	216.04	108
Rented vehicles	37.56	38.57	103
Auto rental	5.99	5.39	90
Auto rental, out-of-town trips	24.44	25.62	105
Truck rental	1.54	1.61	105
Truck rental, out-of-town trips	4.32	4.53	105
Leased vehicles	163.26	177.47	109
Car lease payments	109.24	117.45	108
Cash downpayment (car lease)	13.22	14.05	106
Termination fee (car lease)	0.37	0.41	111
Truck lease payments	36.55	41.17	113
Cash downpayment (truck lease)	3.86	4.35	113
Termination fee (truck lease)	0.03	0.03	100
State and local registration	79.21	84.52	107
Drivers' license	6.96	7.37	106
Vehicle inspection	8.36	8.73	104

(continued)

(continued from previous page)

	average spending of total consumer units	white consumer units	
		average spending	indexed spending*
Parking fees	$25.59	$25.97	101
Parking fees in home city, excluding residence	22.49	22.59	100
Parking fees, out-of-town trips	3.10	3.37	109
Tolls	9.34	10.31	110
Tolls on out-of-town trips	4.63	5.02	108
Towing charges	4.96	4.84	98
Automobile service clubs	7.47	7.94	106
Public transportation	381.05	396.19	104
Airline fares	249.48	269.99	108
Intercity bus fares	11.34	11.65	103
Intracity mass transit fares	47.65	37.99	80
Local trans. on out-of-town trips	10.35	11.27	109
Taxi fares on trips	6.08	6.62	109
Taxi fares	7.70	6.62	86
Intercity train fares	16.24	17.43	107
Ship fares	31.13	33.68	108
School bus	1.07	0.95	89
HEALTH CARE	**$1,754.74**	**$1,859.94**	**106**
Health insurance	**814.95**	**857.77**	**105**
Commercial health insurance	262.44	273.89	104
Blue Cross/Blue Shield	160.50	172.64	108
Health maintenance plans (HMOs)	122.81	128.44	105
Medicare payments	153.65	157.39	102
Commercial Medicare supplements/ other health insurance	115.55	125.42	109
Medical services	**571.04**	**615.01**	**108**
Physician's services	163.63	174.34	107
Dental services	188.04	202.29	108
Eye care services	29.51	31.54	107
Services by professionals other than physicians	31.92	35.34	111
Lab tests, x-rays	24.95	27.13	109
Hospital room	47.81	52.32	109
Hospital services other than room	59.54	64.03	108
Care in convalescent or nursing home	13.49	15.11	112
Repair of medical equipment	0.03	0.03	100
Other medical care services	12.12	12.87	106
Drugs	**285.78**	**300.70**	**105**
Non-prescription drugs	76.19	79.71	105

(continued)

(continued from previous page)

	average spending of total consumer units	white consumer units	
		average spending	indexed spending*
Prescription drugs	$209.58	$220.99	105
Medical supplies	**82.98**	**86.46**	**104**
Eyeglasses and contact lenses	50.99	53.57	105
Hearing aids	0.73	0.82	112
Topicals and dressings	22.94	23.41	102
Medical equipment for general use	2.53	2.67	106
Supportive/convalescent medical equipment	3.83	3.89	102
Rental of medical equipment	0.68	0.75	110
Rental of supportive, convalescent medical equipment	1.28	1.35	105
ENTERTAINMENT	**$1,566.93**	**$1,668.24**	**106**
Fees and admissions	**439.11**	**476.34**	**108**
Recreation expenses, out-of-town trips	20.93	22.77	109
Social, recreation, civic club membership	84.23	92.22	109
Fees for participant sports	73.54	80.61	110
Participant sports, out-of-town trips	26.99	29.72	110
Movie, theater, opera, ballet	76.23	80.75	106
Movie, other admissions, out-of-town trips	36.38	39.75	109
Admission to sporting events	32.42	34.61	107
Admission to sports events, out-of-town trips	12.13	13.25	109
Fees for recreational lessons	55.31	59.90	108
Other entertainment services, out-of-town trips	20.93	22.77	109
Television, radio, and sound equipment	**533.16**	**545.86**	**102**
Televisions	370.56	375.14	101
Community antenna or cable TV	209.60	210.31	100
Black and white TV	1.79	1.95	109
Color TV, console	24.03	23.35	97
Color TV, portable/table model	53.02	54.10	102
VCRs and video disc players	32.24	33.89	105
Video cassettes, tapes, and discs	21.90	23.26	106
Video game hardware and software	19.21	19.02	99
Repair of TV, radio, and sound equipment	8.43	8.97	106
Rental of televisions	0.33	0.29	88
Radios and sound equipment	162.60	170.72	105
Radios	9.21	10.13	110
Tape recorders and players	6.05	6.46	107
Sound components and component systems	30.28	30.75	102
Miscellaneous sound equipment	1.18	1.32	112

(continued)

(continued from previous page)

	average spending of total consumer units	white consumer units	
		average spending	indexed spending*
Sound equipment accessories	$4.75	$4.93	104
Compact disc, tape, record, and video mail order clubs	12.08	12.92	107
Records, CDs, audio tapes, needles	36.16	37.79	105
Rental of VCR, radio, sound equipment	0.36	0.38	106
Musical instruments and accessories	17.02	18.34	108
Rental and repair of musical instruments	1.92	2.05	107
Rental of video cassettes, tapes, films, and discs	43.58	45.66	105
Pets, toys, and playground equipment	**288.73**	**309.24**	**107**
Pets	165.03	180.12	109
Pet food	75.80	82.51	109
Pet purchase, supplies, and medicines	26.15	27.99	107
Pet services	15.53	17.02	110
Veterinary services	47.56	52.61	111
Toys, games, hobbies, and tricycles	121.11	126.20	104
Playground equipment	2.59	2.92	113
Other entertainment equipment, supplies, and services	**305.92**	**336.80**	**110**
Unmotored recreational vehicles	27.76	31.27	113
Boats without motor and boat trailer	5.13	5.78	113
Trailers and other attachable campers	22.63	25.49	113
Motorized recreational vehicles	81.56	91.87	113
Motorized campers	16.55	18.64	113
Other motorized recreational vehicles	22.84	25.73	113
Boats with motor	42.17	47.50	113
Rental of recreational vehicles	2.33	2.60	112
Outboard motors	1.79	2.01	112
Docking and landing fees	5.59	6.12	109
Sports, recreation, exercise equipment	107.91	118.12	109
Athletic gear, game tables, and exercise equipment	51.01	55.68	109
Bicycles	13.36	14.09	105
Camping equipment	3.23	3.63	112
Hunting and fishing equipment	18.99	20.97	110
Winter sports equipment	5.08	5.64	111
Water sports equipment	6.03	6.79	113
Other sports equipment	8.44	9.36	111
Rental and repair of sports equipment	1.77	1.96	111

(continued)

	average spending of total consumer units	white consumer units	
		average spending	indexed spending*
Photographic equipment, supplies, and services	$70.55	$75.61	107
Film	19.61	20.90	107
Other photographic supplies	0.36	0.32	89
Film processing	27.15	29.17	107
Repair and rental of photographic equip.	0.32	0.35	109
Photographic equipment	12.50	13.66	109
Photographer fees	10.60	11.20	106
Fireworks	1.58	1.78	113
Souvenirs	0.51	0.58	114
Visual goods	1.77	2.00	113
Pinball and electronic video games	4.58	4.85	106
PERSONAL CARE PRODUCTS AND SERVICES	**$396.66**	**$401.45**	**101**
Personal care products	**219.22**	**223.28**	**102**
Hair care products	46.35	46.59	101
Nonelectric articles for the hair	6.36	6.58	103
Wigs and hairpieces	0.83	0.67	81
Oral hygiene products, articles	23.10	23.66	102
Shaving needs	12.07	12.25	101
Cosmetics, perfume, and bath preparation	99.46	102.11	103
Deodorant, feminine hygiene products, and misc.	26.87	27.07	101
Electric personal care appliances	4.18	4.34	104
Personal care services	**177.45**	**178.17**	**100**
Personal care services/female	87.44	88.39	101
Personal care services/male	89.89	89.65	100
Repair of personal care appliances	0.12	0.13	108
READING	**$164.80**	**$175.84**	**107**
Newspapers, subscription	52.48	56.16	107
Newspapers, non-subscription	17.83	18.03	101
Magazines, subscription	24.59	26.45	108
Magazines, non-subscription	12.19	12.86	105
Newsletters	0.11	0.13	118
Books purchased through book clubs	$10.51	$11.29	107
Books not purchased through book clubs	45.85	49.59	108
Encyclopedia and other reference book sets	1.23	1.33	108

(continued)

(continued from previous page)

	average spending of total consumer units	white consumer units	
		average spending	indexed spending*
EDUCATION	**$459.88**	**$485.36**	**106**
College tuition	271.59	291.44	107
Elementary/high school tuition	64.79	66.41	103
Other school tuition	14.46	15.42	107
Other school expenses including rentals	18.85	19.80	105
School books, supplies, equipment for college	38.29	39.31	103
School books, supplies, equipment for elementary/high school	9.51	9.39	99
School books, supplies, equipment for day care, nursery, other	3.34	3.46	104
School supplies, etc., unspecified	39.04	40.13	103
TOBACCO PRODUCTS AND SMOKING SUPPLIES	**$258.55**	**$265.68**	**103**
Cigarettes	236.05	241.74	102
Other tobacco products	21.06	22.37	106
Smoking accessories	1.44	1.57	109
MISCELLANEOUS EXPENSES	**$748.51**	**$789.05**	**105**
Miscellaneous fees, pari-mutuel losses	44.69	45.77	102
Legal fees	112.87	122.54	109
Funeral expenses	85.75	91.17	106
Safe deposit box rental	5.69	6.19	109
Checking accounts, other bank service charges	26.49	27.25	103
Cemetery lots, vaults, and maintenance fees	18.48	19.93	108
Accounting fees	43.06	47.19	110
Miscellaneous personal services	22.50	23.34	104
Finance charges, excl. mortgage, vehicles	205.23	212.57	104
Occupational expenses	84.96	88.30	104
Expenses for other properties	93.52	99.27	106
Interest paid, home equity line of credit (other property)	0.42	0.47	112
Credit card memberships	4.87	5.06	104
CASH CONTRIBUTIONS	**$960.31**	**$1,019.31**	**106**
Cash contributions to non-cu member, incl. students, alimony, child support	265.01	278.49	105
Gifts of cash, stocks, and bonds to non-cu member	206.25	228.76	111
Contributions to charities	90.33	98.67	109
Contributions to church	363.85	375.03	103
Contributions to educational organizations	21.24	23.52	111

(continued)

(continued from previous page)

	average spending of total consumer units	white consumer units	
		average spending	indexed spending*
Contributions to political organizations	$7.17	$7.92	110
Other contributions	6.45	6.93	107
PERSONAL INSURANCE			
AND PENSIONS	**$2,957.19**	**$3,099.31**	**105**
Life and other personal insurances			
except health	**397.69**	**407.43**	**102**
Life, endowment, annuity,			
other personal insurance	380.59	388.76	102
Other nonhealth insurance	17.11	18.67	109
Pensions and Social Security	**2,559.49**	**2,691.88**	**105**
Deductions for government retirement	70.79	72.82	103
Deductions for railroad retirement	4.53	4.93	109
Deductions for private pensions	273.66	293.09	107
Non-payroll deposit to retirement plans	298.11	324.21	109
Deductions for Social Security	1,912.40	1,996.82	104
GIFTS*	**$1,007.51**	**$1,072.27**	**106**
Food	**84.05**	**90.42**	**108**
Cakes and cupcakes	2.44	2.63	108
Candy and chewing gum	9.86	10.73	109
Potato chips and other snacks	2.04	2.23	109
Board (including at school)	27.35	28.92	106
Catered affairs	18.48	20.62	112
Housing	**262.20**	**281.12**	**107**
Housekeeping supplies	37.84	40.59	107
Other household products	8.28	8.55	103
Miscellaneous household products	4.99	5.43	109
Lawn and garden supplies	2.14	1.95	91
Postage and stationery	27.69	30.10	109
Stationery, stationery supplies, giftwraps	22.27	24.15	108
Postage	5.42	5.95	110
Household textiles	15.73	16.95	108
Bathroom linens	2.56	2.79	109
Bedroom linens	10.39	11.08	107
Appliances and misc. housewares	26.36	28.33	107
Major appliances	5.46	5.52	101
Small appliances and misc. housewares	20.90	22.82	109
China and other dinnerware	3.43	3.77	110
Glassware	4.29	4.84	113
Nonelectric cookware	2.54	2.43	96

(continued)

(continued from previous page)

	average spending of total consumer units	white consumer units	
		average spending	indexed spending*
Tableware, nonelectric kitchenware	$3.07	$3.46	113
Small electric kitchen appliances	3.79	4.10	108
Miscellaneous household equipment	65.40	72.15	110
Lamps and lighting fixtures	3.66	4.04	110
Other household decorative items	24.59	27.75	113
Lawn and garden equipment	2.30	2.59	113
Indoor plants and flowers	16.77	18.55	111
Computers and computer hardware, nonbusiness use	5.60	5.84	104
Other housing	116.87	123.09	105
Repair or maintenance services	5.00	5.58	112
Housing while attending school	36.93	39.13	106
Lodging on out-of-town trips	2.49	2.72	109
Electricity (renter)	9.95	10.20	103
Telephone services in home city, excl. mobile car phone	12.04	12.86	107
Day-care centers, nursery, and preschools	12.40	11.92	96
Housekeeping services	5.52	6.02	109
Gardening, lawn care services	2.48	2.63	106
Moving, storage, freight express	2.29	2.57	112
Sofas	2.72	2.72	100
Kitchen, dining room furniture	2.26	2.22	98
Infants' furniture	2.18	2.33	107
Apparel and services	**246.23**	**258.17**	**105**
Males, aged 2 or older	64.05	68.24	107
Men's coats and jackets	4.46	5.03	113
Men's accessories	5.71	5.39	94
Men's sweaters and vests	3.26	3.55	109
Men's active sportswear	2.24	2.40	107
Men's shirts	15.44	16.78	109
Men's pants	5.72	6.45	113
Boys' shirts	4.95	5.07	102
Boys' accessories	2.02	2.22	110
Boys' pants	3.73	3.82	102
Boys' shorts and short sets	2.07	2.32	112
Females, aged 2 or older	93.94	96.96	103
Women's coats and jackets	10.55	11.17	106
Women's dresses	9.92	8.02	81
Women's vests and sweaters	6.44	7.25	113
Women's shirts, tops, blouses	14.50	15.98	110
Women's pants	5.12	5.72	112

(continued)

(continued from previous page)

	average spending of total consumer units	white consumer units	
		average spending	indexed spending*
Women's active sportswear	$3.30	$3.63	110
Women's sleepwear	5.85	6.04	103
Women's undergarments	2.30	2.41	105
Women's suits	2.42	2.16	89
Women's accessories	10.27	11.11	108
Girls' dresses and suits	3.23	3.35	104
Girls' shirts, blouses, sweaters	6.04	6.28	104
Girls' skirts and pants	2.23	2.34	105
Children under age 2	34.90	35.87	103
Infant dresses, outerwear	13.81	14.19	103
Infant underwear	14.38	14.92	104
Infant nightwear, loungewear	2.50	2.54	102
Infant accessories	2.78	2.85	103
Other apparel products and services	53.33	57.09	107
Jewelry and watches	25.94	28.67	111
Watches	3.40	3.50	103
Jewelry	22.54	25.17	112
All other apparel products and services	27.40	28.42	104
Men's footwear	8.18	9.21	113
Boys' footwear	4.83	3.72	77
Women's footwear	7.59	8.47	112
Girls' footwear	4.94	5.11	103
Transportation	**56.11**	**54.76**	**98**
New cars	7.43	1.89	25
Used cars	11.40	12.84	113
Gasoline on out-of-town trips	13.14	14.29	109
Airline fares	9.19	9.91	108
Ship fares	4.74	5.15	109
Health care	**34.69**	**38.38**	**111**
Physicians services	2.66	2.83	106
Dental services	3.43	3.76	110
Hospital room	3.66	4.12	113
Hospital service other than room	3.68	4.14	112
Care in convalescent or nursing home	11.30	12.69	112
Prescription drugs	2.28	2.43	107
Entertainment	**83.57**	**89.39**	**107**
Toys, games, hobbies, tricycles	32.48	34.74	107
Other entertainment	51.08	54.65	107
Movie, other admission, out-of-town trips	7.27	7.90	109

(continued)

(continued from previous page)

	average spending of total consumer units	white consumer units	
		average spending	indexed spending*
Admission to sports events, out-of-town trips	$2.42	$2.63	109
Fees for recreational lessons	4.96	5.15	104
Community antenna or cable TV	2.81	3.12	111
Color TV, portable/table model	2.01	2.00	100
VCRs, video disc players	2.67	2.94	110
Video game hardware and software	2.00	2.03	102
Radios	4.70	5.23	111
Sound components and component systems	2.05	2.22	108
Veterinary services	3.48	3.81	109
Athletic gear, game tables, and exercise equipment	3.46	3.79	110
Education	**114.09**	**123.84**	**109**
College tuition	86.94	94.69	109
Elementary, high school tuition	6.43	7.25	113
Other schools tuition	3.09	3.49	113
Other school expenses including rentals	4.72	4.67	99
School books, supplies, equipment for college	6.56	6.79	104
School supplies, etc., unspecified	5.32	5.93	111
All other gifts	**126.58**	**136.20**	**108**

* The index compares the spending of the average white consumer unit with the spending of the average consumer unit by dividing white spending by average spending in each category and multiplying by 100. An index of 100 means that white spending in that category equals average spending. An index of 132 means that white spending is 32 percent above average, while an index of 75 means that white spending is 25 percent below average.
** This figure does not include the amount paid for mortgage principal, which is considered an asset.
*** Expenditures on gifts are also included in the preceding product and service categories. Food spending, for example, includes the amount spent on food gifts. Only gift categories with average spending of $2.00 or more by the average consumer unit are shown.
Note: The Bureau of Labor Statistics uses consumer units rather than households as the sampling unit in the Consumer Expenditure Survey. For the definition of consumer unit, see the Glossary. Expenditures listed for items in a given category may not add to the total for that category because the listing is incomplete.
Source: Bureau of Labor Statistics, unpublished tables from the 1994 Consumer Expenditure Survey

CHAPTER

6

Total Population

■ The U.S. received over 800,000 immigrants in 1994. Thirty-six percent were from Asia, 34 percent from Mexico, and 20 percent from Europe. The largest single ancestry group in the U.S. is German, claimed by 58 million people.

■ Eighty-one percent of Americans had a high school diploma in 1994, up from 69 percent in 1980. The proportion of Americans with a high school diploma did not top 50 percent until the late 1960s, then rose rapidly as the well-educated baby-boom generation entered adulthood.

■ At birth, the average American male can expect to live to age 73, while the average female can expect to live to age 79. At age 65, men can expect to live 15.5 more years, and women 19 more years.

■ Between 1994 and 2005, the total labor force will grow by 12 percent. Labor force participation rates for women are projected to increase from 59 to 62 percent, while those for men should fall slightly from 75 to 73 percent.

■ Seventy-two percent of American children live with both parents, while 24.5 percent live with their mother only. Only 3 percent of children live only with their father. Half of men aged 20 to 24 live with their parents.

■ The median income of American households fell by 5 percent between 1990 and 1994, to $32,264 after adjusting for inflation. Despite this decline, median household income in 1994 was 1 percent greater.

Total Population:
Education

Overall, 81 percent of Americans had a high school diploma in 1994, up from 69 percent in 1980. The proportion of Americans with a high school diploma did not top 50 percent until the late 1960s, then rose rapidly as the well-educated baby-boom generation entered adulthood.

Twenty-two percent of Americans have a college degree, including 25 percent of men and 20 percent of women. Over 30 percent of men in their 40s have a college degree. Among the 50 states, the proportion of people with a college degree is highest in Connecticut and Massachusetts (27 percent), and lowest in West Virginia (12 percent).

Among all families with children aged 18 to 24, 41 percent have a child in college full-time. The proportion of families with a child in college rises steadily with income, to 64 percent among families with incomes of $75,000 or more.

More than 1.1 million bachelor's degrees were awarded in 1992-93, as well as over 368,000 master's degrees and more than 42,000 doctorates. The number of people earning first-professional degrees, at nearly 75,000, is far greater than the number earning doctorates. The most popular first-professional degree is law, with over 40,000 people earning law degrees in 1992-93.

Total High School and College Graduates, 1980 to 1994

(percent of total persons aged 25 or older who are high school or college graduates, by sex, 1980-94)

	total	men	women
High school graduates			
1994	80.9%	81.0%	80.7%
1990	77.6	77.7	77.5
1985	73.9	74.4	73.5
1980	68.6	69.2	68.1
College graduates			
1994	22.2	25.1	19.6
1990	21.3	24.4	18.4
1985	19.4	23.1	16.0
1980	17.0	20.9	13.6

Source: Bureau of the Census, Educational Attainment in the United States: March 1993 and 1992, *Current Population Reports, P20-476, 1994; and Internet web site,* http://www.census.gov

Educational Attainment of the Total Population by Sex, 1994

(number and percent distribution of people aged 25 or older, by educational attainment and sex, 1994; numbers in thousands)

	total		men		women	
	number	*percent*	*number*	*percent*	*number*	*percent*
Total, aged 25 or older	164,512	100.0%	78,539	100.0%	85,973	100.0%
Not a high school graduate	31,422	19.1	14,844	18.9	16,507	19.2
High school graduate or more	133,090	80.9	63,617	81.0	69,380	80.7
Some college or associate's degree	39,976	24.3	18,535	23.6	21,493	25.0
Bachelor's degree or more	36,522	22.2	19,713	25.1	16,851	19.6

Source: Bureau of the Census, Internet web site, http://www.census.gov

Educational Attainment of the Total Population by Age and Sex, 1993

(percent of the total population aged 25 or older who are high school or college graduates, by sex and age, 1993)

	total	men	women
HIGH SCHOOL GRADUATES			
Total, aged 25 or older	80.2%	80.5%	80.0%
Aged 25 to 29	86.7	86.0	87.4
Aged 30 to 34	87.0	86.1	87.9
Aged 35 to 39	88.4	87.8	88.9
Aged 40 to 44	88.8	89.0	88.7
Aged 45 to 49	86.6	86.4	86.7
Aged 50 to 54	82.4	82.2	82.7
Aged 55 to 59	76.7	76.5	76.9
Aged 60 to 64	71.8	71.7	72.0
Aged 65 to 69	67.0	64.8	68.7
Aged 70 to 74	64.5	64.2	64.8
Aged 75 or older	52.1	52.5	51.8
COLLEGE GRADUATES			
Total, aged 25 or older	21.9	24.8	19.2
Aged 25 to 29	23.7	23.4	23.9
Aged 30 to 34	23.9	24.8	23.1
Aged 35 to 39	25.4	26.2	24.6
Aged 40 to 44	28.2	31.2	25.3
Aged 45 to 49	27.1	31.0	23.5
Aged 50 to 54	22.9	26.4	19.7
Aged 55 to 59	19.8	25.8	14.2
Aged 60 to 64	17.5	22.1	13.2
Aged 65 to 69	14.2	18.6	10.6
Aged 70 to 74	12.0	16.7	8.3
Aged 75 or older	10.2	13.2	8.4

Source: Bureau of the Census, Educational Attainment in the United States: March 1993 and 1992, *Current Population Reports, P20-476, 1994*

Educational Attainment of the Total Population by Age and Region, 1993

(percent of the total population aged 25 or older who are high school or college graduates, by age and region, 1993)

	Northeast	Midwest	South	West
HIGH SCHOOL GRADUATES				
Total, aged 25 or older	81.5%	82.1%	76.7%	82.5%
Aged 25 to 34	89.7	89.6	85.1	84.0
Aged 35 to 44	90.2	91.5	86.4	87.3
Aged 45 to 54	85.3	88.3	80.7	86.9
Aged 55 to 64	76.4	75.3	68.3	80.8
Aged 65 or older	61.5	58.2	55.2	70.1
COLLEGE GRADUATES				
Total, aged 25 or older	24.3	19.9	19.9	24.7
Aged 25 to 34	28.6	24.0	21.6	22.7
Aged 35 to 44	30.5	24.6	24.9	28.3
Aged 45 to 54	27.5	23.3	22.3	29.9
Aged 55 to 64	19.2	15.5	16.4	25.6
Aged 65 or older	12.2	8.3	11.5	16.8

Source: Bureau of the Census, Educational Attainment in the United States: March 1993 and 1992, *Current Population Reports, P20-476, 1994*

Educational Attainment of the Total Population by State, 1990

(percent of the total population aged 25 or older who are high school or college graduates, by state, 1990)

	high school graduate or more	college graduate		high school graduate or more	college graduate
United States	75.2%	20.3%	Missouri	73.9%	17.8%
Alabama	66.9	15.7	Montana	81.0	19.8
Alaska	86.6	23.0	Nebraska	81.8	18.9
Arizona	78.7	20.3	Nevada	78.8	15.3
Arkansas	66.3	13.3	New Hampshire	82.2	24.4
California	76.2	23.4	New Jersey	76.7	24.9
Colorado	84.4	27.0	New Mexico	75.1	20.4
Connecticut	79.2	27.2	New York	76.7	23.1
Delaware	77.5	21.4	North Carolina	70.0	17.4
District of Columbia	73.1	33.3	North Dakota	76.7	18.1
Florida	74.4	18.3	Ohio	75.7	17.0
Georgia	70.9	19.3	Oklahoma	74.6	17.8
Hawaii	80.1	22.9	Oregon	81.5	20.6
Idaho	79.7	17.7	Pennsylvania	74.7	17.9
Illinois	76.2	21.0	Rhode Island	72.0	21.3
Indiana	75.6	15.6	South Carolina	68.3	16.6
Iowa	80.1	16.9	South Dakota	77.1	17.2
Kansas	81.3	21.1	Tennessee	67.1	16.0
Kentucky	64.6	13.6	Texas	72.1	20.3
Louisiana	68.3	16.1	Utah	85.1	22.3
Maine	78.8	18.8	Vermont	80.8	24.3
Maryland	78.4	26.5	Virginia	75.2	24.5
Massachusetts	80.0	27.2	Washington	83.8	22.9
Michigan	76.8	17.4	West Virginia	66.0	12.3
Minnesota	82.4	21.8	Wisconsin	78.6	17.7
Mississippi	64.3	14.7	Wyoming	83.0	18.8

Source: National Center for Education Statistics, Digest of Education Statistics 1993, *NCES 93-292, 1993*

School Enrollment of the Total Population by Age and Sex, 1993

(number and percent of the total population aged 3 or older enrolled in school as of October 1993, by age and sex; numbers in thousands)

	total		male		female	
	number	**percent**	**number**	**percent**	**number**	**percent**
Total, aged 3 or older	65,363	26.9%	32,889	27.9%	32,475	26.0%
Aged 3 and 4	3,275	40.4	1,727	41.5	1,548	39.3
Aged 5 and 6	7,298	95.4	3,750	95.5	3,547	95.2
Aged 7 to 9	11,211	99.5	5,754	99.5	5,457	99.4
Aged 10 to 13	14,899	99.5	7,605	99.6	7,295	99.5
Aged 14 and 15	7,011	98.9	3,604	99.0	3,407	98.7
Aged 16 and 17	6,339	94.0	3,286	95.0	3,054	92.9
Aged 18 and 19	4,063	61.6	2,049	61.6	2,014	61.7
Aged 20 and 21	2,810	42.7	1,358	42.6	1,452	42.9
Aged 22 to 24	2,579	23.6	1,369	25.5	1,210	21.8
Aged 25 to 29	1,942	10.2	899	9.6	1,043	10.8
Aged 30 to 34	1,303	5.9	562	5.2	741	6.6
Aged 35 to 44	1,762	4.3	647	3.2	1,115	5.4
Aged 45 to 54	702	2.4	222	1.6	480	3.2
Aged 55 or older	170	0.3	56	0.2	113	0.4

Source: Bureau of the Census, School Enrollment—Social and Economic Characteristics of Students: October 1993, *Current Population Reports, P20-479, 1994*

Total Families With Children in College, 1993

(total number of families, number with children aged 18 to 24, and number and percent with children aged 18 to 24 attending college full-time as of October 1993, by household income in 1992; numbers in thousands)

| | *total* | *with children aged 18-24* | with one or more children attending college full-time | | |
			number	*percent of total families*	*percent of families with children 18-24*
Total families	68,463	10,457	4,278	6.2%	40.9%
Under $20,000	18,714	2,421	515	2.8	21.3
$20,000 to $29,999	10,800	1,435	466	4.3	32.5
$30,000 to $39,999	10,061	1,472	579	5.8	39.3
$40,000 to $49,999	6,876	1,149	551	8.0	48.0
$50,000 to $74,999	10,085	1,850	994	9.9	53.7
$75,000 or more	6,855	1,354	870	12.7	64.3

Source: Bureau of the Census, School Enrollment—Social and Economic Characteristics of Students: October 1993, *Current Population Reports, P20-479, 1994*

College Enrollment of the Total Population by Age, 1993

(total number of persons enrolled in college by age and attendance status, October 1993; numbers in thousands)

| | | undergraduate | | | | | | | graduate | | |
| | total | total | two-year college | | | four-year college | | | total | full-time | part-time |
			total	full-time	part-time	total	full-time	part-time			
Total enrolled, aged 15 or older	13,898	11,507	4,196	2,274	1,922	7,311	5,720	1,591	2,391	1,025	1,366
Aged 15 to 17	123	123	38	21	16	85	80	6	-	-	-
Aged 18 and 19	2,926	2,922	1,039	829	211	1,883	1,802	81	3	3	-
Aged 20 and 21	2,734	2,721	696	483	213	2,025	1,897	129	13	10	3
Aged 22 to 24	2,533	2,020	614	325	288	1,406	1,104	302	514	358	156
Aged 25 to 29	1,867	1,256	551	208	343	705	393	312	611	326	285
Aged 30 to 34	1,227	832	414	152	262	418	174	244	395	143	251
Aged 35 to 39	976	691	381	139	242	310	130	180	285	95	190
Aged 40 to 44	690	439	201	46	155	238	71	168	250	43	207
Aged 45 to 49	457	277	146	52	93	131	34	96	180	21	159
Aged 50 to 54	216	129	62	16	46	67	18	49	87	12	75
Aged 55 to 59	70	41	18	2	16	23	13	10	28	7	21
Aged 60 to 64	29	16	9	-	9	7	2	5	13	6	7
Aged 65 or older	52	39	26	-	26	13	4	9	13	-	13

Note: (-) means number in sample is too small to make a reliable estimate.
Source: Bureau of the Census, School Enrollment—Social and Economic Characteristics of Students: October 1993, Current Population Reports, P20-479, 1994

Bachelor's, Master's, and Doctoral Degrees Earned by the Total Population by Field of Study, 1992-93

(number of bachelor's, master's, and doctoral degrees earned by the total population, by field of study, 1992-93)

	bachelor's	master's	doctoral
Total degrees	1,159,931	368,701	42,021
Agriculture and natural resources	16,778	3,965	1,173
Architecture and related programs	9,167	3,808	148
Area, ethnic, and cultural studies	5,481	1,523	178
Biological/life sciences	47,038	4,756	4,435
Business, management, and admin. services	256,842	89,615	1,346
Communications	53,874	4,754	293
Communications technologies	832	455	8
Computer and information sciences	24,200	10,163	805
Construction trades	69	-	-
Education	107,781	96,028	7,030
Engineering	61,973	27,626	5,823
Engineering related technologies	15,904	1,100	20
English language and literature	56,133	7,790	1,341
Foreign languages and literature	14,387	3,198	830
Health professions and related sciences	67,089	25,718	1,767
Home economics	15,100	2,479	345
Law and legal studies	2,056	2,197	86
Liberal arts and sciences	33,456	2,416	81
Library science	83	4,871	77
Mathematics	14,812	4,067	1,189
Mechanics and repairers	105	-	-
Multi/interdisciplinary studies	23,955	2,498	196
Parks, recreation, leisure and fitness	9,859	1,434	108
Philosophy and religion	7,781	1,425	448
Physical sciences	17,545	5,366	4,393
Precision production trades	388	2	-
Protective services	20,902	1,357	32
Psychology	66,728	10,957	3,651
Public administration and services	16,775	20,634	459
R.O.T.C. and military sciences	11	108	-
Social sciences and history	135,703	13,471	3,460
Theological studies/religious vocations	5,433	4,985	1,417
Transportation and material moving	3,930	495	-
Visual and performing arts	47,761	9,440	882

Source: National Center for Education Statistics, Digest of Education Statistics 1995, *NCES 95-029, 1995*

First-Professional Degrees Earned by the Total Population by Field of Study, 1992-93

(number of first-professional degrees earned by the total population, by field of study, 1992-93)

	number
Total degrees	74,960
Dentistry (D.D.S. or D.M.D.)	3,605
Medicine (M.D.)	15,531
Optometry (O.D.)	1,148
Osteopathic medicine (D.O.)	1,627
Pharmacy (Pharm. D.)	1,904
Podiatry (Pod. D. or D.P. or D.P.M.)	476
Veterinary medicine (D.V.M.)	2,057
Chiropractic medicine (D.C. or D.C.M.)	2,799
Law (L.L.B. or J.D.)	40,302
Theology (M.Div., M.H.L., B.D., or Ord.)	5,447
Other	64

Source: National Center for Education Statistics, Digest of Education Statistics 1995, *NCES 95-029, 1995*

Total Population:
Health

Sixty-six percent of Americans say their health is excellent or good, while just 10 percent rate their health as only fair or poor.

Overall, Americans report an average of two acute illnesses per year. Acute conditions peak in the youngest age group—children under age 5—because they have fewer immunities to many viruses. Chronic conditions peak in the oldest age group, with arthritis affecting over half of people aged 75 or older.

Nineteen percent of Americans are disabled, with 10 percent severely disabled. The average American contacts a physician seven times a year. Fifteen percent of the total population is without health insurance, but this proportion peaks at 27 percent among 18-to-24-year-olds.

Heart disease and cancer are the leading causes of death among all Americans, while AIDS ranks eighth, suicide ninth, and homicide tenth.

At birth, the average American male can expect to live to age 72.5, while the average female can expect to live to age 79. At age 65, men can expect to live 15.5 more years, and women 19 more years.

Health Status of the Total Population by Age, 1993

(percent distribution of self-assessed or parent-assessed health status of the total population, by age, 1993)

	total	excellent	very good	good	fair	poor
Total	100.0%	37.6%	28.3%	23.7%	7.7%	2.8%
Under age 5	100.0	52.6	27.3	16.8	2.9	0.3
Aged 5 to 17	100.0	51.2	27.6	18.4	2.5	0.4
Aged 18 to 24	100.0	41.4	31.2	22.6	4.1	0.8
Aged 25 to 44	100.0	38.6	31.1	22.8	5.9	1.6
Aged 45 to 64	100.0	28.3	27.1	27.5	11.9	5.3
Aged 65 or older	100.0	16.4	22.5	33.1	19.5	8.5

Source: National Center for Health Statistics, Current Estimates From the National Health Interview Survey, 1993, *Series 10, No. 190, 1994*

Acute Health Conditions Among the Total Population by Age, 1993

(number of acute conditions affecting the total population and rate per 100 persons in specified age group, by type of acute condition, 1993; numbers in thousands)

	total		under age 5		aged 5-17		aged 18-24		aged 25-44		aged 45 or older	
	number	rate	number	rate	number	rate	number	rate	number	rate	number	rate
Total acute conditions	484,180	190.4	79,550	399.5	124,131	261.1	45,212	187.3	137,971	169.0	97,317	120.1
Infective and parasitic diseases	54,253	21.3	10,842	54.4	20,042	42.2	4,232	17.5	10,992	13.5	8,145	10.0
Common childhood diseases	5,025	2.0	2,236	11.2	2,543	5.3	111	0.5	135	0.2	–	–
Intestinal virus	11,388	4.5	1,756	8.8	3,782	8.0	837	3.5	3,274	4.0	1,738	2.1
Viral infections	18,102	7.1	3,434	17.2	5,573	11.7	1,336	5.5	4,020	4.9	3,738	4.6
Other	19,738	7.8	3,415	17.1	8,143	17.1	1,948	8.1	3,563	4.4	2,669	3.3
Respiratory conditions	251,551	98.9	36,416	182.9	65,699	138.2	23,575	97.7	77,556	95.0	48,305	59.6
Common cold	68,266	26.8	13,195	66.3	18,905	39.8	6,375	26.4	17,801	21.8	11,950	14.7
Other acute upper respiratory infections	28,637	11.3	4,781	24.0	8,371	17.6	2,361	9.8	7,429	9.1	5,695	7.0
Influenza	132,633	52.2	13,019	65.4	35,058	73.7	13,269	55.0	46,573	57.1	24,714	30.5
Acute bronchitis	12,014	4.7	2,921	14.7	1,895	4.0	974	4.0	3,583	4.4	2,641	3.3
Pneumonia	4,990	2.0	1,271	6.4	683	1.4	183	0.8	1,211	1.5	1,642	2.0
Other respiratory conditions	5,052	2.0	1,228	6.2	788	1.7	414	1.7	958	1.2	1,663	2.1
Digestive system conditions	16,085	6.3	1,978	9.9	3,984	8.4	1,737	7.2	4,990	6.1	3,397	4.2
Dental conditions	3,254	1.3	803	4.0	486	1.0	359	1.5	1,292	1.6	314	0.4
Indigestion, nausea, and vomiting	7,311	2.9	356	1.8	2,837	6.0	1,145	4.7	1,846	2.3	1,127	1.4
Other digestive conditions	5,520	2.2	819	4.1	660	1.4	233	1.0	1,851	2.3	1,956	2.4

(continued)

(continued from previous page)

	total		under age 5		aged 5-17		aged 18-24		aged 25-44		aged 45 or older	
	number	rate	number	rate	number	rate	number	rate	number	rate	number	rate
Injuries	62,120	24.4	4,955	24.9	12,477	26.2	7,369	30.5	21,752	26.6	15,568	19.2
Fractures and dislocations	7,887	3.1	123	0.6	1,637	3.4	1,418	5.9	2,490	3.1	2,220	2.7
Sprains and strains	14,208	5.6	154	0.8	2,561	5.4	1,949	8.1	5,901	7.2	3,643	4.5
Open wounds and lacerations	12,543	4.9	1,798	9.0	2,974	6.3	959	4.0	4,364	5.3	2,447	3.0
Contusions and superficial injuries	12,092	4.8	1,169	5.9	2,930	6.2	1,798	7.4	3,375	4.1	2,819	3.5
Other current injuries	15,391	6.1	1,711	8.6	2,375	5.0	1,244	5.2	5,622	6.9	4,440	5.5
Selected other acute conditions	74,813	29.4	21,775	109.3	17,631	37.1	6,171	25.6	16,173	19.8	13,063	16.1
Eye conditions	3,089	1.2	1,086	5.5	428	0.9	286	1.2	351	0.4	938	1.2
Acute ear infections	27,845	11.0	14,751	74.1	7,501	15.8	1,191	4.9	2,253	2.8	2,150	2.7
Other ear conditions	3,440	1.4	1,033	5.2	927	1.9	-	-	823	1.0	656	0.8
Acute urinary conditions	7,513	3.0	529	2.7	695	1.5	878	3.6	2,294	2.8	3,116	3.8
Disorders of menstruation	796	0.3	-	-	237	0.5	114	0.5	244	0.3	200	0.2
Other disorders of female genital tract	1,776	0.7	-	-	285	0.6	304	1.3	1,068	1.3	118	0.1
Delivery and other conditions of pregnancy	3,884	1.5	-	-	185	0.4	1,220	5.1	2,479	3.0	-	-
Skin conditions	6,522	2.6	1,823	9.2	1,834	3.9	758	3.1	1,164	1.4	942	1.2
Acute musculoskeletal conditions	9,644	3.8	32	0.2	1,071	2.3	648	2.7	3,852	4.7	4,042	5.0
Headache, excluding migraine	4,224	1.7	57	0.3	1,905	4.0	426	1.8	1,320	1.6	516	0.6
Fever, unspecified	6,080	2.4	2,462	12.4	2,563	5.4	346	1.4	326	0.4	384	0.5
All other acute conditions	25,358	10.0	3,584	18.0	4,298	9.0	2,129	8.8	6,508	8.0	8,839	10.9

Note: The acute conditions shown here are those that caused people to restrict their activity for at least half a day, or that caused people to contact a physician about the illness or injury. (-) means not applicable or number in sample is too small to make a reliable estimate.
Source: National Center for Health Statistics, Current Estimates From the National Health Interview Survey, 1993, Series 10, No. 190, 1994

Chronic Health Conditions Among the Total Population by Age, 1993

(number of chronic conditions affecting the total population and rate per 1,000 persons in specified age group, by type of chronic condition, 1993; numbers in thousands)

	total		under age 18		aged 18-44		aged 45-64		aged 65-74		aged 75 or older	
	number	rate	number	rate	number	rate	number	rate	number	rate	number	rate
Selected skin and musculoskeletal conditions												
Arthritis	32,642	128.4	154	2.3	5,439	51.4	11,627	233.5	8,596	461.8	6,827	539.5
Gout	2,304	9.1	-	-	416	3.9	908	18.2	721	38.7	259	20.5
Intervertebral disc disorders	6,078	23.9	37	0.5	2,696	25.5	2,276	45.7	730	39.2	339	26.8
Bone spur or tendinitis	2,411	9.5	31	0.5	826	7.8	947	19.0	485	26.1	121	9.6
Disorders of bone or cartilage	1,677	6.6	86	1.3	440	4.2	562	11.3	272	14.6	316	25.0
Trouble with bunions	2,982	11.7	71	1.1	839	7.9	996	20.0	621	33.4	456	36.0
Bursitis	4,334	17.0	-	-	1,375	13.0	1,961	39.4	594	31.9	404	31.9
Sebaceous skin cyst	1,539	6.1	141	2.1	665	6.3	561	11.3	87	4.7	85	6.7
Trouble with acne	5,663	22.3	1,894	28.1	3,345	31.6	372	7.5	41	2.2	10	0.8
Psoriasis	2,434	9.6	236	3.5	1,105	10.4	757	15.2	193	10.4	143	11.3
Dermatitis	9,896	38.9	2,411	35.7	4,444	42.0	1,959	39.3	674	36.2	409	32.3
Trouble with dry (itching) skin	5,170	20.3	677	10.0	2,090	19.8	1,188	23.9	857	46.0	359	28.4
Trouble with ingrown nails	6,237	24.5	588	8.7	2,476	23.4	1,627	32.7	688	37.0	859	67.9
Trouble with corns and calluses	5,117	20.1	126	1.9	1,883	17.8	1,688	33.9	769	41.3	651	51.4
Impairments												
Visual impairment	9,302	36.6	487	7.2	3,363	31.8	2,461	49.4	1,205	64.7	1,786	141.1
Color blindness	3,173	12.5	253	3.8	1,554	14.7	758	15.2	266	14.3	342	27.0
Cataracts	6,067	23.9	55	0.8	276	2.6	996	20.0	2,122	114.0	2,617	206.8
Glaucoma	2,762	10.9	28	0.4	140	1.3	778	15.6	753	40.4	1,063	84.0
Hearing impairment	24,160	95.0	1,152	17.1	6,040	57.1	7,146	143.5	4,792	257.4	5,030	397.5

(continued)

	total		under age 18		aged 18-44		aged 45-64		aged 65-74		aged 75 or older	
	number	rate	number	rate	number	rate	number	rate	number	rate	number	rate
Tinnitus	8,845	34.8	162	2.4	2,643	25.0	2,979	59.8	1,883	101.1	1,177	93.0
Speech impairment	3,101	12.2	1,348	20.0	953	9.0	412	8.3	212	11.4	177	14.0
Absence of extremities	1,546	6.1	30	0.4	416	3.9	549	11.0	299	16.1	252	19.9
Paralysis of extremities	1,752	6.9	113	1.7	455	4.3	475	9.5	420	22.6	288	22.8
Deformity or orthopedic impairment	31,182	122.6	1,977	29.3	15,044	142.2	8,581	172.4	3,050	163.8	2,529	199.8
Selected digestive conditions												
Ulcer	4,569	18.0	17	0.3	2,184	20.6	1,240	24.9	671	36.0	458	36.2
Hernia of abdominal cavity	4,900	19.3	191	2.8	844	8.0	1,629	32.7	1,223	65.7	1,013	80.0
Gastritis or duodenitis	3,372	13.3	170	2.5	1,253	11.8	1,071	21.5	577	31.0	302	23.9
Frequent indigestion	6,253	24.6	180	2.7	2,957	28.0	1,774	35.6	718	38.6	624	49.3
Enteritis or colitis	2,672	10.5	155	2.3	1,088	10.3	827	16.6	333	17.9	269	21.3
Spastic colon	1,786	7.0	11	0.2	774	7.3	634	12.7	246	13.2	121	9.6
Diverticula of intestines	2,021	7.9	-	-	123	1.2	444	8.9	799	42.9	655	51.8
Frequent constipation	4,460	17.5	368	5.5	1,092	10.3	1,210	24.3	692	37.2	1,098	86.8
Selected conditions of the genitourinary, nervous, endocrine, metabolic, or blood systems												
Goiter or other disorders of the thyroid	4,155	16.3	129	1.9	1,492	14.1	1,328	26.7	697	37.4	509	40.2
Diabetes	7,813	30.7	104	1.5	1,389	13.1	3,081	61.9	1,897	101.9	1,341	106.0
Anemias	3,917	15.4	583	8.6	2,013	19.0	650	13.1	342	18.4	329	26.0
Epilepsy	1,342	5.3	362	5.4	544	5.1	273	5.5	111	6.0	51	4.0
Migraine	11,023	43.3	891	13.2	6,559	62.0	2,968	59.6	374	20.1	230	18.2
Neuralgia or neuritis	684	2.7	12	0.2	145	1.4	216	4.3	134	7.2	176	13.9
Kidney trouble	3,850	15.1	317	4.7	1,668	15.8	1,023	20.5	458	24.6	384	30.3
Bladder disorders	4,024	15.8	226	3.4	1,470	13.9	1,108	22.3	533	28.6	686	54.2
Diseases of prostate	2,024	8.0	-	-	167	1.6	679	13.6	535	28.7	643	50.8
Diseases of female genital organs	5,339	21.0	178	2.6	3,470	32.8	1,341	26.9	174	9.3	177	14.0

(continued)

(continued from previous page)

	total		under age 18		aged 18-44		aged 45-64		aged 65-74		aged 75 or older	
	number	rate	number	rate	number	rate	number	rate	number	rate	number	rate
Selected circulatory conditions												
Rheumatic fever	2,006	7.9	78	1.2	828	7.8	692	13.9	280	15.0	127	10.0
Heart disease	21,255	83.6	1,367	20.3	4,353	41.2	5,926	119.0	5,193	279.0	4,416	349.0
Ischemic heart disease	7,157	28.1	20	0.3	601	5.7	2,265	45.5	2,454	131.8	1,816	143.5
Heart rhythm disorders	9,121	35.9	1,007	14.9	2,909	27.5	2,209	44.4	1,720	92.4	1,276	100.8
Other diseases of heart, excl. hypertension	4,977	19.6	340	5.0	843	8.0	1,452	29.2	1,019	54.7	1,323	104.5
High blood pressure (hypertension)	27,549	108.3	212	3.1	5,630	53.2	10,808	217.1	6,389	343.2	4,510	356.4
Cerebrovascular disease	3,358	13.2	67	1.0	123	1.2	952	19.1	874	46.9	1,342	106.0
Hardening of the arteries	1,789	7.0	-	-	52	0.5	359	7.2	668	35.9	709	56.0
Varicose veins of lower extremities	7,641	30.0	41	0.6	2,651	25.1	2,708	54.4	1,289	69.2	952	75.2
Hemorrhoids	10,111	39.8	14	0.2	4,451	42.1	3,323	66.7	1,406	75.5	916	72.4
Selected respiratory conditions												
Chronic bronchitis	13,820	54.3	3,997	59.3	4,845	45.8	3,048	61.2	1,292	69.4	638	50.4
Asthma	13,074	51.4	4,830	71.6	4,495	42.5	2,242	45.0	986	53.0	521	41.2
Hay fever	23,743	93.4	3,827	56.7	12,326	116.5	5,298	106.4	1,527	82.0	765	60.5
Chronic sinusitis	37,293	146.7	5,371	79.6	18,004	170.2	9,227	185.3	3,180	170.8	1,511	119.4
Deviated nasal septum	1,779	7.0	44	0.7	993	9.4	480	9.6	181	9.7	80	6.3
Chronic disease of tonsils or adenoids	2,796	11.0	1,783	26.4	868	8.2	92	1.8	53	2.8	-	-
Emphysema	1,931	7.6	45	0.7	179	1.7	775	15.6	509	27.3	422	33.3

Note: Chronic conditions are those that last at least three months or belong to a group of conditions that are considered to be chronic regardless of when they began. (-) means number in sample is too small to make a reliable estimate.
Source: National Center for Health Statistics, Current Estimates From the National Health Interview Survey, 1993, Series 10, No. 190, 1994

Total Population With Disabilities, 1991-92

(total number of persons, number and percent with a disability, and number and percent with a severe disability, by selected characteristics, 1991-92; numbers in thousands)

	total	with a disability		with a severe disability	
		number	percent	number	percent
Total persons	251,796	48,936	19.4%	24,117	9.6%
AGE					
Under age 3	11,791	254	2.2	41	0.4
Aged 3 to 5	11,511	597	5.2	75	0.7
Aged 6 to 14	32,766	2,062	6.3	412	1.3
Aged 15 to 17	10,067	933	9.3	309	3.1
Aged 18 to 24	24,695	2,537	10.3	843	3.4
Aged 25 to 34	42,939	5,361	12.5	2,093	4.9
Aged 35 to 44	39,511	6,669	16.9	2,626	6.7
Aged 45 to 54	26,714	6,213	23.3	2,841	10.6
Aged 55 to 59	10,594	3,418	32.3	1,820	17.2
Aged 60 to 64	10,520	4,352	41.4	2,639	25.1
Aged 65 to 69	10,185	4,423	43.4	2,561	25.2
Aged 70 to 74	8,170	3,759	46.0	2,085	25.5
Aged 75 to 79	6,016	3,530	58.7	2,231	37.1
Aged 80 to 84	3,873	2,771	71.6	1,869	48.3
Aged 85 or older	2,445	2,058	84.2	1,672	68.4
HOUSEHOLD TYPE					
Family householder or spouse	119,226	27,421	23.0	13,052	11.0
With children under age 18	56,184	8,359	14.9	3,094	5.5
Married, spouse present	104,654	23,051	22.0	10,607	10.1
With children under age 18	48,342	6,474	13.4	2,200	4.6
No spouse present	14,572	4,369	30.0	2,445	16.8
With children under age 18	7,842	1,885	24.0	895	11.4
Nonfamily householder	28,956	10,366	35.8	6,099	21.1
Living alone	25,309	9,779	38.6	5,898	23.3
REGION					
Northeast	50,751	9,019	17.8%	4,928	9.7%
Midwest	63,757	12,341	19.4	5,460	8.6
South	84,609	17,755	21.0	9,239	10.9
West	52,679	9,821	18.6	4,490	8.5

Source: Bureau of the Census, Americans With Disabilities: 1991-92, *Current Population Reports, P70-33, 1993*

Physician Contacts by the Total Population, 1993

(total number of physician contacts by the total population and number per person per year, by age and place of contact, 1993)

	total places	telephone	office	hospital	other
Total contacts (in thousands)	143,464	19,762	84,319	20,280	18,081
Under age 5	173,325	23,415	103,234	20,365	25,245
Aged 18 to 24	97,528	10,542	49,350	15,355	21,666
Aged 25 to 44	442,488	59,161	251,165	58,414	69,646
Aged 45 to 64	353,912	48,205	196,344	47,028	60,333
Aged 65 to 74	183,589	14,185	100,189	25,144	42,155
Aged 75 or older	156,286	11,006	72,122	16,502	56,220
Contacts per person	7.2	1.0	4.2	1.0	0.9
Under age 5	3.6	0.5	2.2	0.4	0.5
Aged 18 to 24	4.0	0.4	2.0	0.6	0.9
Aged 25 to 44	5.4	0.7	3.1	0.7	0.9
Aged 45 to 64	7.1	1.0	3.9	0.9	1.2
Aged 65 to 74	9.9	0.8	5.4	1.4	2.3
Aged 75 or older	12.3	0.9	5.7	1.3	4.4

Source: National Center for Health Statistics, Current Estimates From the National Health Interview Survey, 1993, Series 10, No. 190, 1994

Health Insurance Coverage of the
Total Population by Age, 1993

(number and percent distribution of persons by age and health insurance coverage status, 1993; numbers in thousands)

	total persons	covered by private or government health insurance							not covered
			private health insurance		government health insurance				
		total	total	group health	total	Medicaid	Medicare	Champus	
Number									
Total	259,753	220,040	182,351	148,318	68,554	31,749	33,097	9,560	39,713
Under 18	69,766	60,192	47,017	39,745	18,696	16,693	48	2,307	9,574
18 to 24	25,475	18,645	15,668	11,133	4,087	2,976	148	1,115	6,830
25 to 34	41,946	32,869	28,629	25,432	5,345	4,002	515	1,176	9,076
35 to 44	41,528	34,537	31,441	28,115	4,189	2,619	647	1,276	6,991
45 to 54	29,522	25,424	23,332	20,654	3,248	1,546	812	1,244	4,098
55 to 64	20,737	17,957	15,938	13,291	3,499	1,204	1,536	1,234	2,781
65 or older	30,779	30,416	20,324	9,947	29,490	2,709	29,390	1,208	363
Percent									
Total	100.0%	84.7%	70.2%	57.1%	26.4%	12.2%	12.7%	3.7%	15.3%
Under 18	100.0	86.3	67.4	57.0	26.8	23.9	0.1	3.3	13.7
18 to 24	100.0	73.2	61.5	43.7	16.0	11.7	0.6	4.4	26.8
25 to 34	100.0	78.4	68.3	60.6	12.7	9.5	1.2	2.8	21.6
35 to 44	100.0	83.2	75.7	67.7	10.1	6.3	1.6	3.1	16.8
45 to 54	100.0	86.1	79.0	70.0	11.0	5.2	2.8	4.2	13.9
55 to 64	100.0	86.6	76.9	64.1	16.9	5.8	7.4	6.0	13.4
65 or older	100.0	98.8	66.0	32.3	95.8	8.8	95.5	3.9	1.2

Source: Bureau of the Census, unpublished tables from the 1994 Current Population Survey

Leading Causes of Death for the Total Population, 1993

(total number of deaths, and number and percent accounted for by ten leading causes of death, 1993)

		number	percent
	All causes	2,268,553	100.0%
1.	Diseases of heart	743,460	32.8
2.	Malignant neoplasms	529,904	23.4
3.	Cerebrovascular diseases	150,108	6.6
4.	Chronic obstructive pulmonary diseases and allied conditions	101,077	4.5
5.	Accidents and adverse effects	90,523	4.0
6.	Pneumonia and influenza	82,820	3.7
7.	Diabetes mellitus	53,894	2.4
8.	Human immunodeficiency virus infection	37,267	1.6
9.	Suicide	31,102	1.4
10.	Homicide and legal intervention	26,009	1.1
	All other causes	422,389	18.6

Source: National Center for Health Statistics, Advance Report of Final Mortality Statistics, 1993, *Vol. 44, No. 7 Supplement, 1996*

Life Expectancy of the Total Population at Birth and Age 65, 1995-2020

(average number of years of life remaining at birth and at age 65 for total males and females, 1995-2020)

	life expectancy (years)	
	males	*females*
At birth		
1995	72.5	79.3
2000	73.0	79.7
2005	73.5	80.2
2010	74.1	80.6
2015	74.8	81.1
2020	75.5	81.5
At age 65		
1995	15.5	19.2
2000	15.9	19.5
2005	16.4	19.7
2010	16.8	20.0
2015	17.2	20.3
2020	17.6	20.6

Source: Bureau of the Census, Population Projections of the United States, by Age, Sex, Race, and Hispanic Origin: 1995 to 2050, *Current Population Reports, P25-1130, 1996*

Total Population:
Households and Living Arrangements

Because the baby-boom generation is now in its 30s and 40s, a large proportion of households in the United States are headed by 30-to-49-year-olds—44 percent in 1994. The number of older Americans heading households has also grown, with 21 percent of all households headed by people aged 65 or older in 1994.

Married couples account for slightly more than half of all households in the U.S. Couples without children at home are a larger share of households (29 percent) than are those with children at home (26 percent). Female-headed families, which have grown rapidly over the past few decades, account for 13 percent of households. Twenty-four percent of all householders are people who live alone.

Seventy-two percent of American children live with both parents, while 25 percent live with their mother only. Only 3.4 percent of children live only with their father. Over half of men aged 20 to 24 still live with their parents.

Among the nation's 54 million married couples, 1.2 million are interracial. In 1993, 2.2 percent of the nation's couples were interracial, up from 1.3 percent in 1980.

Total Households by Age of Householder, 1994

(number and percent distribution of total households, by age of householder, 1994; numbers in thousands)

	number	percent
Total households	97,107	100.0%
Under age 25	5,265	5.4
Aged 25 to 29	8,472	8.7
Aged 30 to 34	11,245	11.6
Aged 35 to 39	11,795	12.1
Aged 40 to 44	10,498	10.8
Aged 45 to 49	9,221	9.5
Aged 50 to 54	7,616	7.8
Aged 55 to 59	6,234	6.4
Aged 60 to 64	5,954	6.1
Aged 65 to 69	6,028	6.2
Aged 70 to 74	5,611	5.8
Aged 75 or older	9,168	9.4

Source: Bureau of the Census, Household and Family Characteristics: March 1994, *Current Population Reports, P20-483, 1995*

Total Households by Household Type, 1994

(number and percent distribution of total households, by type of household, 1994; numbers in thousands)

	number	percent
Total households	97,107	100.0%
Family households	68,490	70.5
Married-couple families	53,171	54.8
With children <18	25,058	25.8
Without children <18	28,113	29.0
Female householder, no spouse present	12,406	12.8
With children <18	7,647	7.9
Without children <18	4,759	4.9
Male householder, no spouse present	2,913	3.0
Nonfamily households	28,617	29.5
Female householder	16,155	16.6
Living alone	14,171	14.6
Male householder	12,462	12.8
Living alone	9,440	9.7

Source: Bureau of the Census, Household and Family Characteristics: March 1994, *Current Population Reports, P20-483, 1995*

Total Households by Type and Age of Householder, 1994

(number and percent distribution of total households, by age of householder and household type, 1994; numbers in thousands)

	total	family households				nonfamily households	
		total	married couples	female householder, no spouse present	male householder, no spouse present	female householder	male householder
Total, number	97,107	68,490	53,171	12,406	2,913	16,155	12,462
Under 20	539	294	78	186	30	146	99
20 to 24	4,726	2,704	1,495	935	274	911	1,111
25 to 29	8,472	5,733	4,021	1,346	366	1,102	1,637
30 to 34	11,245	8,512	6,351	1,765	396	1,007	1,726
35 to 39	11,795	9,402	7,118	1,898	386	872	1,521
40 to 44	10,498	8,401	6,573	1,472	356	863	1,234
45 to 49	9,221	7,285	5,763	1,264	258	950	986
50 to 54	7,616	5,993	4,961	829	203	867	756
55 to 59	6,234	4,715	3,914	654	147	885	634
60 to 64	5,954	4,235	3,651	469	116	1,144	574
65 to 74	11,639	7,237	6,061	953	224	3,276	1,125
75 to 84	7,134	3,312	2,705	482	125	3,034	788
85 or older	2,034	665	481	152	32	1,099	269
Total, percent	100.0%	70.5%	54.8%	12.8%	3.0%	16.6%	12.8%
Under 20	100.0	54.5	14.5	34.5	5.6	27.1	18.4
20 to 24	100.0	57.2	31.6	19.8	5.8	19.3	23.5
25 to 29	100.0	67.7	47.5	15.9	4.3	13.0	19.3
30 to 34	100.0	75.7	56.5	15.7	3.5	9.0	15.3
35 to 39	100.0	79.7	60.3	16.1	3.3	7.4	12.9
40 to 44	100.0	80.0	62.6	14.0	3.4	8.2	11.8
45 to 49	100.0	79.0	62.5	13.7	2.8	10.3	10.7
50 to 54	100.0	78.7	65.1	10.9	2.7	11.4	9.9
55 to 59	100.0	75.6	62.8	10.5	2.4	14.2	10.2
60 to 64	100.0	71.1	61.3	7.9	1.9	19.2	9.6
65 to 74	100.0	62.2	52.1	8.2	1.9	28.1	9.7
75 to 84	100.0	46.4	37.9	6.8	1.8	42.5	11.0
85 or older	100.0	32.7	23.6	7.5	1.6	54.0	13.2

Source: Bureau of the Census, Household and Family Characteristics: March 1994, *Current Population Reports, P20-483, 1995*

Total Households by Size, 1994

(number and percent distribution of total households, by size, 1994; numbers in thousands)

	number	percent
Total households	97,107	100.0%
One person	23,611	24.3
Two persons	31,211	32.1
Three persons	16,898	17.4
Four persons	15,073	15.5
Five persons	6,749	7.0
Six persons	2,186	2.3
Seven or more persons	1,379	1.4

Source: Bureau of the Census, Household and Family Characteristics: March 1994, *Current Population Reports, P20-483, 1995*

Total Married Couples by Age of Householder and Presence of Children, 1994

(number and percent of total married couples, by presence and number of own children under age 18 at home and by age of householder, 1994; numbers in thousands)

	total	< age 20	20-24	25-29	30-34	35-39	40-44	45-54	55-64	65+
Number	53,171	78	1495	4,021	6,351	7,118	6,573	10,724	7,564	9,247
Without children <18	28,113	42	647	1,342	1,307	1,053	1,539	6,111	6,953	9,119
With children <18	25,058	36	849	2,678	5,044	6,065	5,033	4,613	612	128
One	9,452	20	497	1,166	1,539	1,497	1,615	2,614	411	91
Two	10,188	14	277	1,053	2,279	2,801	2,197	1,399	142	26
Three or more	5,418	2	75	458	1,225	1,766	1,221	601	59	10
Percent	100.0%	100.0%	100.0%	100.0%	100.0%	100.0%	100.0%	100.0%	100.0%	100.0%
Without children <18	52.9	53.8	43.3	33.4	20.6	14.8	23.4	57.0	91.9	98.6
With children <18	47.1	46.2	56.8	66.6	79.4	85.2	76.6	43.0	8.1	1.4
One	17.8	25.6	33.2	29.0	24.2	21.0	24.6	24.4	5.4	1.0
Two	19.2	17.9	18.5	26.2	35.9	39.4	33.4	13.0	1.9	0.3
Three or more	10.2	2.6	5.0	11.4	19.3	24.8	18.6	5.6	0.8	0.1

Source: Bureau of the Census, Household and Family Characteristics: March 1994, *Current Population Reports, P20-483, 1995*

Total Female-Headed Families by Age of Householder and Presence of Children, 1994

(number and percent of total female-headed families, by presence and number of own children under age 18 at home and by age of householder, 1994; numbers in thousands)

	total	< age 20	20-24	25-29	30-34	35-39	40-44	45-54	55-64	65+
Number	12,406	186	935	1,346	1,765	1,898	1,472	2,093	1,123	1,587
Without children <18	4,759	37	108	85	75	165	348	1,314	1,052	1,573
With children <18	7,647	149	827	1,261	1,690	1,733	1,124	779	71	13
One	3,566	98	440	468	611	715	603	559	59	12
Two	2,531	42	263	435	629	620	360	169	12	1
Three or more	1,550	8	124	358	449	398	161	51	-	-
Percent	100.0%	100.0%	100.0%	100.0%	100.0%	100.0%	100.0%	100.0%	100.0%	100.0%
Without children <18	38.4	19.9	11.6	6.3	4.2	8.7	23.6	62.8	93.7	99.1
With children <18	61.6	80.1	88.4	93.7	95.8	91.3	76.4	37.2	6.3	0.8
One	28.7	52.7	47.1	34.8	34.6	37.7	41.0	26.7	5.3	0.8
Two	20.4	22.6	28.1	32.3	35.6	32.7	24.5	8.1	1.1	0.1
Three or more	12.5	4.3	13.3	26.6	25.4	21.0	10.9	2.4	-	-

Note: (-) means number in sample is too small to make a reliable estimate.
Source: Bureau of the Census, Household and Family Characteristics: March 1994, *Current Population Reports, P20-483, 1995*

Total Single-Person Households by Age of Householder, 1994

(number and percent distribution of single-person households and single-person households as a percent of total households, by age of householder, 1994; numbers in thousands)

	number	percent	percent of total households
Total households	23,611	100.0%	24.3%
Under age 25	1,126	4.8	21.4
Aged 25 to 29	1,733	7.3	20.5
Aged 30 to 34	1,984	8.4	17.6
Aged 35 to 39	1,864	7.9	15.8
Aged 40 to 44	1,654	7.0	15.8
Aged 45 to 54	3,015	12.8	17.9
Aged 55 to 64	2,952	12.5	24.2
Aged 65 to 74	4,199	17.8	36.1
Aged 75 or older	5,086	21.5	55.5
Median age (years)	56.6	-	-

Source: Bureau of the Census, Household and Family Characteristics: March 1994, Current Population Reports, P20-483, 1995

Living Arrangements of Total Children by Age, 1994

(number and percent distribution of total children by living arrangement, marital status of parent, and age of child, 1994; number in thousands)

	total	under age 6	6 to 11	12 to 17
Number with one or both parents	66,674	23,540	22,349	20,785
Living with both parents	48,084	16,883	16,252	14,949
Living with mother only	16,334	5,861	5,393	5,080
Divorced	5,799	1,166	2,136	2,496
Married, spouse absent	3,838	1,228	1,329	1,281
Widowed	696	102	208	386
Never married	6,000	3,365	1,719	917
Living with father only	2,257	795	704	757
Divorced	1,077	271	340	466
Married, spouse absent	411	82	147	182
Widowed	113	6	54	53
Never married	655	435	163	57
Percent with one or both parents	100.0%	100.0%	100.0%	100.0%
Living with both parents	72.1	71.7	72.7	71.9
Living with mother only	24.5	24.9	24.1	24.4
Divorced	8.7	5.0	9.6	12.0
Married, spouse absent	5.8	5.2	5.9	6.2
Widowed	1.0	0.4	0.9	1.9
Never married	9.0	14.3	7.7	4.4
Living with father only	3.4	3.4	3.2	3.6
Divorced	1.6	1.2	1.5	2.2
Married, spouse absent	0.6	0.3	0.7	0.9
Widowed	0.2	0.0	0.2	0.3
Never married	1.0	1.8	0.7	0.3

Source: Bureau of the Census, Marital Status and Living Arrangements: March 1994, *Current Population Reports, P20-484, 1996*

Living Arrangements of Total Women by Age, 1994

(number and percent distribution of total women aged 18 or older by living arrangement and age, 1994; numbers in thousands)

	total	18 to 19	20 to 24	25 to 29	30 to 34	35 to 39	40 to 44	45 to 54	55 to 64	65 to 74	75 or older
Number	98,764	3,454	9,338	9,861	11,212	11,078	9,906	15,068	10,805	10,163	7,880
Family householder or spouse	65,514	343	3,308	6,323	8,735	9,191	8,247	12,282	8,191	6,224	2,671
Child of householder	8,813	2,441	3,483	1,212	647	434	263	271	91	36	37
Other member of family household	4,611	275	704	517	341	290	208	361	346	553	911
Nonfamily householder	16,150	141	911	1,102	1,007	872	863	1,817	2,029	3,276	4,133
Other member of nonfamily household	3,561	248	892	693	473	286	322	335	139	63	111
Group quarters*	115	6	40	14	9	5	3	2	9	11	17
Percent	100.0%	100.0%	100.0%	100.0%	100.0%	100.0%	100.0%	100.0%	100.0%	100.0%	100.0%
Family householder or spouse	66.3	9.9	35.4	64.1	77.9	83.0	83.3	81.5	75.8	61.2	33.9
Child of householder	8.9	70.7	37.3	12.3	5.8	3.9	2.7	1.8	0.8	0.4	0.5
Other member of family household	4.7	8.0	7.5	5.2	3.0	2.6	2.1	2.4	3.2	5.4	11.6
Nonfamily householder	16.4	4.1	9.8	11.2	9.0	7.9	8.7	12.1	18.8	32.2	52.4
Other member of nonfamily household	3.6	7.2	9.6	7.0	4.2	2.6	3.3	2.2	1.3	0.6	1.4
Group quarters*	0.1	0.2	0.4	0.1	0.1	0.0	0.0	0.0	0.1	0.1	0.2

* The Current Population Survey does not include people living in institutions such as prisons, the military, or college dormitories. It defines people living in group quarters as those in noninstitutional living arrangements that are not conventional housing units, such as rooming houses, staff quarters at a hospital, or halfway houses.
Source: Bureau of the Census, Marital Status and Living Arrangements: March 1994, Current Population Reports, P20-484, 1996

Living Arrangements of Total Men by Age, 1994

(number and percent distribution of total men aged 18 or older, by living arrangement and age, 1994; numbers in thousands)

	total	18 to 19	20 to 24	25 to 29	30 to 34	35 to 39	40 to 44	45 to 54	55 to 64	65 to 74	75 or older
Number	89,693	3,263	8,786	9,767	11,089	10,606	9,298	13,847	10,205	8,114	4717
Family householder or spouse	56,191	88	1,564	4,505	6,784	7,195	7,085	11,116	8,040	6,470	3,098
Child of householder	12,001	2,646	4,408	1,914	1,204	907	399	307	181	36	-
Other member of family household	4,287	280	742	661	556	394	255	343	429	336	536
Nonfamily householder	12,242	92	1,179	1,644	1,720	1,399	1,149	1,725	1,225	1,116	994
Other member of nonfamily household	4,815	145	861	1,012	802	701	402	347	314	150	79
Group quarters*	157	12	32	31	23	10	8	9	16	6	10
Percent	100.0%	100.0%	100.0%	100.0%	100.0%	100.0%	100.0%	100.0%	100.0%	100.0%	100.0%
Family householder or spouse	62.6	2.7	17.8	46.1	61.2	67.8	76.2	80.3	78.8	79.7	65.7
Child of householder	13.4	81.1	50.2	19.6	10.9	8.6	4.3	2.2	1.8	0.4	-
Other member of family household	4.8	8.6	8.4	6.8	5.0	3.7	2.7	2.5	4.2	4.1	11.4
Nonfamily householder	13.6	2.8	13.4	16.8	15.5	13.2	12.4	12.5	12.0	13.8	21.1
Other member of nonfamily household	5.4	4.4	9.8	10.4	7.2	6.6	4.3	2.5	3.1	1.8	1.7
Group quarters*	0.2	0.4	0.4	0.3	0.2	0.1	0.1	0.1	0.2	0.1	0.2

* The Current Population Survey does not include people living in institutions such as prisons, the military, or college dormitories. It defines people living in group quarters as those in noninstitutional living arrangements that are not conventional housing units, such as rooming houses, staff quarters at a hospital, or halfway houses.

Note: (-) means number in sample is too small to make a reliable estimate.

Source: Bureau of the Census, Marital Status and Living Arrangements: March 1994, Current Population Reports, P20-484, 1996

Marital Status of Total Women by Age, 1994

(number and percent distribution of total women aged 15 or older by age and marital status, 1994; numbers in thousands)

	total	never married	married	widowed	divorced
Total, number	104,032	24,645	58,185	11,073	10,129
Under age 20	8,722	8,339	350	3	30
Aged 20 to 24	9,338	6,162	2,931	11	234
Aged 25 to 29	9,861	3,476	5,689	29	667
Aged 30 to 34	11,212	2,228	7,702	80	1,202
Aged 35 to 39	11,078	1,420	7,960	135	1,563
Aged 40 to 44	9,906	909	7,359	146	1,492
Aged 45 to 54	15,068	892	10,977	705	2,494
Aged 55 to 64	10,805	440	7,500	1,501	1,364
Aged 65 to 74	10,163	386	5,520	3,476	781
Aged 75 to 84	5,969	240	1,905	3,577	247
Aged 85 or older	1,911	153	294	1,409	55
Total, percent	100.0%	23.7%	55.9%	10.6%	9.7%
Under age 20	100.0	95.6	4.0	0.0	0.3
Aged 20 to 24	100.0	66.0	31.4	0.1	2.5
Aged 25 to 29	100.0	35.2	57.7	0.3	6.8
Aged 30 to 34	100.0	19.9	68.7	0.7	10.7
Aged 35 to 39	100.0	12.8	71.9	1.2	14.1
Aged 40 to 44	100.0	9.2	74.3	1.5	15.1
Aged 45 to 54	100.0	5.9	72.8	4.7	16.6
Aged 55 to 64	100.0	4.1	69.4	13.9	12.6
Aged 65 to 74	100.0	3.8	54.3	34.2	7.7
Aged 75 to 84	100.0	4.0	31.9	59.9	4.1
Aged 85 or older	100.0	8.0	15.4	73.7	2.9

Source: Bureau of the Census, Marital Status and Living Arrangements: March 1994, *Current Population Reports, P20-484, 1996*

Marital Status of Total Men by Age, 1994

(number and percent distribution of total men aged 15 or older by age and marital status, 1994; numbers in thousands)

	total	never married	married	widowed	divorced
Total, number	96,768	30,228	57,068	2,222	7,250
Under age 20	9,008	8,877	119	2	10
Aged 20 to 24	9,221	7,469	1,658	5	89
Aged 25 to 29	9,765	4,910	4,422	9	424
Aged 30 to 34	11,108	3,298	6,940	6	864
Aged 35 to 39	10,892	2,094	7,603	31	1,164
Aged 40 to 44	9,651	1,255	7,103	31	1,262
Aged 45 to 54	14,454	1,185	11,362	137	1,770
Aged 55 to 64	9,933	539	8,034	327	1,033
Aged 65 to 74	7,924	390	6,353	695	486
Aged 75 to 84	3,888	147	2,925	681	135
Aged 85 or older	924	64	546	299	15
Total, percent	100.0%	31.2%	59.0%	2.3%	7.5%
Under age 20	100.0	98.5	1.3	0.0	0.1
Aged 20 to 24	100.0	81.0	18.0	0.1	1.0
Aged 25 to 29	100.0	50.3	45.3	0.1	4.3
Aged 30 to 34	100.0	29.7	62.5	0.1	7.8
Aged 35 to 39	100.0	19.2	69.8	0.3	10.7
Aged 40 to 44	100.0	13.0	73.6	0.3	13.1
Aged 45 to 54	100.0	8.2	78.6	0.9	12.2
Aged 55 to 64	100.0	5.4	80.9	3.3	10.4
Aged 65 to 74	100.0	4.9	80.2	8.8	6.1
Aged 75 to 84	100.0	3.8	75.2	17.5	3.5
Aged 85 or older	100.0	6.9	59.1	32.4	1.6

Source: Bureau of the Census, Marital Status and Living Arrangements: March 1994, *Current Population Reports, P20-484, 1996*

Interracial Married Couples, 1980 to 1993

(total number of married couples, number of interracial couples by race, and interracial share of total couples, 1980-93; numbers in thousands)

| | | interracial married couples | | | | |
| | | | black/white | | | |
	total	total	total	black husband/ white wife	white husband/ black wife	white/ other race	black/ other race
1993	54,199	1,195	242	182	60	920	33
1992	53,512	1,161	246	163	83	883	32
1991	53,227	994	231	156	75	720	43
1990	53,256	964	211	150	61	720	33
1989	52,924	953	219	155	64	703	31
1988	52,613	956	218	149	69	703	35
1987	52,286	799	177	121	56	581	41
1986	51,704	827	181	136	45	613	33
1985	51,114	792	164	117	47	599	29
1984	50,864	762	175	111	64	564	23
1983	50,665	719	164	118	46	522	33
1982	50,294	697	155	108	47	515	27
1981	49,896	639	132	104	28	484	23
1980	49,714	651	167	122	45	450	34

Percent

1993	100.0%	2.2%	0.4%	0.3%	0.1%	1.7%	0.1%
1992	100.0	2.2	0.5	0.3	0.2	1.7	0.1
1991	100.0	1.9	0.4	0.3	0.1	1.4	0.1
1990	100.0	1.8	0.4	0.3	0.1	1.4	0.1
1989	100.0	1.8	0.4	0.3	0.1	1.3	0.1
1988	100.0	1.8	0.4	0.3	0.1	1.3	0.1
1987	100.0	1.5	0.3	0.2	0.1	1.1	0.1
1986	100.0	1.6	0.4	0.3	0.1	1.2	0.1
1985	100.0	1.5	0.3	0.2	0.1	1.2	0.1
1984	100.0	1.5	0.3	0.2	0.1	1.1	0.0
1983	100.0	1.4	0.3	0.2	0.1	1.0	0.1
1982	100.0	1.4	0.3	0.2	0.1	1.0	0.1
1981	100.0	1.3	0.3	0.2	0.1	1.0	0.0
1980	100.0	1.3	0.3	0.2	0.1	0.9	0.1

Source: Bureau of the Census, Internet web site, http://www.census.gov

Interracial and Interethnic Married Couples, 1994

(number and percent distribution of married couples, by race and Hispanic origin of husband and wife, 1994; numbers in thousands)

	total	race of wife			origin of wife	
		white	*black*	*other*	*non-Hispanic*	*Hispanic*
NUMBER	54,251	48,167	3,718	2,366	49,776	4,475
Race of husband						
White	48,251	47,606	100	544	44,157	4,094
Black	3,852	196	3,598	59	3,761	92
Other	2,148	365	19	1,764	1,859	289
Origin of husband						
Non-Hispanic	49,931	44,188	3,646	2,098	49,212	719
Hispanic	4,320	3,979	72	269	564	3,755
PERCENT	100.0%	88.8%	6.9%	4.4%	91.8%	8.2%
Race of husband						
White	88.9	87.8	0.2	1.0	81.4	7.5
Black	7.1	0.4	6.6	0.1	6.9	0.2
Other	4.0	0.7	0.0	3.3	3.4	0.5
Origin of husband						
Non-Hispanic	92.0	81.5	6.7	3.9	90.7	1.3
Hispanic	8.0	7.3	0.1	0.5	1.0	6.9

Note: Hispanics may be of any race. For a breakdown of the Hispanic composition of racial groups or the racial composition of Hispanics, see the tables in the introduction to this book.
Source: Bureau of the Census, Household and Family Characteristics: March 1994, *Current Population Reports, P20-483, 1995*

Total Population:

Housing

Sixty-four percent of Americans own their homes, which had a median value of $78,300 in 1990. Among the 50 metropolitan areas with the most households, homeownership rates are highest in Nassau-Suffolk, New York (80 percent) and lowest in New York City (33 percent). Housing values are greatest in San Francisco, at $332,400 in 1990.

Sixty-two percent of homes are single-family detached structures. American homes have a median of six rooms, and half have more than one bathroom. Most homes have dishwashers; washing machines; clothes dryers; a porch, deck, balcony, or patio; a telephone; and a garage or carport. Ninety percent of householders own a car or truck.

Fully 74 percent of Americans rate their homes at least an eight on a scale of one to ten. This includes 82 percent of homeowners and 60 percent of renters. Only 7 percent of householders think crime is a problem in their area—just 5 percent of homeowners and 12 percent of renters. Sixty percent of householders say their neighborhoods have no problems.

Homeowners paid a median of $45,295 for their homes. Forty-five percent paid for the downpayment with savings, while 29 percent used the proceeds from the sale of a previous home. Sixteen percent of homeowners had their roof repaired in the past two years, the most common home repair. Another 12 percent installed storm doors or windows, while 10 percent remodeled a bathroom.

Characteristics of Total Households
by Metropolitan Status, 1990

(total number of households, percent owner occupied, and median value of owner-occupied households, by metropolitan status, 1990; numbers in thousands)

	number	owner-occupied percent	owner-occupied median value
Total households	91,947	64.2%	$78,300
Inside metropolitan areas	71,265	61.8	89,100
Central cities	29,794	49.0	71,600
Suburbs*	41,471	71.0	99,000
Outside metropolitan areas	20,682	72.4	50,100

* The suburbs are the portion of a metropolitan area that is outside the central city.
Source: Bureau of the Census, unpublished tables from the 1990 census

Homeownership in the
50 Largest Metropolitan Areas, 1990

(total number of households, percent of total households that are owner occupied, and median value of owner-occupied households, in the U.S. and in the 50 largest metropolitan areas ranked alphabetically, 1990; numbers in thousands)

		owner-occupied	
	number	percent	median value
Total households	91,947	64.2%	$78,300
Anaheim-Santa Ana, CA	827	60.1	252,700
Atlanta, GA	1,056	62.3	88,300
Baltimore, MD	880	63.7	101,200
Bergen-Passaic, NJ	464	63.9	214,400
Boston, MA	1,081	55.9	186,100
Buffalo, NY	377	63.7	74,100
Charlotte-Gastonia-Rock Hill, NC-SC	441	66.8	72,200
Chicago, IL	2,222	58.6	111,200
Cincinnati, OH	548	63.1	70,700
Cleveland, OH	712	65.4	74,100
Columbus, OH	525	60.1	55,600
Dallas, TX	955	55.1	82,100
Denver, CO	649	61.6	86,800
Detroit, MI	1,619	69.8	68,200
Fort Lauderdale-Hollywood-Pompano Beach, FL	528	68.0	89,800
Fort Worth-Arlington, TX	495	60.3	71,800
Greensboro-Winston-Salem-High Point, NC	372	67.3	71,200
Houston, TX	1,186	54.9	63,900
Indianapolis, IN	480	63.8	66,900
Kansas City, MO-KS	602	65.4	66,100
Los Angeles-Long Beach, CA	2,990	48.2	226,400
Louisville, KY-IN	368	67.5	56,000
Miami-Hialeah, FL	692	54.3	85,300
Milwaukee, WI	538	59.4	76,600
Minneapolis-St. Paul, MN-WI	936	68.7	87,400
Monmouth-Ocean, NJ	366	77.4	150,600
Nashville, TN	376	63.2	75,800
Nassau-Suffolk, NY	856	80.3	187,000

(continued)

(continued from previous page)

	number	owner-occupied	
		percent	*median value*
New Orleans, LA	455	58.0%	$69,800
New York, NY	3,252	33.3	209,000
Newark, NJ	652	59.1	191,400
Norfolk-Virginia Beach-Newport News, VA	494	58.9	85,700
Oakland, CA	780	58.8	224,400
Oklahoma City, OK	368	64.3	53,900
Orlando, FL	402	61.9	83,100
Philadelphia, PA-NJ	1,777	69.6	100,800
Phoenix, AZ	808	63.3	84,300
Pittsburgh, PA	820	69.3	54,800
Portland, OR	487	60.7	72,100
Riverside-San Bernardino, CA	867	65.2	133,900
Rochester, NY	374	67.6	85,600
Sacramento, CA	556	59.0	136,700
San Antonio, TX	451	59.2	56,900
San Diego, CA	887	53.8	186,700
San Francisco, CA	643	48.3	332,400
San Jose, CA	520	59.1	289,400
Seattle, WA	788	60.4	136,700
St. Louis, MO-IL	925	68.5	69,700
Tampa- St. Petersburg-Clearwater, FL	869	69.3	71,100
Washington, DC-MD-VA	1,459	60.5	166,100

Source: Bureau of the Census, unpublished tables from the 1990 census

Characteristics of Housing Units Occupied by the Total Population, 1993

(total number and percent distribution of occupied housing units, by selected housing characteristics and homeownership status, 1993; numbers in thousands except for medians)

	total number	total percent	owner-occupied number	owner-occupied percent	renter-occupied number	renter-occupied percent
Total occupied housing units	94,724	100.0%	61,252	100.0%	33,472	100.0%
Region						
Northeast	18,906	20.0	11,751	19.2	7,155	21.4
Midwest	23,031	24.3	15,617	25.5	7,415	22.2
South	32,936	34.8	21,841	35.7	11,096	33.2
West	19,850	21.0	12,043	19.7	7,808	23.3
Units in structure						
1, detached	58,918	62.2	50,490	82.4	8,428	25.2
1, attached	5,375	5.7	2,824	4.6	2,550	7.6
2 to 4	9,279	9.8	1,774	2.9	7,505	22.4
5 to 9	4,724	5.0	409	0.7	4,315	12.9
10 to 19	4,190	4.4	359	0.6	3,831	11.4
20 to 49	3,154	3.3	335	0.5	2,819	8.4
50 or more	3,429	3.6	579	0.9	2,850	8.5
Mobile home or trailer	5,655	6.0	4,482	7.3	1,173	3.5
Median number of rooms in unit	6	-	6	-	4	-
Median square footage of unit	1,725	-	1,805	-	1,273	-
Number of complete bathrooms						
None	526	0.6	171	0.3	354	1.1
One	43,944	46.4	19,604	32.0	24,339	72.7
One and one-half	14,740	15.6	11,345	18.5	3,395	10.1
Two or more	35,515	37.5	30,131	49.2	5,384	16.1
Primary heating fuel						
Total with heating fuel	93,813	99.0	60,886	99.4	32,928	98.4
Electricity	25,107	26.5	14,204	23.2	10,903	32.6
Piped gas	47,669	50.3	32,049	52.3	15,620	46.7
Bottled gas	3,922	4.1	3,107	5.1	815	2.4
Fuel oil	11,168	11.8	7,072	11.5	4,096	12.2

(continued)

(continued from previous page)

	total		owner-occupied		renter-occupied	
	number	*percent*	*number*	*percent*	*number*	*percent*
Kerosene or other liquid fuel	1,021	1.1%	751	1.2%	270	0.8%
Coal or coke	297	0.3	227	0.4	70	0.2
Wood	4,104	4.3	3,195	5.2	909	2.7
Solar energy	30	0.0	23	0.0	7	0.0
Other	496	0.5	257	0.4	238	0.7
Selected equipment						
Dishwasher	49,332	52.1	37,519	61.3	11,813	35.3
Washing machine	73,146	77.2	57,731	94.3	15,414	46.1
Clothes dryer	67,464	71.2	54,334	88.7	13,130	39.2
Disposal in kitchen sink	40,091	42.3	26,828	43.8	13,263	39.6
Central air conditioning	42,183	44.5	30,560	49.9	11,622	34.7
Porch, deck, balcony, patio	73,181	77.3	52,087	85.0	21,094	63.0
Telephone	88,442	93.4	59,383	96.9	29,059	86.8
Usable fireplace	30,254	31.9	25,811	42.1	4,443	13.3
Garage or carport	55,351	58.4	45,219	73.8	10,132	30.3
Cars and trucks available						
No cars, trucks, or vans	9,793	10.3	2,555	4.2	7,238	21.6
1 car, with or without						
trucks or vans	46,430	49.0	29,328	47.9	17,102	51.1
2 or more cars	32,506	34.3	25,505	41.6	7,002	20.9
Overall opinion of housing unit						
1 (worst)	550	0.6	106	0.2	444	1.3
2	334	0.4	67	0.1	267	0.8
3	714	0.8	223	0.4	491	1.5
4	967	1.0	232	0.4	735	2.2
5	6,073	6.4	2,616	4.3	3,457	10.3
6	4,600	4.9	1,958	3.2	2,642	7.9
7	10,700	11.3	5,536	9.0	5,164	15.4
8	22,862	24.1	14,443	23.6	8,419	25.2
9	14,638	15.5	10,518	17.2	4,120	12.3
10 (best)	32,517	34.3	25,167	41.1	7,349	22.0

Source: Bureau of the Census, American Housing Survey for the United States in 1993, *Current Housing Reports, H150/93, 1995*

Neighborhood Characteristics of Total Housing Units, 1993

(total number and percent distribution of occupied housing units by selected characteristics of neighborhoods and homeownership status, 1993; numbers in thousands)

	total		owner-occupied		renter-occupied	
	number	*percent*	*number*	*percent*	*number*	*percent*
Total occupied housing units	94,724	100.0%	61,252	100.0%	33,472	100.0%
Overall opinion of neighborhood						
1 (worst)	1,463	1.5	451	0.7	1,012	3.0
2	896	0.9	338	0.6	559	1.7
3	1,319	1.4	529	0.9	790	2.4
4	1,797	1.9	747	1.2	1,050	3.1
5	7,155	7.6	3,495	5.7	3,660	10.9
6	4,861	5.1	2,598	4.2	2,263	6.8
7	10,172	10.7	5,986	9.8	4,186	12.5
8	20,628	21.8	13,690	22.4	6,938	20.7
9	13,522	14.3	9,607	15.7	3,914	11.7
10 (best)	31,192	32.9	22,785	37.2	8,407	25.1
Neighborhood problems						
No problems	57,019	60.2	38,196	62.4	18,823	56.2
With problems*	35,799	37.8	21,906	35.8	13,892	41.5
Crime	6,828	7.2	2,811	4.6	4,017	12.0
Noise	7,607	8.0	3,669	6.0	3,938	11.8
Traffic	6,920	7.3	4,245	6.9	2,675	8.0
Litter or housing deterioration	3,980	4.2	2,699	4.4	1,281	3.8
Poor city or county services	1,272	1.3	858	1.4	414	1.2
Undesirable commercial, institutional, industrial	1,387	1.5	883	1.4	505	1.5
People	11,825	12.5	6,610	10.8	5,215	15.6
Other	9,898	10.4	6,963	11.4	2,935	8.8
Not reported	684	0.7	447	0.7	237	0.7

* Figures will not add to total because more than one problem could be cited.
Source: Bureau of the Census, American Housing Survey for the United States in 1993, *Current Housing Reports, H150/93, 1995*

Geographical Mobility of the Total Population by Age, 1993-94

(total number of persons aged 1 or older, number and percent of those who moved between March 1993 and March 1994, by age of person and type of move; numbers in thousands)

	total	same house (non-movers)	total	same county	total	same state	total	same region	different region	movers from abroad
							different state			
					different county					
						different house in the U.S.				
Total, 1 or older	255,774	83.3%	16.3%	10.4%	5.8%	3.2%	2.6%	1.4%	1.2%	0.5%
Aged 1 to 4	16,477	78.0	21.5	14.6	6.9	3.6	3.3	1.8	1.5	0.5
Aged 5 to 9	19,365	82.7	16.9	11.2	5.7	3.1	2.6	1.5	1.1	0.4
Aged 10 to 14	19,152	86.8	12.9	8.7	4.2	2.4	1.8	0.9	0.9	0.4
Aged 15 to 19	17,722	82.4	16.9	10.8	6.0	3.2	2.9	1.6	1.3	0.7
Aged 15 to 17	10,806	85.5	14.0	8.7	5.3	2.6	2.7	1.6	1.1	0.5
Aged 18 and 19	6,916	77.7	21.4	14.2	7.1	4.0	3.1	1.5	1.6	0.9
Aged 20 to 24	18,559	64.4	34.4	22.0	12.4	7.4	5.0	2.5	2.5	1.2
Aged 25 to 29	19,622	69.3	29.7	19.1	10.7	6.0	4.7	2.6	2.1	0.9
Aged 30 to 34	22,319	77.1	22.2	14.4	7.9	4.6	3.2	1.7	1.6	0.6
Aged 35 to 39	21,967	83.4	16.3	10.4	5.9	3.0	2.9	1.4	1.5	0.4
Aged 40 to 44	19,557	86.7	12.9	7.9	5.0	3.0	2.0	1.1	0.9	0.4
Aged 45 to 49	16,562	88.6	10.9	6.9	4.1	1.9	2.1	1.1	1.1	0.5
Aged 50 to 54	12,960	90.6	9.1	5.4	3.6	2.0	1.6	1.0	0.6	0.3
Aged 55 to 59	10,730	92.8	6.9	4.0	3.0	1.4	1.6	0.7	0.8	0.3
Aged 60 to 64	10,005	93.6	6.2	3.8	2.4	1.3	1.1	0.6	0.4	0.1
Aged 60 and 61	3,999	94.1	5.8	3.5	2.3	1.5	0.8	0.5	0.3	0.1
Aged 62 to 64	6,007	93.3	6.6	4.1	2.5	1.2	1.2	0.7	0.5	0.1
Aged 65 to 69	9,595	93.4	6.4	3.3	3.1	1.5	1.6	1.1	0.5	0.1
Aged 70 to 74	8,490	94.7	5.2	3.2	2.0	0.9	1.1	0.6	0.4	0.0
Aged 75 to 79	5,979	95.4	4.4	2.7	1.7	0.8	1.0	0.8	0.2	0.1
Aged 80 to 84	3,879	94.5	5.3	3.1	2.2	1.1	1.1	0.6	0.5	0.2
Aged 85 or older	2,835	94.2	5.6	3.4	2.2	1.0	1.2	0.4	0.8	0.1
Median age	33.8	36.0	26.8	26.4	27.5	27.3	27.9	28.0	27.8	26.5

Source: Bureau of the Census, Geographical Mobility: March 1993 to March 1994, *Current Population Reports, P20-485, 1995*

Reasons for Moving Among Total Movers, 1993

(total number and percent distribution of households moving in the previous 12 months, by reason for move and for choosing new neighborhood and house, and by comparison with previous home and neighborhood, by homeownership status, 1993; numbers in thousands)

	total		owner-occupied		renter-occupied	
	number	*percent*	*number*	*percent*	*number*	*percent*
Total households moving in past 12 months	16,603	100.0%	4,850	100.0%	11,754	100.0%
Reasons for leaving previous unit*						
Private displacement	784	4.7	179	3.7	605	5.1
Government displacement	148	0.9	30	0.6	117	1.0
Disaster loss	90	0.5	19	0.4	71	0.6
New job or job transfer	1,764	10.6	397	8.2	1,367	11.6
To be closer to work, school, other	1,612	9.7	307	6.3	1,305	11.1
Other, financial/employment related	878	5.3	175	3.6	703	6.0
To establish own household	2,308	13.9	532	11.0	1,776	15.1
Needed larger house or apartment	2,362	14.2	825	17.0	1,538	13.1
Married	478	2.9	201	4.1	276	2.3
Widowed, divorced, or separated	869	5.2	208	4.3	661	5.6
Other, family/person related	1,752	10.6	419	8.6	1,333	11.3
Wanted better home	1,935	11.7	669	13.8	1,267	10.8
Change from owner to renter	208	1.3	-	0.0	208	1.8
Change from renter to owner	1,167	7.0	1,167	24.1	-	0.0
Wanted lower rent or maintenance	1,018	6.1	103	2.1	915	7.8
Choice of present neighborhood*						
Convenient to job	3,615	21.8	787	16.2	2,828	24.1
Convenient to friends or relatives	2,887	17.4	747	15.4	2,141	18.2
Convenient to leisure activities	730	4.4	262	5.4	468	4.0
Convenient to public transportation	514	3.1	61	1.3	454	3.9
Good schools	1,301	7.8	556	11.5	745	6.3
Other public services	366	2.2	98	2.0	268	2.3
Looks/design of neighborhood	3,302	19.9	1,314	27.1	1,987	16.9
House was most important consideration	3,750	22.6	1,459	30.1	2,292	19.5
Neighborhood search						
Looked at just this neighborhood	6,786	40.9	1,581	32.6	5,204	44.3
Looked at other neighborhoods	9,323	56.2	3,081	63.5	6,242	53.1
Choice of present home*						
Financial reasons	7,055	42.5	2,154	44.4	4,901	41.7
Room layout/design	3,451	20.8	1,486	30.6	1,964	16.7

(continued from previous page)

	total		owner-occupied		renter-occupied	
	number	*percent*	*number*	*percent*	*number*	*percent*
Kitchen	273	1.6%	161	3.3%	112	1.0%
Size	2,668	16.1	842	17.4	1,825	15.5
Exterior appearance	1,261	7.6	621	12.8	640	5.4
Yard/trees/view	1,436	8.6	681	14.0	755	6.4
Quality of construction	895	5.4	541	11.2	354	3.0
Only one available	1,858	11.2	167	3.4	1,691	14.4
Other reasons	5,308	32.0	1,512	31.2	3,796	32.3
Comparison to previous home						
Better home	8,377	50.5	3,165	65.3	5,212	44.3
Worse home	3,184	19.2	479	9.9	2,705	23.0
About the same	4,536	27.3	1,022	21.1	3,514	29.9
Comparison to previous neighborhood						
Better neighborhood	6,611	39.8	2,428	50.1	4,184	35.6
Worse neighborhood	2,603	15.7	370	7.6	2,233	19.0
About the same	5,815	35.0	1,640	33.8	4,175	35.5
Same neighborhood	1,043	6.3	221	4.6	822	7.0

* Figures may not add to total because more than one category may apply and unreported reasons are not shown.
Source: Bureau of the Census, American Housing Survey for the United States in 1993, *Current Housing Reports, H150/93, 1995*

Housing Value and Purchase Price for Total Homeowners, 1993

(total number and percent distribution of homeowners, by value of home, purchase price, and major source of downpayment, 1993; numbers in thousands)

	number	percent
Total homeowners	61,252	100.0%
Value of home		
Under $50,000	14,433	23.6
$50,000 to $79,999	13,569	22.2
$80,000 to $99,999	8,034	13.1
$100,000 to $149,999	11,093	18.1
$150,000 to $199,999	6,284	10.3
$200,000 to $299,999	4,733	7.7
$300,000 or more	3,104	5.1
Median	$86,529	-
Purchase price*		
Home purchased or built	58,492	95.5
Under $50,000	28,152	46.0
$50,000 to $79,999	9,692	15.8
$80,000 to $99,999	4,279	7.0
$100,000 to $149,999	5,111	8.3
$150,000 to $199,999	2,507	4.1
$200,000 to $299,999	1,670	2.7
$300,000 or more	960	1.6
Median purchase price	45,295	-
Received as inheritance or gift	1,564	2.6
Major source of downpayment*		
Sale of previous home	17,855	29.2
Savings or cash on hand	27,703	45.2
Sale of other investment	473	0.8
Borrowing, other than mortgage on this property	1,992	3.3
Inheritance or gift	1,259	2.1
Land where building built used for financing	387	0.6
Other	2,619	4.3
No downpayment	4,660	7.6

* Figures may not add to total because "not reported" is not shown.
Source: Bureau of the Census, American Housing Survey for the United States in 1993, *Current Housing Reports, H150/93, 1995*

Repairs, Improvements, and Alterations by Total Homeowners, 1993

(total number and percent of homeowners performing selected repairs, improvements, and alterations to their homes in the past two years; among those doing work, percent who had most of it done by others; among those doing work, percent spending $500 or more, 1993; numbers in thousands)

	number	percent having work done	percent having most work done by others	percent spending $500 or more
Total homeowners	61,252	-	-	-
Roof replaced (all or part)	9,722	15.9%	74.4%	70.0%
Additions built	2,469	4.0	54.4	79.4
Kitchen remodeled or added	5,033	8.2	47.7	70.3
Bathroom remodeled or added	6,126	10.0	42.5	60.7
Siding replaced or added	3,212	5.2	68.2	60.7
Storm doors/windows bought and installed	7,180	11.7	53.2	41.9
Major equipment replaced or added	6,053	9.9	80.5	76.3
Insulation added	3,827	6.2	43.6	23.0

Source: Bureau of the Census, American Housing Survey for the United States in 1993, *Current Housing Reports, H150/93, 1995*

Total Population:
Income

The median income of American households fell by 5 percent between 1990 and 1994, after adjusting for inflation, to $32,264. Despite this decline, median household income in 1994 was 1 percent greater than in 1980, after adjusting for inflation.

Household income peaks for householders aged 45 to 54, reaching $47,261 in 1994. Among household types, incomes are greatest for married couples, who had a median of $45,041 in 1994. Ten percent of married couples have incomes of $100,000 or more.

For men w ho work full-time, median income peaks in the 45-to-54 age group, at $40,367. Income also peaks in this age group for women who work full-time, at $25,911 in 1994. Since 1980, the median earnings of men who work full-time have dropped by nearly 8 percent, after adjusting for inflation. In contrast, women's median earnings have grown by 10 percent. Consequently, the median earnings of women are now 72 percent as much as the median earnings of men, up from 60 percent in 1980.

Incomes rise sharply with education. Men and women with professional degrees who work full-time earn more than twice as much as the average male or female full-time worker.

Overall, about 12 percent of American families were poor in 1994, a larger proportion than in 1990 or 1980. By age, the nation's children have the highest poverty rate—22 percent of people under age 18 are poor, versus 14.5 percent of the population as a whole.

Median Income of Total Households, 1980 to 1994

(median income of total households, 1980-1994, and percent change in income for selected years; in 1994 dollars)

	median income
1994	$32,264
1993	32,041
1992	32,361
1991	32,780
1990	33,952
1989	34,547
1988	34,106
1987	33,999
1986	33,665
1985	32,530
1984	31,972
1983	31,274
1982	31,269
1981	31,374
1980	31,891

Percent change

1990-1994	-5.0%
1980-1994	1.2

Source: Bureau of the Census, unpublished tables from the 1995 Current Population Survey

Income Distribution of Total Households by Age of Householder, 1994

(number and percent distribution of total households by income and age of householder, 1994; households in thousands as of 1995)

	total	15-25	25-34	35-44	45-54	55-64	65+
Total	98,990	5,444	19,453	22,914	17,590	12,224	21,365
Under $10,000	13,412	1,261	2,173	1,975	1,338	1,658	5,008
$10,000 to $19,999	17,371	1,548	3,078	2,533	1,777	1,717	6,717
$20,000 to $29,999	15,219	1,183	3,408	3,061	1,970	1,843	3,755
$30,000 to $39,999	12,985	686	3,105	3,301	2,118	1,551	2,223
$40,000 to $49,999	10,108	350	2,466	2,823	2,074	1,295	1,102
$50,000 to $59,999	7,917	180	1,808	2,418	1,658	1,029	824
$60,000 to $69,999	6,150	91	1,220	1,964	1,631	793	453
$70,000 to $79,999	4,362	60	767	1,443	1,205	570	318
$80,000 to $89,999	2,795	26	432	839	956	325	218
$90,000 to $99,999	2,089	12	305	584	665	346	180
$100,000 or more	6,581	48	693	1,974	2,198	1,099	570
Median income	$32,264	$19,340	$33,151	$41,667	$47,261	$35,232	$18,095
Percent distribution	100.0%	100.0%	100.0%	100.0%	100.0%	100.0%	100.0%
Under $10,000	13.5	23.2	11.2	8.6	7.6	13.6	23.4
$10,000 to $19,999	17.5	28.4	15.8	11.1	10.1	14.0	31.4
$20,000 to $29,999	15.4	21.7	17.5	13.4	11.2	15.1	17.6
$30,000 to $39,999	13.1	12.6	16.0	14.4	12.0	12.7	10.4
$40,000 to $49,999	10.2	6.4	12.7	12.3	11.8	10.6	5.2
$50,000 to $59,999	8.0	3.3	9.3	10.6	9.4	8.4	3.9
$60,000 to $69,999	6.2	1.7	6.3	8.6	9.3	6.5	2.1
$70,000 to $79,999	4.4	1.1	3.9	6.3	6.9	4.7	1.5
$80,000 to $89,999	2.8	0.5	2.2	3.7	5.4	2.7	1.0
$90,000 to $99,999	2.1	0.2	1.6	2.5	3.8	2.8	0.8
$100,000 or more	6.6	0.9	3.6	8.6	12.5	9.0	2.7

Source: Bureau of the Census, unpublished tables from the 1995 Current Population Survey

Income Distribution of Total Households by Household Type, 1994

(number and percent distribution of total households, by income and type of household, 1994; households in thousands as of 1995)

| | family households | | | | | nonfamily households | | | |
| | total | married couples | female hh, no spouse present | male hh, no spouse present | total | female householder | | male householder | |
total households	total	married couples	female hh, no spouse present	male hh, no spouse present	total	total	living alone	total	living alone
Total 98,990	69,305	53,858	12,220	3,226	29,686	16,496	14,592	13,190	10,104
Under $10,000 13,412	5,634	2,106	3,181	346	7,779	5,447	5,333	2,332	2,154
$10,000 to $19,999 17,371	9,682	6,094	2,959	630	7,690	4,674	4,372	3,016	2,616
$20,000 to $29,999 15,219	10,157	7,479	2,066	612	5,062	2,571	2,237	2,491	1,965
$30,000 to $39,999 12,985	9,680	7,581	1,623	476	3,305	1,526	1,224	1,779	1,343
$40,000 to $49,999 10,108	8,084	6,745	963	375	2,025	872	638	1,153	734
$50,000 to $59,999 7,917	6,628	5,800	562	265	1,289	521	349	769	464
$60,000 to $69,999 6,150	5,352	4,854	330	167	798	294	145	503	286
$70,000 to $79,999 4,362	3,835	3,496	207	132	527	203	113	326	153
$80,000 to $89,999 2,795	2,477	2,314	98	66	319	116	45	203	103
$90,000 to $99,999 2,089	1,909	1,773	91	45	181	51	15	130	65
$100,000 or more 6,581	5,869	5,618	139	112	713	221	122	492	258
Median income $32,264	$39,390	$45,041	$19,872	$30,472	$18,947	$14,948	$13,431	$24,593	$21,216

(continued)

(continued from previous page)

Percent distribution	total households	family households				total	nonfamily households			
		total	married couples	female hh, no spouse present	male hh, no spouse present		female householder		male householder	
							total	living alone	total	living alone
	100.0%	100.0%	100.0%	100.0%	100.0%	100.0%	100.0%	100.0%	100.0%	100.0%
Under $10,000	13.5	8.1	3.9	26.0	10.7	26.2	33.0	36.5	17.7	21.2
$10,000 to $19,999	17.5	14.0	11.3	24.2	19.5	25.9	28.3	30.0	22.9	25.8
$20,000 to $29,999	15.4	14.7	13.9	16.9	19.0	17.1	15.6	15.3	18.9	19.4
$30,000 to $39,999	13.1	14.0	14.1	13.3	14.8	11.1	9.3	8.4	13.5	13.2
$40,000 to $49,999	10.2	11.7	12.5	7.9	11.6	6.8	5.3	4.4	8.7	7.2
$50,000 to $59,999	8.0	9.6	10.8	4.6	8.2	4.3	3.2	2.4	5.8	4.6
$60,000 to $69,999	6.2	7.7	9.0	2.7	5.2	2.7	1.8	1.0	3.8	2.8
$70,000 to $79,999	4.4	5.5	6.5	1.7	4.1	1.8	1.2	0.8	2.5	1.5
$80,000 to $89,999	2.8	3.6	4.3	0.8	2.0	1.1	0.7	0.3	1.5	1.0
$90,000 to $99,999	2.1	2.8	3.3	0.7	1.4	0.6	0.3	0.1	1.0	0.6
$100,000 or more	6.6	8.5	10.4	1.1	3.5	2.4	1.3	0.8	3.7	2.5

Source: Bureau of the Census, unpublished tables from the 1995 Current Population Survey

Income Distribution of Total Men by Age, 1994

(number and percent distribution of total men aged 15 or older by income and age, 1994; men in thousands as of 1995)

	total	< 25	25-34	35-44	45-54	55-64	65+
TOTAL	97,704	18,241	20,589	20,972	15,022	9,878	13,003
Without income	6,450	4,533	613	585	308	237	174
With income	91,254	13,708	19,976	20,386	14,714	9,641	12,829
Under $10,000	20,703	8,319	3,256	2,617	1,670	1,625	3,218
$10,000 to $19,999	21,376	3,661	5,179	3,445	2,040	1,944	5,108
$20,000 to $29,999	16,097	1,216	4,958	3,809	2,378	1,660	2,075
$30,000 to $39,999	11,542	306	3,053	3,557	2,387	1,338	903
$40,000 to $49,999	7,399	109	1,623	2,485	1,865	840	476
$50,000 to $74,999	8,643	61	1,354	2,731	2,624	1,259	614
$75,000 to $99,999	2,616	13	325	826	807	451	195
$100,000 or more	2,878	23	228	917	945	524	240
Median income							
Total men	$21,720	$7,048	$22,606	$30,707	$34,933	$27,075	$15,250
Year-round, full-time workers	31,612	15,860	26,572	35,586	40,367	37,799	35,667
PERCENT DISTRIB.	100.0%	100.0%	100.0%	100.0%	100.0%	100.0%	100.0%
Without income	6.6	24.9	3.0	2.8	2.1	2.4	1.3
With income	93.4	75.1	97.0	97.2	97.9	97.6	98.7
Under $10,000	21.2	45.6	15.8	12.5	11.1	16.5	24.7
$10,000 to $19,999	21.9	20.1	25.2	16.4	13.6	19.7	39.3
$20,000 to $29,999	16.5	6.7	24.1	18.2	15.8	16.8	16.0
$30,000 to $39,999	11.8	1.7	14.8	17.0	15.9	13.5	6.9
$40,000 to $49,999	7.6	0.6	7.9	11.8	12.4	8.5	3.7
$50,000 to $74,999	8.8	0.3	6.6	13.0	17.5	12.7	4.7
$75,000 to $99,999	2.7	0.1	1.6	3.9	5.4	4.6	1.5
$100,000 or more	2.9	0.1	1.1	4.4	6.3	5.3	1.8

Source: Bureau of the Census, unpublished tables from the 1995 Current Population Survey

Income Distribution of Total Women by Age, 1994

(number and percent distribution of total women aged 15 or older by income and age, 1994; women in thousands as of 1995)

	total	< 25	25-34	35-44	45-54	55-64	65+
TOTAL	105,028	18,052	20,799	21,363	15,672	10,878	18,264
Without income	9,881	4,735	1,625	1,232	1,005	867	417
With income	95,147	13,318	19,174	20,131	14,666	10,011	17,847
Under $10,000	42,771	9,481	6,784	6,852	4,724	4,730	10,199
$10,000 to $19,999	24,170	2,736	5,462	4,863	3,554	2,420	5,133
$20,000 to $29,999	13,612	845	3,770	3,659	2,593	1,336	1,411
$30,000 to $39,999	7,231	151	1,822	2,234	1,745	709	571
$40,000 to $49,999	3,490	43	715	1,202	959	379	192
$50,000 to $74,999	2,780	36	477	929	783	323	230
$75,000 to $99,999	542	11	66	197	156	55	57
$100,000 or more	552	14	80	192	153	59	54
Median income							
Total women	$11,466	$5,508	$14,884	$16,189	$17,051	$10,867	$8,950
Year-round, full-time workers	23,265	15,063	22,426	25,744	25,911	22,875	24,498
PERCENT DISTRIB.	100.0%	100.0%	100.0%	100.0%	100.0%	100.0%	100.0%
Without income	9.4	26.2	7.8	5.8	6.4	8.0	2.3
With income	90.6	73.8	92.2	94.2	93.6	92.0	97.7
Under $10,000	40.7	52.5	32.6	32.1	30.1	43.5	55.8
$10,000 to $19,999	23.0	15.2	26.3	22.8	22.7	22.2	28.1
$20,000 to $29,999	13.0	4.7	18.1	17.1	16.5	12.3	7.7
$30,000 to $39,999	6.9	0.8	8.8	10.5	11.1	6.5	3.1
$40,000 to $49,999	3.3	0.2	3.4	5.6	6.1	3.5	1.1
$50,000 to $74,999	2.6	0.2	2.3	4.3	5.0	3.0	1.3
$75,000 to $99,999	0.5	0.1	0.3	0.9	1.0	0.5	0.3
$100,000 or more	0.5	0.1	0.4	0.9	1.0	0.5	0.3

Source: Bureau of the Census, unpublished tables from the 1995 Current Population Survey

Median Earnings of Total Men and Women
Who Work Full-Time, 1980 to 1994

(median earnings of total men and women aged 15 or older who work year-round; full-time, and ratio of total female to total male median earnings, 1980-1994; percent change in earnings and ratio for selected years; in 1994 dollars)

| | median earnings | | ratio total |
	men	women	female/male
1994	$30,854	$22,205	0.72
1993	31,186	22,304	0.72
1992	31,897	22,579	0.71
1991	32,013	22,364	0.70
1990	31,384	22,476	0.72
1989	32,665	22,432	0.69
1988	33,393	22,056	0.66
1987	33,849	22,062	0.65
1986	34,151	21,949	0.64
1985	33,324	21,519	0.65
1984	33,118	21,082	0.64
1983	32,558	20,705	0.64
1982	32,674	20,174	0.62
1981	33,324	19,740	0.59
1980	33,515	20,163	0.60
Percent change			
1990-1994	-1.7%	-1.2%	0.5%
1980-1994	-7.9	10.1	19.6

Note: The female/male ratio is calculated by dividing the median earnings of women by the median earnings of men.
Source: Bureau of the Census, unpublished tables from the 1995 Current Population Survey

Median Earnings of Total Men and Women by Education, 1994

(median earnings of total men and women aged 25 or older by work experience and educational attainment, 1994)

	men		women	
	total	year-round full-time workers	total	year-round full-time workers
Total	$27,689	$32,131	$16,804	$23,165
Less than 9th grade	13,838	17,151	8,056	12,029
9th to 12th grade, no diploma	17,016	21,748	9,441	14,474
High school graduate	24,482	27,237	14,033	19,529
Some college, no degree	27,044	31,344	16,222	22,171
Associate's degree	31,111	35,121	20,113	25,214
Bachelor's degree or more	41,896	46,976	27,588	33,306
Bachelor's degree	39,067	42,049	25,248	30,740
Master's degree	46,096	51,354	32,679	37,546
Professional degree	63,575	72,090	37,056	48,284
Doctoral degree	57,250	60,270	41,127	46,479

Source: Bureau of the Census, unpublished tables from the 1995 Current Population Survey

Total Families Below the Poverty Level, 1980 to 1994

(total number of families, and number and percent below poverty level by type of family and presence of children under age 18, 1980-94; percent change in numbers and rates for selected years; families in thousands as of March the following year)

	total families			married couples			female hh, no spouse present		
		in poverty			in poverty			in poverty	
	total	number	percent	total	number	percent	total	number	percent
With & without									
children <18									
1994	69,313	8,053	11.6%	53,885	3,272	6.1%	12,220	4,232	34.6%
1993	68,506	8,393	12.3	53,181	3,481	6.5	12,411	4,424	35.6
1992	68,216	8,144	11.9	53,090	3,385	6.4	12,061	4,275	35.4
1991	67,173	7,712	11.5	52,457	3,158	6.0	11,692	4,161	35.6
1990	66,322	7,098	10.7	52,147	2,961	5.7	11,268	3,768	33.4
1989	66,090	6,784	10.3	52,137	2,931	5.6	10,890	3,504	32.2
1988	65,837	6,874	10.4	52,100	2,897	5.6	10,890	3,642	33.4
1987	65,204	7,005	10.7	51,675	3,011	5.8	10,696	3,654	34.2
1986	64,491	7,023	10.9	51,537	3,123	6.1	10,445	3,613	34.6
1985	63,558	7,223	11.4	50,933	3,438	6.7	10,211	3,474	34.0
1984	62,706	7,277	11.6	50,350	3,488	6.9	10,129	3,498	34.5
1983	62,015	7,647	12.3	50,061	3,815	7.6	9,896	3,564	36.0
1982	61,393	7,512	12.2	49,906	3,789	7.6	9,469	3,434	36.3
1981	61,019	6,851	11.2	49,630	3,394	6.8	9,403	3,252	34.6
1980	60,309	6,217	10.3	49,294	3,032	6.2	9,082	2,972	32.7
Percent change									
1990-1994	4.5%	13.5%	8.4%	3.3%	10.5%	7.0%	8.4%	12.3%	3.6%
1980-1994	14.9	29.5	12.6	9.3	7.9	-1.6	34.6	42.4	5.8

(continued)

(continued from previous page)

	total families			married couples			female hh, no spouse present		
		in poverty			in poverty			in poverty	
	total	number	percent	total	number	percent	total	number	percent
With children <18									
1994	36,782	6,406	17.4%	26,367	2,197	8.3%	8,665	3,816	44.0%
1993	36,456	6,751	18.5	26,121	2,363	9.0	8,758	4,034	46.1
1992	35,851	6,457	18.0	25,907	2,237	8.6	8,375	3,867	46.2
1991	34,861	6,170	17.7	25,357	2,106	8.3	7,991	3,767	47.1
1990	34,503	5,676	16.4	25,410	1,990	7.8	7,707	3,426	44.5
1989	34,279	5,306	15.5	25,476	1,872	7.3	7,445	3,190	42.8
1988	34,251	5,373	15.7	25,596	1,847	7.2	7,361	3,294	44.7
1987	33,996	5,465	16.1	25,464	1,963	7.7	7,216	3,281	45.5
1986	33,801	5,516	16.3	25,571	2,050	8.0	7,094	3,264	46.0
1985	33,536	5,586	16.7	25,496	2,258	8.9	6,892	3,131	45.4
1984	32,942	5,662	17.2	25,038	2,344	9.4	6,832	3,124	45.7
1983	32,787	5,871	17.9	25,216	2,557	10.1	6,622	3,122	47.1
1982	32,565	5,712	17.5	25,276	2,470	9.8	6,397	3,059	47.8
1981	32,587	5,191	15.9	25,278	2,199	8.7	6,488	2,877	44.3
1980	32,773	4,822	14.7	25,671	1,974	7.7	6,299	2,703	42.9
Percent change									
1990-1994	6.6%	12.9%	6.1%	3.8%	10.4%	6.4%	12.4%	11.4%	-1.1%
1980-1994	12.2	32.8	18.4	2.7	11.3	7.8	37.6	41.2	2.6

Source: Bureau of the Census, unpublished tables from the 1995 Current Population Survey

Total Persons in Poverty by Age and Sex, 1994

(total number of persons, and number and percent below poverty level by age and sex, 1994; persons in thousands as of 1995)

	total	in poverty	
		number	percent
Total	261,616	38,059	14.5%
Under age 18	70,020	15,289	21.8
Aged 18 to 24	25,158	4,538	18.0
Aged 25 to 34	41,388	5,463	13.2
Aged 35 to 44	42,334	4,467	10.6
Aged 45 to 54	30,693	2,381	7.8
Aged 55 to 59	10,844	1,129	10.4
Aged 60 to 64	9,911	1,129	11.4
Aged 65 to 74	18,214	1,842	10.1
Aged 75 or older	13,053	1,821	13.9
Female, total	133,778	21,744	16.3
Under age 18	34,191	7,604	22.2
Aged 18 to 24	12,612	2,833	22.5
Aged 25 to 34	20,799	3,359	16.1
Aged 35 to 44	21,363	2,539	11.9
Aged 45 to 54	15,672	1,348	8.6
Aged 55 to 59	5,680	693	12.2
Aged 60 to 64	5,198	644	12.4
Aged 65 to 74	10,117	1,288	12.7
Aged 75 or older	8,147	1,436	17.6
Male, total	127,838	16,316	12.8
Under age 18	35,830	7,684	21.4
Aged 18 to 24	12,545	1,705	13.6
Aged 25 to 34	20,589	2,104	10.2
Aged 35 to 44	20,972	1,929	9.2
Aged 45 to 54	15,022	1,033	6.9
Aged 55 to 59	5,164	436	8.5
Aged 60 to 64	4,714	485	10.3
Aged 65 to 74	8,097	555	6.8
Aged 75 or older	4,906	385	7.8

Source: Bureau of the Census, unpublished tables from the 1995 Current Population Survey

Total Population:
Labor Force

Sixty-seven percent of Americans aged 16 or older are in the labor force, including 75 percent of men and 59 percent of women. Labor force participation rates peak for men in the 25-to-34 age group, at 93 percent. They peak for women in the 35-to-44 age group, at 77 percent.

Forty-five percent of all households have two or more earners, while 22 percent have no earners—mostly retired elderly. Only one in three households has a single eaner. Among all married couples, 55 percent are dual earners, while 22 percent are traditional—meaning only the husband works.

Just over 28 percent of all employed workers are in managerial or professional specialty occupations. Another 30 percent are technical, sales, or administrative support workers. Nearly 42 percent of women are in technical, sales, or administrative support work, versus 20 percent of men. Conversely, 18 percent of men are precision production, craft, or repair workers versus only 2 percent of women. Overall, 15 percent of employed wage and salary workers are union members, including 17 percent of men and 12 percent of women.

Between 1994 and 2005, the total labor force will grow by 12 percent. Labor force participation rates for women are projected to increase from 59 to 62 percent, while those for men should fall from 75 to 73 percent.

Employment Status of the Total Population by Age and Sex, 1995

(employment status of the civilian noninstitutional population aged 16 or older, by age and sex, 1995; numbers in thousands)

			civilian labor force				not in labor force	
	total	percent of population	employed	percent of labor force	unem- ployed	percent of labor force	total	percent of population
Total persons	132,304	66.6%	124,900	94.4%	7,404	5.6%	66,280	33.4%
Aged 16 to 19	7,765	53.5	6,419	82.7	1,346	17.3	6,746	46.5
Aged 20 to 24	13,688	76.6	12,443	90.9	1,244	9.1	4,176	23.4
Aged 25 to 34	34,198	83.8	32,356	94.6	1,841	5.4	6,600	16.2
Aged 35 to 44	35,751	84.6	34,202	95.7	1,549	4.3	6,503	15.4
Aged 45 to 54	25,223	81.4	24,378	96.6	844	3.3	5,751	18.6
Aged 55 to 64	11,860	57.2	11,435	96.4	425	3.6	8,875	42.8
Aged 65 or older	3,819	12.1	3,666	96.0	153	4.0	27,628	87.9
Total men	71,360	75.0	67,377	94.4	3,983	5.6	23,818	25.0
Aged 16 to 19	4,036	54.8	3,292	81.6	744	18.4	3,331	45.2
Aged 20 to 24	7,338	83.1	6,665	90.8	673	9.2	1,497	16.9
Aged 25 to 34	18,670	93.0	17,709	94.9	961	5.1	1,409	7.0
Aged 35 to 44	19,189	92.3	18,374	95.8	815	4.2	1,611	7.7
Aged 45 to 54	13,421	88.8	12,958	96.6	464	3.5	1,690	11.2
Aged 55 to 64	6,504	66.0	6,272	96.4	233	3.6	3,352	34.0
Aged 65 or older	2,201	16.8	2,108	95.8	94	4.3	10,929	83.2
Total women	60,944	58.9	57,523	94.4	3,421	5.6	42,462	41.1
Aged 16 to 19	3,729	52.2	3,127	83.9	602	16.1	3,415	47.8
Aged 20 to 24	6,349	70.3	5,779	91.0	571	9.0	2,680	29.7
Aged 25 to 34	15,528	74.9	14,647	94.3	880	5.7	5,191	25.1
Aged 35 to 44	16,562	77.2	15,828	95.6	735	4.4	4,891	22.8
Aged 45 to 54	11,801	74.4	11,421	96.8	381	3.2	4,061	25.6
Aged 55 to 64	5,356	49.2	5,163	96.4	193	3.6	5,524	50.8
Aged 65 or older	1,618	8.8	1,558	96.3	60	3.7	16,699	91.2

Note: The civilian labor force equals the number employed plus the number unemployed. The civilian population equals the number in the labor force plus the number not in the labor force.
Source: Bureau of Labor Statistics, Employment and Earnings, *January 1996*

Total Households by Number of Earners, 1994

(number and percent distribution of total households, by number of earners, 1994; numbers in thousands)

	number	percent
Total households	97,107	100.0%
No earners	21,169	21.8
One earner	32,337	33.3
Two or more earners	43,601	44.9
Two earners	33,987	35.0
Three earners	7,186	7.4
Four or more earners	2,428	2.5

Source: Bureau of the Census, Internet web site, http://www.census.gov

Labor Force Status of Total Married Couples, 1994

(number and percent distribution of total married couples, by age of householder and labor force status of husband and wife, 1994; numbers in thousands)

	total married couples	husband and wife	husband only	wife only	neither husband nor wife in labor force
Total, number	53,171	29,279	11,665	3,069	9,158
Under age 20	78	45	27	-	5
Aged 20 to 24	1,495	979	459	32	25
Aged 25 to 29	4,021	2,813	1,048	103	56
Aged 30 to 34	6,351	4,427	1,664	145	115
Aged 35 to 39	7,118	4,923	1,899	157	139
Aged 40 to 44	6,573	4,852	1,384	201	136
Aged 45 to 49	5,763	4,151	1,203	237	172
Aged 50 to 54	4,961	3,297	1,155	297	212
Aged 55 to 59	3,914	2,036	1,037	398	443
Aged 60 to 64	3,651	1,066	830	626	1,129
Aged 65 to 74	6,061	589	760	725	3,986
Aged 75 to 84	2,705	71	173	125	2,336
Aged 85 or older	481	29	26	22	405
Total, percent	100.0%	55.1%	21.9%	5.8%	17.2%
Under age 20	100.0	57.7	34.6	-	6.4
Aged 20 to 24	100.0	65.5	30.7	2.1	1.7
Aged 25 to 29	100.0	70.0	26.1	2.6	1.4
Aged 30 to 34	100.0	69.7	26.2	2.3	1.8
Aged 35 to 39	100.0	69.2	26.7	2.2	2.0
Aged 40 to 44	100.0	73.8	21.1	3.1	2.1
Aged 45 to 49	100.0	72.0	20.9	4.1	3.0
Aged 50 to 54	100.0	66.5	23.3	6.0	4.3
Aged 55 to 59	100.0	52.0	26.5	10.2	11.3
Aged 60 to 64	100.0	29.2	22.7	17.1	30.9
Aged 65 to 74	100.0	9.7	12.5	12.0	65.8
Aged 75 to 84	100.0	2.6	6.4	4.6	86.4
Aged 85 or older	100.0	6.0	5.4	4.6	84.2

Note: (-) means number in sample is too small to make a reliable estimate.
Source: Bureau of the Census, Household and Family Characteristics: March 1994, *Current Population Reports, P20-483, 1995*

Occupations of the Total Population by Sex, 1995

(number and percent distribution of employed persons aged 16 or older in the civilian labor force, by occupation and sex, 1995; numbers in thousands)

	total	men	women
Total employed, number	124,900	67,377	57,523
Total employed, percent	100.0%	100.0%	100.0%
Managerial and professional specialty	28.3	27.3	29.4
Executive, administrative, and managerial	13.8	14.6	12.8
Professional specialty	14.5	12.7	16.7
Technical, sales, and administrative support	30.0	19.8	41.9
Technicians and related support	3.1	2.8	3.5
Sales occupations	12.1	11.3	13.0
Administrative support, including clerical	14.7	5.6	25.4
Service occupations	13.6	10.1	17.7
Private household	0.7	0.1	1.4
Protective service	1.8	2.8	0.6
Service, except private household and protective	11.1	7.2	15.7
Precision production, craft, and repair	10.8	18.3	2.1
Operators, fabricators, and laborers	14.5	20.3	7.6
Machine operators, assemblers, and inspectors	6.3	7.4	5.1
Transportation and material moving occupations	4.1	6.9	0.9
Handlers, equipment cleaners, helpers, and laborers	4.0	6.0	1.7
Farming, forestry, and fishing	2.9	4.3	1.3

Source: Bureau of Labor Statistics, Employment and Earnings, *January 1996*

Union Membership of the Total Population, 1995

(number of employed wage and salary workers aged 16 or older, number and percent who are represented by unions or are union members, and median weekly earnings by union membership status; by sex, 1995; numbers in thousands)

	total	men	women
Total employed	110,038	57,669	52,369
Represented by unions*	18,346	10,868	7,479
Percent of employed	16.7%	18.8%	14.3%
Members of unions**	16,360	9,929	6,430
Percent of employed	14.9%	17.2%	12.3%
Median weekly earnings, total*	$479	$538	$406
Represented by unions*	598	638	523
Members of unions**	602	640	527
Non-union	447	507	386

* Members of a labor union or an employee association similar to a union as well as workers who report no union affiliation but whose jobs are covered by a union or an employee association contract.
** Members of a labor union or an employee association similar to a union.
*** Full-time wage and salary workers.
Source: Bureau of Labor Statistics, Employment and Earnings, *January 1996*

Labor Force Projections of the Total Population by Sex, 1994 to 2005

(number of persons aged 16 or older in the civilian labor force and labor force participation rate in 1994 and 2005, by sex; percent change in number and percentage point change in rate; numbers in thousands)

	1994	2005	percent change 1994-2005
Number in labor force			
Total	131,056	147,106	12.2%
Men	70,817	76,842	8.5
Women	60,239	70,263	16.6

	1994	2005	percentage point change 1994-2005
Labor force participation rate			
Total	66.6%	67.1%	0.5
Men	75.1	72.9	-2.2
Women	58.8	61.7	2.9

Source: Bureau of Labor Statistics, Monthly Labor Review, *November 1995*

Workers Entering and Leaving the Labor Force, 1994 to 2005

(number of persons aged 16 or older in the civilian labor force and projected entrants and leavers, by sex, race, and Hispanic origin, 1994 and 2005; numbers in thousands)

	total labor force, 1994	entrants 1994-2005	leavers 1994-2005	total labor force, 2005
TOTAL PERSONS, NUMBER	131,051	39,343	23,289	147,106
Men	70,814	19,720	13,691	76,842
Women	60,238	19,624	9,598	70,263
White, non-Hispanic	100,463	26,058	18,177	108,345
Men	54,306	12,937	10,814	56,429
Women	46,157	13,122	7,363	51,916
Black, non-Hispanic	14,304	4,871	2,783	16,392
Men	6,981	2,314	1,512	7,783
Women	7,323	2,557	1,271	8,609
Hispanic	11,974	6,085	1,729	16,330
Men	7,210	3,321	1,039	9,492
Women	4,764	2,765	690	6,838
Asian and other, non-Hispanic	4,310	2,329	600	6,039
Men	2,317	1,148	326	3,139
Women	1,994	1,180	274	2,900
TOTAL PERSONS, PERCENT	100.0%	100.0%	100.0%	100.0%
Men	54.0	50.1	58.8	52.2
Women	46.0	49.9	41.2	47.8
White, non-Hispanic	76.7	66.2	78.0	73.7
Men	41.4	32.9	46.4	38.4
Women	35.2	33.4	31.6	35.3
Black, non-Hispanic	10.9	12.4	12.0	11.1
Men	5.3	5.9	6.5	5.3
Women	5.6	6.5	5.5	5.9
Hispanic	9.1	15.5	7.4	11.1
Men	5.5	8.4	4.5	6.5
Women	3.6	7.0	3.0	4.6
Asian and other, non-Hispanic	3.3	5.9	2.6	4.1
Men	1.8	2.9	1.4	2.1
Women	1.5	3.0	1.2	2.0

Note: Hispanics may be of any race and most are white. For a breakdown of the Hispanic composition of racial groups and the racial composition of Hispanics, see the tables in the introduction to this book.
Source: Bureau of Labor Statistics, Monthly Labor Review, *November 1995*

Total Population:
Population

The total U.S. population is projected to grow from 265 million in 1996 to 323 million by 2020, according to the Census Bureau. The rate of population growth, projected at 10.1 percent during the 1990s, should slow to just 8.4 percent from 2000 to 2010.

Nearly 20 million Americans are foreign born, with the largest share from Mexico (22 percent). Overall, only 6 percent of Americans aged 5 or older do not speak English "very well," but among the foreign born, 47 percent do not speak English fluently.

The United States received over 800,000 immigrants in 1994. Thirty-six percent were from Asia, 14 percent from Mexico. The largest single ancestry group in the U.S. is German, claimed by 58 million people.

Thirty-five percent of Americans live in the South. The West should surpass the Midwest in population to become the second most populous region shortly after the turn of the century. California is the most populous state, home to 12 percent of Americans. This share should climb to 15 percent by 2020, due in large part to the immigration of both Hispanics and Asians.

New York is by far the nation's largest metropolitan area, with over 19 million people in 1990. Among the 75 largest metro areas, Asians account for the largest share of the population in San Francisco (15 percent), blacks in Greensboro-Winston-Salem-Highpoint, North Carolina (41 percent), Hispanics in El Paso (70 percent), and Native Americans in Tulsa, Oklahoma (6.8 percent).

Total Population by Race and Ethnicity, 1990 to 2020

(number and percent distribution of persons by race and ethnicity, selected years 1990-2020; numbers in thousands)

	1990		1996		2000		2010		2020	
	number	percent	number	percent	number	percent	number	percent	number	percent
Total persons	249,415	100.0%	265,253	100.0%	274,634	100.0%	297,716	100.0%	322,742	100.0%
White	209,150	83.9	219,641	82.8	225,532	82.1	239,588	80.5	254,887	79.0
Non-Hispanic white	188,559	75.6	194,353	73.3	197,061	71.8	202,390	68.0	207,393	64.3
Black	30,620	12.3	33,611	12.7	35,454	12.9	40,109	13.5	45,075	14.0
Non-Hispanic black	29,400	11.8	31,999	12.1	33,568	12.2	37,466	12.6	41,538	12.9
Asian	7,570	3.0	9,728	3.7	11,245	4.1	15,265	5.1	19,651	6.1
Non-Hispanic Asian	7,096	2.8	9,141	3.4	10,584	3.9	14,402	4.8	18,557	5.7
Native American	2,075	0.8	2,273	0.9	2,402	0.9	2,754	0.9	3,129	1.0
Non-Hispanic Native Amer.	1,806	0.7	1,956	0.7	2,054	0.7	2,320	0.8	2,601	0.8
Hispanic	22,554	9.0	27,804	10.5	31,366	11.4	41,139	13.8	52,652	16.3

Note: Hispanics may be of any race and most are white. For a breakdown of the Hispanic composition of racial groups or the racial composition of Hispanics, see the tables in the introduction to this book. The 1990 population figures are for July 1, 1990.
Sources: Bureau of the Census, Population Projections of the United States, by Age, Sex, Race, and Hispanic Origin: 1995 to 2050, Current Population Reports, P25-1130, 1996; and U.S. Population Estimates, by Age, Sex, Race, and Hispanic Origin: 1980 to 1991, Current Population Reports, P25-1095, 1993

Total Population by Age, 1990 to 2020

(number of persons by age, selected years 1990-2020; percent change 1990-2000 and 2000-2010; numbers in thousands)

	1990	1996	2000	2010	2020	percent change 1990-2000	percent change 2000-2010
Total							
persons	249,415	265,253	274,634	297,716	322,742	10.1%	8.4%
Under 5	18,874	19,403	18,987	20,012	21,979	0.6	5.4
5 to 9	18,064	19,555	19,920	19,489	21,548	10.3	-2.2
10 to 14	17,191	19,096	20,057	20,231	21,334	16.7	0.9
15 to 19	17,754	18,578	19,820	21,782	21,364	11.6	9.9
20 to 24	19,131	17,363	18,257	21,134	21,298	-4.6	15.8
25 to 29	21,229	19,004	17,722	19,710	21,569	-16.5	11.2
30 to 34	21,907	21,370	19,511	18,582	21,365	-10.9	-4.8
35 to 39	19,976	22,536	22,180	18,536	20,534	11.0	-16.4
40 to 44	17,789	20,775	22,479	19,985	19,078	26.4	-11.1
45 to 49	13,819	18,420	19,806	21,884	18,376	43.3	10.5
50 to 54	11,367	13,921	17,224	21,680	19,363	51.5	25.9
55 to 59	10,473	11,359	13,307	19,068	21,165	27.1	43.3
60 to 64	10,618	10,001	10,654	16,215	20,549	0.3	52.2
65 to 69	10,077	9,891	9,410	12,112	17,530	-6.6	28.7
70 to 74	8,021	8,794	8,726	8,945	13,855	8.8	2.5
75 to 79	6,145	6,876	7,415	7,124	9,435	20.7	-3.9
80 to 84	3,932	4,564	4,900	5,557	5,940	24.6	13.4
85 or older	3,050	3,746	4,260	5,671	6,460	39.7	33.1
18 to 24	26,828	24,617	26,258	30,137	29,919	-2.1	14.8
18 or older	185,230	195,874	203,852	225,206	245,138	10.1	10.5
65 or older	31,224	33,872	34,709	39,408	53,220	11.2	13.5

Source: Bureau of the Census, Population Projections of the United States, by Age, Sex, Race, and Hispanic Origin: 1995 to 2050, *Current Population Reports, P25-1130, 1996; and* U.S. Population Estimates, by Age, Sex, Race, and Hispanic Origin: 1980 to 1991, *Current Population Reports, P25-1095, 1993*

Total Population by Age and Sex, 1996

(number of persons by age and sex, and sex ratio by age, 1996; numbers in thousands)

	total	male	female	sex ratio*
Total persons	265,253	129,522	135,731	95
Under age 5	19,403	9,927	9,476	105
Aged 5 to 9	19,555	10,013	9,543	105
Aged 10 to 14	19,096	9,779	9,317	105
Aged 15 to 19	18,578	9,523	9,055	105
Aged 20 to 24	17,363	8,815	8,548	103
Aged 25 to 29	19,004	9,516	9,488	100
Aged 30 to 34	21,370	10,649	10,721	99
Aged 35 to 39	22,536	11,221	11,315	99
Aged 40 to 44	20,775	10,269	10,506	98
Aged 45 to 49	18,420	9,038	9,382	96
Aged 50 to 54	13,921	6,760	7,161	94
Aged 55 to 59	11,359	5,451	5,908	92
Aged 60 to 64	10,001	4,711	5,290	89
Aged 65 to 69	9,891	4,502	5,389	84
Aged 70 to 74	8,794	3,821	4,973	77
Aged 75 to 79	6,876	2,818	4,059	69
Aged 80 to 84	4,564	1,660	2,904	57
Aged 85 or older	3,746	1,050	2,697	39
Aged 18 to 24	24,617	12,516	12,099	103
Aged 18 or older	195,874	93,982	101,892	92
Aged 65 or older	33,872	13,850	20,022	69

* The sex ratio is the number of males per 100 females.
Source: Bureau of the Census, Population Projections of the United States, by Age, Sex, Race, and Hispanic Origin: 1995 to 2050, Current Population Reports, P25-1130, 1996

Foreign-Born Population by Country of Origin, 1990

(number and percent distribution of the foreign-born population and percent of the foreign born aged 5 or older who do not speak English "very well," for the 20 largest foreign-born populations in the United States, ranked by size, 1990; numbers in thousands)

	number	percent of total foreign born	% who do not speak English very well*
Total persons	248,710	–	6.1%
Total native born	228,943	–	2.3
Total foreign born	19,767	100.0%	47.0
Mexico	4,298	21.7	70.7
Philippines	913	4.6	31.8
Canada	745	3.8	5.0
Cuba	737	3.7	60.1
Germany	712	3.6	13.1
United Kingdom	640	3.2	1.1
Italy	581	2.9	42.0
Korea	568	2.9	62.0
Vietnam	543	2.7	66.2
China	530	2.7	72.1
El Salvador	465	2.4	72.4
India	450	2.3	27.1
Poland	388	2.0	46.8
Dominican Republic	348	1.8	68.7
Jamaica	334	1.7	1.7
Former Soviet Union	334	1.7	52.1
Japan	290	1.5	56.2
Guatemala	286	1.4	70.7
Taiwan	244	1.2	57.9
Colombia	226	1.1	61.1

* Among those aged 5 or older.
Note: The 1990 population figures are for April 1, 1990.
Source: Bureau of the Census, The Foreign-Born Population in the United States, 1990, *Census of Population, 1990 CP-3-1, 1993*

Total Immigrants by Country of Birth, 1994

(number and percent distribution of immigrants to the U.S. by world region and country; for countries sending at least 6,000 immigrants to the U.S.; 1994)

	number	percent
Total immigrants	804,416	100.0%
Europe	160,916	20.0
Soviet Union	63,420	7.9
Poland	28,048	3.5
Ireland	17,256	2.1
United Kingdom	16,326	2.0
Germany	6,992	0.9
Asia	292,589	36.4
China, mainland	53,985	6.7
Philippines	53,535	6.7
Vietnam	41,345	5.1
India	34,921	4.3
Korea	16,011	2.0
Iran	11,422	1.4
Taiwan	10,032	1.2
Pakistan	8,698	1.1
Hong Kong	7,731	1.0
Japan	6,093	0.8
Iraq	6,025	0.7
Africa	26,712	3.3
Oceania	4,592	0.6
North America	272,226	33.8
Canada	16,068	2.0
Mexico	111,398	13.8
Caribbean	104,804	13.0
Dominican Republic	51,189	6.4
Cuba	14,727	1.8
Jamaica	14,349	1.8
Haiti	13,333	1.7
Trinidad & Tobago	6,292	0.8

(continued)

(continued from previous page)

	number	percent
Central America	39,906	5.0%
El Salvador	17,644	2.2
Guatemala	7,389	0.9
South America	47,377	5.9
Colombia	10,847	1.3
Peru	9,177	1.1
Guyana	7,662	1.0

Source: U.S. Immigration and Naturalization Service, Statistical Yearbook of the Immigration and Naturalization Service, *1995*

Ancestry of the Total Population, 1990

(number and percent distribution of persons by top 50 ancestry groups, ranked by size, 1990; numbers in thousands)

	number	percent
Total persons	248,710	100.0%
German	57,947	23.3
Irish	38,736	15.6
English	32,652	13.1
Afro-American	23,777	9.6
Italian	14,665	5.9
American	12,396	5.0
Mexican	11,587	4.7
French	10,321	4.1
Polish	9,366	3.8
American Indian	8,708	3.5
Dutch	6,227	2.5
Scotch-Irish	5,618	2.3
Scottish	5,394	2.2
Swedish	4,681	1.9
Norwegian	3,869	1.6
Russian	2,953	1.2
French Canadian	2,167	0.9
Welsh	2,034	0.8
Spanish	2,024	0.8
Puerto Rican	1,955	0.8
Slovak	1,883	0.8
White	1,800	0.7
Danish	1,635	0.7
Hungarian	1,582	0.6
Chinese	1,505	0.6
Filipino	1,451	0.6
Czech	1,296	0.5
Portuguese	1,153	0.5
British	1,119	0.4
Hispanic	1,113	0.4
Greek	1,110	0.4
Swiss	1,045	0.4
Japanese	1,005	0.4

(continued)

(continued from previous page)

	number	percent
Austrian	865	0.3%
Cuban	860	0.3
Korean	837	0.3
Lithuanian	812	0.3
Ukrainian	741	0.3
Scandinavian	679	0.3
Acadian/Cajun	668	0.3
Finnish	659	0.3
United States	644	0.3
Asian Indian	570	0.2
Canadian	550	0.2
Croatian	544	0.2
Vietnamese	536	0.2
Dominican	506	0.2
Salvadorian	499	0.2
European	467	0.2
Jamaican	435	0.2

Note: Since those who reported multiple ancestries were included in more than one group, the sum of the persons reporting an ancestry is greater than the total number of persons.
Source: Bureau of the Census, Detailed Ancestry Groups for States, *CP-S-1-2, 1990*

Total Population by Region and Division, 1990 to 2020

(number and percent distribution of persons by region and division, selected years 1990-2020; percent change in number and percentage point change in distribution, 1990-2000 and 2000-2010; numbers in thousands)

	1990	1995	2000	2010	2020	percent change 1990-2000	percent change 2000-2010
Number							
UNITED STATES	248,710	263,434	276,241	300,431	325,942	11.1%	8.8%
Northeast	50,809	51,440	51,885	53,301	55,352	2.1	2.7
New England	13,207	13,198	13,217	13,754	14,527	0.1	4.1
Middle Atlantic	37,602	38,243	38,668	39,547	40,824	2.8	2.3
Midwest	59,669	61,994	63,837	66,332	68,984	7.0	3.9
East North Central	42,009	43,610	44,806	46,258	47,799	6.7	3.2
West North Central	17,660	18,383	19,031	20,074	21,185	7.8	5.5
South	85,446	91,726	97,241	107,385	117,498	13.8	10.4
South Atlantic	43,567	47,017	50,004	55,321	60,610	14.8	10.6
East South Central	15,176	16,018	16,762	17,941	19,078	10.5	7.0
West South Central	26,703	28,690	30,476	34,124	37,809	14.1	12.0
West	52,786	58,273	63,277	73,412	84,109	19.9	16.0
Mountain	13,659	15,384	16,889	19,094	21,147	23.6	13.1
Pacific	39,127	42,890	46,388	54,318	62,961	18.6	17.1

	1990	1995	2000	2010	2020	percentage point change 1990-2000	percentage point change 200-2010
Percent distribution							
UNITED STATES	100.0%	100.0%	100.0%	100.0%	100.0%	-	-
Northeast	20.4	19.5	18.8	17.7	17.0	-1.6	-1.1
New England	5.3	5.0	4.8	4.6	4.5	-0.5	-0.2
Middle Atlantic	15.1	14.5	14.0	13.2	12.5	-1.1	-0.8
Midwest	24.0	23.5	23.1	22.1	21.2	-0.9	-1.0
East North Central	16.9	16.6	16.2	15.4	14.7	-0.7	-0.8
West North Central	7.1	7.0	6.9	6.7	6.5	-0.2	-0.2
South	34.4	34.8	35.2	35.7	36.0	0.8	0.5
South Atlantic	17.5	17.8	18.1	18.4	18.6	0.6	0.3
East South Central	6.1	6.1	6.1	6.0	5.9	0.0	-0.1
West South Central	10.7	10.9	11.0	11.4	11.6	0.3	0.4
West	21.2	22.1	22.9	24.4	25.8	1.7	1.5
Mountain	5.5	5.8	6.1	6.4	6.5	0.6	0.3
Pacific	15.7	16.3	16.8	18.1	19.3	1.1	1.3

Note: The 1990 population figures are for April 1, 1990. Projections of the total population for 2000, 2010, and 2020 are different from those at the beginning of the population section because they are from an earlier report for states and regions.
Source: Bureau of the Census, Population Projections for States, by Age, Sex, Race, and Hispanic Origin: 1993 to 2020, *Current Population Reports, P25-1111, 1994*

Total Population by State, 1990 to 2020

(number of persons by state, selected years 1995-2020; and percent change 1995-2020; numbers in thousands)

	1995	2000	2010	2020	percent change 1995-2020
United States	263,434	276,241	300,431	325,942	23.7%
Alabama	4,274	4,485	4,856	5,231	22.4
Alaska	634	699	781	866	36.6
Arizona	4,072	4,437	5,074	5,713	40.3
Arkansas	2,468	2,578	2,782	3,005	21.8
California	32,398	34,888	41,085	47,953	48.0
Colorado	3,710	4,059	4,494	4,871	31.3
Connecticut	3,274	3,271	3,412	3,617	10.5
Delaware	718	759	815	871	21.3
District of Columbia	559	537	577	636	13.8
Florida	14,210	15,313	17,372	19,449	36.9
Georgia	7,102	7,637	8,553	9,426	32.7
Hawaii	1,221	1,327	1,551	1,815	48.6
Idaho	1,156	1,290	1,454	1,600	38.4
Illinois	11,853	12,168	12,652	13,218	11.5
Indiana	5,820	6,045	6,286	6,488	11.5
Iowa	2,861	2,930	2,981	3,038	6.2
Kansas	2,601	2,722	2,922	3,130	20.3
Kentucky	3,851	3,989	4,160	4,313	12.0
Louisiana	4,359	4,478	4,808	5,193	19.1
Maine	1,236	1,240	1,309	1,400	13.3
Maryland	5,078	5,322	5,782	6,289	23.8
Massachusetts	5,976	5,950	6,097	6,363	6.5
Michigan	9,575	9,759	10,033	10,377	8.4
Minnesota	4,619	4,824	5,127	5,426	17.5
Mississippi	2,666	2,750	2,918	3,100	16.3
Missouri	5,286	5,437	5,760	6,123	15.8
Montana	862	920	996	1,071	24.2
Nebraska	1,644	1,704	1,793	1,885	14.7
Nevada	1,477	1,691	1,935	2,145	45.2
New Hampshire	1,132	1,165	1,280	1,399	23.6
New Jersey	7,931	8,135	8,562	9,058	14.2
New Mexico	1,676	1,823	2,082	2,338	39.5
New York	18,178	18,237	18,546	19,111	5.1

(continued)

(continued from previous page)

	1995	2000	2010	2020	percent change 1995-2020
North Carolina	7,150	7,617	8,341	9,014	26.1%
North Dakota	637	643	676	719	12.9
Ohio	11,203	11,453	11,659	11,870	6.0
Oklahoma	3,271	3,382	3,683	4,020	22.9
Oregon	3,141	3,404	3,876	4,367	39.0
Pennsylvania	12,134	12,296	12,438	12,656	4.3
Rhode Island	1,001	998	1,034	1,090	8.9
South Carolina	3,732	3,932	4,311	4,685	25.5
South Dakota	735	770	815	863	17.4
Tennessee	5,228	5,538	6,007	6,434	23.1
Texas	18,592	20,039	22,850	25,592	37.7
Utah	1,944	2,148	2,462	2,749	41.4
Vermont	579	592	623	658	13.6
Virginia	6,646	7,048	7,728	8,388	26.2
Washington	5,497	6,070	7,025	7,960	44.8
West Virginia	1,824	1,840	1,842	1,852	1.5
Wisconsin	5,159	5,381	5,629	5,846	13.3
Wyoming	487	522	596	658	35.1

Note: Projections of the total population for 2000, 2010, and 2020 are different from those at the beginning of the population section because they are from an earlier report for states and regions.
Source: Bureau of the Census, Population Projections for States, by Age, Sex, Race, and Hispanic Origin: 1993 to 2020, *Current Population Reports, P25-1111, 1994*

Distribution of the Total Population by State, 1995 to 2020

(percent distribution of the total population by state, selected years 1995-2020; numbers in thousands)

	1995	*2000*	*2010*	*2020*
United States	100.0%	100.0%	100.0%	100.0%
Alabama	1.6	1.6	1.6	1.6
Alaska	0.2	0.3	0.3	0.3
Arizona	1.5	1.6	1.7	1.8
Arkansas	0.9	0.9	0.9	0.9
California	12.3	12.6	13.7	14.7
Colorado	1.4	1.5	1.5	1.5
Connecticut	1.2	1.2	1.1	1.1
Delaware	0.3	0.3	0.3	0.3
District of Columbia	0.2	0.2	0.2	0.2
Florida	5.4	5.5	5.8	6.0
Georgia	2.7	2.8	2.8	2.9
Hawaii	0.5	0.5	0.5	0.6
Idaho	0.4	0.5	0.5	0.5
Illinois	4.5	4.4	4.2	4.1
Indiana	2.2	2.2	2.1	2.0
Iowa	1.1	1.1	1.0	0.9
Kansas	1.0	1.0	1.0	1.0
Kentucky	1.5	1.4	1.4	1.3
Louisiana	1.7	1.6	1.6	1.6
Maine	0.5	0.4	0.4	0.4
Maryland	1.9	1.9	1.9	1.9
Massachusetts	2.3	2.2	2.0	2.0
Michigan	3.6	3.5	3.3	3.2
Minnesota	1.8	1.7	1.7	1.7
Mississippi	1.0	1.0	1.0	1.0
Missouri	2.0	2.0	1.9	1.9
Montana	0.3	0.3	0.3	0.3
Nebraska	0.6	0.6	0.6	0.6
Nevada	0.6	0.6	0.6	0.7
New Hampshire	0.4	0.4	0.4	0.4
New Jersey	3.0	2.9	2.8	2.8
New Mexico	0.6	0.7	0.7	0.7
New York	6.9	6.6	6.2	5.9

(continued)

(continued from previous page)

	1995	2000	2010	2020
North Carolina	2.7%	2.8%	2.8%	2.8%
North Dakota	0.2	0.2	0.2	0.2
Ohio	4.3	4.1	3.9	3.6
Oklahoma	1.2	1.2	1.2	1.2
Oregon	1.2	1.2	1.3	1.3
Pennsylvania	4.6	4.5	4.1	3.9
Rhode Island	0.4	0.4	0.3	0.3
South Carolina	1.4	1.4	1.4	1.4
South Dakota	0.3	0.3	0.3	0.3
Tennessee	2.0	2.0	2.0	2.0
Texas	7.1	7.3	7.6	7.9
Utah	0.7	0.8	0.8	0.8
Vermont	0.2	0.2	0.2	0.2
Virginia	2.5	2.6	2.6	2.6
Washington	2.1	2.2	2.3	2.4
West Virginia	0.7	0.7	0.6	0.6
Wisconsin	2.0	1.9	1.9	1.8
Wyoming	0.2	0.2	0.2	0.2

Source: Bureau of the Census, Population Projections for States, by Age, Sex, Race, and Hispanic Origin: 1993 to 2020, *Current Population Reports, P25-1111, 1994*

Minority Populations of the 75 Largest Metropolitan Areas, 1990

(total population of the 75 largest metropolitan areas ranked by population; and minority shares of the total population, 1990; numbers in thousands)

		total	Asian	black	Hispanic	Native American
1.	New York-Northern New Jersey-Long Island, NY-NJ-CT-PA	19,342	4.6%	17.8%	14.7%	0.2%
2.	Los Angeles-Riverside-Orange County, CA	14,532	9.2	8.5	32.9	0.6
3.	Chicago-Gary-Kenosha, IL-IN-WI	8,240	3.1	19.0	10.9	0.2
4	Washington-Baltimore, DC-MD-VA-WV	6,727	3.7	25.2	3.9	0.3
5.	San Francisco-Oakland-San Jose, CA	6,253	14.8	8.6	15.5	0.7
6.	Philadelphia-Wilmington-Atlantic City, PA-NJ-DE-MD	5,893	2.0	18.4	3.8	0.2
7.	Boston-Brockton-Nashua, MA-NH-ME-CT	5,455	2.5	4.8	4.4	0.2
8.	Detroit-Ann Arbor-Flint, MI	5,187	1.4	20.5	2.0	0.4
9.	Dallas-Fort Worth, TX	4,037	2.4	14.0	13.0	0.5
10.	Houston-Galveston-Brazoria, TX	3,731	3.5	17.9	20.7	0.3
11.	Miami-Fort Lauderdale, FL	3,193	1.4	18.5	33.3	0.2
12.	Seattle-Tacoma-Bremerton, WA	2,970	6.1	4.5	3.0	1.3
13.	Atlanta, GA	2,960	1.8	25.2	2.0	0.2
14.	Cleveland-Akron, OH	2,860	1.0	15.6	1.9	0.2
15.	Minneapolis-St. Paul, MN-WI	2,539	2.6	3.5	1.5	1.0
16.	San Diego, CA	2,498	7.9	6.4	20.4	0.8
17.	St. Louis, MO-IL	2,493	1.0	17.0	1.1	0.2
18.	Pittsburgh, PA	2,395	0.7	7.5	0.6	0.1
19.	Phoenix-Mesa, AZ	2,238	1.6	3.5	17.0	2.2
20.	Tampa-St. Petersburg-Clearwater, FL	2,068	1.1	9.0	6.7	0.3
21.	Denver-Boulder-Greeley, CO	1,980	2.2	5.0	12.8	0.7
22.	Cincinnati-Hamilton, OH-KY-IN	1,818	0.8	11.2	0.5	0.1
23.	Portland-Salem, OR-WA	1,793	3.2	2.5	4.0	1.0
24.	Milwaukee-Racine, WI	1,607	1.2	13.3	3.8	0.5
25.	Kansas City, MO-KS	1,583	1.1	12.7	2.9	0.5
26.	Sacramento-Yolo, CA	1,481	7.7	6.9	11.6	1.1
27.	Norfolk-Virginia Beach-Newport News, VA-NC	1,443	2.4	28.3	2.3	0.3
28.	Indianapolis, IN	1,380	0.8	13.2	0.9	0.2
29.	Columbus, OH	1,345	1.6	12.1	0.8	0.2
30.	San Antonio, TX	1,325	1.2	6.7	47.4	0.4
31.	New Orleans, LA	1,285	1.7	34.8	4.2	0.3
32.	Orlando, FL	1,225	1.7	12.0	8.2	0.3
33.	Buffalo-Niagara Falls, NY	1,189	0.9	10.3	2.0	0.6
34.	Charlotte-Gastonia-Rock Hill, NC-SC	1,162	1.0	19.9	0.9	0.4
35.	Hartford, CT	1,158	1.5	8.3	6.9	0.2

(continued)

(continued from previous page)

		total	Asian	black	Hispanic	Native American
36.	Providence-Fall River-Warwick, RI-MA	1,134	1.8%	3.3%	4.2%	0.3%
37.	Salt Lake City-Ogden, UT	1,072	2.4	1.0	5.8	0.8
38.	Rochester, NY	1,062	1.3	8.9	3.0	0.3
39.	Nashville, TN	1,050	0.7	19.3	0.7	0.3
40.	Greensboro-Winston-Salem-High Point, NC	1,007	0.8	40.7	0.8	0.2
41.	Memphis, TN-AR-MS	985	1.0	15.5	0.8	0.2
42.	Oklahoma City, OK	959	1.9	10.5	3.6	4.8
43.	Dayton-Springfield, OH	951	1.0	13.3	0.8	0.2
44.	Louisville, KY-IN	949	0.6	12.9	0.6	0.2
45.	Grand Rapids-Muskegon-Holland, MI	938	0.9	6.9	3.1	0.6
46.	Jacksonville, FL	907	1.7	20.0	2.5	0.3
47.	Richmond-Petersburg, VA	866	1.4	29.2	1.1	0.3
48.	West Palm Beach-Boca Raton, FL	864	1.0	12.5	7.7	0.1
49.	Albany-Schenectady-Troy, NY	861	1.2	4.6	1.7	0.2
50.	Raleigh-Durham-Chapel Hill, NC	856	1.6	24.2	1.3	0.3
51.	Las Vegas, NV-AZ	853	3.1	8.4	10.4	1.1
52.	Austin-San Marcos, TX	846	2.2	9.4	20.9	0.4
53.	Birmingham, AL	840	0.5	28.7	0.4	0.2
54.	Honolulu, HI	836	63.0	3.1	6.8	0.4
55.	Greenville-Spartansburg-Anderson, SC	831	0.6	17.4	0.7	0.1
56.	Fresno, CA	756	7.7	4.8	35.3	1.1
57.	Syracuse, NY	742	1.1	5.7	1.4	0.6
58.	Tulsa, OK	709	0.9	8.2	2.1	6.8
59.	Tucson, AZ	667	1.8	3.1	24.5	3.0
60.	Omaha, NE-IA	640	1.0	8.0	2.6	0.5
61.	Scranton-Wilkes-Barre-Hazelton, PA	638	0.5	0.9	0.6	0.1
62.	Toledo, OH	614	1.0	11.4	3.3	0.2
63.	Youngstown-Warren, OH	601	0.4	9.4	1.3	0.2
64.	Allentown-Bethlehem-Easton, PA	595	1.1	2.0	4.6	0.1
65.	El Paso, TX	592	1.1	3.7	69.6	0.4
66.	Albuquerque, NM	589	1.4	2.5	37.1	5.1
67.	Harrisburg-Lebanon-Carlisle, PA	588	1.1	6.7	1.7	0.1
68.	Springfield, MA	588	1.4	6.3	8.5	0.2
69.	Knoxville, TN	586	0.8	6.1	0.5	0.2
70.	Bakersfield, CA	543	3.0	5.5	28.0	1.3
71.	Little Rock-North Little Rock, AR	513	0.7	19.9	0.8	0.4
72.	Charleston-North Charleston, SC	507	1.2	30.2	1.5	0.3
73.	Sarasota-Bradenton, FL	489	0.5	5.8	3.1	0.2
74.	Wichita, KS	485	1.9	7.6	4.1	1.1
75.	Stockton-Lodi, CA	481	12.4	5.6	23.4	1.1

Source: Bureau of the Census, Statistical Abstract of the United States 1993

Total Births by Age of Mother, 1993

(total number and percent distribution of births, by age of mother, 1993)

	number	percent
Total births	4,000,240	100.0%
Under age 15	12,554	0.3
Aged 15 to 19	501,093	12.5
Aged 20 to 24	1,038,127	26.0
Aged 25 to 29	1,128,862	28.2
Aged 30 to 34	901,151	22.5
Aged 35 to 39	357,053	8.9
Aged 40 or older	61,400	1.5

Source: National Center for Health Statistics, Advance Report of Final Natality Statistics, 1993, *Vol. 44, No. 3 Supplement, 1995*

Total Births to Unmarried Women by Age, 1993

(total number and percent of births to unmarried women, by age of mother, 1993)

	number	percent of total births in age group
Total births to unmarried women	1,240,172	31.0%
Under age 15	11,467	91.3
Aged 15 to 19	357,432	71.3
Aged 20 to 24	438,538	42.2
Aged 25 to 29	233,776	20.7
Aged 30 to 34	132,263	14.7
Aged 35 to 39	55,570	15.6
Aged 40 or older	11,126	18.1

Source: National Center for Health Statistics, Advance Report of Final Natality Statistics, 1993, *Vol. 44, No. 3 Supplement, 1995*

Total Births by State, 1993

(total number and percent distribution of births by state, 1993)

	number	percent
United States	4,000,240	100.0%
Alabama	61,706	1.5
Alaska	11,073	0.3
Arizona	69,056	1.7
Arkansas	34,289	0.9
California	585,324	14.6
Colorado	54,022	1.4
Connecticut	46,700	1.2
Delaware	10,568	0.3
District of Columbia	10,629	0.3
Florida	192,537	4.8
Georgia	110,622	2.8
Hawaii	19,593	0.5
Idaho	17,440	0.4
Illinois	190,788	4.8
Indiana	83,949	2.1
Iowa	37,826	0.9
Kansas	37,406	0.9
Kentucky	53,000	1.3
Louisiana	69,402	1.7
Maine	15,065	0.4
Maryland	74,988	1.9
Massachusetts	84,668	2.1
Michigan	139,855	3.5
Minnesota	64,648	1.6
Mississippi	42,149	1.1
Missouri	75,253	1.9
Montana	11,365	0.3
Nebraska	23,224	0.6
Nevada	22,403	0.6
New Hampshire	15,436	0.4
New Jersey	117,686	2.9
New Mexico	27,852	0.7
New York	282,392	7.1

(continued)

(continued from previous page)

	number	percent
North Carolina	101,357	2.5%
North Dakota	8,690	0.2
Ohio	158,793	4.0
Oklahoma	46,243	1.2
Oregon	41,576	1.0
Pennsylvania	160,762	4.0
Rhode Island	13,976	0.3
South Carolina	53,835	1.3
South Dakota	10,719	0.3
Tennessee	73,017	1.8
Texas	322,071	8.1
Utah	37,127	0.9
Vermont	7,457	0.2
Virginia	94,944	2.4
Washington	78,645	2.0
West Virginia	21,792	0.5
Wisconsin	69,767	1.7
Wyoming	6,555	0.2

Source: National Center for Health Statistics, Advance Report of Final Natality Statistics, 1993, *Vol. 44, No. 3 Supplement, 1995*

Projections of Total Births, 1995 to 2020

(total number of births, 1995 to 2020, numbers in thousands)

	number of births
1995	3,941
1996	3,921
1997	3,907
1998	3,899
1999	3,896
2000	3,899
2001	3,907
2002	3,920
2003	3,940
2004	3,967
2005	4,001
2006	4,042
2007	4,089
2008	4,140
2009	4,192
2010	4,243
2011	4,291
2012	4,336
2013	4,378
2014	4,415
2015	4,450
2016	4,481
2017	4,509
2018	4,534
2019	4,557
2020	4,579

Source: Bureau of the Census, Population Projections of the United States, by Age, Sex, Race, and Hispanic Origin: 1995 to 2050, *Current Population Reports, P25-1130, 1996*

Total Population:
Wealth

The median net worth of the average American household stood at $37,587 in 1993, down slightly from $38,500 in 1991, after adjusting for inflation.

The most commonly owned asset among Americans is a motor vehicle, owned by 86 percent. But the value of motor vehicles is relatively small, amounting to just over $5,000 in 1993. In contrast, homes are a much more valuable asset for most Americans. Sixty-four percent of householders own their homes, worth a median of $46,669 in 1993. Homes comprise the largest share of net worth for most American households. Twenty-one percent of households own stocks or mutual fund shares, worth a median of $6,960. Twenty-three percent have an IRA or KEOGH account, with a median value of $12,985.

Among all households, 11.5 percent have zero or negative net worth (their debts exceed their assets). Twenty-nine percent have a net worth in excess of $100,000.

For spending data on the total population, see the spending tables in the black, Hispanic, or white chapters.

Distribution of Net Worth Among Total Households, 1993

(number and percent distribution of total households by net worth, 1993; numbers in thousands)

	number	percent
Total households	96,468	100.0%
Zero or negative net worth	11,094	11.5
$1 to $4,999	13,216	13.7
$5,000 to $9,999	6,077	6.3
$10,000 to $24,999	10,419	10.8
$25,000 to $49,999	11,769	12.2
$50,000 to $99,999	15,917	16.5
$100,000 to $249,999	17,847	18.5
$250,000 to $499,999	6,656	6.9
$500,000 or more	3,473	3.6
Median net worth	$37,587	-

Source: Bureau of the Census, Internet web site, http://www.census.gov

Asset Ownership and Value of Assets for Total Households, 1993

(percent of total households owning assets and median value of asset among owners, 1993)

	percent owning	median value
Interest-earning assets at financial institutions*	71.1%	$2,999
Other interest-earning assets**	8.6	12,998
Regular checking accounts	45.9	499
Stocks and mutual fund shares	20.9	6,960
Own business or profession	10.8	7,000
Motor vehicles	85.7	5,140
Own home	64.3	46,669
Rental property	8.4	29,300
Other real estate	9.3	19,415
U.S. savings bonds	18.5	775
IRA or KEOGH accounts	23.1	12,985

* Includes passbook savings accounts, money market deposit accounts, certificates of deposit, and interest-earning checking accounts.
** Includes money market funds, U.S. government securities, municipal and corporate bonds, and other interest-earning assets.
Source: Bureau of the Census, Asset Ownership of Households: 1993, *Current Population Reports, P70-47, 1995*

7

Attitudes

While in many ways Americans are more tolerant than ever toward people of other races and ethnicities, they are also concerned that we are an increasingly divided nation. These attitudes are revealed by the 1994 General Social Survey (GSS), a nationally representative survey of the attitudes of Americans on a wide variety of issues. The GSS, taken annually by the National Opinion Research Center of the University of Chicago, is a window into the hearts and minds of Americans. The window reveals a public sharply divided on some diversity issues, but strongly united on others.

Regardless of race, more than half of Americans believe the country is divided, with blacks and people of "other" race (Asians, Native Americans, and some Hispanics*) most likely to feel this way. Nevertheless, most people think of themselves as American rather than as a member of an ethnic or racial group.

The biggest disagreements are between whites and blacks over the issues of black progress and affirmative action. While most whites think conditions for blacks have improved in the past few years, a minority of blacks agree. A majority of whites think blacks have worse jobs, income, and housing than whites because blacks lack the motivation to pull themselves out of poverty. Blacks, in contrast, are most likely to blame discrimination. Blacks are much more likely than whites to think the government is obligated to help them.

The issue of affirmative action reveals the greatest divide between whites and blacks. While only 8 percent of whites favor preferential hiring and promotion of blacks to make up for past discrimination, fully 55 percent

---

* *Hispanics may be of any race and most are white. For a breakdown of the Hispanic composition of racial groups and the racial composition of Hispanics, see the tables in the introduction to this book.*

of blacks support affirmative action. To whites, reverse discrimination is a very real threat. Over 70 percent of whites think it is somewhat or very likely that a white person won't get a job or a promotion while a less qualified black person gets one instead. Only 23 percent of blacks think reverse discrimination is likely.

Like squabbling siblings battling for their parents' attention, both blacks and whites think the government pays too much attention to the other. About half of whites think blacks get more attention from government than they deserve. Only 5 percent of blacks agree. Conversely, two out of three blacks think whites get more attention from government than they deserve. Only 12 percent of whites agree.

Equal opportunity issues show whites and blacks in strong agreement. Most whites disagree with the statement that "blacks shouldn't push where they're not wanted." Most whites say whites should not be able to keep blacks out of their neighborhood, and most also support fair housing laws. Neither whites nor blacks think political leaders need to be from the same racial or ethnic background as their constituents. Neither group thinks that teachers need to be from the same background as their students. A majority of both races think a person who believes blacks are genetically inferior should be allowed to speak in their community. And neither whites nor blacks favor removing racist books from libraries.

Whites and blacks agree that immigration should not be increased. Over 60 percent of both races say that immigration should in fact be decreased. People who list their race as "other" do not agree. Only one-third want to see immigration decreased, while another third want to see it remain at the same level, and 18 percent would like to see immigration increased.

Nearly two out of three whites favor making English the official language, while a plurality of blacks (45 percent) and "others" (49 percent) agree. There is surprising agreement among all races regarding bilingual education. A majority of whites, blacks, and "others" think children should be taught in their native language for one or two years only. Fewer than one in four of blacks, whites, or "others" think children should be taught in their native language through high school.

Are Americans Divided or United?

"There is a lot of discussion today about whether Americans are divided or united. What is your view about this?"

(percent responding by race, 1994)

	total	white	black	other
United	39.4%	42.7%	22.8%	27.9%
Divided	55.0	51.2	74.1	67.2
Don't know	5.0	5.4	2.5	3.3

Note: Numbers by race may not add to 100 percent because no answer is not shown.
Source: 1994 General Social Survey, National Opinion Research Center, University of Chicago

Ethnic Group Member or American?

"When you think of social and political issues,
do you think of yourself mainly as a member of a
particular ethnic, racial, or nationality group, or
do you think of yourself mainly as just an American?"

(percent responding by race, 1994)

	total	white	black	other
American	89.2%	94.2%	66.5%	63.9%
One ethnic group	7.4	3.3	28.4	21.3
Two or more ethnic groups	0.2	0.2	0.5	0.0
American and ethnic group	1.4	0.7	3.6	8.2
It depends	0.8	0.7	1.0	3.3
Don't know	0.5	0.5	0.0	3.3

Note: Numbers by race may not add to 100 percent because no answer is not shown.
Source: 1994 General Social Survey, National Opinion Research Center, University of Chicago

Melting Pot

"Some people say that it is better for America if different racial and ethnic groups maintain their distinct cultures. Others say that it is better if groups change so that they blend into the larger society as in the idea of a melting pot. Where do you place yourself on the following scale, from: 1) Racial and ethnic groups should maintain their distinct cultures; to 7) Groups should change so that they blend into the larger society."

(percent responding by race, 1994)

		total	white	black	other
1	Maintain distinct culture	13.0%	10.3%	26.4%	23.0%
2		6.9	7.2	6.1	3.3
3		11.3	11.7	8.1	13.1
4		28.8	30.0	21.3	27.9
5		15.6	16.4	11.2	14.8
6		7.7	8.1	6.6	4.9
7	Blend in	14.1	13.5	18.8	11.5
	Don't know	2.2	2.4	1.5	1.6

Note: Numbers by race may not add to 100 percent because no answer is not shown.
Source: 1994 General Social Survey, National Opinion Research Center, University of Chicago

Should Government Help Maintain Ethnic Identity?

"Should it be up to the government to help racial and ethnic groups maintain their distinct cultures, or should this be left up to the groups themselves?"

(percent responding by race, 1994)

	total	*white*	*black*	*other*
Government should help	10.1%	7.5%	18.8%	20.8%
Up to the groups	86.0	88.9	75.0	79.2
Don't know	2.4	1.9	5.0	0.0

Note: Numbers by race may not add to 100 percent because no answer is not shown.
Source: 1994 General Social Survey, National Opinion Research Center, University of Chicago

Should Government Help Blend In?

"Should it be up to the government to help racial and ethnic groups change so that they blend into the larger society, or should this be up to the groups themselves?"

(percent responding by race, 1994)

	total	*white*	*black*	*other*
Government should help	19.4%	16.5%	33.3%	36.8%
Up to the groups	70.6	72.8	58.3	63.2
Don't know	3.9	4.3	2.8	0.0

Note: Numbers by race may not add to 100 percent because no answer is not shown.
Source: 1994 General Social Survey, National Opinion Research Center, University of Chicago

Promote Separatism?

"Political organizations based on race or ethnicity
promote separatism and make it hard for all of us
to live together—do you agree or disagree?"

(percent responding by race, 1994)

	total	*white*	*black*	*other*
Agree, total	66.5%	69.5%	49.8%	59.0%
Agree strongly	24.5	25.7	18.3	19.7
Agree slightly	42.0	43.8	31.5	39.3
Neither agree nor disagree	13.6	13.2	16.8	13.1
Disagree, total	15.0	12.6	27.5	24.6
Disagree slightly	11.9	9.6	23.9	19.7
Disagree strongly	3.1	3.0	3.6	4.9
Don't know	4.1	3.9	5.6	3.3

Note: Numbers by race may not add to 100 percent because no answer is not shown.
Source: 1994 General Social Survey, National Opinion Research Center, University of Chicago

Have Conditions for Blacks Improved?

"In the past few years, do you think conditions for black people have improved, gotten worse, or stayed about the same?"

(percent responding by race, 1994)

	total	white	black	other
Improved	52.8%	56.5%	33.3%	40.0%
Gotten worse	12.0	10.7	21.2	9.1
Stayed the same	32.2	29.6	43.9	49.1
Don't know	2.4	2.6	1.5	0.0

Note: Numbers by race may not add to 100 percent because no answer is not shown.
Source: 1994 General Social Survey, National Opinion Research Center, University of Chicago

Why Do Blacks Have It Worse?

"On the average, blacks have worse jobs, income, and housing than white people. Do you think these differences are..."

(percent responding by race, 1994)

	total	white	black	other
A. Mainly due to discrimination?				
Yes	40.5%	33.8%	77.4%	56.6%
No	54.0	60.2	18.4	42.1
Don't know	5.1	5.5	3.8	1.3
B. Because most blacks have less in-born ability to learn?				
Yes	12.8	12.9	9.6	21.1
No	82.7	82.5	86.6	72.4
Don't know	4.0	4.0	3.1	6.6
C. Because most blacks don't have the chance for education that it takes to rise out of poverty?				
Yes	49.0	46.8	59.4	61.8
No	46.8	49.1	36.8	32.9
Don't know	3.5	3.5	3.1	5.3
D. Because most blacks just don't have the motivation or willpower to pull themselves out of poverty?				
Yes	48.8	51.4	29.1	59.2
No	44.6	42.0	65.5	30.3
Don't know	5.8	6.0	3.8	9.2

Note: Numbers by race may not add to 100 percent because no answer is not shown.
Source: 1994 General Social Survey, National Opinion Research Center, University of Chicago

Is Government Obligated to Help Blacks?

"On a scale of 1 to 5, how much should government help blacks, from: 1) I strongly agree the government is obligated to help blacks; to 5) I strongly agree that government shouldn't give special treatment."

(percent responding by race, 1994)

		total	white	black	other
1	Government obligated to help	8.2%	3.8%	35.4%	13.9%
2		7.3	6.3	13.0	10.1
3	Agree with both	29.0	27.7	37.4	31.6
4		23.1	26.2	4.7	17.7
5	No special treatment	28.9	32.8	5.1	22.8
	Don't know	3.0	2.9	3.5	2.5

Note: Numbers by race may not add to 100 percent because no answer is not shown.
Source: 1994 General Social Survey, National Opinion Research Center, University of Chicago

Should Blacks Work Their Way Up?

"Irish, Italians, Jews, and many other minorities overcame prejudice and worked their way up. Blacks should do the same without special favors—do you agree or disagree?"

(percent responding by race, 1994)

	total	white	black	other
Agree, total	72.1%	76.3%	45.9%	76.3%
Agree strongly	43.5	47.2	21.2	43.6
Agree somewhat	28.6	29.1	24.7	32.7
Neither agree nor disagree	10.0	10.1	9.1	10.9
Disagree, total	15.6	11.6	40.4	10.9
Disagree somewhat	9.7	8.6	16.7	7.3
Disagree strongly	5.9	3.0	23.7	3.6
Don't know	2.0	1.6	4.0	1.8

Note: Numbers by race may not add to 100 percent because no answer is not shown.
Source: 1994 General Social Survey, National Opinion Research Center, University of Chicago

Should Blacks Push?

"Blacks shouldn't push themselves where they're not wanted."

(percent responding by race, 1994)

	total	white	black	other
Agree, total	41.0%	42.7%	30.4%	41.2%
Agree strongly	14.2	14.7	9.6	19.0
Agree slightly	26.8	28.0	20.8	22.2
Disagree, total	55.2	53.3	67.5	54.0
Disagree slightly	24.9	25.6	19.3	28.6
Disagree strongly	30.3	27.7	48.2	25.4
No opinion	3.6	3.8	2.0	4.8

Note: Numbers by race may not add to 100 percent because no answer is not shown.
Source: 1994 General Social Survey, National Opinion Research Center, University of Chicago

Can Whites Keep Blacks Out of Their Neighborhoods?

"White people have a right to keep blacks out of their neighbor-hoods if they want to, and blacks should respect that right."

(percent responding by race, 1994)

	total	white	black	other
Agree, total	15.0%	16.0%	9.2%	12.6%
Agree strongly	5.1	5.7	2.3	2.3
Agree slightly	9.9	10.3	6.9	10.3
Disagree, total	82.5	81.6	88.5	82.8
Disagree slightly	23.6	26.1	10.7	16.1
Disagree strongly	58.9	55.5	77.8	66.7
No opinion	2.2	2.2	1.9	3.4

Note: Numbers by race may not add to 100 percent because no answer is not shown.
Source: 1994 General Social Survey, National Opinion Research Center, University of Chicago

Fair Housing Laws

"Select from: A. One law says that a homeowner can decide for himself whom to sell his house to, even if he prefers not to sell to blacks; or B. The second law says that a homeowner cannot refuse to sell to someone because of their race or color."

(percent responding by race, 1994)

	total	white	black	other
Up to owner	32.4%	35.3%	18.5%	15.2%
Can't refuse	62.2	59.4	76.0	78.5
Neither	2.9	2.9	2.0	5.1
Don't know	1.8	1.7	2.4	1.3

Note: Numbers by race may not add to 100 percent because no answer is not shown.
Source: 1994 General Social Survey, National Opinion Research Center, University of Chicago

Blacks in the Neighborhood

"Are there any black families living close to you?"

(percent responding by race, 1994)

	total	white	black	other
Yes	73.8%	69.9%	88.6%	88.0%
No	22.2	25.8	8.6	8.0
Don't know	0.4	0.6	0.0	0.0

Note: Numbers by race may not add to 100 percent because no answer is not shown.
Source: 1994 General Social Survey, National Opinion Research Center, University of Chicago

Busing

"In general, do you favor or oppose the busing of black and white school children from one district to another?"

(percent responding by race, 1994)

	total	white	black	other
Favor	31.5%	26.8%	57.5%	43.4%
Oppose	62.5	66.9	38.7	50.0
Don't know	5.4	5.7	3.4	6.6

Note: Numbers by race may not add to 100 percent because "no answer is not shown.
Source: 1994 General Social Survey, National Opinion Research Center, University of Chicago

Integrated Schools

"Would you yourself have any objection to sending your children to a school where a few of the children are whites/blacks?"

(percent responding by race, 1994)

	total	white	black	other
Yes	3.6%	3.4%	5.0%	2.6%
No	94.8	95.2	93.1	93.4
Don't know	0.9	0.8	0.8	3.9

Among those who responded "no" or "don't know" to the above question:
Where half of the children are whites/blacks?

	total	white	black	other
Yes	12.1	13.6	1.2	14.9
No	84.8	83.1	96.4	82.4
Don't know	2.4	2.6	0.8	2.7

Among those who responded "no" or "don't know" to the above question:
Where more than half of the children are whites/blacks?

	total	white	black	other
Yes	34.1	38.6	10.2	28.6
No	59.4	54.2	86.5	66.7
Don't know	5.3	5.9	2.0	4.8

Note: Numbers by race may not add to 100 percent because no answer is not shown.
Source: 1994 General Social Survey, National Opinion Research Center, University of Chicago

Interracial Marriage

"Do you think there should be laws against marriages between blacks and whites?"

(percent responding by race, 1994)

	total	white	black	other
Yes	13.4%	15.4%	2.7%	8.0%
No	84.1	82.0	95.0	89.7
Don't know	2.3	2.3	2.3	2.3

Note: Numbers by race may not add to 100 percent because no answer is not shown.
Source: 1994 General Social Survey, National Opinion Research Center, University of Chicago

Do Blacks/Whites Attend Your Church?

"Do blacks/whites attend the church that you, yourself, attend most often, or not?"

(percent responding by race, 1994)

	total	white	black	other
Yes	39.1%	36.5%	54.0%	47.6%
No	43.8	46.1	34.9	23.8
No church	16.2	16.6	9.5	28.6
Don't know	0.2	0.2	0.0	0.0

Note: Numbers by race may not add to 100 percent because no answer is not shown.
Source: 1994 General Social Survey, National Opinion Research Center, University of Chicago

Would You Integrate Your Social Club?

"If you and your friends belonged to a social club that would not let whites/blacks join, would you try to change the rules so that whites/blacks could join?"

(percent responding by race, 1994)

	total	white	black	other
Yes	60.4%	60.0%	60.3%	66.7%
No	29.2	29.8	27.0	23.8
Don't know	9.9	9.9	11.1	4.8

Note: Numbers by race may not add to 100 percent because no answer is not shown.
Source: 1994 General Social Survey, National Opinion Research Center, University of Chicago

Preferential Hiring and Promotion of Blacks

"Some people say that because of past discrimination,
blacks should be given preference in hiring and promotion.
Others say that such preference in hiring and promotion
of blacks is wrong because it discriminates against others.
What about your opinion—are you for or against
preferential hiring and promotion of blacks?"

(percent responding by race, 1994)

	total	*white*	*black*	*other*
Favor, total	15.0%	8.4%	55.3%	16.4%
Strongly favor	8.8	3.7	41.1	6.6
Not strongly favor	6.2	4.7	14.2	9.8
Oppose, total	78.9	86.2	36.0	73.8
Not strongly oppose	18.7	18.8	15.7	27.9
Strongly oppose	60.2	67.4	20.3	45.9
Don't know	5.3	4.7	8.1	8.2

Note: Numbers by race may not add to 100 percent because no answer is not shown.
Source: 1994 General Social Survey, National Opinion Research Center, University of Chicago

Reverse Discrimination on the Job

"What do you think the chances are these days that a white person won't get a job or a promotion while a less qualified black person gets one instead?"

(percent responding by race, 1994)

	total	white	black	other
Very likely	25.4%	29.3%	8.5%	3.0%
Somewhat likely	38.4	42.4	14.9	33.3
Not likely	31.4	23.9	71.3	51.5
Don't know	4.2	3.7	5.3	9.1

Note: Numbers by race may not add to 100 percent because no answer is not shown.
Source: 1994 General Social Survey, National Opinion Research Center, University of Chicago

Reverse Discrimination in College Admissions

"What do you think the chances are these days that a white person won't get admitted to a college or university program while a less qualified black person gets admitted instead?"

(percent responding by race, 1994)

	total	white	black	other
Very likely	26.6%	30.2%	10.6%	9.1%
Somewhat likely	40.4	43.4	25.5	30.3
Not likely	27.1	20.7	60.6	45.5
Don't know	4.9	4.7	3.2	12.1

Note: Numbers by race may not add to 100 percent because no answer is not shown.
Source: 1994 General Social Survey, National Opinion Research Center, University of Chicago

Should Politicians Be from Same Racial/Ethnic Background?

"Do you feel that people are best represented in politics by leaders from their own racial and ethnic background, or doesn't the leader's background make very much difference?"

(percent responding by race, 1994)

	total	white	black	other
Own background	33.7%	31.9%	42.1%	42.6%
Doesn't matter	62.0	63.3	55.8	55.7
Don't know	3.5	3.9	1.5	1.6

Note: Numbers by race may not add to 100 percent because no answer is not shown.
Source: 1994 General Social Survey, National Opinion Research Center, University of Chicago

Should Teachers Be from Same Racial/Ethnic Background?

"What about teachers in public schools or universities? Should they have roughly the same racial or ethnic background as their students, or should they be considered purely on the basis of their ability without regard to their racial or ethnic background?"

(percent responding by race, 1994)

	total	white	black	other
Consider background	7.8%	5.7%	17.8%	18.0%
Consider ability	88.9	91.0	79.7	77.0
Don't know	2.5	2.4	2.5	4.9

Note: Numbers by race may not add to 100 percent because no answer is not shown.
Source: 1994 General Social Survey, National Opinion Research Center, University of Chicago

Would You Vote for a Black President?

"If your party nominated a black for president, would you vote for him if he were qualified for the job?"

(percent responding by race, 1994)

	total	white	black	other
Yes	87.4%	85.7%	98.1%	86.8%
No	8.8	10.1	0.8	9.2
Don't know	3.3	3.7	0.8	3.9

Note: Numbers by race may not add to 100 percent because no answer is not shown.
Source: 1994 General Social Survey, National Opinion Research Center, University of Chicago

Should Minority Experience Be Taught by Minorities?

"Some people say that when the experience of a racial or ethnic minority group is taught in high school or college, it should be taught by a teacher from that group—do you agree or disagree?"

(percent responding by race, 1994)

	total	white	black	other
Agree, total	24.4%	21.2%	42.1%	31.1%
Agree strongly	6.3	3.6	20.8	13.1
Agree	18.1	17.6	21.3	18.0
Neither agree nor disagree	28.2	29.1	21.3	31.1
Disagree, total	42.1	44.3	31.0	34.4
Disagree	36.1	37.8	26.9	31.1
Disagree strongly	6.0	6.5	4.1	3.3
Don't know	4.6	4.5	5.6	3.3

Note: Numbers by race may not add to 100 percent because no answer is not shown.
Source: 1994 General Social Survey, National Opinion Research Center, University of Chicago

Should People Be Allowed to Express Offensive Opinions?

"People should not be allowed to express opinions that are harmful or offensive to members of other religious or racial groups—do you agree or disagree?"

(percent responding by race, 1994)

	total	white	black	other
Agree, total	40.9%	38.7%	53.2%	45.5%
Agree strongly	9.9	8.5	17.0	15.2
Agree	31.0	30.2	36.2	30.3
Neither agree nor disagree	12.0	12.5	10.6	6.1
Disagree, total	44.2	45.8	34.0	45.5
Disagree	34.3	35.1	28.7	36.4
Disagree strongly	9.9	10.7	5.3	9.1
No opinion	1.1	1.2	1.1	0.0

Note: Numbers by race may not add to 100 percent because no answer is not shown.
Source: 1994 General Social Survey, National Opinion Research Center, University of Chicago

Free Speech

"Consider a person who believes that blacks are genetically inferior. If such a person wanted to make a speech in your community, claiming that blacks are inferior, should he/she be allowed to speak, or not?"

(percent responding by race, 1994)

	total	white	black	other
Allowed	61.3%	63.1%	51.3%	56.3%
Not allowed	36.6	35.1	44.8	39.1
Don't know	1.9	1.5	3.8	3.4

Note: Numbers by race may not add to 100 percent because no answer is not shown.
Source: 1994 General Social Survey, National Opinion Research Center, University of Chicago

Freedom to Teach

"Should a person who believes that blacks are genetically inferior be allowed to teach in a college or university, or not?"

(percent responding by race, 1994)

	total	white	black	other
Allowed	42.3%	45.0%	27.6%	35.6%
Not allowed	53.7	51.2	68.6	57.5
Don't know	3.6	3.5	3.8	5.7

Note: Numbers by race may not add to 100 percent because no answer is not shown.
Source: 1994 General Social Survey, National Opinion Research Center, University of Chicago

Book Banning

"If some people in your community suggested that a book, written by a racist, which said blacks are inferior should be taken out of your public library, would you favor removing this book, or not?"

(percent responding by race, 1994)

	total	white	black	other
Favor	31.1%	29.6%	39.8%	34.5%
Not favor	65.8	67.6	55.9	60.9
Don't know	2.9	2.6	4.2	3.4

Note: Numbers by race may not add to 100 percent because no answer is not shown.
Source: 1994 General Social Survey, National Opinion Research Center, University of Chicago

Who Gets the Most Attention from Government?

"Do you think people in the following groups in this country get much more attention from government than they deserve, more attention than they deserve, about the right amount of attention, less attention than they deserve, or much less attention than they deserve?"

(percent responding by race, 1994)

	total	*white*	*black*	*other*
WHITES				
Get more than they deserve	20.4%	12.3%	66.5%	34.4%
About right	54.5	59.0	26.9	52.5
Get less than they deserve	20.9	24.8	1.0	8.2
Don't know	3.6	3.2	5.6	4.9
BLACKS				
Get more than they deserve	43.0	49.9	4.6	29.5
About right	28.2	29.7	18.3	29.5
Get less than they deserve	25.2	16.7	73.6	36.1
Don't know	3.1	2.9	3.6	4.9
HISPANICS				
Get more than they deserve	28.5	31.1	17.8	13.1
About right	35.9	37.5	27.9	29.5
Get less than they deserve	28.0	24.3	44.1	47.5
Don't know	7.1	6.4	10.2	9.8
ASIANS				
Get more than they deserve	23.2	22.5	31.0	14.7
About right	40.4	42.8	26.4	36.1
Get less than they deserve	26.0	24.9	29.4	37.7
Don't know	9.8	9.1	13.2	11.5

Note: Numbers by race may not add to 100 percent because no answer is not shown.
Source: 1994 General Social Survey, National Opinion Research Center, University of Chicago

Which Groups Work Hard?

"Do the people in the following groups tend to be hard working, or do they tend to be lazy?"

(percent responding by race, 1994)

		total	white	black	other
WHITES					
1	Work hard	7.5%	7.1%	10.2%	8.2%
2		17.3	17.6	16.2	14.8
3		25.8	25.7	27.9	23.0
4		37.5	39.2	26.4	39.3
5		5.3	4.7	8.6	6.6
6		2.1	1.6	4.6	3.3
7	Lazy	0.9	0.6	3.0	1.6
	Don't know	2.2	2.1	2.5	3.3
BLACKS					
1	Work hard	3.3	1.7	13.2	3.3
2		6.5	3.9	24.4	1.6
3		11.8	10.6	19.3	11.5
4		33.4	34.8	24.4	34.4
5		21.5	23.6	10.2	16.4
6		13.0	14.2	4.6	16.4
7	Lazy	6.0	6.4	1.5	11.5
	Don't know	3.3	3.4	2.0	4.9
HISPANICS					
1	Work hard	3.6	2.5	8.1	9.8
2		6.7	6.3	7.6	13.1
3		14.4	14.0	17.3	13.1
4		34.3	35.4	26.9	36.1
5		20.1	21.1	16.2	11.5
6		8.2	8.1	9.1	8.2
7	Lazy	3.7	4.0	2.5	0.0
	Don't know	7.8	7.2	11.7	8.2

(continued)

(continued from previous page)

ASIANS		total	white	black	other
1	Work hard	11.9%	9.5%	25.9%	14.8%
2		19.9	18.7	25.4	26.2
3		22.5	23.5	14.2	29.5
4		23.9	25.6	14.7	21.3
5		7.3	7.9	5.6	1.6
6		3.5	3.9	2.0	0.0
7	Lazy	1.0	1.2	0.0	0.0
	Don't know	8.7	8.3	11.7	6.6

Note: Numbers by race may not add to 100 percent because no answer is not shown.
Source: 1994 General Social Survey, National Opinion Research Center, University of Chicago

How Wealthy Are Racial/Ethnic Groups?

"Where would you rate the wealth of the following groups?"

(percent responding by race, 1994)

		total	white	black	other
WHITES					
1	**Rich**	3.8%	1.6%	15.7%	8.2%
2		8.0	5.3	24.4	8.2
3		25.4	25.3	21.8	39.3
4		51.9	56.8	28.4	29.5
5		5.7	6.1	3.6	4.9
6		1.3	1.4	0.0	3.3
7	**Poor**	0.4	0.4	0.0	1.6
	Don't know	2.6	2.0	5.6	4.9
BLACKS					
1	**Rich**	0.3	0.2	0.5	1.6
2		1.2	1.3	1.0	0.0
3		3.1	3.0	5.1	0.0
4		20.2	19.9	22.8	18.0
5		40.9	42.0	37.6	29.5
6		24.4	24.3	19.8	41.0
7	**Poor**	6.2	6.0	8.6	3.3
	Don't know	2.6	2.2	4.1	6.6
HISPANICS					
1	**Rich**	0.3	0.2	0.5	1.6
2		1.2	1.2	2.0	0.0
3		3.6	3.1	6.1	4.9
4		19.1	19.4	17.3	18.0
5		33.9	34.8	25.4	44.3
6		27.1	28.0	23.9	19.7
7	**Poor**	6.9	6.5	9.6	6.6
	Don't know	7.1	5.9	14.7	4.9

(continued)

(continued from previous page)

ASIANS		total	white	black	other
1	Rich	2.7%	1.6%	10.2%	1.6%
2		6.4	5.7	12.2	3.3
3		16.6	16.3	14.7	27.9
4		32.8	34.2	26.4	26.2
5		18.8	20.0	11.2	19.7
6		10.0	10.3	8.1	9.8
7	Poor	2.8	2.6	4.6	1.6
	Don't know	9.0	8.4	12.2	9.8

Note: Numbers by race may not add to 100 percent because no answer is not shown.
Source: 1994 General Social Survey, National Opinion Research Center, University of Chicago

Should the Number of Immigrants Be Increased or Decreased?

"Do you think the number of immigrants from foreign countries who are permitted to come to the United States to live should be increased or decreased?"

(percent responding by race, 1994)

	total	white	black	other
Increased, total	6.0%	4.7%	10.1%	18.1%
Increased a lot	2.4	2.1	3.0	6.6
Increased a little	3.6	2.6	7.1	11.5
Stay the same	26.8	27.2	21.8	34.4
Decreased, total	62.0	63.5	60.4	37.7
Decreased a little	27.6	28.5	24.9	18.0
Decreased a lot	34.4	35.0	35.5	19.7
Don't know	4.7	3.9	7.6	9.8

Note: Numbers by race may not add to 100 percent because no answer is not shown.
Source: 1994 General Social Survey, National Opinion Research Center, University of Chicago

What Will Happen If Immigration Is Increased?

"What do you think will happen as a result of more immigrants coming to this country?"

(percent responding by race, 1994)

	total	white	black	other
Higher economic growth				
Very likely	8.4%	7.0%	15.7%	13.1%
Somewhat likely	21.4	20.0	24.4	41.0
Not too likely	41.3	43.5	33.0	24.6
Not likely	21.1	22.3	16.2	13.1
Don't know	7.2	6.7	10.2	8.2
Higher unemployment				
Very likely	53.9	54.9	52.8	39.3
Somewhat likely	31.1	30.9	32.0	31.1
Not too likely	7.9	7.8	5.6	16.4
Not likely	2.3	2.3	1.0	6.6
Don't know	4.3	3.5	8.1	6.6
Make it harder to keep the country united				
Very likely	33.9	34.0	34.5	31.1
Somewhat likely	33.7	33.2	39.1	26.2
Not too likely	18.0	18.7	10.7	27.9
Not likely	7.5	7.6	6.6	8.2
Don't know	6.3	5.9	8.6	6.6

Note: Numbers by race may not add to 100 percent because no answer is not shown.
Source: 1994 General Social Survey, National Opinion Research Center, University of Chicago

Should Immigrants Work Their Way Up?

"Irish, Italians, Jews, and many other minorities overcame prejudice and worked their way up. Today's immigrants should do the same without special favors—do you agree or disagree?"

(percent responding by race, 1994)

	total	white	black	other
Agree, total	79.6%	82.5%	63.0%	75.4%
Agree strongly	33.9	36.7	17.3	32.8
Agree	45.7	45.8	45.7	42.6
Neither agree nor disagree	10.5	9.9	15.7	6.6
Disagree, total	6.7	5.6	11.6	14.8
Disagree	5.7	4.9	9.1	11.5
Disagree strongly	1.0	0.7	2.5	3.3
Don't know	2.4	1.6	7.6	3.3

Note: Numbers by race may not add to 100 percent because no answer is not shown.
Source: 1994 General Social Survey, National Opinion Research Center, University of Chicago

How Hard Do Immigrants Work?

"On a 7-point scale (1 being hardworking, 7 being lazy), how hard do immigrants work?"

(percent responding by race, 1994)

		total	white	black	other
LEGAL IMMIGRANTS					
1	**Hard working**	5.6%	4.4%	11.7%	9.8%
2		13.4	11.9	21.8	14.8
3		21.9	22.6	15.2	29.5
4		33.0	34.9	23.9	26.2
5		10.4	11.3	6.6	4.9
6		3.9	4.0	3.0	4.9
7	**Lazy**	1.6	1.6	1.5	1.6
	Don't know	8.9	7.8	15.7	8.2
ILLEGAL IMMIGRANTS					
1	**Hard working**	8.6	6.8	16.2	19.7
2		11.7	11.7	11.7	13.1
3		14.2	13.7	17.3	14.8
4		22.1	23.2	15.7	21.3
5		10.8	11.1	10.2	6.6
6		12.3	13.1	7.6	11.5
7	**Lazy**	7.1	7.6	4.1	4.9
	Don't know	11.8	11.2	16.8	8.2

Note: Numbers by race may not add to 100 percent because no answer is not shown.
Source: 1994 General Social Survey, National Opinion Research Center, University of Chicago

Do You Favor Making English the Official Language?

"Do you favor a law making English the official language of the United States, meaning government business would be conducted in English only, or do you oppose such a law?"

(percent responding by race, 1994)

	total	white	black	other
Favor	60.4%	63.5%	44.7%	49.2%
Neither	9.3	8.3	14.7	11.5
Oppose	26.5	24.4	36.5	36.1
Don't know	3.4	3.3	4.1	3.3

Note: Numbers by race may not add to 100 percent because no answer is not shown.
Source: 1994 General Social Survey, National Opinion Research Center, University of Chicago

Bilingual Education

"How do you feel about bilingual education?"

(percent responding by race, 1994)

	total	white	black	other
Favor, total	64.3%	61.7%	75.1%	80.4%
Favor strongly	26.3	24.0	35.0	44.3
Favor somewhat	38.0	37.7	40.1	36.1
Oppose, total	30.7	34.0	13.7	19.7
Oppose somewhat	16.3	18.0	7.1	11.5
Oppose strongly	14.4	16.0	6.6	8.2
Don't know	4.5	3.7	11.2	0.0

Note: Numbers by race may not add to 100 percent because no answer is not shown.
Source: 1994 General Social Survey, National Opinion Research Center, University of Chicago

Best Way to Teach Children Who Don't Speak English

"There are several different ideas about how to teach children who don't speak English when they enter our public schools. Which of the following statements best describes how you feel: 1) All classes only in English; or 2) Children should have classes in their native language just for a year or two; or 3) Students should be able to take many of their classes in Spanish or other languages through high school."

(percent responding by race, 1994)

	total	*white*	*black*	*other*
Only in English	34.7%	36.1%	27.4%	31.1%
Native language for one or two years	46.6	47.0	45.7	42.6
Native language through high school	15.1	13.7	21.3	24.6
Don't know	2.8	2.5	5.1	1.6

Note: Numbers by race may not add to 100 percent because no answer is not shown.
Source: 1994 General Social Survey, National Opinion Research Center, University of Chicago

Glossary

adjusted for inflation Income or a change in income that has been adjusted for the rise in the cost of living, or the consumer price index (CPI-U-XI). The CPI-U-XI adjustment factors are as follows:

year	index
1994	148.2
1993	144.5
1992	140.3
1991	136.2
1990	130.7
1989	124.0
1988	118.3
1987	113.6
1986	109.6
1985	107.6
1984	103.9
1983	99.6
1982	95.6
1981	90.1
1980	82.3

To figure the inflation rate between two years, divide the index in the later year by the index in the earlier year. Multiply the result by the income of the earlier year. For example, to adjust 1990 income for inflation through 1994, divide 148.2 by 130.7 to arrive at the ratio 1.1339. Multiply that figure by income in 1990 to arrive at 1990 income expressed in 1994 dollars.

Asian In this book, the term "Asian" includes both Asians and Pacific Islanders. The Current Population Survey classifies as Asian or Pacific Islander anyone who identifies his or her race as "Asian or Pacific Islander." The 1990 census goes further, asking respondents to specify their Asian or Pacific Islander ethnic origin, such as Chinese, Filipino, Japanese, Asian Indian, Korean, Vietnamese, Samoan, Tahitian, and so on. All those who name a Far Eastern or Pacific Island nation as their origin is classified as "Asian or Pacific Islander." The only exception to this definition of Asian is in the immigration tables in the Asian and Total Population sections. The Immigration and Naturalization Service includes people from the Middle East—such as Israel, Lebanon, Iran, and so on—as immigrants from the Asian world region. They are included as Asian immigrants in the immigration tables.

baby boom Americans born between 1946 and 1964.

baby bust Americans born between 1965 and 1976, also known as Generation X.

black The black racial category includes those who identify themselves as "black" on the Current Population Survey, or as "black or Negro" on the 1990 Census, or who wrote in an ancestry or ethnic origin on the 1990 census that included African-American, Jamaican, Nigerian, West Indian, or Haitian.

central cities The largest city in a metropolitan area is called the central city. The balance of the metropolitan area outside the central city is regarded as the "suburbs."

complete income reporters Survey respondents who told government interviewers how much money they received from major sources of income, such as wages and salaries, self-employment income, and Social Security income.

consumer unit For convenience, the term consumer unit and households are used interchangeably in the spending tables of this book, although consumer units are somewhat different from the

Census Bureau's households. Consumer units are all related members of a household, or financially independent members of a household. A household may include more than one consumer unit.

dual-earner couple A married couple in which both the householder and the householder's spouse are in the labor force.

employed All civilians who did any work as a paid employee or farmer/self-employed worker, or who worked 15 hours or more as an unpaid farm worker or in a family-owned business, during the reference period. All those who have jobs but who are temporarily absent from their jobs due to illness, bad weather, vacation, labor management dispute, or personal reasons are considered employed.

expenditure The transaction cost including excise and sales taxes of goods and services acquired during the survey period. The full cost of each purchase is recorded even though full payment may not have been made at the date of purchase. Average expenditure figures may be artificially low for infrequently purchased items such as cars because figures are calculated using all consumer units within a demographic segment rather than just purchasers. Expenditure estimates include money spent on gifts for others.

family A group of two or more people (one of whom is the householder) related by birth, marriage, or adoption and living in the same household.

family household A household maintained by a householder who lives with one or more people related to him or her by blood, marriage, or adoption.

female/male householder A woman or man who maintains a household without a spouse present. May head family or nonfamily households.

full-time, year-round Indicates 50 or more weeks of full-time employment during the previous calendar year.

geographic regions The four major regions and nine census divisions of the United States are the state groupings as shown below:
Northeast:
• *New England:* Connecticut, Maine, Massachusetts, New Hampshire, Rhode Island, and Vermont
• *Middle Atlantic:* New Jersey, New York, and Pennsylvania
Midwest:
• *East North Central:* Illinois, Indiana, Michigan, Ohio, and Wisconsin
• *West North Central:* Iowa, Kansas, Minnesota, Missouri, Nebraska, North Dakota, and South Dakota
South:
• *South Atlantic:* Delaware, District of Columbia, Florida, Georgia, Maryland, North Carolina, South Carolina, Virginia, and West Virginia
• *East South Central:* Alabama, Kentucky, Mississippi, and Tennessee
• *West South Central:* Arkansas, Louisiana, Oklahoma, and Texas
West:
• *Mountain:* Arizona, Colorado, Idaho, Montana, Nevada, New Mexico, Utah, and Wyoming
• *Pacific:* Alaska, California, Hawaii, Oregon, and Washington

Hispanic The Hispanic statistics in this book include those who identified themselves as Hispanic on the Current Population Survey or on the 1990 census. Hispanics include those who identify themselves as Mexican, Puerto Rican, Cuban, or of "other" Spanish/Hispanic origin. Persons of "other" Hispanic origin include those from Spain, the Spanish-speaking countries of Central and South America, or the Dominican Republic. They also include those who identify themselves as Spanish, Spanish-American, Latino, and so on. The only exception to this definition of Hispanic is in the immigration table in the Hispanic section, where people from Brazil are classified as Hispanic because they are from South America. Persons of Hispanic origin may be of any race. In other words, there are black Hispanics, white Hispanics, and Asian Hispanics.

household All the persons who occupy a housing unit. A household includes the related family members and all the unrelated persons, if any, such as lodgers, foster children, wards, or employees who share the housing unit. A person living alone is counted as a household. A group of unrelated people who share a housing unit as roommates or unmarried partners is also counted as a household. Households do not include group quarters such as college dormitories, prisons, or nursing homes.

household, race/ethnicity of Households are categorized according to the race or ethnicity of the householder only.

householder The householder is the person (or one of the persons) in whose name the housing unit is owned or rented or, if there is no such person, any adult member. With married couples, the householder may be either the husband or wife. The householder is the reference person for the household.

householder, age of The age of the householder is used to categorize households into age groups such as those used in this book. Married couples, for example, are classified according to the age of either the husband or wife, depending on which one identified him or herself as the householder.

income Money received in the preceding calendar year by each person aged 15 or older from each of the following sources: (1) earnings from longest job (or self-employment); (2) earnings from jobs other than longest job; (3) unemployment compensation; (4) workers' compensation; (5) Social Security; (6) Supplemental Security income; (7) public assistance; (8) veterans' pay-

ments; (9) survivor benefits; (10) disability benefits; (11) retirement pensions; (12) interest; (13) dividends; (14) rents and royalties or estates and trusts; (15) educational assistance; (16) alimony; (17) child support; (18) financial assistance from outside the household, and other periodic income. Income is reported in several ways in this book. Household income is the combined income of all household members. Income of persons is all income accruing to a person from all sources. Earnings is the amount of money a person receives from his or her job.

industry Refers to the industry in which a person worked longest in the preceding calendar year.

labor force The labor force includes both employed workers and the unemployed—people who are looking for work.

labor force participation rate The percent of a population that is in the labor force, which includes both the employed and unemployed.

married couples with or without children under age 18 Refers to married couples with or without children under age 18 living in the same household. Couples without children under age 18 may be parents of grown children who live elsewhere, or they could be childless couples.

median The median is the amount that divides the population or households into two equal portions: one below and one above the median. Medians can be calculated for income, age, and many other characteristics.

median income The amount that divides the income distribution into two equal groups, half having incomes above the median, half having incomes below the median. The medians for households or families are based on all households or families. The median for persons are based on all persons aged 15 or older with income.

metropolitan area An area qualifies for recognition as a metropolitan area if: (1) it includes a city of at least 50,000 population, or (2) it includes a Census Bureau-defined urbanized area of at least 50,000 with a total metropolitan population of at least 100,000 (75,000 in New England). In addition to the county containing the main city or urbanized area, a metropolitan area may include other counties having strong commuting ties to the central county.

Native American The Native American statistics in this book include people who indicated they were American Indian, Eskimo, or Aleut in the 1990 census. Some of the tables in the Native American chapter do not include Eskimos or Aleuts, a fact noted at the bottom of those tables. The American Indian category includes persons who reported their race as American Indian and/or entered the name of an American Indian tribe. The tribal data shown in this book are from the written entries on the 1990 census questionnaire.

nonfamily household A household maintained by a householder who lives alone or who lives with people to whom he or she is not related.

nonfamily householder A householder who lives alone or with nonrelatives.

non-Hispanic People who did not indicate that they were Hispanic on the Current Population Survey or on the 1990 Census are classified as non-Hispanic.

nonmetropolitan area Counties that are not classified as metropolitan areas.

occupation Occupational classification is based on the kind of work a person did at his or her job during the previous calendar year. If a person changed jobs during the year, the data refer to the occupation of the job held the longest during that year.

outside central city The portion of a metropolitan county or counties that falls outside of the central city or cities; generally regarded as the suburbs.

percent change The change (either positive or negative) in a measure that is expressed as a proportion of the starting measure. When median income changes from $20,000 to $25,000, for example, this is a 25 percent increase.

percentage point change The change (either positive or negative) in a value which is already expressed as a percentage. When a labor force participation rate changes from 70 percent of 75 percent, for example, this is a 5 percentage point increase.

poverty level The official income threshold below which families and persons are classified as living in poverty. The threshold rises each year with inflation and varies depending on family size and age of householder. In 1994, the poverty threshold for a family of four was $15,719.

proportion or share The value of a part expressed as a percentage of the whole. If there are 4 million people aged 25 and 3 million of them are white, then the white proportion is 75 percent.

race Race is self-reported and appears in four categories in this book: white, black, Native American, and Asian. A household is assigned the race of the householder.

rounding Percentages are rounded to the nearest tenth of a percent; therefore, the percentages in a distribution do not always add exactly to 100.0 percent. The totals, however, are always shown as 100.0. Moreover, individual figures are rounded to the nearest thousand without being adjusted to group totals, which are independently rounded; percentages are based on the unrounded numbers.

suburbs *See* Outside central city

tenure A housing unit is "owner occupied" if the owner lives in the unit, even if it is mortgaged or not fully paid for. A cooperative or condominium unit is "owner occupied" only if the owner lives in it. All other occupied units are classified as "renter occupied."

white The white racial category includes those who identify themselves as "white" on the Current Population Survey, or as white on the 1990 census. In addition, those who report an ancestry or ethnic origin that includes Canadian, German, Italian, Lebanese, Near Easterner, Arab, or Polish, or another country that is made up primarily of whites. The only exception to this definition of white is in the immigration tables in the Asian and Total Population chapters where the Immigration and Naturalization Service classifies people from the Middle East as from the Asian world region. They are included as Asian immigrants in the immigration tables, though the Census Bureau would classify them as white.

index

total population, 537
whites, 419

Net worth. *See* Wealth

Physician contacts. *See* Health

Population
ancestry of, 569
by ability to speak English
Asians, 45
Hispanics, 269
Native Americans, 361
by age
Asians, 38-45
blacks, 145-148
Hispanics, 262-269
Native Americans, 356-358
total population, 564-565
whites, 444-450
by country of birth, 567
by ethnicity
Asians, 43-45
Hispanics, 265, 268-269
total population, 563
by foreign-born status
Asians, 42, 47
Hispanics, 269, 271
total population, 566
by geography
Asians, 48-64
blacks, 149-158
Hispanics, 272-288
Native Americans, 362-373
total population, 571-576
whites, 451-458
projections
Asians, 38-40
blacks, 145-147, 149-155
Hispanics, 262-263, 275, 282-286
Native Americans, 356-358, 363, 367-372
total population, 563-564, 571-574
whites, 445-448, 451-457
by race, 563
by sex
Asians, 41
blacks, 148
Hispanics, 264
Native Americans, 359
whites, 449
by tribe, 360-362

Poverty
families
Asians, 30
blacks, 130
Hispanics, 247
Native Americans, 349
total population, 551
whites, 433
persons
blacks, 132
Hispanics, 248
total population, 553
whites, 435
tribes, 350

Projections
births
Asians, 70
blacks, 162
Hispanics, 297
Native Americans, 377
total population, 581
whites, 463
labor force
Asians, 36
blacks, 143
Hispanics, 260
whites, 442
population
Asians, 38-40
blacks, 145-147, 149-155
Hispanics, 262-263, 275, 282-286
Native Americans, 356-358, 363, 367-372
total population, 563-564, 571-574
whites, 445-448, 451-457

Sex
education
Asians, 3-4, 7
blacks, 74-75, 78
Hispanics, 192-193, 196
Native Americans, 327, 330
total population, 494-495, 498
whites, 382-383, 386
income
Asians, 28-29
blacks, 126-129
Hispanics, 242-245
Native Americans, 348
total population, 547-550
whites, 429-432

Make your demographic research more efficient with the

AMERICAN CONSUMER SERIES

The Official Guide to
American Attitudes

Find out who thinks what about the issues that shape our lives—marriage and family, sex, work and money, religion, the environment, race and immigration, personal outlook, and the public arena. The nationally representative data are broken out by the variables that are most important to you—age, sex, race (black and white), and education. It's a must-have book that gives you a complete picture of what your customers want out of life. (ISBN 1-885070-02-0; April 1996)   **$89.95**

The Official Guide to
Racial & Ethnic Diversity

An in-depth guide to the most important trend in the U.S.—the growing diversity of our population. You get the latest data on Asians, blacks, Hispanics, Native Americans, and whites—their education, health, households and living arrangements, housing, income and poverty, labor force participation, population, spending and wealth. You also get demographics on the largest ethnic groups among Asians and Hispanics, such as Chinese Americans and Mexican Americans. (ISBN 1-885070-03-9; April 1996)   **$89.95**

The Official Guide to
the Generations

Here is *the* sourcebook for researchers who want to improve their accuracy in targeting adult consumers—Generation X, born 1965-76; the Baby Boom, born 1946-64; the Swing Generation, born 1933-45; and the World War II Generation, born before 1933. You get detailed numbers on the current and projected size of each generation, plus complete information on their demographics and spending patterns. (ISBN 0-9628092-8-4; May 1995)   **$69.95**

The Official Guide to
the American Marketplace, 2nd ed.

The consumer researcher's bible, written by Cheryl Russell, a nationally recognized trend spotter. You get an in-depth look at the trends that define who we are as consumers—our education, health, incomes, occupations, living arrangements, racial and ethnic makeup, spending patterns, and wealth, all accompanied by the author's insightful analysis. *The Wall Street Journal* said this book "should be on your bookshelf." (ISBN 0-9628092-4-1; Jan. 1995)   **$79.95**

The Official Guide to
Household Spending, 3rd ed.

(formerly Consumer Power: How Americans Spend Their Money)

This classic guide has helped thousands of businesses find out what consumers do with their money. Widely praised when the first edition appeared in 1991, it gives you specific answers to the most important questions you can ask about consumers...who buys? what do they buy? how much do they spend? You get spending data on almost 1,000 products, broken out by scores of demographic variables. (ISBN 1-885070-01-2; Oct. 1995)   **$89.95**

The Official Guide to
American Incomes

This remarkable guide, which was selected as a Best Reference Source by *Library Journal*, is a must for anyone seriously interested in the ultimate key to what consumers buy—their incomes. A storehouse of information, it gives you income trends, household and personal income, discretionary income, household income projections, spending and wealth data, and poverty trends. (ISBN 0-9628092-2-5; July 1993)   **$69.95**

Also from New Strategist Publications...

WISE UP TO TEENS
Insights Into Marketing & Advertising to Teenagers

by Peter Zollo

Find out how to get your share of the big-spending and fast-growing teen market from America's #1 teenage marketer. Based on extensive surveys and focus groups with teens around the country, *Wise Up to Teens* gives you an in-depth look at teen lifestyles and values, where teens get their money, how and why they spend it, and proven, hands-on techniques that you can use to research and advertise to teens.

(ISBN 0-9628092-9-2;Oct. 1995)   **$34.95**

MOVING POWER & MONEY
The Politics of Census Taking

by Barbara Everitt Bryant & William Dunn

Here is a rare inside look from a former Census Bureau director at the goings-on behing the 1990 census. Naming names and without pulling punches, Dr. Bryant provocatively details how things should—and must—be changed for the 2000 census. Only then can we get an accurate count for an economical price. Don Dillman, director of the Social & Economic Sciences Research Center says it's "a must read."

(ISBN 0-9628092-7-6;April1995)   **$24.95**

Order today!

CALL 607/273-0913
FAX 607/277-5009
MAIL to
New Strategist,
P.O. Box 242,
Ithaca, NY 14851

qty.	book title	price	total
	Official Guide to American Attitudes	$89.95	$
	Official Guide to Racial & Ethnic Diversity	$89.95	$
	Official Guide to the Generations	$69.95	$
	Official Guide to the American Marketplace	$79.95	$
	Official Guide to Household Spending	$89.95	$
	Official Guide to American Incomes	$69.95	$
	Wise Up to Teens	$34.95	$
	Moving Power & Money	$24.95	$
	Shipping—add $4.75 for 1st book; $1 for each add'l book		$
	Subtotal		$
	New York State deliveries add sales tax		$
	TOTAL		$

Money-Back Guarantee
If you are not 100% satisfied with the books you order from New Strategist, just return them in good condition within 15 days for a full refund

Name

Company

Street Address

City   *State*   *Zip*

Charge to: ☐ *MasterCard* ☐ *Visa* ☐ *American Express*

Account no.   *Exp. date*

Signature

☐ *Check enclosed made payable to New Strategist*

0296